Philosophical Foundations of the Law of Equity

Philosophical Foundations of the Law of Equity

Edited by

DENNIS KLIMCHUK, IRIT SAMET,
AND HENRY E SMITH

OXFORD
UNIVERSITY PRESS

OXFORD
UNIVERSITY PRESS

Great Clarendon Street, Oxford, OX2 6DP,
United Kingdom

Oxford University Press is a department of the University of Oxford. It furthers the University's objective of excellence in research, scholarship, and education by publishing worldwide. Oxford is a registered trade mark of Oxford University Press in the UK and in certain other countries

First Edition published in 2020

Published in the United States of America by Oxford University Press
198 Madison Avenue, New York, NY 10016, United States of America

British Library Cataloguing in Publication Data
Data available

Library of Congress Control Number: 2019911426

ISBN 978–0–19–881765–9

Contents

List of Contributors

Samuel L Bray, Professor of Law, Notre Dame Law School

Simone Degeling, Professor of Law, Faculty of Law, University of New South Wales

James Edelman, Justice, High Court of Australia

Evan Fox-Decent, Professor and Canada Research Chair in Cosmopolitan Law and Justice, Faculty of Law, McGill University

Andrew S Gold, Professor of Law, Brooklyn Law School

John CP Goldberg, Deputy Dean, Carter Professor of General Jurisprudence, Harvard Law School

Matthew Harding, Deputy Dean, Professor of Law, University of Melbourne

Larissa Katz, Associate Professor and Canada Research Chair in Private Law Theory, Faculty of Law, University of Toronto

Dennis Klimchuk, Associate Professor, Department of Philosophy, Western University

Ben McFarlane, Professor of English Law and a Fellow of St John's College, University of Oxford (formerly Professor of Law, University College London)

Paul B Miller, Professor of Law and Associate Dean for International and Graduate Programs, Notre Dame Law School

Aruna Nair, Associate Professor of Law and Fellow of Hertford College, University of Oxford

JE Penner, Kwa Geok Choo Professor of Property Law, Faculty of Law, National University of Singapore

Irit Samet, Professor, Dickson Poon School of Law, Kings College London

Emily Sherwin, Frank B Ingersoll Professor of Law, Cornell Law School

Henry E Smith, Fessenden Professor of Law and Director of the Project on the Foundations of Private Law, Harvard Law School

Lionel Smith, Sir William C Macdonald Professor of Law, Faculty of Law, McGill University

Robert Stevens, Herbert Smith Freehills Professor of English Private Law, University of Oxford

Charlie Webb, Professor, Department of Law, London School of Economics and Political Science

Benjamin C Zipursky, James H Quinn '49 Chair in Legal Ethics and Professor of Law, Fordham Law School

List of Contributors

Introduction

In his celebrated *Lectures* on Equity, FW Maitland famously declared that all that could be said in answer to what is distinctive of the law of Equity is that it comprises 'that body of rules administered by our English courts of justice which, were it not for the operation of the Judicature Acts, would be administered only by those courts which would be known as Courts of Equity'.[1] On this view, 'Equity' merely collects a body of judge-made law originating in a particular set of courts, dissolved by statute in the nineteenth century. If Maitland was right, then there is no reason to think the law of equity names something about which there could be *philosophical* foundations.

The contributors to this volume share, for the most part, and in various degrees, the view that Maitland was wrong, or at least overstated the point: that, though certainly bearing the mark of historical contingency, there are, as it happened, conceptually distinctive features to that body of rules administered in common law courts that, were it not for the operation of the Judicature Acts, would be administered only by those courts which would be known as Courts of Equity. So, there is *something* about whose philosophical foundations we can fruitfully inquire.

There is a certain element of recovery to this claim: Maitland's view is commonly held.[2] But it was not always so. In *The Earl of Oxford's Case*—'the wellspring of equity in modern English law',[3] reported, symbolically enough, at 1 Chancery Rep 1[4]—Lord Ellesmere articulated an earlier orthodoxy when he claimed that '[t]he Cause why there is Chancery is, for that Mens Actions are so divers and infinite, That it is impossible to make any general Law which may aptly meet with every particular Act, and not fail in some Circumstances.'[5] The idea is Aristotle's: 'the nature of the equitable', Aristotle tells us, is 'a correction of law where it is defective owing to its universality'.[6]

This volume opens with a sceptical note on this theme: In 'Discretionary Justice', Charlie Webb asks whether Equity's distinctive role is to do equity in the Aristotelian sense of doing justice where law, by virtue of its generality, would do an injustice, and concludes it is not. Some paradigmatic cases of Equity's interventions are not, Webb argues, corrections for the generality of a rule, but rather for its being simply a bad rule. This is the case, for example, with the rule that grants rescission in cases of innocent

[1] FW Maitland, *Equity, Also, the Forms of Action at Common Law: Two Courses of Lectures* (CUP 1909) 1

[2] Mike MacNair recently suggested it 'has become substantially the current orthodoxy'. MacNair, 'Equity and Conscience' (2007) 27 OJLS 659, 664.

[3] Gary Watt, *Equity Stirring* (Hart 2009) 67.

[4] Though, as David Ibbetson has argued, the text is not a judgment in the ordinary sense. See David Ibbetson, '*The Earl of Oxford's Case*' in Charles Mitchell and Paul Mitchell (eds), *Landmark Cases in Equity* (Hart 2012) 1–32.

[5] 1 Chan Rep 1, 6; 21 ER 485, 486.

[6] *NE* 5.10, 1137b27–28.

Introduction In: *Philosophical Foundations of the Law of Equity*. Edited by: Dennis Klimchuk, Irit Samet, and Henry E Smith, Oxford University Press (2020). © The several contributors.
DOI: 10.1093/oso/9780198817659.003.0001

misrepresentation (whereby common law contracts could be set aside only when misrepresentations were made fraudulently), and in Chancery's response to the common law rule that a sealed bond was incontrovertible evidence of a debt. There are cases that do call for correction for over-generality, such as *Riggs v Palmer*, in which the New York Court found that a grandson could not assert his claim as the named beneficiary of the estate of the grandfather he'd murdered, notwithstanding the silence of the relevant statutes on the point. But there is no reason to say that the techniques used by Equity could not have been adopted by the common law. Furthermore, Webb argues, a case can be made that the common law tradition is especially unneedful of a distinct Equitable jurisdiction, owing to the central role played by judge-made law. The common law is, in a sense, made in its application, always first indexed to the particular facts of the case. Nonetheless, Webb suggests, when later judges clarify implicit rules by distinguishing present cases, this might be seen as a kind of equitable exercise. But, again, this is not unique to Equity but is something we find across the common law. Thus, Webb concludes, if there is something distinctive about Equity, it will be found in its substantive principles rather than its corrective (or any other) function.

In 'Aristotle at the Foundations of the Law of Equity', Dennis Klimchuk also argues that equity in the Aristotelian sense of correcting for errors arising from the generality of law is no less available in common law than in equity. Indeed, Aristotle's account is reflected, in remarkable details, in the common law interpretive doctrine of equitable construction. Lord Ellesmere's appeal to Aristotle in *The Earl of Oxford's Case*, then, would seem to undermine rather than support the claim to the jurisprudential independence of equity and jurisdictional independence of Chancery. However, Klimchuk argues, there is another current in Aristotle's account of equity, substantive rather than functional, that fares much better as the basis of an account of Equity's distinctiveness. This is the idea that equity enjoins persons from being sticklers for their rights in a bad way. In his chapter, Klimchuk unpacks this idea and argues that it makes sense of two illustrative cases. The first is a classic illustration of Chancery's jurisdiction, discussed also by Webb: the defendant discharges a debt owed to the plaintiff under a bond, but either fails to secure an acquittance or loses it. By common law he will be compelled to pay again, but Chancery would enjoin the re-enforcement of the debt. The second is *The Earl of Oxford's Case* itself, which, as well as being a pivotal case in this history of Equity is an important early case in the prehistory of proprietary estoppel. So, Lord Ellesmere's invocation of Aristotle was borne out, in the end, though perhaps not for reasons he had in mind.

Though ranging across a number of other themes, such as the relationship between justice, virtue, and equity, and the place of equity in the distinction between private and public law, the next four chapters each engage in different ways the strengths and limits of the idea that Equity is characterized by a concern to prevent persons from being sticklers in a bad way or, as Henry Smith has argued, from opportunistically exploiting their legal rights.[7]

[7] Henry E Smith, 'Fusing the Equitable Function in Private Law' in Kit Barker, Karen Fairweather, and Ross Grantham (eds), *Private Law in the 21st Century* (Hart 2017) 173, 175–85.

Aristotle's account of Equity is the background of James Penner's exploration of the question whether equity employs a distinctive moral criterion when it intervenes in people's legal rights. Penner approaches the question via three avenues which lead him to answer 'yes, but rarely, and in an unsystematic way'. Starting with the fierce anti-fusion classic of Meagher, Gummow, and Lehane's treatise, he finds in their treatment no evidence for intellectual or moral principles that underlie the historical separation between Law and Equity which they so faithfully record. Penner concludes that to unearth any thread that runs through Equity we need to look for a defect in the Common Law that it sets out to correct. Like Klimchuk, Penner finds that the first sense of equity mentioned by Aristotle—as a source of exceptions to under- or over-exclusive rules—cannot explain in what way reforms that originated in English Equity are materially different from the way(s) in which the common law constantly corrects and refines its own rules. But Penner offers a different account about the extent and justification for the way in which English equity maps onto Aristotle's second sense of equity. For him, combating the stickler for justice is a legitimate reason for state coercion, but it explains only a small number of equitable doctrines, for example estoppel and mistaken payment. Working within a Kantian framework, Penner argues that the state is justified in forcing on some claimants an ethical duty to refrain from sticking to their rights in a bad way in order to protect the legal system from the damage this practice may cause. But while Equity's interventions in the parties' rights in Aristotle's second sense are legitimate, they are too few and far between to be counted as the intellectual foundation that sets Equity apart from the Common Law.

In his chapter, Andrew Gold also argues that the 'stickler-enjoining' account of Equity has important limits, but different ones from those Penner identifies. While many distinctive doctrines of Equity can be understood to limit stickler behaviour, Gold argues, Equity in fact often turns a blind eye to, and sometimes even enables, stickler behaviour. For example, tort defendants can insist on damages from minimally negligent plaintiffs where we might think an apology is adequate; plaintiffs can bring claims for disgorgement in cases of breach of fiduciary duty against parties who acted in good faith and did them no material harm (and perhaps even benefited them). Gold argues that we can sort cases in which equity restrains sticklers from those in which it is indifferent to (and even enables) stickler behaviour if we attend to the role of the state in private litigation. Sometimes the state's responsibilities require it to protect plaintiffs against sticklers—for example, when they engage in wrongfully opportunistic behaviour. Other times, it requires it to protect the stickler, as a means, for example, of keeping as open as possible each person's sphere of choices. Gold argues that the self-regarding account of equity, as he calls it, sheds light on the question of the relationship between equity and justice: from the distinct perspective of the judgment, sometimes equitable justice is better than legal justice and sometimes legal justice is better than equitable justice.

Paul Miller argues that implicit in the idea that equity intervenes to prevent persons from being sticklers for their rights in a bad way or from opportunistically exploiting their legal rights is what he calls a remedial conception of equity, according to which its distinctiveness issues from the way it corrects for injustices arising from the strict application of law. While shedding important light on the nature of Equity, the exclusive focus on its remedial aspect—shared, Miller argues, among many contemporary theorists of Equity, notwithstanding other important differences among them—has obscured a second, no less significant role played by Equity, namely as a source of supplemental law. Equity does not only restrain or qualify the exercise of primary rights; it is also the source of such rights. Some such rights fill gaps remedially by establishing constraints on existing rights, for example the equity of redemption. Others fill gaps interstitially and so expand by adding to existing legal rights, as in rights granted by Equity to remainder-persons against persons who hold life estates in their property. In a third category, Equity fills gaps by developing novel rights, as, for example, with the myriad rights held by the beneficiary of an express trust against the trustee, other beneficiaries and third parties. So, while many doctrines of Equity are remedial, part of what makes Equity distinct, on Miller's view, are the distinctive resources it brings to the task of supplementing law.

Evan Fox-Decent also argues that a remedial conception of Equity is incomplete, at least in the forms that cast its aim as enjoining opportunists and those who are sticklers for their rights in a bad way. Along with what he calls its anti-opportunist domain, Fox-Decent argues, Equity has a jurisdictional sphere. In its jurisdictional sphere, Equity's concern is determining the rightful scope and exercise of other-regarding powers. An opportunist or a stickler in a bad way is just someone who has abused an other-regarding power. In this respect, Equity and its doctrines exhibit a number of striking parallels with the jurisdiction and doctrines of administrative law. From this, Fox-Decent draws two striking conclusions. First: both domains express what he calls jurisdictional justice. Like corrective, but unlike distributive justice, jurisdictional justice structures the juridical relationship between parties who exhibit a relationship of reciprocity; while in corrective justice the relationship at issue is that between rights and duties, in jurisdictional justice is that between powers and liabilities. Second: Equity is either closely related to public law, or is really just a branch of public law. This second lesson, Fox-Decent argues, explains a number of distinctive features of Equity, for example its second-order structure, its historical deployment of the concept of conscience, and the characteristic properties of equitable remedies.

As a phenomenon, Equity is most interesting if it offers something distinctive, whether substantive or formal or both. Is Equity rooted in a moral notion of equity? In addition to the variety of doctrines going under the heading of 'Equity', the kinds of normative sources that might plausibly be associated with equity are if anything more multifarious.

In light of this variegated picture, Lionel Smith sounds a note of caution. In his contribution, Smith explores the foundations of Equity as a living body law, taken from the perspective of jurists who work to implement, develop, and systemize its doctrines. From this point of view, the law of trusts stands out as a central case of Equity. And since much of the law of trusts comprises rules, ie norms that are clear, predictable, and lend themselves to formalistic interpretation, Smith's analysis sharply contrasts with other accounts of Equity that highlight the discretionary open-ended nature of its norms, and/or the category of conscience. Taking trust law as a focal point leads him to advance a pluralist account: Equity has no single underlying normative idea, only characteristic principles. Smith's chapter concentrates on the unique ways in which Equity understands obligations that relate to the benefit of specific assets. Thus, he finds that the famous *in personam* nature of Equity is revealed not in norms that are ad hoc and flexible, but in the unique relationship between trustee and beneficiary. Unlike in both the common law and in the civil law, the core trust obligation may bind any person who acquires the trust property, making such a person into a trustee, but it binds only the person who is trustee at any given time. In this way it blurs the line between property and obligation. The rules of trust law likewise set Equity apart for the way in which it responds to breaches of obligations by generating further *primary* obligations with regards to substitutive assets that were illicitly acquired. From these and many other examples, Smith concludes that while Equity features a series of characteristic approaches to obligations, these approaches cannot be attributed to a single normative root.

Taking a somewhat more optimistic approach to locating distinct but limited normative foundations of Equity, Larissa Katz in her chapter develops an account of Equity that aims to expose its normative foundations without losing sight of the great diversity of rights that originate in the Courts of Chancery. In difference with theories that view Equity as a general concern with fit between legal and moral norms, Katz finds that a distinctive feature of Equity that also unites many of its doctrines is the way Equity works to preserve and regulate the pathways to acquiring a legal right. The Courts of Equity identified a particular kind of injustice that may affect human interactions: the inevitable gap between embarking on a course to acquire a legal right, and the completion of the procedure for acquisition generates an opportunity for forfeiture. Equity, Katz suggests, intervenes to ensure that no such forfeiture takes place. In doing so, the Courts of Equity fulfil the role of the state to protect the citizens against oppression and injustice that is produced by the very nature of the processes through which legal rights are acquired. Equity functions by conscripting rights holders as agents of equity to do as equity would have done in the exercise or assertion of their legal rights. The conscience invoked by Equity is thus the political conscience of the *state* that generates demands of justice its members are bound to assist it to discharge. A big advantage of this normative framework, Katz claims, is that it explains many seemingly disconnected doctrines of equity like trusts, equity of redemption, restrictive covenants, and substantial performance, while remaining faithful to the doctrinal details and the role they play in the big picture of Equity.

An emphasis on doctrinal details offers another avenue to the distinctiveness of Equity—not in its normative foundations or its substance but in its form. While joining other authors in this volume in finding that equity has a distinctive function, Ben McFarlane and Robert Stevens offer a unique *formal* account of what it amounts to. Equitable rights, they say, often take the form of rights in relation to other rights.

Acknowledgement of this unique structure of Equitable rights sheds light on the way they interact with common law rights, on the normative basis for creating them, as well as on the way we assess the common law rights against which they arise. The authors exemplify the advantages of their formal account by reference to two (out of many) equitable rights in which they identify such a right-against-right structure: the beneficiary's rights under a trust, and equitable assignment. What both the beneficiary under a trust and the equitable assignee have is a right against a right held by another; and it is the distinctive formal nature of the entitlement thus recognized by Equity, rather than a different set of substantive values brought to bear by Equity, that explains Equity's intervention. Such intervention also carries commercial benefits: for example, in allowing the right of the assignor against the debtor to be encumbered by a right held by the (equitable) assignee, Equity enables commercial entities to capitalize on debts owed to them without thereby undermining the principle of privity of contracts. Like some other authors in this volume, McFarlane and Stevens focus on what Paul Miller calls the supplemental aspect of Equity. What they find from this perspective are rights that, far from being mere shadows of common law 'equivalents', share a distinctive structure and respond to reasons for restricting certain legal rights by being engrafted on those rights.

The debate over whether Equity possesses any distinctness plays out in the ongoing process of the fusion of law and Equity. Although statutes effecting fusion (or merger, as it is sometimes known) provided for the unification of courts and the melding of legal and equitable procedures, such legislation left its substantive implications, if any, implicit. If Equity is not distinct from the law or not distinct in any deep sense, then fusion would leave little trace of Equity at the end of the day. If, however, Equity has been—or continuous to be—distinct, the question arises whether such differences as exist are worth preserving, and if so in what way.

Taking a functional view of Equity, Henry Smith argues for viewing equity as a second-order system—law about law, or meta-law—whose loss through fusion has created a variety of jurisprudential quandaries. On this view, equity serves as a second-order safety valve particularly suited to problems of great variability and uncertainty—including opportunism, conflicting rights, and multipolar conflicts—and although such problems were not the exclusive preserve or the only focus of equity courts, the former jurisdictional divide did much to highlight the second-order equitable function. In response to specific triggers like bad faith and disproportionate hardship, equity sometimes supplemented and overrode law in the name of a more open-ended considerations sounding in morality, and in this way did a kind of Aristotelian equity, correcting law when it fails on account of its generality. Smith argues that the flattening out of this second-order equitable function though fusion of law and equity has intensified numerous jurisprudential controversies, including the debate between formalism and contextualism and the distinction between rules and standards, in contrast to the older less polarized path of hybrid law-equity. Effacing distinctive second-order equity also leads to extreme views about the supposed death of contract and all-consuming tort, and even the relationship of law and morality tends to be more fraught when equity as meta-law is taken off the table.

Distinguishing substance and form as sources of potential distinctiveness in Equity, Samuel Bray refracts controversies over fusion and the contemporary relevance of equity through the lens of translation. How and to what extent should we—or under the US Constitution 'must' we—translate traditional equity into current law? Drawing on John Dryden's account of varieties of translation as well as modern theories of translation, Bray shows how disagreements over fusion and equity often appear to be about past versus present when they are really about whether to follow the form and substance of equity or the substance only. Distinguishing two axes of translation produces a typology of approaches to equity, which then allows us to recognize that virtually all approaches to equity fall in the middle between the poles of literal tracking of the original on the one hand and loose recreation on the other. Rather than acting as a metaphor, translation is useful as a fiction—evaluating equity as if it were an exercise in translation. When equity is seen as in need of 'translation', we are prompted to consider genuine questions about the place of equity in the current legal system: what is the importance of the form of equity—its distinctiveness, its relation to law, and its discretionary character—and what is the relevance of the equity's substance against the background of changed conditions. Thinking of equity in terms of translation promises to expand the possibilities in the search for the best way to carry equity into current and future law.

Whether to carry Equity forward depends on background conditions that are constantly changing. In a more sceptical view of equity and its continued viability, Emily Sherwin highlights how equity can undermine a system of well-crafted rules and shows how American legal realism has impeded equity from correcting the law in its traditional fashion. The baseline is 'good' rules, which are those that produce better results by being followed across the board. Yet even good rules will sometimes lead to bad results. If, at the point of application a decision-maker, possessing less information than the lawmaker and suffering from cognitive biases, is empowered to deviate from the rule, rules' coordination benefits—stemming from their stability—can quickly dissipate. Such undermining of the rules of the common law is one of the dangers of equity, which Sherwin sees as having been dampened at one time by the less-than-overt operation of equity when it was separate from law. With the rise of American legal realism towards the end of the process of fusing law and equity, courts and commentators became more sceptical about rules and averse to less-than-transparent legal doctrine, and so equity could no longer limit itself to correcting the law without doing undue damage. No solution to this realist-inspired dilemma presents itself, and the best that can be asked of judges is to tone down the realist-style enthusiasm for judicial guesswork.

For many of those who believe that Equity plays a distinctive role in the legal systems in which it operates, this role features some special connection to moral norms. For Aristotle, and the many who followed his footsteps, equity is a response to a deficiency of justice in a system whose purpose is to do justice. But the adverse outcome of this defect is dependent on the willingness of cunny individuals to forgo their duties to other members of the community by taking advantage of deficiencies in the legal system. The courts of Equity, right from its inception, targeted the immorality that is involved in the actions of such sticklers via flexible legal standards which they carefully built around accessible moral norms. By harnessing the familiarity of moral norms, Chancery judges managed to make law that was relatively predictable, in spite of the open-ended formulae they employed. The most conspicuous link between the law of Equity and morality is the standard of conscience. The linchpin of many doctrines of Equity, the unconscionability element affords the court an opportunity to determine liability in Equity in light of the moral norms that apply in the circumstances. The risks of overuse or abuse of this powerful concept have been noted by many, but other writers celebrate the way in which Equity promotes a better fit between legal and moral norms, and the potential of the conscionability standard to answer both justice and efficiency considerations in complex situations.

A prime example of Equity's daring use of a conscience standard at the heart of commercial law is discussed in Aruna Nair and Irit Samet's chapter on 'Equity's darling'. One way of revealing the distinctiveness of Equity is comparing its *mode d'emploi* with that of the Common Law in similar circumstances. The authors set out to do so with regard to conflicts between an owner of assets, a purported purchaser of those assets under an unauthorized transfer, and the community that has a stake in the outcome of the dispute. In common law, even an innocent and cautious purchaser cannot defeat a legal owner's title—with a few limited well-defined policy-driven exceptions—whereas Equity allows a purchaser with clean conscience to defeat even the neediest beneficiary. The authors argue that the central explanatory principle which underlies the choices made by Equity is the battle against unconscionability that reflects its distinctive nature as a body of law that is highly responsive to interpersonal morality. But the flexibility that typifies equitable doctrines allows it to go beyond justice as between the parties and appeal also to aspects of communal justice. The authors explore how considerations of distributive justice, need, desert, and efficiency play out in such conflicts when the property is held on trust. The deep consternation that necessarily accompanies a binary solution to a conflict between innocents makes this area of law a perfect test case for assessing the potential of Equity to utilize its unique features to address the incommensurable values at play. Taking the concept of conscience as the centre of gravity, and employing a flexible standard for fine-tuning, Equity tackles perplexing conflicts with solutions that are responsive to many, if not all, the values and interests that are typically involved.

In their contribution, John Goldberg and Benjamin Zipursky offer further insight into the way in which Equity adjusts legal liability to fit better with considerations of justice and morality. Equity's engagement with mismatches between the solutions offered in common law and the requirements of morality and justice again proves to be a useful anchor for exploring its distinctive nature. Thus, while the authors distinguish law and equity in terms that are connected to historical practice, they highlight the function of the equitable jurisdiction as providing discretionary relief to persons who suffer serious injustices by virtue of the operation of legal rules. The discussion is set within the framework of their claim that private law affords those who have suffered wrongs such as torts or breaches of contract 'recourse'. Recourse consists of courts validating claims for damages and other relief to which claimants are entitled as a matter of right. In contrast, claimants seeking to benefit from the exercise of a court's equitable powers, because they claim on the basis of justice or moral right rather than legal rights strictly speaking, can only expect a discretionary form of relief that is often issued through the issuance of command-like orders. The authors show how this conception of equity plays out in decisions unwinding unjust transactions, ordering the transfer of unjustly held assets, and refusing to validate unjustly brought claims—as well as in issuing orders, notably injunctions, that vindicate legal rights when as-of-right legal remedies fail. They then argue that equity (on the foregoing account) is at the core of landmark judicial opinions issued in cases that are not traditionally categorized as cases 'in equity', including *Riggs v Palmer* (the murdering-heir case) and *Shelley v Kraemer* (concerning state action through court enforcement of restrictive covenants). In view of the important role that equity plays, including in changing law for the better, Goldberg and Zipursky conclude that more attention to the distinctiveness of equity—more than is typically paid in the post-realist United States—promises to improve the overall legal system.

The attention-grabbing standard of conscionability, and the sometimes-dramatic ways in which Equity intervenes to bring legal responsibility up to standard with moral norms should not obscure the other important ways in which Equity serves morality. The willingness of the Courts of Equity to engage in serious moral deliberation about the law they make, and their proactive attitude led them to develop new forms of legal relationship which are deeply informed by moral values. Thus, as two chapters in the volume demonstrate, the Courts of Equity had a special concern for the way in which the law they make promotes the autonomy of those who come under its reign.

In one chapter, Simone Degeling highlights the role of Equity in preserving the autonomy of vulnerable members of the community. Taking as her starting point the perspective of consent requirements, she extrapolates a more general thesis about the concept of autonomy that is employed by Equity. Degeling focuses on the equitable domains of trusts, fiduciary relationships, undue influence, and unconscionability, where an imbalance of power exists in which one party has only limited or bounded ability to make decisions. What can we learn about the way Equity conceives of autonomy from the way it acts to protect the vulnerable party from non-consensual actions on her behalf? Working within a Razian perception of autonomy, the author finds that Equity takes great care to protect the independence aspect of autonomous decision, but is less concerned about the availability of choice between meaningful options. A party will be deemed by Equity as consenting if her (outer) agreement is anchored in (negative) freedom and information. Thus, great care is taken by the Courts of Chancery to ensure that no impediment to the exercise of the claimant's will was present in the circumstance. In addition, relevant information must be provided, and at times nothing less than independent advice from a third party would satisfy this requirement. Equity thus conscripts its particularistic nature to offer strong protection for two elements that are crucial for autonomous decision-making: freedom from coercion and information. This vigorous defence of two elements from Raz's scheme allows the author to argue that despite Equity's leniency when it comes to the existence of a range of options, we can attribute to Equity a commitment to protect autonomy in the liberal sense of the word.

The goal of assisting members of the community to become the authors of their life permeates not only the way Equity protect individual from predatory practices tolerated by the Common Law, but also the development of wholly equitable modes of arranging one's affairs. One prime example is the charitable trust. In developing the law of charity, as Matthew Harding shows in his chapter, the Courts of Equity have taken bold measures that were designed to ensure that a morally commended intention to give to charity does not fall foul of formalistic legal requirements, or the donor's own misconceptions about the best way of realizing her intention. Harding joins Paul Miller and others in taking issue with the view that equity is primarily remedial, drawing attention to the significant facilitative role it occupies. Among Equity's main concerns are institutions, understood as arrangements or frameworks for human action that have some distinctive normative identity and are oriented to some purpose or goal. The key example is the trust. Many core trust doctrines, Harding argues, have been developed to ensure the integrity of the institution of trusts themselves, rather than to bring about remedial justice in the setting of adjudication. Furthermore, in developing new forms of trust, courts in Equity do not remedy but rather facilitate, making possible more options through which donors can express their intentions. In this way, Harding argues, Equity serves a compelling view of liberalism, according to which a measure of the justification of state action lies in its contribution to a social, economic, and political order in which people are able to live autonomous lives. One mode of autonomy-enhancing state actions is the multiplication of institutional options from which persons can chose. Equity serves autonomy, as well, by sometimes limiting options, as when through the cy-pres doctrine courts vary the terms of charitable trusts to undo their discriminatory ends and effects. In defacilitating the use of law as an instrument of discrimination, here Equity serves the end of securing the conditions of self-respect, itself a condition of autonomy.

However, not all writers, in and outside this volume celebrate the tendency of Chancery judges to appeal to moral reasoning when applying and interpreting standards of Equity. Concerned by the adverse effects of departure from the rule of law that appeal to moral reasoning may imply, they recommend that standards and concepts of Equity be detached from the moral baggage they carry in ordinary language and interpreted as legal standards. James Edelman's contribution to this volume is an excellent example of this strand of thought. Edelman focuses on the doctrine of the 'equity of the statute' according to which courts can go beyond the literal meaning of a statute—either narrowing or broadening—in order to avoid perverse results. Edelman distinguishes two versions of the equity of the statute, an older one in which some external standard of morality is brought to bear to override the normal operation of a statute and a more modern version of the equity of the statute in which statutory language is interpreted in a contextual manner and construed with a view to its purposes. This latter kind of equity of the statute, which eschews recourse to a standpoint outside that of participants in the legislative speech act, is not strictly speaking equitable at all, if by equity is meant a kind of law with its own standards. Famous examples of the equity of the statute, in both versions, can be found in the courts' treatment of the Statute of Frauds. Although traces here and there of the older, independently moral, version of the equity of the statute can still be found, Edelman argues on grounds of separation of powers, rule of law, and judicial legitimacy, that the modern view is defensible and desirable, whereas new applications of the older version would be neither. Similar issues of equity arise with respect to all other instruments, notably including contracts, wills, and treaties.

Since at least the time of Aristotle, equity has captured the interest of philosophers, and that fascination continues today. As Equity's place in the legal system continues to evolve, equity's correction of the law, equity's distinctiveness, and equity's moral dimensions will continue to remain central questions. Philosophical analysis of these aspects of equity in general and Equity in common law legal systems promises to help us understand and better shape these developments. The chapters in this volume are an important and exciting new instalment in the long tradition of philosophical analysis of equity.

1

Discretionary Justice

Charlie Webb

I. Equity and equity

One enduring idea is that Equity's job is to do equity: to do justice where law, by virtue of its generality, would do injustice.[1] For some, this image of Equity is an anachronism, true to Equity's origins but out of step with its modern reality. Certainly, Equity today looks very different to the Equity first administered by the medieval Chancellors. Equity is now marked less by wide-ranging discretion than by precision and technicality. If we look to, say, the law of trusts we see a complex and highly systematized body of rules, rules which, in much of their detail, neither do nor aspire to any particular justice. So, many of the rules regulating the creation of trusts—setting the certainty requirements trusts must meet, the range of purposes for which trusts may be established—express no discernible principle of justice, and for good reason since these are questions on which general principles of justice and morality have little or nothing to say. Raw morality doesn't demand that a legal system have a law of trusts at all; it's not likely to tell us what law of trusts it should then adopt.

Nonetheless we might doubt whether these characteristics of modern Equity mark any change in its function. What became the express trust arose where property was conveyed on the undertaking of the recipient that he'd apply it as the transferor had directed. In such cases it would be unjust if the recipient could breach that undertaking and take the property for himself. Once Equity determined, rightly, that such undertakings should create enforceable obligations, a series of further questions arose as to the proper content of those obligations and the remedies which should attend their breach. Should the recipient in all cases be required to do as he had undertaken? What if the terms of the undertaking aren't fully clear? How far should we go in supplementing those terms in order to ensure that the transferor's intentions aren't defeated? Who should be empowered to take action in the event of the recipient breaching these obligations? Should these undertakings also impose obligations or liabilities on others who come into contract with the property?

There may be little, if anything, to choose between alternative answers to some of these questions. Where this is so, we won't find arguments of justice which support the choice of one solution over all others. Nonetheless, just as considerations of safety

[1] Here I follow the convention of using capitalization to distinguish the law of Equity from the broader idea of equity.

Charlie Webb, *Discretionary Justice* In: *Philosophical Foundations of the Law of Equity*. Edited by: Dennis Klimchuk, Irit Samet, and Henry E Smith, Oxford University Press (2020).
DOI: 10.1093/oso/9780198817659.003.0002

justify a rule which directs us to drive on one side of the road though they don't tell us what side that should be, so considerations of justice support a body of rules imposing obligations on those who undertake to hold property on trust even if they don't dictate the full content of those rules and obligations. The same is true elsewhere. That there may be a range of reasonable measures that Equity could adopt to correct some common law injustice or that the correction of that injustice may require a technical solution doesn't, therefore, mean that Equity is no longer in the business of correcting such injustices nor that the rule it adopts is not such a corrective. And this justice continues to be done where the application of these rules becomes settled, so that no continued appeal to the injustice that first prompted the need for these, or some such, rules is made.

It doesn't follow, however, that these rules of Equity do equity. To see why, take a clearer example of Equity correcting injustice. The common law held that contracts could be set aside for misrepresentation only where the misrepresentation was made fraudulently. This rule worked injustice, an injustice which Equity remedied when it granted rescission in cases of innocent misrepresentation. But the injustice of the common law rule wasn't attributable to its generality. It was just a bad rule. There was, and is, nothing to stop us adopting a general rule which says: all misrepresentations make a contract voidable. Indeed, this is just the rule Equity adopted. This isn't an isolated instance. The same is true of what is often taken as the paradigmatic example of Equitable intervention, in response to the common law rule that a sealed bond was incontrovertible evidence of a debt.[2] If the debtor paid but failed to see that the bond was cancelled, he had no defence to a claim for payment. This rule was not senseless but the simplicity and certainty it provided was not worth the injustice it caused. Equity therefore intervened to see that the debtor didn't have to pay twice, and in so doing supplanted a bad, or at least imperfect, rule with a better one.[3]

So, it may be true to say that all Equity operates as a corrective to common law injustice. This, however, leaves us some way short of Equity's job being to do equity. The alternative, and I think far more common, source of such injustice is the law's adoption of what are simply bad rules and the principal Equitable function, though a function hardly unique to Equity, is the correction or offsetting of such rules. How much of Equity can be accounted for on this basis? How much Equity is left for equity? I won't

[2] See eg JH Baker, *An Introduction to English Legal History* (4th edn, OUP 2007) 102–03.

[3] I don't, therefore, share the view that the common law rule was a 'good rule' (Charles M Gray, 'The Boundaries of the Equitable Function' (1976) 20 American Journal of Legal History 192, 220, quoted in JE Penner's chapter in this volume). Perhaps, once Equity had determined that evidence of payment was admissible, it became possible to defend the rule on the basis that it was 'not meant literally' (Gray, ibid 220), with the common law courts denying such evidence in the knowledge that the debtor would get a different answer in Equity. Nonetheless the common law rule adopted—one adopted not in concert with Equity and so not on terms that its unjust effects would be avoided—was indeed a bad one, a conclusion hardly undermined if common law judges came to see the merits of Equity's mitigation of that rule. Now, it may be that the resulting arrangement—the common law refusing such evidence, Equity admitting it—allowed for some of the benefits of the common law rule to be preserved, without all its attendant costs.

The distinctive law-changing technique Equity provides, leaving the common law rule in place, adding a supplementary rule which reverses or mitigates its unjust effects, sometimes brings gains that the common law could not, or could not so easily, have achieved alone (see Penner, ibid 55). Still this is a beneficial, and only occasional, side effect of Equity, not institutional design.

conduct the sort of survey of Equitable doctrine which would be needed to answer these questions fully. Instead I want to focus on the idea of equity, so that we might get a clearer sense of when and why a legal system might have need for an equitable jurisdiction or capacity.

II. Rules, Discretion, and Justice

Some rules do injustice because they have been badly framed.[4] The argument for equity is that rules may do injustice even where there is no deficiency in their framing. How so? The argument goes back to Aristotle:[5]

> [A]ll law is universal but about some things it is not possible to make a universal statement which will be correct. In those cases, then, in which it is necessary to speak universally, but not possible to do so correctly, the law takes the usual case, though it is not ignorant of the possibility of error. And it is none the less correct; for the error is not in the law nor in the legislator but in the nature of the thing, since the matter of practical affairs is of this kind from the start. When the law speaks universally, then, and a case arises on it which is not covered by the universal statement, then it is right, when the legislator fails us and has erred by over-simplicity, to correct the omission—to say what the legislator himself would have said had he been present, and would put into law had he known. . . . And this is the nature of the equitable, a correction of law where it is defective owing to its universality.

This passage can be read in different ways. Here is one reading. On occasion it's impossible to formulate a rule which will do justice across the full range of cases to which the rule is to apply. Whatever rule we adopt will, therefore, sometimes do injustice, and, if we look to revise the rule to avoid injustice in a particular case, it will only result in injustice elsewhere. The equitable solution is not to abandon the rule but for the judge to have a discretion to disapply or to override the rule where it would do injustice and so come to a just decision instead.

We can get a clearer sense of this idea of equity and the sort of problem to which it responds by contrasting it with other cases which might call for the exercise of judicial discretion. We've touched on one already. Sometimes the law does injustice for reasons other than its generality, with the common law rule limiting rescission to cases of fraudulent misrepresentation one example. Here, too, one response to the injustice that would come from application of the rule is to give the judge a discretion not to

[4] The terms 'just', 'unjust', and their cognates are used in different ways, so it's worth saying something here about how I am using them. What I want to capture is a sort of complaint that one may make about the law: that it gives the wrong result, when judged by the norms (of justice or morality) which, law aside, bear on one's case. This in turn explains the sense in which one might say that a justified rule may nonetheless do injustice (for an example, see text to n 23).

[5] Aristotle, *Nicomachean Ethics*, V.10, 1137b13–27. The translation is from Jonathan Barnes (ed), *The Complete Works of Aristotle: The Revised Oxford Translation—Volume 2* (Princeton UP 1984) 1795–96.

apply it. Now, it doesn't follow from the fact that applying a rule would do injustice that it would be better not to apply it. Departing from a rule of law is rarely cost free. In some cases, we can't do justice on the facts without compromising other ends to which the law is reasonably directed. Hard cases, cases where a rule's application leads to unjust outcomes, may sometimes be the price of good law. Even less-than-fully reasonable rules may create reasonable expectations and trigger reliance which would cause harm if those rules weren't applied. Moreover, the law's effectiveness as a means of resolving problems of social coordination is reduced if the solutions it offers are too often subject to review and revision. For these reasons, though the application of a rule would do avoidable injustice, it will sometimes be better to apply it.

The case for exercising a discretion not to apply the rule is likely to be stronger, however, where there is at least a better rule to be had. Where there is, adopting the better rule allows for justice to be done not only in the case at hand but in future cases without the need for further discretionary exemptions. If the exercise of a judge's discretion not to apply the rule where it would do injustice is treated as governing not just this case but also future like cases, the effect is a change in the law, with the old rule now amended or replaced with one new and improved. In common law systems, judicial powers to change the law are extensive, embracing both cases where old rules are expressly overruled and those where they are merely distinguished. We can add to these Equity's distinctive model of lawmaking, by which the relevant common law rule is not removed but is undercut. Notwithstanding the trope that Equity only supplements and does not supersede the law, it is plain that the effect of such Equitable rules and rulings is that the applicable rules of the common law are no longer decisive, and the parties' all-things-considered legal entitlements are changed. So, Equity's contribution to the law of misrepresentation means that, in place of a rule which says that misrepresentations have to be made fraudulently before they empower a contracting party to rescind, we have one which says that they don't.

Judicial lawmaking isn't limited to cases where old rules are removed or replaced. A rule is set down: no vehicles in the park. What this rule means is clear in some cases but not in others. Does it cover wheelchairs? Mobility scooters? Skateboards? As at least some of these examples bring out, the rule has what Hart called an open texture, a penumbra of uncertainty.[6] A combination of inevitable linguistic imprecision and indeterminacy of aim and intention means that, for any rule of positive law, there will be cases where the rule's content is itself indeterminate. As Hart saw it, where a rule is indeterminate, those charged with applying it have a discretion, meaning that they must make their own determination, their own choice, as to what is to be done in such cases.[7] Where that choice is then treated as settling the question of what the rule requires not just for this case but for future cases, it adds to that rule, making the indeterminate rule

[6] HLA Hart, *The Concept of Law* (3rd edn, OUP 2012) 123, 251.

[7] ibid 127–29. Saying that the decision maker has a choice doesn't entail that it is a choice between equals and so doesn't imply that there are no considerations which make one choice better (more just, more reasonable) than others. The existence of discretion signals not the reasonableness of all available options but that responsibility for assessing their reasonableness is for the decision maker.

more determinate. When judges do this with legal rules, they make law. So, say, 'No vehicles in the park' is a rule of law and a court must determine whether this prohibits the use of wheelchairs. Looking to the ordinary meaning of the words provides no answer. Wheelchairs could, but need not, be described as 'vehicles'; neither conclusion would involve an abuse of language. Of course, the law has rules of interpretation to assist in such cases, but these rules, like all rules of law, will have their own indeterminacies and may in any case be designed so as to preserve some discretion in their application. So, we might imagine that there are rules directing the judge to attend to the legislator's intentions, to the purpose of having such a rule and to the broader framework of laws, and of their supporting principles and policies, into which the rule must fit. Imagine, however, that the legislator never considered how the rule should apply in such cases, that the goal of the rule—say, to ensure that the park remains peaceful and safe for those using it—would be advanced in some degree if the rule extended to wheelchairs but would not be significantly compromised if it didn't, that no disability legislation exists which would render a ban on wheelchairs unlawful, and so on.

In such a case, the judge can only consider the alternative solutions on their merits and choose.[8] Once a solution has been chosen—say, that the prohibition does not extend to wheelchairs—it becomes incorporated into the rule and the gap that hitherto existed is filled. Now judges called on to apply the rule in such cases aren't confronted with the choice this judge faced: the correct application of the rule to wheelchairs is settled. In this way, the sort of discretion the judge exercises here is self-exhausting. That discretion empowers the judge to fix the content of the rule in the case before him and in all materially like cases. Once he's made his choice and its relevant content has been fixed, that discretion is spent. No doubt, other questions, and so other choices, remain. No decision or combination of decisions can make the rule fully determinate. We may now know that the prohibition doesn't extend to wheelchairs, but it may not be clear whether a particular object is properly classed as a wheelchair. Even if we are clear about what counts as a wheelchair, what about mobility scooters? Moreover, laws can be changed, and so questions settled in previous decisions may later be reopened. It may be decided that the prohibition should be extended to wheelchairs after all. Nonetheless, unless and until the rule is amended in the exercise of some such law-changing discretion, a judge called on to apply the rule to wheelchair users has no choice to make.

Neither of these cases of judicial lawmaking are cases of equity. In cases of indeterminacy, the problem is not that the law gives an unjust answer but that it gives none. In the case of badly framed rules, the problem is injustice, but this injustice isn't attributable to the rule's generality. In each, the problem can be resolved by the adoption of a new, or newly determinate, general rule. But it appears that this can't be the solution to the distinctive problem of injustice to which equity responds. The cases which call

[8] No doubt, the division between discerning a rule's content as settled by previous determinations and giving it content where it is indeterminate will often be unclear and, given the scope of judicial lawmaking powers, it may be unnecessary in practice to identify where one ends and the other begins. As such, we can see why it is common and, in the main, harmless to see both described as going to the correct interpretation of the rule. Nonetheless, the division exists.

for equity are those in which it is impossible to frame a general rule which will be 'correct'. If so, we don't have the option of adopting some alternative rule which will avoid injustice: any rule which does justice in this case will only do new injustice elsewhere. It follows that it is a mistake to seek to abstract from the just rulings that equity gives in individual cases to just rules of general application. (If we *can* generalize the exercise of 'equitable' discretion in this case into a new and improved rule to be applied in other cases too, the problem is revealed not to be with the *generality* of the rule after all.) Instead the result of the exercise of equitable discretion is that the rule remains in place, unchanged and unqualified, for the resolution of all future cases, the equitable determination not to apply that rule in this instance settling nothing but the case at hand.

On this view, equity offers a brand of particularism, one which rejects the idea that just rulings in individual cases can always be generalized into just rules for other cases. Should we reject this idea? It is commonly thought that a central tenet or aspect of justice is that like cases are treated alike. The idea of treating like cases alike presupposes, however, that we can generalize from individual cases to classes of non-identical but nonetheless materially like cases, which then merit the like treatment that a general rule providing that cases of *this* kind fall to be dealt with in *this* way would accord. This is what grounds Hart's suggestion that there is, 'in the bare notion of applying a general rule of law, the germ at least of justice'.[9] Some read this as claiming that some measure of justice is done whenever general rules are regularly applied. So understood, the claim looks implausible: there are bad, unjust rules and why think that the injustice of these rules is lessened by their regular application? But the better reading is not that there is justice, or even a potential for justice, in all general rules but that there can be no justice without them; the commitment to generalizability—to treating like cases alike—which rules represent a necessary, though by itself plainly insufficient, condition for justice.

This idea is, at the least, implicit in much of the way we reason and think about reasons. Suppose I ought to pay you £100, or that a court ought to order me to pay you £100. If we ask why, we might pick out some aspect of our case which supports this conclusion: say I promised you £100. Now, the promise I made to you is, in a sense, unique. Even if the express terms of my promise match promises I or others have made before or may make again, the full circumstances of this promise repeat no previous promise and will themselves never be repeated. No two cases are in all respects identical. In

[9] Hart (n 6) 206, see also 161. cf Frederick Schauer, *Playing by the Rules: A Philosophical Examination of Rule-Based Decision-Making in Law and in Life* (OUP 1991) 136–37: 'When we entrench a generalization [through a rule] ... we do not further the aim of treating like cases alike. On the contrary, it is *particularism* that recognizes relevant unalikeness, drawing all the distinctions some substantive justification indicates ought to be drawn. And it is particularistic rather than rule-based decision-making that recognizes all relevant similarities.' For Schauer, however, particularism is marked simply by its attention to particulars not by a rejection of the generalizability of those particulars and the judgements they support. In turn, his understanding of rules is limited to what one might call rule-formulations—rules as in fact posited and understood by rule-makers and rule-addressees—and which are then treated as entrenched, so as not to be malleable to their background justifications. As such, Schauer's account simply excludes, rules out, rules of morality or justice. The concept of a rule I am using here isn't tied to this, or any such, style of real-world decision-making but instead identifies a distinct kind of norm: conclusive (or would-be conclusive) norms of general application (for this idea of a rule, see Ronald Dworkin, *Taking Rights Seriously* (Harvard UP 1977) 24–25.) For what it's worth, I think that it is this concept of a rule which tends to be assumed in most talk of common law rules.

identifying my promise as the reason that I should pay you, or as the reason a court should order me to pay you, we therefore isolate one feature of our case as salient over countless others: that I made the promise on Monday, that today is Wednesday, that it's raining, that a bad paper on land registration is being given downstairs ... Moreover, I can be sure that it is only some of these facts which determine what I should do even when unsure exactly which ones do or why they do: is it my act of promising? Your understanding of the promise? How you acted on it? That few of the facts of any individual case have any bearing on the normative questions which arise from them is what enables us to identify cases which are factually non-identical as nonetheless materially alike. It means too that the questions of justice and reasonableness which arise in individual cases are far more likely to be not simply repeatable but repeated.

More than this: the fact of my promise to pay you £100 provides a reason for me to pay you £100 only with the support of some additional, evaluative premise, one which identifies some good promoted or value served by my keeping this promise. By identifying my promise as the reason I should pay you, we imply some such good. It doesn't tell us what this good is. Perhaps there are diverse reasons for keeping promises, each applicable to some promises but not to others. Perhaps there are stronger reasons for keeping some promises than others. Nonetheless, for all the diverse views on the morality of promise-keeping and the normative differences that may exist between different promises, we don't think that the reason for keeping my promise now is unique to *this* promise and all its particulars: that the good of me keeping this promise to you is the distinct good of keeping a promise to pay £100, made by the author of this chapter, on a Monday ... Instead the reason I should keep this promise is a reason for me to keep at least some other promises and for you to keep at least some of yours. Indeed, the existence of some such general reason is implied, when, in response to an inquiry into reasons, we describe the salient facts as an instance of the act-type 'making a promise', rather than some unqualified, and endless, list of these particulars, or as an instance of some other act-type ('uttering an eight-word sentence', 'making a noise').

Other cases are more complex. Many moral questions involve a blend of diverse considerations, differing in force and direction. The idea that moral judgements are always generalizable doesn't presuppose that we will in fact find other cases in which the applicable reasons recur in the same combination and in the same measures. It means only that our judgement on these facts is justified on reasons which apply generally, such that our judgement here is a judgement as to how these reasons balance out *in every case like this.*[10] If the material facts of this case were repeated, they would accordingly

[10] See Neil MacCormick, *Rhetoric and the Rule of Law: A Theory of Legal Reasoning* (OUP 2005) 91, 97–100. Sometimes the balance of reasons leaves us with a range of options, each no better than the others. Here the broader point about the generalizability of reasons and the maxim that like cases be treated alike come apart. Generalizability says only that if there is a range of options open to us on these facts, the same will be true in all like cases. The like cases maxim directs that, once we've chosen between those options, we should make the same choice in all like cases. But it's not clear why this should be, unless the choice made in the first case supplies an additional, and decisive, consideration which bears on the choice faced in other cases. And, if it does, it is no longer true to say that the balance of reasons leaves us with a range of options. For discussion, see Andrei Marmor, 'Should Like Cases Be Treated Alike?' (2005) 11 Legal Theory 27.

merit the same conclusion; any differing conclusion in a superficially similar case must be attributable to a material difference in the facts of the two cases, a difference which is likewise generalizable and which likewise represents some difference in the general reasons applicable to these cases and/or in their operation. The idea that all conclusions in individual cases are generalizable in this way doesn't require that we are able to offer determinate formulations of the general rules they instantiate. Not all rules are bright-line. That judgements in individual cases can be generalized into rules doesn't mean that, when judging, we must be following or applying some such rule. In deciding that this is what I should do here, I may be committing to the idea that this is also what I should do *in cases like this*. But I don't need to have any firm grasp of, or indeed given any thought to, what counts as a case like this, and so I will often have no general rule in mind.

I haven't sought to establish the generalizability of individual moral judgements here so much as to bring out what it is that this sort of generalism claims. If that claim looks pretty thin, it highlights what the stakes are for those who wish to endorse an understanding of equity opposed to it. For this thin idea of generalizability is enough to suggest that the problem of unjust rules is never their generality—never, that is, that there is no general truth about the matters these rules address—but always the specific content they have been given. And, if this is true, the solution is not equity's solution of simply disapplying the rule where it would do injustice but rather to use such cases to help flesh out a new and improved general rule. It is in any event clear, I think, that there is little, if any, evidence of this sort of equity in modern Equity. Though it is common for Equity to be presented as distinctively discretionary in its operation, in contrast to the common law's reliance on rules, Equity, as much as the common law, shows, and frequently expresses, an unqualified commitment to the idea that rulings in individual cases are to be made and justified by reference to rulings in other cases and to norms of general application and, with it, a commitment to treating like case alike.

III. Making Just Laws

I'll say no more about this reading Aristotle's account of equity and, from here on, will simply assume that moral judgements in individual cases are indeed generalizable in the way I have described. Instead, I want to focus on an alternative reading, one suggested by the sole example of equity Aristotle gave.[11] A rule penalizes assaults with weapons. I strike you, while wearing a ring on my finger.[12] My case is captured by the rule but, for Aristotle, it would be inappropriate—unjust—were it to be applied here. Equity sees that it isn't. Now, the point of this example can't be to show that it is impossible to make

[11] Aristotle, *Rhetoric*, I.13, 1374a32–b2.

[12] Shiner describes the relevant example as involving 'a person who brushes past another while wearing a finger-ring', making the application of the rule potentially inappropriate in respect of not only the identity of the 'weapon' but also the nature of the 'assault' (Roger A Shiner, 'Aristotle's Theory of Equity' (1994) 27 Loyola of Los Angeles Law Review 1245, 1252).

any general statement about whether those who hit others while wearing rings on their fingers should be penalized under a rule prohibiting assaults with weapons. On the contrary, the example assumes that the answer to such cases is clear: they shouldn't. This isn't, therefore, equity as we have been describing it. To understand what equity means here, we can start by considering where the need for this equity comes from.

We want a law which penalizes a particular class of serious assaults. Accordingly, we look for a form of words which captures the sorts of cases we want to cover, identifying a general act-type, such as 'assaults with weapons'. But language is inexact. There may be no form of words which fully and precisely captures the idea we want the rule to express. Accordingly, the terms we choose also extend to cases which don't merit the treatment the rule would give them. My striking you while I wear a ring on my finger *is*, as a matter of language, an assault with a weapon. Yet this isn't the sort of case which this rule penalizing assaults with weapons is meant to capture. Of course, if we'd been sufficiently far-sighted, we could have said so much when first framing the rule. But even if express provision were made for ring-wearers, we would only find other cases where the same basic problem arose. What if I hit you while wearing a glove? Or while holding my shopping list, causing you a paper cut? What if I prod you with the bread-stick which I am munching on as I traverse the agora? It may be that we could give answers—general answers, answers which would be correct in all cases of the relevant description—to all these examples. The problem is that it is, in practice, impossible to contemplate, let alone to make provision for, all such eventualities. As Aristotle put it: 'a lifetime would be too short to make out a complete list'.[13] We, therefore, end up with rules framed in general terms but which fail to do general—that is: universal—justice.

A further example of equity, illustrating a rather different problem, is given by Aquinas. The law requires the return of deposited items. Though returning deposits is ordinarily just, there are times where it would be better not to: for instance, 'if a madman were to put his sword in deposit, and demand its delivery while in a state of madness'.[14] The problem here is not, at root, a problem of language. The letter of the law, absent any express provision for such cases, suggests, no doubt, no exception for them. But this doesn't come from any mismatch between the thinking behind the rule and the language in which it is expressed. The principle the rule is designed to capture is that deposited items should be returned to their owners. The injustice, or harm, that would result from the rule's application in this instance isn't attributable to any failure of the rule to give accurate expression to this principle, or indeed to any deficiency in the principle itself. It comes instead from the fact that this principle, though sound, is sometimes overridden or defeated by additional considerations which the rule fails to accommodate.

We see a real-world illustration of this problem in a case sometimes identified as an example of courts doing equity: *Riggs v Palmer*.[15] Elmer Palmer murdered his

[13] Aristotle (n 11) 1374a34.

[14] Thomas Aquinas, *Summa Theologiae* II-II, q 120 a 1.

[15] 115 NY 506 (1889).

grandfather, Francis, so that he could secure an inheritance before Francis changed his mind. Was Elmer entitled to the property? The statutory formalities had been complied with. There was no provision in the statute excluding murderous heirs. Nonetheless the court held that Elmer didn't inherit, and justice was done. Again, this isn't the equity of the previous section. The reasons for thinking it unjust if Elmer inherited apply beyond this murder and this inheritance. If we want a rule which does justice in all such cases, we can have one: 'Murderers can't inherit', which then qualifies the statutory rules on testamentary dispositions accordingly. Nor was it a case like that of Aristotle's ring-wearing assailant, in which the language in which the relevant rule was expressed failed to capture the rule's intended meaning or purpose. Rather the problem which faced the court in *Riggs* came from the rules not accommodating, or not accommodating expressly, considerations which weighed against the sound policy of the statute, accurately expressed in those rules. So, all else equal, a testator's property *should* go to the beneficiaries named in a will which has been duly signed and witnessed. But, exceptionally, this verdict is overridden by other concerns, as it is where the beneficiary kills the testator to secure the property under the will.

Here then we see a distinct idea of equity, responding to a distinct problem or set of problems. The equity we started with rejected the idea that we can generalize from just rulings in individual cases to just rules governing a range of like cases. The idea of equity we see here, by contrast, assumes we *can* so generalize and is directed instead to the practical difficulties of formulating such rules *ex ante*. These different problems in turn invite different solutions. On the first understanding of equity, equitable rulings are a series of one-offs, settling nothing but the case at hand, precisely because there is no way to generalize, or to generalize accurately, from that case to others. This isn't true of equity in this second sense. The examples of the ring-wearing assailant and the madman seeking the return of his sword are themselves generalizations, their force comes from the evident injustice of applying the rule in such cases whatever their additional particulars. The same considerations as make it unjust to punish this ring-wearer make it unjust to punish the next. So, though the question for the court is whether the rule should be applied on *these* facts, the answer equity gives reflects the general justice of applying the rule in all like cases, the same justice which demands those like cases receive like treatment. It doesn't follow that the fact of the decision not to apply the rule in this case stands as authority for future cases. That is a matter on which different legal systems differ. But where that decision given on these particular facts is then treated as governing such like cases, we have a new rule. In these conditions, therefore, the exercise of equitable discretion is just a particular example of the exercise of lawmaking, or law-changing, discretion. What distinguishes cases of equity from other cases where judges have discretion to change the law is the reason for the change: the practical impossibility of formulating in advance a rule which does justice across the board led to the initial adoption of a rule which does occasional injustice.

We might, however, wonder whether this problem is all that common, indeed whether it need ever arise. No doubt it is often impossible to anticipate the full range of circumstances to which a rule will apply and to make just provision for them when deciding on the rule's formulation. But that's not enough to make the case for equity. The need for equity arises only if the law's response to these problems is the adoption of rules which overshoot their justifications. This is what we see in Aristotle's example: it's impossible to list all the items which we want to treat as weapons, so we formulate a rule in general terms which capture not only those items but also others which we wouldn't want to see classed as weapons for the purposes of the rule. It is only because a finger-ring *does* count as a weapon 'by the letter of the law' that we need equity to do justice in this case.

But why think that this is what the letter of the law requires? There are contexts in which we might describe a ring as a weapon. But it is also possible to understand 'weapon' in a way which excludes finger-rings. Styles and practices of legislation and rules of interpretation will differ across legal systems. If a legal system favours legislation framed in broad terms and adopts rules of interpretation which read those terms literally or expansively, with little or no scope for appeals to legislative purpose or context, we might get to the conclusion that the finger-ring is included. But it would be a curious practice to choose such an expansive approach to interpretation—for it is indeed a choice—only then to insist that interpreting rules so expansively does injustice which we can't let stand.

If we don't want a rule prohibiting assaults with weapons to end up capturing the case where I hit you while wearing a ring, we can do this without equity's help. The injustice done by rules of law having consequences the lawmaker didn't intend, indeed which no reasonable lawmaker could have intended, and which are not necessary for the rule to have its intended effect is more easily avoided by legislation which consciously leaves some questions open and by rules of interpretation which direct judges to attend to these intentions and to broader legislative purpose and context. As Hart remarked:[16]

> [W]e should not cherish, even as an ideal, the conception of a rule, so detailed that the question whether it applied or not to a particular case was always settled in advance, and never involved, at the point of actual application, a fresh choice between open alternatives.

Why? Because, as we have seen, there are necessary limits to our ability to anticipate the circumstances in which the rule may be invoked. Better then to acknowledge this and not to seek to settle all such questions blind. Adopting such an approach in Aristotle's example, the *least* likely conclusion, if we share Aristotle's assumptions about the merits, is that the rule applies determinately to treat my hitting you when wearing a ring as an assault with a weapon. Rather, we would conclude that either the rule is, in this instance, indeterminate, empowering the judge to determine how it should apply on such facts, or that the rule *does* have a determinate application here, but the answer it gives is that it doesn't cover this case. In neither event is there any need or role for equity.

[16] Hart (n 6) 128.

Indeed, this is how the court dealt with the problem raised in *Riggs*. Earl J, giving the majority judgment, accepted that, if the statutes regulating the making of wills were to be construed literally, Elmer would inherit. But this, he contended, isn't the approach the courts take:[17]

> It is a familiar canon of construction that a thing which is within the intention of the makers of a statute is as much within the statute as if it were within the letter; and a thing which is within the letter of the statute is not within the statute unless it be within the intention of the makers.

Earl J described this as 'equitable construction', explicitly tying it to Aristotle's account of equity.[18] But the approach described in this passage has no particular connection to equity. Does 'No vehicles in the park' extend to wheelchairs? Well, was the prohibition intended to apply to them? What is the purpose of the rule? We ordinarily ask questions like these not to justify some derogation from the true meaning of the statute or because we think interpreting the rule without this information would result in injustice (it may, it may not) but to determine what its meaning really is. No rule of positive law is ever wholly free of ambiguity and equity's role, as a corrective to injustice done by law, begins only once the content of the law is known. Indeed, the conclusion in *Riggs* was that the injustice of Elmer inheriting was one which the applicable legal rules, when properly construed, already avoided. Far from providing an example of judicial equity, the majority's approach in *Riggs* suggests its redundancy.

Yet we might think there is an important difference between the sort of problem raised by Aristotle's example of the rule prohibiting assaults with weapons and the problem which the court faced in *Riggs*. In Aristotle's example, the potential for injustice arises from the fact that legislative intention and legislative language come apart: the rule was only intended to capture a certain class of serious assaults, yet the language in which it is expressed is capable of extending to other cases too.[19] Here we can see how an appeal to legislative intent and purpose—to the concerns which motivated the lawmaker when formulating this rule in these terms—provides a solution. In cases like *Riggs*, however, there is no such mismatch: the statute says what the lawmaker intended it to say. Instead, the problem arises because the lawmaker, and hence the law as made, failed to take into account some consideration which weighs against the principle or policy accurately expressed in that rule. Against this backdrop, attempts to find answers in legislative intent and purpose look a recourse to fiction. So, in *Riggs*, legislative intention was invoked to justify a result which found no support in the text of the statute and which the legislature appears never to have contemplated. The conclusion that the

[17] *Riggs* (n 15) 509.

[18] ibid 510.

[19] For another, indeed better, illustration of this class of case, see the example given in *Riggs* (ibid 511): a statute in Bologna which stated that whoever drew blood in the streets would be severely punished and its possible application to a street barber who cut his client. Earlier uses of this example are found in Pufendorf (Samuel von Pufendorf, *Of the Law of Nature and Nations* (1672) V.12.8) and, replacing barber with surgeon, Blackstone (1 Bl Comm 60).

legislature didn't intend murderers to inherit was the implication of the majority's view that this is a result no legislature could have intended. Here 'the intention of the makers of the statute' slides from choices the legislature *did* make to choices it *would have* made, if only it had considered these questions. And if the conclusion as to what the legislator would have intended is itself grounded, as was the case in *Riggs*, on little more than the plain injustice of any other result, we don't look to be so far from equity after all.[20]

The picture is further complicated by three additional factors. First: laws are made not only in the knowledge that they will often require interpretation at the point of application but also against the backdrop of existing interpretative rules and practices, some of which may themselves be sourced in legislation. A legislator, enacting a statute of wills, who has given no thought to murderous heirs, may nonetheless be aware that there are likely to be questions he has failed to consider and contingencies for which the statute fails to make any, or adequate, provision. And he may, therefore, intend that the courts, when charged with applying that statute, interpret it, in keeping with judicial practice, so as to consider not only what the legislator did intend but also what he *would have* intended, or, perhaps, to seek an interpretation which is compatible with, say, certain basic principles of justice.[21] Courts may in turn conclude that, absent some express provision to the contrary, when interpreting statutes in this way, they are acting in accordance with the legislator's intentions, even if the application of the rule to which this leads them is not one the legislator can be said to have specifically intended.[22]

Second: we cannot, however, always infer from the fact that a given law sometimes does, or permits, injustice that the lawmaker would have intended it to operate differently. That the law fails to do perfect justice doesn't mean that the law is itself imperfect and not every injustice done by law is one the law should seek to avoid or correct. So, it is not only in cases of murderous heirs that testamentary formality rules may work unjustly. Formality requirements will sometimes defeat a testator's intentions, benefiting those he didn't wish to benefit, depriving those he did. Nonetheless these rules may be justified. They steer testators towards expressing their intentions more clearly and ensure that those intentions are better evidenced; disputes over wills are resolved more easily; though some testators will then find their intentions thwarted, it may be that these rules see more testamentary preferences fulfilled than if the law required no formality and instead identified testamentary intent on the balance of all possible evidence. In such cases, equitable intervention threatens to undermine choices reasonably made by law, compromising its pursuit of such goods and goals.[23]

[20] It is worth noting that the New York Court of Appeals soon departed from the approach taken in *Riggs*: see *Ellerson v Westcott* 148 NY 149 (1896). There the court held that the murderer *did* inherit but would be enjoined from enforcing the rights acquired under the statute. This approach is more clearly equitable (and indeed Equitable) in form. But the two approaches are functionally equivalent and there is no reason to think one more respectful of legislative will or supremacy, or of their supporting values, than the other.

[21] For this reason, the distinction Edelman draws (James Edelman, 'The Equity of the Statute' in this volume) between two meanings, or aspects, of the doctrine of the equity of the statute may not be as sharp as he thinks.

[22] cf *Riggs* (n 15) 511–13.

[23] A criticism that can be levelled at much of Equity's circumvention of legal formality rules.

Third: in a similar way, though there are benefits of legislative and interpretative strategies which leave more questions to be settled by courts at the point of application, there are also costs. Appeals to unspoken, or indeed imagined, legislative intent or purpose, and to the law's broader aims and commitments, are likely to bring with them greater uncertainty and unpredictability, perhaps too greater inconsistency in application. An approach which adheres more closely to literal meaning and to the purposes identified explicitly in the legislation takes us closer to the democratic ideal of laws made by elected representatives and not by judges. If this means greater injustice, it might yet be a price worth paying. And so, here too, equity, with its standing invitation to do justice on the facts, risks upsetting a broader balance the law has reasonably struck between competing goods and values.

Where does this leave us? The practical problems of lawmaking to which equity, on this understanding, is a response are real enough. But equity isn't the only solution to these problems and it is a solution needed, and indeed available, only where a legal system has failed, reasonably or not, to avail itself of other possible solutions. No legislator can anticipate the full range of circumstances in which a rule may be invoked and there will be questions which legislators cannot be expected to settle, or settle well, from their vantage point. But all the more reason, therefore, to reject any model which treats the legislator as settling all such questions in advance, leaving courts with no 'fresh choice', save to depart from the law as given. So, there is no justice done by equity which could not be done by law, no technique that equity—in contrast to Equity—provides which law could not have adopted as its own. Adopting these techniques comes, however, at a cost. A legal system may accordingly choose not to give its courts wide discretion when interpreting laws, limiting their freedom to respond justly when cases arise which the legislature failed to consider and for which it failed to make adequate provision. And so there may be justice that the law failed to do, and which equity can then secure. But, in all cases, this justice can't be done without undermining choices the law has made.

Of course, sometimes the law chooses badly, and it is sometimes reasonable to undermine, indeed to reverse, these choices. But, by this point, equity might appear to have lost much of its distinctiveness. We started with an idea of equity as a response to a specific kind of injustice: one brought about not by rules which are badly chosen but by the practical impossibility of formulating rules which do justice across the board, and so where 'the error is not in the law nor in the legislator but in the nature of the thing'. But there is no inevitability about this. The impossibility of framing rules which do perfect justice doesn't entail rules that do injustice. The operation of any given rule of law is set not only by the choice of lawmakers to adopt *this* rule expressed in *these* terms but by a series of further choices—some pre-dating the adoption of this rule, others coming only at the point of its application—which determine how this rule and others like it are to be interpreted. Any injustice that rule does is, therefore, a function not only of that framing but also of the law's interpretative rules and practices. If there is no error or deficiency in its framing, such that the rule is not itself badly chosen, any injustice resulting from that rule's application sufficient to justify equitable reversal might suggest at least some deficiency in the background rules which govern its proper interpretation.

IV. Judge-Made Law

Though Equity is a distinctive feature of English law and the jurisdictions which grew from it, it may be that it is such common law jurisdictions that have least need for equity. One reason for this is the status of judicial decisions as sources of law. A court determining that, notwithstanding the general law requiring that deposits be returned, this madman isn't entitled to the return of his sword also establishes a rule for other like cases. The next time a court is confronted with a madman wanting his sword back, it doesn't need to do equity again. It just applies the rule established in the first case. The preceding account of equity also suggests a second reason. The problem, or range of problems, to which equity responds comes where we are looking to set down a rule on a given subject matter. What we want is a good rule, one which, in its diverse applications, effectively promotes the goods and goals to which it is directed. One difficulty we face, however, is that we are not likely to be able to anticipate all of its potential applications and, if we are unable to anticipate them, we may well be unable to make adequate provision for them. However, not all law is made like this and one example of this is common law.

While common law is judge-made, the way it is made is in clear contrast to the way law is made by legislators.[24] Unlike legislation which is first made, then applied, common law is, we might say, made in its application. By this I don't mean that, within common law systems, cases provide the occasion both for the making of new law and for its first application, but that there is no stage of lawmaking prior to or independent of the court's resolution of the case on the facts. Of course, judges deciding a particular case will, rightly, consider how their decision fits within the broader system of rules already in place. This may, though it need not, lead them to consider what rule should govern cases of this kind, reasoning from their conception of the appropriate rule for such cases generally to the appropriate ruling in this case. Where they do, they may attempt to formulate that rule expressly when explaining their decision. Nonetheless the rule of law that decision then stands for need not be the rule, if any, that the judge had in mind and its content is not determined or constrained by any formulation of that rule given in his judgment. In this way, the rules of law which derive from judicial decisions are not set down or declared but should instead be considered implicit or implied.[25] This then suggests a further reason why common law systems need less equity: since judges, even when they attempt to formulate legal rules, don't make law through the

[24] For one account of the difference, in line with the argument I am sketching out here, see John Gardner, *Law as a Leap of Faith: Essays on Law in General* (OUP 2012) 74–82.

[25] ibid 77.

express formulation of authoritative rules, the problems which arise from attempts to formulate such rules don't arise in relation to judge-made law. And, since these problems don't arise in relation to judge-made law, there is, so we might think, no need—indeed no room—for the solution equity provides for these problems.

Is this argument a good one? While judicial lawmaking isn't the same as legislating and judges making law do not and need not formulate legal rules in the same way, and with the same effects, as legislators do, it may nonetheless create similar problems. So, if judge-made law is not to be identified with any judicial formulation of that law, we still face the question of how that law is to be identified. One answer to that question looks to the rule the judge's decision instantiates. Again, a judge determining what ruling would be appropriate on the facts of the case before him need have no such rule in mind. Nonetheless whatever considerations make this the appropriate ruling on these facts will also justify like rulings in like cases. This is just the same point made earlier about the generality of the reasons that bear on these decisions and hence the generalizability of decisions on particular facts. Accordingly, when determining that this is indeed the appropriate ruling here, the court cannot but be committing to this being the appropriate ruling in all like cases. In this way and in this sense, legal rulings necessarily presuppose some such general rule. What rule? The rule implied in or presupposed by that decision, with the decision encompassing not simply the end verdict but the reasoning which took the judge from the facts of the case to that verdict.

Imagine a case where the claimant seeks the return of casks of wine he had left with the defendant for safekeeping. The court holds that the wine must indeed be given up. The court's reasoning, let's suppose, is as follows: it was for the claimant, as owner, to set the terms on which the defendant received and retained the wine; the claimant didn't choose to part with the wine out and out but only to leave it with the defendant for the time being and until he requested its return; the defendant's retention of the wine was authorized, therefore, only up to the point at which the claimant asked for it to be returned; having now requested its return, the defendant ought to give it up, and, if he doesn't, the court ought to see that this is done. Now, though this case concerned wine, what matters in this line of reasoning is not that the items deposited were casks of wine but that they belonged to the claimant. So we might say that the decision stands for a rule that all items an owner deposits with someone else must be returned when the owner demands; this reflecting the reasoning that supports the return of *these* items to *this* owner on *this* occasion.

This rule is, of course, the rule Aquinas employed to illustrate the need for equity. No doubt it is, all else equal, appropriate for such items to be returned to their owners. But what if all else isn't equal? Does the rule entitle a madman to the return of his sword? Well, if that rule is the rule implicit in the initial decision, we might well think so. The reasoning of the court in that case applies here too: it is the madman's sword, he didn't intend to part with it outright, and he has now demanded its return. Of course, there *is* a good reason not to return it. But this isn't a reason we find expressed or implied in the court's decision. Little wonder: the question just didn't arise.

So we might conclude that judge-made law, no less than legislated law, calls for the sort of supplement that a judicial discretion to modify the rule at the point of application gives. This view gets further support from a popular view of how the doctrine of precedent in fact operates, a central feature of which is the power of later courts to distinguish the precedent case. On this view, the power to distinguish is a judicial power to adjust judge-made laws which overreach in this way by imposing additional restrictions on their application.[26] Moreover, this argument shows why these powers are extensive, far more extensive than other forms of judicial lawmaking power. Not only will judges deciding cases have no particular rule in mind when coming to their decision, any rule they do adopt will be adopted through the frame of the particular case and without the same opportunities to consider wider concerns and implications which are available to legislators. So, as Raz puts it:[27]

> Judge-made law is constantly subject to potential (though modest) revision on all occasions on which its application is litigated (and it can be litigated in almost all cases to which the law applies). In this sense it can be metaphorically said that judge-made law is less 'binding' than enacted law.

So, if this account of how judges make law is true, we might see the power to distinguish as equitable. Whether it is true is, in the end, a matter of a given legal system's positive laws and practices. And one lesson from the preceding discussion is that it may well be reasonable for a legal system which has a doctrine of precedent *not* to understand precedents in this way. We all agree that the sword shouldn't be returned to the madman. Why then treat the decision that a sane claimant is entitled to the return of his wine as standing for a rule that says the madman gets his sword? Distinguishing gives us a way of avoiding this result, but it is not a result which a legal system is otherwise compelled to reach. Judicial decisions, on the facts of concrete disputes, may well be effective at identifying principles which support the grant or denial of relief on such facts. But they aren't so likely to be effective at identifying considerations which don't bear on these facts, but which might elsewhere weigh against those principles. Accordingly, we might think it better to see those decisions as standing for rules which don't assume the absence of such considerations. Rather, the fact that such decisions will, as a matter of practical necessity, miss some of these considerations is reason to treat the rules established by these decisions as leaving their possible existence open. This result—one consistent with the reasoning in the precedent case—can be achieved by seeing all common law rules as subject to an implicit *ceteris paribus* qualification. So viewed, distinguishing becomes, to this extent, not a matter of revising the precedent rule but rather of filling in its gaps.

In any event, say we do take judicial decisions as standing for rules which don't operate *pro tanto* or *ceteris paribus* and which therefore need to be read down in later cases

[26] See Joseph Raz, *The Authority of Law: Essays on Law and Morality* (2nd edn, OUP 2009) 183–89.
[27] ibid 195.

which raise concerns the precedent case failed to address and which the precedent rule fails adequately to accommodate. We might now see a firmer connection between equity and Equity. Much of the need for Equity arose out of common law judges' self-denial, or their simple refusal to avail themselves, of powers to amend common law rules which worked injustice. While some of these rules were just bad rules, requiring replacement or override, others needed only qualification and refinement, the sort of refinement that comes through distinguishing. But if the power to distinguish is distinctively equitable, it is not distinctively Equitable. And so, while this might allow us to see much of Equity as equitable in its origins, the same goes for much of the common law, which has developed through the very same process of decision upon decision, refinement upon refinement. If Equity has its own distinct philosophy or values, these aren't to be found in equity.

V. Form and Substance

No legislature can hope to identify and formulate a set of rules which will secure justice across the full range of cases to which those rules are to apply. No legal system will, accordingly, be able to see that this justice is done without granting its judges some measure of discretion at the point these rules fall to be applied. This discretion can come in different varieties and can have different effects. It may be limited to cases where the applicable rules are indeterminate, or it may extend to departing from rules of determinate application. The exercise of such discretion may be treated as resolving nothing beyond the dispute at hand or it may be taken also to settle future like cases, making new law. Not all judicial discretion is equitable and the extent to which a legal system has need for equity will turn, in large measure, on the extent to which it recognizes courts as having other, non-equitable, discretions. The greater courts' powers to fix the law's content, the less need, we might expect, for discretion to correct it. The need for correction may arise simply from the law being badly chosen.

There is, in any case, no clean divide separating equitable discretion from other judicial discretionary powers. Few, if any, contingencies are wholly unforeseeable. What contingencies we might reasonably expect a lawmaker to anticipate, and hence to make just provision for when formulating a rule, is not only context-sensitive but a matter of degree. As a result, we will find no sharp division between injustices arising from rules which are badly chosen from those arising from rules which were chosen reasonably, given the limitations of the lawmaker's vantage point. Moreover, the existence of judicial discretion to adjust or to depart from these rules when unanticipated cases arise and injustice is threatened provides context to, and reflects back on the reasonableness of, these choices: a lawmaker who knows such cases can be dealt with as and when they arise has less need to seek a formulation which does justice across the board. There is, in turn, a functional equivalence between an established equitable discretion to disapply a legal rule where it would do injustice and, say, a legal rule of interpretation which, exceptionally, permits courts to appeal to justice when a rule, interpreted in the usual way, would work unjustly. The 'equitable construction' of *Riggs* is equitable in substance if not in form.

In doing equity, a court necessarily looks beyond the facts of positive law. The justice equity does is justice the law fails, or fails otherwise, to do. No doubt, the determination that the application of some rule of law would do injustice and that the court should, therefore, rule differently may be supported by appeal to choices and commitments evident elsewhere in the law. Nonetheless questions of justice are never simply a matter of the law's own internal coherence and the considerations of justice which bear on the exercise of equitable discretions aren't limited to goods and values already identified within its practices. But so much is true of all judicial discretion. Wherever such discretion exists, the judge faces a question to which the positive law provides no answer and, in giving an answer, he cannot but be guided by considerations which are, in this sense, external to law.[28] At the same time, the fact that the exercise of any such discretion takes a judge beyond the positive law doesn't mean that he is acting contrary to law. Judicial discretions, including discretions to depart from existing law, are often law-given. Common law judges exercising their powers to distinguish or overrule precedents aren't acting unlawfully. The upshot of the exercise of these discretionary powers is a *legal* ruling and, where that ruling is taken to bind other decision makers, new *law*. It is, or need be, no different when courts do equity.

The same goes for Equity. No doubt, in its origins, Equity was not law and Equitable discretion wasn't law-given. At what point the practices of Equity became sufficiently regularized and respected that Equity could be said to be (a source of) law isn't a question which can be answered with precision. But the matter was settled long before the Judicature Acts and their merger of the administration of common law and Equity. Those persuaded that Equity remains something distinct from law are, I think, too taken by the idiomatic opposition of 'law' and Equity. This looks a simple mistake. Law here is *the common law*, and Equity, it is true, is not the common law. That Equity is not the common law doesn't mean, however, that it isn't law, and indeed common law, in another sense of that term. More importantly: something doesn't cease to be law just because we call it by a different name. Equity is a body of general rules directly parasitic upon, supplementary to and contiguous with the wider system of rules which is, within such legal systems, routinely identified as 'law', a body of rules which is likewise endorsed and applied by state officials—indeed now the very same officials who administer 'the law'—likewise backed by the state's coercive machinery.

None of this means that there is nothing distinctive about Equity as a body of law. Indeed, Equity's only role was to differ from the law, every Equitable rule, every ruling a qualification or addition to the rights and duties, powers and liabilities set by the common law. That some remain uncertain of this is largely attributable to Equity's distinctive technique of supervening upon, rather than simply replacing, the applicable common law rules. So Equity does not deny the creditor who has promised not

[28] For more on this, see Charlie Webb, *Reason and Restitution: A Theory of Unjust Enrichment* (OUP 2016) 20–23; Charlie Webb, 'The Myth of the Remedial Constructive Trust' (2016) 69 CLP 353, 360–63.

to enforce the debt—a promise given without consideration but on which the debtor reasonably relied—his legal (ie, common law) right to payment but rather enjoins him from enforcing that right. This way speaking has some benefits.[29] It provides, for instance, a neat way of capturing how Equity may only postpone, or place some condition upon, any claim by the creditor. (It may also suggest that equity's intervention leaves untouched the rights and duties of the parties *inter se* but only the creditor's 'second-order' right/power to obtain an order for payment. But while there are times when it is reasonable for the law to recognize duties which it won't enforce, saying to the obligor: 'this is what you should do, but we won't make you do it', this isn't the case here, with the reasons which count against the court ordering payment also counting against the law directing or expecting payment.)[30]

Nonetheless, the upshot of Equity's intervention is, at the least, that the creditor is no longer entitled as of right to an order, here and now, that the debtor pay up. And so, wherever Equity intervenes, whatever that intervention—whether suspensory or extinctive, directed to the parties or to the court hearing their cases—the effect is a change in the parties' all-things-considered rights, duties, powers, and liabilities. Moreover, in effecting these changes, Equity's jurisdictional separation prompted distinctive corrective techniques and devices, the trust first among them. Does Equity's distinctiveness go further? Can it be said to articulate a morality, a set of principles and priorities, distinct from the common law's, advancing goods and values marginalized or ignored by the common law? It's possible. If so, Equity's true, and ongoing, distinctiveness would come not from its role as a corrective to law but from the content of its corrections. Certainly, this is a more promising line of inquiry than one which seeks to locate Equity's present-day significance in the historic jurisdictional divide from which it emerged and the various formal features of Equitable doctrine which resulted from this. Whether this line of inquiry is likely to bear such fruit is a separate question. I have my doubts. But if modern Equity has distinctive philosophical foundations, this is where they'll be found. At present, too many of those eager to establish Equity's continued significance are looking in the wrong place.

[29] But also its limitations. There is, I think, no sense in which the common law rule providing that only contracts can be set aside only where a misrepresentation is fraudulent endures in any form or degree.

[30] And so the suggestion that we need first to recognize the form of Equitable rules and rights before we can usefully consider their rationale gets things exactly wrong (see Ben McFarlane and Robert Stevens, 'What's Special about Equity? Rights about Rights' in this volume). The formal divide between common law and Equity meant that Equity was limited in what it could say and do, but not—or not in the same way—in the reasons upon which it acted. So, often, all Equity could do was to leave the common law rule formally in place but to undo its unjust consequences by denying or conditioning the enforcement of the rights it provided. But the reasons which ground that intervention needn't be so circumscribed, and so the considerations which justify denying an *assertion* of some common law right frequently justify the denial of the right itself. That Equity could not, and so did not, take this second step is not a reason for thinking that these aren't the considerations on which Equity was acting or that the injustice which Equity thereby avoided might not be better addressed more directly and completely.

2

Aristotle at the Foundations of the Law of Equity

*Dennis Klimchuk**

I. Introduction

It is a difficult question what, conceptually speaking, ties together the doctrines collected in the law of equity. One answer is: nothing, really. This view, which we might call equity nominalism, was sharply expressed in Maitland's famous claim that the best one could say is that Equity[1] is 'that body of rules administered by our English courts of justice which, were it not for the operation of the Judicature Acts, would be administered only by those courts which would be known as Courts of Equity'.[2]

Another well-known answer was given by Lord Ellesmere in *The Earl of Oxford's Case* [*Oxford*], 'the wellspring of equity in modern English law'.[3] 'The Cause why there is Chancery', Ellesmere claimed, 'is, for that Mens Actions are so divers and infinite, That it is impossible to make any general Law which may aptly meet with every particular Act, and not fail in some Circumstances'.[4] The idea is Aristotle's—'The nature of the equitable', Aristotle tells us, is 'a correction of law where it is defective owing to its universality' (*NE* 5.10, 1137b27–28)[5]—though Ellesmere does not give Aristotle credit for it. A possible source was St German's *Doctor and Student*, to which Ellesmere explicitly refers elsewhere in *Oxford*. If that is the case, then the link is doubly indirect. Aristotle's view is clearly echoed in the Doctor's description of equity:

> It is not possible to make any generall rewle of the lawe/ but that it shall fail in some case . . . And therefore to folowe the wordes of the lawe/ were in some cas both against Iustyce & the common welth: wherefor in some cases it is *good and even* necessary

* This chapter descends from another, read (via Skype) at a conference on private law and ethics at King's College London and at a meeting of the Law and Philosophy Workshop at UCLA. A later draft was read at the workshop held at King's College London for this volume. I am very grateful to these audiences for their many excellent questions, to Seana Shiffrin for her commentary at the UCLA workshop, to Ben Zipursky for his at the King's College workshop, and to James Penner, Irit Samet, Henry Smith, and Lionel Smith for years of discussion about equity.

[1] I am adopting the common convention of using 'Equity' to refer to the law of equity and 'equity' to the idea that, on some accounts, it expresses.

[2] FW Maitland, *Equity; Also, the Forms of Action at Common Law: Two Courses of Lectures* (CUP 1909). Maitland's view, Mike MacNair recently suggested, 'has become substantially the current orthodoxy'. MacNair, 'Equity and Conscience' (2007) 27 OJLS 659, 664.

[3] Gary Watt, *Equity Stirring* (Hart 2009) 67.

[4] 1 Chan Rep 1, 6; 21 ER 485, 486.

[5] This and all other quotations from the *Nicomachean Ethics* are taken from JO Urmson's revision of WD Ross's translation in Jonathan Barnes (ed), *The Complete Works of Aristotle* vol 2 (Princeton UP 1984).

Dennis Klimchuk, *Aristotle at the Foundations of the Law of Equity* In: *Philosophical Foundations of the Law of Equity*. Edited by: Dennis Klimchuk, Irit Samet, and Henry E Smith, Oxford University Press (2020).

DOI: 10.1093/oso/9780198817659.003.0003

> to leue the wordis of the lawe/ & to folowe that reason and Justyce requyreth/ & to that intent equytie is ordeyned/ that is to say to temper and myttugate the rygoure of the lawe.[6]

But St German too does not cite Aristotle, or anyone. His source seems to have been Jean Gerson.[7] But, however complex the path from Aristotle to St German[8] and from St German to Ellesmere,[9] we can fairly say that we find in *Oxford* the idea that what unifies the doctrines upheld by Chancery (and thus justifies its jurisdictional independence) is that these doctrines do equity in Aristotle's sense.

Was Ellesmere right? Is he still? That is: is Equity equitable in Aristotle's sense? My goal here is to take a preliminary step to answering this question by articulating an answer to another question we must ask first: what features must a rule or doctrine of law exhibit to be equitable in Aristotle's sense? A short answer suggests itself: it must serve to correct the law when it errs owing to its generality. But that, at least by itself, won't do. As we will see, as Aristotle explains it, the procedure by which a judge corrects for the generality of rules describes almost exactly the traditional account of 'equitable construction', an approach to statutory interpretation defended and deployed by no less a champion of the common law against Equity than Coke. The appeal to Aristotle, then, would seem to undermine rather than support the claim to the jurisprudential independence of equity and jurisdictional independence of Chancery.[10]

But this is too quick. There is more to Aristotle's account of equity—a second current, introduced in the *Nicomachean Ethics* in his characterization of the equitable person and given emphasis in his treatment of equity in the *Rhetoric*. When conjoined with the idea invoked by Ellesmere this second current narrows the scope of equity on Aristotle's account in a way that, I will argue, makes plausible his uncredited invocation of Aristotle in defence of the conceptual autonomy of Equity.

Let me clarify that my claim is not that Ellesmere had this enriched version of Aristotle's account in mind; nor, more broadly, am I making any claim about his motives or goals, which arguably were, at least among other things, political.[11] But I do mean to make the case that the outcome of the litigation of which *Oxford* was the near final chapter can be illuminatingly cast in terms of the Aristotelian model as I will reconstruct it. And I will make that case by working through Ellesmere's argument not

[6] TFT Plucknett and JL Barton (eds) *St German's Doctor and Student* (Selden Society 1974) 97.

[7] See Paul Vinogradoff, 'Reason and Conscience in Sixteenth-Century Jurisprudence' (1908) 46 LQR 373, 374–75; Zofia Rueger, 'Gerson's Concept of Equity and Christopher St. German' (1982) 3 History of Political Thought 1.

[8] Aquinas is almost certainly part of this part of the story. See Barton's introduction to *St German's Doctor and Student* (n 6) xlv–xlvi; David Ibbetson, 'A House Built on Sand: Equity in Early Modern English Law' in E Koops and WJ Zwalve (eds), *Law and Equity: Approaches in Roman Law and Common Law* (Martinus Nijhoff 2014) 55, 58.

[9] On which see Ibbetson (n 8) 62–74.

[10] As Georg Behrens argues in respect of St German's invocation of Aristotle, in 'An Early Tudor Debate on the Relation between Law and Equity' (1998) 19 Legal History 143, 158. See too MacNair (n 2) 661.

[11] The judgment in *The Earl of Oxford's Case* was a chapter in Ellesmere's and Chancery's dispute with Coke and the common law courts, itself part of a larger political story. See John Dawson, 'Coke and Ellesmere Disinterred: The Attack on the Chancery in 1616' (1941) 36 Ill L Rev 127; Charles M Gray, 'The Boundaries of the Equitable Function' (1976) 20 American Journal of Legal History 192; JH Baker, *An Introduction to English Legal History* (4th edn, Butterworths 2002) 108–109.

only because it is that text that serves as 'the wellspring of equity in modern English law', but also because doing so is particularly illuminative of the questions raised in seeking to determine what features a doctrine must exhibit to be equitable in Aristotle's sense.

I will begin by filling in the details of the generalization-correcting current of Aristotle's treatment of equity, and then show how well it is tracked in the classic formulations of the common law doctrine of equitable construction. Next, I'll return to Aristotle and fill in the missing element from his account, and then turn to consider the text of *Oxford* and the eventual conclusion of the story of which it was a part. In conclusion, I will consider what lessons may be drawn in reply to the Equity nominalist.

II. Aristotle on Equity

Equity, Aristotle tells us in the *Nicomachean Ethics* (*NE*), is a kind of justice, 'not the legally just but a correction of legal justice' (*NE* 5.10, 1137b11–12). Correction is sometimes necessary because all law is universal and, owing to its universality, can lead to error in particular cases. Legal justice, then, seems to be that justice upheld, or that can be upheld, through legislation or general legal rules.[12] Later in the same passage Aristotle says something slightly different: 'the equitable is just, and better than one kind of justice—not better than absolute justice but better than the error that arises from the absoluteness of the statement' (*NE* 5.10, 1137b25–26). Here Aristotle claims that equity is better not than legal justice but rather than what we would be led to if we upheld legal justice come what may. There is a subtle difference here. Saying that equity is a correction of, and to that extent better than, legal justice invites the thought that equity comprises a set of principles independent of any particular regime of positive legislation and to which any such regime is subject. Saying instead that equity is better than the errors to which we would be led if we upheld legal justice come what may invites the familiar idea that equity invites us to go by the spirit rather than the letter of the law, and so to realize something implicit in the positive law. Let's say that the first expresses an external account of equity and the second an internal account. Aristotle's account, I will argue, is not quite either.

For Aristotle, again, '[t]he nature of the equitable is a correction of law where it is defective owing to its universality' (*NE* 5.10, 1137b27–28). There are two possible sources of this defect. The first is the legislator. Sometimes a case arises for which the relevant legislation fails to provide an answer it could have had it been more carefully crafted. In such cases, Aristotle says, we ask what the legislator would have said had he been present, and treat that answer as law. Sometimes, however, the source of the equity-correcting defect is not in the legislator, but in the nature of the matter of practical affairs (*NE* 5.10, 1137b19). In the *Rhetoric*, Aristotle describes two circumstances in which legislators knowingly find themselves required to cast laws imperfectly. First,

[12] Aristotle seems to have legislation in mind, but he sometimes just talks about the law and in any case, nothing in his account, it seems to me, resists application to common law.

they sometimes must formulate laws 'as if that held good always which in fact only holds good usually' (*Rh* 1.13, 1374a31),[13] stipulating, for example, that borrowed goods must be returned to their owners, notwithstanding that this is not always the case (when, for example, the owner has since gone mad).[14] Second, they sometimes must choose a general term notwithstanding that its extension cannot be precisely fixed, 'such as the kinds and sizes of weapons that may be used to inflict wound—a lifetime would be too short to make out a complete list of these' (*Rh* 1.1.3, 1374a33–34). Imagine someone is accused of assault with a weapon because he was wearing a ring when he lifted his hand to strike or actually struck someone else. According to the letter of the law (the text of which Aristotle does not provide) he is guilty of assault with a weapon. But, Aristotle says, 'he is innocent really'—presumably only of the more serious wrong of assault with a weapon and not of assault *simpliciter*—'and it is equity that declares him to be so' (*Rh* 1.13 1374b1–2).

Sometimes, Aristotle argues, the indeterminacy of the object of a particular piece of legislation is such that it resists subsumption under general rules. In such cases equity requires that the judge issue a fact-specific decree, '[f]or when the thing is indefinite the rule is also indefinite, like the lead rule used in making the Lesbian moulding; the rule adapts itself to the shape of the stone and is not rigid, and so too the decree is adapted to the facts' (*EN* 5.10, 1137b29–33). In such cases no law will do. (He unfortunately does not give us an example.) The weapon example, however, does not seem to be like this. There the wrongdoer's innocence of the greater offence follows from a correct interpretation of, rather than a departure from, the law. So it seems that in at least some cases in which the equity-correcting defect arises owing to the nature of the matter of practical affairs the solution is found by asking what the legislator would say if she were there (just as it is in cases in which the problem could have been avoided by more careful legislation). This is because we can imagine the legislator to have the end of the legislation in mind. In Aristotle's example, if the aim of the law was to single out more violent assaults for more serious treatment, then we could reasonably conclude that the fact that the defendant was wearing a ring should not bring him under the provision.

We can now return to the question whether Aristotle held an external or an internal account of equity. I suggested that the answer was not quite either. Let's begin by seeing why it cannot be the second. As we saw above, in cases in which the equity-correcting defect in the law is owed to the legislator and in at least some cases in which it is owing to the nature of the matter of practical affairs the solution is to ask ourselves what the legislator would say in the present case were she asked. This sounds like an internal account. But if, as we saw Aristotle holds, what is equitable necessarily is just, we must suppose that the legislator seeks to do the kind of justice equity upholds. So 'the legislator' here is not, or not necessarily, the particular author of the particular law, because she may not in fact have sought and would not now seek to do the kind of justice equity

[13] This and all other quotations from the *Rhetoric* are taken from W Rhys Roberts's translation in Barnes (ed) (n 5).

[14] The example isn't Aristotle's (he does not give one) but rather Plato's: see *Republic* 1, 331c.

upholds. Instead, by asking what the legislator would do we must be invoking an objective standard. This is not, on the other hand, quite as external an account as I characterized it because the standard is formal rather than substantive: it takes what we can discern to be the aims of the legislation as found. In Aristotle's assault example, the judge in the particular case realizes equity not by determining what ends the law ought to pursue but rather by ensuring that the burdens imposed by and benefits realized through their pursuit fall as they ought.

Now, here is the problem with treating the account sketched to this point as comprising all of the Aristotelian account of Equity: in this account, we see in nearly all its details a kind of equity that was, at the time of *The Earl of Oxford's Case*, expressly the responsibility of common law judges to see done.

III. Equitable Construction

Especially striking for our story,[15] given that Coke wrote the King's Bench judgment in favour of the side that appeared as defendants in *Oxford*, is the fact that an often-quoted formulation of this non-Equitable sense of equity comes from Coke's first *Institute*. He writes:

> '*Equitie*' is a construction made by the judges, that cases out of the letter of a statute, yet being with the same mischiefe, or cause of making of the same, shall be within the same remedie that the statute provideth: and the reason hereof is, for that the law-makers could not possibly set downe all cases in expresse terms.[16]

Coke here echoes, and I would guess drew upon, Edmond Plowden's annotation to *Eyston v Studd*, a 1574 case in the second volume of his Reports.

Eyston, Plowden argues, illustrates the principle that 'it is not the words of the law, but the internal sense of it that make the law'.[17] He continues:

> And it often happens that when you know the letter, you know not the sense, for sometimes the sense is more confined and contracted than the letter, and sometimes it is more large and extensive. And equity, which in Latin is called equitas, enlarges or diminishes the letter according to its discretion.[18]

There are, then, two kinds of equity on Plowden's account. The first, which on his telling comes from Aristotle, diminishes the letter of law—that is, it corrects for a law's overgenerality by excepting someone who seems to be caught by it. An example is excusing a sheriff for selling perishable goods gathered from a shipwreck before a year and a day

[15] See James Edelman's contribution to this volume (Chapter 17) for more of the story of equitable construction.
[16] Sir Edward Coke, *Commentary on Littleton* 21.24.b.
[17] 2 Plowden 465, 75 ER 695.
[18] ibid.

had passed, contrary to statute. By the letter of the law, he is guilty. '[B]ut on the other hand', Plowden argues

> if we follow the sense and meaning of the Act, he has done well, and shall not be punished, for the meaning of the Act is, that such things as could be kept for a year without spoil or damage should be kept so long, but if the things are so perishable that they cannot be preserved a whole year, not perhaps two days, then it was not the intent of the makers of the Act that the sheriff should let them fall into decay, but rather than he should immediately make the most of them he could: so that although the sheriff has done contrary to the words of the law by selling the goods within a year, yet he has not broken the law, but has punctually observed it, inasmuch as he has observed the intent and meaning of the makers of the law.[19]

This sort of equity is necessary, Plowden argues, because no lawmaker can foresee all things which may happen.

The second kind of equity has the opposite effect. It extends the reach of statutes to cases not covered by their letter. Here Plowden's authority is Bracton, according to whom '[e]quity is the bringing together of things, that which desires like right in like cases and puts all like things on an equality'.[20] Plowden could have invoked Aristotle on this point as well: when Aristotle describes a legislator erring by oversimplicity, the problem he has in mind is a case outside of the letter of the law (*NE* 5.10 1137b19–24). An example (from Plowden) is a case in which a plaintiff was allowed a remedy provided by statute for someone ejected from his land when the defendant had through nuisance made the plaintiff's property unusable, on the ground that that was an effect 'in like degree' with the harm explicitly contemplated by the letter of the law.

How do we tell whether the letter of the law ought to be restrained or enlarged by equity? When interpreting a statute, Plowden writes, 'it is a good way' to ask ourselves what the lawmaker 'being an upright and reasonable man' would say.[21] Plowden, then, follows Aristotle here on every point, down to representing the legislator objectively.

Here, then, is the problem. Aristotle's account of equity has served as the basis of a particular kind of statutory interpretation, a matter squarely in the responsibility of judges of the common law. And it had done so since well before *Oxford*. Lord Ellesmere was well aware of this. In a passage of the judgment in which he emphasized the harmony between common law and Equity he wrote 'Judges themselves do play the Chancellors Parts (upon Statutes, making Construction of them according to Equity, varying from the Rules and Grounds of Law.'[22] So how does Aristotle's account of equity support the distinctiveness of claims in Equity (if it does)?

[19] 2 Plowden 466, 75 ER 697.

[20] Samuel Thorne (ed), *Bracton on the Laws and Customs of England* vol 2 (Harvard UP 1968) 25. Coke quoted the same passage following his definition of equity.

[21] 2 Plowden 468, 75 ER 699.

[22] 1 Chan Rep 13; 75 ER 488. There is no closing parenthesis in the paragraph. Ellesmere continues: 'and enlarging them [statutes] *pro bono publico*, against the Letter *and Intent* of the Makers'. I have added emphasis at the point at which his characterization of equitable construction departs from Plowden, Coke, and Hale (and, I've argued, Aristotle). I do not know whether too much should be made of this. We might imagine Ellesmere was

IV. Aristotle on Equity, Again

In *NE*, after articulating the account of equity as a corrective to the problem caused by the generality of law, Aristotle concludes that 'it is evident also from this who the equitable man is ... [he] is no stickler for justice in a bad sense but tends to take less than his share though he has the law on his side' (*NE* 5.10, 1137b28–1138a1). Here is a puzzle. According to the account to this point, equity gets the law right: the ring-wearing assailant, Aristotle tells us, 'is innocent *really*'. But here, according to Aristotle, equity asks you to take *less* than your share, though you have the law on your side.

The tension is reproduced in a passage in the *Rhetoric* in which Aristotle enumerates a series of what we might call maxims of equity. Some align with the idea that, when faced with what seems to be an error brought about by the generality of law, we ought to ask ourselves what the legislator would do were she present. For example, equity bids us, Aristotle says, 'to think less about the laws than about the man who framed them, and less about what he said than about what he meant' (*Rh* 1.13, 1374b10–11). On the other hand, equity also 'bids us remember benefits rather than injuries, and benefits received rather than benefits conferred [and] to be patient when we are wronged' (*Rh* 1.13, 1374b16–17), which sounds like advice on how not to be a stickler for justice in a bad way. How do we square these two currents in Aristotle's treatments of equity?

The first step of the solution lies in noticing that the directives issued in each have a different addressee. The injunctions from *NE* to not be a stickler for one's rights in a bad way and to not always insist on one's share though one has the law on one's side, and from the *Rhetoric* to remember benefits rather than injuries or to be patient when wronged must be addressed to a claimant rather than an arbitrator or judge. By contrast, the maxims from the *Rhetoric* that direct us to the legislator and her intentions, and the current of the *NE* account explicating the sense in which equity corrects for the generality of law, could only be addressed to an arbitrator or judge.

One might worry that there is still a tension here: how can equity at once ask that complainants be content with less than their due and enable judges to give each party exactly what they are due? The tension is resolved if we say that with 'the law' we have on our side, despite which we take less than our due, Aristotle refers to the strict letter of the law. What equity asks us to forgo is that to which legal justice, uncorrected by equity, entitles us. This suggests a way to understand the relationship between the characterization of equity as a correction to the generality of legal justice and the claim that it requires claimants to take a particular attitude towards their claims and those against whom they raise them. The *Rhetoric* example of the ring-bearing assailant illustrates one possible problem with general rules. They can be over-inclusive, and so if strictly applied can lead, for example, to the conviction of the innocent. A second possible

representing the common law judges as more activist (as we'd now say) than their own self-description would suggest, so as to make the Chancellor's interventions seem less dramatic. That would be consistent with the spirit of the surrounding passages. There is a second sense in which, according to Ellesmere, common law judges 'play the Chancellor's parts': see below, p. 41.

problem with general rules is that they can be exploited by those who are sticklers for their rights.[23] Equity, on Aristotle's account, serves to correct for this problem.

Does this solution require us to cast equity as a correction of law in favour of morality? The thought is invited by the fact that Aristotle introduces the stickler as he turns to the question of who the equitable person is. Perhaps the equitable person is someone whose virtue checks her pursuit of her legal rights. Two considerations, however, count against this interpretation. The first is that the idea that equity is a moral constraint on law casts equity as an external standard and, as we saw above, that is not Aristotle's view. The second is that, again, on Aristotle's telling, equity gets *the law* right (the ring-wearing assailant, he says, is innocent *really*).

But, while it is not a moral idea in the narrow sense in which morality is sometimes contrasted with law, there is, in a more inclusive sense of it, a distinct morality to equity as it bears on the stickler in a bad way—a distinct normative structure, implied by the very idea of being a stickler for one's rights. A stickler stands on her rights, the boundaries of which she therefore must be understood to get correct. She acts intra vires, within, but in abuse of, right. Two important points follow from this. First, on Aristotle's account, equity in this setting therefore operates as a second-order constraint on the exercise of the stickler's first-order legal rights.[24] What equity makes more precise here is not the boundaries of the defendant's rights but rather the conditions under which in which she is entitled to exercise them. Second, for the distinctive normative structure to obtain in any particular case, there must be some compelling reason to find that the rights on which the stickler stands are cast at the right level of generality. If the problem is, in Aristotle's terms, in the (actual) legislator's imprecision rather than in the matter of practical affairs, then it can be resolved at the first order, by reformulating the law.[25] The result would be that the stickler would be revealed to be an ordinary wrongdoer, someone who acts simply outside of right, rather than within but in abuse of it.

So, in sum: there are two currents in Aristotle's account of equity. In the first we can find the conceptual structure of the common law doctrine of equitable construction. Here equity seeks to clarify the law despite its letter, which misleads (or fails to prevent misreadings) owing either to the legislator's imprecision or to the matter of practical affairs, which sometimes resists subsumption under general rules. In the second current, equity seeks to prevent the defendant from being a stickler in a bad way. Here equity must, in a sense, take and leave the law as it is found, else the defendant will turn out not to be a stickler but rather an ordinary wrongdoer. It follows that a doctrine is equitable in this second of Aristotle's senses only if the problem for which it is a solution arises for

[23] I owe this idea to Henry Smith's observation that the generality of a law might facilitate its opportunistic exploitation. See 'An Economic Analysis of Law versus Equity' (unpublished), at 4 (n 10) and 'Equity as Second Order Law: The Problem of Opportunism' (unpublished) at 23. Many opportunists are sticklers in a bad way, and many sticklers in a bad way are opportunists, though I don't think the ideas overlap exactly.

[24] And so Aristotle anticipates a number of recent formulations of what is distinctive of equity. See for example Henry Smith, 'Equity as Second Order Law: The Problem of Opportunism' and Ben McFarlane and Robert Stevens, 'The Nature of Equitable Property' (2010) 4 J Equity 1.

[25] Though, as Henry Smith argues, ibid, and in this volume (Chapter 10), there may be pragmatic reasons for preferring a two-order structure. For example, more details can sometimes just multiply opportunities for sticking with the letter while evading the spirit of the law.

a good reason (approaching, at least, the very matter of practical affairs) and not simply owing to the legislator's imprecision. It is in this current of Aristotle's account, I will argue, that we can find the conceptual structure of the doctrine on which basis matters were settled in the plaintiffs' favour in *Oxford*.

V. *The Earl of Oxford's Case*

The facts of *Oxford* and the judicial history of the litigation to which those facts gave rise are very complex, and have been detailed elsewhere.[26] Here I will retell only what is necessary to frame the elements of the judgment that I want to consider.

The case centred on a dispute over a piece of land in London. The land had been sold by Magdalene College, Cambridge to Benedict Spinola, a merchant to whom the college was in debt, by way of an intermediate transfer to Queen Elizabeth. This contrivance aimed to avoid a statute (13 Eliz c 10) that provided that 'all leases, gifts, grants, reoffends, conveyances or estates, to be made, had, or suffered by any master and fellows of' inter alia 'any college, dean, and chapter of any cathedral or colleagiate church' to 'any person or persons, bodies politic or corporate, other than for the term of 21 years, or three lives, shall be utterly void'.[27] The thought evidently was that, the statute notwithstanding, a transfer from the Queen would grant unimpeachable title to the transferee. This, it seems, was taken to be the case in good faith by Spinola and, in turn, by Edward de Veer, the 17th Earl of Oxford, to whom he sold the land in 1580. The Earl and his tenants developed the property, building some 130 houses. One of these houses came to be leased to John Warren, by way of a number of intermediaries.

The dispute that began the litigious story started when Barnaby Goche, Master of Magdalene, claimed to lease the same land and house to John Smith. Warren brought an action of ejection against Smith. It seems his lease expired before judgment could be rendered, but the court decided the question of title anyway. In a lengthy and careful opinion, Chief Justice Coke held that the initial transfer of land was void on the grounds, among others, that it was caught by the prohibition in 13 Eliz c 10.[28] It was immaterial to whom the property was transferred: the College did not have the power to transfer it. But even setting that aside, the contrivance they deployed could have no legal effect, because, as 'the fountain of justice and common right', the Queen could not be exempted by construction from a statute that aims at the public goods of the maintenance of religion, the advancement of learning, and the sustenance of the poor.

In the meantime, Edward de Vere had died and was succeeded as Earl of Oxford by his son Henry de Vere, still a minor. The new Earl of Oxford and Thomas Wood,

[26] See Mark Fortier, 'Equity and Ideas' in Daniel Fischlin and Mark Fortier, *Royal Subjects: Essays on the Writings of James VI and I* (Wayne State UP 2002) 268–74; Mark Fortier, *The Culture of Equity in Early Modern England* (Ashgate 2005) 4–5; Watt (n 3) 67–72; and, for an especially detailed account, David Ibbetson, '*The Earl of Oxford's Case*' in Charles Mitchell and Paul Mitchell (eds), *Landmark Cases in Equity* (Hart 2012) 1–32.

[27] *The Case of the Master and Fellows of Magdalene College in Cambridge* 11 Co Rep 66b, 67a, 77 ER 1235, 1236–37.

[28] The Court also considered and rejected the argument that the transfer was saved by later statutory provisions.

another tenant dispossessed by Magdalene College, brought the case to Chancery. The defendants Goche and Smith refused to answer the bill, arguing that the initial conveyance to Spinola was void by statute. Two Masters in Chancery ordered them to appear, but they refused on grounds that, in their view, the matter was not in Chancery's jurisdiction. They were then committed to Fleet Prison for contempt.

Here is the point in the story that the text '*The Earl of Oxford's Case*' appears: on the first page Ellesmere reports that the defendants 'do now stand [in Fleet] bound over to answer their Contempts, they refusing to answer'.[29] The text does not conclude with Chancery's judgment. It is not, in fact, a judicial opinion in the typical sense, but seems rather, as David Ibbetson argues, to be a text aimed at justifying Chancery's standing to intervene in the proceedings, and to imprison Goche and Smith.[30] While Ellesmere addresses the substantive issues of the litigation, the core of *Oxford* is a defence, in principle, of the conceptual independence of Equity from the common law and so of the jurisdictional independence of Chancery. The plaintiffs did win soon after: on 6 May 1616, Ellesmere issued an injunction granting the Earl and his tenants quiet enjoyment of the land and staying all common law suits against them. I will get to that below. First, let's see how the argument of *Oxford* (that is, the document) unfolds.

It begins with a prima facie case for the Earl and his tenants. According to Ellesmere, both the law of God and Equity support the plaintiffs' claim, and nothing in law opposes it. By the Law of God (glossing Deuteronomy 28:30), 'He that builds a House ought to dwell in it; and he that plants a Vineyard ought to gather the Grapes thereof'. Here defendants claim houses and gardens they have neither built nor planted: less metaphorically, in asserting title to the disputed land they claim too the benefit of the improvements made by the Earl and his tenants. But just as the common law will not recognize a contract to be good without consideration, here Equity insists that persons in the defendants' position render quid pro quo. (This, note, is all that the plaintiffs sought, that is, to be compensated for the improvements they had made to the land. Below I will consider the conceptual significance of the distinction between this and the remedy they eventually were granted.) Against this, Ellesmere tells us, the defendants 'would silence Equity', on two grounds: they have a judgment at law and that judgment is based upon a statute. His answer to each comprises the defence of the independence of Equity for which the case is famous. I'll take them up in reverse order, because the really important work is done in the first.

Ellesmere rejects the argument that the plaintiffs' claim cannot be heard because the defendant's judgment at common law was based on a statute on two grounds. Each seeks to show that in entertaining the plaintiffs' bill, Chancery would not be disrespecting the authority of statutes any more than common law judges do. First, just five years earlier Coke had, in *Dr Bonham's Case*, declared that the common law can control acts of parliament and declare them void if they are against common right or reason.[31] Chancery

[29] 1 Chan 1, 1; ER 485.
[30] Ibbetson (n 26) 28.
[31] *Thomas Bonham v College of Physicians* (1610) 8 Co Rep 107; 77 Eng Rep 638.

was not proposing to do anything so drastic. Second, as noted above, Ellesmere claims that common law judges themselves 'play the Chancellors Parts' in taking the equitable construction of statutes to be law properly speaking.

More basic is the argument that, because the defendants have a judgment at common law, Chancery has no jurisdiction. The background is a statute, 4 Henry 4 c 22, that declared that judgments in the king's courts are final. In *Doctor and Student*, St German's student supports 4 Henry 4 c 22 on the ground that '[y]f Iugemenmtes gyen in the kynges courtes shulde be examined in the Chauncerye/*or* byfore the kyngis counceyll or in any other place/the playntyfes or demaundauntes shuld seldom come to the effecte of they suyte ... ne the lawe shulde neuer haue ende'.[32] Thus, though he did later acknowledge that Chancery did sometimes entertain suits after judgments given in common law,[33] through the character of the student in *Doctor and Student*, St German expressed the view that Chancery's jurisdiction was limited to intervening at an earlier stage.

Ellesmere begins by arguing that in the case before the court, 'upon the Matter there is no Judgment, but only a Discontinuance of the Suit, which gives no Possession'— by which he meant, as I understand it, that the Court in *Magdalene College* did not end up deciding the specific dispute before it. (He might have added that the parties in Chancery were different from those who argued before King's Bench.) Recognizing, I suspect, that the point is rather fine—*Magdalene College* did after all establish who held title to the disputed land—Ellesmere agreed to 'take it as a Judgment to all Intent' and, granting that, defend Chancery's jurisdiction nonetheless.[34]

He has two main arguments. The first is that, in revisiting a dispute after judgment has been rendered, Chancery only does something common law courts do as well, via the writ of *audita querela*: here too 'the Judges also Play the Chancellors'. The second argument engages the main conceptual point of *Oxford*: 'in this Case there is no Opposition to the Judgment; neither will the Truth or justice of the Judgment be examined in this Court, not any Circumstance depending thereupon'; nor are they in Chancery's dealings with common law judgments generally. How exactly this can be so, Ellesmere does not say, but he illustrates with an example.

It is a staple, discussed in *Doctor and Student*.[35] The defendant discharges a debt owed to the plaintiff under a bond, but either fails to secure an acquittance (a written receipt) or loses it. By common law he will be compelled to pay again, but Chancery will enjoin the creditor from seeking or, depending on the timing, enforcing a judgment. It will do so 'not for any Error or Defect in the Judgment but for the hard Conscience of

[32] Plucknett and Barton (eds) (n 6) D1 Ch 18, 107.

[33] In *A Little Treatise Concerning Writs of Subpoena*. See JA Guy (ed), *Christopher St German on Chancery and Statute* (Seldon Society 1985) 119–20. The *Little Treatise* was written in reply to *The Replication of a Serjeant at the Law of England*, itself a reply to *Doctor and Student*. See Guy (ed) 68–69 for the evidence concerning how often Chancery was used as a court of appeal.

[34] *Magdalene College* (n 27).

[35] Plucknett and Barton (eds) (n 6) D1 Ch 12, 76–79. The example is then taken up by the author of *The Replication of a Serjeant at the Law of England* and again in reply by St German in *A Little Treatise Concerning Writs of Subpoena*. See Guy (ed) (n 30) 99–100, 110–12, respectively. See Baker (n11) 331–32 on the doctrinal background to the careless debtor case.

the Party',[36] and so in exercise of the Office of the Chancellor, which 'is to correct Mens Consciences for Frauds, Breach of Trusts, Wrong and Oppressions, of what Nature soever they be, and to soften and mollify the Extremity of the Law'.[37] So, in this sense, Chancery leaves the judgment undisturbed. Acting *in personam*, Equity prevents the defendant from enforcing rights no one denies he has.

In doing so, does Equity do equity in Aristotle's sense? A key element seems easily made out: the creditor is pretty clearly a stickler for his rights in a bad way. But here there is arguably an important qualification, one that shows a link between the procedural and substantive sides of the issue before Chancery. How well Chancery's intervention in the careless debtor case can be cast as a matter of preventing someone from being a stickler in a bad way arguably depends in part on the timing of the intervention. The example serves well to illustrate a nice distinction on this point drawn by Charles M Gray. While enjoining the execution of judgments at common law seems to imply that common law courts are themselves capable of working injustices, 'enjoining a party from seeking to use the law for unjust advantage', by contrast, 'implies no more than that the common law, like any other conceivable system, is not airtight against abuse by the unscrupulous'.[38] In the latter case, Chancery's intervention is more clearly directed at the claimant—at the stickler. In the former it seems directed at least in part to the common law court as well, which seems now cast as the stickler's enabler.

Here, then, we see the sense in the worry, raised forcefully by the anonymous author of *The Replication of a Serjeant at the Law of England*, written in reply to *Doctor and Student*, that in acting as it did Chancery was *simply* contradicting the judgments of the common law courts.[39] The answer to the worry is to take seriously the idea that Equity operates at the second order: the stickler is correct about her rights; her mistake is in undertaking to enforce them.

The plausibility of this answer depends on there being some reason to find that the first-order rights are cast at the right level, that there isn't simply an error, here, on the part of the legislator in failing to carve out an exception in the careless debtor's favour. We find three main ideas, or groups of ideas, among judges and commentators then and recent historians of Equity now. The first is about evidence. Parol evidence could not be admitted against the fact of the uncancelled bond to show the debt had been paid, the arguments go, because in its form the debt was of such a 'high nature',[40] and because it would then be too insecure, too vulnerable to dishonest debtors.[41] Second, there are consequentialist considerations: though an individual debtor may have to bear the cost of the rule, it would thereby serve to encourage care in business,[42] and, in any case, 'although the truth be, that the plaintiff is paid his money, better to suffer a mischief to

[36] 1 Chan Rep 9; ER 487.

[37] 1 Chan 6–7; ER 486. For a recent treatment and defence of the place of conscience in Equity, see Irit Samet, 'What Conscience Can Do for Equity' (2012) 3 Jurisprudence 13.

[38] Gray (n 11) 193.

[39] *Replication*, Guy (ed) (n 33) 100.

[40] St German, *Little Treatise*, Guy (ed) (n 33) Ch 5 (110).

[41] St German, *Doctor and Student*, Plucknett and Barton (eds) (n 6) D1 Ch 12 (77).

[42] Gray (n 11) 220.

one man than an inconvenience to many, which would subvert the law'.[43] And, finally, there is a culpability of the debtor himself: 'it is not reasonable', the anonymous author of the *Replication* argued through the Serjeant, 'that for a particular mannes cause, whiche hathh hurte hym self by his owne negligence and by his owne folly, that this good commen lawe of the realme ... shulde be made voyde or sette at noughte by the suyte of any poarticuler personne may yn the chancerie or yn any other place'.[44]

So, the collective idea is that the rule is morally sound, and does good work—work it can do if only understood, in some sense, to be unqualified. But then how would Chancery, in admitting parol evidence, not *simply* be rejecting the rule? Part of the answer is that it would not be subverting it. This is what St German argues in reply to the *Replication*. Though the rule requiring an acquittance 'is goode and reasonable, and also profitable to ye common welth', the availability of a remedy in Chancery does not undo the incentive to follow the common law rule, because doing as the rule requires is still the easier path to take.[45] The rest of the answer is that even the common law judges know that the fact of payment discharges the debt in conscience.[46] The plaintiff has a claim, but it would be contrary to conscience to press it. Put another way: the rule grants a right that, at least in some circumstances,[47] only a stickler in a bad way would seek to uphold. In intervening on the debtor's behalf, Chancery would do equity in Aristotle's sense.

What about in *Oxford*? There are two questions here: would Chancery have done equity in Aristotle's sense if it had awarded the plaintiffs what they requested, and did it do equity in Aristotle's sense in awarding them what it did? I'll consider each in turn.

VI. Unjust Enrichment

The Earl's claim in *Oxford*, recall, was not for title to the disputed property but rather for the increased value represented by the improvements that he and his tenants had made to it. So cast, it sounds like a claim in unjust enrichment. Of course, the suggestion that it was so is anachronistic. Though antecedent forms of some of the legal and equitable doctrines that form its prehistory were in place, the development of unjust enrichment as a cause of action or domain of private law as such was over three hundred years in the

[43] *Waverley v Cockerel* (1542) 1 Dyer, 51b.

[44] *Replication*, Guy (ed) (n 33) 100.

[45] Gray puts the thought this way: 'If equity is permitted to undercut the [common law] rule [about acquittances and bonds], it is not because the rule is faulty by a moral standard above the law, but because it is not meant literally. The common law itself does not hold that careless people should always or even usually have to pay twice, but one that a deterrent price should be attached to carelessness. The price consists in having to bring a suit in equity, with the trouble and risk of failure and lawsuit involves; in having to sue in time or lose the chance (given the common law position in the judgements controversy); in having—one may hope, even if one is willing to leave the determination to equity—to convince the court of equity that the carelessness was in some way excusable or the hardship of double payment an undue penalty in the circumstances' ((n 11) 220). See James Penner's contribution to this volume (Chapter 3) for more on the view that we can see this kind of harmony in the early history of the relationship between the courts of common law and Equity.

[46] Guy (ed) (n 33) 111.

[47] Here's an unambiguous example: the debtor pays and receives the bond; the creditor steals it back and sues on it. The creditor would win at common law (Baker (n 11) 325).

future. Further, at the time, the candidate antecedent doctrine, the claim in *quantum meruit*, required that the defendant have requested the plaintiff to have perform some service, whose value he now seek to recover.[48] But our interest here is conceptual, and so long as we are careful to guard against errors invited by the anachronism implicit in the question, it will be illuminating to ask the question whether, if cast as a claim in unjust enrichment, the plaintiffs' claim in *Oxford* seeks that equity be done in Aristotle's sense.

We are invited to think it may well be the judgment in a pivotal case in the prehistory of unjust enrichment, *Moses v Macferlan* (1760). *Moses* concerned a claim in money had and received, which like *quantum meruit* would come to be collected under unjust enrichment. While squarely a common law action, money had and received was in the eighteenth century cast in terms strikingly similar to the way in which Ellesmere cast Equity. There is first of all the language in which it was formulated. In *Moses*, Lord Mansfield—who elsewhere called it an action 'in the nature of a bill in equity'[49]—wrote that '[i]n one word, the gist of this kind of action is, that the defendant, upon the circumstances of the case, is obliged by the ties of natural justice and equity to refund the money'.[50] More telling is Mansfield's argument that finding in the plaintiff's favour in this case is consistent with the lower court's finding in the defendant's favour. Mansfield wrote:

> The ground of this action is not, 'that the judgment was wrong:' but, 'that, (for a reason which the now plaintiff could not avail himself of against that judgment,) the defendant ought not in justice to keep the money' . . . Money may be recovered by a right and legal judgment: and yet the iniquity of keeping that money may be manifest, upon grounds which could not be used by way of defence against the judgment.[51]

The parallels with the case of the careless debtor are striking. If the plaintiff's claim in the latter can be plausibly reconstructed a claim that equity in Aristotle's sense be done, then the same analysis would apply to the action for money had and received as Mansfield reckoned it.

The reasoning, however, does not carry over to the present-day understanding of the paradigmatic case of unjust enrichment, the claim for the value of money paid under a liability mistake.[52] (We see its history here: the first example in Lord Mansfield's canonical list of cases in which the action for money had and received would lie is money paid by mistake.)[53] A liability mistake is a mistake as to one's legal obligations. P forgetfully repays a debt to D twice over, for example. Let me sharpen the example a bit and

[48] JH Baker, 'The History of Quasi-Contract in English Law' in WR Cornish, Richard Nolan, Janet Sullivan, and Graham Virgo (eds), *Restitution Past Present and Future* (Hart 1998) 42–44.

[49] *Clark v Shee* (1774) 1 Cowp 197, 199; 98 ER 1041, 1042.

[50] 2 Burr 1005, 1012; 97 ER 676, 681. Telling as well, perhaps, is the full name of the cause of action: money had and received to the use of the plaintiff. It's tempting to think this is the trust-precursor 'use'.

[51] 2 Burr 1010; 97 ER 679.

[52] In his final work on the topic, Peter Birks defined the law of unjust enrichment as 'the law of all events materially identical to the mistaken payment of a non-existent debt'. Peter Birks, *Unjust Enrichment* (2d edn, OUP 2005) 3.

[53] 2 Burr 1013; 97 ER 681.

add that the payment was by electronic bank transfer, in an amount small enough that D reasonably enough didn't notice it. There is no claim in law that P has to defeat to win recovery: that is the difference with Mansfield. But, conceptually speaking, it can be said that the distinctiveness of unjust enrichment as a ground of recovery rests on there being a sense in which P's recovery would be despite something about D's legal position post-transfer. That is that D will now have legal title to the money. So P's claim cannot lie in tort; nor can it in contract: thus, as Birks put it, there is here a *teritium quid*, a distinct ground of recovery.[54] Does the claim for recovery of the liability mistaken payment thus exhibit—if perhaps in an attenuated sense and as a conceptual matter only—the structure of a claim in equity in Aristotle's sense?

The answer depends, in part, on how compelling are the grounds on which we can say that P's claim proceeds *despite* D's title to the impugned payment. D's claim to title is in fact overdetermined. On one of its two bases, the point is nearly literally about the matter of practical affairs: there is no *thing* post-transactionally to which a claim in tort could be attached. But the outcome would be the same had P paid with paper money (as long as the notes were used as currency—that is, as fungible tokens of a medium of exchange rather than, say, as valuable collectable artefacts). That is because liability mistakes do not prevent title to money passing derivatively. The point is often drawn in contrast with mistakes as to the identity of the transferee and the identity or quantity of the subject matter of transfer, which mistakes are 'fundamental' and so prevent title from passing.[55] Is the contrast here a matter of principle? Arguably yes. Two possibilities suggest themselves. The first is that the distinction is respectful of the transferor's agency. So long as I intend to transfer *this* to *you*, it is yours to accept (on whatever conditions the transfer was made under, sale or gift for example). *Why* I chose to transfer it is another matter. Alternatively, we might say that the transferor's knowledge of the identity of the transferee and of the subject matter of the transfer is constitutive of the event's being a transfer. Her motives for undertaking the transfer are a separate matter.

If this is sound, then one feature of the liability mistaken payment in virtue of which we can say P's claim arises *despite* D's post-transaction legal position is invariant across forms of currency. Nonetheless, there is something essential to the Aristotelian account missing from the claim in unjust enrichment as it is now understood. Recall that the defendant may be utterly unaware of being in receipt of the disputed enrichment: in my example, she has received a bank transfer in an account she rarely checks, in an amount that would not trigger her suspicion.[56] She could not, therefore, be said to be a stickler for her rights in any way.

[54] Birks (n 52) 5–9.

[55] See D Fox, 'The Transfer of Legal Title to Money' (1996) RLR 60; G Virgo, *The Principles of the Law of Restitution* (OUP 1999) 607–10.

[56] You might think that she couldn't at that point be liable, either on point of principle ('ought' implies 'can') or doctrine (the defence of change of position). I address this worry in 'What Kind of Defence Is Change of Position?' in A Dyson, J Goudkamp, and F Wilmot-Smith (eds), *Defences in Unjust Enrichment* 76–78 (Hart 2016).

VII. Proprietary Estoppel

Recall that in the end the plaintiffs in *Oxford* were not awarded the value of the improvements that they had made to the land (ownership of which, again, the King's Bench held had remained with Magdalene College all along). Instead Ellesmere issued an injunction that the Earl and his tenants have quiet enjoyment of the land and that all suits at common law be stayed. We can't understand this as a remedy for unjust enrichment, because it awards more than restitution would require. It is instead a remedial response to different element of the facts. Here is how Ellesmere describes the situation at the beginning of *Oxford*: 'This Conveyance having been in Peace forty Years, and thus advanced by the Purchasers from a Thing of Little Value to a great and considerable one; and it being a general Case wherein Persons of all Degrees and Callings have made Purchases, they resting secure on its Passing thro' the Crown, the greatest Protection'.[57] The Earl and his tenants *had* improved the disputed property, but the more basic point was that the plaintiffs had relied in good faith on the representation that they had acquired rights via a transaction to which the defendants, on those terms, had unquestionably consented[58] and which had been to their benefit but that they now sought to be declared void.

It was on this basis, in effect that the College was estopped from reclaiming its land, that Ellesmere eventually granted the injunction in the defendant's favour.[59] Indeed, while celebrated as a case concerning the relationship between law and equity, *Oxford* is also an important case in the history of estoppel, in particular proprietary estoppel.[60] So reckoned, I will argue, we can see the Aristotelian account of equity expressed in Chancery's judgment, bearing out Ellesmere's uncredited invocation of Aristotle at the opening of his argument.

Now, the claim that *Oxford* was a case of proprietary estoppel requires qualification on more than one count. To begin, it is no less anachronistic than would be casting it as a case of unjust enrichment, and in just the same way. The idea that there is such a thing as a claim in proprietary estoppel is relatively new; Ben McFarlane begins his recent authoritative treatment of the law of proprietary estoppel by remarking that '[f]ifty years ago, the term "proprietary estoppel" was essentially unknown'.[61] But, as with 'unjust enrichment' as we now use it, 'proprietary estoppel' names a set of principles and doctrines that pre-date its present assemblage by, in some cases, hundreds of years—and

[57] 1 Chan 1; 75 ER 485.

[58] The Earl held the land in fee farm, a form of estate by which title transferred to him but rent was due to the college, which rent they had been accepting annually.

[59] As recorded in the Chancery rolls (C 78/291 no 17), on which see Ibbetson (n 25) 26–27. The litigation continued, and the estoppel argument continued to win. See Ibbetson ibid.

[60] For example, it is invoked by counsel for the respondents in *Ramsden v Dyson* (1865) LR 129, 134, 'the foundation of proprietary estoppel' in the words of Lord Neuberger of Abbotsbury, in 'The Stuffing of Minerva's Owl? Taxonomy and Taxidermy in Equity' (2009) 68 CLJ 537, 541.

[61] Ben McFarlane, *The Law of Proprietary Estoppel* (OUP 2013) 1.

what is interesting is whether the reasoning and outcome of the case can be reconstructed as issuing from any of these doctrines or principles.

A further complication is that it is by no means settled just what proprietary estoppel consists in, what sort of relationship it bears to promissory estoppel, and indeed whether we ought to forgo this distinction, however it should be cast, in favour of a more general doctrine of equitable estoppel.[62] These issues we can set aside here, where again our interest is whether the doctrine or principle on the basis of which *Oxford* was decided was equitable in Aristotle's sense. The question is what the doctrine was, and the starting point of the current hypothesis is that it is one now found under the heading of proprietary estoppel.

On this question there seems to be some consensus. McFarlane identifies three principles collected in the present-day law of proprietary estoppel and finds in *Oxford* the operation of the first, 'estoppel by acquiescence',[63] and it is in the history of this doctrine in particular that Ibbetson places the case.[64] On McFarlane's account, estoppel by acquiescence

> applies where B adopts a particular course of conduct in reliance on a mistaken belief as to B's current rights and A, knowing both of B's belief and of the existence of A's own, inconsistent right, fails to assert that right against B. A then comes under a liability to B if B would suffer a detriment, as a result of B's reasonable reliance on that mistaken belief, were A wholly free to enforce A's right against B.[65]

But is it unambiguous that this structure fits the story of *The Earl of Oxford's Case*? I'm not sure that there was any point during which time the Earl and his tenants were developing the disputed property that anyone at the College *knew* of the existence of its inconsistent right.[66] There is good reason to believe that it would have been a lawyer's opinion at the time that the contrivance through which the College sold the disputed property to Spinola would have secured him unimpeachable title to it.[67] So the facts at least suggest that in asserting that the land was still the College's, Goche had been hoping for the best, rather asserting a bona fide belief, and things just worked out in his favour.

Perhaps *Oxford* sits more comfortably in what McFarlane calls the 'representation-based' strand of proprietary estoppel, which

> applies where A make a representation to B as to a matter of fact, or mixed fact and law, and B reasonably believes that A intends B to adopt a particular course of conduct in

[62] For, for example: Elizabeth Cooke, *The Modern Law of Estoppel* (OUP 2000); against, for example: Ben McFarlane, 'Understanding Equitable Estoppel: From Metaphors to Better Laws' (2013) 66 Current Legal Problems 267.

[63] McFarlane (n 61) 3.

[64] Ibbetson (n 26) 27.

[65] McFarlane (n 61) 3.

[66] As the law seems, on the best reconstruction to require. For a review of recent cases that appear to relax the requirement of actual knowledge and an argument that they are 'inconsistent with authority and unjustifiable in principle' see McFarlane (n 61) 31–33.

[67] Ibbetson (n 26) 22.

> reliance on the truth of that representation. If B then does adopt that course of conduct and, as a result, would suffer a detriment if A were free to deny the truth of the representation, A will be precluded from doing so.[68]

The problem here, however, is that the College did quite a bit more than merely represent the disputed matter of fact and law (that it had transferred title to the disputed property). Instead its agents had gone to extraordinary lengths to effect the transfer.

Need this be settled? I don't think so. While McFarlane shows that the two principles come apart, and so there is clarity gained by distinguishing them, for present purposes I think it's enough that the facts in *Oxford* satisfy the more general statement of the basis of a claim in proprietary estoppel—one that I believe captures both of McFarlane's principles as well—articulated by Lord Neuberger. 'In very summary terms', he writes, the ingredients of proprietary estoppel are the following:

> (1) a statement of action (which can include silence or inaction) by the defendant, who ought to appreciate that the claimant will rely on it;
> (2) an act by the claimant in the reasonable belief that he has or will get an interest in land, induced by that statement or action;
> (3) consequent detriment to the claimant if the defendant is entitled to resile from the statement or action.[69]

Here (1) the College and its agents contrived to sell the disputed property to Spinola notwithstanding statutory barriers to it and subsequently received payments as per the terms of the transfer; (2) upon which basis Spinola and subsequent owners and tenants improved the property; (3) to a degree that would cause a great loss had their evictions been upheld.

So: thus understood, is the Earl's claim equitable in Aristotle's sense? To begin: were Goche and the College being sticklers in a bad way? I think so, though we need to be careful. While certainly exhibiting a kind of bad faith in its moral neighbourhood, it perhaps can't quite be said that they were sticklers in asserting that the initial transfer of the disputed land was void. In asserting title there was no right within which they were acting and on which they were standing. What made Goche a stickler was his refusal to answer the Earl's petition,[70] with the implication that the value by which the land had been improved by the Earl, his father and their tenants was a windfall in the College's favour, captured by the decision in *Magdalene College*.

So far so good. The next question is whether we can understand proprietary estoppel as serving to correct for the generality of a rule, and doing so in such a way that does

[68] McFarlane (n 61) 5.
[69] Neuberger (n 60) 538.
[70] As he evidently did right to the end. Ibbetson (n 26) 21.

not amount to simply making the rule more precise. The answer depends on which of two ways we think about the operation of proprietary estoppel. The first is as supplying a mode of the acquisition of property. So understood, estoppel might correct for something in the law (as a whole, that is, comprising common law and equity), namely its incompleteness, but not its generality. And it's not clear how there would be anything distinctly equitable in this correction: we just now add an entry to the list of modes of property acquisition.

The second way is reflected in the remedy ordered by Chancery, which again was that the Earl and his tenants have quiet enjoyment of the land and that all suits at common law be stayed. This does not so much grant rights to the plaintiff as it, rather, prevents—that is, estops—the defendant from exercising his. The remedy works at the second order: Chancery's judgment corrects the generality of the law not by refining it, but rather by spelling out a condition under which the rights it assigns cannot be exercised. Ellesmere's insistence that Equity leaves the common law undisturbed means that the judgment in effect vindicates Coke's holding in *Magdalene College* that the College's initial transfer of the disputed property was void on grounds that it was caught by the prohibition in 13 Eliz c 10. In the background of this holding are basic constitutional principles: contested, so perhaps, in one sense, more contingent than the nature of the matter of practical affairs, but foundational, nonetheless.

Thus, Lord Ellesmere's invocation of Aristotle was borne out, in the end, though perhaps for reasons he did not have in mind. In granting the relief it did on the basis on which it did, Chancery did equity in Aristotle's sense.[71]

VIII. Conclusion

On my reconstruction, it is a claim of Aristotle's account of equity that a legal system cannot get by only with a set of rules that specify the rights and duties persons hold and bear. It will also need a set of rules that constrain the manner in which and the ends for the sake of which persons exercise their rights. Chancery was, of course, not established with the end of upholding a set of rules that have the properties of this set. Its jurisdictional independence and association with equity pre-date Ellesmere's invocation of Aristotle's account in the justification of both. But this analysis shows how apt that invocation was.

The Equity nominalist certainly has at least two things right: the collection of doctrines that eventually fell within the jurisdiction of the courts of Equity is conceptually heterogeneous and it is a matter of historical contingency that the institutional division between common law and equity came to be. Nothing in the Aristotelian account,

[71] You might think the remedy was inequitable because over-generous: things would have been set well aright, one might argue, had Chancery given the Earl only what he asked for, recovery of the value of the improvements rather than in effect title to the land. But this equivocates on 'equitable': even if the Earl got more than equity required, in giving him what it did, Chancery's judgment had the form of equity in Aristotle's sense.

certainly, requires otherwise. But the Aristotelian account promises to make some sense of this complexity and contingency, at least in part, and in interesting ways. How well it delivers on that promise depends on how well the structure identified by the Aristotelian account is reflected in throughout the doctrines of Equity, an investigation into which is beyond the scope of this chapter.[72]

[72] I argue that the structure I claim to find in Aristotle's account of equity is reflected in four characteristically equitable doctrines in 'Equity and the Rule of Law' in Lisa Austin and Dennis Klimchuk (eds), *Private Law and the Rule of Law* (OUP 2014) 247–68. See Andrew Gold's contribution to this volume (Chapter 4) for an argument that sometimes equity enables sticklers, even those who are so in a bad way.

3

Equity, Justice, and Conscience

Suitors Behaving Badly?

*JE Penner**

To be a stickler for your rights in a 'bad' way does not, ipso facto, mean in an 'unjust way'.

I. The Operations of Equity

Here are two typical characterizations of the moral[1] basis for equitable intervention:

> Equity intervened where the common law rules, in particular owing to their rigidity, would give rise to injustice.
>
> Equity intervened where a party would otherwise be able to rely upon her common law rights in a such a way as to act against conscience.

Do these amount to the same thing? They do if 'acting against conscience' just is acting unjustly, acting unjustly because the rules of common law allow one to do so. This seems to be the idea lying behind equity's intervention in the case of someone who pays a debt undertaken under a covenant, but who fails to take possession of the deed, ensure it is destroyed, or get a deed of acquittance, thereby making himself liable to be sued on the debt a second time. A similar thought seems to operate where a trustee commits a breach of trust.

* I must thank Samuel Bray, Larissa Katz, Dennis Klimchuk, Irit Samet, Henry Smith, Lionel Smith, Rob Stevens, Bill Swadling, and the participants at the Philosophical Foundations of the Law of Equity conference held at King's College London, on 29 and 30 June 2017, for comments on earlier drafts. Dennis and Henry's comments on the penultimate version were of especial help. I also owe particular thanks to Peter Turner for extensive comments on a first draft. I regret that I was unable to explore all the interesting avenues for further investigation he suggested which, had I been able to pursue them, would undoubtedly have enriched what you have before you. And made it considerably longer.

[1] I am adopting the standard Razian/Gardnerian line that in so far as the law's demands are legitimate, this is so because they are morally legitimate. To put this another way, law has whatever genuine normativity it has only in so far as it embodies moral as opposed to, say, aesthetic normativity; the standards by which we evaluate the legitimacy of legal norms are moral standards not, say, aesthetic standards. For a recent elaboration of this view in the context of private law, see John Gardner, 'Private Authority in Ripstein's *Private Wrongs*' (2016) 14 Jerusalem Review of Legal Studies 52. Justice is one moral criterion (albeit a central one), amongst others, with which the law can comply.

JE Penner, *Equity, Justice, and Conscience* In: *Philosophical Foundations of the Law of Equity*. Edited by: Dennis Klimchuk, Irit Samet, and Henry E Smith, Oxford University Press (2020).
DOI: 10.1093/oso/9780198817659.003.0004

> [T]he growing strength of the substantive law could also work injustice, because the judges preferred to suffer hardship in individual cases than to make exceptions to clear rules. The stock example was that of the debtor who gave his creditor a sealed bond [a formal paper document recording the obligation to pay the debt], but did not ensure that it was cancelled when he paid up. The law regarded the bond as incontrovertible evidence of the debt, and so payment was no defence. Here the debtor would suffer an obvious hardship if he was made to pay twice; but the mischief was a result of his own foolishness, and the law did not bend to protect fools ... Again, if someone granted land to others on trust to carry out his wishes, he would find that at law the grantees were absolute owners who could not be compelled to obey him. *Now it was not that the common law held that a debt was due twice, or that a promise or trust could be broken; such propositions would have been dismissed as absurd.* Yet those were the results which followed from observing strict rules of evidence, rules which might exclude the merits of the case from consideration but which could not be relaxed without destroying certainty and condoning carelessness.[2]

In cases such as this, it would seem that equity took no different view about the justice of the case than would a court of common law vis-à-vis *the justice as between the parties*. The difference was that, for the reasons stated, the common law refused to intervene to make exceptions to its rules for fear that the rules would become too complicated and uncertain.

The case of the trust is particularly instructive. Enforcing trusts is not a good example of equity's doing anything other than regular justice, that is applying the principle of *pacta sunt servanda*.[3] Trusts are voluntarily undertaken obligations and in that respect are no different from obligations under the law of covenants or the general law of contract. At the time Chancery started enforcing uses it was clear to all parties concerned that uses would not, and should not, be enforced at common law. It is sometimes thought, and taught, that this failure of the common law to recognize the use is indicative of the harshness or rigidity of the common law, a harshness and rigidity so severe that it would deprive A, his wife, and their children of their rights in land, thwarting the clear agreement between A and X, Y, and Z, his feoffees to use. But this is a profound misunderstanding. The common law's blindness to the use was essential

[2] JH Baker, *An Introduction to English Legal History* (4th edn, OUP 2002) 102–03 (emphasis added). For a statement of the principle in a case, see *Waberley v Cockerel* (1542) 1 Dyer 51a. I thank Dennis Klimchuk for the reference.

[3] Lionel Smith (this volume, Chapter 7), places great weight on the idea that equity specifically *enforced* obligations, while the common law, because of its standard remedy of money damages, typically allowed a defendant to escape her obligations by breaching them (and thus becoming liable to an award of damages, of course). I agree with Smith that this is a very important feature of equity, in particular concerning the nature of trusts. The point I am making in the text is that this doesn't, to my mind, reveal a different idea about what a voluntarily undertaken obligation *is*. This would only be so if the common law actually adopted the Holmesian 'bad man' view of the law, ie that an obligation amounted to an option to perform or pay damages. Leaving Holmes aside, this is not the way a typical common law judge (or academic) understands contractual obligations. For discussion, see Daniel Friedmann, 'The Performance Interest in Contract Damages' (1995) 111 Law Quarterly Review 628; JE Penner, 'The Beneficiary's Performance Interest in a Trust: AIB v. Redler and the *March of the Compensatory Principle*' in Kelvin Low, Richard Nolan, and Hang Wu Tang (eds), *Trusts and Modern Wealth Management* (CUP 2018) 277.

for the benefits of the use to be achieved.[4] It was only because the cestuis que use had no recognized common legal title to or other common law legal interest in the land that the various schemes to avoid the incidents of feudal landholding would work. If the common law had recognized in the use a new kind of legal estate,[5] then it would not have put the cestuis's interests in the land beyond the reach of the very legal rules that the use was engineered to avoid. It was the very rigidity of the common law in refusing to recognize a new legal estate in the use that made the use effective.

The problem of enforcing uses against legal title holders was a real, but secondary, problem, which appears to have been met differently as time went on,[6] before the Chancellor's jurisdiction became the normal, then exclusive, means of enforcement, ultimately leading to the rules governing uses, now trusts, that make up such a large part of equity doctrine.

It is important, therefore, to make clear that at the time the use originated, the feoffor to uses could not be anything other than a 'legal risk'-taker. He had to really trust his feoffees to use. By the way, even today settlors are often 'legal risk'-takers vis-à-vis their trustees. Consider this description by Lord Hoffmann of a typical offshore trust:[7]

> It was a typical offshore trust and since a number of these trusts feature in these proceedings, it may be useful to describe their general characteristics. The named settlor is usually a stranger to the transaction who has been requested to lend his name to a document which records (in many cases truthfully) that he has provided a nominal sum as the initial trust fund.... The name of the person providing the assets subsequently added to the fund, whom I may call 'the real settlor', does not appear..... The trustees are given a wide discretion to pay income and capital to the beneficiaries, but the persons actually contemplated as beneficiaries are not necessarily named in the document. Instead, a local charity or some other person will be named and the trustee given a discretionary power to add to the list of beneficiaries.... Sometimes the trustee will be given a 'letter of wishes' by the real settlor saying whom he wishes to benefit. Sometimes the real beneficiary, who may be the real settlor himself, will remain a matter of oral understanding between him and the trustee. These trusts therefore reveal very little *and depend upon trust and confidence reposed in the trustee to give effect to expectations and understandings which may not be legally enforceable*. The business of providing offshore financial services requires a reputation for probity, efficiency and discretion in executing such trusts in accordance with the confidential wishes of clients.[8]

[4] As Baker ((n 2) 249–50) points out, a feoffor *could* have embodied the form of the trust into the feoffment itself by way of condition, but the rules governing conditions would have defeated the purpose of the exercise.

[5] Which would have, roughly, had the effect that the Statute of Uses 1536 actually had in the case of most uses.

[6] Baker (n 2) 250, mentions the case of feoffees to uses who were excommunicated by an ecclesiastical court for breach of use.

[7] *Re T R Technology Investment Trust plc* [1998] BCLC 256, 263–64 (emphasis added).

[8] See also *Schmidt v Rosewood Trust Ltd* [2003] 2 AC 709, 724, [36] per Lord Walker:

> The Board have to consider what rights or claims to disclosure the appellant has, either personally or as his father's personal representative, under two badly drafted settlements whose terms have been

Moreover, common law judges might well have been perfectly at ease with the unhappy common law litigant's having to resort to equity. As Gray says[9]

> it is a good rule that a sealed bond can only be defeated by a sealed acquittance, for the rule will encourage care in business and diminish factual controversies about whether debts have been paid. If equity is permitted to undercut the rule, it is not because the rule is faulty by a moral standard above the law, but because it is not meant literally. The common law itself does not hold that careless people should always or even usually have to pay twice, but only that a deterrent price should be attached to carelessness. The price consists in having to bring a suit in equity, with the trouble and risk of failure any lawsuit involves; in having to sue [in equity] in time or lose the chance [ie, at the time, sue before common law judgment was given ordering payment of the debt a second time];[10] in having—one may hope, even if one is willing to leave the determination to equity—to convince the court of equity that the carelessness was in some way excusable or the hardship of double payment an undue penalty in the circumstances.

The thought that the law allows individuals to 'do it the easy way', such as comply with the rules about formalities, or 'do it the hard way', having to go to court and engage in a time-consuming and inefficient exploration of all the circumstances, should be given more prominence today than I think it generally has. I think the treatment of informal trusts of the family home[11] and the application of the *Re Rose*[12] principle[13] very much gives rise to just the sort of uncertainty, and consequent likelihood of a need to resort to litigation, which in practice does amount to a penalty for failing to comply with clear rules about property transactions.

The takeaway point at this juncture is simply that the law has more concerns than doing justice, or perfect justice, as between the parties. Other values come into play, in particular 'rule of law' values which also shape the structure of laws, some of which, at least, may have the consequence of excluding, or diminishing, the justice that can be

> moulded by the sort of influences mentioned above. One possible reaction would be that Mr. Schmidt and his colleagues have made their bed and they must lie on it; if they have deliberately entered into a web of camouflage, it is hardly for anyone claiming through them to complain that the position is not transparent. As Lord Greene MR observed, giving the judgment of the court in *Lord Howard de Walden v Inland Revenue Comrs* [1942] 1 KB 389, 397 if a taxpayer plays with fire it scarcely lies in his mouth to complain of burnt fingers.

[9] Charles M Gray, 'The Boundaries of the Equitable Function' (1976) 20 American Journal of Legal History 192, 220.

[10] As Gray, ibid, explores in detail, the crux of the issue in the controversy between Lord Coke and the Chancery was whether the Chancery could issue injunctions restraining a successful common law litigant from enforcing a common law judgment *after* final judgment was given in the common law courts. The common law judges led by Coke did not object to, or at least accepted, Chancery's right to issue 'common injunctions' restraining common law litigants from initiating or pursuing actions at common law. What Coke objected to was litigants who did not act in a timely fashion to stop the common law process, and who sought to restrain successful litigants at common law after final judgment, ie after the losing party had allowed the full common law process to have been completed. See also Baker (n 2) 108–09.

[11] See, eg, *Stack v Dowden* [2007] UKHL 17; *Kernott v Jones* [2011] UKSC 53.

[12] [1952] Ch 499.

[13] See, eg, *Pennington v Waine* [2002] EWCA Civ 277.

done as between the parties.[14] To the extent that the common law's concern with certainty can be seen as an element of the rule of law virtues of 'clarity' and 'prospectivity', which I think it can,[15] then certainty itself has a moral value, albeit a moral value that constrains as between the legal system and the individual, not individuals qua subjects of a legal system inter se. This leads us to enquire whether equitable intervention is really just a matter of a different balancing of the values underlying justice as between the parties versus 'rule of law' values, than the balancing undertaken by the common law (or, indeed, by statute).

In light of these preliminary considerations, I am going to consider whether there are other grounds for holding that equity has, at least in some cases, a different moral criterion for taking action than does the common law, one perhaps based upon 'conscience'. I will pursue this from several different angles. I shall consider the 'equitable' maxims; I shall consider Aristotle's notion of equity; I shall consider a Kantian 'doctrine of virtue' spin on the issue. But first I want to consider Meagher, Gummow, and Lehane's[16] Part 1, 'The Background of Equity'.

II. Meagher, Gummow, and Lehane: Fusionism versus Abstractionism

I have been reading through the several prefaces of MGL and the first part of the book, 'The Background of Equity'. MGL is famously an anti-fusionist or 'equity purist' tract,[17] so I approached these pages with a somewhat wary fascination, given that I have long thought of myself as an equity pragmatist and fusionist. What do I take being a fusionist to mean? By that I mean that the law should more or less use all of the intellectual resources at its disposal to iron out apparent inconsistencies, in particular inconsistencies arising from the path-dependent development of legal doctrine in different, though related, areas of the law, inconsistencies which lead to like cases not being decided alike. Because of the obvious path dependence of the development of legal doctrine, I am naturally suspicious of the idea that the historical provenance of a doctrine is itself a reason for keeping that doctrine in some way immune or insulated from rational investigation. But although MGL place weight on historical origins, there is nothing, so far as I can tell, in these pages to suggest that the equitable doctrines reflect some different orientation towards justice than do common law doctrines. MGL's chief concern

[14] For two explorations of the relationship between rule-of-law values and equity, see Henry E Smith, 'Property, Equity, and the Rule of Law' in Lisa M Austin and Dennis Klimchuk (eds), *Private Law and the Rule of Law* (OUP 2014) 224; Dennis Klimchuk, 'Equity and the Rule of Law' in Lisa M Austin and Dennis Klimchuk (eds), *Private Law and the Rule of Law* (OUP 2014) 247.

[15] See, eg, John Gardner, *Law as a Leap of Faith* (OUP 2012) 199–201.

[16] JD Heydon, MJ Leeming, and PG Turner, *Meagher, Gummow & Lehane's Equity: Doctrines & Remedies* (5th edn, LexisNexis Butterworths 2015) (hereafter MGL; all such citations are to this, the fifth, edition).

[17] Lionel D Smith, 'Book Review of Equitable Damages by Peter M McDermott; Equity: Issues and Trends by Malcom Cope, ed; Commercial Equity: Fiduciary Relationships by John Glover' (1996) 75 Canadian Bar Review 388, 388–90, discussing the second edition of *Meagher, Gummow & Lehane*. For a somewhat less bleak purist view, see MGL, [2-325]–[2-400].

is to show that the Judicature Acts did not suggest that there should be some collapse of different legal and equitable doctrines on the basis that merely analogous elements between them should lead judges to move to higher levels of abstraction so as, for instance, to gather all examples of 'civil wrongs' in some overarching category such that genuinely different legal doctrines should be simplified and generalized. With that sentiment I find myself in entire agreement.

At certain places MGL seem to suggest that there is some kind of moral, intellectual perspective which is native, or proprietary, to equity. Kitto's foreword to the first edition states:[18]

> What is Equity? For no crisp answer will satisfy the earnest inquirer. He must be told a long story, if he has the patience to listen. He must learn how Equity emerged from the mists of the Middle Ages an amorphous and unruly thing, *and must be made to see the single bright thread running through the whole of Equity's dealing with the topics*, and for that purpose he must be taken back, as we are in the pages of this book, to the time when the Chancellors of England found themselves entrusted with a wider power of exercising the King's prerogative of administering justice between subjects than was enjoyed by the King's Judges.

Kitto does not elaborate on what that 'single bright thread' amounts to.

Here, from the 'Preface—Second Edition', we have:[19]

> The truth is, as we have endeavoured to show in the First Edition, that equity remains as vital and fruitful a source of principle as it has ever been, *because the fundamental notions of equity are universal applications of principle to continually recurring problems; they may develop but they cannot age or wither.*

Nowhere are these universal, fundamental principles of equity ever given anything like a precise formulation. Indeed, I don't find any later passages in which the topic of equity's universal, fundamental principles, is returned to.

For the most part, just as I have suggested above, MGL seem to express the same idea that given its historical path dependent origin, equity is nothing more than an assemblage of different areas of doctrine arising in those cases where equity 'glossed' the common law, to use Maitland's phrase.[20]

> [1-005] Equity can be described but not defined. It is the body of law developed by the Court of Chancery in England before 1873. Its justification was that is corrected, supplemented and amended the common law. It softened and modified many of the injustices in common law, and provided remedies where at law they were either inadequate or non-existent.

[18] MGL, v (emphasis added).
[19] ibid xv (emphasis added).
[20] FW Maitland, *Equity; Also the Forms of Action at Common Law: Two Courses of Lectures* (CUP 1910) 18–19.

> [1-010] ... its growth progressed in a haphazard ad hoc manner, never travelling on any given course or developing any clear doctrinal basis. As one writer put it:
>
> the accidents of history make equity a fragmentary thing. First one point, then another was developed, *but at no time was it the theory or the fact that equity would supplement the law at all places where it was unsatisfactory; consequently it has not been possible to erect a general theory of equity.* In the last resort, we are always reduced to a more or less disguised enunciation of the historical heads of equity jurisdiction.[21]

This fragmentary character of equity, and the idea that chancery judges and common law judges had no different ideas of justice, is supported by MGL's discussion of the early development of equity in the mediaeval period.[22]

MGL point out that at this time equitable relief was available in the many courts that existed, and was not restricted to Chancery. As they say, 'Chancery was, to a considerable extent, not dispensing really novel or unique remedies'. Other courts did the same; common law courts at the time issued injunctions, awards of specific performance, etc.[23] At this time there was common membership of the courts; common law judges, for example, regularly sat in Chancery.[24]

There then followed a formative period in which the common law courts began more and more to emphasize the certainty of rules, and this development overlapped with the 'the almost complete refusal of the courts of law to recognise that equitable rights, titles and interests entitled their holders to any relief at law'.[25] This latter refusal seems to cohere with Gray's observation, above, that the common law courts were happy with equity's discretionary[26] jurisdiction to afford relief in individual cases as a kind of penalty for failing to comply with common law rules.

In view of these considerations, the character of MGL's characterization of the 'fusion fallacy'[27] seems less to be about the idea that equity takes a particular, proprietary[28] view of what justice requires, but is rather about showing that the fusion of the administration of equity and the common law in a single high court did not give judges any 'abstractionist' marching orders. That is, it did not initiate some programme of law reform in which different doctrinal areas of law and equity were to be reassessed so as to create a reformed body of law at which higher-level abstractions such as 'unjust enrichment'

[21] MGL, 5 (emphasis added).

[22] MGL, 6 [1-020]: MGL notice that early pleas sometimes referred to conscience, others merely that there was no, or no sufficient, remedy at law.

[23] ibid 7 [1-040].

[24] ibid [1-045].

[25] ibid 24, [1-200].

[26] 'Discretionary' may not be the right word. What I mean by it here is that the Chancellor was not required to apply particular equitable rules to justify relief in the formative stages of equity; the equitable rules came later with the systemization of equity (see ibid 9 [1-070]). Rather, he was able to afford relief for any reason of justice or more broadly, any good moral reason, which seemed to arise on the facts as revealed by his personal interrogation of the parties. That is to say, 'discretionary' does not here mean 'unprincipled'.

[27] ibid 47–66.

[28] 'Proprietary' in the philosophical sense, ie a view of justice properly 'belonging' to equity which distinguishes it from the law. Not 'proprietary' in the sense of property law.

were to lead to grouping together areas of doctrine which were heretofore separate, on the basis of particular ideas about the rational reconstruction of the law. This anti-fusionist/anti-abstractionist stance seems to have nothing to do with defending some peculiar, proprietary ideas of justice entertained by equity, as opposed to different such ideas in the common law.

So, the authors say in 'Preface—Third Edition':[29]

> The invocation of general principle is all very well so long as it is done in a way which is consistent with what Sir William Deane has called 'the legitimate processes of legal reasoning': *Muschinski v Dodds* (1985) 160 CLR 583 at 615.

And in 'Equity in the Twenty-First Century':[30]

> [The] orthodoxy [of regard to the historical continuity of equity] is antithetical to radical reformulations of dogma, even those advanced with the justification that they seek greater clarity, coherence, and consistency in some part of the existing legal system. These formulations seek to re-write history, and in a way which jars with the well-established processes of incremental legal change. They do so in a manner which is destructive of an essential element of the legal system, namely, its historical continuity. . . . [Equity's] unifying themes are, or ought to be, widely recognised.

As far as I can see the examples MGL cite[31] of cases where the fusion fallacy was at work in generating bad decisions are cases in which courts borrowed ideas from common law areas of doctrine and applied them to equitable areas of doctrine without noticing significant differences between these areas of doctrine which make the borrowing not only suspect, but gave rise to errors of legal development in the learned authors' opinion. I am wholly in agreement with the authors in the examples they cite, and I could supplement them with examples of my own, where *Tinsley v Milligan*,[32] *Shell UK v Total UK*,[33] and *AIG v Redler*[34] would top the list.

Along these lines, I feel somewhat uneasy with MGL's favourable opinion of McLachlan J's judgment in *Canson Enterprises*.[35] In order to avoid fusion-fallacious reasoning all McLachlan needed to say was that while fiduciary obligations may be

[29] ibid xvii.

[30] ibid xxii.

[31] ibid 51–66, [2-190]–[2-400].

[32] [1984] 1 AC 340. In mentioning *Tinsley v Milligan*, I do not mean to imply that a kind of fusion could not have been justified in that case. At first glance, it seems to me that the standard of moral turpitude necessary to deny a plaintiff an otherwise valid claim should, in principle, be the same whether the claim was legal or equitable. But to say this is not to say that the court in *Tinsley* dealt with this well, because it didn't (see JE Penner, *The Law of Trusts* (10th edn, OUP 2016) [5.33]–[5.40]); *Patel v Mirza* [2016] UKSC 42, which supersedes *Tinsley*, only makes things worse.

[33] [2010] EWCA Civ 180. See Penner (n 32) [2.29].

[34] [2014] UKSC 58; see JE Penner, 'Falsifying the Trust Account and Compensatory Equitable Compensation' in Simone Degeling and Jason NE Varuhas (eds), *Equitable Compensation and Disgorgement of Profit* (Hart 2017); Penner (n 4) for detailed criticism.

[35] MGL, 63–64, [2-360].

undertaken by contract, as they were in that case, fiduciary obligations have different features from contractual obligations, the relevant obligation in this case being the obligation to disclose a conflict of interest, to which obligation contractual parties are not generally subject. McLachlin could have said this without adding the high-minded guff about 'an obligation which betokens loyalty [and] good faith', notions which were irrelevant to the decision and needlessly suggest some different notion of justice proprietary to equitable doctrine.

Let me summarize. The basic point here is that nothing of intellectual interest concerning the moral basis of equitable intervention appears to tie the doctrines of equity together, and MCG makes no real claim that there is. Despite the mention of 'the single bright thread' by Kitto, in the subsequent prefaces and in the section on the fusion fallacy, one hears a complaint that I find personally resonant because of my jealous attitude towards the law of trusts (which I have made, to the extent my limited acuity allows, one of the subjects of my study), in the face of the fusionist unjust enrichment/restitution enthusiasts[36] whose destructive tendency, happily limited so far in Australia, is wreaking much havoc in England. But there is no claim that equity has an intellectual or moral foundation that is distinct from that found in the common law, as a philosopher might find in those distinct moral views one of which founds itself on the right, another on the good, as a Kantian might distinguish himself from a utilitarian. The complaint is rather that the subsumption of equity under one 'fused' law simply assumes that what legal doctrines equity covers could be more or less *replaced* by an extension of the reasons which derive from principles of the common law and/or vice versa, depending on the particular area of doctrine. If that is the complaint, then the complaint is, to my mind, fully justified.

But the fusionist complaint, I hasten to add, is not one which ought to be restricted to the equity–common law divide. Perhaps that line is more easily seen there, and the dangers more clearly apparent. Trusts and contracts are both voluntarily undertaken obligations.[37] But they are not the same kind of voluntarily undertaken obligations, in the same way as a bailment is not the same voluntarily undertaken obligation as is the undertaking to act as someone's executor or act as their power of attorney holder. But the same kind of bad fusionist thinking works within the common law as well, for example in the developing idea that some uniform, abstract 'compensatory principle' should inform the calculation of damages across different cases of damages at common law.[38]

One last thought. The idea promulgated here is that equity just dealt with a bunch of different things, and it would be a matter of investigating its historical, path-dependent development to determine which of those it decided to address and why. The driving

[36] Perhaps the most obvious candidate for this description would be Professor Andrew Burrows: see, eg, 'The Australian Law of Restitution: Has the High Court Lost Its Way?' in Elise Bant and Matthew Harding (eds), *Exploring Private Law* (CUP 2010).

[37] While trusts can be imposed by operation of law, the obligation of positive trusteeship cannot; 'negative trusteeship', the obligation not to dishonestly act inconsistently with the rights of beneficiaries in respect of a title one has acquired, is merely the imposition of a duty not to act wrongfully in respect of another's property.

[38] See Penner (n 3).

feature of equity's development was not so much its own vision of justice, but rather the particular failures of the common law. To try to find whether equity had its own vision of justice, ie to find out whether there indeed is or was any 'bright common thread' to equity, we would have to look in the opposite direction, trying to discern if there was a systematic, common law deficiency, to which equity responded and which shaped whatever proprietary outlook on justice that equity, in this reactive mode, came to embody. As a matter of the substantive common law, finding such a deficiency seems unlikely, at least as matter of common law judges' views about justice, although one might easily cite systematic institutional attitudes about 'rule of law' values which led to *adjectival* deficiencies of common law justice, as the case of sealed bonds seems to illustrate.

This is an interesting question, which, given my inadequacy as an intellectual historian, I am unable to answer, but it is obvious that the common law was substantially shaped by its procedure, as was equity by its, so that when that gave rise to substantive moral deficiencies, equity not similarly constrained might address them. In the interstices of these procedural rules, both at law and in equity, one *might* find a substantive view of justice distinguishing the former from the latter. For instance, the rules of pleading may have embraced a certain attitude about 'worthy' claims as opposed to unworthy ones. Consider the quotations above from Baker and Gray. Consider also Lionel Smith's contrast between equity's view that obligations should be performed, and cannot be escaped by breaching them, whereas the common law typically only provided for judgments in the form of money damages for breach, not specific enforcement.[39] Or let us say, for example, that equity took a more lenient attitude towards those who failed to comply with, for example, the formalities for the creation or transfer of rights at common law than did the common law itself. Would such a greater leniency reveal a different *conception* of justice, or would it merely reflect *leniency* per se, a leniency of which equity was capable because of its different procedure? At first glance it does not seem that such leniency, in so far as it has any substantial distinguishing moral content, is captured by the notion of conscience.[40] These are interesting avenues for further inquiry, but to the present point, nothing we have seen in MGL suggests that they have found anything like that or, for that matter, are even interested in asking the question.

III. Equitable Maxims

Here is a conventional list of the equitable maxims:[41]

1. Equity will not suffer a right to be without a remedy.
2. Equity regards that as done which ought to be done.

[39] Smith (n 3).

[40] I thank Peter Turner for helping to organize my thinking about this.

[41] See Wesley Newcomb Hohfeld, 'The Relations Between Equity and Law' (1913) 11 Michigan Law Review 537; JE Penner, 'Hohfeld's Equity' in Shyam Balganesh, Ted Sichelman, and Henry E Smith (eds), *The Legacy of Wesley Hohfeld: Edited Major Works, Select Personal Papers, and Original Commentaries* (CUP, forthcoming).

3. Equity looks to the intent rather than to the form.
4. Equity imputes an intent to fulfil an obligation.
5. Equality is equity.
6. He who seeks equity must do equity.
7. He who comes into equity must come with clean hands.
8. Where there are equal equities the first in time shall prevail.
9. Where equities are equal the legal title will prevail.
10. Equity aids the vigilant, not those who slumber on their rights.
11. Equity follows the law. (That is, in, dealing with 'equitable estates' equity follows in large measure the analogy of legal estates.)

It is difficult to find in this list any 'single bright thread' which shows equity to have any particular notion of justice distinct from that of the common law.

As regards 1, there is an identical idea in the common law, expressed in the Latin phrase *ubi ius, ibi remedium*; 6 and 7 most obviously concern the suitor's conscience, but as I adverted to in the last section, the common law has a very similar principle in the *ex turpi causa* doctrine. The rest, except for 10, have nothing to do with anything like 'conscience' at all; they merely reflect rules equity has developed to deal with particular substantive issues, in particular issues of legal certainty (5, 8, 9, 11). Maxim 10 is perhaps an exception. It embodies the equitable doctrine of laches, the doctrinal contours of which are complex, including an 'estoppel' justification.[42] I shall return to the question of estoppels, below.[43]

IV. Aristotle's Equity

The moving ideas in Aristotle's brief discussion of equity are two. The first is the problem of general rules: 'the error is not in the law nor in the legislator but in the nature of the thing', that is, in the nature of general rules being under- or over-inclusive, prima facie applying to particular cases in which the rule would work an injustice. The departure from the rule, equity, is 'not a different class of thing'; it is just 'a correction of legal justice'.[44]

The second is the idea of the 'equitable man', who is 'no stickler for his rights in a bad sense'.[45]

As to the former, there is nothing here about the correction of the law in individual cases which is a departure from justice, in particular no special kind of moral norm referring to something like 'conscience'.[46]

[42] See Klimchuk (n 14) 263–64. For two recent decisions discussing the doctrine in detail, see *Re Estate of Tan Kow Quee (alias Tan Kow Kwee)* [2007] SGHC 19; [2007] 2 SLR(R) 417; *Chng Weng Wah v Goh Bak Heng* [2016] SGCA 9.

[43] Pt VI.

[44] Aristotle, *The Nicomachean Ethics* (OUP 2009) 98–99, 1137b–1138a.

[45] ibid.

[46] See further Klimchuk, this volume (Chapter 2, section III), a common law doctrine which echoes Aristotle's first characterization of equity.

The second moving idea offers more promise in this vein. One might say that the equitable person, being conscious of the unjust advantage the law might give him in a particular case, has his conscience affected. So understood, equity is a foil for 'opportunism',[47] a distinctly 'second-order' way of framing equity.

In recent work Dennis Klimchuk has sought to develop this idea by tying the two aspects of Aristotle's equity together in two kinds of case. In the first the idea is this: a judge corrects the generality of the law, in some cases at least, because the litigant wishes to rely upon a law which, strictly construed as to its letter is in her favour, shows by doing so that she is a stickler for her rights in a bad way. In this way she seeks to stand on the generality of the right on one construal of its content.[48] As Klimchuk points out, when this intervention of equity occurs, equity recognize a new exception to the rule (albeit only one enforced by a suit in Chancery), and the stickler just amounts to an 'ordinary wrongdoer'.[49] There is a second sort of case, however, which can be related to the idea that equity 'acts *in personam*', in the sense[50] that equity does not generate new rule-like exceptions to common law rules, but deals with each case as a one-off, in which the common law (or equitable) rule stands, but where the stickler is held to abuse her undoubted rights, and equity's personal order against her prevents her from doing so. Let us call this equity's true 'stickler jurisdiction', to distinguish it from the 'ordinary wrongdoer' one.

There would seem to be two ways of conceiving of this *in personam* 'stickler' jurisdiction: (1) a merely (practical) jurisdiction where the *in personam* order is not really different from one where a rule-like exception *could* be made to deal with the case, but because of matters of practicality and perhaps ideology, the result is not stated as such. As we shall see, this is a breach of the principle of legality, but perhaps in the early days of Chancery that was a cost worth bearing. On this footing, the equitable jurisdiction collapses into the 'ordinary wrongdoer' stickler jurisdiction in substance, though not in form. The second view, which I take to be Klimchuk's, is that it is an essential conceptual feature of equity's stickler jurisdiction that the orders are genuinely *in personam*, and are not to be understood as creating new exceptions to the rule at stake. Only on this conception is the stickler acting *within her rights* but in a bad way. Although Klimchuk recognizes that the stickler jurisdiction is not the whole of the equitable jurisdiction, pockets of this jurisdiction remain to this day.[51]

[47] See Smith (n 14) 232–46; Henry E Smith, 'Fusing the Equitable Function in Private Law' in K Barker, K Fairweather, and R Grantham (eds), *Private Law in the 21st Century* (Hart 2017);; HE Smith, 'Equity as Second-Order Law: The Problem of Opportunism' (unpublished MS, 15 January 2015), http://ssrn.com/abstract=2617413.

[48] Klimchuk (n 14) 254, 255, 260, 268.

[49] Klimchuk, this volume (Chapter 2) p. 39.

[50] The other meaning of 'equity acts *in personam*' is that equity acts upon one's body, via subpoena and the power to jail recalcitrant individuals for contempt, unlike the common law, which by contrast, enforced its judgments by empowering officials to act upon one's property.

[51] Such as proprietary estoppel (see Chapter 2 47–50).

Although Klimchuk seeks to develop this account as a version of Aristotle's, Aristotle himself does not address whether the application of equity to the stickler may generate precedents, thus creating exceptions with a rule-like character, which then form part of a more complex rule, ie a rule with exceptions. But this is clearly not an idea foreign to English equity per se. The idea that equity intervenes in individual cases against individual persons, without 'changing the law' in the sense of generating an equitable exception, an equitable 'rule-like' exception, may have once been true of the early unsystematic jurisdiction of the early Chancellors, but this has not been true, or at least true generally, of equity since the time of the great systematizers of equity, from Lord Nottingham onwards.[52] In my own view this must have something to do with the principle that like cases ought to be decided alike, ie one formulation of the principle of the rule of law. As Gardner puts the point:

> And under the heading of 'generality' [the rule of law] requires not only that the law regulate by rules capable of regulating an indeterminate class of people and cases, but also that rulings against particular people in particular cases be made according to those rules (*sometimes, according to rules made in the making of those rulings*). It is a violation of the requirements of the rule of law for a judge to separate the rule from the ruling by declaring what the rule is (or henceforth will be) while declining to apply it; *or likewise by denying that there is a rule (in other words, claiming that the case under decision is being decided only 'on its particular facts')*.[53]

If Klimchuk is right about the true stickler's jurisdiction, then it would suggest that whatever the 'abuse of right' idea has going for it in terms of addressing unconscientiousness, it suffers at the same time a deficiency in conforming to the rule of law.

V. Some Distinctions: Kantian Right and Virtue, and the Moral and the Ethical

Kant begins his discussion of the law with the thought that where people cannot avoid coming into contact, and therefore coming into possible conflict, they must leave the state of nature where their rights vis-à-vis each other are only imperfect and provisional, and enter into a civil condition, which perhaps most importantly involves both creating an authority that, through legislation (including judicial lawmaking in systems where that occurs) crystallizes laws, and creating an authority to adjudicate disputes.[54] This is all in the way of ensuring the freedom of individuals conceived of as the independence from the choices of others with respect to one's 'means'—that is, one's body and one's appropriated property.

[52] See MGL, 6–10, [1-025]–[1-070].

[53] Gardner (n 15) 210, footnotes omitted (emphasis added).

[54] Immanuel Kant, *The Metaphysics of Morals* (CUP 1996) 29, [6:237]; 86, [6:308]. See also Arthur Ripstein, *Force and Freedom: Kant's Legal and Political Philosophy* (Harvard UP 2009).

As regards private law, on this account the law concerns both those forms of law that promulgate primary rules that make explicit each person's right to independence from the unilateral choices of others with respect to each person's means (such as tort, contract, property); and, secondary, adjudicative rules that provide for the resolution of disputes between citizens.

As regards public law, this seems, as far as I can tell, for Kant to amount merely to various rules which create the offices of the state as well as state prerogative law—such as the power to appoint individuals to offices and to declare war—all of which are directed to preserving the civil condition within the state's jurisdiction.[55]

On the Kantian account the ontology of rights is such that true right can only be achieved in a civil society with such a political authority. Although we can appreciate the norms of private right in the pre-civil condition,[56] in the absence of a regime of enforcement to which all are committed, right as such does not exist. If this is correct, then on the Kantian account all legislation that follows the initial institution of the state and the basic private law is essentially 'law reform'—that is, refining or adjusting of the rules of private law, contract, tort, property, and so on, for example to adapt to changing circumstances.[57]

Perfectly in keeping with this picture is the first notion of equity we find in Aristotle, the need for exceptions to general rules to be created. The law will adjust and modify its rules, in particular creating necessary exceptions, as time goes on. But the second notion, that of the equitable person, would seem to breach a divide which Kant places much weight upon, the divide between duties of right and duties of virtue.

The classic example of a duty of virtue is the Kantian duty of 'beneficence'.[58] This duty can be variously described, but for our purposes here I think we can say, to 'act beneficently' is to advance the happiness of others, with their happiness in mind, or their happiness being the motivation for the act, or with the pursuit of their happiness serving as the principle underlying the act.[59] It is essential to the 'meaning' or significance of

[55] Kant (n 54) 89–110, [6:311]–[6:338]. There is one very controversial addition to these: a state's duty to support the poor (ibid 100–01, [6:326]–[6:327]). But it is far from clear that a state duty to support the poor can be sustained as a justified application of state power on Kant's own premises. For detailed criticism, see James Penner, 'The State Duty to Support the Poor in Kant's Doctrine of Right' (2010) 12 British Journal of Politics & International Relations 88.

[56] Kant, ibid 51–52, s 15, [6:264]–[6:265].

[57] This might be called the 'libertarian Kantian' account (see James R Otteson, 'Kantian Individualism and Political Libertarianism' (2009) 13 Independent Review 389), which may be contrasted with the 'liberal Kantian' account, most forcefully pressed by Ripstein, under which the state may legislate to distribute resources to the poor and to guarantee equality of opportunity; see A Ripstein, *Force and Freedom: Kant's Legal and Political Philosophy* (Harvard UP 2009) ch 9. For reasons too detailed to go into here it seems to me that as a matter of Kant exegesis, the libertarian account rings truer. See Penner (n 51).

[58] Kant (n 54) 151–52 [6:387]–[6:389], 155–56 [6:393]–[6:394]. Kant, ibid 26–27, [6:234]–[6:235] posits his own definition of equity 'considered objectively', denying that it has anything to do with fulfilling ethical duties. But his characterization of equity is an odd one, making it essentially inert as a matter of law or 'right'. Equity, on his account, reflects reasons *of right* which cannot be proved before a judge because of a lack of evidence or because it would overturn the written terms of a contract. Somewhat oddly, he concludes that this sort of 'right' binds only in a 'court of conscience', which seems to muddy his first claim that equity has nothing to do with equitable duties. I thank Dennis Klimchuk for asking me to address this point.

[59] On O'Neill's narrower formulation, the agent's concern is for the needs of others rather than their flourishing: see Onora O'Neill, *Constructions of Reason: Explorations of Kant's Practical Philosophy* (CUP 1989) 230, 233.

imperfect duties that they (1) are not correlated with rights, and (relatedly) (2) that their discharge cannot be coercively enforced.[60]

The non-correlativity of imperfect duties to rights is conceptual. Duties of virtue, it is said, are 'agent-centred' while duties of right are 'action-centred'. Both sorts of duties are, as O'Neill emphasizes,[61] duties concerned with the agency of others, but these duties address different aspects of our agency in distinct ways. To the extent you are needy, your agency is diminished or imperilled, and this evokes my moral concern. Imperfect duties of virtue capture our moral obligation to concern ourselves with how the lives of others go—they reflect how we act as agents properly attuned to the moral law so as to reflect this concern for others who are also agents, but whose agency may be imperilled or diminished by their circumstances. Perfect duties, by contrast, relate us to each other in so far as we are rational, not needy. To the extent we are rational, we can exercise freedom, pursue meaningful projects and so on. Perfect duties are action-centred in that they prohibit interference with the agency of others irrespective of our moral motivation. The very *raison d'être* of perfect duties of right is that their observation prevents hindrances to freedom, and their coercive enforcement can be justified as the hindrance of hindrances to freedom, whereas to fail to fulfil an imperfect duty does not *constitute an interference* with the freedom (agency) of others in any sense.

It is because they are agent-centred that it can be argued that coercing the discharge of duties of virtue is conceptually impossible: if the act is coerced, then it is no longer the discharge of a duty of virtue, for it then does not involve, much less require, my 'adopting an end'. If I am forced to give money as charity, it is no longer really an act of charity by me: because I do not give it freely, it no longer manifests my virtue or expresses my benevolence towards the recipient, any more than an obligatory 'gift' really counts as a gift, or a forced apology counts as an apology.[62]

So for the Kantian, then, when the court of equity conceives of its role as not changing the rights, ie not making an equitable exception to the rules which institute the corresponding rights, changing the rights as a consequence, but acts *in personam*, requiring an individual not to stand on her rights, this appears to be the case of a state official, here the Chancellor, enforcing a duty of beneficence. On the picture just set out this is plainly illegitimate.[63] Equity comes across as a moralistic busybody, requiring the individual defendant to act beneficently. Perhaps out of considerations of this kind equity chose more and more over time to treat its own decisions as precedents, *rule-generating* precedents which were to be conceived of as corrections to the injustices of the common law, giving rise to the better specification of actual duties *of right*, not coercively enforcing duties of virtue.

[60] Kant (n 54) 152–53 [6:389]–[6:391]. I am here endorsing what I have called a 'robust' notion of duties of virtue. For discussion of an alternative, 'thin', view of such duties under which they are merely contingently applicable duties of right, see JE Penner, 'We All Make Mistakes: A "Duty of Virtue" Theory of Restitutionary Liability for Mistaken Payments' (2018) 81 MLR 222, 230–34.

[61] O'Neill (n 59) 162, ch 12.

[62] Which is not to say that in any of these cases, adverse criticism cannot be responded to in a thoughtful manner so that one may then proceed, in the right spirit, to give to charity, to make a gift, or to apologize.

[63] See again (n 58) above, discussing Kant's brief discussion of equity.

I now want to explore a slightly different distinction which may be of relevance here, that between the 'moral' and the 'ethical'.[64]

The distinction is largely intuitive, and cannot be perfectly sharp. It is sometimes framed as a distinction between the 'right' and the 'good' in morality generally, or in political morality specifically. Rawls famously argued that states should stand neutral as between different conceptions of the good, or 'the good life'.[65] More specifically, in virtue of his discussion of what individuals would choose behind a 'veil of ignorance'—that is, not knowing their own personal attributes—he argued that in providing for the rights of individuals in a just society, no recourse should be made to particular conceptions of the good life. What results is a distribution of rights, not goods.[66] In later work he either refined or elaborated his position to say that in a liberal democracy the realm of political discourse—ie, 'public reason'—could not admit of reasons which drew upon comprehensive doctrines of the good.[67]

But regardless of whether or not the distinction is ultimately sound, and whether or not Rawls's own use of it stands up to scrutiny, I want to proceed on the basis that there is something in it. I do however want to recast it in terms of the non-negotiable (the peremptory) and the negotiable. In terms of political theory, what distinguishes the two is that in the absence of the institutionalization of norms that can be characterized as norms of the 'moral' or the 'right', individuals remain in a Hobbesian state of nature, one of war of all against all.[68] This is the sense in which the moral is simply non-negotiable. I am not concerned about what particular norms fall within this class, about which there is obviously a measure of disagreement. It is that whatever view anyone takes, everyone takes the norms generated by their 'moral' views as being 'non-negotiable'—as being peremptorily demanded by morality.

Most obviously, the basic norms of criminal law under which murder, assault, fraud, theft, and so on are recognized as offences are the obvious sorts of candidates for this sort of non-negotiable norm, as would be the basic norms of private law, such as tort, property, contract, which more or less reflect the same underlying ideas.[69] By contrast, the ethical is precisely that part of moral and political discourse which considers norms that *are* negotiable, in the sense of not being peremptory. For liberals such as Rawls, there are many valuable ways of living a good—or ethical—life, and there is no single, true vantage point from which one life is to be chosen over any of the others. Nor is there a principle by which these various lives can be ranked. This need not, of course, be framed in terms of lives or life plans. Ethics, in this sense, applies to evaluative judgments concerning all activities, for all activities realize values or disvalues in various ways. Nor is it the claim that there are no possible objective

[64] For a more extended discussion of this distinction in the context of political philosophy more generally, see JE Penner, 'Private Law, Potentia and the Ethical: On What Justification Does the State Coercively Tax Its Subjects in Order to Build Bridges, Fund the BBC, and Subsidise Charities?' in M Dowdle and M Wilkinson (eds), *Questioning the Foundations of Public Law* (Hart 2018).

[65] John Rawls, *A Theory of Justice, Revised Edition* (Belknap Press 1999) s 50, 68.

[66] The 'difference principle' allocates economic *rights*, not the goods that flow from having such rights (ibid s 13).

[67] John Rawls, *Political Liberalism, Expanded Edition* (Columbia UP 2005) xvi–xi.

[68] Thomas Hobbes, *Leviathan. Revised Student Edition* (CUP 1991) 88.

[69] cf HLA Hart, *The Concept of Law* (2nd edn, OUP 1994) 193–200, on the minimum content of natural law.

standards in these evaluations. The point is simply that the realm of the ethical is, in an important sense, second order, presupposing adherence to a non-negotiable morality, the peremptory or non-negotiable sort of norms I have mentioned.

Before I proceed, in light of these considerations, to explore the role of equity in all of this, the relationship between the law and the moral/ethical distinction needs to be refined somewhat.

In the first place, the state, in exercising its Kantian duty to legislate the non-negotiable norms of right, cannot do so by simply reading the 'non-negotiable' off some natural law book of morality, such that the ethical is not brought into play. The ethical permeates the private and criminal law in its every legal detail. By this I mean that it is straightforwardly not true that any modern private law is simply the realization of a private ordering determined by basic moral principles. These are not principles that can be spelled out more or less uncontroversially, whether on a state of nature model of pre-political right or on the basis of any other heuristic. The law of trusts, the law governing insolvency, security interests, wills, estates, and the law of probate, to say nothing of company law, and much more that would fall within private law conceived of as the law of private ordering, cannot be treated as directly reflective of natural rights. In particular, they are not the sorts of rights one could glean from a state-of-nature story. The long natural law debates over what made a contract usurious and the particularities of the doctrine of the just price establish this point. In the view advanced here, these are controversies of ethics. They reflect all sorts of controversial evaluations about what sorts of property laws we should have, how we understand the ethical behaviour of contracting parties, and so on. A more or less identical story could be told about the criminal law, in particular the criminal law power of punishment. To take but one example: I do not know whether capital punishment is immoral in all circumstances, in the sense that it is never justified for any crime however heinous, and I am not sure what the form of the argument aiming to establish that would be. But I do understand what people mean when they say capital punishment is barbaric. Whether I agree with them or not, it seems to me that such a claim advances an evaluable ethical position, roughly along the lines that we as a society are degraded if we adopt this form of punishment, in the same way (though to a much greater extent) we should be degraded if we used torture as a form of punishment.

The upshot of these considerations is that we cannot simply map the non-negotiable positive law directly onto the moral side of the moral/ethical distinction as I have described it. The positive law will invariably reflect both the moral and the ethical. But equitable intervention on the basis of conscience, of requiring the equitable person not to be a stickler for her rights in a bad way, can be framed as an evocation of the ethical in a different way.

I have argued elsewhere that the legal duty to repay a mistaken payment is best seen as the institutionalization in law of an imperfect duty of beneficence.[70] The law is not, strictly speaking, morally required to institute such a duty, but if doing so appears to

[70] Penner (n 60).

be an obvious intuitive choice for the law to make, that is so, I suggested, because of the sorts of considerations Ripstein raises in discussing the duty of easy rescue. I want now to consider whether a similar analysis might apply so as to generate an equitable jurisdiction to enforce what would appear to be duties of virtue on the second aspect of Aristotelian equity, an equitable jurisdiction which in a sense acts because of the individual's conscience being affected, but not so as to come across as moralistic busybody.

Ripstein endorses the private law distinction between nonfeasance and misfeasance: 'When persons pursue their ends separately, private law only requires that they avoid interfering with each other. When they pursue them jointly, private law requires that they honour the terms of their arrangements.'[71]

> Thus within the realm in which parties bear a special responsibility for their own lives, parties are entitled to equal freedom, each allowed to pursue his or her own ends as he or she sees fit, secure against interference by others, provided that others are also entitled to a like liberty and security. Equal freedom can also be described as the idea that one person's liberty will not be limited unilaterally by another's vulnerability, nor one person's security limited by another's choices.[72]

To my mind, this notion of freedom under private law does not generate any duty to go beyond the rules and act beneficently towards others, in particular requiring someone not to enforce his legal rights, just because his conscience is affected (whether in fact he feels the pull of conscience or not), as for example, when a creditor faces the question whether he should sue upon a sealed bond a second time because his debtor failed get an acquittance when he paid the first time round. The rules are the rules, the creditor might say, pounding the table and thundering out passages from the *Metaphysics of Morals*.

But that is not the end of the story. Ripstein also argues that one may have duties to contribute to important institutions that underpin the freedom of all, like a legal system or a system ensuring that people have sufficient material resources to live as free agents. In general, such an institution doesn't single out any one person to perform a specific duty in favour of a specific other. One would normally contribute to the institution itself via taxation. But, as with a duty of easy rescue, a person may be singled out on the basis of their immediate availability, or 'salience'. Thus conceived, the duty is not a private law duty that the available rescuer owes to the person in need, who has a correlative right to aid; rather, the duty of rescue is a public law duty which is just a specification of a duty to contribute to just institutions that support the freedom of all. Being a public law duty of this kind, according to Ripstein an available rescuer who failed to act would

[71] Arthur Ripstein, 'Three Duties to Rescue: Moral, Civil, and Criminal' (2000) 19 Law and Philosophy 751, 758–59. For an elaboration of the misfeasance–nonfeasance distinction throughout the law of torts, see A Ripstein, *Private Wrongs* (Harvard UP 2016).

[72] Ripstein 'Three Duties to Rescue' (n 71) 759.

not be liable to the person in need in private law damages, but could justifiably be criminally sanctioned.

Translating this sort of thought to the case, for example, of the mistaken payment, one would argue that the institution which allows us collectively to evince a concern for the welfare of others might, in the right circumstances, be embodied in private law—not as a reflection of fundamental perfect duties of right, but as the creation of conventional, *ethical*, duties, evincing the same sort of concern. The concern is about what sorts of people we regard ourselves as being, about what good, as opposed to right, might reasonably require of us in keeping with our collective self-conception of the kind of people we are (eg compassionate and kind rather than, say, competitive and individualistic).

Such duties are a kind of hybrid. Their resonance is with imperfect duties of virtue, for their source is the ethical, not the non-negotiable moral. But by dint of legislation, which includes judicial lawmaking, here the lawmaking of the judges of Chancery, the duties are made perfect and enforceable. Equitable intervention on the basis of 'conscience' would fall into the same conceptual ball park as doctrines such as 'good faith' in contract, or 'abuse of rights', which prevent people from taking advantage of others even when the available advantage does not result from any illicit interferences with those others' means. Such doctrines arise from a social, institutional, *ethical* choice we make about the rigour with which we treat ourselves as responsible and autonomous.

On this story it is perfectly justifiable for a legal system to legislate in this way (including by way of judicial legislation), because it falls within the range of reasonable options we can pursue under this collective, social, ethical motivation.[73]

If this is right, then 'conscience' as it is used in equity doctrine serves as a kind of short hand for the recognition of the ethical in the law, of non-legal but conventional ethical rules or principles of the society in question, conventional ethical rules and principles which might have been otherwise.

VI. Conclusion

This leaves a fairly small province for genuine equity of this kind, the equity which relates to the equitable person who is made not to be a stickler for her rights in a bad way, such as in the cases of mistaken payments or proprietary estoppel cases (especially the 'standing by' cases). But that seems to be the right result. As we have seen from the first two sections of this chapter, it seems very implausible to say that equity doctrine for the most part concerns this. Most of equity doctrine seems to fall within Aristotle's first take on equity, the correction of rules when they cause injustice or fail to provide a remedy (or at least an adequate remedy), or a right necessary for the legal process to

[73] I have not, here, of course *justified* the state's being able to do so. I have merely tried to describe what appears to me to be the 'story' of morality and the ethical underlying what the state is doing here. See further Penner (n 51). For what it is worth, I am not convinced that anyone has provided a satisfactory answer to the justificatory question.

operate fairly, for example the equitable right to discovery of documents. English equity, then, we may say, mostly cleaves to Aristotelian equity in its first aspect, but the second aspect has found its place, here and there, in no obviously systematic fashion. That is why, I would suggest, that these here-and-there manifestations of Aristotelian equity in its second aspect, such as in the case of the mistaken payments and proprietary estoppel, have proved so controversial, controversial, that is, in trying to fit them neatly within some general principles of private law or corrective justice. They don't neatly fit because they involve ethical considerations that cannot be framed in terms of justice, where 'justice' is that which is concerned with matters of right. Of course, one can develop a more capacious notion of justice in which abusing one's rights, eg by trying to enforce a property right where an estoppel lies, counts as a person acting unjustly. But it seems to me that 'injustice' is not happily invoked here. To be an equitable person, is, I would say, to see beyond the rights and the wrongs, and to understand that there is more to morality than right, or justice, or giving to each her 'due'. To be sure, the property owner who is estopped has *done something* in regard to her *rights* (in making a representation about them, for example). That lays her open to the estoppel defence. But to speak about the parties' relative 'rights' in such a circumstance may already be to give too much to 'right' or 'justice', and not enough to other sorts of moral considerations such as sympathy, solidarity, or neighbourliness.

4

Equity and the Right to Do Wrong

*Andrew S Gold**

I. Introduction

On Aristotle's view, the equitable person is someone who is not a stickler for justice 'in a bad sense'.[1] Recent work on the theory of equity has built on this insight, and equitable reasoning is readily understandable as a limit on stickler behaviour.[2] The difficulty is that equity also turns a blind eye to cases in which people obstinately insist on their rights, indeed, to cases that involve sticklers in a bad sense. Law and equity interact in a complex fashion, and equity's role is circumscribed. The result is that sticklers sometimes have carte blanche if they want to stand on their rights.

Another way to explain the interaction between law and equity is to see equity as a safety valve, with equity addressing a functional concern about the operation of legal systems. For example, equity may be an anti-opportunism device which addresses savvy but undesirable manipulations of legal rules.[3] On this view, equity responds to a vulnerability in legal systems, given the endless variety of ways in which innovative opportunists can misuse legal doctrine. While this account offers an excellent functional explanation of the relation between law and equity, equity is not always concerned with opportunism. This chapter will consider whether the relation between law and equity—in particular, its safety valve aspect—can be accounted for by additional principles of interpersonal morality.[4]

* I thank Charles Barzun, Samuel Bray, Evan Fox-Decent, Kim Ferzan, Ezra Friedman, Jamie Glister, John Goldberg, Michael Grynberg, Matthew Harding, Heidi Hurd, Dennis Klimchuk, Christian List, Paul Miller, Michael Moore, James Penner, Arden Rowell, Irit Samet, Frederick Schauer, Henry Smith, Deborah Tuerkheimer, and Laura Valentini for helpful conversations about ideas discussed in this chapter. This chapter benefited especially from Dennis Klimchuk's and Henry Smith's editorial comments. I also thank conference and workshop participants at King's College London, the University of Illinois, the University of Southern California, and the University of Virginia for helpful suggestions, as well as Bharath Palle for excellent research assistance. Finally, I am grateful to my mother, Estella Gold, who told me years ago how interesting equity is. As usual, she was right. Any errors, however, are my own.

[1] Aristotle, *Nicomachean Ethics*, in Jonathan Barnes (ed), *The Complete Works of Aristotle*, vol 2 (Princeton UP 1984) 1796 (bk 5.10 1137b35–1138a1). On an Aristotelian account, however, equity has a broader role than addressing rights sticklers. See ibid 1795 ('What creates the problem is that the equitable is just, but not the legally just but a correction of legal justice. The reason is that all law is universal but about some things it is not possible to make a universal statement which will be correct'). For an insightful application to modern legal systems, see Dennis Klimchuk, 'Equity and the Rule of Law' in Lisa Austin and Dennis Klimchuk (eds), *Private Law and the Rule of Law* (OUP 2014) 247.

[2] See, eg, Klimchuk (n 1).

[3] See Henry E Smith, 'Equity as Second-Order Law: The Problem of Opportunism' https://ssrn.com/abstract=2617413

[4] In focusing on this role, I will be addressing equity in functional terms—as a decision-making mode—and not providing a historical account of equity as practiced by the chancery courts. See Smith (n 3) 3–4 (adopting a functional approach along these lines).

Andrew S Gold, *Equity and the Right to Do Wrong* In: *Philosophical Foundations of the Law of Equity*. Edited by: Dennis Klimchuk, Irit Samet, and Henry E Smith, Oxford University Press (2020). © The several contributors.
DOI: 10.1093/oso/9780198817659.003.0005

I will begin with the idea that equity addresses rights sticklers. This account is accurate in a range of cases. Yet without more it does not tell us enough about equity's tendency to permit stickler behaviour, both in ordinary legal settings and in equitable spheres, like fiduciary law. Equity's apparent blind spots offer an interpretive puzzle, for they are hard to predict if equity is designed to prevent sticklers from misbehaving. Equity prevents people from being sticklers in a bad way, but only some of the time—and this suggests there is something more to equity's function.

This chapter suggests we shift our focus to the state's role in enforcing individuals' legal rights. Norms of interpersonal morality do govern a plaintiff's conduct with respect to a defendant, but they also govern a judge's conduct with respect to a plaintiff. Judges have good reasons to assist plaintiffs when they pursue a valid private right of action, even when the plaintiff is being a stickler. Yet the reasons for a judge to help these parties can be outweighed under the right circumstances, and equity allows the state to choose not to assist in the right holder's behaviour. In the ordinary case, courts owe their support to right holders, even if those right holders are insisting on their rights in a harsh, stubborn, or otherwise unappealing fashion. In more egregious or exceptional cases, the calculus changes and equitable reasoning takes over. As a safety valve, equity is enabling courts to better align their own conduct with the state's moral obligations.

The above account also provides another angle from which to assess equity as a type of justice. A court's shift between legal and equitable reasoning indicates a shift between two different types of justice: a more rule-like or context-insensitive kind of justice, and a potentially more desirable context-sensitive type of justice. Aristotle's understanding suggests that the equitable type is in some sense 'better' than the legal type.[5] But if equity's safety valve function tracks the account offered here, then the question whether equity is a better kind of justice will depend on the agent who brings about an equitable outcome. The stickler who chooses not to insist on her rights may indeed be equitable, and if so the justice that results is ordinarily better than the justice that would result from a strict enforcement of her legal rights. Still, it could often be true that the better kind of justice for *courts* to apply—to the extent a right holder insists—is the legal kind. On this view, equity is only sometimes the better kind of justice.

This chapter's argument will proceed as follows. Section II will discuss the problem of rights sticklers, and assess some key settings in which equity intervenes to address stickler behaviour. Section II also develops the idea that equity sometimes allows people to insist on their rights even when they ought not to—equity's response appears inconsistent. Section III will begin with a discussion of rights to do wrong. Moral rights to do moral wrong can help explain contexts in which legal systems provide support for sticklers. On the other hand, such rights to do wrong will not adequately explain why equity also prevents people from insisting on their rights. This section will then discuss

[5] See Aristotle (n 1) 1796 ('It is plain, then, what the equitable is, and that it is just and is better than one kind of justice. It is evident also from this who the equitable man is; the man who chooses and does such acts, and is no stickler for justice in a bad sense but tends to take less than his share though he has the law on his side, is equitable, and this state is equity, which is a sort of justice, and not a different state'). For helpful analysis of Aristotle's language on the relation between equity and legal justice, see Klimchuk, this volume (Chapter 2, secs. II and IV).

judicial obligations to assist right holders, and the potential for exceptions to this responsibility. These obligations (and the contexts in which they are overcome) can help explain variations in the law's approach. Section IV will discuss how a focus on such judicial obligations can support a distinctive safety valve account of equity's role. Section V will then consider how the law–equity divide implicates different types of justice. As will be developed, equity is sometimes the better type of justice, but not in all cases. Section VI will conclude.

II. The Rights Stickler Problem

Equity does a number of things, and it plausibly has more than one function.[6] Yet a core feature of equity is its responsiveness to cases in which individuals misuse their rights. This aspect of equity can be traced back to Aristotle. In Aristotle's words, the equitable person 'is no stickler for justice in a bad sense but tends to take less than his share though he has the law on his own side'.[7] Dennis Klimchuk has ably shown how this type of equity—equity that is concerned with people who are sticklers in a bad way—plays a major role in present-day legal systems.[8] When courts do equity, they are often responding to people who are insisting on their rights when they ought not to.

For purposes of this chapter, I will define a stickler as someone who insists on her rights to their full extent when there are good reasons not to do so. This definition leaves room for such behaviour to qualify as legitimate or even desirable behaviour, while still capturing the sense that a stickler is doing more than simply laying claim to what she has a right to claim. Consider a contract case where Jill has repeatedly dealt with a counterparty, Jack, who has regularly underperformed under their prior agreements. Assume that Jack has taken advantage of Jill's willingness to accept minor breaches in the past, and she knows it. Even if Jill usually prefers to compromise, at some point it is appropriate for Jill to insist on a perfect performance, to the letter. If she does so with respect to the current contract, Jill will qualify as a stickler. This matches a common understanding of what a stickler is, even though we may sympathize with Jill's perspective.

This relatively expansive understanding is also allowed for by a broadly Aristotelian account; Aristotle refers to being a stickler in a *bad* way, and this presumably leaves room for being a stickler in a good way or an indifferent way. As Klimchuk recognizes, '[s]ometimes, one might argue, one ought to be a stickler for one's rights'.[9] Indeed, Kant can be read in support of this idea.[10] While describing

[6] For helpful discussion of the ways in which equity's role varies, see Smith, Chapter 7 and Miller, Chapter 5, both in this volume.

[7] See Aristotle (n 1) 1796 (bk 5.10 1137b35–1138a1).

[8] See Klimchuk (n 1).

[9] See ibid 260.

[10] See ibid, citing Immanuel Kant, *Metaphysics of Morals* (M Gregor tr, CUP 1996) 188 (6:436). cf Stephen L Darwall, 'Two Kinds of Respect' (1977) 88 Ethics 36, 47 ('To acquiesce in the avoidable denial of one's rights is to fail to respect one's rights as a person'). The risk is thus not always that one is being a stickler; it is sometimes that one is being a pushover. I thank Arden Rowell for suggesting the pushover category.

someone as a stickler usually carries negative connotations, not every case in which people stubbornly insist on their rights should worry us, and certain cases might even be celebrated.

Granting that people who stubbornly insist on their rights are not always acting inappropriately, the Aristotelian account offers deep insights into equitable doctrines and remedies. Sometimes, as when they act out of spite, people vehemently insist on their rights when it would be much better for them to forgive and forget. And, irrespective of any tensions between equity and the judicial role—or between equity and law—equity may expect such people to accept less than their rights provide them. From a legal perspective, there is a sense in which people often receive less than their due when equity prevails, and this gap between what one has a legal right to and what one will actually receive calls for an explanation.

In some cases, equity remedies legal wrongs that result from a right holder's overreaching conduct,[11] but this is not always how equity works. Commonly, equity withholds assistance to a right holder, or even impedes a right holder's conduct, without the added conclusion that the right holder's overreaching conduct constitutes a legal wrong. In these cases, the stickler may very well possess the right on which he insists, but it is not a right that he is given help in enforcing (or at least not equitable help). Klimchuk insightfully captures this in his analyses of estoppel and laches—both of which he has suggested are doctrines impeding the exercise of second-order rights.[12] These are doctrines that qualify rights to enforce one's rights.[13] Here, equity is doing something other than bringing legal wrongs to the surface. It is making it harder to be a stickler by preventing the enforcement of rights, even though these rights are legally recognized.[14]

In fact, equity often prevents people from enforcing their legal rights, while still making clear that those rights exist in other respects. Good illustrations show up in contract law settings. For example, a broadly equitable doctrine—the doctrine of unconscionability—limits enforcement of contract rights without displacing the existence of those rights. As Seana Shiffrin has noted:

> The unconscionability doctrine, famously, operates as a shield and not as a sword. One may protect oneself against enforcement of an unconscionable contract, but one may not obtain damages for having been subject to an unconscionable offer; nor may one seek restitution for compliance with an unconscionable contract.[15]

[11] For an example, see Klimchuk (n 1) 257 (discussing *Hollywood Silver Fox Farm v Emmett*, [1936] 2 KB 468).

[12] Klimchuk indicates he would now view these doctrines as second-order constraints on first-order rights. I do not think the distinction affects the analysis here, but I am inclined towards the original formulation.

[13] See ibid 263–64.

[14] For a classic discussion of this role for equity, see FW Maitland, *Equity: A Course of Lectures* (AH Chaytor and WJ Whittaker (eds), revised by JW Brunyate, 2nd edn, CUP 1936) 9. For helpful recent discussion, see Matthew Harding, 'Equity and the Rule of Law' (2016) 132 LQR 278, 301.

[15] See Seana Valentine Shiffrin, 'Paternalism, Unconscionability Doctrine, and Accommodation' (2000) 29 Philosophy & Public Affairs 205, 229.

This is not a scenario where the underlying rights have been exceeded, nor is it an independent legal wrong to seek enforcement of such contracts. Courts may still refuse to assist the drafter of an unconscionable contract in enforcing its terms, thus protecting the counterparty. Equity is doing something here, but it is not the same thing it does in a case where a purportedly improper exercise of a right constitutes a legal wrong.[16]

Indeed, this tendency to leave legal rights intact is central to the interplay between law and equity. As Henry Smith has emphasized, equity has a second-order quality. Equity famously presupposes the common law,[17] and as Smith notes it can be understood as 'law about law'.[18] When courts act equitably, they are exercising a power vis-à-vis the law, working a change with respect to legal rights.[19] An important feature is the way in which that power preserves what it acts upon. While the possibility of equitable intervention may always be present, the impact equity has on existing legal rights is often an impact that leaves those rights in place, in some form.

These second-order applications of equity are a good match for the idea that equity responds to right holders who improperly insist on their rights. Yet there is also an explanatory challenge: while equity's impediment to stickler behaviour is prominent in certain settings, other features of the law–equity relationship don't appear to fit. In many contexts, equity ignores or even facilitates stickler behaviour.

Frequently, equity is quite permissive towards plaintiffs who insist on their rights even when it is morally questionable for them to do so. For example, a tort plaintiff may seek a very large damages award against a defendant who was minimally negligent, in contexts where forgiveness would seem appropriate. Equity is generally not responsive to such fact patterns. And, this phenomenon is particularly evident in the equity-based field of fiduciary law, where plaintiffs are able to bring claims for disgorgement against parties who acted in good faith and (arguably) caused them no harm, or even benefited them.[20] While these claims are legitimate if our focus is on the underlying rights themselves,[21] the fact remains that as a matter of morality some of these suits ought not to be brought. Various extralegal concerns—mercy, compassion, friendship, and a range of other considerations—bear on these cases. Often, such plaintiffs are classic sticklers,

[16] Estoppel has similar features. For discussion of how estoppel is a shield and not a sword, as well as the significance of this aspect, see Henry E Smith, 'Equitable Defenses as Meta-Law' in Paul S Davies, Simon Douglas, and James Goudkamp (eds), *Defences in Equity* (Hart 2018); Mark P Gergen, 'Towards Understanding Equitable Estoppel' in CEF Rickett and Ross Grantham (eds), *Structure and Justification in Private Law: Essays for Peter Birks* (Hart 2008) 319, 319–20.

[17] See Maitland (n 14) 19.

[18] See Henry E Smith, 'Fusing the Equitable Function in Private Law' MS, 11 https://ssrn.com/abstract=2783483

[19] See Andrew S Gold and Henry Smith, 'Scaling up Legal Relations' forthcoming in Shyam Balganesh, Ted Sichelman, and Henry Smith (eds), *The Legacy of Wesley Hohfeld: Edited Major Works, Select Personal Papers, and Original Commentaries* https://ssrn.com/abstract=3091652.

[20] A classic example is *In re Will of Gleeson*, 124 NE2d 624 (Ill App 1955). In the UK, a well-known instance is *Boardman v Phipps*, [1967] 2 AC 46 (HL). For recent discussion of such cases, see Andrew S Gold, 'Justice, Redress, and the Right to Do Wrong' in Simone Degeling and Jason Varuhas (eds), *Equitable Compensation and Disgorgement of Profit* (Hart 2017) 47; Emily Sherwin, 'Formal Elements of Contract and Fiduciary Law' in Paul B Miller and Andrew S Gold (eds), *Contract, Status, and Fiduciary Law* (OUP 2016) 167, 180. It should be noted that there is a sense in which a harm exists even in these contexts, if these cases are viewed from the perspective of a beneficiary's rights.

[21] For a helpful explanation of such remedies, see Paul B Miller, 'Justifying Fiduciary Remedies' (2013) 63 University of Toronto Law Journal 570.

and in some cases we may even say that they are sticklers in a bad way. Equity, however, is largely unperturbed.[22]

In certain settings, equity thus turns a blind eye to rights sticklers. In other cases, equity takes note of their behaviour, but its primary response is that it refuses to help them out by means of an equitable remedy. Or, as with the unconscionability doctrine in contract law, equitable reasoning effectively impedes sticklers without displacing their underlying legal rights. On occasion, equitable reasoning may police misconduct in a more expansive way. Applications clearly vary. It does not make sense, however, to think that each case of non-intervention involves virtuous right holders, and it is worth asking why equity would give legal rights such deference even when a right holder is wrongly insisting on her rights. I will turn to a potential answer in the next section.

III. The Right to Do Wrong and the Role of the State

A. The Right to Do Wrong

One reason courts might allow right holders to wrongly insist on their rights is if courts think it is morally appropriate for right holders to have that choice. If so, this isn't to say that the right holder is doing a good thing from the court's point of view—quite the contrary. Rather, a court could find that the right holder ought not to be interfered with even if she is acting wrongfully in standing on her rights. On this understanding, a stickler may have a moral right to do a moral wrong, with respect to conduct that qualifies as the misuse of a legal right.

Some might question whether moral rights to do moral wrongs can exist at all, but the idea is not as counter-intuitive as it might sound. Jeremy Waldron argues that, conceptually, it is quite reasonable to recognize a moral right to commit a moral wrong. As he notes: 'To assent to the proposition that I have a right to perform some action is not thereby to acknowledge any reason for my performing that action.'[23] The key effect of a right to perform an action is simply that others may not prevent performance of that action.[24] In turn, 'the wrongfulness of an act does not by itself entail the moral permissibility of interfering with it.'[25] Rights to do wrong are possible because the moral undesirability of a course of conduct is distinct from the legitimacy of preventing that conduct. While there is lingering debate over the merits of a right to do wrong in this sense, I will assume that such rights can exist in theory.[26]

[22] Indeed, there is an irony here, for equity is less responsive to these moral concerns in the fiduciary setting (where we are dealing with a historically equitable field) than it is in the contract law setting. See Sherwin (n 20) 176–81 (comparing the strictness of fiduciary remedies to the flexibility of contract law remedies).

[23] See Jeremy Waldron, 'The Right to Do Wrong' in *Liberal Rights: Collected Papers 1981–1991* (CUP 1993) 71.

[24] See ibid 73 ('The cutting edge of the claim that P has a right to do A is the correlative claim that other people are morally required to refrain from interfering with P's performance of A').

[25] See ibid 74.

[26] The conceptual possibility of such rights does not mean they actually exist in the moral realm. For discussion on this point, see David Enoch, 'A Right to Violate One's Duty' (2002) 21 Law & Philosophy 355, 378–80. There are, however, arguments grounded in integrity or in autonomy that support their existence. See Waldron (n 23) 81; Ori J Herstein, 'Defending the Right to Do Wrong' (2011) 31 Law & Philosophy 343 (2011).

Such moral rights may plausibly implicate many of the legal rights found in private law. Indeed, moral rights to do moral wrong could help explain their counterpart legal rights.[27] Ownership rights, rights of beneficiaries in fiduciary relationships, the rights of contractual promisees, the remedial rights of tort victims, and a range of similar legal rights are sufficiently tied to individual autonomy that they make for good candidates. This isn't to say that each and every legal right in these spheres corresponds to a moral right to do moral wrong, but some of these legal rights are at least plausible settings for that to be true. For example, suppose one thinks that a property owner should have a moral right to exclude potential invitees to a party she is hosting on her property, even if doing so would be morally wrongful. If she has a legal right to arbitrarily exclude unwanted party guests, this legal right might be justified in light of her moral right to do a certain kind of moral wrong. More importantly, courts could think this way even if there is no such moral right.

Yet this potential justification for judicial enforcement of a stickler's rights presents us with a new interpretive problem. Now, the puzzle may not be why there are contexts in which right holders get to be sticklers for their rights in a bad way. Instead, we may wonder why there are contexts in which courts refuse to assist them. A legal system that takes rights to do wrong seriously could plausibly allow all manner of immoral exercises of legal rights. The way in which law and equity interact, however, means that some people get to be sticklers in a bad way, some of the time. It is an intermediate result that merits further exploration.

B. The Self-Regarding Account of Judicial Conduct

The real challenge is to account for a hybrid regime, a regime in which stickler behaviour is occasionally hindered and at other times left alone or even facilitated. This intermediate result suggests that we have not quite captured the basis for the legal phenomena at issue. By focusing on the state's role, however, we can locate a reason for courts to sometimes assist people who wrongly insist on their rights and sometimes choose not to.

Seana Shiffrin's analysis of unconscionability doctrine points us in the right direction. Shiffrin claims that unconscionability doctrine need not rely on a paternalist grounding; instead, she suggests that the doctrine may be 'self-regarding'. In other words, her account sees unconscionability doctrine from the perspective of judicial morality. A court's moral obligations will not always require assistance to a right holder even where the rights at issue would appear to decide a case in her favour.

As Shiffrin notes in the contract setting, 'unless we assume that one must ensure that others' obligations are met, the promisor's genuine responsibility does not entail that

[27] cf John Gardner, 'What Is Tort Law For? Part 1. The Place of Corrective Justice' (2011) 30 Law & Philosophy 1 (contending that legal norms of corrective justice could be explained in light of counterpart moral norms of corrective justice).

unaffected parties or the community at large must take it upon themselves to enforce promises'.[28] On her view, 'refusal to enforce would . . . make sense when the content and outcome of the contract were morally objectionable in such a way as to implicate the judge's and the state's moral stature'.[29] The court's proper focus, then, is not solely on what the contracting parties owe each other, but also on the moral responsibilities of the judge and state. While Shiffrin references both judge and state, I will focus on the state's conduct for present purposes. And, as she argues, '[t]he state has at least a permission and perhaps a deontological commitment not to assist grossly unfair treatment of one of its citizens by another'.[30]

This seems broadly right, and the insight is applicable well beyond the unconscionability doctrine.[31] Suppose we extend the argument further. There is a range of settings in which individuals treat each other in a grossly unfair or otherwise immoral manner by means of exercising their legal rights. We can then think of equity as a mechanism for the state to avoid assisting citizens in immoral behaviour, and even as a way that the state seeks to undermine such behaviour: the motivation, however, would be a concern for the morality of the state's conduct. Adopting Shiffrin's terminology, I will refer to this as a 'self-regarding' account of equity's role. The justification for equity's intervention, if we extend the argument, would be that the state has a permission, or sometimes a deontological commitment, not to help out a stickler. The state may even have a permission or a deontological commitment to interfere in the more extreme cases.

The problem, then, is whether the state should in fact get to stay out of it, or in some cases even impede a stickler's conduct.[32] Figuring this out, in turn, may require a balancing of reasons pro and con in individual cases. Part of the moral backdrop includes a court's obligation to assist right holders who possess legitimate legal rights. But this obligation may be defeasible. The state may also owe moral obligations to third parties, and what is owed to right holders may be in tension with what is owed to others. Depending on context, different parties may deserve the court's assistance (or nonintervention), and this can help justify a system in which equity is part of a hybrid regime instead of providing an overarching limit on any and all rights stickler behaviour.

[28] See Shiffrin (n 15) 222.

[29] See ibid 231. As Shiffrin indicates, her argument is analogous to the argument made in the constitutional case of *Shelley v Kraemer*, 334 US 1 (1948) (in which the court refused to enforce a racially discriminatory restrictive covenant). See Shiffrin (n 15) 233 n 34. It is an interesting question how to draw the line between cases like the dinner party example discussed above, and the more egregious fact patterns. Resolving this sometimes-difficult question may require not only an analysis of the underlying moral landscape, but also an assessment of how the relevant legal doctrines will operate within a larger-scale system. For further discussion, see Andrew S Gold and Henry E Smith, 'Sizing Up Private Law' (forthcoming, University of Toronto Law Journal). This set of concerns quickly brings us to the polycentric challenges discussed later in this chapter.

[30] See Shiffrin (n 15) 235.

[31] Note that there is some debate how well the argument works in the unconscionability setting. See Nicolas Cornell, 'A Complainant-Oriented Approach to Unconscionability and Contract Law' (2016) 164 University of Pennsylvania Law Review 1131, 1154 (suggesting that '[i]n an unconscionable contract, it is not that one party truly has a moral complaint and yet the state will not give damages'). See also Rebecca Stone, 'Unconscionability, Exploitation, and Hypocrisy' (2013) 22 Journal of Political Philosophy 27 (raising questions concerning state hypocrisy).

[32] There could also be cases in which the state should assist a right holder, but only if a right holder meets certain conditions first. Equity appears responsive to this concern as well. I thank Jamie Glister for noting this possibility.

From this perspective, the moral concerns of private law extend beyond what the plaintiff and defendant may owe to each other, although that concern is relevant. There are also important questions regarding the proper responsibilities of additional parties—in particular the state and its judges—with respect to the interactions of the plaintiff and defendant. Some cases in which equity refuses to assist may simply reflect attention to judicial economy, or perhaps epistemic challenges that courts wish to avoid. A classic reason why expectation damages are readily provided—but not specific performance—is that specific performance can be costly to monitor.[33] But other considerations sound more directly in interpersonal morality, and these will be the focus here.

Moral concerns that might justify a refusal to assist a stickler (or a decision to actively impede one) come in distinct types, and their features do not easily boil down to a single worry.[34] In addition, they are moral concerns that are sensitive to specific contextual details (indeed, the fine-grained moral analysis prominent in equitable reasoning makes sense from this perspective). While equity does develop rules over time, the open-textured features of equitable reasoning are understandable as a response to difficulties in *ex ante* rule-making.[35] Space constraints thus preclude a detailed assessment of the morality involved in injunctions, estoppel, laches, or unclean hands—among others. We can, however, discern rough categories of equitable doctrine that match up with a self-regarding account of equity's role.

For example, equity's sensitivity to cases of extreme hardship is well recognized.[36] As Henry Smith notes, building encroachments are a good illustration.[37] A similar idea is at work in contract law, in cases like *Jacob and Youngs v Kent*.[38] While for Smith these examples fit an anti-opportunism model of equity, these fact patterns likewise fit into an analysis of when we ought to assist others (or when we should feel free not to assist, or to assist only in a modified form).[39] In such cases, the consequences of the remedy

[33] See Emily L Sherwin, 'Law and Equity in Contract Enforcement' (1991) 50 MLR 253, 254 (noting that equitable defences to specific performance include both the practical difficulties of administration as well as moral standards).

[34] cf Irit Samet, 'What Conscience Can Do for Equity' (2012) 3 Jurisprudence 13, 16 ('Each doctrine identifies a particular *fault* that triggers equity to fasten on to the defendant's conscience, eg taking advantage of special personal relationships in undue influence or failing to warn the other not to rely on your word to her detriment in estoppel').

[35] cf Smith (n 3) 4 (discussing how equity is 'open-textured'); ibid 10 (describing a context in which equity is partly crystallized into a rule, but with equity 'left over for new hard-to-foresee variants on the theme'); Henry E Smith, 'Why Fiduciary Law Is Equitable' in Andrew S Gold and Paul B Miller (eds), *Philosophical Foundations of Fiduciary Law* (OUP 2014) 270 (noting how equity shows 'open-endedness at the margin').

[36] See, eg, Smith (n 3) 9 ('[E]quity courts got at opportunism by employing proxies and presumptions that typically sounded in disproportionate hardship or other dramatic harmful surprises, bad intention, and vulnerability of the victim'). See also ibid 49 (discussing the equitable maxim that 'equity abhors a forfeiture').

[37] See ibid 17–18.

[38] 129 NE 889 (NY 1921). Smith notes the similarity in Henry E Smith, 'The Equitable Dimension of Contract' (2012) 45 Suffolk Law Review 897, 910. For additional analysis of such remedies, see Samuel L Bray, 'The System of Equitable Remedies' (2016) 63 UCLA Law Review 530, 577–78 (discussing the potential asymmetric effects of equitable remedies).

[39] Another factor in equitable reasoning concerns the availability of alternative remedies that are almost as good as what an equitable remedy would offer. Although this remedial analysis may not have perfect extralegal analogues, the relevant moral considerations also exist outside the law. cf Neil MacCormick, 'The Obligation of Reparation' in *Legal Right and Social Democracy: Essays in Legal and Political Philosophy* (OUP 1982) 213 (describing a related problem in the morality of promising).

are sufficiently extreme that plaintiffs ordinarily ought not to insist on their rights to the fullest extent. But the hardship that will be suffered by the other party is also such that courts will quite reasonably hesitate before assisting the right holder. If assisting another person will do sufficient damage to a third party, we often should be reluctant to assist, even if we would otherwise have a duty to help them out. For example, if we promise to help someone move out of their apartment, and then discover that doing so will have horrendous effects on a third party, our moral obligation to help this person move could be outweighed. Similar moral considerations have bearing on a court's conduct.

Other doctrines impede right holder claims by focusing on the prior history between the parties. A whole set of equitable maxims addresses the history of a right holder's behaviour, and for these purposes the degree of hardship that the other party will suffer is less significant. For example, consider equitable maxims such as: equity will not allow someone to profit from her own wrong; she who seeks equity must do equity; one who comes into equity must do so with clean hands. Estoppel is an equitable approach that emphasizes prior conduct as well. For that matter, laches is sensitive to a plaintiff's failure to act.[40]

These doctrines often show linkages to opportunism concerns, and even where opportunism is not clearly demonstrated, the applicable doctrines may still serve as proxies. Nonetheless, equity's maxims and applications also correspond to moral factors that go well beyond opportunism. Someone might seek to profit from their own wrong, for example, without ever having shown any *ex ante* awareness that the wrong at issue would enable the subsequent profit. A laches fact pattern may not involve advantage-taking, yet the context can still undercut a right holder's claim to help from the state. Likewise, we don't need to believe that opportunism has occurred or even is likely in order to find estoppel appropriate.[41] From this perspective, we can see a stickler as the genus, and the opportunist as a species.[42] In each of these cases, these doctrines can be understood in terms of what courts and the state owe to their citizens.

C. Explaining the Law's Allowance for Sticklers

A self-regarding account of equity offers an explanation for why courts would interfere with sticklers, or at least refuse to assist them despite the validity of their rights.

[40] While the overarching concern with the morality of state assistance is a common factor, note that the moral principles implicated by these doctrines may be different from those operating in a disproportionate hardship case. In cases involving unclean hands, for example, we may confront a question of moral standing. For analysis of unclean hands in standing terms, see Cornell (n 31) 1161–63; Ori J Herstein, 'A Normative Theory of the Clean Hands Defense' (2011) 17 Legal Theory 171.

[41] We might, however, think that allowing people to take inconsistent positions is an invitation to opportunism. That is surely a valid concern. But if estoppel covers situations where that risk is unlikely (compare classic agency by estoppel fact patterns), or if estoppel would be independently justifiable even if we doubted the opportunism risk, these features are worth our attention. Estoppel may ultimately have more than one grounding, or serve more than one function. I thank Henry Smith for emphasizing that estoppel fact patterns may involve an invitation to opportunism.

[42] I thank Dennis Klimchuk for this formulation.

We once again need insight into those cases in which courts facilitate the right holder's behaviour. Perhaps sometimes the state's responsibilities will call for it to help sticklers enforce their rights, but then we need an account of why. Yet a self-regarding account is consistent with—indeed supportive of—enforcement of rights on behalf of sticklers as long as there are sufficiently compelling moral reasons to provide this assistance.

As a starting point, it may help to recognize that assisting moral wrongdoers isn't always problematic—the context matters. As Shiffrin recognizes, '[n]ot all participation or assistance renders one fully complicit in the ends with which one participates.'[43] But that does not get us far enough. What we want to know is if there is a plausible moral basis for the state to actually owe sticklers its assistance. This is a necessary component if we are to explain a hybrid regime.

One possibility is that the state's conduct in enforcing certain legal rights is a means to accommodate the foibles of its citizens, giving these citizens a greater sphere of unfettered choices. This kind of analysis overlaps with concerns about tolerance in a liberal society. As Shiffrin notes, '[i]n social, highly connected groups, respect for autonomy may involve lending assistance to behavior we disagree with.'[44] This also means more than just getting out of the way: 'citizens should tolerate some level of burdensome other-regarding behavior. Even further, they should go beyond mere tolerance and they should subsidize some such behavior.'[45] Such subsidies can include state assistance in the enforcement of rights.

We can look to civil recourse theory for an alternative justification of the state's obligation to help right holders—including sticklers. In modern societies, the state has largely scaled back individuals' ability to engage in self-help, and this has moral consequences. In the state of nature it is quite plausible to think that people not only have a range of moral rights, but also legitimate mechanisms of private enforcement.[46] On this view, individuals could originally engage in self-help to protect themselves, and they could likewise engage in self-help to seek redress. By curtailing these self-help remedies, the state arguably takes on a responsibility to fill the gap with alternative mechanisms for seeking redress. Civil recourse theorists have shown that the private right of action can be explained in light of this understanding. This approach, however, also has the resources to make sense of the state's responsibility to assist sticklers, even sticklers in a bad way.

Notice that the state's responsibilities may include an obligation to assist right holders who wish to enforce their rights, even when it would be better for those right holders to forgive and forget. We can see why if we modify the civil recourse account slightly. In

[43] See Shiffrin (n 15) 236 n 37.

[44] See ibid 250.

[45] See ibid 239.

[46] See John Locke, *The Second Treatise of Government* in *Political Writings of John Locke* (David Wootton ed, 1993) 261, 265–66. An important exposition of this idea is in Benjamin Zipursky, 'Philosophy of Private Law' in Jules Coleman and Scott Shapiro (eds), *The Oxford Handbook of Jurisprudence & Philosophy of Law* (OUP 2002) 623, 637. For further development in connection with the US legal system, see John CP Goldberg, 'The Constitutional Status of Tort Law: Due Process and the Right to a Law for the Redress of Wrongs' (2005) 115 Yale Law Journal 524.

some contexts, individuals may have more than a pre-legal right to self-help; they may have a moral right to do moral wrong by means of that self-help. In the pre-legal setting, then, such right holders would have the option to be sticklers in a bad way. Yet the state in most contexts precludes exercises of self-help (for both sticklers and non-sticklers). If individuals' pre-legal rights allow them not only to enforce their rights, but also to be sticklers in doing so, the state may at least presumptively owe these individuals a venue in which to insist on their rights.[47]

To the extent that the state has moral obligations to assist rights sticklers in some cases, but moral obligations not to assist them in other cases (or at least permissions not to assist them), there is reason for a hybrid regime.[48] Indeed, we might expect a hybrid regime something like the mixture of law and equity that we presently have: one in which equity operates in limited contexts to curtail or modify the enforcement of legal rights. If the reasons for assisting right holders are sufficiently robust—whether from an accommodationist perspective, from a civil recourse perspective, or perhaps based on some other justification—then a safety valve approach is a natural fit. From this angle, equity's seemingly inconsistent interest in stickler behaviour may simply reflect the morality of state intervention on behalf of private parties. Sometimes a self-regarding account requires assistance to people who are sticklers for their rights, other times it does not. On occasion, equity should impede them, but not in every case.

IV. Revisiting the Safety Valve Structure

We can now compare the existing safety valve accounts of equity's role. Most prominently, a safety valve account has been developed in Henry Smith's recent work. A core idea on Smith's view is that law serves as a default, with equity intervening in exceptional cases as a way of policing and deterring opportunism. Smith suggests, however, that there are multiple safety valve justifications, and not all of these emphasize opportunism as their central concern. For example, he also suggests a safety valve may be justified by polycentric tasks (described below) and in conflicting rights contexts.[49] The self-regarding account of the relation between law and equity offers a distinctive perspective on why equity should operate as a safety valve—but, as we will see, an overlapping one. In the default case, courts are called on to enforce right holders' rights,

[47] One way of understanding this relationship might draw on a social contract metaphor (cf Zipursky (n 46) 642 (offering a social contract analysis of civil recourse)). One could alternatively adopt a remedial picture of the state's obligations. See Andrew S Gold, 'The State as a Wrongful Fiduciary' in Evan Criddle and others (eds), *Fiduciary Government* (CUP 2018). See also Andrew S Gold, *The Right of Redress* (OUP forthcoming) chapter 6. I will leave the broader political theory questions open for present purposes.

[48] Civil recourse theorists have also recognized that the state's responsibilities incorporate a concern for objectionable right holder claims. See Zipursky (n 46) 650 ('In the legal and political setting, as in the non-legal, there is sometimes a gap between what one ought to do oneself, and what one ought to permit or facilitate others' doing, if they so choose. Conversely, in both domains, there are classes of cases in which the objectionability of the underlying action destroys the individual plaintiff's claim to have any right to the state's empowerment or permission to do it').

[49] See Smith (n 3) 3.

even if those right holders are being sticklers. In the exceptional case, this default obligation to enforce legal rights is overcome by moral considerations.

To illustrate how equity works as a safety valve, let's begin with Smith's account. As Smith indicates, there are two different ways to interpret equity's proper scope. On an expansive reading, equity's role is capacious: 'equity corrects any flaw in the law in the interest of justice; it closes any gaps between the terms of the law and its purpose'.[50] But there is also a more constrained account of equity. As Smith argues: 'equity, even historical equity, is susceptible to another narrower interpretation—one that does not threaten to swallow all of law'.[51] Equity still draws on morality, but 'in a constrained fashion'.[52] Not every case of inappropriate behaviour is an invitation for equitable reasoning—it is in the exceptional cases that equity steps in. On this latter reading, equity is a safety valve.

The safety valve account is compelling, and an anti-opportunism concern fits this structure very well.[53] Equity is an anti-opportunism device, and frequently so. Yet we might wonder how often opportunism is the overarching consideration supporting equity's safety valve features, with various equitable doctrines addressing proxies for opportunism. Opportunism may be one of the most important considerations, while still coexisting with several others. And at times there is cause to doubt opportunism's centrality, as certain contexts in which equity intervenes may stem from moral concerns that are distinct from opportunism.[54]

As noted, Smith has suggested that equity operates as a safety valve to address not only opportunism concerns, but also polycentric tasks and cases of conflicting rights. The moral questions that this chapter is centrally concerned with may raise polycentric tasks for legal institutions, whether or not they involve opportunism. Such tasks show a complexity that is very hard to address *ex ante* in a cost-effective manner; they are well suited to second-order law that steps in when primary legal rules and principles have not adequately anticipated a given fact pattern.

As Lon Fuller describes polycentric problems, they are highly complex due to the many ways in which different components of a situation may interact with each other:

> We may visualize this kind of situation by thinking of a spider web. A pull on one strand will distribute tensions after a complicated pattern throughout the web as a whole. Doubling the original pull will, in all likelihood, not simply double each of the resulting tensions but will rather create a different complicated pattern of tensions.

[50] See Smith (n 50) 264.

[51] See ibid 266.

[52] See Smith (n 3) 5.

[53] The degree to which equity is constrained in practice is a matter of dispute. For some, equity is not as exceptional as the safety valve picture suggests. See, eg, Douglas Laycock, 'The Triumph of Equity' (1993) 56 Law & Contemporary Problems 53, 53. It might also be the case that equity is more safety valve-like in some settings or jurisdictions than in others.

[54] See Klimchuk (n 1) 254 n 26 (suggesting a non-opportunistic case of spite). See also Sherwin (n 20) 169 ('[T]he moral pressure that strict enforcement of determinate rules places on judges is not limited to cases of likely opportunism: it also arises whenever determinate rules lead to outcomes that are out of line with the rules' purposes or otherwise unjust to the parties').

> This would certainly occur, for example, if the doubled pull caused one or more of the weaker strand to snap. This is a 'polycentric' situation because it is 'many centered'—each crossing of strands is a distinct center for distributing tensions.[55]

Many of the problems that equity can help solve show this type of complexity, with cross-cutting individual incentives, context-sensitive moral principles, and administrative costs of various types all potentially in play.[56]

Even where the challenges that arise under a self-regarding account of equity do not have polycentric features, they may nonetheless be hard to anticipate and regulate *ex ante* due to their fact-specific nature. If delineation costs are high enough, we can locate a reason for second-order law as a response. There is always some risk that a given exercise of legal rights will raise doubts about the propriety of state assistance, and no easy way to figure out ahead of time which fact patterns will look like that—or at least not in a comprehensive way.

We might wonder whether the moral questions underlying these cases are really so intricate; many of the cases in which equitable reasoning plays a role seem obvious enough once they arise (think of a slayer case like *Riggs v Palmer*). In addition, moral principles are plausibly understood to take into account informational complexity for the parties who must comply with them.[57] Even so, determinations of when parties ought or ought not to insist on their legal rights—and by extension, when courts should intervene—will often call for a very fine-grained analysis, and it is hard to see how courts or legislatures could make such determinations *ex ante* in a cost-effective way. *Ex ante*, there are often immense challenges involved in determining who might count as a stickler in a bad way.

Sometimes, stickler behaviour that is sufficient to undercut judicial assistance will be easily recognizable over time. These cases may repeat with enough frequency to merit a clear ex ante rule. The law understandably produces rules in such contexts—and when this happens there is a sense in which these rules are no longer 'equitable' even though they originate in equitable concerns.[58] This is an ongoing process, however, and not the kind of process that will foreseeably come to an end. The infinite variety of fact patterns that could have bearing on the state's responsibility to assist with, or even permit, legal claims means that there will always be a need for second-order law.

Opportunism fits comfortably into this picture, with a caveat. The self-regarding account of equity covers a broad range of contexts, commonly implicating novel fact patterns. Each raises the spectre of intractable complexity and potential difficulty in delineation *ex ante*. The equitable safety valve on this account is understandable as a

[55] See Lon L Fuller, 'The Forms and Limits of Adjudication' (1978) 92 Harvard Law Review 353, 395.

[56] For helpful discussion of polycentric problems in private law, see Henry E Smith, 'Property, Equity, and the Rule of Law' in Lisa Austin and Dennis Klimchuk (eds), *Private Law and the Rule of Law* (OUP 2014) 224, 230–31.

[57] See TM Scanlon, *What We Owe to Each Other* (Harvard UP 1998) 205 (describing pressure against finer-grained moral principles in light of informational burdens); Smith (n 56) 231 ('It is hard to see how human beings would adopt a morality that is too informationally demanding, and the fact that a system has been internalized and institutionalized as a moral system makes it easier to implement in terms of generality, stability, and notice').

[58] For helpful discussion of the way equity crystallizes into rules, see Smith (n 56) 244.

response to context-sensitive moral concerns, inclusive of opportunism and also neighbouring forms of undesirable yet hard to capture behaviour. With these points in mind, it is still important to recognize that there are differences between opportunism cases and other stickler cases that justify equity's role.[59]

Some spiteful behaviour—arguably, most of it—is not about opportunism but simply about spite.[60] Dennis Klimchuk suggests an important example: *Hollywood Silver Fox Farm v Emmett*.[61] There, a landowner had his son fire a gun near his land's boundary so that a neighbour's foxes would not breed. The firing of the gun was otherwise legal, but the motive was problematic. While we cannot know with certainty what was going on inside the landowner's head, Klimchuk concludes that this was a non-opportunistic case:

> [T]he defendant in *Hollywood Silver Fox* ... was, it seems to me, a stickler in a bad way but not an opportunist. He did not seize a chance made available by the letter of the law. He just acted badly, and then sought immunity under a strict and narrow interpretation of his rights.[62]

This is a reasonable interpretation, and it is not hard to imagine that it will match a substantial subset of spite cases. Particularly if we link opportunism to some form of deception, and/or to strategic conduct, there will be instances of spite that are a questionable fit.[63]

Other cases may represent sheer obstinacy, or a finicky insistence on the letter of a contract. People may be sticklers out of pride, or because they seek revenge. In laches fact patterns, we may see someone who just regrets their own sloth or forgetfulness, and now seeks late in the day to make up for it. Human vices take a range of shapes, and often they are at least as plausible as opportunism (if not more so) when we seek to explain why people are acting as sticklers for their rights in a bad way. In many of these cases, it is reasonable to think that the state does not owe a stickler its assistance (and in some, that the state should intervene against the right holder), even if the state is convinced that something other than opportunism is involved.

This doesn't necessarily point us to the self-regarding account in all contexts. Arguably, there are other bases for a morality-grounded safety valve. For example, Irit Samet claims that equity should be understood in terms of conscience, in particular in terms of a Kantian perspective on conscience.[64] A conscience-based account might

[59] With the caveat that opportunism is itself a behaviour that implicates the self-regarding account.

[60] At one point, Smith describes opportunism in a way that is expansive enough that it may cover such cases. See Smith (n 3) 14 ('Let me suggest that opportunism is behavior that is undesirable but that cannot be cost-effectively captured—defined, detected, deterred—by explicit ex ante rulemaking'). However, most of his analysis of equity's role suggests that opportunism involves strategic behaviour. See, eg, Smith (n 35) 264 ('[O]pportunism by its nature—a strategic interaction between the opportunist and other actors including courts—cannot be dealt with purely through *ex ante* rules').

[61] [1936] 2 KB 468.

[62] See Klimchuk (n 1) 254 n 26. See also Sherwin (n 20) 169 ('[T]he moral pressure that strict enforcement of determinate rules places on judges is not limited to cases of likely opportunism: it also arises whenever determinate rules lead to outcomes that are out of line with the rules' purposes or otherwise unjust to the parties').

[63] cf Smith (n 56) (suggesting that '[s]ome notion of deception is somehow involved' in opportunism).

[64] See generally Irit Samet, 'What Conscience Can Do for Equity' (2012) 3 Jurisprudence 13.

readily cover cases of opportunism while also indicating why courts would care about non-opportunistic instances of spite or other undesirable behaviour. In addition, such an account could be developed in a way that results in a safety valve.

On Samet's view, equity addresses conduct whose immorality is accessible to us. If we emphasize consensus, this gives us a reason why courts would not intervene in every case where a party is acting immorally. As Samet notes:

> If the court stays on the safe side, allowing defendants to enjoy the benefit of the doubt, we can be confident that the decision will echo the voice of the defendant's conscience, and, indeed, that of any thinking person.[65]

This account of equity provides a prudential reason why courts would not act against rights sticklers in every case.

Yet Samet's account faces a challenge: plaintiffs often get to insist on their rights in settings where their behaviour is, by moral consensus, questionable behaviour. Rich plaintiffs can bankrupt poor defendants who were slightly careless (or in the fiduciary setting, even acted in good faith to benefit them)—and in some of these cases, plaintiffs are acting rightfully yet contrary to moral consensus. Granted, moral consensus is not always clear to a given judge. There is room to debate how much caution is the right amount of caution in this area, and courts might be more or less tentative in discerning a moral consensus. Still, equity allows for a substantial number of sticklers to insist on their rights, often in areas where an existing moral consensus would condemn the right holder's behaviour. If caution about finding moral consensus is the reason for judicial reluctance, courts are being very, very cautious.

Finally, we might see equity as a safety valve designed (perhaps ironically) to provide support for the predictability of legal doctrine. This position is developed in Lawrence Solum's work. On Solum's view, '[i]f equitable departure from legal rules is an accepted and acknowledged (but limited) exception within a general practice in which legal rules determine outcomes, then judges can tolerate the constraint of binding rules'.[66] In the absence of equity's role, the legal rules might be modified considerably. As Solum continues: '[w]ithout this safety valve, judges will have good reason to engage in interpretive practices that give them considerable freedom of choice in every case and not just the exceptional one'.[67]

This view dovetails with the arguments in this chapter, for presumably many of the cases in which judges feel pressure to moderate the law's effects are going to be cases in which it is morally questionable for them to be assisting a stickler. Solum's approach is nonetheless providing a different type of argument, and it is dependent on predictions

[65] See ibid 31.

[66] See Lawrence B Solum, 'Equity and the Rule of Law' in Ian Shapiro (ed), *Nomos XXXVI* (1994) 140.

[67] See ibid. In turn, Solum suggests that 'the open practice of equity in a limited class of cases is likely to increase the adherence of the system as a whole to the requirements of the rule of law'. See ibid. Once again, there is room for disagreement on the descriptive side. Some might argue that courts have already found ways to give themselves such freedom. cf Laycock (n 53) 54 ('Perhaps most important, the discretion once associated with equity now pervades the legal system').

about what judges would do in equity's absence. On a self-regarding account, courts have a moral permission or responsibility not to assist in certain cases where individuals engage in an extreme insistence on their rights. This is tied to what courts owe right holders in individual cases, and it stands independent of the possibility that judges without a safety valve would loosen up their overall approach to legal interpretation.[68]

The self-regarding account gives room for equitable reasoning in contexts that are not about opportunism, and it does so without reliance on prudence about moral consensus to explain equity's constraints. In addition, while system effects may help to justify equity as a safety valve, the present account offers an explanation of these features that is drawn from a smaller-scale moral analysis.[69] Such micro-level reasoning may produce macro-level benefits, but these larger-scale effects are not necessarily part of the moral reasoning itself. In other words, while alternative safety valve accounts offer important steps forward, they offer different insights and cover different ground. Equity as a safety valve may be justified on multiple, overlapping bases, but the present account offers distinct explanatory benefits.

V. Equity as a Type of Justice

The above analysis also offers insights into equity's connection to justice. Equity is ordinarily seen in justice terms; people commonly think that bringing about an equitable result is a way of being just.[70] Yet one might wonder whether being equitable is always what justice requires. It could be thought that equity is imposing a moral outcome in place of justice:[71] recall how equity at times seems to require that right holders receive less than their due. Isn't receiving less than one's due a description of an injustice?

That depends on what we mean. Courts might still do a form of justice in such cases, even if we assume that equity is displacing the justice that results from a strict enforcement of legal rights. It might turn out that a different norm of justice is in operation when equity applies, distinct from the more stilted type that results from following the letter of the law. The justice we get through equity may then diverge from the justice we get through law, yet still count as a genuine instance of justice—and private law would simply be incorporating two different norms of justice.

[68] Note also that some of the safety valves found in legal interpretation may have a different, non-equitable basis. The absurdity doctrine, for example, may be a product of a textualist interpretive mode under the right circumstances. See Andrew S Gold, 'Absurd Results, Scrivener's Errors, and Statutory Interpretation' (2006) 75 University of Cincinnati Law Review 25.

[69] It might be thought that this micro-level perspective is at a disadvantage, if a safety valve is an unlikely outcome of courts' ground-level moral reasoning. Yet safety valves appear to play a recurring role in at least some moral deliberations. For examples—described in terms of a 'standby' mode of deliberation—see Philip Pettit, *The Robust Demands of the Good: Ethics with Attachment, Virtue, and Respect* (OUP 2015) 218–24.

[70] See Estella Gold, 'Does Equity Still Lack Jurisdiction to Enjoin a Libel or Slander?' (1982) 48 Brooklyn Law Review 231, 238 ('Equitable remedies, as a reflection of their ecclesiastical origin, seek to do justice between the parties'); Klimchuk (n 1) 253.

[71] But see Martha Nussbaum, 'Equity and Mercy' (1993) 22 Philosophy & Public Affairs 83, 96 ('[I]t seems wrong to make a simple contrast between justice and equity, suggesting that we have to choose between the one and the other').

Consider John Gardner's suggestion that equity could be justice's 'rebellion against law'.[72] As he argues:

> Not every manifestation of justice is an act of following a sound rule. For some, just rulings are not governed by nor capable of being elevated to any sound rule of justice. They are based on a weighing of allocative considerations in their raw, unruly form. Solomon's justice was justice ad hoc.[73]

Arguably, receiving less than one's due—in the legal sense—is what a more desirable category of justice will sometimes require. In such cases, the justice in equity may be the category of justice we should seek, while the justice we get from following a legal rule strictly is an undesirable justice.

Yet, if we accept that equity is justice's rebellion against law, does this mean that when legal rules are strictly applied in support of sticklers, we are not following sound norms of justice? Perhaps, but this is not our only option; law's justice and equity's justice can both be sound even if equitable justice is (in a sense) better than the justice provided by the law. In addition, a safety valve account of equity can be consistent with the idea that equity's justice is better than the alternative, if we take context into account. To see why, we need to look more closely at the settings in which equity comes into play.

Authorship matters for the relationship between law and equity, and it matters in terms of legitimacy. Recall that Aristotle speaks of the 'equitable man' as someone who 'is no stickler for justice in a bad sense'.[74] This equitable person demonstrates a kind of justice when he accepts less than his due—he 'tends to take less than his share though he has the law on his side'.[75] The equitable judge is a different author, and the distinction is significant.

Notice that an equitable plaintiff who accepts less than what his legal rights allow for is being just in a way that (ordinarily) is consistent with the moral obligations he owes to others. It's up to him if he wants to settle for less than he has a right to. The equitable judge, on the other hand, could very well be violating a moral obligation owed to all of the state's citizens if she gives the plaintiff less than his legal rights require, or even simply fails to assist. In such a case, it could be morally appropriate for the plaintiff to accept less than his legal due (perhaps by settling the case),[76] yet morally inappropriate for the judge to give him less than his due. The equitable right holder acts as he ought, while the equitable judge, potentially, does not. When this divide will occur is a contingent matter, but it is not difficult to imagine cases of divergence.

[72] See John Gardner, 'The Virtue of Justice and the Character of Law' in *Law as a Leap of Faith* (OUP 2012) 254.
[73] See ibid.
[74] See Aristotle (n 1) 1796.
[75] See ibid.
[76] cf Aristotle, *Rhetoric*, in Jonathan Barnes (ed), *The Complete Works of Aristotle*, vol 2 (Princeton UP 1984) 2189 (bk 1.13 1374b) (indicating that equity 'bids us ... to be patient when we are wronged; to settle a dispute by negotiation and not by force'). For further discussion of the ways authorship impacts justice, see Andrew S Gold, *The Right of Redress* (OUP forthcoming) chapters 2 and 3.

Equitable plaintiffs are ordinarily engaging in a better kind of justice when they choose to act equitably.[77] Whether equitable *judges* are engaging in a type of justice that is better than legal justice is dependent on context. Sometimes the imposition of equitable justice is merited, while at other times it is not. This can be the case, moreover, even if a voluntary equitable act by a right holder would be the ideal outcome.

Turning to equity's safety valve structure, we now face a question of institutional design. If both legal and equitable types of justice are sound, and if the exercise of one type will displace the other type, legal systems may need to engage in justice trade-offs.[78] They may need to choose which justice category should apply to which fact patterns, in the process foregoing another type of justice. This doesn't necessarily require courts to leave the realm of justice in making their choice: a justice-allocating norm of justice may tell us when equity should prevail.[79] These trade-offs do, however, call for some mechanism to determine when courts should pursue a more rule-based, legal approach to justice and when a more fine-grained, equitable approach to justice is appropriate. This is where a safety valve approach can make sense.

From the perspective of judges deciding cases, legal justice may sometimes be better than equitable justice, and equitable justice may sometimes be better than legal justice. Yet, although either type of justice could potentially supplant the other within a legal system, it is often thought that equity runs a risk of swallowing up the law. Equally important, if rights to do wrong are robust enough, or if reasons to accommodate are sufficiently compelling, the cases in which courts ought to apply equitable reasoning probably should be exceptional. The challenges of polycentricity and high delineation costs also give us reason to avoid trying to pick out the exceptional cases *ex ante*. A safety valve approach to equity may then be justifiable as a method for allowing courts to avoid assisting rights sticklers where equity's justice is better, while leaving a wide scope for contexts in which legal justice is still preferable. That is, a safety valve can respect those settings in which sticklers should legitimately be able to stand on their rights—and even call on the state for its assistance—while still permitting equity to step in when the right holder goes too far.

[77] Equitable justice may cover multiple subcategories of justice, and for that reason I am hesitant to define it in a comprehensive fashion here. That said, the above analysis suggests that equitable justice may, in some cases, be the kind of justice that results when people exercise their rights as they ought to be exercised. For discussion of this idea, see Andrew S Gold, 'The Relevance of Wrongs' in Paul B Miller & John Oberdiek (eds), *Civil Wrongs and Justice in Private Law* (OUP forthcoming). This possibility also suggests a tension between equitable justice and some accounts of private law fields. cf Arthur Ripstein, *Private Wrongs* (Harvard UP 2016) 15 ('The law does not make a global assessment of whether you should stand on your rights; it leaves that question to you. Neither the person who wronged you nor a court has standing to impose any all-things-considered judgment about how you should respond to a wrong against you').

[78] For discussion of such justice trade-offs, see Andrew S Gold, 'Private Rights and Private Wrongs' (2017) 116 Michigan Law Review 1071, 1092–93.

[79] See ibid 1093. See also John Gardner, 'What Is Tort Law For? Part Two. The Place of Distributive Justice' in John Oberdiek (ed), *Philosophical Foundations of the Law of Torts* (OUP 2014) 335, 340–41 (describing how distributive justice may govern institutional allocations of corrective justice).

VI. Conclusion

Equity does prevent people from being sticklers in a bad way. Yet the relationship between law and equity is not easily explained by focusing on this feature alone. It is true that equity concerns itself with sticklers, but one of the interesting aspects of equity is precisely the way in which it also frequently allows people to abuse their rights. On the other hand, focusing on cases in which such right holder conduct is permitted is of limited help. Cases in which people may abuse their rights can be explained, at least in part, by the law's recognition of a moral right to do moral wrong. But then the instances in which equity steps in grow puzzling. It is a striking feature of common law systems that they mix law and equity together, and it is hard to illuminate this hybrid aspect if we emphasize either law or equity at the expense of the other.

We can make more headway if we look to the tripartite relation of plaintiff, defendant, and state. Sometimes the law supports sticklers, despite their overreach. The value of accommodation could be a reason to enforce legal rights in these cases, as a subsidy for behaviour we disapprove of but ought to tolerate. Or, perhaps, the state may owe citizens enforcement of their rights in light of the state's limitations on self-help. This latter picture fits well with a civil recourse account, given appropriate adjustments. The key insight, in either case, is that the state may have a default responsibility to enforce its citizens' rights on their behalf barring some feature of the moral landscape that has overcome that responsibility.

From this perspective, a number of distinct moral concerns enter into the analysis. Opportunism, disproportionate hardship, spite, estoppel, substitute remedies, and laches may all raise relevant moral doubts about the state's responsibility to assist a right holder. The common feature is that these fact patterns can give the state permission not to assist a stickler, and in some cases may even support interference in that right holder's efforts to enforce her rights. The state's obligation to enforce private rights is lifted or at least modified.

These insights also provide another perspective on the idea that equity involves a justice that is 'better than' another type of justice. This chapter suggests that the merits of this claim can hinge on the authorship of an equitable result.[80] The equitable right holder who accepts less than his due is being just, and this justice is better than the justice we would get if he were a stickler. On the other hand, the judge who imposes an equitable outcome by limiting a right holder's enforcement options is an importantly different author. She may be bringing about a better kind of justice, but this won't always be the case. Sometimes the justice we get from equity is better than the justice we get from law, but, then again, the reverse also holds true.

[80] That is not, however, the only justice-related consideration. There may also be a different concern: that equity will be used as a tool for one party to inflict injustice on another. I thank Henry Smith for emphasizing this point.

5

Equity as Supplemental Law

Paul B Miller[*]

I. Introduction

Equity theory is dominated by the question of equity's substantive distinctiveness. The implications of this question are manifold. They bear on the conceptual structure, doctrinal expression, and normative underpinnings of equity. In contemporary work, theorists have bracketed this question from others going to equity's institutional distinctiveness. It is taken as given that equity *was* institutionally distinctive in its administration and procedure.[1] It is likewise accepted that equity's institutional distinctiveness has been eroded since the passage of the Judicature Acts. Equity theorists instead query whether equity performs unique functions in modern private law; whether, and if so, how, equitable concepts are distinctive; and whether equity serves a unique set of values, or preserves values underlying the law in ways the law itself cannot.

The interest in these questions is understandable. Apart from the fact that they are more philosophically compelling than those going to equity's institutional history, the burden of establishing that equity is substantively distinctive is more important to modern private law. This is because fusionists and other equity sceptics are given to attack equity partly on the basis that it is *not* substantively distinctive. Equity sceptics deny that equity makes any contribution that could not be made in law.[2] Proof of equity's redundancy is a pillar of the fusionist's case: if equity is not substantively distinctive, what need have we for it in modern private law?

Preoccupation with the substantive distinctiveness of equity is evident in recent scholarship. For example, Henry Smith seeks to establish a distinctive functional contribution made by equity as a safety valve responding to polycentric problems and protecting against opportunistic abuse of the formal or modular structure of law.[3] Dennis

* I am very grateful for comments from Sam Bray, Paul Davies, Josh Getzler, Matthew Harding, Larissa Katz, Dan Kelly, Dennis Klimchuk, Ian Lee, Charles Mitchell, Jeff Pojanowski, Irit Samet, Bill Swadling, and Henry Smith. I am also grateful for comments from participants at a Faculty Colloquium at Notre Dame Law School and a workshop on Legal and Theoretical Aspects of Equity and Commercial Law at St Hugh's College, University of Oxford.

[1] Of course, some believe that equity has only ever possessed institutional distinctiveness. See especially Frederick Maitland, *Equity: A Course of Lectures* (CUP 1936) 1: 'What is Equity? . . . if we were to inquire what it is that all of these rules [of Equity] have in common and what it is that marks them off from all the other rules administered by our courts, we should by way of answer find nothing but this, that these rules were until lately administered, and administered only, by our courts of equity.'

[2] See Peter Birks, 'Equity, Conscience, and Unjust Enrichment' (1999) 23 Melbourne University Law Review 1, 20. See also the works cited (n 8).

[3] See, for example, Henry E Smith, 'The Equitable Dimension of Contract' (2012) 45 Suffolk University Law Review 897 (2012); Kenneth Ayotte, Ezra Friedman, and Henry E Smith, 'A Safety Valve Model of Equity as

Paul B Miller, *Equity as Supplemental Law* In: *Philosophical Foundations of the Law of Equity*. Edited by: Dennis Klimchuk, Irit Samet, and Henry E Smith, Oxford University Press (2020). © The several contributors.
DOI: 10.1093/oso/9780198817659.003.0006

Klimchuk's writings aim to show how equity prevents sticklers from standing on their rights in a way inconsistent with the law's ambition to serve justice.[4] Irit Samet's work suggests that equity is distinctively concerned with the conscience of legal actors.[5] Matthew Harding has suggested that equity is distinctive in part in its concern to restrain unconscionable reliance on legal rights.[6] And Samuel Bray has argued that equitable remedies are unified by distinctive functions not performed by legal remedies.[7]

This body of work is effective in answering most of the charges laid against equity by its sceptics.[8] Each of the theorists mentioned has made important contributions that are hard to accommodate within a fusionist agenda. Nevertheless, preoccupation with the sceptics has led many to make overbroad and therefore untenable claims about equity. These claims bear on the province of equity as well as its functions, relationship to law, and justification.

There are important differences in the views of contemporary theorists. Nevertheless, as I'll explain, their central claims reflect a shared commitment to a *remedial conception of equity*. Briefly, the remedial conception suggests that the substantive distinctiveness of equity is a product of the way in which it rectifies or ameliorates injustices generated by strict enforcement of legal rights. On this view, equity is a handmaiden to law in the pursuit of justice. Equity intervenes in the law in aid of our ambition to do justice through law, and it does so primarily by way of remedies properly so-called, or by devices that restrain the enforcement of legal rights.

The remedial conception emphasizes important facets of equity. But it excludes other, equally important, facets: those that indicate that equity is an important source of supplemental law. Equity, as a source of law, generates legal principles, rules, and associated constructs. These constructs are formal or modular in nature and (like laws sourced elsewhere) operate generally, prospectively, and in a way that is typically invariant to context.

For the sake of convenience, we can call the view that emphasizes these facets the *conception of equity as supplemental law*. Most sources of law produce law in a variety of forms. I cannot presently show that equity is a source of law in this encompassing

Anti-Opportunism' Northwestern Law and Economics Working Paper No. 13–15 (2013) http://papers.ssrn.com/sol3/papers.cfm?abstract_id=2245098; Henry E Smith, 'Why Fiduciary Law Is Equitable' in Andrew S Gold and Paul B Miller (eds), *Philosophical Foundations of Fiduciary Law* (OUP 2014); Henry E Smith, 'Equity as Second-Order Law: The Problem of Opportunism' Harvard Public Law Working Paper No. 15–13 (2015) http://papers.ssrn.com/sol3/papers.cfm?abstract_id=2617413; Henry E Smith, 'Fusing the Equitable Function in Private Law' in Kit Barker, Karen Fairweather, and Ross Grantham (eds), *Private Law in the 21st Century* (Hart 2016).

[4] Dennis Klimchuk, 'Equity and the Rule of Law' in Lisa M Austin and Dennis Klimchuk (eds), *Private Law and the Rule of Law* (OUP 2014).

[5] Irit Samet, 'What Conscience Can Do for Equity' (2012) 3 Jurisprudence 13 (2012). See also Irit Samet, 'Fiduciary Law as Equity's Child' in Paul B. Miller and Andrew S. Gold (eds), *Contract, Status, and Fiduciary Law* (OUP 2016).

[6] Matthew Harding, 'Equity and the Rule of Law' (2016)132 LQR 278.

[7] Samuel Bray, 'The System of Equitable Remedies' (2016) 63 UCLA Law Review 539.

[8] Including prominent English private law scholars like Peter Birks and Andrew Burrows, who have criticized equity on the basis of its alleged redundancy with law, that it remedies wrongs differently, and that it shelters particularly opaque concepts. See Peter Birks, 'Equity in the Modern Law: An Exercise in Taxonomy' (1996) 26 University of Western Australia Law Review 1; Andrew Burrows, 'We Do This at Common Law But That in Equity' (2002) 22 OJLS 1.

sense. Nevertheless, note that a key function of private law is the articulation and enforcement of primary rights (especially rights which protect interests of persons as such, interests in property, and interests in personal relationships and associations). This being so, the conception of equity as supplemental law may reasonably be thought well founded if it can be shown that equity is a source of primary rights. My aim presently is to make this important but partial case for viewing equity as a source of supplemental law.

The chapter will unfold as follows. In section I, I explain the remedial conception of equity. In section II, I introduce the conception of equity as supplemental law. Consistent with my focus on equity as a source of primary rights, in section III, I discuss equitable rights in general terms and by illustration. In section IV, I situate the present account relative to the debate about equity's substantive distinctiveness. Finally, in section V, I canvas some implications for broader questions concerning the relationship between law and equity.

II. The Remedial Conception of Equity

Recent scholarship adopts a remedial conception of equity. Remedial theories identify the distinctive substantive characteristics of equity in its remedial purpose(s) or function(s). These purposes or functions are remedial not (or not merely) in the familiar and narrow *interpersonal* sense of effectuating relief or redress between persons. Instead, they are remedial in a *systemic* sense in so far as they are concerned with case-by-case remediation of the impact of defects in the law on aggrieved individuals.

A. Remedialism in Historical Perspective

The remedial conception is powerful because it is familiar. It draws on some of the most well-known characterizations of equity. Consider the following statements, several of which have been so influential that they are now treated as truisms.

1. Equity is a branch of the law of remedies

The most straightforward expression of remedialism is the view that locates equity within the law of remedies.[9] On this view, equity's signal contribution lies in supplying remedies that the law cannot, or has not, provided, but which (for one reason or another) ought in justice to be provided. This view suggests further that, in supplying remedies, equity corrects for law by providing a more perfect measure of relief from civil wrongs. Equitable remedies may be more perfect because they are better able to achieve restorative equilibrium or because they are better able to protect interests

[9] The *locus classicus* is Langdell's survey of equity, which asserts that: 'Equity jurisdiction is a branch of the law of remedies'. CC Langdell, 'A Brief Survey of Equity Jurisdiction I' (1887) 1 Harvard Law Review 55, 55.

secured by primary rights. Either way, on this view, equity perfects the law *interpersonally* by providing a more suitable remedy to a person with just cause for one, and *systemically* by providing society with a set of remedies better suited to protection of important interests.

This view of equity is plainly implausible. It ignores large swaths of doctrine that do not implicate remedies. However, it was (and is) attractive for at least two reasons. First, it is based in truth. Remedies occupy a significant part of the doctrinal landscape of equity and equitable remedies often provide a more perfect measure of relief. Second, it promises resolution of the criticism that equity frustrates the rational classification of jural relations in private law.[10] If equity is simply a branch of the law of remedies, it should have no impact on higher order categories (especially categories of primary right and duty).

2. Equity corrects for inherent defects of law

Another view is that the *sine qua non* of equity lies in its correction of inherent defects of law. This view of is normally traced to Aristotle, who said that equity involves the 'correction of law where it is defective owing to its generality'.[11]

Consistent with Aristotle's view, in some cases equity appears to correct for harsh consequences of strict enforcement of legal rules while in others it seems to respond to abuse or evasion of the spirit or purpose of the law. However one might understand the law's inherent defects and the ways in which they may be exposed, the Aristotelian view implies that equity has a fundamentally remedial character that is necessitated by the nature of law as law, and that equitable correction of law is essential to the realization of the law's ends.

The Aristotelian view of equity is widely regarded as plausible. It makes sense of equitable doctrines other than remedies, including, for example, principles that condition the enforcement of contracts (eg, mistake, unconscionability, and undue influence). The difficulties with the Aristotelian perspective are that it ignores those parts of equity that supplement rather than correct for the law, and therefore mistakenly suggests that equity is responsive only to *inherent* defects in the law (ie, those that, being the product of an essential characteristic of law, cannot be addressed through supplementation of law).

[10] Birks (n 8).

[11] Aristotle, *Nicomachean Ethics* 1137b in 2 *The Complete Works of Aristotle* (J Barnes, ed, WD Ross, tr, Princeton UP 1984). See also Aquinas, *Summa Theologica*, Second Part of the Second Part, q.120, art 1:

> since human actions, with which laws are concerned, are composed of contingent singulars and are innumerable in their diversity, it was not possible to lay down rules of law that would apply to every single case. Legislators in framing laws attend to what commonly happens: although if the law be applied to certain cases it will frustrate the quality of justice and be injurious to the common good, which the law has in view ... On these and like cases it is bad to follow the law, and it is good to set aside the letter of the law and to follow the dictates of justice and the common good. This is the object of 'epikeia' which we call equity.

See also Dennis Klimchuk's careful analysis in this volume (Chapter 2). Klimchuk suggests that while Aristotle is best known for his remedial view of equity, he also allows that equity contributes law (eg, in delineating levels of fault attributable to wrongdoers and/or third parties).

3. Equity intervenes through ex post discretionary judicial review

A key feature of legal systems that instantiate the rule of law is that legal rules are announced *ex ante* and operate prospectively, supplying normative guidance to persons subject to them. Equity, it is commonly said, is different. Whereas law *governs* behaviour through relatively sharp rules that operate prospectively, equity *sanctions* behaviour through relatively fuzzy standards that ground *ex post* judicial review.[12] This characterization is sometimes coupled with the claim that equity has a distinctive function. Unlike legal rules, equitable standards do not supply terms of conduct but instead function in a superordinate way, constraining the way in which legal rules are enforced.

This view is attractive in part because it lends specificity to Aristotle's account, explaining equity's characteristic mode of intervention upon the law. It therefore seems well equipped to explain equitable doctrine that has arisen alongside contract law (eg, unconscionability, mistake, and undue influence) as well as certain equitable defences and remedies. It also resonates with the common platitudes that equity 'follows' or 'assumes' the law and that it operates beyond law (eg, by holding law to an aspiration to justice that cannot be achieved through law).[13] Not incidentally, it is consistent with the origins of equity in personal pleas for prerogative relief.[14] As I will explain, however, this view cannot account for many of the products of mature systems of equity, especially those that take the form of law (eg, rules announced *ex ante*, that apply prospectively, establishing terms of interaction).

4. Equitable intervention is based in conscience

Another common view is that equitable intervention is premised on the demands of morality on conscience in the administration of justice.[15] This view can be ambiguous, for example in respect of the nature and bases of the demands morality makes on

[12] See Emily Sherwin, 'Equity and the Modern Mind' https://papers.ssrn.com/sol3/papers.cfm?abstract_id=2817803

[13] See Pound's claim that equity pursues 'justice without, or beyond, law'. Roscoe Pound, 'The Decadence of Equity' (1905) 5 Columbia Law Review 20.

[14] Consider the following account by Pound:

> Equity both at Rome and in England, *began* as executive justice. *It was a reversion to justice without law.* The praetor interposing by virtue of his imperium, the emperor enforcing fide-commissa because, as the Institutes say, he was 'moved several times by favor of particular persons', the Frankish king deciding, not according to law, but secundum aequitatem for those whom he had taken under his special protection, and the Chancellor granting relief 'of almes and charitie', *acted without rule* in accordance with general notions of fair play and sympathy for a wronged or weaker party.
>
> Roscoe Pound, *Jurisprudence* (Lawbook 1959) (emphasis added)

At its dawn, equitable relief was clearly purely remedial and discretionary. A person with a grievance brought it, couching it explicitly as an appeal to the conscience of the king, and prayed for the charity of his assistance. This person asserted no cause of action. He was a supplicant. According to Maitland this state of affairs persisted until the late thirteenth century: 'Though these great courts of law have been established there is still a reserve of justice in the king. Those who cannot get relief elsewhere present their petitions to the king and his council ... The petition is often couched in piteous terms, the king is asked to find a remedy for the love of God and in the way of charity' ((n 1) 3 and 5).

[15] See, for example, Ryan's suggestive claim that 'Equity is a mode of giving morality a juridical character'. Philip A Ryan, 'Equity: System or Process?' (1956) 45 Georgetown Law Journal 213, 217. See also Lord Cowper's famous dictum: 'Now equity is no part of the law, but a moral virtue, which qualifies, moderates, and reforms the rigour, hardness and edge of the law ... [it] defends the law from crafty evasions, delusions, and new subtleties, invented and contrived to evade and delude the common law, whereby such as have undoubted right are made remediless' (*Dudley v Dudley* (1705) 24 ER 118, 119 (Ch)).

conscience and the identities of those upon whom these demands may be made in equity.[16] It is also unclear whether equity has worked with a fixed conception of conscience over its history.[17] However, many think that equity's basis in conscience is a critical point of substantive distinction between law and equity.[18]

The notion that equity is conscience-based does not imply remedialism. Indeed, one might allow that equity supplements the law but maintain that its contributions reflect demands of conscience. For present purposes, however, it is useful to consider this view as aligned with remedialism, for one typically sees this alignment in the literature. From this perspective, it is suggested that equity intervenes upon the law and corrects for its defects on the basis that this is what morality demands of conscience (whether of the conscience of the judge, who hears an appeal in equity; the conscience of the claimant, who makes that appeal in conscience, and in so doing implicates her own conscience; and/or the conscience of the respondent, whose entitlements are varied on the basis either that he has acted contrary to conscience or that dictates of conscience require the variation).[19]

This view of equity is powerful because of the role undeniably played by conscience in the history of equity. In early equity, petitions for equitable intervention were plainly pleas made upon the conscience of the Crown. The pleas invoked principles of natural law and the notion that posited law is subordinate to God's will that human interactions and institutions comport with the requirements of natural justice.[20] Further, many procedures and substantive doctrines of equity imply a concern with matters of conscience in the administration of justice. This seems patently true of prominent equitable maxims (eg, 'one who seeks equity must do equity' and 'one who comes to equity must do so with clean hands'). This said, discernment of the precise relationship between conscience and equity depends on: the characterization given to the moral demands that are heard in equity; how one locates these demands, interpersonally and institutionally; and how one traces their positive development in equitable doctrine and procedure. Each of these points merits further study.

5. Equity aims for particular justice

One can debate the norm(s) of justice to which private law is responsive, but few would question that it includes norms of interpersonal justice. Our final statement on equity draws a distinction between law and equity in terms of the forms of justice apposite to each. It claims that while law aims for general justice, equity aims for particular justice.

[16] Dennis R Klinck, 'The Unexamined "Conscience" of Canadian Equity' (2001) 46 McGill Law Journal 571.

[17] ibid.

[18] Indeed, in *Soulos v Korkontzilas*, McLachlin J (as she then was) expressed the view that 'the concept of "good conscience" ... lies at "the very foundation of equitable jurisdiction"' ([1997] 2 SCR 217, 232–33).

[19] This is one interpretation of Lord Ellesmere's famous characterization of the two 'offices' of the Chancellor as implying a jurisdiction 'to correct men's consciences for frauds' and 'to soften and modify the extremity of the law'. *The Earl of Oxford's Case* (1615) 1 Ch Rep 4. See also Aquinas, *Summa Theologica* (n 11) q.120, art 1; art. 2: 'to follow the letter of the "strict Common Law" when it should not be followed is sinful'.

[20] As explained by Brian Simpson: '[T]o a fifteenth-century ecclesiastic, sitting as a judge of conscience, in a court of conscience "for the love of God and in way of charity", "conscience" ... connoted what we now call the moral law as it applied to particular individuals for the avoidance of peril to the soul through mortal sin'. AWB Simpson, *A History of the Common Law of Contract: The Rise of the Action of Assumpsit* (Clarendon 1975).

It is not entirely clear what is meant by this. However, a plausible interpretation is that whereas law aims for general justice by articulating norms of general application that, *ceteris paribus*, seem most likely to secure conditions of justice between persons, equity aims for particular justice by adjusting the application of these norms where their ordinary application would bring about injustice.

The notion that equity aims for particular justice is not patently remedial. But if one considers that intervention in service of such a conception of justice cannot be premised on general norms (the latter being the way in which requirements of general justice are expressed), it is clear that a kind of remedialism is implied. That is, it is implied that equity intervenes upon the law (by altering its ordinary operation) in order to achieve particular justice because this is necessary to prevent a perversion of the law in its aim for general justice.

Unsurprisingly, the basis in positive law for this view of equity is less easily identified. However, it has the endorsement of eminent scholars [21] and is reflected in the commonplace observation that equitable intervention is tailored to suit the exigencies of particular cases.[22]

B. Remedialism in Contemporary Scholarship

The statements that we have just considered are among the most influential of efforts to encapsulate our subject. It is thus not surprising that contemporary scholars—and particularly those who wish to defend equity from the charges laid by equity sceptics—are given to remedialist thinking, as well.

Consider the work of Henry Smith. In a series of essays, Smith has developed a theory of equity as a 'safety valve' for law.[23] Drawing on insights from history, philosophy, and economics, the safety valve theory is strikingly original. Smith's account is developed, in part, through his drawing of several sharp contrasts between law and equity. The result is a dichotomous representation of the roles respectively for law and equity in private law.[24] This makes it easier for Smith to highlight equity's substantive

[21] For example, Ryan has expressed the view that that equity supplies '*individualized* justice by the use of well-tempered judicial discretion illuminated by moral principles' ((n 15) 217).

[22] As reflected in Story's encomium: 'The beautiful character, or pervading excellence . . . of Equity Jurisprudence is, that it varies its adjustments and proportions, so as to meet the very form and pressure of each particular case in all its complex habitudes' (Joseph Story, *Commentaries on Equity Jurisprudence* (Hilliard, Gray & Co 1836) s 439).

[23] See works cited above (n 3). Smith has focused primarily on articulating the 'safety valve' theory and usually frames the relationship of law and equity in dichotomous terms, but he has also occasionally pointed to non-remedial functions of equity, including its role in enforcing custom. See, for example, Henry Smith, 'Community and Custom in Property' (2009) 10 Theoretical Inquiries in Law 5; Henry Smith, 'Custom in American Property Law: A Vanishing Act' (2013) 48 Texas International Law Journal 507.

[24] Henry Smith, 'Property, Equity, and the Rule of Law' in Lisa M Austin and Dennis Klimchuk (eds), *Private Law and the Rule of Law* 244 (OUP 2014): 'equity points to something beyond the more formal parts of law . . . even if equity is part of the law, it cannot be a part of a formal part of the law'. See also Smith, 'Equity as Second-Order Law' (n 3) 5: 'Functionally, equity is part of the law broadly conceived, *but outside the more formal part of the law*' (emphasis added). Smith acknowledges that equitable intervention as he understands it sometimes results in law, but he asserts that the resulting law is—seemingly simply by virtue of being law—not equity: 'equity is *only* a safety valve . . . [certain equitable responses, which were once] purely equitable [can become] partially crystallized, or sedimented, into a well-known rule. Equity is left over for new hard-to-see variants on the theme and is reserved

distinctiveness, and so to throw off the fusionists. It also makes it easier for him to convince the reader of the value of equity, for his account suggests that equity performs functions that the law cannot.

The safety valve theory claims that law and equity stand to one another as first- and second-order normative systems.[25] Law is the first-order system, establishing general rules of conduct on a formal or modular basis. Equity, by contrast, is a second-order system necessitated by law. It operates upon the law and exists in order to ensure that the law actually meets its ends.

Smith explains: 'Private law sets up simple and stable structures as platforms upon which people can coordinate.'[26] Law facilitates coordination by providing (and, where necessary, coercively securing) general terms of conduct. The generality of law is reflected in its formal or modular expression and is essential to the law's capacity to support coordination. Equity, by contrast, is impliedly not formal or modular and does not *directly* support coordination. It is instead second order, or, 'law about law'.[27] Equity permits exceptional suspension or modification of first-order law to ensure the proper overall functioning of law as a complex normative system.

Smith characterizes equity as a 'safety valve' because it releases pressure that builds within law. A dominant source of this pressure lies in sophisticated individuals' exploitation of opportunities for evasion or abuse of law entailed by its generality.[28] Smith explains: 'One reason law fails is that the need for general rules leaves loopholes wide open for opportunists to exploit.'[29] Equity exists principally to remedy this particular kind of defect inasmuch as it 'counters opportunism'.[30]

The safety valve theory clearly articulates a remedial view of equity. If the safety valve metaphor was not suggestive enough, Smith is quite explicit about it. He says that 'Equity is exactly what theorists from Aristotle's day to that of the Legal Realists assumed: an intervention into the law, a qualification of the law when it was inadequate on account of its generality.'[31] Smith suggests further that equity operates through vague standards[32] (including 'rules of thumb' and 'shifting presumptions') that allow for 'targeted' intervention upon first-order law.[33] In his own words, 'equity is a safety valve with its built-in limits, in being called upon to intervene *only* when the law is inadequate and *only* in a targeted *in personam* fashion'.[34] Furthermore, Smith says that this intervention

for as-yet-undreamed-of opportunism' (ibid 10). See also Samuel Bray, 'Equity: Notes on the American Reception' in John CP Goldberg, Peter Turner, and Henry Smith (eds), *Equity and Law: Fusion and Fission* (CUP 2019) 3–4.

[25] Smith (n 24).
[26] Smith, 'Economic Analysis of Law Versus Equity' (n 3) 3.
[27] Smith, 'Equity as Second-Order Law' (n 3) 1.
[28] As Smith notes, 'the problem with ... simple modular structures is that they are sometimes vulnerable to people with *too much* information' (ibid 6).
[29] ibid. See also Smith, 'Property, Equity, and the Rule of Law' (n 24) 225; Smith, 'Equitable Dimension of Contract' (n 3) 903.
[30] Smith, 'Equitable Dimension of Contract' (n 3) 6.
[31] ibid 2.
[32] Smith, 'Equitable Dimension of Contract' (n 3) 904: 'equity employs ex post standards rather than ex ante rules'.
[33] Smith, 'Equity as Second-Order Law' (n 3) 25–26.
[34] ibid 33 (emphasis added, in part). See also: 'Equity seeks *individualized* justice in which opportunism has no scope for exploiting the defects of the law that stem from its generality' (ibid 42).

occurs through *ex post* judicial review: 'equity is a needed ex post intervention to keep the ex ante environment safe from opportunists' misuse and manipulation'.[35]

Remedialism is also evident in Dennis Klimchuk's important work.[36] Klimchuk aims to excavate equity's normative foundations by considering what equitable intervention implies about the morality of the behaviour of a person against whom an intervention is made. Like Smith, Klimchuk believes that Aristotle got equity basically right. The lodestar for equity is concern for a particular kind of mischief. According to Klimchuk, equity offers relief from the inequity of the 'stickler'—the person who insists on his rights in order to oppress, coerce, or otherwise dominate the person subject to liabilities or duties relative to those rights.[37]

The stickler theory is powerful because it articulates reasons for equitable intervention in the enforcement of legal rights that are consistent with reasons thought to justify those rights. This is important because it supplies the basis for an original argument for equity's consistency with the rule of law.[38] Under the stickler theory, equity is consistent with the rule of law (and, indeed, is an entailment of it) because the law cannot countenance abuses of right (via the general form of law) that would undermine its underlying values, including the values of independence and equality.

Consistent with remedialist thinking more broadly, Klimchuk generally positions equity not as a *source* of rights but as focused on justice in the *enforcement* of rights.[39] The problem with the stickler is not that he is asserting rights that he does not have or seeking enforcement on terms not provided by law. It is, rather, that he is standing on his rights in a way that is permitted by law but antithetical to its values. Equity's response is not to vary the rights of the stickler, or recognize rights in persons who suffer for his behaviour, but to limit him in the enforcement of his rights. In this way, equity is positioned beyond law, in a distinctive and non-rivalrous relationship with it, in a way that recalls Smith's characterization of equity as second-order law. Equity is not itself law but is essential to the realization of our ambitions for law, whether those ambitions are framed in terms of function or in terms of value.

C. Beyond Remedialism

The remedial conception of equity is dominant for good reason. For centuries, equitable intervention was strictly remedial. Furthermore, significant parts of equity continue to fit the remedial view. Much of equity consists in vague standards, engaged *ex post*, that

[35] ibid 6.

[36] Klimchuk (n 4).

[37] Following Aristotle's characterization of the equitable person as one who: 'is no stickler for justice in a bad sense but tends to take less than his share though he has the law on his own side' ((n 11) 1796).

[38] Klimchuk (n 4).

[39] For example, Klimchuk explains that remedial equity is consistent with, and indeed implied by, the rule of law because '[r]espect for the rule of law . . . requires imposing constraints on the manner in which rights are exercised' (ibid 250). However, note that Klimchuk's analysis of proprietary estoppel suggests that equity can sometimes be a source of rights (Klimchuk (n 11)).

permit courts to check the ordinary operation of legal norms in order to achieve particular justice. Enrichment of the remedial view has also enabled contemporary theorists to effectively answer the equity sceptics. However, equity theory ought now to move beyond remedialism. This is important because a substantial part of modern equity consists in doctrine that is best understood as supplemental law.

II. Equity as Supplemental Law

Modern equity performs key remedial functions, but it also serves as an important source of supplemental law, expanding the reach of the common law and improving its responsiveness to salient interests. Where equity has supplemented law, it has improved the law by completing or extending it. Recognition of the latter contribution is important to understanding how equity facilitates the renewal of private law. It is also essential to the development of a suitably capacious interpretive theory of equity.[40]

In what follows, I introduce the idea of equity as supplemental law, explain how equity supplements law, and point to some evidence supporting supplementation as a core function of equity. This will set the stage for the analysis of equitable rights in section III, and reflection on the value of equity's supplemental function in section V.

A. The Basic Idea

The basic idea of equity as supplemental law is that equity contributes to law in part by adding to, or supplementing, it. It does so by serving as a unique source of law.

This idea has two elements. The first is that, in so far as equity supplies law, it is itself law. This implies that it won't do to describe equity broadly in contradistinction to law; ie, as something other than law, such as a body of supervening moral principles. If those parts of equity that belong to it as supplemental law are to be distinguished from ordinary common law, they will be distinguished as a different *kind* of law (eg, as a kind of law that has a distinctive conceptual structure or normative signature), or else as law derived from a different *source*. The second element is that, as a body of supplemental

[40] In work interpretive legal theory, one must take the law as found. Which means that the analysis provided here will focus on the *results* of equity's supplementation of law. One cannot interpret that which is not yet available for interpretation. But there is obvious interest in the question whether equity *continues* to function—here, in remedying the law, there in supplementing it—in the ways that I and others have suggested it *has*. One can ask—and many have—whether equity is past the age of 'childbearing'. Judges have often insisted that it is not. See, for example, *Eves v Eves* [1975] 1 WLR 1338, CA (per Lord Denning, MR). But the question is not easily answered partly because different jurisdictions feature markedly different attitudes toward the salience of equity in modern law. Australians, for example, tend to be proud defenders of traditional equity. See, for example, Michael Tilbury, 'Fallacy or Furphy? Fusion in a Judicature World' (2003) 26 UNSW Law Journal 357. And, so, one might hypothesize, Australian jurists generally remain alive to equity's generative potential. Americans, by contrast, have largely forgotten or become indifferent to equity's various contributions. See generally Smith, 'Fusing the Equitable Function in Private Law' (n 3); Bray (n 24). And so, one might hypothesize, American equity might now be rather less generative. Various commonwealth jurisdictions likely fall within these extremes, but assessing the current generativity of equity can't be easy in any case. I am grateful to Henry Smith for raising this issue.

law, equity bears a particular relationship to ordinary common law. Being a supplement to something implies not just the existence of that something (the thing supplemented), but also a contribution to it—one which enhances its value, utility, or suitability for a purpose. This, in turn, suggests that while equity is a source of law, it is not a *primary* source of law, and that it assumes law attributable to one or more primary sources.[41]

I have said that equity supplements ordinary common law by adding to it in order to improve it. In my view, equity makes three broad kinds of contribution.

First, equity supplements the law by filling gaps that, for one reason or another (and perhaps purely by chance), have not been filled otherwise. In many cases, these gaps may not have been recognized at all—or as salient—at common law, but ultimately came to be recognized as such in equity (ie, as bona fide gaps, rather than idiosyncratic cases in which enforcement of law would entail inequitable results).

Second, equity supplements the law by supplying terms that modify or adjust common law rules in order that the law may better comport with norms of general justice. As will be discussed in section V, in some cases supplementation of this sort might follow from equity's repeated remedial intervention in the law. Where equity might, for a time, intervene remedially by suspending the operation of certain legal rules, it may eventually—as the basis for intervention is repeatedly invoked, generating a pattern suggestive of a generic problem—alter the rules, supplementing them through recognition of a right, duty, or some other jural construct that has the effect of changing (and, from the perspective of equity, repairing) the law.

Third, equity supplements law by supplying and comprehensively specifying distinctive forms of transaction, relationship, or association. While equity has made narrow, tailored contributions by amending or adding to a set of legal rules otherwise comprehensively specified at common law, it has also made broad contributions by establishing rules for forms of transaction, relationship, or association that equity alone, or principally, recognizes. Some of equity's best-known contributions are of this sort.[42]

Equity adds significantly to law through each of these three modes of supplementation. I have characterized the first as 'gap filling' on the basis that equity here fills occasional lacunae, but it should be appreciated that equity's supplementation of law more broadly implicates a gap-filling function. Just as the various remedial operations of equity are encapsulated by Henry Smith's safety valve metaphor, so too are its various supplemental operations tidily illustrated by thinking of equity as an especially plastic gap filler. Each of equity's three modes of supplementation involves the closure of gaps by provision of new law. In some cases, the gap-filling role of equity is obvious; in others, the presence of the gap can be inferred only by imagining our law without supplementation by equity, or by considering legal systems that have not devised constructs like those supplied by equity.

[41] As was recognized by Maitland, who explained that equity is 'not a self-sufficient system' and that it has 'presupposed the existence of the common law' in its development ((n 1) 19).

[42] Some of the most prominent of these contributions involve equity's provision for the formation and governance of institutions, as explained by Matthew Harding (see this volume, Chapter 16).

We may now return to my claim that equity is a source of law. To many lawyers, the idea that one should have to demonstrate that modern equity is body of law might seem strange. While centuries ago one might have maintained that equity is a discretionary fount of justice that subsists beyond law, most lawyers accept that modern equity is a body of law, even if they think it an embarrassingly shambolic one. Yet it should be remembered that remedialists characterize equity as non-law or as meta-law. This makes it important to pause over the claim that equity is, in part, supplemental *law*.

I mean here to highlight equity's contributions that take the usual form of law. Again, where equity supplements law, it does so by generating new law to fill in gaps in existing law. Equity's successes in supplementation are arguably, if ironically, most notable where least discernible. Where equity succeeds, the seams between 'old' and 'new' law—this part, of common law, that part, of equity—will fade over time to the point that one might only see fused law. Equity's contributions can, with time, be overlooked precisely because it operates from *within* the law, as a conjoint body of judge-made law administered simultaneously with the common law.

As section III will show, equity's contributions often reflect the deontic structure for which private law is well known.[43] That is, equity articulates interpersonal primary rights and conditions governing their ascription. These rights give rise to correlative equitable obligations. Violation of such an obligation is a civil wrong[44] and the commission of such a wrong usually founds a secondary right in the victim to an equitable remedy. Where equity supplements the law in this way, equitable intervention occurs not by way of petition for discretionary relief from the enforcement of legal rules but instead through recognition of a cause of action in which a wrong is alleged as the basis of an action and associated claims for relief.[45]

B. Provenance

The notion that equity supplements law can be traced to developments in the institutional history of equity in England. Particularly pertinent is the practice that arose in the Chancery of responding to injustices wrought by the rigid system of writs at common law by creating new writs, and thereby establishing new causes of action. In drafting these writs, Chancery officials clearly believed that equity jurisdiction extends to supplementation of law.

[43] See Birks (n 8) 8: 'Private law concerns the persons who bear rights, the rights which they bear, and the actions by which they protect those rights.'

[44] ibid 10: 'A wrong is an infringement of a right, or which is ultimately synonymous, a breach of duty. Every wrong therefore supposes a prior right infringed and duty broken.' See also Peter Birks, 'The Concept of a Civil Wrong' in David G Owen (ed), *Philosophical Foundations of Tort Law* (OUP 1995) 31, 33: 'A civil wrong is no more nor less than a breach of a legal duty owed to a plaintiff.'

[45] Here, I part ways with John Goldberg and Ben Zipursky, who emphasize judicial discretion in their account of equity and suggest that equity generally does not facilitate civil recourse for wrongs. See John CP Goldberg and Benjamin C Zipursky, 'Judicial Power in Law and Equity' in this volume.

Accounts of this practice vary, but according to Maitland the Chancery was promulgating new writs by the end of the thirteenth century. Describing the position of the Chancellor at this point in history, Maitland says:

> He is not yet a judge, but already he by himself or his subordinates has a great deal of work to do which brings him into a close connexion with the administration of justice. One of the duties of that great staff of clerks over which he presides is to draw up and issue those writs whereby actions are begun in the courts of law … A man who wishes to begin an action must go to the Chancery and obtain a writ. Many writs there are which have been formulated long ago … But the Chancery has a certain limited power of inventing new writs to meet new cases as they arise … Thus the Chancellor may often have to consider whether the case is one in which some new and some specially worded writ should be framed.[46]

Of course, the issuance of new writs implicated a limited lawmaking power: the writs developed by the Chancellor were subject to acceptance by the royal courts.[47] Nevertheless, the practice provides important precedent for the view that equity jurisdiction extends to supplementation of law. Indeed, Maitland suggests that the Chancery might have been emboldened in their remedial interventions due to frustration over power struggles with the royal courts over supplementation of the writs system:

> [O]ne thing that the Chancellor may do … is to invent a new writ and so provide the complainant with a means of bringing an action in a court of law. But in the fourteenth century the courts of law have become very conservative and are given to quashing writs which differ in material points from those already in use. But another thing that the Chancellor can do is to send for the complainant's adversary and examine him against the charges made against him. Gradually a procedure [for doing so] is established.[48]

[46] Maitland (n 1) 3.

[47] As Maitland explains: 'This … is not judicial business. The Chancellor does not hear both sides of the story, he only hears the plaintiff's application, and if he grants a writ the courts of law may afterwards quash that writ as being contrary to the law of the land' (ibid). See also Duncan Kerly, *History of Equity* (CUP 1890) 10–11:

> The form of the writ [issued by the Chancery] was debated upon before, and its sufficiency determined by the judges, not by its framers, and they were, as English judges have always been, devoted adherents to precedent. In the course of centuries, by taking certain writs as starting points, and accumulating successive variations upon them, the judges added great areas to our Common Law, and many of its most famous branches, assumpsit and trover and conversion, for instance, were developed in this way; but the expansion of the Common Law was the work of the 15th and subsequent centuries, when, under the stress of eager rivalry with the growing equitable jurisdiction of the Chancery, the judges strove, not only by admitting and developing actions upon the case, but also by use of fictitious actions … to supply the deficiencies of their system.

[48] (n 1) 5. The power of the Chancellor to issue new writs, and so to supplement or support the growth of forms of action at law, was explicitly set forth in the Statute of Westminster II (3): 'And whensoever from henceforth it shall fortune in the Chancery, that in one case a writ is found, and in like case falling under law, and requiring like remedy, is found none; the clerks of the chancery shall agree in making the writ.' See also Edward Jenks, *A Short History of English Law* (Little, Brown 1912) 45: 'The invention of writs was really the making of the English Common Law; and the credit of this momentous achievement, which took place chiefly between 1150 and 1250,

Whatever the historical relationship between equity's remedial and supplemental functions, both are of considerable vintage. It is less clear when, and for what reasons, the Chancery came to assert the jurisdiction to liberally supplement the law after the writs system was done away with. Some point to the enforcement of uses as a key moment. Maitland, for instance, suggests that by the fourteenth century, it is becoming increasingly clear that 'the Chancellor is doing some convenient and useful works that could not be done, or could not as easily be done by the courts of common law. He has taken to enforcing uses or trusts ... [and] [t]hus one great field of substantive law fell into his hand.'[49]

Maitland further explains that until the end of the fifteenth century, while the Chancery habitually enforced uses, the bases for its practices were inchoate. He notes that 'with the idea of a law of nature in their minds they decided cases without much reference to any written authority, now making some analogy drawn from the common law, and now of some great maxim of jurisprudence which they have borrowed from the canonists or the civilians.'[50] But, as of the sixteenth century, 'the jurisprudence of the court is becoming settled' with the result that 'from the Restoration or thereabouts ... we may regard equity as administered in the Chancery as a recognized part of the law of the land.'[51]

It is, unfortunately, unusual to find scholarly discussion of equity's supplementation of law. However, an important exception is found in Hohfeld's survey of equity.[52] Interestingly, Hohfeld framed his survey as a response to Langdell's assertion that equity is a branch of the law of remedies. Hohfeld rejected this view, calling it 'inadequate and misleading', and observed that 'from the time of the very earliest cases now available down to the present, equity has always recognized and vindicated what would now be called, as a matter of analysis, exclusively equitable antecedent (or primary) rights.'[53] Hohfeld, in turn, provided a detailed catalogue of equitable rights, categorized according to their relationship to legal rights.[54] We needn't be detained here by

must be shared between officials of the royal Chancery, who framed new forms, and the royal judges who either allowed or quashed them.'

[49] Maitland (n 1) 6–7. See Holmes's observation that in developing the use, equity can be seen to have supplied 'an improvement invented in a relatively high state of civilization which the common law was too archaic to deal with'. Oliver Wendell Holmes, 'Early English Equity' (1908) 1 LQR 162. See also Ames on the 'transformation of the honorary obligation of the feoffee into a legal obligation'. James Barr Ames, 'The Origin of Uses and Trusts' (1908) 21 Harvard Law Review 261, 265.

[50] (n 1) 9.

[51] ibid 9–10. See also Birks (n 8) 24: 'Already in the 16th century St German was playing down the differences [between law and equity]. Law was not deaf to reason, and equity had to be orderly ... As the story comes down through the centuries, past Nottingham in the 17th century and Eldon in the first quarter of the19th, it offers no support for the view that the chancery judges thought themselves peculiarly free to pursue a refined justice tailored to the particular case"; Birks (n 2) 22: 'Sir Edward Coke saw the Chancery under Lord Chancellor Ellesmere as an instrument of Stuart prerogative power, and the Court of Chancery came within a whisker of being swept away with the Star Chamber. It escaped and, having long forgotten Aquinas, it settled into a quest for regularity indistinguishable from that of the common law"; Megarry and Baker: 'By the time Lord Eldon retired, the rules of equity were as fixed as those of the common law.' RE Megarry and PV Baker, *Snell's Principles of Equity* (26th edn, Sweet & Maxwell 1966) 10.

[52] Wesley N Hohfeld, 'The Relations Between Equity and Law' (1913) 11 Michigan Law Review 537.

[53] ibid 543, n 7.

[54] See Hohfeld's discussion of the concurrent operation of equitable and legal rights and duties, privileges, and 'no rights', powers and liabilities (ibid at 553–54), and his discussion of exclusive operation of equity through the

the particulars of his scheme. But advertence to his work provides a suitable point of departure for our discussion of equitable rights.

III. An Illustration: Equitable Rights

I have suggested that equity supplements law by filling gaps in the law with new legal rules. Of course, legal rules take a variety of forms. As Hart explained, primary rules are those through which law facilitates and regulates behaviour.[55] Secondary rules, in turn, govern the operation of primary rules, providing for their enactment, alteration, and enforcement.[56] The rules with which we are presently concerned are primary rules.[57] Following Hohfeld's scheme, some are expressed as rights, privileges and powers, while others are correlative or standalone duties, no-rights and liabilities.[58] There is no a priori reason to think that the menu of primary rules supplied by equity is more limited than that supplied by law, but for present purposes we needn't explicate all manner of primary rules originating in equity. Instead, we need only to establish what Hohfeld tried to show: that equity supplies primary rights.

A. Seeds of Doubt

As is true of my general claim that equity supplements law, so too this narrower claim that it supplements the law through recognition of primary rights might seem obvious to those who see equity as Hohfeld did. One thinks especially of lawyers working in trust and corporate law. Who, they might think, could doubt that equity is a source of primary rights?

Actually, a number of people have. Indeed, some have flatly denied that equity supplies primary rights.[59] Of these, none was more insistent than Hohfeld's foil, Christopher Langdell. Langdell favoured the common, binary view of law and equity. According to Langdell, the articulation of primary rights is within the province of law alone. Equity, by contrast, is a site for achievement of discretionary justice. Langdell expressed these

same jural categories (ibid 555–56). Hohfeld explained: 'When a jural relation is such as to be recognized and vindicated only in equity, it is, according to general usage, called "exclusively equitable",—for instance, the right of a cestui against his trustee' (ibid 570, n 34).

[55] HLA Hart, *The Concept of Law* (3rd edn, OUP 2012) 79–99.

[56] ibid.

[57] To the extent that it is expressed in rules, much of remedial equity consists of secondary rules. This way of understanding remedial equity is consistent with Smith's framing of equity as second-order law. See works cited ((n 3)).

[58] Wesley N Hohfeld, 'Fundamental Legal Conceptions as Applied in Judicial Reasoning' (1917) 26 Yale Law Journal 710.

[59] See, for example, John Adams, *The Doctrine of Equity* (T & JW Johnson & Co 1890) xxix: 'The principle by which [the powers of the Chancery] was regulated appears to have been the one above stated, viz., that of affording an effectual remedy when the remedy at common law was imperfect, but not, as has sometimes been erroneously supposed, that of creating a right which the common law denied.'

views most clearly in an ambitious paper in which he set out a classificatory scheme of rights and wrongs. Explaining equity's exclusion from the scheme, he said:

> What has thus far been said of rights and their infringement has in it no element of equity. The rights which have been described may be defined as original and independent rights, and equity has no voice either in the creation of such rights or in deciding in whom they are invested. Equity cannot, therefore, create personal rights which are unknown to the law.[60]

While others have not expressed scepticism about equitable rights as forcefully, Langdell's conclusions are entailed by any theory that explains equity in strictly remedial terms.

B. Examples of Equitable Rights

As Hohfeld recognized, Langdell and his followers are wrong. Equity supplements the law and has routinely done so by generating primary rights. I'll presently provide some examples that involve equity (1) filling gaps remedially by establishing constraints on legal rights; (2) filling gaps interstitially and so expanding law by adding to existing legal rights; and (3) filling gaps comprehensively through gradual development of novel modular or formal frameworks of rights.

We begin by considering equitable rights that remedy defects arising in the enforcement of legal rights. In such cases, gaps are filled by equity through provision of a novel right, presumably on the basis that it affords the best protection for an underlying general interest (ie, an interest imperilled or left unprotected at common law). An excellent example is the right of redemption held under a mortgage.

The right of redemption entitles a debtor to reclaim mortgaged property from a lender—even after foreclosure—where the debtor has secured the funds needed to pay off the mortgage.[61] As is well known, the lender's security in mortgaged property is usually held by way of a claim upon title. The lender is expected to exercise rights attached to this claim—up to and through foreclosure—in good faith, relinquishing the claim freely where debtor is prepared to pay off the mortgage.

Lenders sometimes try to exercise their rights under mortgage contracts in lawful but sharp ways in order to advance their extra-contractual self-interest. The right of redemption (otherwise referred to as the equity of redemption) came to be recognized in equity in cases where this behaviour was found unfair, exploitative, or predatory.[62] The motivations of lenders who obstruct debtors in the redemption of mortgages vary.

[60] CC Langdell, 'Classification of Rights and Wrongs (II)' (1900) 13 Harvard Law Review 659; see also CC Langdell, 'Classification of Rights and Wrongs (I)' (1900) 13 Harvard Law Review 537.

[61] See Fiona Burns, 'Clogs on the Equity of Redemption: A Story of Changing Equitable Intervention' in Jamie Glister and Pauline Ridge (eds), *Fault Lines in Equity* (Hart 2012).

[62] ibid 64, noting the concern of equity 'to protect necessitous borrowers from unscrupulous lenders'.

But, in many cases, lenders are alleged to have had an undisclosed collateral purpose in entering the mortgage, and to have acted on that purpose in frustrating redemption. In doing so, the lender acts within its legal rights but with indifference to the debtor's interests and expectations. Equity refused to countenance this behaviour, even where the parties purported to derogate from the right of redemption through contract. It has historically deemed 'clogs' on the right of redemption unenforceable.[63]

What is one to make of the right of redemption? I see it as a clear example of equity supplementing law by filling a gap for the purpose of remedying a defect in the law—a defect that is not inherent but instead remediable through improvement of the law. The right of redemption is of particular interest because it involves an intricate intervention at an intersection of property and contract law. The right of redemption supplements property law by protecting owners' interests in continued ownership of real property they have mortgaged.[64] It also supplements contract law by limiting lenders' contractual rights to exercise their security in a particular type of contract.

We may now consider equitable rights that fill interstitial gaps in the law. By 'interstitial' I mean sporadic gaps in sets of rules otherwise comprehensively specified at common law. These gaps, being interstitial, bear no obvious relationship with one another. It is thus difficult, possibly pointless, to survey the results of this mode of supplementation. Little may be said of it in general terms other than that (1) equity here supports the law's ends by improving the protection of interests that engage those ends; and (2) equity's ability to close interstitial gaps shows its elasticity as a source of supplemental law.

An illustration of equity's interstitial gap filling is found in the law of estates, particularly in its contribution to the law's definition of the rights and obligations *inter se* of those with lesser interests in real property through estates other than the fee simple absolute. There are, for example, a number of points of potential conflict between persons with interests in property subject to a life estate.[65] The life tenant can expect full use and enjoyment during his lifetime. But the manner in which he exercises associated legal rights will impact the interest of the remainder-person. Equity has intervened to address the potential for conflict. It has done so by supplying certain equitable rights to adjust the balance struck between the life tenant and remainder-person. These include the remainder-person's right that the life tenant properly maintain the property and not commit waste. Through filling interstitial gaps in the law of estates in land, equity provided needed clarification of what the life tenant and remainder-person owe one another.

We may now consider equity's comprehensive supplementation of law; that is, its wholesale additions to law in the form of frameworks of rules that establish novel kinds of transaction, relationship, or association.

[63] *Jennings v Ward* (1705) 2 Vern 520, 23 ER 935. See also Burns, ibid 46: 'The Court of Chancery considered the equity of redemption as an important right in property and the anti-clog doctrine was ultimately protective of it.'

[64] AM Honoré, 'Ownership' in AG Guest (ed), *Oxford Essays in Jurisprudence* (OUP 1961).

[65] See generally Kevin Gray and Susan Francis Gray, *Land Law* (6th edn, OUP 2009) 397–400.

The equitable rights that we are now to consider are elements of complex formal or modular structures devised entirely or primarily in equity. Accordingly, most are bundled with other equitable rights, duties, powers, and liabilities within of one of these structures. Consider, for example, the equitable rights of the beneficiary of an ordinary donative trust. The position of the beneficiary, his interest in the trust corpus, and his claims relative to the trustee, other beneficiaries, and third parties, are all defined by interlocking jural relationships defined over centuries in equity. In many cases, the equitable interests of the beneficiary are at once defined and secured by equitable rights. Thus, for example, his interest in faithful administration of the trust is secured by a right to loyalty, correlative to which is the trustee's duty of loyalty. His interest in understanding the present condition of the trust and the record of trust administration is secured by a right to an account, correlative to which the trustee has a duty to render an account. And so on. One could undertake a similar exercise in delineating rights that contribute to equity's specification of the positions of beneficiaries *inter se* and of beneficiaries vis-à-vis third parties. The important point is that equity has elaborated the trust in part by creating and defining equitable rights.

C. Form and Foundations

Having established that equity has generated primary rights in each of its characteristic modes of supplementation (remedial, interstitial, and comprehensive), we may now entertain two general questions about equitable rights.

The first goes to form. Are equitable rights formally distinctive? It would appear not. Equitable rights, like other legal rights, have a fixed formal or modular character.[66] This may be seen in the content of equitable rights as well as ancillary conditions (eg, rules governing the incidence or alteration of the right). Consider, for example, the right of redemption. This right places uniform demands on mortgage lenders (notably, they must effectuate a transfer of title upon redemption, and must not impair redemption). The prohibition on clogs limits alteration of the right and does so by way of general rules. The modularity of the right and ancillary conditions is essential to the capacity of the right of redemption to reliably protect the interests of debtors and to enable social and economic coordination in relation to mortgages.

A second question goes to foundations. Let us assume that rights are justified by the protection they provide for valued human interests. These interests and their relation to underlying values could be simple or complex. Furthermore, the relative value of various interests and associated rights may vary, with this variation expressed formally in secondary rules establishing the relative priority of rights. With this complexity in mind, is there anything to suggest that the foundations of equitable rights differ fundamentally from those of legal rights? Again, it would appear not. Equitable rights, like legal rights, are justified by reasons reflecting values attached to human interests.

[66] As Smith has recognized: 'the structure of rights tends to be modular' ('Equity as Second Order Law' (n 3) 15).

In some cases, equitable rights are justified by the very reasons that underlie the legal rights that they supplement.

An implication is that the common law imperfectly serves interests and values that it can, does, and should protect. When equity supplements law with equitable rights, it does so (1) to protect interests that would otherwise be left exposed to setback in the ordinary operation of legal rules (remedial equitable rights); (2) to provide better protection for interests underlying existing legal rights, or to provide protection for interests implicated alongside those that underlie existing legal rights (interstitial equitable rights);[67] and (3) to provide comprehensive protection for, or a means of advancement of, important interests not equivalently served at common law (comprehensive equitable rights).

IV. Is the Law Supplied by Equity Distinctively Equitable?

As noted earlier, contemporary scholarship is preoccupied with the question of equity's substantive distinctiveness. Haunted by the spectre of fusion, someone who has been so preoccupied will surely ask: is the law supplied by equity distinctively equitable?

Though I share my contemporaries' interest in uncovering the value of equity's contributions, I fear that pursuit of concerns like this can lead one into blind alleys. It is, for example, not clear what is meant by 'fusion' and whether the integration of law and equity should always be considered a loss by equity's defenders. Further, concern over fusion reflects a false assumption that equity can make an important contribution only if it is substantively distinctive. As I will explain in section V, this ignores the possibility that equity has succeeded in part because of its comparative functional advantages. That said, given the likely interest in the question, I shall briefly assess possible bases of the distinctiveness of the supplemental law provided by equity.

Most remedialist views of equity are unable to account for equity's supplemental functions. However, one view—that recourse in equity is conscience-based—might, depending how it is developed. Manifest concern with matters of conscience might, then, seem a promising basis upon which to establish equity's substantive distinctiveness. As I will explain in section V, it is likely that, in many instances, equity has supplemented the law for reasons of conscience. Indeed, equity's institutional identification with matters of conscience may partly explain its comparative advantage relative to other sources of supplemental law.

[67] An excellent example is presented by Webb:

> The common law held that misrepresentation could support the setting aside of a contract only when made fraudulently. This rule worked an injustice, an injustice which Equity remedied when it granted rescission in cases of innocent misrepresentation. But the injustice of the common law rule wasn't attributable to its generality. It was just a bad rule. There was, and is, nothing to stop us adopting a general rule which says: all misrepresentations make a contract voidable. Indeed this is just the rule Equity adopted.
>
> Charlie Webb, this volume, Chapter 1, p 13

The difficulty is that it is hard to determine whether equity's supplementation of law is *uniquely* grounded in conscience. The difficulty arises partly because equity has worked with different conceptions of conscience. It arises also because, while conscience is clearly central to certain equitable doctrines (eg, unconscionability), it is not as obviously significant for others (eg, equity's creation of new security interests). Finally, it arises because when considerations of conscience are detached from practices relating to the enforcement of legal rights and are offered as justification for new legal rules, it is hard to understand why equity should be thought to occupy a unique position of moral authority in addressing demands of conscience upon the content of the law. The lowly common lawyer or judge might reasonably protest that many common law rules also reflect demands of conscience, and that the common law generally has as much reason to be responsive to these demands as does equity.[68] We would thus do well to consider other possible grounds of the distinctiveness of law supplied by equity.

Bearing in mind our focus on equitable rights, one might naturally wonder whether they have any structural properties that differentiate them from legal rights. In my view, it is doubtful that they do. Equitable primary rights imply a deontic relational structure that parallels that of legal primary rights. They can be ascribed to persons or personified groups. Likewise, they can operate bilaterally (between two persons), multilaterally (between members of a group in virtue of their legal identification with that group), or omnilaterally (binding all).

More promising is the possibility that equitable rights are uniquely situated relative to surrounding legal rules. I have suggested that equity supplements the law remedially, interstitially, and comprehensively. Further analysis of these modes of supplementation suggests that some equitable rights may be substantively distinctive in their situation relative to surrounding legal rules because of the kinds of problem they solve.

Where equity fills interstitial gaps, it is difficult to see anything uniformly distinctive in the rights it supplies. Indeed, there may be no reason to think these gaps incapable of being closed—and closed precisely as they have been by equity—through incremental development of the common law. It is, however, easier to discern something distinctive in rights that arise in equity's remedial gap-filling mode. The distinctiveness of these rights is a product of characteristic features of the gaps they address and the manner in which closure is achieved.

Recall that some equitable rights operate remedially to fill gaps that arise in the ordinary operation of legal rules. These rights often correct law by establishing a condition or limitation on legal rights implicated in the gap. They accordingly bear the *remedial signature*—or distinguishing mark—of being in the nature of *a right against a right*.[69] Conceptually and doctrinally, this suggests that remedial equitable rights are

[68] See generally James Penner, in this volume, Chapter 3.

[69] Interestingly, and somewhat ironically, Langdell articulated something quite like this view in attempting to show that equitable jural relations are subordinate to legal ones: 'An equitable obligation ... can bind the obligor only in respect of some right vested in him; and, therefore, every right created by an equitable obligation is derived from, and dependent upon, some other right vested in the obligor. Moreover, every original equitable right is derived from, and dependent upon, a *legal* right vested in the obligor' ('Classification of Rights and Wrongs (II)' (n 59) 674).

derivative of legal rights. Normatively, it suggests that remedial equitable rights give recognition to previously unrecognized interests implicated by the ordinary operation of legal rights.

From this, we may conclude that what is distinctively equitable about *some* equitable rights is that they are held against other legal rights. I will explain the qualification in a moment. I want first to acknowledge that this may strike some as a familiar and, partly for that reason, odd statement. It is familiar because it recalls a debate over the nature of beneficial interests in trusts. The long-established view is that beneficiaries have a kind of property interest (ie, equitable title to, or ownership of, trust property).[70] However a new line of analysis suggests an obligational rendering according to which beneficiaries' interests are *in personam* and in the nature of a 'right against a right'.[71] By this it is meant that beneficiaries enjoy equitable rights (eg, rights to loyalty, care, and accounting) that are held relative to, and that constrain, the trustee's exercise of legal rights of ownership of trust property.

How does my account square with the obligational view? The short answer is that it comports well with it, but that this shows that (1) trust theorists have still to explain what distinguishes the interests of beneficiaries from those whose interests are secured by (different) remedial equitable rights; and (2) the remedial signature borne by some equitable rights may be discerned even where those rights have become incorporated within complex modular structures developed by equity.

While we have hopefully arrived at a deeper understanding of equitable rights, we have also come up with modest conclusions about equity's substantive distinctiveness. Some, but not all, supplemental law generated by equity is distinctively equitable in that it bears a remedial signature. While this conclusion may disappoint some, I don't think it should. For, as we shall see, equity can be defended on other grounds, including its comparative advantage as a source of supplemental law.

V. Why Equity as a Source of Supplemental Law?

We must now confront scepticism about equity from a different point of view. It is one that can best be rendered by imagining the questions that might be put about equity by lawyers from traditions—notably, civilian traditions—to which equity is foreign. From this vantage point, one is forced to confront the reality that in some legal systems, equity's functions must be carried out by other means if they are to be carried out at all, and one is thus led to query why we rely on equity, specifically, to perform the functions it does. Remedialists really ought to consider this perspective, but so

[70] James Penner, 'The (True) Nature of a Beneficiary's Equitable Proprietary Interest under a Trust' (2014) 27 Canadian Journal of Law & Jurisprudence 473.

[71] Ben McFarlane and Robert Stevens, 'The Nature of Equitable Property' (2010) 4 Journal of Equity 1; Lionel Smith, 'Trust and Patrimony' (2014) 38 Revue générale de droit 379. McFarlane and Stevens have since extended their argument and now claim that equity more generally implicates rights held in relation to other rights. See McFarlane and Stevens, this volume, Chapter 9.

must we as well. The puzzled observer will ask: why *equity* as a source of supplemental law? Why not other, more familiar, alternatives?

The outside observer's vantage point is important because it underscores the fact that equity enjoys no monopoly or special privilege as a source of supplemental law. It does not make a *unique* contribution by filling gaps in the law, even where it has done so comprehensively and, indeed, ingeniously. Civilian systems, like all other legal systems, are constructed and so gap-prone. These gaps must be addressed other than by equity. And, so, of course, they are (notably, by legislative supplementation). Indeed, the effectiveness of alternative mechanisms for supplementing law is neatly demonstrated by the prevalence of 'transplants' in civilian systems (ie, supplementation through adaptation of common law constructs). The point that equity's supplemental function is generic holds even if, as I will suggest is also true, equity is a particularly rich and responsive source of supplemental law.

Before considering its advantages, it is important to recognize that equity is not an exclusive source of supplemental law even in systems in which equity traditions were or are robust. While some suppose otherwise, the common law is not an inelastic system that simply instantiates abstract, universal principles of practical reason. It is a dynamic source of law that embeds collective, contextualized moral judgment. It is gap-prone, yet routinely supplemented from within as judges extend and amend the law through ordinary devices, including interpretation and analogical reasoning. That being said, doubtless judges sometimes fail to recognize and address the gaps that have arisen within the common law. In such cases, it will be in need of extrinsic supplementation.

Reflecting on the prospects for supplementation, it bears notice that some have queried whether equity recognizes and protects interests that tort (and, by extension, the common law) cannot.[72] The honest answer, I think, is that equity has no exclusive jurisdiction over the interests it has come to protect. Rather, it has simply come to recognize and protect interests that the common law, for one reason or another, neglected or failed adequately to protect. Of course, it should also be noted that the common law is routinely supplemented by other extrinsic sources, notably legislation. Even in common law systems, equity has competition, and in many cases legislated schemes displace rules supplied by common law *and* equity.

The fact that equity has competition raises interesting questions about the interaction of various sources of private law. However, I am interested principally in the question why equity has been relied upon for supplementation given the alternatives. Again: why equity as a source of supplemental law?

A full answer to this question would require one to address historically and culturally conditioned features of particular legal traditions. However, several factors might make equity an especially rich and adaptive source of supplemental law.

[72] The common law has proved more and less elastic in recognizing gaps by establishing new primary rights and causes of action. Birks suggested that tort law can and should be able to supplant equity, and predicted that 'One day the law of torts (meaning the law of wrongs rooted in the common law) will be transformed into the law of civil wrongs, by the addition of wrongs rooted in the jurisdiction of the Court of Chancery such as abuse of confidential information and breach of fiduciary duty. No special difficulties impede that integration' (Birks (n 2) 19).

First, for a variety of reasons (eg, judicial temperament and systemic considerations favouring status quo arrangements) the common law may be slow to innovate. While we could simply trust that incremental reform will close the most significant gaps and permit modest expansion of the common law's modular structures, society might be better served by extrinsic supplementation, particularly from a system that has supplementation as one of its core functions.

Second, relative to other sources of supplemental law (notably, legislation), equity has the advantage of providing for judge-made supplementation of law that is also judge-made. This may be advantageous for reasons of *institutional competence* (judges may be better situated than other lawmakers to notice and respond to gaps in law they routinely administer), *simultaneity* (procedural fusion allows common law courts to assert equitable jurisdiction and to consider issues of law and equity in a single case), *parsimony* (one can reasonably expect judges to favour narrowly crafted gap-filling rules, and to amend or expand these rules on a gradual, as-needed, basis), *fit* (narrow gap-filling rules crafted by lawmakers with superior institutional competence would seem, *ceteris paribus*, to promise better integration with surrounding law), and *efficiency* (a choice of narrow gap-filling rules devised simultaneously with the administration of a primary source of law by officials expert in both systems, who have the power and opportunity to revisit and adjust those rules, would appear to promise efficiency gains relative to broader legislated frameworks of rules developed by officials who operate at some remove from adjudication and are subject to processes that are costly, time-consuming, and politically uncertain). Indeed, particularly where remedial or interstitial gap filling is required, it is hard to imagine a circumstance in which an alternative source of supplemental law would prove superior (ie, more likely to produce an apt, alterable, and cost-justified rule) to equity.

These factors might suffice to explain equity's comparative advantage as a source of supplemental law. However, there may be another. It lies in a hypothesized productive dynamic between equity's core functions.

Thus far I have explained equity's supplemental function and shown how it differs from its remedial function. One might think that, being distinct, remedial, and supplemental equity are also functionally independent. In fact, I think that they have often been intertwined. While in many cases equity may have supplemented the law without prior remedial intervention, it seems reasonable to think that in others equity has shifted from a remedial to supplemental mode.[73] In these cases equity has, over time, come to recognize and fill a gap after a period in which it merely suspended the

[73] Others have speculated that parts of modern equity have developed in just this way. For example, Mike Macnair has said that the Chancery's power to issue writs implies two things: 'The first was that the Chancellor's jurisdiction extended to wherever the common law was defective in point of justice. The second was that ... equity should in due course become ordinary law, displacing the defective rules of law it was designed to deal with.' Mike Macnair, 'Equity and Conscience' (2007) 27 OJLS 659. See also Lord Evershed's remarks: 'in the course of the growth of equity, what had started as being no more than the grant in a number of similar cases of a particular remedy had ended in the creation of rights—a principle of which perhaps the most obvious instance is the trust.' Lord Evershed, 'Reflections on the Fusion of Law and Equity after 75 Years' (1954) 70 LQR 326, 331, citing reasons given by Lord Parker in *Sinclair v Brougham*, [1914] AC 398, 441–42.

ordinary operation of legal rules. This shift may be long in coming. For a considerable period, equity might operate in strictly remedial guise, providing case-by-case relief. Gradually, recognition of a gap in the law and definition of its contours will generate an imperative to close it. In shifting to its supplemental mode, equity might initially prefer narrow, remedial, or interstitial, gap filling. If, with time, it appears that the gap is larger, or that there might be value in the development of new modular structures, equity might shift again to comprehensive supplementation.

If one accepts that remedial equity might be an important driver of supplemental equity, there remains the question how this might help to explain equity's comparative advantage as a source of supplemental law. Briefly, certain features of remedial equity make it especially well suited to the identification of gaps in the common law. To begin with, remedial equity is premised on the recognition that the law suffers infirmities that impair its ability to serve justice. Indeed, error detection may well be a functional excellence of remedial equity. Second, remedial equity offers remediation of these errors by channelling grievances and requiring judges to consider, define, and ultimately resolve them. Third, while in responding to these grievances a court may decide that a supplemental rather than strictly remedial approach is required, the fact that equity is judge-made law ensures that its products will be subject to testing and verification in subsequent cases. Fourth, remedial equity's focus on particular justice encourages judges to be more sensitive than they might otherwise be to the need for calibration of any new rules devised by them. These properties of remedial equity enable equity more broadly to reliably detect gaps in the law and to gradually arrive at durable solutions in the form of supplemental law.

VI. Conclusion

In this chapter I have addressed facets of equity that have been unattended but lie in plain view. Scholars have lavished attention upon equity's remedial functions, and for good reason. Nevertheless, equally important to our understanding of equity and its relationship to law are its supplemental functions. I have aimed presently to elucidate these functions. I have explained the limited sense in which law supplied by equity is distinctively equitable. I have also suggested that even where equity's supplementation of law is not distinctive, it nonetheless reveals the importance of equity to private law.

6

The Constitution of Equity

Evan Fox-Decent[*]

I. Introduction

I will defend three related ideas regarding the law of Equity, and will discuss another that is much more speculative. The first two related ideas are that Equity has the characteristic form of public law, and that Equity shares public law's basic concern, which is to regulate power held by one party for the benefit of another. Equity and public law alike are structured by the presence of other-regarding power in the legal relations they govern. The third related idea is that the legal form of Equity and public law answers to a particular kind of justice that is neither corrective justice nor distributive justice, but what I will call *jurisdictional justice.* The speculative idea is that Equity is best regarded as a species of public law. I will refer to the conjunction of the first three ideas as the *weak* public law theory of Equity. This theory is consistent with Equity belonging on either side of the private law–public law divide. I will refer to the conjunction of all four claims as the *strong* public law theory of Equity. On this account, Equity is a species of public law. My aim is to defend the weak public law theory, identify some of the obstacles that stand in the way of the strong theory, and then nonetheless offer some tentative arguments that aim to show some of the features and possible merits of the strong theory.

Let me start by stipulating what I mean by 'Equity' and 'public law'. By 'Equity', I mean the rules, principles, doctrines, maxims, and remedies that would eventually fall under the jurisdiction of the Court of Chancery during the fourteenth and fifteenth centuries,[1] and then subsequently be applied and developed by that court until the Judicature Acts of the nineteenth century. The Judicature Acts brought together or 'fused' courts of common law and Equity. Since that time, these fused courts have applied Equity alongside the common law.

By public law I mean judicial review of administrative action in the common law tradition, or what is commonly called administrative law. Judicial review in this context typically involves, on one side, a public entity with statutory or prerogative

* For very helpful comments, I owe a debt to Paul Miller, Joanne Murray, Lionel Smith, Mark Walters, Andrew Gold, Dennis Klimchuk, Irit Samet, and Henry Smith. I owe special thanks to my colleague Lionel Smith, for years of conversation and discussion of many of the topics touched on in this chapter. I thank also the Social Science and Humanities Research Council for financial support that helped make this chapter possible.

[1] There were exceptions, such as the law of bankruptcy. See Ben McFarlane and Robert Stevens, in this volume, Chapter 9, citing J Hackney, *Understanding Equity and Trusts* (Fontana Press 1987).

Evan Fox-Decent, *The Constitution of Equity* In: *Philosophical Foundations of the Law of Equity*. Edited by: Dennis Klimchuk, Irit Samet, and Henry E Smith, Oxford University Press (2020). © The several contributors.
DOI: 10.1093/oso/9780198817659.003.0007

decision-making powers, and on the other, an individual or group under a liability to have their legal position changed by an exercise of those powers (usually liberty rights denied or claim rights withdrawn). An immigration officer's decision to revoke a permanent residence visa, for example, usually results in the termination of the visa holder's statutory liberty right or privilege to remain in a country. The general aim of administrative law is to ensure that public decisions have legal warrant (ie, that they are made using fair and impartial procedures) and that their outcomes and reasons are faithful to a reasonable interpretation of the letter and underlying purpose of their legal authorization.

At the root of my claim that Equity has the form of public law is the thought that its fundamental mission is to govern the exercise of public or other-regarding powers, and to do so irrespective of whether those powers are held by public or private actors. Equity of course has manifold rights and duties. But, I will argue, Equity's real target is the proper exercise of other-regarding powers. Trustees, agents, and statutory bodies, among others, have legal and other-regarding powers. The harder cases for public law theories of Equity are private actors who appear to possess only self-regarding powers, such as the power to seek redress for a wrong. These cases include the creditor in the medieval and early modern period who under the common law could collect a debt a second time if the debtor neglected to have his sealed bond cancelled.[2] At common law a sealed bond was incontrovertible proof a debt was owed. Equity would relieve the debtor of the second payment. I will argue that the creditor's power to seek redress takes on a public, other-regarding character in fact situations that trigger Equity's intervention. Under the weak public law theory, Equity in these contexts regards the creditor as someone endowed with other-regarding powers. The strong theory builds on this foundation to claim that the possession of such powers is characteristic of public law, and so Equity may be classified as a branch of public law.

Part of the argument for both kinds of public law theory is to explain why Equity must presuppose that individuals such as the creditor are to be understood to hold other-regarding powers. Another part of the argument will be to show that the possession of these powers renders the power holder amenable to well-established doctrines and principles from private law and public law that govern the exercise of discretionary power. As we shall see, courts of Equity exercise their jurisdiction in a manner akin to courts engaged in judicial review of administrative action: in both cases, the legality of an exercise of other-regarding power is subject to scrutiny. In both cases, the overarching concern is the lawfulness of an exercise of other-regarding power.

The point of these public law arguments is not to attach a new label or qualification to Equity. The point, rather, is to expose Equity's deep conceptual and normative structure so as to discern a persuasive theory that can explain and justify its core features. In section II, I suggest that theorizing Equity is especially challenging because its doctrines, parties, and remedies traverse large swaths of both private and public law. From this perspective, Equity's constitution—in the sense referring to its features or

[2] Timothy S Haskett, 'The Medieval English Court of Chancery' (1996) 14(2) Law & History Review 245, 252.

properties—is avowedly heterogeneous. I suggest we can distinguish between what I will call Equity's *anti-opportunist* domain, which involves cases of rights sticklers and equitable constraints on claims otherwise available at common law (eg, the sealed bond cases),[3] and Equity's *jurisdictional* sphere, which is mainly composed of cases involving fiduciary relations, such as trusts or agency relations. This distinction, however, reveals the difficulty of the task of theorizing Equity. Not only must one's theory help us understand two realms of law that contain very different doctrines, it must also explain why Equity (at least on its anti-opportunist side) trumps the common law in the event of conflict. The strong theory offers a path through the thicket, while the weak theory is consistent with other theories of Equity that purport to explain its supremacy vis-à-vis the common law without adopting a strong public law theory.[4]

Section III begins to develop the thought that Equity has the form of public law by comparing trust law and administrative law. It is in virtue of its public law form that Equity is a kind of constitutional law. This is the second sense of 'constitution' to which the chapter's title refers. In the private sphere, there is a good sense in which Equity is to legal relations between private parties what administrative law is to relations between public bodies and individuals. And administrative law, in the common law tradition of Sir Edward Coke and AV Dicey, simply is constitutional law, albeit of an 'unwritten' constitution that lacks an entrenched bill of rights. Both Equity and administrative law prevent abuses of power that law itself makes possible. We might think of this as the negative side of Equity's constitution. But Equity as constitutional law has a positive side, too, a dimension that exposes the way its shares the concerns of public law and the rule of law. In public law, judicial review of administrative action provides a bulwark against arbitrary state action, and to that extent provides a bulwark against domination and abuse. Equity likewise resists domination and abuse, bringing a measure of the rule-of-law ideal to private relations. To this extent, Equity and the rule of law contribute to a framework for legal order that makes possible freedom from domination and abuse; that is, freedom from the looming threat of arbitrary choices (domination), and the realization of arbitrariness in particular cases (abuse).[5]

In section IV, I discuss other-regarding powers. These powers are a defining and structural feature of Equity. Their significance to Equity is the principal basis for thinking that Equity has the form of public law. The form itself is suggestive, since implicit to an other-regarding power is a concern for others who are subject to the power. This is paradigmatically the kind of power held and exercised under statute in public law settings.

[3] Some theorists have sought to explain Equity generally in terms of its resistance to rights sticklers, while others have pointed to the protection Equity provides against a limited range of opportunistic behaviour. For exemplars of such accounts, see in this volume Dennis Klimchuk, Chapter 2 (Equity as a constraint on abusive rights sticklers), Henry Smith, Chapter 10 (Equity as a safety valve constraint on opportunism made possible by law), and Andrew Gold, Chapter 4 (Equity as an ambivalent, moral constraint on rights sticklers).

[4] See eg MacFarlane and Stevens (n 1); Klimchuk (n 3); Smith (n 3); Gold (n 3).

[5] For contemporary accounts of neo-Roman or republican accounts of freedom as non-domination, see Philip Pettit, *Republicanism: A Theory of Freedom and Government* (OUP 1999);; Quentin Skinner, *Hobbes and Republican Liberty* (CUP 2008).

In section V, I argue that Equity is not structured by corrective or distributive justice, but rather by *jurisdictional justice*. This is the form of justice apposite to supervisory review of other-regarding powers. Its structure is plainly evident in Equity's jurisdictional sphere.

In section VI, I argue that jurisdictional justice is also the prevailing form of justice within Equity's anti-opportunist domain. In Equity's jurisdictional dimension, doctrine explicitly recognizes the presence of other-regarding power, and that power reflects the jural or conceptual level that posits a power–liability relation between other-regarding power holder and beneficiary. In Equity's anti-opportunist sphere, however, we shall see that doctrine does not explicitly recognize other-regarding powers, but that those are nonetheless implicit and discernible at the jural level. Distinguishing doctrinal and jural levels of inquiry is thus crucial to this argument.

In section VII, I discuss some of the advantages of weak and strong public law theories and their explanatory potential. I also set out the features of a possible strong public law theory and some of the arguments that would have to be made to establish and sustain such an account.

First, however, we need to have in view the range and diversity of Equity's features—the first sense of Equity's constitution—because these elements are the subject matter we aim to theorize, and because their diversity and complexion pose a serious challenge to theorizing Equity.[6]

II. The Challenge of Theorizing Equity

A series of obstacles confronts the scholar who aims to theorize the philosophical foundations of Equity. In many cases, Equity of the early modern period sought to correct injustices made possible by the formality and strictness of the common law and its evidentiary rules. On Aristotelian accounts, equity served as 'a correction of law where it is defective owing to its universality' (*EN* 5.10, 1137b27–28).[7] Equity protected individuals who found themselves vulnerable to opportunists or sticklers who sought to enforce their legal rights when the generality or strictness of the common law enabled them to do so, but their doing so was nonetheless unconscionable. This is what I am calling Equity's anti-opportunist dimension.[8] As Lord Ellesmere put it in *The Earl of Oxford's Case*, the reforming mission of Equity was 'to soften and mollify the extremity

[6] Some scholars suggest that the diverse and open-ended nature of equitable doctrines befuddle attempts to provide a unified account of Equity. Maitland famously defined Equity as simply the rules that originated in the Court of Chancery, 'a collection of appendixes between which there is no very close connection'. Frederick Maitland, edited by AH Chaytor and WJ Whittaker, *Equity; Also, The Forms of Action at Common Law: Two Courses of Lectures* (CUP 1929) 1, 19. See also, in this volume, Lionel Smith, Chapter 7 (asserting with Maitland that Equity lacks quiddity).

[7] Aristotle, *Nicomachean Ethics*, JO Urmson's revision of WD Ross's translation in Jonathan Barnes (ed), *The Complete Works of Aristotle* vol 2 (Princeton UP 1984).

[8] In Paul Miller, in this volume, Chapter 5 Miller refers to the 'remedial conception of equity' as one that emphasizes (more or less) the role that Aristotle's sense of equity has played in Equity.

of the law'.[9] Thus, as noted above, Equity offered relief to the common law debtor who repaid the debt but failed to have her sealed bond cancelled. Equity did not deny or annul in some way the common law right holder's entitlement to collect the debt a second time. The common law right remained intact. Instead, Equity intervened by acting *in personam* and on the conscience of the right holder, thereby preventing the right holder from enforcing his rights against the debtor.[10]

Equity would also enforce certain oral agreements and order discovery of documents necessary to enforce legal rights, measures generally unavailable at common law.[11] When justice required, Equity would grant specific performance of contracts, reform or rescind contracts tainted by fraud or mistake, and enjoin torts such as trespass and nuisance before they were committed.[12] And Equity would protect partial payers of mortgages who fell behind on payment via the equity of redemption.[13] In these and other ways, Equity emerged as a distinctive body of law that was guided by considerations of conscience and substantive justice, and which aimed to provide relief from sticklers and opportunists eager to take advantage of the generality and rigors of the common law.[14]

Because a significant part of Equity's mission was to address injustices produced by or through the common law, in principle its breadth was as far and wide as the common law could travel. Moreover, historically the equitable jurisdiction was understood to be discretionary rather than rule-bound, driven by particularities rather than abstract ideas and precedent, and guided by a murky idea of conscience. The wide scope of Equity's reforming mission, its aversion to formalism, and the apparent fuzziness of its theoretical basis led to John Selden's infamous barb:

> Equity is a roguish thing: for law we have a measure, know what to trust to; equity is according to the conscience of him that is Chancellor, and as that is larger or narrower, so is equity. 'Tis all one as if they should make the standard for the measure we call a foot, a Chancellor's foot; what an uncertain measure would this be? One Chancellor has a long foot, another a short foot, a third an indifferent foot: 'tis the same thing in a Chancellor's conscience.[15]

[9] (1615) 1 Ch Rep 1 at 7; 21 ER 485.

[10] For discussion of the rationale underlying the common law rule on bonds and acquittances, see Klimchuk's contribution in this volume (n 3).

[11] Haskett (n 2) 252.

[12] Thomas O Main and Timothy Haskett, 'Traditional Equity and Contemporary Procedure' (2003) 78 Washington Law Review 429, 443.

[13] See *Vernon v Bethell* (1762) 23 ER 838 (upholding a mortgagor's equity of redemption). For discussion of this doctrine and the similar contract doctrine of substantial performance, see Larissa Katz, in this volume, Chapter 8. In section VI, I will use the equity of redemption to help illustrate the structural similarity between Equity's anti-opportunist and jurisdictional dimensions.

[14] For a more formal account of Equity, see MacFarlane and Stevens (n 1). The account of early Equity I briefly sketch in the text is intended to reflect a conventional understanding of the shape and content of early Equity's anti-opportunist doctrines. For lucid discussion from this perspective, and of the relationship of morality and conscience to Equity in particular, see Dennis Klinck, *Conscience, Equity and the Court of Chancery in Early Modern England* (Ashgate 2010);; Irit Samet, *Equity: Conscience Goes to Market* (OUP 2018).

[15] John Selden, *Table Talk*, quoted in M Evans and RI Jack (eds), *Sources of English Legal and Constitutional History* (Butterworths 1984) 223–24.

On Selden's view, Equity's reliance on a vague sense of conscience meant that it was uncertain and unpredictable.

Equity's reforming mission and its context-sensitive approach are also evident in public law cases involving the exercise of a statutory power. In *A-G v Wandsworth District Board of Works*,[16] for example, Jessell MR had to determine whether the Wandsworth Board of Works had wrongly charged the general fund of local taxpayers for the paving of a road, and if so, whether this charge could be treated as a mistake that Chancery could remedy. Under the Metropolis Management Act, 1855, if paving or other road work created a 'new street', the Board had no authority to charge the general fund, but instead had to charge the property owners with homes adjacent to the street. Prior case law had determined that the street in question was a 'new street' under the Act. The crucial issue was whether Chancery could order an effective remedy, which it had never done before in like circumstances. The Master of the Rolls treated the case as one of innocent mistaken payment involving trust property, and ordered the Board to rectify the mistake by charging the adjacent homeowners for the paving work so as to restore the general fund. In reaching this conclusion, Jessell MR held the following:[17]

> This case only shews that new cases require, not the application of new law, but the application of old principles of law in a new way; nothing more.... The Board of Works for the Wandsworth District holds the funds really as a trustee for the ratepayers of the district, to be laid out in accordance with the terms of the Act of Parliament. They are bound to raise the funds according to those terms, and apply them according to those terms.

In short, the Court in *Wandsworth* explains its jurisdiction by reference to trust law and mistaken payment, areas of law within Equity's domain.[18] Commenting on public law's sharing of doctrinal resources and structure with Equity, Sir Anthony Mason has observed that '[i]n the field of public law, equitable relief in the form of the declaration and the injunction have played a critical part in shaping modern administrative law which, from its earliest days, has mirrored the way in which equity has regulated the exercise of fiduciary powers'.[19] In the next section I consider administrative law cases involving broad discretionary powers and some of the ways in which, to turn Mason's thought on its head, Equity mirrors them.

There is, however, a final and important branch of Equity that is important to have in view: the law of fiduciaries, and in particular, trust law. Equity has a rich history of regulating relationships of trust and confidence. On Lionel Smith's view, the law of trusts

[16] [1877] 6 Ch D 539 (*Wandsworth*).

[17] ibid 541, 543.

[18] For insightful discussion of many such public law cases, see Chief Justice Robert French, 'The Interface between Equitable Principles and Public Law' (Speech to the Society of Trust and Estate Practitioners: Sydney, 2010) www.hcourt.gov.au/assets/publications/speeches/current-justices/frenchcj/frenchcj29oct10.pdf (last viewed 22 April 2018).

[19] Anthony Mason, 'The Place of Equity and Equitable Remedies in the Contemporary Common Law World' (1994) 110 LQR 238, 238.

'stands as the signal contribution of Equity jurisprudence to the legal landscape of the world.... the trust itself is characteristic of and peculiar to Equity'.[20] He points out that trust law is not replete with rules that are 'non-discretionary, clear and hard-edges' and norms that are 'generally precise and technical in nature'.[21] Paul Miller similarly characterizes the trust as part of Equity's 'supplemental law', by which he means that part of Equity which is a different kind of law when compared to the common law or is derived from a different source.[22] The supplemental facets of Equity, Miller claims, reveal Equity as a source of law that 'generates legal principles, rules, and associated normative constructs' which are 'formal or modular in nature and (like laws sourced elsewhere) operate generally, prospectively, and in a way that is typically invariant to context'.[23]

In the next section I'll try to explain why fiduciary relations may be thought to lie at the core of Equity. I will refer to this core as Equity's jurisdictional law, because at its heart is a concern to regulate the exercise of other-regarding powers. Some of these powers, on some accounts, may not be fiduciary in a private law sense. To avoid a quarrel over what is or isn't fiduciary, I use 'jurisdictional' instead of 'fiduciary' to label the category.[24] By 'jurisdictional' I mean simply those relationships or interactions such as one finds in trust or agency law that have the character they do in part because one party to them has discretionary and other-regarding power in relation to some other person or persons, or possibly in relation to an impersonal purpose where there is no determinate beneficiary (eg, a public purpose or charitable trust).[25]

In summary, my suggestion is that Equity's salient doctrinal features can be understood to pertain to either its anti-opportunist or jurisdictional dimensions.

One question that arises is whether the relatively well-defined norms of Equity's jurisdictional law can find a common organizing principle with the more discretionary doctrines of Equity's anti-opportunist law. A further puzzle is the following: if private law is structured by corrective justice, and public law is structured by distributive justice, what structures Equity?[26] Corrective justice, distributive justice, one or the other depending on context, or some other form of justice? My claim is that Equity's

[20] Smith (n 6) 145.

[21] ibid 145. Smith gives as an example the second branch of the Rule in *Howe v Lord Dartmouth* that requires trustees to treat equally or with an even hand income and capital beneficiaries of a trust.

[22] Miller (n 8) 101.

[23] ibid 93.

[24] The label 'jurisdictional law' may not be ideal, since jurisdictional review in commonwealth administrative law is closely associated with conservative judicial activism hostile to the administrative state generally. See, eg, Lord Hewart, *The New Despotism* (Ernest Benn 1929). Yet it is hard to find another term as fitting to analysis of a power's scope and exercise, and so I'll use 'jurisdictional' with the hope that this conceptual project won't be tarred with that historical brush.

[25] For the view that fiduciary relations with beneficiaries are to be distinguished from fiduciary cases in which the power is directed towards an abstract purpose and no specific, ascertainable beneficiary, see Paul B Miller and Andrew S Gold, 'Fiduciary Governance' (2015) 57 William & Mary Law Review 513. For the view that fiduciary cases of both kinds are explicable by paying attention to the other-regarding purpose or purposes for which a power is conferred on a fiduciary, see Evan Fox-Decent, *Sovereignty's Promise: The State as Fiduciary* (OUP 2011) 37.

[26] Scholars sympathetic to critical legal studies may question the alignment of private law with (merely) corrective justice, while theorists with libertarian sympathies may doubt the legitimacy of distributive justice and thereby deny its purported connection to public law. I cannot enter these debates here, and would simply point out that I am calling on corrective and distributive justice simply to draw a contrast with the form of justice I will argue is inherent to Equity.

distinctive quality lies in its recognition and regulation of other-regarding powers. The form of justice that structures Equity is one that emulates the form of justice constituted by public law doctrines that govern the scope and exercise of discretionary powers held by public bodies. We will canvass some of these public law doctrines immediately below as we compare them to their trust law analogues (eg, doctrines that prohibit decision-making on the basis of irrelevant considerations and improper purposes). I will refer to the form of justice they embody as *jurisdictional justice*, since its concern is determining the rightful scope and exercise of other-regarding powers. It is worth underscoring from the outset that review of jurisdictional questions is a central concern of administrative law. A majority of the Supreme Court of Canada affirms in *Dunsmuir v New Brunswick*, a leading Canadian administrative law case, that 'the rule of law is maintained because the courts have the last word on jurisdiction', and they characterize 'the inherent power of the superior courts' to include 'a power to review administrative action and ensure that it does not exceed its jurisdiction'.[27]

I begin now the argument that Equity has the characteristic form of public law with a comparison of some of the core doctrines of trust law and administrative law. Their striking similarity to one another is explained, I claim, by the structure they share, which in turn makes both amenable to jurisdictional justice.

III. Trust Law vs Administrative Law

Consider the doctrine from *Re Hastings-Bass*,[28] known commonly to trust lawyers as 'the rule in *Re Hastings Bass*':[29]

> [W]here … a trustee is given a discretion as to some matter under which he acts in good faith, the court should not interfere with his action notwithstanding that it does not have the full effect which he intended unless: (1) what he has achieved is unauthorized by the power conferred upon him, or (2) it is clear that he would not have acted as he did (a) had he not taken into account considerations which he should not have taken into account, or (b) had he not failed to take into account considerations which he ought to have taken into account.

Put more concisely, Buckley LJ cautioned courts not to 'interfere' with a trustee's disposition of trust assets unless (1) the trustee acted in a manner beyond the scope of his power, or (2) in exercising his discretion (a) he took into account irrelevant considerations or (b) he failed to take into account all relevant considerations. Buckley did not

[27] [2008] 1 SCR 190 paras 30–31 (per Bastarache and LeBel JJ) [*Dunsmuir*]. See also *Anisminic Ltd v Foreign Compensation Commission* [1968] UKHL 6, [1969] 2 AC 147, 171 (distinguishing between jurisdiction in a 'narrow' sense of 'the tribunal being entitled to enter on the inquiry in question', and jurisdiction in a 'wide sense' where 'although the tribunal had jurisdiction to enter on the inquiry, it has done or failed to do something in the course of the inquiry which is of such a nature that the decision is a nullity', per Lord Reid).

[28] [1975] Ch 25.

[29] ibid 41.

specify, however, the nature or form of a court's intervention if a trustee's decision were caught by one of the rule's two branches. Were the trustee's impeachable acts void, or merely voidable if the beneficiary makes a successful claim, and therefore valid until a court rules favourably on such a claim?

The legal effects of the two branches were considered in two tax cases heard together: *Pitt v Holt-Futter v Futter*.[30] Concerning the first branch, Lloyd LJ held that '[t]he purported exercise of a discretionary power on the part of the trustees will be void if what is done is not within the scope of the power'.[31] As examples, his lordship said there could be a procedural defect, 'such as the use of the wrong kind of document', or a substantive defect, 'such as an unauthorized delegation or an appointment of someone who is not within the class of objects' or a 'fraud on the power'.[32] Regarding the second branch of the rule, Lloyd LJ said that 'if an exercise by trustees of a discretionary power is within the terms of the power, but the trustees have in some way breached their duties in respect of that exercise, then ... the trustees' act is not void but it may be voidable at the instance of a beneficiary who is adversely affected'.[33]

The rule in *Re Bass Hastings* is literally identical to black-letter administrative law governing the exercise of discretionary public powers. And with a very minor *mutatis mutandis* qualification, the legal effects of the rule, as specified by Lloyd LJ in *Pitt-Futter*, are also found in judicial review of administrative action. The first branch of the rule is what administrative lawyers refer to as jurisdictional review.[34] In public law, this is typically an inquiry to determine whether the frontline decision-maker acted beyond or outside her statutory authority. As in the case of trusts, errors going to jurisdiction can be procedural or substantive, with the result that the decision, as with trusts, is treated as void *ab initio*.

The second branch of the rule in *Re Bass Hastings* is likewise identical to administrative law doctrine governing discretion. In fact, a central device reviewing courts' use to test the legality of public discretionary decisions is inquiry into whether the administrative decision-maker took into account all relevant considerations while excluding from deliberation all irrelevant considerations. In a leading UK public law case on discretion, *Padfield v Minister of Agriculture, Fisheries and Food*,[35] Lord Upjohn found that the minister would unlawfully exercise his discretionary power 'by taking into account some wholly irrelevant or extraneous consideration' or 'by wholly omitting to take into account a relevant consideration'.[36] A finding on either of these two grounds would typically result in the court making an order of *certiorari*, which has the effect

[30] [2011] EWCA Civ 197, [2012] Ch. 132. On appeal, Lord Walker described 'the rule in *Hastings-Bass*' as a 'misnomer' because *Re Hastings Bass* concerned 'only the scope of the power itself, rather than the nature of the decision making process which led to its being exercised in a particular way', but given the expression's familiar usage, his Lordship concluded that 'it is best to continue to use it'. *Pitt v Holt-Futter v Futter* [2013] UKSC 26, para 1. The Supreme Court qualified the rule such that a decision *intra vires* the trustee's discretionary power would be declared void only if the trustee could be said to have breached her duty in the exercise of her power (para 93).

[31] *Pitt-Futter* (n 30) 96.

[32] ibid.

[33] ibid 99.

[34] See, eg, *Dunsmuir* (n 27) paras 31–32; *Anisminic* (n 27) 171.

[35] [1968] UKHL 1.

[36] ibid 23.

of setting aside the decision (ie, declaring it void) and sending it back to the administrative decision-maker for redetermination. It follows that in these circumstances the decision is voidable at the behest of the complainant, and so voidable in a manner that parallels trust law.

Numerous other doctrines in trust law and administrative law also bear a striking resemblance to one another. In both spheres, there are doctrines of fettering and non-delegation. These doctrines aim at preserving the integrity and independence of the decision-maker's deliberative process. I'll use non-delegation to illustrate. Trustees may only delegate ministerial or non-discretionary decisions that do not involve an exercise of judgment.[37] In the public sphere, legislatures cannot delegate their legislative powers to administrative officials.[38] And, within the administration itself, the rule is the same as the one that governs trustees: agencies can delegate only ministerial decisions that do not require the exercise of discretion. If an agency delegates a decision that requires judgment, the agency would give to another body or person a power that it (and it alone) has authority to exercise.

In *Vic Restaurant Inc v Montreal (City)*,[39] for example, the city passed a bylaw that made the issuance of permits conditional on the authorization of the director of police. A majority of the Supreme Court of Canada held that this was a wrongful delegation because the bylaw did not provide precise guidance to the director, in effect conferring on him the city's power to issue permits. In both trust law and public law, the decision-maker must use her own judgment to exercise the power confided to her;[40] otherwise, the entrusted power is exercised by someone not authorized to use it. The legal regimes in the two spheres can rightfully hold their decision-makers to account precisely because their decisions are indeed *their* decisions.

One also finds in both trust law and administrative law similar doctrines regarding the purposes for which entrusted legal powers can be exercised.[41] In both domains, the entrusted power must be used exclusively for the purpose or purposes for which it was conferred.[42] In trust law, 'fraud on a power' refers to the precept that 'a power can only be used for the purpose for which it is conferred, and not for any extraneous or ulterior purpose'.[43] Thus, in *Courage Group*, Millet J held that it was possible to amend

[37] Lionel Smith, 'Can We Be Obliged to Be Selfless?' in Andrew S Gold and Paul B Miller (eds) *Philosophical Foundations of Fiduciary Law* (OUP 2014) 141, 149.

[38] See, eg, *In re the Initiative and Referendum Act* [1919] AC 935, 945 (a provincial legislature cannot 'create and endow with its own capacity a new legislative power not created by the [British North America Act]', per Viscount Haldane); *JW Hampton, Jr & Co v United States*, 276 US 394, 409 (1928) (to avoid unconstitutional delegation of legislative power, Congress must provide to administrative agencies an 'intelligible principle' to guide their creation of regulations).

[39] [1959] SCR 58.

[40] I'm much indebted to Lionel Smith's careful elaboration of this idea, in the context of trusts and fiduciary relationships more generally. See Smith (n 37); Lionel Smith, 'Fiduciary Relationships: Ensuring the Loyal Exercise of Judgement on Behalf of Another' (2014) 130 LQR 608.

[41] Additionally, administrative law and fiduciary law disclose duties of good faith. In the fiduciary context, good faith is especially salient in Delaware corporate law: see, eg, Strine Jr and others, 'Loyalty's Core Demand: The Defining Role of Good Faith in Corporation Law' (2010) 98 Georgetown Law Journal 629.

[42] For discussion of trust cases, see C Mitchell, 'Stewardship of Property and Liability to Account' (2014) 78 Conv 215.

[43] *Re Courage Group's Pension Schemes v Imperial Brewing and Leisure Ltd* [1987] 1 All ER 537, per Millet J [*Courage Group*]. See also, *Vatcher v Paull* [1915] AC 372, PC 378; *Andco Nominess Pty Ltd v Lestato* (1995) 17 ASCR 239 262; *Hillsdown Holdings plc v Pensions Ombudsman* [1997] 1 All ER 862.

provisions of a pension scheme provided the amendments were consistent with the purposes of the scheme. The doctrine of improper purposes in administrative law is identical.

In *Smith & Rhuland Ltd v The Queen*,[44] the Supreme Court found that a labour board with power to certify a union could not refuse certification on grounds that the union's secretary-treasurer was a communist. And in *Roncarelli v Duplessis*,[45] an iconic judgment on the rule of law, Rand J found that an unqualified discretionary power had been used for an improper purpose.[46] The Quebec liquor commissioner, at the behest of Quebec Premier and Attorney General Duplessis, revoked Roncarelli's liquor permit because Roncarelli had guaranteed bail of fellow Jehovah's Witnesses. His fellow congregants were in conflict with Quebec's Catholic establishment and were being arrested for petty municipal offences. Dennis Klimchuk suggests that the reasoning in *Roncarelli* exhibits a structure akin to the reasoning of the rights stickler cases of Equity's anti-opportunist law.[47] I agree with Klimchuk's conclusion, and also with the idea of unifying anti-opportunist cases with jurisdictional cases, but propose that the jural route for getting there runs through abused other-regarding powers rather than abused rights.[48]

The point of immediate interest, however, is the similarity and nature of the doctrines discussed above; ie, review for relevant and irrelevant considerations; fettering; non-delegation; good faith; and proper/improper purposes.[49] These doctrines are constitutive of much of trust law and administrative law, so much so that those bodies of law would not be what they are—they would lose their character as trust law and administrative law respectively—were these doctrines not part of them. Something the doctrines have in common is that they regulate the relevant decision-making power by ensuring that it is exercised by the party authorized to exercise it (fettering, non-delegation), and that the actual exercise of the power is consistent with the reasons for which the power was conferred in the first place (good faith, proper purposes, no

[44] [1953] 2 SCR 95.

[45] [1959] SCR 121 [*Roncarelli*].

[46] In Canadian administrative law courses, *Roncarelli* is often the case students read first to give them a sense of how courts supervise executive discretion. The case, however, was actually brought as a claim against Duplessis personally for extra-contractual damages. The revocation of Roncarelli's liquor permit had driven him into bankruptcy, and he sought damages from Duplessis. The former premier pleaded that as a public servant exercising the powers of his office in good faith, he was immune from suit. The majority found that Duplessis's actions constituted such an egregious abuse of power that he could not be understood to have taken them as a good-faith public servant. The immunity-stripping discussion of good faith in *Roncarelli* is identical in structure to the reasoning of 'improper purpose' cases on discretion in administrative law, where there is no claim for damages but merely a challenge to the validity of the decision. This is why *Roncarelli*, despite being a claim for damages, is a central fixture of Canadian administrative law.

[47] Dennis Klimchuk, 'Equity and the Rule of Law' in Lisa Austin and Dennis Klimchuk (eds), *Private Law and the Rule of Law* (OUP 2014) 247, 250–51, 257–58.

[48] Klimchuk has clarified to me in comments that he was using 'rights' in a 'non-disaggregated, pre-Hohfeldian sense'. I take him to mean he deployed a conception of rights that includes powers, these powers were abused in *Roncarelli*, and so his analysis is consistent with mine. If that is right, then my argument might be construed as bringing to the surface something that is already implicit in Klimchuk's work.

[49] These similarities were noticed and discussed explicitly in *Edge v Pensions Ombudsman* [2000] Ch 602 and *Equitable Life Assurance Society v Hyman* [2002] 1 AC 408. But for reservations, see *Abacus Trust Co (Isle of Man) v Barr* [2003] Ch 409 (distinguishing the discretionary nature of relief on judicial review, judicial review's approach to nullity, and time limits, per Lightman J para 29).

irrelevant considerations, all relevant considerations). One way to explain this constellation of doctrines across both trust law and administrative law is to suppose that (1) they are designed to govern powers, and (2) those powers are other-regarding rather than self-regarding. In the next section I sketch what I mean by 'powers' and 'other-regarding'.

IV. Other-Regarding Powers

The paradigmatic sorts of powers I mean to specify are legal powers in the Hohfeldian sense. These denote a normative capacity ordinarily exercised through an intentional act of the power holder to change someone's legal position.[50] Whereas the jural correlative of a claim right is a duty, the jural correlative of a power is a liability. Trust beneficiaries and persons subject to administrative bodies alike are generally under a liability to have their legal positions changed by those who hold legal powers in relation to them. When the Quebec liquor commissioner cancelled Roncarelli's liquor permit, Roncarelli lost the privilege or liberty right (in Hohfeld's sense) of selling liquor. So, the exercise of a power can result in a change of jural position involving, for example, privileges or immunities, as well as a change of claim rights and duties. It is a live question whether Hohfeld's own analysis of powers is best.

Raz suggests that the exercise of powers can result in a wider set of legal consequences than Hohfeld envisioned.[51] These consequences, Raz says, include 'a change in the existence, content or application of a law or legally recognized norm', such as consequences that follow from 'norm-creating' powers like the power to make a contract.[52] These consequences show the facilitative and enabling side of powers. Elaborating on Raz, Lisa Austin argues that in the case of property, exclusive possession can be understood as a 'legal power that confers exclusive control in relation to the object of property', which in turn facilitates future uses by an owner who doesn't presently possess the object.[53] A payoff to this approach, Austin says, is that it reveals a variety of actions that law makes possible, and in that sense discloses some of the ways law makes the realization of freedom possible, and not merely secure.[54]

Adult individuals typically have personal legal powers that reflect their legal capacity, and those powers allow them to act in ways to change their legal position or produce legal consequences related to themselves as private parties. If I sign a contract, I now personally owe an obligation to the counterparty that I didn't owe before. My personal legal power to contract for myself is *self-regarding*. I hold and exercise it for my purposes. I can include others within my purposes, and I can elect to exercise the

[50] Neil MacCormick and Joseph Raz, 'Voluntary Obligations and Normative Powers' (1972) 46 *Proceedings of the Aristotelian Society*, Supplementary Volumes 59, 81 (underscoring the normative and not factual aspect of a legal power, and its intentionality).

[51] Joseph Raz, *Practical Reason and Norms* (OUP 1975).

[52] ibid 103, 82.

[53] Lisa Austin, 'The Power of the Rule of Law' in Austin and Klimchuk (eds), (n 47) 269, 276, 278–79.

[54] ibid 280.

power for their benefit.[55] But the power is personal and self-regarding because, ordinarily, as a matter of private law I alone am entitled to decide how to use it and the ends to be pursued with it. Other legal powers, however, such as the powers of trustees and administrative agencies, are not self-regarding: they are not held for the purposes or benefit of the person who possesses them. They are held for the benefit of someone else, or for many others, or for the advancement of an impersonal purpose. These powers are *other-regarding*. They are brought into existence and conferred on their possessor for the benefit of some person or persons other than the power holder, or to advance an impersonal purpose.[56]

Public decision-makers necessarily hold *powers*, and the powers they hold are necessarily *other-regarding*. They necessarily hold *powers* because that is what makes them decision-makers—ie, their possession of statutory or prerogative power to make decisions in a given field. And those powers are necessarily *other-regarding* because it is definitional of a public actor qua public actor that she make decisions and take other actions in the public interest. She must do so (and be seen to do so) impartially and free from corrupting influences such as conflicts of interest.[57] If she uses a public position to rent-seek, she engages in corruption. If she favours without justification a friend or family member, she participates in nepotism. And if she favours without justification a particular group, she advances sectionalism. Corruption, nepotism, and sectionalism are all wrongful uses of public power because they capture power conferred for public purposes and turn it to private ends.[58] Put another way, these practices are manifestly wrongful because they egregiously breach the requirements of role that inhere in and follow from the public actor's possession of other-regarding power.

Mutatis mutandis, the same story can be told with respect to private fiduciaries. The private law duty of loyalty and the prophylactic rules against unauthorized conflicts and profits reflect the fact that the fiduciary's powers are necessarily other-regarding rather than self-regarding. Lionel Smith's discussion of equitable remedies in his contribution to this volume makes this clear.[59] Smith notes that '[i]n respect of trust property held by the trustee, a trust is always automatically specifically enforceable', and as a consequence, there is 'no inquiry into whether damages would be adequate as a remedy.... there is no option to pay compensation: you have to do what you are obliged to do'.[60]

[55] Agents present complications. My preferred thumbnail analysis of agency relations is that, typically, a contract-based agency relationship between principal and agent is formed through mutual consent, with each party exercising their own legal power to contract. Once the agency relationship is created, however, the agent is authorized to act as the principal's representative, and this means that the agent uses the principal's legal power to contract with third parties on behalf of the principal, creating contractual relations between the principal and the relevant third parties.

[56] Partnerships, joint ventures and like associations may appear to present complications, since the duty bearers (eg, partners) profit directly from the association. The complications are merely apparent, since the relevant power can be understood to be held in the service of the joint interest embodied by the association (eg, a partnership), rather than in the service of any one member's separate and personal interest (discussed in section V).

[57] *Dimes v Grand Junction Canal Co* [1852] Eng R 789, 10 ER 301, 2 HLJ 759 (decision of the Lord Chancellor set aside because he had shares in the canal company that was a party to the dispute).

[58] See, eg, *A-G Hong Kong v Reid* [1994] AC 324, [1993] 3 WLR 1143, [1994] 1 All ER 1 (PC, NZ) (a Director of Public Prosecutions breached his fiduciary duty to the Crown by accepting bribes, becoming a debtor in equity to the Crown for the amount of the bribes as well as criminally liable).

[59] Smith (n 6).

[60] ibid 00.

In contract law, on the other hand, the duty is one of performance rather than loyalty, and expectation damages—the net value the breachee expected to receive under the contract—are the norm. Specific performance is the exception. At contract, one has a duty to perform, but failure to perform is not usually met with a court order to perform on pain of being held in contempt. The usual remedy is damages, and so at the remedial stage of contract law there is a good sense in which one need not do what one is obliged to do; one usually pays damages instead.[61]

In my view, the different kinds of powers in play under contract law and fiduciary law respectively explain the different default duties and remedies, and this is because the difference in the powers makes a difference to the structure of the two kinds of relation. In contract, typically two parties with separate interests and separate self-regarding powers to contract come together and make a contract.[62] The parties are understood to have entered into the contract to advance their own interests, and not the interests of the counterparty. Hence, there is no default prophylactic rule against conflicts in contract law. Such a rule would be nonsensical in light of the basic, self-regarding presuppositions of contract. The law does not expect them to act *for* each other, but rather expects them to perform their contractual obligations, possibly for self-interested reasons, in the expectation that the other party will do the same. Thus, if one party breaches her obligation to deliver a chattel, ordinarily the breachor is not treated as a constructive trustee who holds the chattel for the benefit of the breachee. In the standard case, a court will order payment of expectation damages rather than impose a trust on the chattel for the breachee's benefit. If our contractor finds a buyer for her chattel at a higher price, she can choose to breach the original contract and then be held liable to pay damages.

Trustees do not have this choice. As Samuel Bray points out, historically Equity has been characterized by judicial commands that order parties to do what they are obligated to do on pain of contempt and imprisonment.[63] This divergence from contractual norms is explained by the fact that fiduciary relations involve other-regarding powers and mandates that enable and direct fiduciaries to act *for* their beneficiaries—in their names or on their behalves—whereas contract relations *as such* typically do not have these features.[64] Contractors act jointly with each other, but in the typical case the law

[61] I do not mean to endorse the theory of efficient breach under which contractual duties are viewed as optional; ie, contractors are allegedly entitled to choose between performance and paying damages. I doubt contractors are so entitled. In the standard case, contractors have duties to perform, failure to perform is a breach of duty, and it is for the court (not the contractor) to set the remedy. The contractor has factual power to decide whether or not to perform, and ordinarily the court will not order a breachor to perform (expectation damages are the norm). But this does not imply that the contractor can breach her duty without doing wrong, or that the law's attitude towards contractors is that they may treat their contractual obligations as merely placeholders for what they might do in the future if it is maximally in their interest to do so.

[62] Ernest Weinrib articulates a similar relational scheme of classification, although he doesn't distinguish fiduciary from contractual relationships with reference to the different kinds of powers in play in each domain: Ernest J Weinrib, 'The Juridical Classification of Obligations' in Peter Birks (ed) *The Classification of Obligations* (OUP 1998) 37.

[63] Samuel L Bray, 'Equity: Notes on the American Reception' in John CP Goldberg, Peter Turner, and Henry E Smith (eds), *Equity and Law: Fusion and Fission* (CUP 2019).

[64] Contracts that establish fiduciary relations, such as agency, are not counterexamples to this claim, because in these cases it is not the contract *as such* that explains the legal effect of the other-regarding power, but rather (on my view anyway) its inherent character as an other-regarding power. Further, even if one imagines that

recognizes that ultimately they are acting for themselves. Fiduciaries, on the other hand, possess other-regarding and discretionary powers that are to be used *for* their beneficiaries, triggering norms of loyalty rather than mere performance.[65]

To summarize: both public entities and private fiduciaries are subject to a wide range of regulative doctrines that closely resemble each other because in both cases the proper exercise of other-regarding power is at stake and subject to judicial review.[66] This is the characteristic form of public law, the doctrines of which jointly comprise 'unwritten' constitutional law in the domain of public law. Equity's jurisdictional law shares this form transparently, and therefore has the form of public, unwritten constitutional law; ie, the form of judicial review of administrative action. Of course, the matter can be viewed the other way round, using the private law of Equity's jurisdictional dimension as the starting place and analysing the ways public law shares its form. There is now a burgeoning literature that looks to private fiduciary law to explain and understand national and international public law.[67] In my view, public law and private fiduciary law in fact share the same relational structure, as suggested by the foregoing comparison of trust law to administrative law. They each have the form of one another, and from this it follows that Equity's jurisdictional law has the form of public law, and vice versa. Let's consider briefly the kind of justice that responds to this form of law—jurisdictional justice—before turning to the task of explaining how Equity's anti-opportunist law can be understood to possess the form of public law and Equity's jurisdictional law.

contract can somehow explain the nature and legal effect of other-regarding powers in agency and like cases, we can still distinguish contractual relations that vest other-regarding powers from contractual relations that don't, such as an ordinary transaction involving a sale of goods. This is enough to let us see that the default legal norms in cases animated by self-regarding powers are different than the usual norms in cases structured by other-regarding powers. For arguments of a similar nature, see Daniel Markovitz, 'Sharing *ex ante* and Sharing *ex post*: The Non-Contractual Basis of Fiduciary Relations' in Gold and Miller (eds) (n 37) 209; Lionel D Smith, 'Contract, Consent, and Fiduciary Relationships' in Paul B Miller and Andrew S Gold (eds) *Contract, Status, and Fiduciary Law* (OUP 2016).

[65] The absence of a duty of mitigation in fiduciary law is also striking, for it speaks to the way Equity treats the subject matter of the fiduciary duty as something belonging to the beneficiary such that a faithless fiduciary's gains will be disgorged and responsibility for loss will lie solely with the breaching fiduciary.

[66] I have just scratched the surface of both administrative law and trust law. In the case of trust law, I have said nothing about how its regulation of other-regarding power may or may not serve as an organizing principle with respect to the law governing the constitution of trusts, effects on third parties, the three certainties, and issues related to enforcement. Still, I hope to have said enough to lend credibility to the thought that the presence of other-regarding power and its regulation is constitutive of the legal form of the relationship between trustee and beneficiary, even if the form alone cannot supply an exhaustive account of all trust law's particulars.

[67] See, eg, Paul Finn, 'The Forgotten "Trust": The People and the State' in Malcolm Cope (ed) *Equity: Issues and Trends* (Federation Press 1995) (discussing the historical role of fiduciary principles in commonwealth public law); Fox-Decent (n 25) (arguing that the state is a fiduciary of the people amenable to its jurisdiction, and that this fiduciary relationship explains administrative law); Evan J Criddle and Evan Fox-Decent, *Fiduciaries of Humanity: How International Law Constitutes Authority* (OUP 2016) (affirming that states are fiduciaries humanity as well as their people, and that this dual fiduciary role explains international law); Evan J Criddle and others (eds), *Fiduciary Government* (CUP 2018) (fourteen essays assessing and developing fiduciary public law); (Ethan J Leib and others, 'A Fiduciary Theory of Judging' 101 California Law Review 699 (2013) (analysing judging from a fiduciary perspective); Paul Miller, 'Principle of Public Fiduciary Administration' in A Scolnikov and T Kahana (eds), *Boundaries of State, Boundaries of Rights* (CUP 2016) (defending a parsimonious account of public fiduciary authority).

V. Jurisdictional Justice

The kind of justice that best responds to the form of public law is neither corrective nor distributive justice, but jurisdictional justice. Corrective justice is an awkward fit with the form of public law because the fundamental relationship between power holder and power subject is structured by an other-regarding power and a correlative liability rather than a self-regarding claim right and a correlative duty. The power–liability structure leads Lionel Smith to claim that the (so-called) fiduciary duty of loyalty is not a duty in the strict Hohfeldian sense, because it is in the nature of the fiduciary's discretionary powers that 'they neither forbid nor require action'.[68] On Smith's view, the beneficiary does not have a claim right to a particular outcome, but rather has standing to challenge whether the power has been exercised in the required manner; ie, loyally. The norm of loyalty, on this construal, is a requirement of valid decision-making that flows from the possession of other-regarding discretionary powers. Smith compares the requirement of loyalty to the requirements of making a valid contract, such as an absence of mistake and pressure.[69] There is no duty on contractors to avoid mistakes or pressure, but if they can show that mistake or pressure vitiated consent, they can avoid the contract.

The validity-assessing doctrines from public law discussed above support Smith's theory. Judges typically apply those doctrines to discretionary decisions without reference to whether the decision-maker breached a duty to the affected individual. The issue for the reviewing court is whether the decision has legal warrant (is it within the agency's jurisdiction?), and if so, whether the power was used reasonably (eg, was the power exercised for a proper purpose and without regard to irrelevant considerations?). The classic wrongs of public law are not the violation of an individual's claim right (though that is possible, particularly in an era of enshrined human rights), but rather the exercise of power either without legal authority or in a manner that constitutes an abuse of authority. Whereas corrective justice seeks to restore a normative balance between private parties such that both enjoy what they are due, jurisdictional justice seeks to ensure that every exercise of other-regarding power is intelligible as action taken in the name of or on behalf of the persons subject to it.[70]

Some might think that distributive justice is up to the task of explaining public law. Distributive justice can specify the goods of public law (eg, public and accessible education, healthcare, housing, basic income and insurance), as well as the criteria to be used for their distribution across a given population (eg, need, merit, expected benefit, relative social position). But distributive justice is not chiefly concerned with the delineation and regulation of other-regarding powers. In the sphere of public law, distributive justice is

[68] Smith (n 37) 154.

[69] ibid 153.

[70] Evan Criddle and I develop this latter thought as a 'criterion of legitimacy' for assessing the lawfulness and legitimacy of state action from the perspective of international law (Criddle and Fox-Decent (n 67) 3, 99–100, 131, 217, 240, 268, 288).

chiefly concerned with how the benefits and burdens of society are to be equitably distributed. Naturally, legislation can put the dictates of distributive justice into effect. But assessing the validity of exercises of discretionary public power is a task that calls on judicial review doctrines about which considerations of distributive justice may have little to say, and most importantly, will not have the right things to say. Consider again *Roncarelli*.

Let's assume that distributive justice concerns justify the prescribed conditions on which one could obtain and hold a liquor permit in Quebec in the 1940s. Let's take for granted as well that Roncarelli at all times met those conditions, including when the liquor commissioner revoked his permit. The wrong from the standpoint of distributive justice, on the assumptions we've made, is that someone deserving of a liquor permit had his taken away. But what is missing from this characterization of the wrong is precisely the quality of the wickedness that makes *Roncarelli* an iconic rule-of-law case: ie, the fact that Roncarelli's permit was revoked for an improper purpose wholly unrelated to the statutory regime, and therefore in what was an egregious abuse of power. Distributive justice would have to undergo significant contortions to explain the nature of this wrong, whereas abuses of power of this kind are paradigm cases for jurisdictional justice and the institutional framework it provides for the rule of law. Distributive justice looks at actual distributions of goods. Jurisdictional justice looks at the manner in which public power is exercised so as to distribute goods through law. Jurisdictional justice is thus keenly attuned to the terms on which public power is held and used in a way that distributive justice is not. To put the contrast another way, distributive justice cares about the ends of policy whereas jurisdictional justice cares about the manner in which powers are used and decisions are made to bring those ends about.

The regulative doctrines from Equity's jurisdictional law and public law alike suffuse jurisdictional justice with juridical content. These doctrines aim at the regulation of other-regarding powers with a view to assessing the legality of their exercise. This is the distinctive kind of justice that explains the structure of public law relations in a manner analogous to the way corrective justice explains the structure of tort law relations. The point of both corrective justice and jurisdictional justice is to structure tort law and public law respectively so that the relevant jural relations—right and duty in tort law, power, and liability in public law—provide the salient and foundational conceptual structure apposite to each domain. We turn now to the question of how Equity's anti-opportunist law might fit within jurisdictional justice.

VI. Equity's Anti-Opportunist Law and Jurisdictional Justice

Consider first the equity-of-redemption cases from Equity's anti-opportunist law. These cases featured a mortgagee who held title in a 'deed by mortgage' as security for the debt.[71] The title was subject to a condition subsequent that gave the debtor the right

[71] For a summary of the mechanics of mortgages in common law jurisdictions and lucid discussion of the doctrine of equity of redemption, see Katz (n 13).

to regain title once the mortgage debt was paid. If the mortgagor defaulted, the creditor would become the owner with title clear of the condition subsequent. Equity, however, through the doctrine of equity of redemption, allowed the mortgagor to redeem her property (ie, to get it back from the mortgagee, its legal owner) by paying down the debt—even after default—so long as she was paying the debt and signalled her intention and ability to continue doing so. The creditor was entitled at common law to take full ownership of the property from the defaulting debtor, but Equity didn't let her do so. Why not?

One explanation might proceed by pointing to the non-fungible value of land and one's home, the security and independence a home gives its occupants, and the disproportionate harm caused by evicting willing but late mortgage payers. Independently of these kinds of reasons, however, an important challenge from a legal point of view is to explain why the creditor—who had a legal right to evict and had committed no wrong—bears the burden of this doctrine. Ideally, the explanation should specify the jural relations between the parties in a way that helps to show how Equity could justifiably impose the cost of its doctrine on the creditor.

The creditor, as title holder of the mortgaged property, had legal powers that came with the title. These powers were limited by both the condition subsequent in favour of the debtor and the equity of redemption. The creditor's powers were not fiduciary powers, however, that had to be exercised exclusively for the benefit of the mortgagor. If the debtor became a recalcitrant defaulter, the equity of redemption would yield, and the creditor could take free and clear ownership of the land. And, at common law, the creditor could exercise the power of foreclosure if the debtor failed to make payment when she was supposed to do so. In other words, at law the creditor held a *power* of foreclosure in relation to the debtor's equity of redemption (the creditor could foreclose on the possibility of redemption and gain clear title) to which the debtor was *liable* in the event of *recurrent* non-payment. This power–liability relationship is the relevant jural relation that obtained between the parties.

It is important here to distinguish the doctrinal level of analysis from the jural or conceptual level. In contract, for example, we would distinguish doctrines relating to formation (eg, offer, acceptance and consideration) from the conceptual idea that parties can form a binding contract through the use of self-regarding legal powers. Likewise, in property law we can distinguish doctrines relating to real estate and security, such as condition subsequent or equity of redemption, from the power–liability jural relation that obtains between creditor and debtor. Roughly, the jural level provides the relevant legal form, whereas the doctrinal level provides content that inhabits the form. Sometimes the doctrinal level explicitly declares what is happening at the jural level. Equity's jurisdictional law, such as trust law, does this: trusts doctrine expressly recognizes the presence of an other-regarding legal power in the hands of the trustee. Trust law doctrine therefore explicitly mirrors the power–liability relation between trustee and beneficiary at the jural level. But Equity's anti-opportunism law, such as the equity of redemption, generally does not wear explicitly its jural form on its doctrinal sleeve. As with contract law, the underlying power–liability jural form of Equity's anti-opportunism law is implicit. With doctrinal and conceptual levels of analysis thus distinguished, we can now sharpen the substantive question we need to answer with respect to the equity of redemption, which is: How can we explain Equity's restriction on the creditor's otherwise lawful use of his power of foreclosure against the mortgagor's equity of redemption in the event of non-recurrent default?

I will argue that we can understand the creditor to occupy a public position in the service of Equity. Of course, Equity does not formally or explicitly assign its burden bearers a public role. Nonetheless, I will claim that Equity treats them as possessing the obligations and status ordinarily possessed by public actors. This alone does not imply that they ought to be considered public officials per se, or that the law of Equity is public law rather than private law. Three significant obstacles stand in the way of these claims, which each implicitly assert a strong public law theory of Equity. First, competing theories of Equity that situate its doctrines squarely within private law would have to be considered and found wanting. These include accounts that expressly aim to explain how Equity can operate as both a distinctive and second-order law vis-à-vis the common law,[72] and theories that take on board an other-regarding-powers interpretation of Equity but question why this interpretation cannot be accommodated within private law.[73] Second, substantive theories of private law that include organizing principles such as substantive equality may be able to absorb the other-regarding aspects of Equity, so one would need to show that such theories are unpersuasive or that the move to public law was worthwhile even taking a theory of this kind on board.[74] Third, criteria pertaining to the classification of legal obligations would need to be adduced and considered before a strong public law theory could be endorsed. I cannot address fully these issues here, but will offer some arguments that both strengthen the weak public law theory and lay groundwork for the strong account.

Returning to the equity-of-redemption case, let's consider the possibility that Equity calls on the creditor to occupy a public role when the equity of redemption is available to the debtor. For so long as the creditor occupies that public role, her private power of foreclosure assumes the character of a public, other-regarding power. Consequently, in this context, her power is potentially subject to the doctrines of jurisdictional justice that regulate the exercise of other-regarding powers (eg, jurisdictional inquiry, improper purposes, irrelevant/relevant considerations). And concretely, her power of foreclosure is constrained by the equity of redemption to allow the debtor to make good on the mortgage debt and ultimately redeem her land.

The weak public law theory of Equity holds private actors accountable to public law standards, and in that respect resembles key elements of the theories defended by Larissa Katz and James Penner in this volume.[75] The idea of clothing private actors in

[72] See eg MacFarlane and Stevens (n 13); Klimchuk (n 3).

[73] I thank Andrew Gold and Dennis Klimchuk for raising this latter objection to the strong public law theory.

[74] See eg Hanoch Dagan and Avihay Dorfman, 'Just Relationships' 116 Columbia Law Review 1395 (2016) (defending self-determination and substantive equality as organizing principles of private law).

[75] Katz (n 13); James Penner, in this volume, Chapter 3. See also Tony Honoré, *The South African Law of Trusts* (4th edn, 1992 Juta) (characterizing significant elements of trust law, such as the courts' supervisory jurisdiction, as public law).

public garb also enjoys a venerable pedigree. Hobbes uses it to bring within public authority the putatively private 'right of zeal' under scriptural Judaic law; ie, the right of a private party to execute an offender under prescribed circumstances. Hobbes claims that the execution becomes lawful 'upon subsequent ratification'.[76] More central to Hobbes's political project is his claim that in some contexts individuals must be able to count on the 'presumption of a future ratification ... as in a sudden rebellion any man that can suppress it by his own power ... without express law or commission, may lawfully do it, and provide to have it ratified or pardoned whilst it is in the doing or after it is done'.[77] This resonates with Katz's conscription idea regarding 'the state's prerogative to enlist our help in discharging the burdens of government',[78] and with Penner's view that there's a 'public law duty to contribute to just institutions'.[79]

However, whereas Hobbes was anxious to relieve certain actors of liability by showing that apparently private acts of violence were really lawful acts of public authority, Equity, I suggest now, may be interpreted to treat private actors as occupants of public roles for three other reasons: (1) to preserve their equality as private legal actors, (2) to provide a distinctive institutional home for Equity, and (3) to make them amenable to jurisdictional justice and its norms. Regarding (3), bringing private actors into a public role helps explain how they can be held accountable to public law values, including the collective commitments those values express or signal. It is noteworthy that for Penner the public law dimension of Equity includes ethical norms 'about what sorts of people we regard ourselves as being, about what good, as opposed to right, might reasonably require of us in keeping with our collective self-conception of the kind of people we are, eg, compassionate and kind rather than, say, competitive and individualistic'.[80] In this sense, Equity might be thought to have an expressive as well as accountability dimension as it seeks to bring public law values to private legal order.

Consider now how Equity's treatment of private actors as occupants of public positions (1) preserves equality at private law and (2) carves out an institutional space for Equity. When Equity calls on individuals to fulfil public roles, it arguably treats them as occupying a public position, in part, because that position is consonant with them holding an other-regarding power (ie, the power to foreclose limited by the equity of redemption). Were the creditor a mere private actor rather than someone occupying a public role, the demands of Equity would confront him as authoritarian fiats, as demands arising from the unilateral needs of another private party, and in a context in which the bearers of Equity's burdens have law on their side. As Equity's public servants,

[76] Thomas Hobbes, *Leviathan with Selected Variants from the Latin Edition of 1668* (first published 1651, Edwin Curely ed, Hackett 1994) 493 (Review and Conclusion, para 11).

[77] ibid 493–94 (Review and Conclusion, para 11).

[78] Katz (n 13).

[79] Penner (n 75). Penner credits Arthur Ripstein who developed the idea in relation to the duty to rescue: Arthur Ripstein, 'Three Duties to Rescue: Moral, Civil, and Criminal' (2000) 19 Law & Philosophy 751 (the state can rightfully enforce a duty to rescue through criminal law because through legislation we all give law to ourselves, but private law cannot rightfully demand performance of this kind of duty, since private law's doing so would vindicate allowing the need of one individual to set unilaterally the terms of interaction with another).

[80] Penner (n 75).

on the other hand, they are brought within a hierarchically superior institution (public law) that is legally entitled to modify or extinguish private law entitlements for the sake of public law concerns.

Let's consider now a second doctrine from Equity's anti-opportunism law, the well-worn rights stickler case of the debtor who didn't get his bond cancelled and is liable at common law to pay the creditor a second time. The case can serve as a model for other doctrines from Equity that lend themselves to rights stickler or opportunist explanations, such as estoppel. The creditor who held a debtor's sealed bond did not have a first-order legal power over the debtor's assets. But she did have the power to compel the debtor to enter litigation, or the power of redress or civil recourse.[81] Unlike a trustee's power, however, the power to seek redress is a second-order power in that, for it to be effective, a plaintiff has to convince a court of the merits of her claim and get the court to change the legal position of the defendant through a remedial order. The power is thus not, strictly speaking, a Hohfeldian power, as Hohfeld understood powers, since an exercise of it alone (eg, by serving a statement of claim) does not change the defendant's legal position. Nonetheless, we might think of it as a legal power in an extended sense, in the way Raz and Lisa Austin mean, since its exercise does produce legal consequences: the party served with a claim must defend the action in court or (ordinarily) face summary judgment. And, even if we think of the power as factual, we shall see now that there is reason to interpret the power as other-regarding, which then lets us explain the doctrine from the standpoint of Equity.

As in the case of equity of redemption, a puzzle here is explaining why a common law right holder should bear the burden of Equity's doctrine. One way to resolve this puzzle is to suppose that the creditor who receives payment from the debtor, but retains the debtor's sealed bond, is called on by Equity to occupy a public position vis-à-vis the debtor, and to act on a public law mandate rather than her private law entitlement.[82] In these circumstances, Equity can be understood to transform the creditor's self-regarding power to seek redress into a public, other-regarding power. This public power is subject to the principles of Equity, including the principle that Equity favours substance over form. From this principle and the public position of the creditor we can identify at least four routes to the conclusion that a creditor's opportunistic exercise of the power to seek redress is invalid.[83] The first is to treat the substance-over-form principle as a condition precedent to the exercise of the power; ie, where the substantive basis of a claim is no longer applicable, one cannot rely on the peculiarities of form to

[81] The power to seek redress against an alleged wrongdoer lies at the core of the civil recourse theory of private law. See, eg, John CP Goldberg and Benjamin C Zipursky, 'Civil Recourse Theory Revisited' (2011) Florida State University Law Review 341.

[82] This stratagem may appear to have a cost that would be unappealing to theorists with voluntarist or libertarian sympathies, since it may appear to enlarge the scope of the state's authority to direct individuals to contribute to the pursuit of public ends. However, the theory mooted is merely an explanatory theory of what is already there in the relevant legal practices of Equity, and so the theory itself is inert with respect to the question of whether individuals should or should not be asked to hold their rights in abeyance for others. Equity is already making this demand. The theory merely seeks to explain the demand in a way that is consonant with the public form of Equity and its quality as hierarchically superior second-order law.

[83] Another way to think of the subsequent points in the text is that they lend substance and texture to what it means for a court to find that the creditor has acted in a manner that is unconscionable, and therefore suitable for Equity's intervention.

bring a suit. The second is to treat the substance-over-form principle as a mandatory relevant consideration of the creditor's decision-making process, a consideration she must take into account for her decision to be lawful. Since she cannot plausibly take that principle into account in any meaningful way *and* bring an action for a second payment, a reviewing court would find her decision to bring the suit invalid. Third, a reviewing court could find that the creditor exercised the power of redress in bad faith, since the power was never devised or conferred to enable egregious opportunism. And, fourth, the creditor's decision to seek 'redress' could be impugned on the grounds that it was exercised for an improper purpose, since in substance there is no wrong here to be redressed, and the power exists exclusively for the purpose of redressing wrongs.

A sceptic may think that what I've said about jurisdictional justice fits trusts and fiduciary relations from Equity's jurisdictional law, but that it is awkward in relation to the equity of redemption, sealed bonds, and other cases from Equity's anti-opportunist law. In the next section I'll spell out various advantages to seeing Equity's anti-opportunist law as part of a wider public law and jurisdictional theory of Equity. For now, I've a few brief replies. First, since my main concern is to explain Equity as it is today, trusts and fiduciary law arguably lie at its core while the anti-opportunist dimension (or large parts of it) are more peripheral. Given my contemporary purpose, there is a reason to start with Equity's jurisdictional law and, if possible, bring Equity's anti-opportunist law within it, rather than vice versa.

Moreover, the nature of the explanation I'm seeking is philosophical and conceptual. Consistency with the internal point of view of Equity's historical anti-opportunist law is (or would be) a virtue. That said, we should bear in mind that Selden's complaint was essentially that there was no meaningful internal point of view; there were just the Chancellor's palm-tree intuitions applied in a given case. But more importantly, and constructively, the conceptual explanation offered by the weak public law theory is juridical because it proceeds from a certain kind of jural relation—the power–liability relation—that is common to both Equity and the common law. In this respect, the theory takes seriously the relational precepts of legal order.

Some may balk at the power-based interpretation of Equity on the grounds that it may seem to mix unacceptably self-regarding powers with other-regarding powers. The sceptic might say that the creditor/mortgagee is not in a trustee-like position, but rather is a particular kind of contractor limited by certain equitable side constraints when the possibility of foreclosure arises. If we can make sense of these side constraints through reference to public policy or conscience, why twist the contractor into something altruistic he is not? While it is true that the mortgagee is not a fiduciary, it is instructive that some fiduciaries are also beneficiaries of the assets they administer. Partnerships are structured this way. Partners owe duties to the partnership, and in return benefit from their membership in the partnership. The interest protected by fiduciary duty in this case is a *joint* interest, which is an interest that is collective and separate from the direct personal interests of the partners. The discretionary decision-making power that partners have with respect to this interest is therefore other-regarding in nature, notwithstanding the (indirect) benefit partners are entitled to gain from their use of the power.

Something similar can be said of the mortgagee, despite the fact that exercising the power to foreclose on the debtor's equity of redemption inevitably will benefit the creditor and harm the mortgagor. Unlike partners, the interests of the mortgagee and mortgagor are not aligned. Yet, it is common, perhaps the norm, for public powers to be exercised across classes of persons with divergent interests. On the view under consideration, property law allocates the power of foreclosure for public purposes. Those purposes permit foreclosure in the event of incorrigible non-payment, but do not permit foreclosure if a defaulting debtor begins repayment and demonstrates a preparedness to continue doing so (the equity of redemption bars foreclosure in these circumstances). Notwithstanding the clash of interests, there is nothing awkward or incongruous about calling a power of foreclosure regulated by the equity of redemption an other-regarding power: to the extent it answers to public purposes that include but are not exhausted by the power holder's interest, the power to foreclose is a public and therefore other-regarding power.

Finally, the argument regarding the applicability of jurisdictional justice to anti-opportunist law is wholly severable from the argument that jurisdictional justice is the mode of justice apposite to Equity's jurisdictional law. If at the end of the day the sceptic cannot accept the weak public law theory as an explanation of Equity's anti-opportunist dimension, she could still accept it as an explanation of Equity's jurisdictional law. Let's consider now some of the merits of the weak and strong public law theories.

VII. The Merits of Public Law Theory

A merit of the weak public law theory is that it has at its disposal the entire arsenal of public law doctrines relevant to review of discretionary power. We have seen several of these in the preceding discussion: eg, relevant considerations, good faith, and improper purposes. These and other doctrines can offer substantial, varied, and legal explanations of Equity's interventions. A common complaint against Equity's anti-opportunist law—Selden's complaint—was that its criterion of conscience was too amorphous to provide meaningful guidance. Yet some contemporary commentators continue to use conscience as an organizing principle that strives to lend unity to Equity.[84] The difficulty with conscience is not that it is incapable of covering the varied doctrines its proponents say it can cover, but rather that it is not obvious why it could not also cover a multitude of common law doctrines. It seems, for example, that unconscionability or duress in contract law could be explained by conscience.

Some may wonder whether weak public law theory offers any comparative advantage if, as I argued in section III, private law doctrines such as we find in trust law offer essentially the same arsenal of discretion-regulating doctrines. Recall that weak public

[84] See, eg, Patrick Parkinson, 'The Conscience of Equity' in Patrick Parkinson (ed), *The Principles of Equity* (Law Book Co 1996) 28; Irit Samet, 'What Conscience Can Do for Equity?' (2012) 3 Jurisprudence 13; references at (n 13).

law theory denotes only that Equity and public law share the same form. An advantage of strong public law theory, under which Equity is a species of public law, is that Equity can help itself to public law purposes and mandates or, as Penner puts it, considerations of the good.[85] The equity of redemption could thus be interpreted as a doctrine that seeks to embody, in limited fashion, a public law concern for the non-fungible value of someone's home as well as a broader concern to ensure the availability of housing. Here too the comparative advantage of the strong public law theory could be questioned from the standpoint of a conception of private law that includes substantive equality, such as Hanoch Dagan's and Avihay Dorfman's account of private law. Under their theory, private law can serve as a vehicle for interpersonal human rights,[86] and so resort to public law may not be necessary. A challenge that confronts their approach is specifying the domain of public law, or conversely, the limits of private law. I cannot address these large questions here.

Returning now to the possible advantages of weak and strong public law approaches to Equity, public law doctrines (improper purposes, irrelevant considerations, fettering, etc) helpfully connect Equity's substantive conception of legality to the chief requirement of its form; ie, that decision-makers respect the purpose for which other-regarding power was conferred on them. Resort to public law doctrines brings the further benefit of providing public means for testing decisions through inquiry into the considerations the decision-maker took into account. Through this toolkit, public law doctrines help us see what it means to be a stickler or opportunist in a bad way: you're a stickler or opportunist in a bad way if you abuse an other-regarding power, as revealed through the doctrines we've considered. And, conversely, if you use a power for a purpose for which it was conferred, taking all relevant and no irrelevant considerations into account, ordinarily you will not be a stickler in a bad way, even if you set back the interests of a person for whom the power is held.

Weak and strong public law theories also offer an explanation of why conscience could properly be, for all its theoretical infelicities, a significant fixture of Equity. While breaching certain contracts or entering into them on certain terms may be unconscionable, the parties to contractual relations ordinarily are under no illusions about whose interests they are seeking to advance through contract—their own. In Equity, on the other hand, the wrongdoer under a public law approach is someone who has abused an other-regarding power. Even if an abuse does not rise formally to the level of breach of trust or breach of the fiduciary duty of loyalty, it carries with it always the scent of betrayal, since the wrong depends intimately on the use of a power meant to benefit someone else. As a general matter, betrayals are unconscionable in a way that inflicting negligent harm or failing to perform a contract is not, because betrayals denote the corrupt abuse of an other-regarding power.

[85] Penner (n 75).

[86] Hanoch Dagan and Avihay Dorfman, 'Interpersonal Human Rights' (2018) 51 Cornell International Law Journal 361.

The strong public law theory offers a ready account of the sense in which, as many commentators suggest, Equity is an hierarchically superior second-order law[87] or 'laws about laws'.[88] These scholars point out that Equity's anti-opportunist dimension works as second-order and superior law with respect to the common law, as we saw in the sealed bond and equity-of-redemption cases. On Equity's jurisdictional side, here too there is a sense in which Equity piggybacks on the common law while controlling its reach. In a land trust, for example, the beneficiary has a right (and power) to force a reluctant trustee to use his legal right to enforce exclusive possession of the land held in trust. If the trustee refused to remove squatters from trust land, the beneficiary could go to court to compel him to do so.[89] The public law theory explains the second-order quality of Equity as simply an instance of private law being subject to, and displaceable by, public law, even if the 'legislation' that does the displacing is 'judicial legislation'.[90]

Additionally, a strong public law theory helps make sense of the way Equity addresses wrongs and orders remedies. Ordinarily, judges in Equity do not make orders that by themselves and without more will have the effect of transferring title or discharging a debt or otherwise acting at first instance.[91] Instead, they order the burden bearer to do what needs to be done to respect the maxim that Equity regards as done that which should be done. So, if a trustee is found to have misapplied trust funds, he will be liable to restore the trust. In this respect, courts of equity are much like courts that exercise supervisory jurisdiction over administrative actors: in both cases, judges assess the legality of the relevant decision, and if the decision is found to be invalid, the matter is returned to the first-instance decision-maker for redetermination or some form of remedial action, since the court has supervisory but not first-instance decision-making authority. Unlike an appeal proceeding, where an appellate court can simply replace the trial court's decision with its own, the remedial orders of Equity and administrative law alike commonly come in two parts: (1) a review of the impugned decision and possibly a finding of invalidity or a setting aside of an impugned decision,[92] and (2) an order for redetermination or an order for the frontline decision-maker to take whatever remedial action is necessary to make done that which should be done. In Equity, remedial orders are backed up by the threat of contempt and prison, which is distinctively public,

[87] See eg Smith (n 3).

[88] MacFarlane and Stevens (n 1).

[89] Thanks to Lionel Smith for this example. For a dissenting view, see James Penner, 'The (True) Nature of a Beneficiary's Equitable Proprietary Interest under a Trust' (2014) 27 Canadian Journal of Law and Jurisprudence 473.

[90] Penner (n 75).

[91] An important exception is the court's supervisory jurisdiction in trust. If a trustee dies, or is removed, the court has discretion to manage the trust. But it is an exception that proves the rule, in that it places the court in a truly public-law-like administrative position. Courts exercising supervisory jurisdiction to administer a trust themselves assume an executive position to comply with the requirements of the enabling or facilitative side of the judicial supervisory role. Like the mortgagee and the creditor with the debtor's sealed bond, courts too can be called on to help Equity fulfil its mission.

[92] In trust law, sometimes the reviewing court will deem a decision to embezzle to have been made on behalf of the beneficiary and therefore will allow it to stand and the property to remain in trust for the beneficiary if the embezzled funds were invested in a way that produced a profit. *Re Oatway* [1903] Ch 356.

since contempt is a wrong against the state.[93] A strong public law theory can explain effortlessly these features of Equity.

I have discussed already how weak and strong public law theories accord with jurisdictional justice, which (to recall) is the kind of justice that applies to relations in which one party holds an other-regarding power in relation to another. Seeing the structure of jurisdictional justice helps to resolve another puzzle, this one with respect to the interests Equity protects. On some views of private law, private legal rights enable individuals to relate to each other on terms of formal equal freedom, with the implication that no party's choices or needs are permitted to dictate unilaterally the terms of interaction with another.[94] The puzzle, which we have seen with both the sealed bond and mortgage debtor cases, is that Equity seems to let a claimant's practical interest dictate terms against others whose own interests are protected by legal rights. The mortgager who falls behind but later discovers the means of paying may deserve sympathy, but consider again: why should the mortgagor's need or wish to retain the property tell against the mortgagee's legal right to take full ownership of it? Isn't the mortgager dictating terms to the mortgagee that were not part of the original loan agreement? How is this not impermissible unilateralism?

It is not unilateralism because the creditor's power to enter a mortgage agreement was always limited by the equity of redemption, which was always there as a background term of the mortgage. But, the Equity sceptic might press, this doesn't explain why the doctrine was there in the first place. Earlier on I pointed to the non-fungible nature of land and the importance of one's home, and the inhumanity of evicting someone who has fallen behind but can now make good. The contemporary legal principle most apt to assist the debtor is the public law principle of proportionality. Under this principle, public decision-makers need to consider the effects of their decisions on the people directly affected by them, and more specifically, whether the deleterious effect of a given decision is proportionate to the good that is to come from pursuit of a policy. In the typical equity-of-redemption case, it is likely that the cost to the debtor of eviction and losing her land far outstrips the cost to the creditor of a delay in payment. As a matter of private law, however, where the parties are assumed capable of negotiating the terms of the mortgage ahead of time, proportionality is usually irrelevant. The disproportionate effect is just hard cheese for the debtor who made an agreement and is liable under it. Yet, from a public law perspective, one can sensibly ask questions about the proper minimal content and protections appropriate to a mortgage. While from a private law perspective enforcing one's rights under a valid contract, ordinarily, is perfectly legitimate, from a public law perspective the very power to do so in certain circumstances may smack of domination, and the exercise of that power, arbitrariness, and abuse. What a strong public law approach can deliver that a doctrinal private law approach cannot is the legal salience of important practical interests to which contract and tort

[93] Katz (n 13).

[94] See, eg, Arthur Ripstein, *Force and Freedom: Kant's Legal and Political Philosophy* (Harvard UP 2009); Evan Fox-Decent, 'Unseating Unilateralism' in Austin and Klimchuk (eds), (n 47) 116.

doctrine are in practice blind (if they were not so blind, the space left for Equity, if any, would be much diminished).

Let me conclude this section with a thumbnail sketch of how Equity and the common law may be thought to fit together. I assume a rights-based conception of the common law of tort, contract, and property, a conception that finds its grounding in an assumption of formal equal freedom. I assume as well that this conception, properly elaborated and institutionalized, provides its subjects with a regime of secure and equal freedom. The principal kind of freedom available in this regime, in my view, is freedom as non-interference: generally, individuals have or can acquire rights to property, physical integrity, and contractual promises with which others may not interfere. People can cooperate through contract, and they can fashion life plans assisted by the self-regarding powers that come with property and the independence that comes with non-interference.

Equity, on the other hand, regulates the possession of other-regarding power. Its characteristic legal relations are fiduciary in nature, though I have tried to show that even its anti-opportunist doctrines presuppose the possession of other-regarding power on the part of Equity's burden bearer. Equity is concerned with the terms on which other-regarding power is held, such as the terms on which a mortgage can be given. Equity monitors those terms, providing a rule-of-law measure of security against arbitrariness by ensuring that other-regarding powers are exercised within their limits and in a manner consistent with their purpose. By supervising the terms on which power is held in addition to the way it is exercised, Equity answers mainly to the ideal of freedom as non-domination.

The common law and Equity together create the institutional conditions for a hybrid conception of freedom—freedom as independence. Under this conception, freedom as non-interference relates to actual uses of force whereas freedom as non-domination relates to the threat of the use of force. Or, put another way, freedom as non-interference controls uses of power whereas freedom as non-domination controls the terms on which power is held and *may* be used. Evan Criddle and I suggest that this hybrid conception of freedom underlies a relational conception of contemporary international human rights law.[95] The strong public law theory of Equity hints that Equity and international human rights law may share foundational commitments, with doctrines such as the equity of redemption serving as inchoate versions of contemporary social rights (eg, the rights to an adequate standard of living and housing).[96]

VIII. Conclusion

I have argued that Equity's jurisdictional law and public law share cognate doctrines and the same legal form, a form based on the possession by one party of an

[95] Evan Fox-Decent and Evan J Criddle, 'A Fiduciary Conception of Human Rights' (2009) 15 Legal Theory 301.

[96] See, eg, International Covenant on Economic, Social and Cultural Rights (1976) 993 UNTS 3, Can TS 1976 No 46, art 11. See also Robert Walker, 'Equity and Human Rights' in PG Turner (ed), *Equity and Administration* (CUP 2016) 380 (drawing connections between human rights and Equity's protection of both personal privacy and women's property rights prior to the Married Women's Property Acts of the late nineteenth century).

other-regarding power to which another is subject. I have also suggested that the kind of justice that responds to this legal form is not corrective or distributive justice, but jurisdictional justice. This is the type of justice concerned with how an other-regarding power is exercised. The similarity of the ways Equity's jurisdictional law and public law embody jurisdictional justice suggests that these two bodies of law share the same basic concern—the legal regulation of other-regarding power. None of this establishes that Equity's jurisdictional law is public law per se (the strong theory of public law), but rather is evidence of the weak theory according to which Equity shares the characteristic form and basic concern of public law.

I subsequently argued that Equity's anti-opportunism law can be understood at the jural level to regulate a power–liability relation in which the relevant power is other-regarding. And, thus, Equity's anti-opportunism dimension also shares the form of public law, and is also amenable to jurisdictional justice. It follows that Equity *in toto* has the form of public law and is amenable to jurisdictional justice.

I offered a number of arguments in favour of the strong public law theory of Equity. I underline again that these are tentative and preliminary, and that for them to be persuasive one would have to consider (at least) whether jurisdictional justice within private law is not adequate to the task, whether a substantive conception of private law could not accommodate Equity's concern for the good, and general criteria regarding the classification of legal obligations. One argument in favour of the strong public law theory, I suggested, is that the anti-opportunist law of Equity can be understood to assume the status of public law because public law can displace rightfully the otherwise valid norms of private law.

More substantively, I suggested that the strong public law theory is attractive because it can explain the legal salience of considerations of the good in Equity, considerations to which the common law of property, tort, and contract are generally blind. Public law consists in the laws we give ourselves collectively, and therefore does not oppress when it asks us to contribute to the well-being of others and public goods that answer to a wider range of values and concerns than one finds in private law. But, again, this and other arguments in favour of the strong theory of public law are necessarily speculative.

The claim I wish to assert with more confidence is that at the heart of both Equity and public law is other-regarding power amenable to jurisdictional justice. If this claim is sound, then public law scholars and Equity scholars alike may have much to learn from one another.

7

Equity Is Not a Single Thing

Lionel Smith[*]

I. Introduction

The goal of this chapter is to say something about the philosophical foundations of 'the law of equity'. What does it mean to seek the philosophical foundations of some area of law? My project finds its inspiration in a tradition that asks whether it is possible to articulate the normative foundations of a living body of legal doctrine, as the body of doctrine is understood by those who participate in its elaboration and its application; in other words, as it is understood by jurists.[1] One might, for example, seek the philosophical foundations of contract law, and be led into debates about whether contracts are enforced because they are agreements, or because they involve promising, or because people should fulfil the reliance they have induced in others.[2] In this perspective, part of the point of the inquiry is that the field of study is delineated by established juridical categories. In other words, it would be a very different project to seek the philosophical foundations of promising. That would be a philosophical inquiry that could dispense entirely with law. Philosophers making such an inquiry could rightly be utterly unconcerned with the law of contracts. Those who seek the philosophical foundations of contract law, by contrast, must necessarily pay attention to what jurists mean by 'contract law'.

II. Which Equity?

I cannot begin without clarifying what I mean by the 'equity' whose philosophical foundations I seek to explore.

Equity has many meanings. Aristotle's idea of equity is found in many places; Aristotle himself placed it in the context of ancient Greek law. It was recognized as part of Roman law, just as it is recognized as part of modern civil law.[3] The common law, in

[*] I thank the editors for their invitation to participate in this project, and King's College London and Harvard University for their hospitality and financial support. I thank my friend and colleague Stephen Smith for many helpful and thought-provoking comments. This research is part of a project on 'Conflicts of Interest and Fiduciary Obligations', funded by a Killam Research Fellowship during 2014–2016. I acknowledge with gratitude the support of the Killam Trustees.

[1] A classic example of scholarship in this tradition is HLA Hart and T Honoré, *Causation in the Law* (2nd edn, OUP 1985).

[2] G Klass, G Letsas, and P Saprai (eds), *Philosophical Foundations of Contract Law* (OUP 2015).

[3] See in this volume J Edelman (Chapter 17).

Lionel Smith, *Equity Is Not a Single Thing* In: *Philosophical Foundations of the Law of Equity*. Edited by: Dennis Klimchuk, Irit Samet, and Henry E Smith, Oxford University Press (2020). © The several contributors.
DOI: 10.1093/oso/9780198817659.003.0008

the narrow sense that excludes the law of the Court of Chancery, has often had recourse to equity.[4] Even non-legal normative systems implement Aristotelian equity. If something totally unforeseen happens in an improvised children's game, the usual recourse is a 'do-over', although there is no explicit rule providing either for what happened or for such a remedy.

The Equity of the common law tradition may have begun as a kind of Aristotelian equity, albeit in a form founded on a particular set of religious beliefs; but it did not stay that way. My goal is not to theorize an Equity of the past. It is to say something about the philosophical foundations of Equity, and by Equity I mean the living body of legal doctrine that is identified by that name and that is peculiar to the common law tradition.[5] This is important because it means that the subject matter of my analysis is not the same as that of some other contributions to this volume.

It is also important to my project that Equity as I take it includes all of the law of trusts, which stands as the signal contribution of Equity jurisprudence to the legal landscape of the world. A discussion of Equity, as I have defined it, that did not take account of the trust would be like a discussion of *Hamlet* that did not refer to the Prince of Denmark. And many of the rules of the law of trusts are non-discretionary, clear, and hard-edged. Speaking generally, they do not react to opportunism or to unforeseen cases, or to helping people to finish what they have started. They might do all these things, but no more than any set of legal rules does all of these things. Moreover, the particular role of conscience in the operation of Equity mostly disappeared centuries ago. Far from being based on broad generalities, Equity's norms are generally precise and technical in nature.[6] They are rules of Equity that, in the modern world, owe nothing to equity.

The Equity of my project is therefore Equity as Maitland defined it:

> Equity now is that body of rules administered by our English courts of justice which, were it not for the operation of the Judicature Acts, would be administered only by those courts which would be known as Courts of Equity. This, you may well say, is but a poor thing to call a definition.[7]

[4] Famously in *Moses v Macferlan* (1760) 2 Burr 1005, 97 ER 676 (KB), discussed in ET Bishop, 'Money Had and Received, an Equitable Action at Law' (1933) 7 Southern California Law Review 41. Another example is found in Pennsylvania, which for a substantial period lacked any court of Equity and whose courts of common law modified the common law in order to do equity (and to do Equity): SR Liverant and WH Hitchler, 'A History of Equity in Pennsylvania' (1933) 37 Dickinson Law Review 156, 165–79.

[5] For this reason, I will say 'Equity' when I refer to the body of law within the common law tradition, and (more rarely in this chapter) 'equity' when I refer to the wider Aristotelian notion.

[6] A representative example is the so-called second branch of the rule in *Howe v Lord Dartmouth*, which could be formulated in an if–then form as follows: *if*, in a trust of successive interests, the trustees have a duty to convert the trust property from its original form into another form that holds an even hand between the different classes of beneficiaries (those entitled to income and those later entitled to capital), *then* in relation to the period of time before that duty to convert is fulfilled, the trustees must allocate trust property (capital and income) between the income and capital beneficiaries in such a way that each class will receive the same benefit as if the duty to convert had been fulfilled from the moment of the trust's constitution. See DWM Waters, M Gillen, and L Smith, *Waters' Law of Trusts in Canada* (4th edn, Thomson/Carswell 2012) 1041–48; D Hayton, P Matthews, and C Mitchell, *Underhill and Hayton: Law Relating to Trusts and Trustees* (19th edn, LexisNexis 2016) 760–72, noting a statutory change for English trusts created after 2013.

[7] FW Maitland, *Equity; Also, the Forms of Action at Common Law: Two Courses of Lectures* (AH Chaytor and WJ Whittaker (eds), CUP 1929) 1.

I do not deny that Equity, as I take it, still has the ability to do equity. In 1975 Lord Denning rightly observed that 'Equity is not past the age of childbearing'.[8] In 1993 the Supreme Court of Canada was faced with a case in which an unjust enrichment claim was brought in relation to the division of property between unmarried cohabitants. One defence was that the province had enacted a comprehensive framework for property division, but it applied only to married persons. The argument was that this implied that the legislative intention was that no such division should be available between those who were not married. The majority of the Court disposed of this argument in a single sentence: 'It is precisely where an injustice arises without a legal remedy that equity finds a role.'[9]

But just because Equity is not past the age of childbearing, it does not follow that we should ignore her adult children. It is important to have a theory of equity, such as the one articulated by Aristotle which has been handed down to us through the centuries. That kind of equity can find a role in any system of rules, legal or not. But since Equity is about much more than equity, and since equity is found far and wide, inside and outside of Equity, the philosophical foundations of equity have very little to do with the philosophical foundations of Equity.

Indeed, it is impossible to posit a single normative idea that underlies all of Equity. As Maitland went on to say: 'I do not think that any one has expounded or ever will expound equity as a single, consistent system, an articulate body of law. It is a collection of appendixes between which there is no very close connection.'[10] This is the sense in which Equity is not a single thing. It lacks quiddity.

This is not at all surprising, since Equity and Equitable doctrines and principles deal with such a wide range of matters, across the whole system of private law. Just like the common law or the civil law, Equity is concerned to implement multiple normative principles.[11] And, indeed, Equity implements many of the very same normative principles that are implemented by the common law and the civil law, such as enforcing promises and protecting reliance.

In a sense, my chapter could end here. Equity, as I have defined it, is not a single thing. Of course, some might say, I have made that true by my choice of definition. But first, the definition is far from unusual or radical. Maitland was a legal historian, and his definition was a historical one; but it is also one which very many lawyers use, reflectively or not. Most legal books on Equity use Maitland's idea of Equity, and most of them talk about trusts; and every book on trusts says that trusts come from Equity. As I said in my introduction, to seek the philosophical foundations of some area of the law, one must use a jurist's and not a philosopher's conception of an area of law; otherwise, one

[8] *Eves v Eves* [1975] 1 WLR 1338 (CA) 1341.

[9] *Peter v Beblow* [1993] 1 SCR 980, 101 DLR (4th) 621, 994 (SCR). It is not totally clear whether the Court was referring to equity or to Equity, nor whether the Court always appreciates the difference. The Court often refers to the equitable nature of unjust enrichment, but in many cases this is equity, not Equity (n 5). On the other hand, the Court in *Peter* imposed a constructive trust, which is a creature of Equity.

[10] Maitland (n 7) 19.

[11] See in this volume B McFarlane and R Stevens (Chapter 9).

is seeking the philosophical foundations of a philosophical notion, which is a different enterprise. And, secondly, a similar charge could made in relation to accounts that use a different definition of equity. If one defines equity in terms of some particular normative concern or principle, it will hardly be surprising if that principle is found to infuse equity so defined.

I choose to continue the chapter by asking the following question. Even if Equity is not a single thing, what approaches does Equity bring to normativity that are *not* found in other legal orders, such as the common law (in the narrow sense that excludes Equity) or the civil law tradition? In other words, even though there is no normative principle that underlies all of Equity, are there normative principles that are *characteristic* of Equity?

Consider, for example, the ways in which the Chancery interfered with freedom of contract in respect of mortgages, as well as in the law relating to penalties and relief against forfeiture. One could make a fairly strong case that these principles show that Equity developed a characteristic approach to contracts. As far as the philosophical foundations, one could argue that Equity's characteristic contribution is that although parties are free to create such *primary* contractual obligations as they wish, they are not entirely free to stipulate the consequences of a breach of those primary obligations; they are not allowed to contract out of corrective justice.[12] This idea can explain the development of the law of mortgages, penalties and forfeitures in Equity, and it is characteristic of Equity in the sense that such an idea is not found in the common law or in the civilian tradition.[13]

If one adopted this strategy, one could aim to identify philosophical foundations of Equity that are characteristic of Equity, even while accepting that Equity is not a single thing. Each characteristic contribution so identified might have only a narrow range of operation in the law, but would still be a peculiarly Equitable contribution to legal normativity.[14]

It is an argument of this more modest kind that I make in the remainder of this chapter. I will argue that Equity has a characteristic way of understanding obligations that relate to the benefit of particular assets; and, that to a significant extent, this understanding is *peculiar* to Equity.[15] It is not by accident that my argument will concentrate on Equity's articulation, over the years, of different elements of the trust, because the

[12] See the argument in L Smith, 'Relief Against Forfeiture: A Restatement' (2001) 60 CLJ 178.

[13] Of course, every generalization is risky. The civil law may impose restrictions on the lender's remedy called 'taking in payment' which is similar to foreclosure: the collateral is taken in payment of the debt (see art 2779 of the Civil Code of Québec, forbidding taking in payment and requiring sale if the debtor or a junior secured creditor objects). But the conceptual structure of the equity of redemption is a unique creation of Equity.

[14] Another example might be the rules about undue influence. B McFarlane, 'Understanding Equitable Estoppel: From Metaphors to Better Laws' (2013) 66 CLP 267, 281–90 argues that what is often called promissory estoppel is made up of three distinct principles. Each of those may be a characteristic creation of Equity (though some aspects of them might be implemented in a civilian system by an undifferentiated doctrine of good faith).

[15] In this respect I differ from JE Penner, 'An Untheory of the Law of Trusts, or Some Notes Towards Understanding the Structure of Trusts Law Doctrine' (2010) 63 CLP 653, 662: 'disagreement in trusts law is overwhelmingly about error, not clashes of value, or clashes of theoretical disagreement'. I suspect many examples of what he or I would call errors do in fact arise from theoretical disagreements, in the sense of disagreements about what it means to owe certain kinds of obligation in Equity.

trust itself is characteristic of and peculiar to Equity. I am well aware that civilian systems, modern and ancient, have or had their own trusts;[16] and that even the common law courts sometimes took an interest.[17] And of course, there is more to Equity than trusts. This is the way in which my argument is modest in the sense mentioned above: it identifies some features that are characteristic of Equity, but does not claim that these features are all there is to Equity.

But because of the centrality of trust law, it is less modest than my earlier example of the rules relating to mortgages, penalties, and relief against forfeiture. Although there is more to Equity than trusts, and although there are trusts outside of Equity, it remains true that the trust, as it was conceived, articulated, and (especially) juridically conceptualized by Equity, is a unique contribution. It is not at all surprising that the norms that developed in this context remain characteristic of Equity.[18] Many of them, as I will discuss, have migrated to other roles; but they also remain where they started, constituting the core of the trust and of what is special about it, and therefore of what is special about Equity. Together, these norms constitute a unique conceptual toolkit for the juridical apprehension of relationships in which a person is charged with conducting herself unselfishly, in the pursuit of the interests of another or of some impersonal goal.[19]

III. Fiduciary Relationships

In an earlier text I tried to say what I thought was fundamentally different about Equity, as compared to the common law, in the context of asking why the question of the 'fusion' of common law and Equity is still a challenge.[20] I said there were two crucial differences. One was that in the context of fiduciary relationships, Equity systematically inquires into a person's reasons for acting, whereas in the common law this is almost always immaterial. This concern with reasons for acting is the foundation of the control of fiduciary powers, including the norms about conflicts of interest.[21] The other crucial difference is that in the context of obligations relating to the benefit of property, Equity has always been willing to impose those obligations on perfect strangers who never agreed to be bound by them. I argued that these two features together constitute

[16] See for example L Smith (ed), *The Worlds of the Trust* (CUP 2013).

[17] JH Baker, 'The History of Quasi-Contract in English Law' in WR Cornish and others (eds), *Restitution: Past, Present and Future: Essays in Honour of Gareth Jones* (Hart 1998) 37; see also the Pennsylvania experience, mentioned above (n 4). For examples of common-law courts giving effect to the incidents of Chancery trusts before the fusion of the courts, see L Smith, 'Tracing in Taylor v. Plumer: Equity in the Court of King's Bench' [1995] LMCLQ 240; L Smith, 'Simplifying Claims to Traceable Proceeds' (2009) 125 LQR 338.

[18] My argument will frequently make reference to legal history. As I said earlier, my goal in this chapter is to discuss Equity as it exists today, but in my view an understanding of the history is essential to an understanding of many aspects of modern Equity.

[19] Other traditions, notably the civil law, have their own conceptual toolkits for these situations, but they are different from Equity's. See for example G Gretton, 'Trusts without Equity' (2000) 49 ICLQ 599; L Smith, 'Droit et pouvoir' in A-S Hulin and R Leckey (eds), *L'abnégation en droit civil* (Éditions Yvon Blais 2017).

[20] L Smith, 'Fusion and Tradition' in S Degeling and J Edelman (eds), *Equity in Commercial Law* (Thomson/Law Book Co 2005) 19.

[21] For the full argument, see L Smith, 'Fiduciary Relationships: Ensuring the Loyal Exercise of Judgement on Behalf of Another' (2014) 130 LQR 608.

the core of the law of trusts, because they concern the regulation fiduciary relationships and the protection of the beneficiary's interest against third parties. And the trust, in turn, as I have also argued here, is the core of Equity.

In this chapter, I will not discuss the control of discretions in fiduciary relationships, although I still think that Equity's willingness to investigate reasons for action is a crucial and distinctive feature of Equity.[22] I will, however, address some other aspects of fiduciary relationships.[23] I also still believe that a crucial and distinctive feature of Equity is its willingness to impose certain obligations on people who never agreed to be burdened by them. I will say something about these third-party effects in a later section.[24] But the main focus of the current chapter will be different: it will be on showing that even in relation to the original parties to such an obligation, Equity took, and still takes, a distinctive approach.

IV. The Nature of an Obligation

Oliver Wendell Holmes Jr may inadvertently have launched a thousand ships of American legal realism when he said:

> The duty to keep a contract at common law means a prediction that you must pay damages if you do not keep it—and nothing else.[25]

This was an application to contract law of his 'bad man' theory of law, which itself was presented not as a way of understanding what the law is, still less what it should be, but only as a way of learning it.[26] Moreover, Holmes himself was too good a lawyer to believe that this was an accurate statement of the law as a whole; he was not talking about Equity, and he was aware that his statement about damages was not accurate in a case in which Equity would intervene.[27]

[22] Maitland (n 7) 7, referring to procedure in the old common law courts, said: 'A system of law which will never compel, which will never even allow, the defendant to give evidence, a system which sends every question of fact to a jury, is not competent to deal adequately with fiduciary relationships.' This description is of course no longer accurate, if only because we have a unified system of civil procedure. But it remains distinctive of the regulation of fiduciary powers that the courts will intervene not just in cases of bad faith (which today's common law may also do for non-fiduciary powers: *Paragon Finance plc v Pender* [2005] 1 WLR 3412 (CA)) but also in cases where the power holder has been motivated by irrelevant considerations (*Klug v Klug* [1918] 2 Ch 67; *Turner v Turner* [1984] Ch 100 (ChD); *Fox v Fox* (1996) 28 OR (3d) 496 (CA)).

[23] Sections V.B.3.(a) and V.B.3.(b).

[24] Section V.A.

[25] OW Holmes, 'The Path of the Law' (1897) 10 Harvard Law Review 457, 462; reprinted (1998) 78 Boston University Law Review 699, 702; see also OW Holmes, *The Common Law* (Little, Brown & Co. 1881) 299–301.

[26] See L Smith, 'Understanding Specific Performance' in E McKendrick and N Cohen (eds), *Comparative Remedies for Breach of Contract* (Hart 2005) 221, 222–23.

[27] Holmes (n 25) 462–63, 703. He described contractual cases in which Equity would grant specific performance as 'relatively few'. Whether this is accurate today, I leave aside; but I will suggest that in the law of trusts, matters are and have always been different. It has also been held that in some cases, the Equitable remedy of an accounting of the defendant's profits can be ordered: *A-G v Blake* [2001] 1 AC 268 (HL). Quite apart from specific performance, this remedy also falsifies the Holmesian prediction.

His statement about contractual obligations, however, serves to focus the mind on an issue that should preoccupy jurist and philosopher alike. To say that a person is obliged to do something invites us to define what this means, but the task may not be finished until we say what is the consequence of the person's not doing it. In other words, part of the nature of an obligation is what happens if you do not perform it. Turning that around, from a normative system's reaction to breach, one can infer something about that system's understanding of an obligation. The Holmes line about contractual obligations at common law is premised on an understanding as to the consequences of a breach, and from that understanding, it invites the inference that a contractual obligation is really a kind of option belonging to the debtor of the obligation.[28]

Of course, one could argue about whether Holmes's claim is correct, even leaving Equity to one side as he did. First, some contractual obligations are obligations to pay a fixed sum of money, such as the obligation to pay the agreed price of goods sold and delivered. Here I doubt that Holmes would say that the debtor has the option whether to perform (which means, in this case, to pay the debt), or pay damages; the debtor has to perform.[29] The *creditor* might choose to claim damages in such a case, which would open up inquiries into causation, remoteness and mitigation; but it must be the case that he can instead directly enforce the primary obligation to pay the debt.[30] Holmes might say that in such a case, the damages claim will always be the amount of the debt owing, but this seems fictional; a genuine damages claim is a claim for the loss suffered as a result of a breach of duty, and so it requires an assessment of the actual loss suffered by the actual plaintiff that was actually caused by the breach. By contrast, a claim in debt is a claim to enforce the primary obligation, not a claim to recover losses caused by its breach; no causal inquiry into loss is needed or appropriate.[31] In this sense the debtor of an obligation to pay fixed amount of money does not possess Holmes's option.

Secondly, and more significantly, even if we focus on other contractual obligations, it is doubtful that judges deciding cases involving damages for breach of contract would agree with Holmes's characterization of what it means to have a contractual obligation.[32] Long ago, the courts of common law specifically enforced contractual promises, at least if they were made formally.[33] Somewhat later, beginning in the fourteenth

[28] In the English of the common law we usually use the word 'debtor' only in reference to obligations to pay an ascertained sum of money. In this chapter, I adopt the civil law English practice of using the words 'creditor' and 'debtor' more generally, in relation to any kind of obligation. I have always found the terms 'obligor' and 'obligee' to be unintuitive and ugly.

[29] R Stevens, *Torts and Rights* (OUP 2007) 60 n 21.

[30] By 'primary' obligation, I mean an obligation that arises apart from the breach of an obligation. Examples include the obligation to perform a contract, the obligations not to defame or assault people, and the obligation to repay a mistaken payment that one has accepted. By contrast, an obligation to pay damages as a result of committing a wrongful act (that is, a breach of an obligation, usually primary) is a secondary obligation.

[31] Indeed, English law used to say that in the case of an obligation to pay a fixed sum, a creditor *could not* claim damages, but the law has changed: A Burrows, *Remedies for Torts and Breach of Contract* (OUP 2005) 153–55.

[32] SA Smith, *Contract Theory* (OUP 2004) 119.

[33] In the thirteenth century, the form of action in covenant could be brought in the courts of common law without a deed, and the court could order either damages or specific performance. A deed was required in those courts by 1321, meaning that informal agreements could only be enforced in other courts, such as local courts or merchants' courts. The possibility of specific performance in covenant at common law of non-money obligations then fell away through desuetude: JH Baker, *An Introduction to English Legal History* (4th edn, Butterworths 2002) 318–21.

century, those courts allowed informal promises to be actionable in *assumpsit*, and this became the common law for all promises not recorded in deeds; in other words, the vast majority. But *assumpsit* was a subcategory of the form of action in trespass, and a trespass claim was always a claim for damages. In other words, *assumpsit* was a claim for the past wrong of breaching an undertaking; the idea of imposing specific performance in a claim in trespass was conceptually impossible.[34] The 'bad man' theory, like one strand at least of legal realism, points to what the courts actually do, and what the courts of common law have actually done for a long time is only to award compensatory damages for the breach of an obligation other than an obligation to pay a debt. This, then, is a historical and pragmatic basis for the Holmesian argument that at common law, a contractual obligation (other than one to pay a fixed amount of money) is a kind of option.

One response to Holmes would be along these lines: the choices that the common law courts have made regarding court-ordered remedies for breach of contract do not actually tell us much about the common law's understanding of the juridical nature of such obligations. The reason is that, as Stephen A Smith has argued, when courts turn to remedies, they can and rightly should consider the institutional and resource implications of the decisions that they make.[35] Courts and their officials are organs of the state, and the supervision of remedial orders expends public resources. Hence courts' decisions on remedies should take account of public concerns such as efficiency and effectiveness. This is one way to understand why the common law courts took the position that they would not order specific performance, without necessarily reaching Holmes's conclusion that according to the common law, a contractual obligation is only an option held by the debtor. Moreover, this kind of argument can assess the law as a whole—common law and Equity together—in suggesting that cases where Equity *does* intervene by enforcing contracts specifically are cases in which the balance of public concerns about efficiency and so on—as well as other relevant concerns—comes out differently.[36]

One distinct feature of Equity is that it always took a different approach from that of the common law inasmuch as obligations relating to the benefit of particular property—that is, trust obligations—were, and are, always specifically enforceable by default where this is possible. Where it is not possible, Equity's traditional aim is to

[34] Although the courts could, and did systematically after 1602, allow debt claims to be enforced through trespass, via *indebitatus assumpsit*: Baker ibid 341–45. This not only led to the decline of the form of action in debt, but also meant, somewhat paradoxically, that debts were enforced through a claim that was formally a claim for damages. After the abolition of the forms of action, the distinction between debt and damages survives not as a procedural distinction but as a conceptual one, as described in the previous paragraph of the text.

[35] SA Smith, 'Form and Substance in Equitable Remedies' in A Robertson and M Tilbury (eds), *Divergences in Private Law* (Hart 2014) 321, 330–33.

[36] Thus, this approach might speculate that even if English law never had the common law-Equity duality, a single system of courts might eventually have arrived at the position that in certain cases, a plaintiff would not be confined to compensatory damages. One difficulty with this, however, is that it would suggest that the civilian tradition (which has never had a formal law-Equity duality) should have similar results in relation to the question of specific enforcement, which is not the case (see for example, in relation to contract law: JP Dawson, 'Specific Performance in France and Germany' (1959) 57 Michigan Law Review 495; K Zweigert and H Kötz, *Introduction to Comparative Law* (T Weir tr, 3rd edn, Clarendon Press 1998), 472–83).

get as close as possible to specific performance, not to award compensatory damages. I will discuss these points in the next section. One might say that Equity has a different understanding than does the common law of what an obligation is, since Equity rejects the Holmesian approach that an obligation gives the debtor a kind of option. On the other hand, if one took the view about remedies outlined in the previous paragraph, one might say that the common law also rejects the Holmesian approach; but then, one would have to say that Equity is different from the common law when it comes to the question of what remedy is appropriate in a case of non-performance.[37] Either way, Equity's approach to trust obligations is characteristic and is distinct from that of the common law.

V. Obligations Relating to the Benefit of Property

The signal contribution of Equity to the law is the trust. The origins of the trust lie in the 'use' of land that began to be enforced by the Chancellor in the fifteenth century. At this time, the Chancellor was not understood to be enforcing a system of legal rules, and the use was understood to be outside of the law.[38] Well into the sixteenth century, it was orthodoxy that the use was 'nothing in law'.[39] And yet, in a case argued in 1502 counsel stated that by 1489, the greater part of land in England was held to uses.[40] Why would most people set up structures in which their rights to their own land were not fully recognized by the legal system? The reason is that their interests, although not understood to be legal, were reliably and systematically enforced in the Chancery.

In the use, an estate in land was transferred to persons who were obliged to hold the benefit of that estate for others; these transferees were called 'feoffees to uses' and are now called trustees.[41] Usually, they were obliged to hold the benefit of the estate for the original transferor while he lived, and then according to his instructions when he died. What created the trust, as we now know it, was the Chancellor's understanding of what it meant to have an obligation relating to the benefit of an estate that had been transferred to one. The principles developed in the fifteenth century are still foundational in modern Equity.

[37] In this perspective, the thought experiment mentioned in the previous note seems to be focused on contract law. Could that hypothetical single system have arrived at the position that trust obligations are always specifically enforceable, on the basis of considerations relating to public resources?

[38] JH Baker (ed), *The Oxford History of the Laws of England* (OUP 2003) vol VI, 1483–1558 654–55.

[39] ibid, citing Fitzherbert J in a case of 1536–37, that is, contemporaneous with the Statute of Uses 1536 that aimed to abolish most uses which had by then become so universal as to deprive the Crown of various sources of revenue. As Baker shows, however, the story is more complicated than this orthodoxy suggests; already by 1484 it was made possible by statute for a beneficiary to convey the legal estate, that he did not hold, to a third party. Courts of common law were thus forced, increasingly, to take account of uses.

[40] ibid 654.

[41] 'Feoffor' and 'feoffee' were the transferor and transferee, *inter vivos,* of an estate in fee, that is an inheritable estate; a fee is always a freehold although not every freehold is a fee.

A. Third-Party Effects

Almost immediately after the Chancellor began enforcing uses, it was necessary to address third-party effects. Wills of freehold estates were not permissible at this time, and indeed this was a primary reason to deploy uses. The desires of the feoffor to uses, as to what should happen to the land after his death, were implemented by his feoffees to uses after the death of the feoffor. Since this was done via *inter vivos* transactions carried out by the feoffees, the prohibition on wills was not infringed.

But the rule against making wills of freehold estates created a problem if there was a single feoffee to uses and he died. The estate would descend, by operation of the common law, to his heir. This person had never agreed to be under any obligation and, according to the common law, the estate was his. And yet, the Chancellor decided, he was bound by the use; he could not take the estate with a clear conscience. From this case it was not difficult to say that a donee (*inter vivos*) was also bound by the use; so too, one who bought the estate, if he knew or ought to have known about the use. Putting it the other way, a person was *not* bound by the use only if that person acquired the legal estate, giving fair value for it, and without knowing or having reason to know of the use.[42] This remains a basic and distinctive principle of Equity today, that any equitable interest survives a transfer of the relevant asset, unless the transferee is a good faith purchaser of a legal interest, who gives value without notice of the equitable interest.[43]

These third-party effects arise from a specific understanding of the nature of an obligation that relates to the benefit of particular property. An obligation is, on its face, a bond between two persons. The early development of the law of uses made the use into a strange kind of obligation: one that could bind a new debtor. The feoffee to uses was the original debtor, but anyone in the world could end up being the debtor of that obligation, should they acquire the relevant property otherwise than as a good faith purchaser of a legal interest for value without notice. This is what the legal historian SFC Milsom meant when he said that 'equity has proved that from the materials of obligation you can counterfeit the phenomena of property'.[44] It is also arguable, although I do not explore the question in this chapter, that the early development of the law of uses also underlies the modern position that trusteeship is an office that is understood to exist separately from the person who may hold the office from time to time. This is exactly because the burden of the trust obligation binds the person who holds, from time to time, the trust property. And trusteeship as office, in turn, may be the foundation of the Court of Chancery's supervisory jurisdiction over trusts: since the role of trustee is impersonal, it can be given to another if need be, and even the Court itself can

[42] For an analysis of this principle in today's law, see A Nair and I Samet this volume (Chapter 13).

[43] Unsecured creditors, even if they had lent money in good faith, were never considered to be protected by this principle; they had not purchased an interest in any property. This is why such creditors could not, and cannot, access property held in trust by their debtor.

[44] SFC Milsom, *Historical Foundations of the Common Law* (2nd edn, Butterworths 1981) 6.

act as trustee. Both of these features of the trust remain foundational, and are among the many deep conceptual differences between trusts and contracts.

In earlier work, I have tried to explore the philosophical foundations of this understanding of an obligation relating to the benefit of property; namely, how such an obligation can rightly be seen to bind some third parties.[45] It is important to say that this understanding of obligations is wider than the law of trusts in which it originated. It now applies to all equitable interests, including equitable charges (which are privileges and powers granted over defined property)[46] and negative covenants (which are promises relating to the use of defined property).[47] All these interests can bind third parties according to the same logic. So the approach, as it developed, was not confined to obligations relating to the benefit of property, but was extended to at least some obligations relating to the use of property.

B. Effects between the Parties

1. In relation to the original trust property

But even if we look only at the obligation as between creditor and debtor, Equity's approach to obligations represents the most thoroughgoing rejection that one could imagine of the Holmesian description of a contractual obligation, as something that gives the debtor an option as to whether to perform or pay compensatory damages.[48]

A feoffee to uses held a legal estate in fee—let us say the fee simple, being the typical case. As we have already noticed, the common law did not generally recognize the use. Assume that a feoffee to uses—the trustee, in modern terms—took proceedings to eject the feoffor, the beneficiary. Since the feoffee/trustee held the fee simple, he could do this successfully in the courts of common law. The feoffor/beneficiary must go to Chancery and plead the use. The Chancellor would examine the parties under oath to learn the truth of the matter.[49] Let us assume that he found that the estate was indeed held to uses. What would he do? He would issue an injunction against the feoffee, to cease the proceeding at common law, and if necessary, to restore the possession or fruits of the land to the feoffor/beneficiary.

[45] L Smith, 'Transfers' in P Birks and A Pretto (eds), *Breach of Trust* (Hart 2002) 213; L Smith, 'Philosophical Foundations of Proprietary Remedies' in R Chambers, C Mitchell, and J Penner (eds), *Philosophical Foundations of Unjust Enrichment* (OUP 2009) 281. In the latter paper I speculated that the early Chancellors may have been influenced by the writings of Thomas Aquinas regarding how third parties may be properly liable in respect of the obligations of others, including by innocently receiving the property of another, and by participating in the wrong of another through receiving property improperly taken by that other.

[46] LD Smith, 'Powership and Its Objects' in A Steven, R Anderson, and J MacLeod (eds), *Nothing So Practical as a Good Theory: Festschrift for George L Gretton* (Avizandum 2017) 223.

[47] B McFarlane and R Stevens, 'The Nature of Equitable Property' (2010) 4 Journal of Equity 1.

[48] This is true whether we are considering the original debtor or a new one, who is bound according to the logic discussed in the previous section.

[49] At common law the parties were incompetent to give evidence (n 22), an incompetency that lasted until 1851 (Baker (n 33) 91). More importantly, in general a deed could never be contradicted by parol (non-deed) evidence (Baker ibid 324–25), a rule that still leaves traces in the modern law (*Friedmann Equity Developments Inc v Final Note Ltd* [2000] 1 SCR 842). None of this was true in Chancery.

And what was the nature of this obligation that the Chancellor discovered? In a sense it was contractual, arising as it did out of the promise that the feoffee made when the feoffment was made to him.[50] Was it a Holmesian option? Only in a very different sense. The defendant did not have the option of paying compensatory damages; he had the option of going to prison, for contempt, until such time as he was willing to comply with the order.[51]

I will argue that this reveals two important things. One is that the Equitable remedy works, in a sense, not against the defendant, but through him. The other is that, directly contrary to the Holmesian view, in Equity you cannot get rid of your obligations by breaching them and paying compensation.

(a) *Equity acts in personam*

The first point is fundamental historically, and it is part of what is captured by the idea that 'Equity acts *in personam*'. If you got an order at common law against the defendant to pay money—damages, or a debt—and it was not complied with, you could get your money in the teeth of the defendant's intransigence, and without his cooperation.[52] Court officers would physically take the defendant's goods and sell them.[53] Imprisonment of the defendant might be possible, but it was the creditor's last choice, when there were no assets on which to execute, because imprisonment did not produce money to pay the judgment debt. Similarly, if you got an order at common law for the recovery of land, the intransigent defendant could be physically removed by officers of the court. The reason that Equity was systematically different on this point is not specifically related to the trust, but rather to the historical relationship between Equity and the common law. Since, as we have seen, Equity was originally not a legal system at all, the Chancellor's orders had to respect the legal system even while defendants were given orders as to how they must, or could not, use their legal rights, powers, privileges, and immunities.[54]

So the order against the faithless feoffee was not in the nature of an order in ejectment, that could allow court officers to throw the defendant off the land. That would too directly contradict the common law. It was an order to him, that he do what he was obliged in conscience to do. Non-compliance was contempt that led to imprisonment, but not to direct enforcement of the order. In a decision of 1748, Lord Hardwicke LC mentioned an extreme case: Chancery can order a party to convey an interest in

[50] cf Maitland (n 7) 28: 'a use, or in modern terms, a trust generally has its origin in something that we can not but call an agreement'.

[51] Holmes did not consider that such a choice revealed an option, but rather a true duty: Holmes (n 25) 462–63, 703. I am not sure whether his distinction on this point is philosophical or merely pragmatic, because either way, the defendant has a choice. It is just that in one case, the consequences of not performing are much more unpleasant.

[52] As Stephen A Smith has noted, it was not, strictly speaking, an *order* against the defendant that he should pay money to the plaintiff; it was a *judgment* that the plaintiff 'shall recover' money from the defendant, which leaves open the possibility of recovery without the defendant's cooperation. See Smith (n 35) 322–29.

[53] Things were more complicated if the relevant asset of the defendant was an estate in land, or (as can be imagined) an Equitable interest under a trust, in which case execution itself required recourse to Chancery.

[54] For more on this point, see LD Smith, 'Law and Equity: Chunk and Permeate' in HP Glenn and LD Smith (eds), *Law and the New Logics* (CUP 2017) 181, 182–86.

land; '[b]ut if he will not, choosing to lie all his life in prison, as Mr. *Savil* did, the court cannot carry it into execution'.[55]

This *in personam* aspect of Equity is crucial, in my view, to understanding the relationship between Equity and the common law, and how two different legal orders could have developed together in the same jurisdiction. To illustrate this, we can consider a classic example of the Chancellor's intervention, one which shows that the *in personam* nature of Equitable obligations was not confined to trust obligations that related to particular property. This is the case of a debtor who gave his creditor a sealed deed as evidence of the debt, and who paid the debt but neglected to recover or destroy the deed. The creditor could sue at common law, and the problem facing the debtor would be that the deed was effectively incontrovertible evidence of the debt in the common law courts.[56] If the common law case were to proceed to judgment, the debtor would lose and would have to pay the debt a second time.[57] To prevent this, the debtor would commence a proceeding in Chancery, where the rules of evidence were different. The Chancellor would investigate what had happened (including via the sworn testimony of the parties), and if he were convinced that the debtor had paid, he would order the creditor to hand over the deed and to cease the proceeding at common law. This example has nothing to do with uses or trusts. The reason that the Chancellor's order had to operate *in personam,* with imprisonment for non-compliance, is that the Chancellor did not make any order that was understood to bind, override, or contradict the common law courts. He had no jurisdiction to do that. He made orders against the parties, orders relating to how they must use or not use their legal rights, powers, privileges, and immunities.

The *in personam* nature of Equitable jurisdiction is somewhat paradoxical when we consider the nature of the beneficiary's interest under a trust: as we have seen, that interest can potentially bind an unlimited number of persons. In this sense it seems strange to call it *in personam.* But the label makes more sense when we realize that while the beneficiary's interest has proprietary effects because it can be enforced against any trustee, including transferees of the trust property who become trustees by operation of law, it is nonetheless *in personam* in the sense that it only binds one person at a time. It is not an interest *in rem* that simultaneously binds everyone.[58] In this sense, the beneficiary's interest does not contradict or compete with the trustee's interest in the same property; on the contrary, the beneficiary's interest depends upon the existence of the trustee's interest. The *in personam* aspect of Equitable remedies still frequently reveals itself. For example, a court may declare that the defendant holds a legal estate on constructive trust for the plaintiff. Even today, speaking generally, while this declaration may include, or may lead to, a separate order that the defendant transfer the legal

[55] *A-G v Day* (1748) 1 Ves Sen 218, 27 ER 992, at 224, 996.

[56] (n 49).

[57] Baker (n 33) 102.

[58] If there is wrongful interference with or damage to trust property, it is the trustee who must sue the wrongdoer; the beneficiary can force the trustee to do so, but the beneficiary has no direct claim against the wrongdoer. See McFarlane and Stevens (n 47) 3–4; J Edelman, 'Two Fundamental Questions for the Law of Trusts' (2013) 129 LQR 66, 67–75.

estate to the plaintiff, such an order is needed. This is because still today, the court generally cannot, in its Equitable jurisdiction, itself effect the transfer of legal rights. The defendant must make the transfer, just as Mr Savil had to.[59]

In the modern world, the *in personam* aspect of Equity is not likely to be important in relation to the execution of a money judgment, even if the judgment is founded on an Equitable obligation. We will see that that there are multiple foundations for such orders, and not all of them are or were based on compensation for loss. But when a money order is made in the modern world, we can expect that the execution of the judgment, in the case of an intransigent defendant, is likely to occur in the same way whether the foundation of the order lies in common law or in Equity, due to the unification of enforcement procedures. But the *in personam* nature of Equitable jurisdiction is of continuing importance in understanding the nature of the beneficiary's interest under a trust.

(b) In Equity you cannot get rid of your obligation by breaching it

What are the implications of the enforcement of uses via contempt of court? Where the feoffee still had the estate, the use was automatically specifically enforceable. This is also true of the modern law of trusts, whether of land or of any other asset.[60] If the trustee has the trust property, he is not given the option of keeping it and paying compensation. In respect of trust property held by the trustee, a trust is always automatically specifically enforceable. There is no appeal to the discretion of the court, and no inquiry into whether damages would be adequate as a remedy.[61] This is one of those things that is so foundational that people sometimes do not notice how interesting it is. It constitutes, in respect of the nature of those obligations, a complete rejection of the Holmesian description. In relation to trust obligations, there is no option to pay compensation: you have to do what you are obliged to do.[62]

2. When the defendant no longer holds the trust property

This imperative, that you have to do what you are obliged to do, is applied even when it might seem to be impossible for the trustee to perform. What do I mean by this? Take a simple case: a trustee holds $1,000 in trust. By an honest mistake, the trustee uses the

[59] For a more recent example of a defendant who refused to comply with a declaration of constructive trust, see RJ Sharpe and K Roach, *Brian Dickson: A Judge's Journey* (Osgoode Society 2003) 185–91. The court's powers may be changing in some jurisdictions. For discussion, see L Smith, 'Unravelling Proprietary Restitution' (2004) 40 CBLJ 317, 335–37.

[60] R Chambers, 'Liability' in P Birks and A Pretto (eds), *Breach of Trust* (Hart 2002) 1, 2–11.

[61] In a contract, the victim of a breach has a right to compensatory damages at common law, and so if a decree of specific performance is refused, the victim is not left empty-handed. The breacher owes a common law obligation, and Equity intervenes only if it is shown that the common law remedy is inadequate. In a trust, speaking generally, the beneficiary has no rights at common law. Even though (as we will see below) the Chancellor could make orders to pay money, there is no practise of asking whether a money order might be sufficient, as a precondition to specific enforcement of the trust.

[62] As Holmes himself acknowledged (n 27), there is no option to pay damages even in contract law where the victim of a breach obtains a decree (an Equitable decree) of specific performance. See *Semelhago v Paramadevan* [1996] 2 SCR 415, 136 DLR (4th) 1, [22], questioning the routine availability of specific performance, but acknowledging that where it is available the plaintiff need not mitigate its loss because the plaintiff is not claiming for loss caused by breach.

$1,000 to buy an unauthorized investment, which falls to $500 in value. Assume further that this was part of a general fall in the market, so that the trustee might wish to argue that his actions have caused no loss: the argument would be that even if he had bought an authorized investment, it too would have fallen in value by half. Trust law traditionally does not allow this argument to be made, even if it be plausible on the facts. It works this way: the beneficiaries, when they learn of what has happened, can disallow the unauthorized investment, and demand the reconstitution of the trust fund. The disallowance has the effect that the trustee has no ground for saying that he properly spent *any* of the trust property. The trustee held $1,000 in trust, and now he has no justification for saying that he does not still hold $1,000 in trust. This makes the trustee personally liable to restore $1,000 into the trust fund. (Conversely, once he has done that, he will be the owner of the rejected, unauthorized investment.)

This is what was meant by James LJ when he said, with the concurrence of Baggallay LJ:

> The Court of Chancery never entertained a suit for damages occasioned by fraudulent conduct or for breach of trust. The suit was always for an equitable debt or liability in the nature of debt. It was a suit for the restitution of the actual money or thing, or value of the thing, of which the cheated party had been cheated.[63]

It is an exaggeration to say that Chancery never awarded damages.[64] But the distinction between debt and damages is sound.[65] The beneficiaries in my example do not (or do not need to) sue for damages; that is to say, they need not frame their claim as a claim for the loss caused by a wrongful act.[66] A claim in debt is a claim for a fixed amount. The amount is very often fixed by agreement, such as the amount of money lent, the contractual monthly rent, the agreed wages, or the price of property sold. But it is not always fixed by agreement; if I pay you $100 by mistake, you owe me $100; this is not a claim for damages, nor is it based on wrongdoing. All of these debt claims are the enforcement of a primary obligation to pay a determined sum, an obligation which does not arise from a wrongful act.

In the case of the trust, the logic is very simple. The trustee held $1,000 in trust. He was a kind of manager, with an authority which was limited in various ways. He then did something unauthorized, and since it was unauthorized, the beneficiaries are entitled to say that it was of no legal effect. So, he is required still to hold $1,000 in trust. In other words, the beneficiaries are allowed to enforce his original obligation (which did not arise by wrongdoing), to hold $1,000 in trust. In this case, they are allowed to enforce it by substitution: by demanding an equivalent amount of money. But because they are enforcing the original, primary obligation, the measurement of their claim is

63 *Ex parte Adamson* (1878) 8 Ch D 807 (CA), 819.

64 PM McDermott, *Equitable Damages* (Butterworths 1994) ch 1.

65 Above, section IV.

66 For more detail, see L Smith, 'The Measurement of Compensation Claims Against Trustees and Fiduciaries' in E Bant and M Harding (eds), *Exploring Private Law* (CUP 2010) 363.

not determined by calculating any loss suffered. That is why, in my example, the trustee would not (according to the traditional law) be allowed to make any argument about the general fall in the investment market. That is an argument about loss, and the claim is not founded on loss.[67]

In my view, this is another example of the approach of Equity to trust obligations: you have to do what you are obliged to do, *even if it be necessary to enforce by substitution.* You cannot plead your own breach in diminution of that. You cannot get rid of, or reduce, your obligations by breaching them. There is no room for Holmes' view of contracts in the law of trusts.

We can see the same effect in Equitable orders arising in the contractual context. A decree of specific performance of a contract may be over-compensatory. Assume that A has agreed to sell his house to B, but then A reneges. A's house doubles in value, but so does B's house, which B has kept because of A's breach. An order for compensation for breach of contract would take account of the gain that B has realized but that he would not have realized if A had performed the contract. But if a court orders specific performance, as well it might to protect B's rights, then A has no Holmesian option to pay compensation. B will get the increase in both properties. That is because an order for specific performance is not a compensatory order; it is the enforcement of the original contractual obligation. And if the court is willing to make such an order, but for whatever reason it chooses to turn it into a money order in substitution, the same effect will follow: B will be overcompensated, but that is because the order does not aim to compensate.[68] It aims to enforce the original obligation.

In the law of trusts, the UK Supreme Court seems to have adopted a new approach, which implies that sometimes it is the court, not the beneficiaries, that decides whether the measure of the award shall be the original obligation or not.[69] Whatever the merits of this new approach, it is demonstrably incorrect to think that all monetary remedies aim to compensate the plaintiff for loss suffered by a wrongful act. The only live question is, which plaintiffs (if any) are allowed to enforce the original obligation, specifically or by substitution in money? The answer to that will tell us which plaintiffs can be forced to settle for compensation when they would rather not do so.

Much of the critique of the new approach has been based on its failure to respect the ancient proceeding of trustee accounting.[70] A trustee is always accountable, in both a wide and a technical sense. In a wide sense, he is responsible for his actions and must explain what he has done, and why. This is because he is a kind of manager. He must produce information about the trust, about conflicts of interest, about unauthorized profits, and so on. In a technical sense, he is liable to render an account of what he has done

[67] C Mitchell, 'Stewardship of Property and Liability to Account' [2014] Conveyancer and Property Lawyer 215, 221–28.

[68] *Semelhago* (n 62), discussed in Smith (n 26). In this context, where the defendant was not already required to render an account of property to the plaintiff, the jurisdiction to make the substitutional order comes from nineteenth-century legislation (Lord Cairns' Act of 1858).

[69] *AIB Group (UK) plc v Mark Redler & Co Solicitors* [2014] UKSC 58.

[70] For example, L Ho, 'An Account of Accounts' (2016) 28 Singapore Academy of LJ 849.

with the trust property that was vested in him.[71] The beneficiaries can call into question the truthfulness of this account. Even once its factual accuracy is established, they may disallow unauthorized expenditures (as in the example above, of the unauthorized investment). If they do so, it will leave the account out of balance, making the trustee personally liable to restore the trust fund in order to make the account balance.[72]

I am not sure that the most pertinent critique of the UK Supreme Court is one that is based on the way the trustee accounting process works. Trustee accounts are traditionally in the form of 'charge–discharge' accounting: when a trustee receives trust property, it is an item of charge, and when she makes an authorized disbursement, it is an item of discharge. This is a very old system of accounting. It is also a rather simple one.[73] It is a mix of a factual inquiry and a set of rules, rules which determine, for example, which expenditures are lawful. But in my view, the norms that differentiate the Holmesian approach to contracts from the law of trusts are not tied to the accounting process. The crucial differences are that in trusts, the original primary obligation is (1) specifically enforceable as a matter of course, and (2) enforceable by substitution in money where it is not enforceable *in specie*.[74] Those propositions could be true whether or not there was a formal accounting process, and they could be true whatever form it took. Those propositions involve the rejection of the Holmesian approach that posits an option in the breaching defendant and a restriction to compensatory orders for the plaintiff.

And conversely, accounting can make room for compensatory orders. If a trustee is unreasonably incompetent in choosing investments, so that the value of trust investments is below what it would be if she had taken reasonable care, she is liable. Traditionally, this is via accounting 'on the basis of wilful default', which imports an inquiry into fault. Let us assume that the trust fund is worth $1,000 less than it should be; once this is determined, via accounting on the basis of wilful default, then the account is 'surcharged' with $1,000, so it does not balance, making the trustee personally liable. But this measure of liability is compensatory; it is compensation for a loss caused via a breach of a duty.[75] Accounting, therefore, is not tied exclusively to the enforcement of the primary obligation, nor to compensation for breach. Accounting is procedure, not

[71] J Penner, 'Distinguishing Fiduciary, Trust, and Accounting Relationships' 8 Journal of Equity 202 discusses the incidence of accountability in this technical sense. All fiduciaries are accountable in the wide sense, but as Penner explains, only some are accountable in the narrower sense. A fiduciary adviser, for example, does not receive property and is not required to keep accounts. But he is responsible for his actions: he must account for unauthorized profits and disclose all relevant information to his principal.

[72] An excellent example is in *Campbell v Hogg* [1930] 3 DLR 673 (PC), which reveals not only the mechanics of adjusting the account, but the traditional order when the account ends up out of balance: namely, a declaration that the trustee 'does hold' in trust the amount that he should be holding in trust.

[73] One might even say, simplistic. The story of 'double-entry' accounting is that of a more sophisticated system that more reliably allows the identification of mistakes. In most commercial contexts, double-entry accounting supplanted charge–discharge accounting hundreds of years ago: MJ Jones, 'The *Dialogus De Scaccario* (c.1179): The First Western Book on Accounting?' (2008) 44 Abacus 443. In many trusts, moreover, where there are income beneficiaries and capital beneficiaries, trustees' accounts may become very complicated as a result of the need to allocate receipts and outgoings between the two: see the rule mentioned in (n 6), and for more detail, *Waters' Law of Trusts* (n 6) 1023–1119.

[74] To close a circle: it is possible to see the second branch of the Rule in *Howe v Lord Dartmouth* (n 6) as an example of exactly the same approach, except that in this case it operates to regulate the position between classes of beneficiaries, rather than between beneficiaries and trustee.

[75] *Hall v Libertarian Investments Ltd* [2013] HKCFA 93, [2014] 1 HKC 368 [170].

substance. The substance that is important is the ability to enforce the primary trust obligation, specifically or if necessary by substitution in money. That can be articulated, in both philosophical and juridical registers, without any reference to accounting.

One reason to be wary of the celebration of accounting as the unique characteristic of money remedies in Equity is that in some versions, it leads to seemingly fictional claims. Joseph Story said that '[a] Court of Equity will presume that the party meant to act in pursuance of his trust and not in violation of it'.[76] It is not by accident that this may be called a 'good man' theory, in direct opposition to Holmes's 'bad man' theory.[77] Some support is lent to this approach by the traditional order that might be made after an accounting, if the account did not balance. Assume that a trustee had received $1,000 in trust property, and he no longer has it, but he can only validly discharge himself of $500 in disbursements. He is liable for $500, to make the account balance, without inquiry into loss caused by breach. The traditional order, however, was in the form of a finding that he 'does hold' $500 in trust.[78] That order does not do the law much credit. It is more direct to say that he is personally liable.

In my view, rather than reasoning in terms of estoppels or irrebuttable presumptions, it is better simply to say that the beneficiary can enforce the primary obligation; it is clearer to focus on the rights of the plaintiff than on what the defendant is not allowed to say or do. If I lend you $1,000 and you do not repay when the debt is due, you are liable for $1,000. I do not have to sue you for compensation for breach of contract, trying to establish the loss I have suffered. Perhaps I mitigated somehow and my loss is less than $1,000. Perhaps it is more, because I missed some business opportunity, but I cannot be bothered to try to lead evidence to establish my loss.[79] But, on any view, I can sue you for $1,000. No one says that this represents a 'good man' theory of contract or of debt. No one says that you are presumed to pay your debts, or that you are not allowed plead that you breached our contract. It is merely the case that you have to pay the debt.

The trust case is different from the debt case because trusts, although they involve obligations, are not simply debt relationships where the obligation is only to pay an equivalent amount. Trusts, on the contrary, are trusts of particular property, and it is not lawful for the trustee to use other property to satisfy her trust obligations. But the tradition of Equity, that turns the primary obligation into a substitutional obligation to pay an equivalent amount of money, bridges this gap. It refuses to allow a defendant to get rid of, or reduce, his obligation by not performing it.[80] As stated by James LJ, if the

[76] As quoted by Lord Peter Millett, 'Bribes and Secret Commissions Again' (2012) 71 CLJ 583, 591. For his part, Millett states (ibid) that a 'fiduciary is not allowed to say that he received the bribe for his own benefit'.

[77] P Millett, 'Bribes and Secret Commissions' [1993] Restitution Law Review 7, 19–20: 'Equity insists on treating him as a good man, despite all the evidence to the contrary; it will not allow him to say that he is a bad one.'

[78] (n 71).

[79] See also (n 31).

[80] I would argue that many cases that are discussed as damages cases are in fact examples of substitutional performance of the original obligation. In *Estate of Rothko* (1977) 372 NE2d 291 (NY), executors (who are like trustees in this respect) sold estate assets while in a conflict of interest. This made the sales voidable and they were set aside. Ideally the assets would have been recovered, but not all of them could be. The executors had to restore to the estate the value of the assets that could not be recovered. This may be described as a claim in damages (see AW Scott, WF Fratcher, and ML Ascher, *Scott and Ascher on Trusts* (4th edn, Aspen Publishers 2007) vol. 4, 1709–11). In my view, once the sales were set aside, the executors were restored to being required to hold the assets for the estate; where

primary obligation cannot be performed *in specie*, it is transmuted into a debt, not into damages.[81]

The possibility of making substitutional money orders also exists at common law, and not only in relation to obligations to pay a sum of money. Robert Stevens argues that such orders are used frequently, in both contract and tort, as a means of measuring damages that is not based on the calculation of the plaintiff's loss.[82] It is also true that the common law used to have an action of account, which presumably allowed the enforcement of primary obligations by substitution.[83] If that is so, it would mean that Equity's practice of making such orders is not peculiar to Equity. The question remains, however, whether Equity's practices do reveal a unique approach in that the accountability of trustees grew to reach even further.

3. When the defendant acquires a new asset that is subject to a trust obligation

(a) Traceable proceeds

Earlier I gave the example of a trustee who acquires an unauthorized investment which falls in value. Not so different is the case of tracing into the proceeds of misappropriated trust property. Assume the trustee uses misappropriated trust property to buy a racing car. As with the investment, this is not authorized, and the beneficiaries need not accept it. But they may wish to: either because the trustee is insolvent, or perhaps because the car is now worth more than he paid for it. Equity says that they are allowed to treat the car as trust property, even though its purchase was unauthorized, and even though the trustee never intended it to be trust property.[84]

Why this should be the case is a matter of some dispute.[85] Here, unlike in the cases discussed in the previous section, the beneficiary is asserting a new right, and it is this new right that needs to be justified. The original property was held on trust. The trustee has, in a sense, 'invested' it; he has used it to acquire a different asset. That asset was acquired by the trustee with the rights (and powers) that he held in trust and so it is not surprising, on an anti-Holmesian view, that the new property should be seen as held in trust. And this has been the law ever since there were uses and trusts.[86] I would suggest that the decision that the obligation extends to the proceeds

this was no longer possible, they were liable to perform that original obligation by substitution in money (with evidentiary uncertainties as to valuation resolved against the wrongdoer, according to general principle).

[81] (n 63).

[82] Stevens (n 29) 59–91.

[83] Baker (n 33) 363–65, noting that the action fell into desuetude for procedural reasons in the sixteenth century. See also Jones (n 72), describing medieval accounting to the Crown in the English Exchequer.

[84] It is a fortiori in the case of the unauthorized investment which was intended to be trust property: the beneficiaries do not need to accept it as trust property, but they may do so.

[85] T Cutts, 'Tracing, Value and Transactions' (2016) 79 MLR 381; A Nair, *Claims to Traceable Proceeds* (OUP 2018).

[86] The earliest case I know is *Bale v Marchall* (1457) 10 SS 143, decided by the Lord Chancellor in consultation with the judges of the common law. The case is discussed in Smith 'Philosophical Foundations of Proprietary Remedies' (n 45) 299–303. Of course, the finding of such a trust has adverse effects on unsecured creditors of the trustee. But the logic of trust obligations has always been worked out through the analysis of the bilateral relationship between trustee and beneficiary. Whether or not there is a trust *affects* the trustee's creditors, not the other way around.

is not based on providing a remedy for wrongdoing. It is an approach that extrapolates from the original relationship and says that in the light of that relationship and of what the trustee has done with trust property, the rightful conclusion is that the proceeds are held in trust.[87]

In this sense, such claims may best be understood as having arisen from the accountability of a trustee. When the trustee *lawfully* spends trust property to acquire some other asset, the account needs to show this, and the trustee's obligation in relation to the new asset is of course not a remedy for wrongdoing but a primary obligation. Allowing beneficiaries to claim the traceable proceeds of an *unlawful* disposition is effectively allowing them to insist that the transaction be entered into the trust accounts even though the trustee was intending to act unlawfully. In other words, his intention in this respect is not determinative; the decision of the beneficiaries is. As discussed above, accounting does not itself justify Equity's approach to these obligations, but it frames that approach and underscores that the trustee's obligation in respect to the traceable proceeds is, if the beneficiaries so choose, a primary obligation, not a remedy for wrongdoing.

It is the latter point that reveals something that may be peculiar to Equity. Above we noted, in the context of the unauthorized investment, that the beneficiaries can enforce the original primary obligation of the trustee, specifically or by substitution. The tracing case shows a willingness to recognize a new obligation, in relation to the traceable proceeds, and to characterize it as also a primary obligation. This approach shows a particular understanding of the fiduciary accountability that exists in the trust relationship. In a contract, the parties have primary obligations to perform the contract, and a breach of those obligations may generate secondary remedial obligations. Equity's understanding of the trust is as a juridical relationship that is capable of generating new obligations that are primary obligations. The primary obligations of the trustee go beyond what was expressly contemplated. This makes sense inasmuch as the parties are understood to be in a relationship in which one party acts for and on behalf of another.[88]

The case just discussed involved the acquisition of new property with trust property; in this case, according to Equity, the new asset is subject to a trust obligation because it was itself acquired with trust property. The same philosophy is revealed in other rules of Equity.

[87] *Hall* (n 74) [169]. Sometimes beneficiaries may instead claim a security interest or lien over the proceeds, to secure their personal claim for reimbursement. For example, if the proceeds have been acquired only partly with trust money, and have then gone down in value, the lien may secure full recovery, whereas a proportional trust interest would be worth less than the original misappropriated property. This option is based on the logic of combining the ability to claim a trust with the principle that in cases of mixed substitutions, evidentiary difficulties are resolved against one who wrongfully created them: L Smith, *The Law of Tracing* (Clarendon Press 1997) 348–49. In effect, beneficiaries who assert a security interest in some asset are laying a claim to the (not yet existing) proceeds of the disposition of that asset.

[88] Beginning in the nineteenth century, the ability to claim a trust interest over the proceeds of an unauthorized disposition has evolved to be available in fiduciary relationships outside of trusts, and, in the twentieth century, outside of any fiduciary relationship (Smith ibid 342–47).

(b) The no-profit rule

It is revealed, for example, in Equity's rule against the acquisition of unauthorized profits by those in fiduciary relationships. This rule is puzzling when viewed as a remedy for wrongdoing. Like claims based on tracing, it pays no attention to the loss suffered by the plaintiff, and like those claims, it may lead to the plaintiff's being better off than if the relevant events had never happened. This has led to speculation that the no-profit rule must be based on deterrence. But this approach is unpersuasive.[89]

In fact, the no-profit rule is just another example of the philosophy that we have already seen. A person who owes fiduciary obligations is in a relationship in which he is required to act for and on behalf of another person. If and when the fiduciary extracts some advantage from the situation (whether it be in the form of valuable rights, or information), he is obliged to surrender that advantage to the person on whose behalf he is acting. This is not a remedy for having done something wrong; it is just the rightful implication of the pre-existing relationship. It is a new, primary obligation. If a fiduciary acquires an unauthorized profit, she is obliged to hold it for her beneficiary. She does not get a choice to keep it and pay compensation. And because an unconditional obligation to hold property for another person is, in Equity, a trust (with the relevant third-party effects), unauthorized profits are held on constructive trust.[90] In the same way, if a fiduciary acquires information that is relevant to her beneficiary, she comes under a duty of disclosure. That is a primary duty growing out of the other-regarding nature of the relationship.

Once again, the accountability of trustees is traditionally deployed to frame this approach to unauthorized profits. Equity says that the trustee is 'accountable' for such profits. What this means is that the beneficiaries are entitled to enter such profits onto the 'charge' side of the account, just like any other receipt of property that is held for the benefit of the beneficiaries. The profit is thus understood to be held in trust, as a matter of primary obligation. But again, the account is procedural machinery. The substance is that a particular kind of relationship is understood to be capable of generating new primary obligations that go beyond anything that was agreed or contemplated by the parties. This is clear because even a fiduciary who is not accountable in the strict sense—that is, who is not obliged to keep accounts of property—is accountable for unauthorized profits. This is the case, for example, for corporate directors and managers, and for fiduciary advisers.

The machinery so developed by Equity was to some extent applied outside of its original home in the context of fiduciary or other-regarding relationships. In the nineteenth century, it became possible to demand an 'accounting of profits' in relation to some profitable breaches of intellectual property rights.[91] More recently, it has been suggested that it can be used for at least some profitable breaches of contract.[92] In these settings, it has become a gain-based remedy for wrongdoing.

[89] L Smith, 'Deterrence, Prophylaxis and Punishment in Fiduciary Obligations' (2013) 7 Journal of Equity 87.
[90] *FHR European Ventures LLP v Cedar Capital Partners LLC* [2014] UKSC 45.
[91] J Edelman, *Gain-Based Damages* (Hart 2002) 233–34.
[92] *A-G v Blake* (n 27).

(c) *After-acquired property*

Another dimension of this philosophy is revealed in relation to after-acquired property. 'Equity treats that as done which ought be done' is a potentially misleading phrase. But it describes something very important. If you are unconditionally obliged to hold some property for another, then Equity views this obligation as a trust, attaching all of the consequences discussed above. This happens, for example, where a vendor has agreed to sell an estate in land to a purchaser, and the purchaser has paid the full price.[93] If a person has agreed to grant or convey a lesser interest, and has received full counter-performance so that their obligation is unconditional, then the principle operates by creating whatever Equitable interest is necessary to fulfil the unconditional obligation.[94]

Where the person has agreed, for value given, to transfer or create such an interest in property that he does not yet hold, then what happens is that as soon as he gets it, the relevant Equitable interest will arise.[95] Once again, one is not offered the choice as to whether one will, or will not, fulfil one's obligation.[96] In this context, 'Equity treats that as done which ought to be done' takes away that choice. This principle can apply to a promise to grant or transfer any interest, including security interests. It allows a charge (security interest) to bind after-acquired property, where the chargor was unconditionally obliged to charge that property. The common law has no such principle: if you don't do what you are obliged to do, that may be a breach of contract. On this point, civilian systems are traditionally like the common law, although in recent years some have been legislating to adopt the Equitable approach to security interests.[97] The reason is that a security interest that automatically binds after-acquired property is a very commercially useful tool.[98]

[93] I am not here addressing the much more limited Equitable interest that can arise where a contract of sale is specifically enforceable, but the price has not been fully paid. Although that is sometimes called a 'constructive trust', it is really only a security interest: K Gray and SF Gray, *Elements of Land Law* (5th edn, OUP 2009) 1057–63; EH Burn and J Cartwright, *Cheshire and Burn's Modern Law of Real Property* (18th edn, OUP 2011) 980–81; A Oakley, *Parker and Mellows: The Modern Law of Trusts* (9th edn, Sweet & Maxwell 2008) 482; PG Turner, 'Understanding the Constructive Trust between Vendor and Purchaser' (2012) 128 LQR 582, 586–88. For a full history, see DWM Waters, *The Constructive Trust* (Athlone Press 1964) ch 2. Once the price has been paid, a genuine trust arises: Gray and Gray, *Elements of Land Law* 1063: 'Full beneficial ownership of the land … passes to [the buyer] only upon payment of the full purchase price'; Oakley, *Parker and Mellows* 482: 'as soon as the purchase price has been paid in full, the qualified nature of the vendor's trusteeship will disappear since he no longer has any interest to protect; from that moment onwards he will be a bare trustee of the property for the purchaser'. See also N Hopkins, 'Acquiring Property Rights from Uncompleted Sales of Land' (1998) 61 MLR 486, 492–94; Turner, 'Understanding the Constructive Trust' 587, 598.

[94] If the person has promised to create an Equitable interest, such as a trust or an Equitable mortgage or an Equitable charge, that interest will arise. If they have promised to create or convey a legal interest, an Equitable interest will arise that aims to fulfil the promise: an obligation to convey a legal estate will create a trust of that interest, an obligation to grant a lease will create an 'Equitable lease', and an obligation to grant a legal mortgage will create an Equitable mortgage.

[95] The most striking example I know is *Pullan v Koe* [1913] 1 Ch 9. In 1859 a woman promised to transfer, to trustees of her marriage settlement, any property that she should receive in excess of £100. In 1879 she received £285, some of which she used to buy bonds in her husband's name. In 1912, after her death, the trustees were able to recover the bonds. She held the money in trust as soon as she received it, and neither the purchase of proceeds, the donative transfer to her husband, or the passage of time got rid of the trust. Her promise was treated as one given in exchange for value under the doctrine of 'marriage consideration', which I do not address here.

[96] The law is different if the obligation was not assumed for value. This is discussed in Smith (n 45) 294–5.

[97] See for example Civil Code of Québec, arts 2715–23.

[98] In many common law jurisdictions, for various reasons, it has been put on a statutory footing, as in UCC Article 9 and Canadian Personal Property Security Acts. But the root is in Equity.

In a way, this phenomenon is not that different from trust interests in unauthorized profits or in traceable proceeds. Both of those are kinds of after-acquired property.[99] In the cases discussed in this section, just as in interests in unauthorized profits or in traceable proceeds, the interest in the after-acquired property arises as a primary obligation, not as a remedy for wrongdoing. The difference is the source of the obligation. In the examples in this section, the obligation relating to the property, whether currently held or after-acquired, was consensually adopted. In tracing claims and in unauthorized profits, it is imposed by law as an implication of the relationship between the parties. But in all of these situations, it is a primary obligation.

VI. Conclusion

'Equity is not a set of rules but a state of mind.'[100] That is another way, perhaps, of saying that Equity is not a single thing.

I have suggested that Equity's approach to obligations displays a series of features that evolved centuries ago in the context of uses and trusts, institutions that dealt with obligations relating to the benefit of particular property. These obligations were impersonalized, so that they could bind an unlimited number of third parties. This gave the interest of a trust beneficiary a proprietary character that it retains to this day.

Equitable obligations relating to the benefit of particular property are always specifically enforceable. Where this is impossible, Equity demands the substitutional enforcement of those primary obligations, rather than imposing an obligation to pay compensation. This amounts to a wholehearted rejection of the Holmesian 'option' view of contractual obligations.

Treating trust obligations as impersonal is perhaps what led to trusteeship's being conceptualized as an impersonal office. The official role of the trustee, moreover, was seen as an other-regarding one, not one in which the trustee was free to act selfishly. One result of this is the willingness of Equity to impose new primary obligations on a trustee to hold in trust any asset acquired with trust property. In the same way, any fiduciary must hold unauthorized profits derived from his other-regarding role for the benefit of the beneficiary. The same logic means that any relevant or valuable information acquired by a fiduciary from his or her role must be disclosed to the beneficiary. In short, what Equity does is to create new, primary obligations in order to give effect to a relationship in which one party is bound to act for and on behalf of another. The result is a much more robust protection for the beneficiary of such a relationship than would be given by attempting to define the primary obligations in advance, leaving the beneficiary to claim compensation for loss caused by breach.

[99] Equity, and the statutory reforms, allow security interests to be asserted in the traceable proceeds of collateral that was subject to a security interest.

[100] Lord Peter Millett, 'The Common Lawyer and the Equity Practitioner' (2016) 6 UK Supreme Court Yearbook 193, 193.

Some aspects of these approaches of Equity may be found in other legal orders, such as the common law or the civil law. But taken as a whole, this interrelated suite is unique. The evolution of Equity's approach to the use, and later to the trust and to fiduciary relationships more generally, grew out of its characteristic way of understanding obligations, and of understanding other-regarding relationships. The outcome has been the elaboration of a conceptual toolkit that is uniquely suited to the juridical apprehension of such relationships. It is not by accident that in today's world, the label 'fiduciary' is ever more frequently invoked by those who aim to describe any legal relationship in which one person is bound to act for unselfish ends.[101]

[101] See for example E Fox-Decent, *Sovereignty's Promise: The State as Fiduciary* (OUP 2011); EJ Criddle, PB Miller, and RH Sitkoff (eds), *The Oxford Handbook of Fiduciary Law* (OUP 2018), identifying 'fiduciary principles' in legal orders from around the world, ancient and modern; EJ Criddle and others (eds), *Fiduciary Government* (CUP 2018).

8

Pathways to Legal Rights

The Function of Equity

Larissa Katz

Equity was once widely understood to have an important domain of its own in relation to law: a distinctive body of doctrine and principles administered by its own courts.[1] Today, as courts of equity have largely disappeared, it is no longer obvious what keeps this traditional cluster of equitable doctrine and principles together. Without a clear normative idea picking out what is distinctively equitable about equity as an institution, we have lost our grip on why equity matters. In this chapter, I set out to revive the idea of equity as a morally significant—indeed, a morally required—companion to a rights-based system of law.[2] I offer a new account of Equity as an institution that preserves and regulates the pathways to legal rights.

The obvious and proper starting point in a search for Equity's normative foundations is the long-standing philosophical discussion of the idea of equity and its relation to law. The conventional way to think about equity in the philosophical tradition is as a response to problems arising out of the generality of rules.[3] Say there is a rule in my house that children must never awaken adults before 7 am (and dire sanctions await those who do). That rule might even list a few exceptions, eg, if there is blood or fire, children can wake up adults anytime. Now imagine a child wakes me up one morning at 5 am because there is a flood in the bathroom, something no one in my household had foreseen. It seems unjust to treat her as a wrongdoer in the circumstances. The rule seems to require an *ex post facto* correction to ensure its equitable application in that case.[4] We might say then that my child had no obligation to forebear from awaking me to warn me of the flood. Equity in this broad sense is the practice of allowing for exceptions where a particular application of a general rule produces results at odds with the purposes or normative ideals to which that rule is committed.

[1] See John Norton Pomeroy, *Equity* (1914) 6.

[2] In doing so, I do not follow philosophical accounts of equity as a matter of ethics, a softening of claims of right with appeals to virtue and conscience. Nor do I suggest that equity is primarily concerned with behaviour that is *unethical*, such as opportunism in a bad sense.

[3] Aristotle is the source of this view of equity. See Book V, *Nicomachean Ethics*, in 2 The Complete Works of Aristotle (J. Barnes, ed, WD Ross, tr, Princeton UP 1984) 1796 ('And this is the nature of the equitable, a correction of law where it is defective owing to its universality').

[4] Suárez, following Aristotle, thought that equity was a process of interpreting the will of the legislator to allow that a legal obligation had lapsed, 'although it will be necessary for some extrinsic circumstances to arise which will force one to make such an interpretation'. See Francisco Suárez, 'A Treatise on Laws and God the Lawgiver', in Thomas Pink, (ed), *Selections from Three Works* (Gwladys L. Williams et al, tr, Liberty Fund, Inc. 2014) 367.

Larissa Katz, *Pathways to Legal Rights* In: *Philosophical Foundations of the Law of Equity*. Edited by: Dennis Klimchuk, Irit Samet, and Henry E Smith, Oxford University Press (2020). © The several contributors.
DOI: 10.1093/oso/9780198817659.003.0009

There are two ways that this philosophical idea of equity might relate to law: one conceives of equity as bound up with the very idea of legal concepts. HLA Hart's account of the defeasibility of legal concepts reflects something like this idea. Hart wrote that legal concepts are compounds of law and fact and as such are inherently subject to defeating conditions (if x, then y, unless p).[5] Equity in the broad sense concerns an inherent feature of legal concepts: their defeasibility in circumstances that are not knowable *ex ante*.

A second way to see the relation of equity to law is in terms of the judicial role and its relation to law more generally. John Gardner has written about equity, not as a feature of law or legal concepts but rather as a role-based responsibility of judges, something judges do. For Gardner, whereas law aims at many things, judges are charged with doing justice first.[6] Equity is the idea of the judge acting as arbitrator, doing justice as between the parties when the demands of law and justice are at odds.[7] Equity stands outside of law on this account, supplying justice in the particular case where law fails to do so.

Equity, in this philosophical sense we trace to Aristotle, is not a difficult idea to go along with. The basic story and its normative significance seem relatively uncontroversial. For who would deny that there is a place for particularized justice in our legal institutions and in the work of courts in particular? If equity means justice in the particular case, then equity surely is a bedrock value of any legal system.

The real challenge is to figure out the extent to which equity in this broad sense sets out the philosophically significant core of Equity as an institution as we know it in common law systems, and, if not, what does. By core, I mean the ideals that give the institution as a whole its normative bearing, allowing us to determine the justifiability (or not) of various accretions to that core by reference to it. By Equity as an institution, I mean both the agents (or agencies) with the special power to make and enforce equitable rules and also the product of these agents: the equitable rules that agents of equity make and the juridical relations that they regulate.

Now, most lawyers, quite properly, recognize that Equity does much more, or maybe much other, than require judges to aim for justice in a particular case or to recognize the inherent defeasibility of legal concepts. Equity has given us all kinds of very specific rights, such as restrictive covenants, securities (such as the equity of redemption, which makes a mortgage really a mortgage rather than a conveyance of property to the bank), equitable shares in partnership assets, trusts, options to purchase, fancy interests in future rights to property or contract, inter alia.[8] The systematicity of Equity, and its trade in the language of rights and obligations, gives it more of the feel of law and juridical relations than the feel of equity as justice in the particular case.

[5] HLA Hart, 'The Ascription of Responsibility and Rights' (1948) 49 Proceedings of the Aristotelian Society 171, 175–187. Note that Hart himself did not intend this to be an account of equity but an account of legal concepts generally. *See also* Suárez supra at 368: '... the precept is no binding... because under the conditions stated it is improbable that the intention of the lawgiver extended to the case in question.'

[6] John Gardner, *Law as a Leap of Faith* (OUP 2014) 257.

[7] Aristotle drew the connection between equity and arbitration but did not go on to suggest that equity was a feature of the judicial role or something built into law. See *Rhetoric* Bk 1 sec 13 (we 'prefer arbitration to litigation—for an arbitrator goes by the equity of the case; a judge by the law and arbitration was invented with the express purpose of securing full power for equity').

[8] For instance, rights to undeclared dividends on shares or rights to contractual rights to payment for doing something in the future.

Most lawyers recognize, moreover, that doing equity in the sense of meting out justice in the particular case has never been uniquely the province of Equity as an institution. Although courts of chancery, the primary agents of Equity for a time, did quite a lot of equity in the philosopher's sense, at least in early days, the common law, too, has the tools within it to promote justice in the particular case even if common law courts did not always deploy them. The view that the common law courts too could do equity in the philosopher's sense accounts for Thomas More's famous challenge to the common law courts: courts of chancery would interfere less, he said, if the common law courts themselves took their responsibility to do equity more seriously.

What might we make of the looseness of the relation between the philosopher's equity and Equity as an institution? We might double down on the idea that equity in the broad sense is all that is philosophically interesting about Equity as an institution and dismiss the rest as normatively insignificant. Or we might find in this looseness a reason to deny that Equity has its own normative core (taking equity in the broad philosophical sense to be the only possible contender), perhaps concluding that that equitable rights are just more private rights that we have against others.[9] Equitable rights appear from this viewpoint as components of private law, itself a modular thing, to be justified in terms of what they add to the range of private law relations available to us.

An alternative to both of these approaches is to investigate equity's normative significance in terms of its place within our larger institutional arrangements.[10] This is my aim in this chapter: to offer a different perspective on what equity[11] does and the kind of injustice it targets. Equity 'sees' and protects against a kind of injustice visible only from the equitable standpoint: interruptions on the pathways to legal rights, leading to a loss or forfeiture of position. Vulnerability to forfeiture through interruption arises out of the very nature of acquired rights. All acquired rights presuppose procedures for acquisitions, temporally extended ways of satisfying law's criteria for the successful acquisition of that kind of right. As we will see, procedures, no matter how truncated they may be, take place over time and so are always potentially interruptible. That preserves and regulates the pathways to legal rights. This account of Equity enables us to identify and explain what is equitable about the traditional core of Equity. It accounts for the distinctive conceptual structure of equitable rights as rights in respect of other people's rights.[12] Equity always has these legal rights in view but concerns a domain necessarily outside of the private law framework: the ways in. Finally, it also has important implications for the application of equity into new domains.

This account of equity as an institution protecting pathways to legal rights draws on political and moral ideas about the state and its status as a public authority. The integrity of a system of law as a blueprint for our lives together, requires that the state

[9] As Henry Smith has pointed out, this is the view of many American scholars and may be the view that lies behind the idea at many American schools that equity is not a subject to be taught on its own.

[10] See also Henry Smith in this volume (Chapter 10), offering an institutional account in terms of opportunism.

[11] From now on, I will use capital 'E', because I intend only to refer to Equity as an institution.

[12] Ben McFarlane and Robert Stevens, 'The Nature of Equitable Property' (2010) 4 Journal of Equity 1 (rights against rights). See also Glanville Williams, ed, *Salmond, on Jurisprudence* (11th edn, Sweet & Maxwell 1957) 268–69 (describing rights in respect of other rights as one of the categories of rights we might have and includes here equitable rights arising by agreements of purchase and sale).

attend to the potential for oppression and injustice that is produced by the very nature of acquired rights. There are limits to what the state can tolerate while maintaining its status as a legitimate public authority: injustice outside of the framework of acquired rights weighs on what I will call the political conscience of the state. There is a role then for the state to play in setting out pathways to legal rights and in protecting us against injustice and tyranny as we traverse them. This is the role I think equity is meant to fill.

There are two aspects of equity, on my account. The first, concerning the protection of pathways to legal rights, is the foundation for equitable rights. This is what I will focus on in this chapter. There is another side to my account of equity that concerns the allocation of the burden of equitable rights—equitable duties—to specific private actors. Equity almost always lays that duty upon the person who holds the very legal right towards which the petitioner in equity is moving. And yet there are cases where equity intervenes to constrain the exercise of some other right, power or privilege that might have the effect of triggering a forfeiture. Equity, I will argue, conscripts private actors as participants in the legal order to do as equity would have done, and so to avoid or mitigate the forfeiture.[13]

My account of an equitable burden, ie the duty to do as equity requires done, draws on ideas about the state's prerogative to enlist our help in discharging the burdens of government. Equity enlists the service of the legal right holder—by making a personal demand that she avoid or mitigate the forfeiture in the exercise of her legal rights.[14] It is a matter of political or civil conscience for each of us to serve the state in discharging its core obligations to protect its citizens against tyranny and injustice.[15] Equitable duties can be understood as accessions of a public burden to a legal right.[16] Equity usually allocates the burden of that public right and responsibility to guard against forfeiture to the person best placed to carry it out, the person in a position to interrupt through the exercise of legal rights.[17] The bearer of the burden is answerable to the state personally in contempt if she refuses to do as equity would have done.[18]

Both in its aims (guarding against forfeiture along the pathways to rights) and in its *modus operandi* (enlisting legal rights holders in service of this protection), equity represents a political ideal of proper state–citizen relations. This normative ideal of proper

[13] This account then departs from those who have argued that conscience in a moral, rather than political or institutional sense, accounts for equity's work. See Irit Samet, *Conscience Goes to Market* (OUP 2019); P Nyuk Chin, 'Relieving against Forfeiture: Windfalls and Conscience' (1995) 25 Western Australia Law Review 110, 111 (offering doctrinal grounds for the view 'improper or shabby behavior on the part of the party against whom relief is sought has much less to do with relief than is believed').

[14] Thus, it is often said that 'Equity always acts *in personam*' (RE Megarry and PV Baker, *Snell's Principles of Equity* (25th edn, Sweet & Maxwell 1960) 38).

[15] 'The conscience by which I am to proceed is merely civilis and politica' (*Cook v Fountain* 3 Swan 585 (Ch 1733) 600).

[16] Compare other public burdens that accede to private rights, like the duty to shovel snow on public sidewalks. See Larissa Katz, 'Governing Through Owners: How and Why Formal Private Property Enhances State Power' (2012) 160 University of Pennsylvania Law Review 2029.

[17] I examine in more depth the role of conscience, opportunism, and unclean hands in equity's conscription of private actors in another paper, LM Katz, 'Conscience and Conscription' (work in progress).

[18] Note the state can take over this function, by itself arranging for the exercise of a legal right in the manner that equity requires: equity regards as done what ought to have been done and a court can make whatever orders it needs to see to it that fact aligns with this fiction. That is in effect to take the proportionate exercise of rights out of private hands altogether.

state–citizen relations has an unmistakably premodern flavour.[19] It may be helpful in understanding why that is so to remember how equity as an institution emerged in common law jurisdictions: not from the judiciary's understanding of its role (eg to do justice first), but from the executive's understanding of its role within the constitutional order.[20] Historically, equity was one of a bundle of prerogative powers that constitute the executive (or the Crown) as the fountain of justice and honour.[21] Prerogative power—or reasons of state, as it is sometimes called—is often described as an arbitrary power to decide the exception, shielded from review by courts or the legislature.[22] This description (at best) sets out only negatively the jurisdiction the executive claims as its prerogative power.[23] The prerogative power defined a role for the executive as the source of justice and honour within its realm, with ultimate responsibility for peace, order, and good government.[24] We can make sense of equity as one aspect of the prerogative alongside other powers, including the common law idea that the executive had exclusive jurisdiction to create offices and an ancient right to command the service of its subjects in those offices;[25] the power to pardon and to grant dispensations; authority and responsibility to hear pleas from the poor.[26] Equity's origins within the executive branch are evident in the way that equity continues to operate in the twenty-first century.

[19] My view overall is that there is more than a trace of the premodern in the common law generally: the continued importance of roles and offices in ascribing rights and responsibilities is one indicator. See Katz (n 16); Leif Wenar, 'The Nature of Claim-Rights' (2013) 123 Ethics 202 (on roles).

[20] See Thomas Poole, *Reason of State: Law, Prerogative and Empire* (CUP 2015) (on the nature of the prerogative).

[21] Charles Barton, *Elements of Conveyancing* (1815) 282 ('Nor can the King ... grant to any one authority to hold a court of equity for the dispensation of equity is a special trust committed to the King himself and not to be entrusted to any other save only his Chancellor').

[22] See AV Dicey, *The Law of the Constitution* (OUP 2013) 240, 256 (comparing Equity to *droit administratif* in France, concluding it might have but did not continue on as a source of arbitrary discretion). There is a strand of constitutional thought according to which rule by royal prerogative made its own distinctive a claim of public justifiability. Michael J Braddick makes an argument that rule by king makes a claim of legitimacy based on wise counsel (*State Formation in Early Modern England* (CUP 2000) 21–6). Hobbes may mean something like that when he says: 'The King's reason, *when it is publicly upon Advice and Deliberation declared* ... is all that is or ever was the Law of England'. (Thomas Hobbes, 'A Dialogue between a Philosopher and a Student of the Common Laws of England', in Sir William Molesworth (ed) *Thomas Hobbes: The English Works* (London 1860) VI 15 (emphasis added)).

[23] This view of the prerogative implies that it stands outside the legal order rather than within it and constrained then by requirements of legality. I leave to one side here what I take to be obvious normative problems with this view.

[24] One interesting application of this view of the prerogative is set out in Eric Nelson, *The Royalist Revolution* (Harvard UP 2014). Nelson argues that American revolutionaries first turned to the Crown and the royal prerogative as a sufficient source of governmental power and as a protector against the tyranny of the British Parliament.

[25] The idea that the state is entitled to the service of its subjects is an old idea in law and in philosophy. See '*Case of Non Obstante*' in Steve Sheppard (ed), *The Selected Writings of Sir Edward Coke* (Liberty Fund, Inc. 2003) I, 423 (this essentially sets out the right of the sovereign to the service of any of his subjects 'for the publick Weal'). Maitland also mentions the ancient common law power to conscript subjects to serve. FW Maitland, *The Constitutional History of England* (CUP 1920) 504 ('[I]t is a very general if somewhat antiquated doctrine of the common law that a person is bound to serve the crown in all manner of offices'). See also DEC Yale (ed.), *Sir Matthew Hale's The Prerogatives of the King* (Selden Society 1976) 268 (the compulsion of men to do those things that are in aide and subservient to the dispensation of justice). Suarez talked about the right of the prince to the liberty (but not the life) of his subjects, ie, a right to their service. More recently, see OW Holmes, 'Early English Equity', in *Collected Legal Papers* (Harcourt, Brace and Howe 1921) 1 ('[Equity] had a form of decree requiring personal obedience') and 'The Path of the Law' ibid at 175–176 on equity as the exceptional case allowing to speak of the 'civil liabilities as imposing duties in an intelligible sense' when 'equity will grant an injunction, and will enforce it' 6 ('the personal command of obedience is the only real duty' the rest is just a set of options, with prices, that does not convey *duty* at all).

[26] JH Baker, *An Introduction to English Legal History* (Butterworths 1971) 209.

In what follows, I set out the basic contours of this account of equity and the moral ideas that animate it. I will first explain how pathway problems arise out of the very nature of acquired rights. I will then explain what forfeiture means in this context and the kind of moral problem it presents. I will then go on to show how many central and well-known equitable interventions can be explained in terms of pathway problems and also how equitable forms of reasoning help us to identify and work through new pathway problems. I will show how core equitable rights—including restrictive covenants, mortgages, the trust—share this rational structure. And I will show how equity retains its promise to act as a force of innovation in the law, allowing us to identify and solve new pathway problems.

I. Pathway Problems and the Nature of Acquired Right

Pathway problems are inextricably connected to the very nature of some kinds of legal rights. An obvious but important feature of some private rights, traditionally property and contract rights, is that they are not rights we are born with but rather stand to be acquired. Property and contract law supply the success conditions for the acquisition of rights, what must already have been done for a right to have been acquired. These success conditions define the point at which a procedure for acquiring rights has been completed. But procedures for acquiring rights are always temporally extended: it takes action to complete a procedure, and action is never instantaneous. The very nature of acquired rights, then, produces an intuitive moral problem: acquisition requires procedures, procedures are always temporally extended, and so there is always the potential for interruption after a procedure has begun but before it is completed. By looking at equity in terms of pathway problems, it should become clear why equity 's traditional focus was always property (only later extended to contract).[27] Property rights are acquired in a way that our rights stemming from the idea of the person, eg rights to our bodies or our political rights, are not.[28] On my account, there is simply no call for equitable intervention with respect to rights associated with personhood: we cannot acquire rights in respect of others' rights to their bodies or to a voice in government, etc, and so we cannot suffer the kind of forfeiture on the way to rights that attracts equity's concern.

[27] This makes sense of Lord Eldon's 'Equity protects property' dictum. Criticized as unduly restrictive in cases like *Berrien v Pollitzer* 165 F 2d 21 (DC 1947) 22. Oliver W Holmes writing for the majority in *Giles v Harris*, 189 US 475 (1903) 189 was concerned that 'The traditional limits of proceedings in equity have not embraced a remedy for political wrongs. See *Scandinavian Trading Tanker Co v The Scaptrade*, 1 Lloyd's Rep 146 (CA Civ 1982) denying Equity's jurisdiction to relieve against forfeiture in case where there is no right to property or possession of vessel: time charter cases involved contract for services: charterer provides services to shipowner through use of ship by employees of charterer. No path to anything in these cases (no specific performance possible). Therefore, withdrawal of ship for non-payment might cause economic loss but does not dislodge the plaintiff from path to rights.

[28] There are some interesting in-between cases, like copyright, that requires some event, like creation to trigger the applicability of the right but is closely connected to the idea of a person. See Abraham Drassinower, *What's Wrong with Copying?* (Harvard UP 2015).

Of course, procedures for acquisition of property rights vary widely, and pathways problems are more obvious in some contexts than others. Some procedures require very little action and leave very little scope then for interruption in fact. Imagine a very simple procedure for acquisition: a right acquired simply by taking something in hand, as when I acquire a right to an apple on the ground simply by picking it up. The time from beginning to completion of the procedure is limited. The potential for interruption is there, nonetheless. Someone might snatch the very apple I was reaching for, seconds before my hand closes around it.

Other procedures are more obviously temporally extended, and the actual risk of interruption is higher. In these contexts, we should expect to see and do see more scope for equitable intervention. Many of these are extended and complicated, some requiring multiparty action for their completion. These generate substantial pathway problems. The most established forms of equitable rights, the trust, the mortgage, the equitable interest in specifically performable contracts, all concern pathway problems that take place over longer periods of time.[29] It stands to reason that equity has more actively intervened in protecting these pathways to legal rights than those that are simpler and shorter. But there is always a procedure for acquisition of property rights, and it is always potentially interruptible even if the actual risk of interruption as it turns out is very low. Pathway problems are inherent in the very nature of acquired right, even if many do not rise to the level of seriousness to attract equitable intervention.

As we will see, equity properly distinguishes between pathways and mere hopes of acquiring rights. A nephew who has spent years cultivating an ageing aunt in the hope that she may leave him her fortune might consider himself to have taken significant steps in the direction of that inheritance. I have no doubt that in many cases there is a likelihood of that person's succeeding in what he has set out to do: he may in the end inherit. And yet it should be clear that there is no pathway to legal rights that the nephew is traversing from equity's standpoint. A pathway to his aunt's fortune is not his to build in that way, and his acts are just so much unilateralism. It may seem surprisingly formalistic for equity to refuse to assist someone who has real hopes of acquiring a right and who may even have expended resources in order to make it more likely that the right comes her way. Why does equity not intervene?

As will emerge in the overview and analysis of equitable rights that follow, equity's aim is to protect the pathways that are presupposed by the conditions law itself has set down for the acquisition of rights. Equity, in ensuring the integrity of the legal order as a whole, is concerned with the potential injustice thrown up by the legal order itself. The particulars of a procedure will reflect what seems salient and obvious to us, given the nature of the right and how it is acquired. As a general matter, equity draws a connection between the success criteria the law has set down for the acquisition of that right and the procedures that these criteria presuppose (and that equity construes as the pathways to rights). Take for instance transfer as a mode of acquiring a right to

[29] First-possession cases, where capture is a success criterion, show just how potentially interruptible that pathway to acquisition really is.

land. The criterion for B's successful acquisition of the land from A is A's exercise of her power to transfer in accordance with the relevant formalities, eg Statute of Frauds, Land Titles Act. The pathways B has to ownership of the land all implicate the various ways in which A can have initiated the procedure presupposed by that success criterion. For B to have any claim actually to be on the way to ownership, A must having taken steps to initiate and yet not to have completed that transfer, including A's representations to B that A will indeed transfer, and on which B detrimentally relies, A's contractual commitments to transfer, A's actual exercise of her authority to transfer, waiting for its completion only on some third-party C's or B's own registration of the transfer.

Where the success criteria for acquisition relate to some other mode of acquisition, such as original methods of acquisition like first possession or adverse possession or the fulfilment of a condition within the control of the petitioner, other pathways emerge. There we see that the petitioner herself, in taking steps to capture or acquire possession of land, or to fulfil a condition, has propelled herself forward along the pathway to rights, in precisely the way presupposed by the success criteria law set down.

The location of pathways is thus very much tied with equity's concern for the integrity of a framework of rights. Equity is not an escape from the blueprint for our shared lives together, a way that we can each act unilaterally and demand the assistance of the state: on the contrary, it is a way that the state secures against all avenues of oppression within that blueprint.

Equity brings into focus a specific kind of injustice visible only from the standpoint of equity: the forfeiture of one's position on the way to legal rights.[30] On my account, what I mean by forfeiture is an interruption along a completable but as yet incomplete pathway to rights. As we will see in the next section, equity takes its cues from law as to what counts as a plausible pathway to rights, given the success criteria for acquisition that law itself has set down. Equity's determination of whether there is a pathway and whether someone in particular is on it is a yes/no determination. In the context of derivative modes of acquisition, where the exercise of a power of transfer is required, equity can see the pathway and identify the person on it much more clearly. Think, for instance of an agreement for purchase and sale of land, where equity intervenes by finding a constructive trust in favour of the buyer after the agreement but before the closing of the deal. By contrast, where a person is traversing the way in to rights presupposed by an original mode of acquisition, like first possession, substantiality plays an important role in equitable reasoning: a person who is substantially on the way to capturing a ball or a fox,[31] or the profits from the news[32] or the treasure from a shipwreck[33] as real-life steps taken along a completable path to capture, has a much better claim to equity's protection than the person who has just set out. Substantiality is what brings

[30] It is consistent with this that Equity developed the action to quiet title, to remove what we might think of as threats of forfeiture—clouds on title. (See also *Rumsey v City of Buffalo*, 97 NY 114 (1884); *Bishop v Moorman*, 98 Ind 1 (1884).)

[31] See section II. C. below.

[32] *International News Service v Associated Press*, 248 US 215 (1918).

[33] *The Tubantia*, [1924] P 78.

the forfeiture in these cases properly to Equity's attention. Equity ensures that our positions on the pathways to legal rights are not something for which we are dependent on the courtesy or good grace of another.[34] It does so by protecting us against the power of others to interrupt a person during that period of unavoidable vulnerability between the initiation of a procedure for acquisition and its completion, at which point she enjoys the security and protection of the legal right itself.

I wanted briefly to raise and then reject an alternative interpretation of what it might mean for equity to guard against forfeiture, one that is a variation on the idea of forfeiture in the usual sense of the loss of rights we already have. There are some grounds for thinking about equitable rights as conditional rights (to property or contract) that are already ours, but subject to forfeiture should we fail to meet private law's requirements for acquisition. This suggests that equity's contribution is to move the 'finish line' backwards so that as soon as you start on a pathway to legal rights it is already yours, subject to forfeiture for failing to meet the success conditions for acquisition. This view is moderately attractive because it seems to capture the idea that a person on the way to a right is in some sense slotted for it; and because to think of equitable rights as conditional legal rights would bring equity within the private law framework of acquired rights. It also suggests that the central moral problem is justifying the loss of rights in terms of our personal claims to them, the merits or demerits of retaining that legal right. This strikes me, however, as an artificial way of looking at the problem that also conceals what is morally salient about it. It seems odd to say that as soon as you set off to acquire a right, you already have it. This puts the right before the acquisition: the failure to complete the acquisition would be a condition subsequent to the right (the success conditions for acquisition themselves an axe that cuts short the right) rather than a procedure you have to have completed first.

This alternative account of 'forfeiture' strikes me as a very distorted way to account for the phenomenon of acquiring rights. But the deeper problem is that the forfeiture of conditional rights suggests that equity is concerned with something that it is not: a real concern that the person slotted for a right actually gets it, rather than a concern just to see to it that once she is on a completable pathway she has a fair opportunity to complete the procedure for acquiring it.

II. Pathway Problems and Equitable Doctrine

A concern with pathway problems actually explains the nature and structure of well-known forms of equitable rights, in the law of trusts, the law of mortgages, the law of contracts, and bankruptcy law. I will show how in each of these areas there are cognizable pathways to legal rights. The idea of a pathway implies a destination,

[34] Some have taken this to capture an idea of bare property, where property is the word 'being used for that right which we have both to land or tenements, goods or chattel, *which in no way depends on another [person's] courtesy*' (*Jackson v House*, 17 John's 281 (NY 1820) (emphasis added))

and the destination in each of these contexts is the vesting of a different kind of legal right.

Some of these pathways are well established and hardened into general, juridified, regularized rights.[35] This talk of pathways is not just a metaphor for regular patterns of equitable relief for petitioners who find themselves outside of private law's protection. There is a built quality to these Equitable pathways: in other words, they harden into categories of equitable rights for which we have names and settled doctrine (eg trusts). Equity as an institution sets out a network of pathways that works to secure the full, free, and equal membership of all of us in the private law order.

In what follows, I propose to analyse a number of conventional equitable rights in ways that reveal the pathways structure behind them and that also reveal the connection to law and its integrity as a system that marks equity's interventions.

A. Mortgages

In common law jurisdictions, mortgages were created in the following way: an owner would transfer title in land in a 'deed by mortgage' to the creditor to secure repayment of debt. The creditor would then have legal title to the land, subject to a condition subsequent: on repayment of the mortgage debt, the debtor would have a right to regain ownership of the land. This is roughly what the conveyance looked like: 'To my Creditor A in fee simple, but if I pay him £1,000 by 1 Jan, then I may re-enter Blackacre.' The law strictly construed such conditions subsequent, which cut short the vested interest of a present owner to make way for the future-interest holder. So, it would happen time and again that when debtors defaulted, that is, failed to repay at the appointed time, the creditor would get the property free and clear of the future interest.

Equity intervened to preserve a debtor's right to redeem her property by repaying the loan even after default, putting the debtor essentially in the position she held immediately before her time in law ran out for the repayment of the debt. This equity of redemption protected a debtor only so long as she remained on the path to repayment (ie one who is actively paying her debt and who evinced a clear intention and ability to continue to do so).[36] Should she fail to progress in this way, she has in effect vacated the position on the pathway to legal rights. Equity in that case properly allows her creditor to bring an action to foreclose the equity of redemption, and so to resort to the security.

What a mortgagor/debtor has, in a secured loan context, is a clear pathway to legal rights in her land. The point of a mortgage is to be an arrangement whereby a debt is

[35] Neil McCormick found it absurd to deny the generality of equitable rules and the insistence by some that Equity as an institution traded in individualized justice (*Legal Reasoning and Legal Theory* (OUP 1994) 97). There is a concern for individualized justice in the structure of Equitable rights but of course it is not open to a king to do purely individualized justice, any more than a king could create an office for one person, or a crime for one person. It is not in the nature of the royal prerogative that gave rise to Equity as an institution to work like a dictator's fiat.

[36] Here we sometimes find countervailing reasons of justice not to throw the burden of equity on some particular private actor: for instance, a '[creditor's] ruin, notwithstanding all the court can offer as compensation' (*Hill v Barclay* 18 Ves 56 (Ch 1811) 60, Lord Eldon cited in Joseph Story, *Commentaries on Equity Jurisprudence* (Simon Greenleaf ed, Arno Press 1972) II 548).

paid off and property is regained. As the debtor pays more and more of the underlying mortgage loan, she moves closer and closer to the terminus, the discharge of her loan and the revesting of her rights to land. Her position on the pathway is established by the substantiality of the proportion of debt that she has repaid.

It is well established in the law of mortgages that there can be no secured interest relationship without a mortgage loan: the contractual and the property relationships are linked in equity's view. Without a mortgage loan, a conveyance to the bank is just the conveyance of a defeasible fee (defeasible on the happening of an event, namely, paying £X), and the taking of a future interest by the original owner. This is the perspective of law. From a legal point of view, the conveyance of a defeasible fee is one thing; the debt relationship is another thing, independent of the first. In law, a payment of money at a specific time, £1,000 on 1 January, may stand as the trigger for the vesting of the future interest. But this is not a pathway to a legal right: it is rather a moment of reckoning.

One way to make sense of equity's linking the loan and the secured interest is in terms of the integrity of the mortgagee's (the creditor's) claim: a person cannot reasonably claim a security interest without an underlying debt relationship where the *raison d'être* of the mortgagee's interest is to secure the repayment of a loan. That must be right, but I do not think it is the whole story. The underlying loan is also, I think, crucial to equity's formulation of the mortgagor's interest, the equitable right it actually protects. It is revealing of the nature of equitable interests generally to consider how. The loan and so its repayment mark the path to the revesting of the legal right in the debtor. Without that underlying debt relationship, there is no basis for equity to preserve an equitable right on the part of the original owner in the property conveyed to her creditor: in the absence of an underlying loan, there is no pathway to a future legal right and so no position along it that equity might protect against forfeiture. There would be merely a hope or expectation that the interest would vest at the relevant time in law.

B. Trusts

Equity's most famous intervention is on behalf of the beneficiary of a trust. A trust is an arrangement whereby a legal owner is obligated to hold property for the benefit of someone else, the beneficiary. Equity enables the beneficiary to enforce the obligation against the owner of the property subject to the trust, the trustee.[37] As we will see, the beneficiary for the duration of the trust does not have *in rem* property rights in the subject matter of the trust but rather an *in personam* right that the trustee carry out the trust. Like many rights of action (think of debt), a beneficiary's interest in a trust is assignable. To the extent that a beneficiary of a trust has property at all, it is property in the right to bring action to compel the trustee's performance of her obligation. The beneficiary, like the owner of debt, has what we technically call a 'chose in action'.[38]

[37] See eg, Oliver Wendell Holmes, *The Common Law* (Little, Brown, and Company, Boston, 1881) 408–09 (describing the *in personam* nature of the trust and noting that, as a personal right as against the trustee, it was not originally assignable).

[38] See Walter R Warren, *Choses in Action and Assignability at Law and in Equity* (Sweet & Maxwell 1899) 20.

The philosopher's formulation of equity as a response to problems arising out of the generality of rules is especially unhelpful in explaining the trust: there is very little in the law of trusts to connect with the conventional idea of equity as the making of exceptions in particular cases, as justice requires. There have been some attempts recently to explain the trust as an instance of private law's modularity or as an illustration of Equity's concern with opportunism.[39] I do not attempt to disprove or to discredit either such approach, but I see reason to avoid both. The first view sees the law of trusts as building on to private law, an expansion set if you like. But we need not give up so quickly on the idea that Equity does something distinctive in relation to law that is not just more law. We have *pro tanto* reasons to favour an approach that accounts for Equity as equity, which is just the way it presents itself.

From another viewpoint, Equity's protection of the beneficiary's interest is a curb on opportunism, the exploitation of a kind of defect in legal forms or legal rules whereby a person can gain advantages that the law had not intended to hand out. There is quite a lot of intuitive appeal to this idea: we can see the room for opportunism in a trust arrangement where a trustee as the legal owner could enjoy a far greater benefit from ownership than the settlor intended for them to enjoy. But there is an equivocation here between two kinds of opportunism. The first kind of opportunism concerns taking an advantage that the legislator did not intend to convey in setting out the law or legal form in general terms (but could not anticipate or rule out *ex ante*). This I take to be the kind of opportunism with which, on Henry Smith's account, equity is concerned. So, for example, where your debtor has already paid you but the bond securing repayment was not discharged, you may not sue on the bond to enrich yourself. A bond is by design meant just to guarantee the promise to repay. In a legal system that allows you to collect on a valid bond and does not admit evidence that might contradict the validity of the bond, there is the opportunity for abuse: for the use of that right for an illegitimate purpose, not as security for a debt but to enjoy a windfall.

The second kind of opportunism concerns taking precisely the advantage that the legislator intended the law or legal form to deliver but in circumstances that the actor who put you in a position to enjoy it did not intend you to have. To treat these two forms of opportunism as attracting equity in the same way is in effect to confuse a private actor and legislator. There may well be a gap between the kind of decisional authority the transferor wanted to convey and the kind of decisional authority the transferee acquired through such a conveyance. But owners do not have the power to create new offices and new kinds of authority: ownership is an office of decisional authority and the incumbent merely appoints the successor.[40] We see this idea, that private actors do not have the power to create new forms of decisional authority, in the restrictions on subinfeudation since the time of Edward I.[41] We see an extension of this idea in courts'

[39] Smith supra note 10 in this volume's chapter 10 and sources cited there.

[40] We see this principle limiting the creation of new offices for private purposes in Lord Coke's famous decision in *Sir Walter Chute's Case*: 'as for how people get appointed to office, it is by law or by prescription. No new rules of appointment can be created by the king' (or presumably by anyone else acting privately). See Coke (n 26) I 492–93.

[41] The Statute of Quia Emptores, 1290. There is, I think, a much larger political and moral idea here, that no one can in any case create offices for purely private ends. Lord Coke had it out with the James I on this point in *Walter*

treatment of certain restrictions as repugnant to a grant of ownership, an attempt in effect to reshape the nature of the decisional authority; for example, 'to my wife in fee simple. Anything she has left on her death to my daughters in equal shares.'[42] So former owners/settlors do get to appoint successors. But it is as a matter of constitutional principle, not for them to determine the kind of decisional authority associated with the office of ownership itself. Equity, which operates within—not outside—our political-legal order, will not help them to that power.[43]

A settlor who transfers property to a dear friend to hold for the benefit of his daughter may have in mind a different kind of authority than the legal form is intended to convey. But the form itself is doing exactly what it was designed to do: to transfer decisional authority outright to the new owner to exercise as she sees fit. The scope of an owner's authority in law thus allows advantages to be taken that the settlor may have never intended for the trustee to have, but Equity's target insofar as it is opportunism at all is not this kind of opportunism, a defect in the form of authority owners have relative to the prior owner's intentions. Rather, it is the kind of opportunism that is made possible by a defect in the legal concept that is at work relative to a legislator's[44] intentions (for private actors' intentions matter only with respect to the powers they actually have, eg, whom to appoint, not the scope of authority and the office to which it is attached.) This kind of opportunism though is not at work in the trust.

So, what explains equity's insistence that the new owner nonetheless hold for the benefit of the intended beneficiary? The trust is fertile ground for thinking more specifically about equity's role in protecting against forfeiture. We can profitably think about the beneficiary's equitable interest in terms of equity's role in regulating the pathways to legal rights. The settlor's intentions matter not in the creation of a new kind of property authority in the trustee/transferee, which I maintain is not her place, as a private actor to create; rather, the settlor's intentions bear on her exercise of her power to appoint her successor: she never intended to appoint the trustee her successor but rather to appoint the beneficiary, by way of the trust.[45] This requires us to think of the trust as a kind of delayed appointment of a beneficiary to the office, delayed during the trust and achieved by way of the trust. The trust arrangement is in effect a pathway to the vesting of rights in the beneficiary. The beneficiary's position on that pathway is vulnerable to forfeiture where a trustee or anyone else in receipt of trust property exercises or enforces legal

Chute's Case ((n 26) I 492). This was a case involving a petition to the king to create a new office and to appoint one, WC, to hold it. Coke considered and said that actually no new offices could be created for private persons for private ends. (Office *for* x as opposed to an office, to which X might be appointed.)

[42] *Re Taylor* 19 Sask R 361 (1982).

[43] As I said above, equity is an aspect of a prerogative power, which is itself lodged within our constitutional order. For a more general account of prerogative power as itself subject to rule of law constraints, see eg, David Dyzenhaus, 'The Compulsion of Legality' in Victor Ramraj (ed), *Emergencies and the Limits of Legality* (OUP 2008) 31–59.

[44] I don't mean legislator in any narrow sense: I mean the constitutional processes and mechanisms by which society decides what decisional authority is available, how, and to whom.

[45] Maitland sometimes used the term 'destinatory' to describe the position of beneficiaries, connoting the idea of the beneficiary as the ultimate recipient of the property. FW Maitland, *THE COLLECTED PAPERS OF FW MAITLAND* (HAL Fisher (ed), CUP 1911) 343.

rights or acts with respect to the trust *res* so as to dislodge the beneficiary from that position in relation to the terminus. What the beneficiary has that equity protects, is a position in relation to the legal right but not of course the legal right in the property itself. All the beneficiary can do is petition equity's assistance in guarding against forfeiture, in ensuring her position on the way to the vesting of legal rights. The constraints on what the trustee can do in the office of ownership are not curbs on her opportunism but protection of the beneficiary's position as the property passes through the trustee to its ultimate owner, the beneficiary. It falls to the trustee, who is in the position to trigger forfeiture of this position by appropriating, wasting, destroying, or otherwise mishandling the thing, to ensure that the beneficiary's position is throughout maintained. Equity will conscript others too to do its work where the trust property falls into another's hands although it is sensitive to avoid disproportionate losses to others, bona fide purchasers without notice, who cannot be seen as authors of their own misfortune (as the bona fide purchaser with notice surely is).

What evidence is there that the trust is in effect a delayed transfer, a way that a settlor in divesting herself of rights sets the beneficiary on a pathway to legal rights? Here are at least two doctrinal indicators. The first is found in the attitude judges take and have taken to their role in relation to trusts (fixed and discretionary): a trust by design is something capable of executing; if it is not, it is not a trust. In other words, a trust is a pathway that admits of a beginning and an end: the vesting of the property in the beneficiary. This idea, that trusts are by their nature mechanism for disposing of property to beneficiaries, also explains the gist of the statute often credited with giving rise to the modern law of trusts, Henry VIII's famous Statute of Uses, still in effect in many common law jurisdictions today.[46] Through the Statute of Use, Henry VIII aimed to abolish the early form of the trust, the 'use', in order to prevent the evasion of feudal burdens. The statute provided that 'where any person stands seised of land to the use of any other person or body politic', that beneficiary shall stand in 'lawful seizen of the same lands in such estates as they had in use in the same'. The statute made the cestui que use—the equivalent of today's beneficiary—the legal owner. The statute executed the use: it in effect fast-tracked the beneficiary along the pathway to legal rights in the property that was subject to the trust. The Statute of Uses saw to it that the beneficiary was fast-tracked along the pathway to legal rights by cutting out the middle man, the trustee, and effectuating the transfer of the property by treating the beneficiary as owner. The Statute of Uses, in demanding the quick execution of the trust, was always consistent with the nature of the trust, merely accelerating its operation. If a judge must take over from a trustee, she does not go about managing property; the judge either appoints a new trustee or she simply executes the trust herself—which means transferring the property to the ultimate owners, the beneficiaries.

The idea that a trust stands to be executed, at which point the property rights vest in the beneficiary is also behind the famous nineteenth-century rule in *Saunders v Vautier*, a rule now abolished in America but still mandatory in other common law

[46] 27 Hen 8 (1536).

jurisdictions.[47] The gist of the rule to come out of *Saunders v Vautier* is this: if a beneficiary is absolutely entitled to a gift and *sui juris*, then the trustee is dispensable. The beneficiary can demand the conveyance of the property straight away. What is more, in those jurisdictions that still have the rule, it is not up to the settlor to do away with *Saunders v Vautier* rights: she cannot set up a trust that attracts equity's protection without *Saunders v Vautier* rights because it is the essence of the trust as a pathway to legal rights that the beneficiaries as ultimate owners ought at some point to be in a position to proceed to the terminus on their own initiative: to demand the conveyance of rights to them where they are *sui juris* and where there is no one else with a beneficial interest who might claim equity's protection.

American courts departed from the rule in *Saunders v Vautier* but not in any way that would deny the executory nature of trusts but rather so as to dispute the terminus, the point at which the beneficiary is in a position to call for the conveyance of the trust property. The American approach, set out in *Claflin v Claflin*,[48] does not contradict the view that the beneficiary is ultimately slotted for the legal right to the thing held on trust; rather, the case stands for the view that the beneficiary only reaches the terminus, at which point he can demand conveyance from the trustee, when the purpose of the trust has been exhausted.

Equity's role to set out and preserve pathways to rights also explains Equity's intervention in a related area, in which a legal transfer is in progress, the incumbent owner having done everything possible to appoint his successor, but yet the transfer is incomplete pending some third-party's exercise of a power. A leading case in this area is *Re Rose*[49] in which a husband made a gift of shares to his wife. The husband, the original owner of the shares, had done everything he could to divest himself of rights to the shares and yet the vesting of legal rights in the wife depended on a further exercise of a legal power by a third party, the corporation itself, which had to approve and register the transfer. He had made a transfer under seal, declaring his wife and trustee to be owners, and further leaving the burdens of ownership to his wife immediately after. He was further estopped in law from going back on the gift (by for example claiming the dividends for himself during this interval or marching into the corporation's head office and demanding that they not register the transfer). Although the husband had exhausted his power to transfer, there was in law a gap in time between his doing everything he could do and the completion of the transfer by the corporation. Pending the registration of the transfer, the wife was not yet legal owner: her husband remained the owner in law. The idea of property in shares presupposes the possibility that people move in and out of the position of owner. Property law indeed sets out a way by which that might occur. But, by requiring a third-party's ratification of the transfer, the law

[47] 49 ER 282 (Ch 1841). See Gregory Alexander, 'The Dead Hand and the Law of Trusts in the Nineteenth Century' (1985) 37 Stanford Law Review 1189 (courts in America followed the rule in the nineteenth century, taking a different tack after 1889). See also Paul Matthews, 'The Comparative Importance of the Rule in Saunders v. Vautier' (2006) 122 LQR 266.

[48] 149 Mass 19 (1889).

[49] *Re Rose*, [1952] Ch. 499.

also created a potentially problematic sphere of human interaction, in which the wife/ donee would be in transit, as it were, on her way into legal rights but not fully protected by law. It is this sphere that calls for an equitable standpoint. From an equitable standpoint, the wife was clearly on a pathway to legal rights in the shares after the husband exhausted his power of transfer but before the corporation completed the transfer. Equity protected her position by finding that her husband held on constructive trust—that is, held legal title for her benefit—until she took legal title herself.

Equity's intervention here might strike us as surprising in light of equity's more general refusal to assist volunteers or perfect imperfect gifts.[50] What explains the difference between a case like *Re Rose*, where equity recognizes and regulates a clear pathway to legal rights, and cases where equity sees only a failed or imperfect gift? Equity intervenes only to regulate a sphere beyond the reach of law. Insofar as property law itself has allocated a power to appoint a successor, which is sufficient to effect the transfer, the way into property rights is accounted for within that legal framework. You are slotted as the next owner if and when someone with the relevant power appoints you as the next owner. An owner has the power to dispose of property by gift in law or by way of a trust. If the owner does not in fact exercise that power fully in your favour, your disappointment does not register as a forfeiture or disproportionate loss that might justify equity's intervention. And so the man who has a deed drafted in favour of his friends but fails to deliver it has not put the intended recipient on a pathway to legal rights.[51] Nor does the father who dies before signing over his cheque to his baby.[52] There is a way in to property rights in the land in the one case and to the cheque, but the friends and baby are only on their way—are only in effect slotted for those rights—once the current owners have done everything they can to appoint them as successors. What distinguishes a case like *Re Rose* is that there the donor had exhausted his legal power to appoint a successor, and yet still there was some way to go before his wife fully moved into the position of owner. In *Re Rose*, the husband and original owner of the shares had exhausted his power in law to appoint his wife as his successor in title—there was nothing more in law for him to do—and yet his wife, the donee, was left on her way to but just short of full ownership. It was this pathway that equity could recognize and her position on it that equity would protect against forfeiture by imposing a temporary constructive trust on the legal owner (the husband) in her favour. The constructive trust was in effect a bridge allowing the wife to maintain her position between the divesting of legal rights and the completion of the transfer in law when the corporation registered the shares.

The factual situation we see in *Re Rose* introduces a problem we do not find in circumstances where an owner has a power to select a successor and simply fails to exercise it fully in favour of the would-be donee. Equity does not help people to pathways but only preserves them against forfeiture once they are on their way.

[50] *Milroy v Lord*, 45 ER 1185 (QB 1862) 1189; *Richard v Delbridge*, LR 18 Eq 11 (1974).
[51] *Carson v Wilson* (1961) OR 113 (CA).
[52] *Jones v Lock* (1865) 1 Ch App 25.

C. Possession

Equity's concern is engaged also in cases of original acquisition, where there may be more than one person on the way to acquiring rights through capture. In multiparty scenarios, where there is more than one person in hot pursuit of the thing, an interruption counts as an injustice only where there has been something like unfair competition along the way.

A case ripe for equitable intervention is the famous fox case, *Pierson v Post*.[53] Equitable reasoning (as I account for it) reveals what the injustice was in that case, an injustice that the common law lacked the tools to identify and redress. (Equitable reasoning was not available to the court quite simply because the case was decided in the early nineteenth century before the Fields Code, merging common law and equitable jurisdiction in New York State.)[54] *Pierson v Post* involved a contest between hunters in hot pursuit of a fox and a beachcomber who stepped in at the last moment to capture the fox from under their noses. The beachcomber as the first to capture the fox (meaning in this context, mortal wounding), thereby acquired the better right to it by first possession. The majority began and ended with the question of who actually had acquired the right to the fox according to the common law rules. The dissent, however, was alive to the injustice of the interruption by the saucy intruder. In a judgment so over the top it is often taken for a joke, the dissenting judge described the progress the hunter had made towards the acquisition of the property right in the fox, detailing the cost and effort it took to prepare for and mount the hunt, and the long, exhausting pursuit that followed, peremptorily terminated by the beachcomber's capture of the fox as the hunters were closing in. In the end, the dissenting judge could not account for the injustice using traditional common law reasoning: his most coherent proposal amounted to moving the finish line, ie what counts as capture, forward so that the hunter could be recognized as the possessor in law long before mortally wounding the animal. Equity offers a cleaner and more coherent solution: from an equitable standpoint the injustice that equity cures just is in the interruption along a substantially completed and still completable, but undeniably incomplete, pathway to acquiring the fox by first possession.

A more recent first-possession case, *Popov v Hayashi*,[55] yields a much clearer view of what I think is the equitable standpoint on a person in 'hot pursuit' of a thing. Popov like many fans had bought a ticket to a game in which it was widely expected that Barry Bonds would hit a record-breaking home run. Barry Bonds did as expected: his 73rd home-run ball went into the arcade and landed in or on Popov's glove and stopped in

[53] *Pierson v Post 2*, Am Dec 264 (NY 1805); cf *INS v AP*, 248 US 215 (1918).

[54] 'The distinctions between actions at law and suits in equity, and the forms of all such actions and suits, heretofore existing, are abolished; and there shall be in this state, hereafter, but one form of action, for the enforcement or protection of private rights and the redress or prevention of private wrongs, which shall be denominated a civil action' (NY Laws (1848) c 379).

[55] *Popov v Hayashi* (2002) WL 31833731 (Cal).

its path. What happened next was poorly documented but something like the following happened. Popov was tackled and thrown to the ground by a mob, and at some point, the ball left his glove, rolled onto the ground. Popov was unable to establish whether at some point the ball had been secured in his glove. Another fan, Hayashi, who was also knocked over by this mob, saw and pocketed the ball. Hayashi clearly took control of the ball and had proof of control—his capture of it was caught on camera. Hayashi was not at all implicated in the mob activity that had deprived Popov of his chance to complete the catch. The court found that Popov had not established that he actually caught the ball and so had not met the success criteria for acquiring property through first possession.

What is fascinating about the case is that the court switched midway to analyse Popov's interest from a point of view that I think is best described as an equitable standpoint, concerned with Popov's position on a pathway to legal rights. The court reasoned thus: 'where an actor takes significant but incomplete steps to achieve possession of a piece of abandoned property and the effort is interrupted by the unlawful acts of others, the actor has a cognizable pre-possessory interest in the property'. When that pathway actually begins is not something the court tells us: was it at the point when Popov first started to research Bonds's batting record, or studying the layout of the stadium? Was it when he bought his ticket to the game? Was it when he packed his binoculars and his glove to take with him? The substantiality requirement dispenses with the need to ascertain with precision when the pathway begins, allowing equity to determine that the petitioner is certainly on the pathway now. Equity engaged when Popov had substantially completed the procedure for acquisition, and stood near the finish line, having moved out ahead of other legitimate competitors by being the first to make contact with the baseball. The loss of that position so near the finish line would have in the court's view constituted a forfeiture. In finding Popov had a protected interest in his position prior to, but on the cusp of capture, the court placed the burden of mitigation on Hayashi, whose capture ended the contest for the ball, and not the mob whose fault it was that Popov had fumbled: Hayashi was the one best placed to mitigate the loss.

D. Substantial Performance

Leaving property, the traditional domain of equity behind, we can see how equitable reasoning might explain the pathways to contractual rights that are construed in contract law as contingent. The doctrine of substantial performance is explicable in terms of pathway problems.[56] There is always the potential for forfeiture[57] and so injustice when someone has substantially but not fully performed a promise that the parties have made a condition precedent to the right of payment. That is because, as Justice Cardozo

[56] See Cardozo J's famous decision in *Jacob & Youngs v Kent* 230 NY 239 (1921).

[57] Or, as Cardozo J put it, 'oppressive retribution' (ibid 242). See also Samuel Williston, *The Law of Contracts* (Baker, Voorhis & Co., New York 1924) II 1527 ('That justice requires relief against the condition where a forfeiture will be caused, without fault on the part of the builder, may be admitted').

put it, 'the courts never say that one who makes a contract fills the measure of his duty by less than full performance'. To make sense of a right to payment for substantial performance in terms of traditional contract reasoning, we would have to resort to a legal fiction about the party's intentions to make a promise a condition. We see something like this in Cardozo J's attempt to formulate the rule at least in part as a rule of contractual interpretation:[58] '[Some promises], though dependent and thus conditions, when there is departure in point of substance will be viewed as independent and collateral when the departure is insignificant'.[59]

A more coherent foundation for the doctrine of substantial performance is in equity.[60] Where a right to another's performance (eg, payment for services) is subject to fulfilling a promise to perform, the criterion for acquiring a right to be paid is clear: perform in full! Where the obligor has performed substantially all the work, she can be understood to be on the way to a right to payment. In circumstances where she has in some small insignificant way failed to completely perform, the obligee may trigger a forfeiture simply by enforcing the contract according to its terms. Someone who has performed 99 per cent of the work is entitled to no more in law than the person who has not performed at all: a failure to complete is a failure to satisfy what the law treats as a condition precedent to payment. But where the obligor has covered substantially all of the ground, leaving just a 'defect insignificant in relation to the project', she is in a different position than someone who has not set out at all: she stands to suffer a much greater setback relative to a much smaller deficiency. What is unfair about denying the obligor a right to payment for her work in this case is the lack of proportionality: all the ground she has covered is lost, a setback out of proportion to the small distance she failed to go. Equity sees to it that the other side avoids the forfeiture or mitigates it by requiring that the obligee pay for the incomplete performance.

The doctrine of substantial performance trains our attention on an important factor in equity's regulation of the pathways to rights. Where the basis of the claim to protection is the injustice of forfeiture, it is important to establish that one actually has a position that is vulnerable to forfeiture. A contractual right to payment conditional on performance indicates how a party is to go about acquiring the right to payment (perform in full), and the procedure that it presupposes (taking all the steps that together constitute performance in full). A person who merely has the contractual duty to perform but has failed to perform at all is clearly not on a completable pathway at all and

[58] Cardozo J (n 57) at 242 ('Considerations of justice and partly of presumable intentions are to tell us whether this or that promise shall be placed in one class or another').

[59] ibid.

[60] Indeed, Equity clearly is the driving force of Cardozo J's decision although his notion of equity lacks specificity: it is just the idea of Equity as an instrument of justice. He writes

> Those who think more of symmetry and logic in the development of legal rules than of practical adaptation to the attainment of a just result will be trouble by [the classification he suggests]. Something doubtless may be said on the score of consistency and certainty in favor of a stricter standard. The courts have balanced such considerations against those of equity and fairness and found the latter to be the weightier.

And later he says, 'the rule that gives a remedy in cases of substantial performance ... has been developed by the courts as an instrument of justice' (*Jacob & Youngs* (n 56) 242, 245).

has no claim to equity's protection against forfeiture in respect of the right to payment. A person who has just begun performance is not clearly on the pathway. The substantiality requirement allows equity to make the yes/no determination that a person is clearly on the pathway to the right to payment, such that it would count as a forfeiture if she lost that position and was treated exactly as though she had not set out at all. Substantiality, here, like substantiality in the possession cases, matters where there may be doubt about whether the claimant is on the pathway to a right.[61]

III. Pathway Problems: Not Always a Bad Problem to Have

Talk of pathway problems seems to suggest a design flaw in a system of private law: if rights were acquired instantaneously or at least very, very quickly, there would be little call for equitable intervention. Are equitable rights a sign of a defect in the private law framework, something we should try to patch up with an aim to eliminating equity's role completely? Of course this line of thinking is bound to be unproductive in the end because there will always be a before and an after to the acquisition of rights as people move in and out of legal relations: we cannot do without procedures for acquisition, the pathways in and out of legal rights. But let's put to one side the impossibility of doing away with procedures that are interruptible to ask whether this is the kind of problem that we would want to fix at source if we could, if only by shortening the pathways as much as possible. As it turns out, pathway problems are not always bad problems to have because temporally extended pathways to rights are valuable features of the legal landscape.

There are some pathways that we have every reason to stretch out. The trust, the mortgage (like the shareholder's interest in the property of the corporation at the time of dissolution)[62]—all can be understood as extended pathways to legal rights that introduce significant pathway problems. In principle, pathways must all be completable: corporations are all in principle dissoluble, trusts, collapsible by the beneficiaries; mortgaged property, redeemable by repayment of the mortgage loan, etc. Indeed, if any of these pathways were not completable, they would not really be pathways at all, and equity would have nothing to manage. But in many situations, the aim is clearly not to complete in as short a time as possible. Take for instance the mortgagor's interest in the mortgaged property. The mortgagor is on a pathway to the legal property right in the

[61] 'Rent to own' contracts illustrate this point, in particular cases like *Williams v Walker* Thomas, 350 F2d 445 (DC Cir 1965). In that case, the seller required payment in full for all purchased items before title to any of them passed. The buyer, who had made a number of purchases from the seller over the years, had been making payments towards ownership for years before defaulting. The seller reclaimed all the furniture, on the grounds that the buyer through the default had not met the requirements to acquire ownership even for the earlier purchases. The court treated the contract as unconscionable but might have found for the buyer on the basis of pathways reasoning: the buyer has a claim to equity's protection against forfeiture on the pathways to rights presupposed by the success criteria for acquiring rights set down in the contract. By making payment he was traversing the pathway, and it was unjust of the seller to use the contract to trigger the forfeiture of his position.

[62] See Larissa Katz, 'Corporate Shares as Shares' in Sinead Agnew and Ben McFarlane (eds), *Modern Studies of Property Law* (Hart 2019) 107, 117–123.

land and moves closer to the finish line with each repayment. The problem of forfeiture through interruption is plain enough here in the absence of equitable intervention: any breach of the conditions for repayment would trigger a forfeiture of her position no matter how close she is to the finish line. And yet it would be perverse to accelerate the procedure for acquisition by shortening the time that she had to traverse the pathway. That would mean in its most extreme form the repayment in full of the loan the minute it was taken out. In the context of the trust, there are obvious reasons why we might not want to accelerate the execution of the trust—time for a child to grow up, the settlor's purposes to be carried out, etc. Similarly, shareholders have reason not to press for the dissolution of the corporation, even though this would be required for the completion of their pathway to the assets of the corporation on dissolution.[63]

Some of that value comes from the extended nature of the pathway: the more extended the pathway to rights, the more scope there is for others to hook up to that pathway and to use it to connect to the legal right itself. I am referring here not just to the assignability of an equitable interest (and of course equity invented the very idea of *in personam* assignment) but also to the possibility of adding further segments, eg, a right in relation to a right in relation to the ultimate (stand-alone) right. Because these segments do not carve out independent paths but simply add to existing ones, they depend for their completion on the completability of the original path. A good example of the expandability of pathways and the value this generates is found in the law of mortgages. Equity protects the mortgagor's pathway to redeeming mortgaged land (by preserving her right to continue repaying even if after a default. It also protects a second (third, fourth, etc) mortgage, by protecting the path for later mortgagees to the land itself, via the mortgagor's equity of redemption. The interests of later equitable mortgagees are all vulnerable in the same way to a blockage or an interruption in the main path, eg, the default of the mortgagor and the foreclosure of her equity of redemption by the legal right holder or the sale of the mortgaged land to bona fide purchase for value (BFPV) without notice of the equity of redemption (more on BFPV status shortly). Crucially, the value of those subsequent equitable mortgages depends in an important way on the mortgagor's own continuing path to the legal right: the value of the equitable mortgage depends on the existence of an open pathway to the legal right in the land, which the equitable mortgagee negotiates one segment at a time.

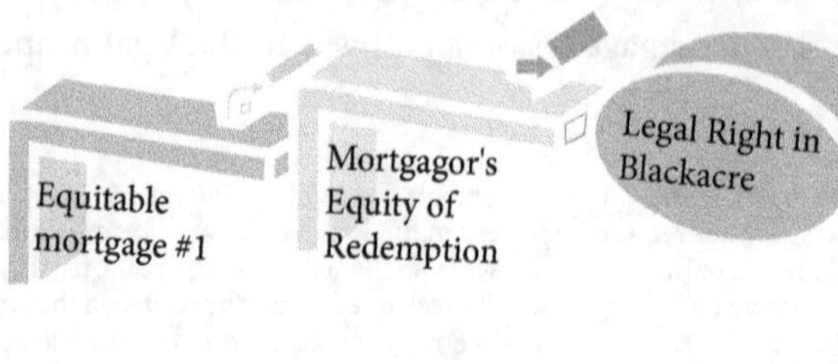

[63] In some contexts, all the value is in the traversing rather than the completing of the pathway. A share in a distressed company, which will have no value if dissolved, might hold value for someone seeking a seat at the restructuring table in a bankruptcy context, which serves to redirect the positions of those on the pathway to rights in corporate assets at the time of dissolution. See Katz (n 63).

The equitable mortgagee has rights in respect of the mortgagor's right in respect of the legal right to Blackacre. So, if the mortgagor with the equity of redemption subsequently loses the capacity to redeem, she no longer has a completable pathway to legal rights before her. The equitable mortgagees would as a result no longer have a completable pathway to the legal right either. Pathways, like roads, are valuable means of connecting everyone to everyone else. Just as roads enable us to associate with people who are not our immediate neighbours, pathways enable us to connect to people with whom we do not stand in relations of bilateral right. Equity's aim then ought not to be to eliminate pathways, to hasten us into relations of right, but rather to regulate the problems they present.

IV. Conscripting Private Actors to Do Equity's Work

Equity is engaged where there is a claim to the state's protection and there is a mechanism in place for the state to offload that burden to private actors: by placing it as a burden or a charge on how they exercise their legal rights. The duties that secure equitable rights are superadded burdens of a public nature. Equity's demand that legal right holders avoid or mitigate disproportionate loss in this way shifts a public law burden to private actors. The trustee forbears from exercising her legal rights or powers as owner in any way that undermines the integrity of the beneficiary's position throughout the duration of the trust; the mortgagee holds off on selling the property to satisfy their claim in debt, to preserve the mortgagor's right to redeem; and so on. In charging legal right holders to bear the burden of satisfying the demands of justice (avoiding forfeiture), Equity invokes an ancient common law right to service: to assist the state in the dispensation of justice.[64]

Equity exacts this service from legal right holders not at first instance by calling them out on interpersonal wrongdoing but by regarding as done what ought to have been done: private actors sometimes have a role, in virtue of being best placed as legal right holders to play it, and that concerns the regulation of pathways to legal rights. Equity's response at first instance is to act as though each of us lives up to the role we are meant to play. This sort of response can be illustrated by an exchange between Anatole France and an academician who had promised to support France's bid for election to the Academy, only to break his word (and so fail to live up to the role of promisor). France was eventually elected to the Academy anyway. The academician then wrote to France to apologize for his perfidy. France would have none of it. His response was: 'You are a gentleman and a person of your word and so you are mistaken. You did vote for me.'[65] That is, the academician, having promised his support, had a role to play: no position inconsistent with it would be countenanced. The selfish, deceitful, perfidious position was simply not open to him to claim. Similarly, equity takes as far as it is able the view

[64] See '*Case of Non Obstante*' (n 25) 423 (this essentially sets out the right of the sovereign to the service of any of his subjects 'for the publick Weal').
[65] Edmund Wilson, *To the Finland Station* (Harcourt, Brace and Company 1940) 57.

that everything has been done as it ought to have been done. That is because the point of equity is not to uncover new ways of wronging each other but rather to use its available levers of power to guard against forfeiture. Thus, the trustee who uses trust money without authorization to buy a painting is taken to have bought it for the trust if it turns out to have been a good investment; if the painting turns out to be worthless, to have used his own money to buy himself a worthless painting. The trustee is regarded as having done what ought to have been done, as abiding within her role, even as in fact she palpably did not. In its accounting process, equity fills in the hole the withdrawal obviously left in the trust fund by requiring the trustee personally to top it up. This leaves the corpus of the trust, what ultimately the trustee holds on account of another, intact and available ultimately for conveyance to the beneficiary.

Equity's first concern is administrative: to see to it that the public right and responsibility to avoid forfeiture is carried out. If it so happens that a trustee or some other legal right holder, called on to do as equity requires, instead withdraws her service, she has committed much more than a personal wrong against the person with the equitable right: she is in effect in contempt of the state.[66] Contempt is a disregard of public authority. It is a form of contempt for public authority to refuse to serve the state where there is a public right to that service.[67] It is then on pain of contempt, that the holders of legal rights are commanded to do as Equity requires.

V. Conclusion

This account of Equity as an institution suggests a different place for equity in relation to law. It is not that equity is built into the very legal concepts we find in private law, concepts of right or obligation that are inherently defeasible then on equitable grounds (as Hart would have it). Nor is it that law and equity come apart, so that we can understand equity as an appeal to judges to put law to one side and to act as arbitrators in the particular case (as Gardner would have it). Equity on my account adds an important dimension to the legal order, by setting down and regulating the ways we move in and out of legal relations.

[66] 'Equity: Contempt: Duration of Imprisonment' (1938) 36 Michigan Law Review 1016.

[67] It was contempt to fail to provide services to the king. It is contempt to fail to require to do as equity requires. See Yale (n 25) 268 ('on the compulsion of men to do those things that are in order and subservient to the dispensation of justice'); Pomeroy (n 1) 9 (explaining that equity acts *in personam*, meaning equity compels obedience, and disobedience is contempt of court punishable by fine or imprisonment) 131 ('a trustee's . . . failure to obey the directions as interpreted by the court will expose him to punishment for contempt').

9

What's Special about Equity?

Rights about Rights

Ben McFarlane and Robert Stevens

I. Introduction

On one view, the theme of this book makes no sense at all. Equity is a body of rules that has its historical source in the Courts of Equity, what is now the Chancery Division in England. It is a body of judge-made law, distinguished by its historical source. One would no more expect it to have any specific philosophical interest than any other body of law distinguished by the body positing it. Nobody would write a book on the philosophical foundations of the law created by statutory instruments, or on the theory of the Queen's Bench Division.

Our thesis is that much, although not all, of the law of Equity is distinguished by its *form*. Equitable rights concern rights in relation to other rights. It is, *in this sense*, a form of second-order, or meta law. This formal difference is a product of its historical origin, and an important part of its present function. A characteristically equitable right is one that has as its subject the right of another party. An example is the right of a beneficiary of a trust. Where T holds a legal freehold of land on trust for B, it is T's legal estate, not the land itself, that is the subject matter of the trust. B's right thus has T's right as its subject. In contrast, where O simply holds an unencumbered legal freehold of land, O's right does not have any other person's right as its subject.

We argue that it would be dangerous to accept the claims made from a variety of perspectives, from legal realism[1] to classical doctrinalism,[2] that we should move on from the 'bizarre common law dualist legal system, with its separate bodies of Common Law and Equitable rules'.[3] The danger lies in the risk of losing sight of the special nature of rights that relate to other rights. Recognizing this category of rights is important for at least three reasons.

First, the interaction of common law and equity may be easier to understand if equity is seen, in many cases at least, as intervening so as to allow a claimant to control

[1] See eg C Clark, 'The Union of Law and Equity' (1925) 25 Columbia Law Review 1; D Laycock, 'The Triumph of Equity' (1993) 56 Law and Contemporary Problems 53. For discussion of the legal realist stance towards fusion of law and equity, see H Smith, 'Fusing the Equitable Function in Private Law' in K Barker and others (eds), *Private Law in the 21st Century* (Hart 2017) 173–196.

[2] See eg P Birks, 'Equity in the Modern Law: An Exercise in Taxonomy' (1996) 26 University of Western Australia Law Review 1.

[3] S Worthington, *Equity* (2nd edn, OUP 2006) 19.

Ben McFarlane and Robert Stevens, *What's Special about Equity?* In: *Philosophical Foundations of the Law of Equity*. Edited by: Dennis Klimchuk, Irit Samet, and Henry E Smith, Oxford University Press (2020). © The several contributors.
DOI: 10.1093/oso/9780198817659.003.0010

the defendant's acquisition or enforcement of a particular right. For example, we argue in section II that the possibility of equitable assignment is not inconsistent with the common law's general and traditional refusal to allow for the transfer of a chose in action. This is because an equitable assignment does not involve the transfer of the assignor's right, but rather consists of the assignor retaining that right, but coming under a duty to the equitable assignee in relation to the right. Certainly, our analysis is consistent with the idea that many equitable rights are secondary, in the sense of depending for their existence on other rights. [4]

Second, the kinds of reason that may justify the existence of a right that relates to another right may differ from the kinds of reason needed to justify the acquisition of other rights. To the extent that the substance of equitable rules is distinctive, the different form of the rights to which they give rise might explain this substantive difference. Such an explanation, we suggest, is more satisfying than the claim that equitable rules are different because judges in Chancery had a different moral world view, or greater discretion,[5] than their common law counterparts. For example, if the reason for the common law's general prohibition on the transfer of a chose in action is the need to prevent the imposition on a debtor of a new creditor, then the concept of equitable assignment does not ignore that need. Rather, it respects the concern through the insistence that the equitable assignee can reach the debtor only through the assignor.[6]

Third, we argue that a full account of many common law rules, including their justification, can be made only if we recognize that a right acquired by a party under such rules may be limited, in favour of a particular claimant, by the recognition of a right that relates to that common law right. To stay with the same example, the traditional common law prohibition on the transfer of a chose in action may seem very inefficient, and unduly restrictive, but it carries the advantage of preventing the imposition on the debtor of a new creditor, and its disadvantages are reduced by the possibility of an equitable assignment.

It is true that there are many areas of law where the labels used by the courts suggest that particular equitable doctrines are simply variants of a common law equivalent, and so are ripe to be treated as part of a broader, unified whole. Yet, as we will show by considering the trust and equitable assignment, while the equitable rules may sometimes have a similar practical effect to their supposed common law counterparts, they

[4] The nature of many equitable rights as dependent on common law rights is reflected in Maitland's observation that: 'equity without common law would have been a castle in the air, an impossibility':FW Maitland, *Equity: A Course of Lectures* (AH Chaytor and WJ Whittaker, eds, revised by John Brunyate, 2nd edn, 1936, CUP 1909) 19. See too H Smith, 'Equitable Defences as Meta-Law' in PS Davies and others (eds), *Defences in Equity* (Hart 2018) 17, 26.

[5] The law of trusts, for example, is entirely a creation of equity yet is notorious for its technicality, with its difficult rules often tripping up even experienced Chancery judges, as noted by J Penner, 'An Untheory of the Law of Trusts' (2010) 63 CLP 653. Conversely, there are many areas of common law where discretion is prominent: see eg the multifactorial approach taken to the impact of illegality by the majority of the Supreme Court in *Patel v Mirza* [2017] AC 467. Significantly, much of the discretionary nature of equity is associated with its law of remedies, and there are some similarly discretionary elements to be found in remedial rules at common law: see eg the 'legitimate interest' test applied in determining the availability of the action for the agreed sum (see eg *White & Carter (Councils) Ltd v McGregor* [1962] AC 413). The concept of 'legitimate interest' also has a role to play in determining whether an agreed contractual remedy is valid (see *Cavendish Square Holding BV v Makdessi* [2016] AC 1172).

[6] See section II below.

have a quite different form. Our argument, which also applies beyond the areas examined here,[7] although of course not to every area of modern equity,[8] is that the formal distinctiveness of such equitable rules needs to be emphasized, as it provides the key to justifying those rules.[9] We are thus in agreement with those other contributors to this volume who emphasize the continuing *formal* distinctiveness of much equitable intervention. Our view is closest to that of Henry Smith,[10] who highlights the second-order nature of many equitable rules, while also noting that common law rules can, and sometimes do, share that nature.[11] While benefiting greatly from his work, we argue that many key equitable rules have a *specific* second-order role to play, which seems to be absent from the common law[12] and from any non-equity systems.[13] That role consists in imposing duties and liabilities which have a content *specifically related* to a particular right or rights held by a defendant. For example, where T holds a legal freehold of land on trust for B, the content of some key duties, such as the duty not to use the freehold for T's own benefit, relate specifically to the trust property. This can be seen at the remedial stage too. As noted by Lionel Smith in this volume: 'If the trustee has the trust property, he is not given the option of keeping it and paying compensation'.[14] The identity of the trustee, as Smith notes, is relatively unimportant:[15] the key claim of the beneficiary is to the specific *right* held by the trustee. In contrast, while the law of defamation, for example, may be said, in some cases at least, to play a secondary role,[16] balancing and adjusting in a more fine-grained way the basic freedoms of individuals,

[7] See too B McFarlane, 'Form and Substance in Equity' in Robertson & Goudkamp (eds) *Form and Substance in the Law of Obligations* (Oxford: Hart, 2019); R Stevens, 'Set-off and the Nature of Equity' in Davies and others (eds) (n 4) 41–51; B McFarlane, 'Understanding Equitable Estoppel: From Metaphors to Better Laws' (2013) 66 CLP 267, 271–80.

[8] There are some areas where equity has intervened not to control the acquisition or enforcement of rights, but rather directly, for example by imposing primary duties or liabilities: see eg the development of the equitable doctrine of breach of confidence as a means to control invasions of privacy. In such cases, the courts are surely correct to regard privacy claims as simply a form of tort claim: see eg *Campbell v MGN Ltd* [2004] 2 AC 457 at [14], where Lord Nicholls, in the context of a claimed infringement of privacy, described breach of confidence as a tort; for an earlier similar argument, see P North, 'Breach of Confidence: Is There a New Tort?' (1972) 12 Journal of the Society of Public Teachers of Law 149; for judicial advocates of a fused action, see too eg Lac Minerals Ltd v International Corona Resources Ltd [1989] 2 SCR 574, 615–18 (Sopinka J).

[9] See eg L Smith, 'Fusion and Tradition' in S Degeling and J Edelman (eds), *Equity in Commercial Law* (Lawbook Co 2005) 19–39; H Smith, 'Fusing the Equitable Function in Private Law' in Barker and others (eds) (n 1).

[10] Smith (n 1) and Chapter 10 in this volume.

[11] H Smith, 'Equity as Second-Order Law: The Problem of Opportunism' Harvard Public Law Working Paper (2015) 3 gives the law of nuisance as an area, inter alia, where common law rules regulate the interaction of rights; the law of defamation provides another example.

[12] The common law doctrines that come closest to sharing the form of the equitable intervention considered in this chapter include the law of waiver and the power to rescind a transaction entered into because of duress or fraud. As to the former, it has the effect of extinguishing A's right against B, and so does not merely limit A's enforcement of that right. As to the latter (see eg *Load v Green* (1846) 15 M & W 216), it may well have been influenced by the form of the equitable power to rescind for eg a non-fraudulent misrepresentation and thus be an example of the common law following equity, and in any case the effect of the rescission in eg a sale of goods is directly to revest title in B and not merely to give B a right in relation to a right held by A: see too p. 202 below.

[13] While this is too large a point to consider properly here, it may be worth noting, for example, the apparent absence from civil law systems of rights with the same form as equitable property rights: R Valsan, 'Rights against Rights and Real Obligations' in L Smith (ed), *The Worlds of the Trust* (CUP 2013) 481–511 considers the *obligation propter rem* to be the closest analogy in French law to the right-against-a-right model discussed in this chapter, but the obligation there is attached to a thing rather than a right.

[14] L Smith, Chapter 7 in this volume, p. 157.

[15] ibid, noting that 'the Equitable remedy works, in a sense, not against the defendant, but through him'.

[16] See H Smith, Chapter 10 in this volume.

the duties imposed do not relate to a specific right held by the defendant, but are rather duties to refrain from specific conduct.

The role we attribute to equity in the cases examined here is thus more narrow than a general second-order function: we do not regard equity as giving judges power to fill in the details of open-textured common law rules, or as a means to give more refined effect to the aims behind those common law rules. A focus on rights that relate to other rights is narrower than a focus on rules that relate to other rules. On the other hand, our analysis is broader than one which sees equitable rules as preventing a defendant from unfairly taking advantage of common law rules,[17] or as assisting a party who is in the process of acquiring rights.[18] This is because there may be a number of quite different principles which can each justify the acquisition of a right that relates to another right. Indeed, the courts may not yet have identified all such principles, and this provides perhaps the most convincing reason for continuing to recognize the distinctiveness of equity: the special form of much equitable intervention may continue to generate special reasons for such intervention.

II. Equity in Practice: Two Examples

A. The Trust

The trust is the *locus classicus* of Equity's second-order operation. As we,[19] and others,[20] have previously argued, where T is trustee for B, the subject matter of B's equitable rights consists of a particular right or rights held by T. For example, where T holds a legal freehold of land on trust for B, it is T's legal estate, not the land itself, that is the subject matter of the trust. That legal estate includes, for example, the power to transfer, and the power to grant a lease, and Penner is correct to point out that, by virtue of the trust, B also has rights in relation to those powers of T.[21] The fact that B's rights relate to the rights of T is perhaps most clear where the subject matter of the trust is a personal right held by T, such as a bank account, or other chose in action. In such a case, T's right does not relate to any specific physical thing, and to that extent would not be described as a proprietary right: it would not, for example, have any protection in the insolvency of the bank or other counterparty. The existence of T's personal right, however, means that it is possible for T to hold that right on trust for B.[22] It is the existence of T's primary

[17] See D Klimchuk, 'Equity and the Rule of Law' 247–268 and H Smith, 'Property, Equity and the Rule of Law' 224–246 each in L Austin and D Klimchuk (eds), *Private Law and the Rule of Law* (OUP 2014); H Smith, Chapter 10 in this volume.

[18] See L Katz, Chapter 8 in this volume.

[19] B McFarlane and R Stevens, 'The Nature of Equitable Property' (2010) 4 Journal of Equity 1.

[20] See eg R Chambers, *An Introduction to Property Law in Australia* (3rd edn, Thomson Reuters 2013) 3.90; L Smith, 'Unravelling Proprietary Restitution' [2004] Canadian Business Law Journal 317; J Edelman, 'Two Fundamental Questions for the Law of Trusts' (2013) 129 LQR 66.

[21] J Penner, 'The (True) Nature of a Beneficiary's Equitable Proprietary Interest Under A Trust' (2014) 27 Canadian Journal of Law & Jurisprudence 473.

[22] See eg Briggs LJ in *re Lehman Bros International (Europe) (in administration)* [2010] EWHC 2914 at [241]: '[N]o-one doubts the beneficial interest of clients in a solicitor's client account. Yet the subject matter of that fund consists entirely of the solicitor's purely personal rights as a customer of the client account bank or banks.'

right that permits equity to control T's assertion of that right and, by so doing, to impose a duty on T that relates specifically to the particular right held by T. It is, therefore, not the case that each of T and B holds wholly distinct and competing entitlements to an asset independent of each of them; rather, B's rights depend on T's rights. It is commonplace to speak of B as having an 'equitable property right', and this suggests that such a right may simply be an equitable equivalent of a 'legal property right'.[23] Our view is that while there are of course some important analogies between equitable property rights and legal property rights,[24] it is crucial to see that the two types of right have a quite different structure, and bind third parties in quite distinct ways.

1. Differences between legal and equitable property rights: a recent example

The different nature of equitable property rights and legal property rights is recognized by the way in which conflict of laws rules are applied to the trust. This topic was addressed recently by the Supreme Court in *Akers v Samba Financial Group*.[25] The court's analysis proceeded on the assumption that T had purported to declare himself a trustee for B, a Cayman Islands company, of shares in a Saudi company, and to have Cayman law govern the trust. After a winding-up presentation had been presented in the Cayman Islands against B, T had transferred the shares to C. It appeared that under Saudi law, C would therefore receive good title to the shares, free from any claim of B. B's liquidators, however, relied on s 127 of the Insolvency Act 1986, which states that, in a winding up by the court, 'any disposition of the company's property ... made after the commencement of the winding up is, unless the court otherwise orders, void'.

In *Akers*, the Supreme Court confirmed that, even if it were the case that Saudi law, as the *lex situs* of the shares, had no concept of the trust, or of a division between legal and equitable entitlements, a common law court could still uphold the validity of a trust of such shares. Lord Mance, for example, noted that 'the English courts have regularly stated their willingness to enforce in personam trusts in respect of property abroad'.[26] The explanation consistently provided by the authorities is that the recognition of a trust does not, in itself, undermine the position under the *lex situs*, as it does not deny that T has a proprietary entitlement, but simply recognizes that T is under a duty to B in relation to T's assertion of that entitlement.[27] The relationship of English law to the *lex situs* provides a modern parallel to the relationship of equity to common law in the early development of the use, and then the trust. There is a sense in which the common

[23] See eg *R v Tower Hamlets LBC, ex p von Goetz* [1999] 1 QB 1019 (CA), 1023 where the right of a party with an equitable lease is described by Mummery LJ as 'for all practical purposes, an interest as good as a legal interest'; *Shell UK Ltd v Total UK Ltd* [2011] QB 86 (CA), [132] where the beneficiary of a trust is described by Waller LJ as 'the "real" owner' of the trust property.

[24] For example, each type of right is 'depersonalized' to some extent as neither is confined to a specific duty-bearer: a legal property right can be defined by reference to a thing (and so bind third parties who interfere with the thing: see H Smith, 'Emergent Property' in J Penner and H Smith (eds), *Philosophical Foundations of Property Law* (OUP 2103) 338), and an equitable property right can be defined by reference to a right (and so affect others who acquire that right).

[25] [2017] AC 424 (SC).

[26] ibid [24].

[27] The same analysis applies to other equitable property rights, such as the equity of redemption: see eg *British South Africa Co v De Beers Consolidated Mines Ltd* [1910] 2 Ch 502, 513–14

law recognized T as simply an unencumbered holder of a property right. As Maitland noted,[28] equity did not contradict or undermine the common law, as it did not deny that T held that property right, but rather imposed a duty on T in relation to it. On this view, the reason why Cayman law can recognize a trust of Saudi shares without undermining the *lex situs* also explains why a court of equity can recognize a trust of English land without undermining the common law. The same reason also explains why, notwithstanding some criticism,[29] the English courts[30] and the Court of Justice of the European Union[31] can be defended in having found that B's claim that A holds A's title to land in France on trust for B is *not* a claim to which the French courts have exclusive jurisdiction under (what is now) the Recast Brussels I Regulation.[32] Such a claim does not involve any denial of the validity of the title held by the supposed trustee, but rather seeks to impose a duty on that party. As a result, it falls outside the rule that applies to 'proceedings which have as their object rights in rem in immovable property' and gives exclusive jurisdiction in such cases to the Member State in which the property is situated.

2. Beneficial interests as property rights?

In *Akers*, the Supreme Court clearly accepted the view that a claim to a beneficial interest under a trust, unlike a claim to legal title to property, is not one that is prima facie governed by the *lex situs* of the asset that is the subject matter of the trust. As regards the nature of such a beneficial interest, however, there may appear to be a tension in at least some of the judgments in *Akers*. One question as to the applicability of s 127 of the 1986 Act was whether B could be regarded as having 'property' in the shares. While that point did detain the lower courts, in truth, as made clear in the Supreme Court, it was not a difficult one—the Act defines 'property' in extremely wide terms,[33] including, for example, 'things in action' and it thus encompasses even a mere personal right, such as a licence. Lord Sumption, however, went further than was strictly necessary on this point, and stated that B:[34]

> [H]ad a true proprietary right. The proprietary character of an equitable interest in property has sometimes been doubted, but in English law (which is in this respect the same as Cayman Islands law), the position must be regarded as settled. An equitable

[28] Maitland (n 4) 17.

[29] See eg A Briggs, *The Conflict of Laws* (3rd edn, OUP 2013) 68: 'The conclusion of the Court that a beneficiary under a resulting trust has only an interest *in personam* and not one *in rem* was wrong, at least as a matter of English law, by several centuries.' See now (4th end, OUP 2019) 59-60.

[30] *Webb v Webb* [1991] 1 WLR 1410.

[31] Webb v Webb [1994] ECR I-1717, [1994] QB 696.

[32] Art 24(1), which is identical to Art 16(1) of the Brussels I Regulation, the provision discussed in the Webb litigation, and confers exclusive jurisdiction to the court of the situs in proceedings which 'have as their object rights in rem in immovable property'. That provision does apply in the different case where a claim is made by one legal co-owner against another for the sale of the property (as in eg *Magiera v Magiera* [2016] EWCA Civ 1292 and Komu v Komu (Case C-605/14), [2016] 4 WLR 26 (ECJ)), as the claim in such a case is not for the recognition of an equitable interest but rather concerns the extent and enforcement of the parties' rights of legal co-ownership.

[33] See eg *Akers* (n 25) [87], where Lord Sumption refers to the 'exceptionally wide words' of s 486.

[34] ibid [82].

> interest possesses the essential hallmark of any right in rem, namely that it is good against third parties into whose hands the property or its traceable proceeds may have come, subject to the rules of equity for the protection of bona fide purchasers for value without notice.

On its face, this analysis may seem close to the view that a trust involves a division between legal and equitable ownership,[35] and it appears inconsistent with the view of the English court and the European Court of Justice that a claim for the imposition of a trust over foreign land is not a claim to a right *in rem* in such land.[36]

Lord Sumption's view can, however, be reconciled with our analysis, once account is taken of an ambiguity in his reference to 'property', and the somewhat unusual approach that he takes to identifying a right *in rem*. The term '*in rem*' usually refers to a right that imposes a prima facie duty on the rest of the world, whether or not such a person is a successor in title. If, for example, O simply has ownership of a chattel, then O's right to the chattel can be described as *in rem* as it imposes a prima facie duty of non-interference on the rest of the world. It does not matter if the chattel 'comes into the hands of' the third party: any deliberate or careless physical interference, whether or not it involves taking possession, can give rise to liability.[37] Similarly, an intellectual property right can be described as *in rem*: a prima facie duty, preventing particular conduct, is imposed on the rest of the world, even though it is difficult to think of any asset which may 'come into the hands of' the defendant.

Lord Sumption's focus seems instead to be on a particular class of third parties: successors in title. It is certainly the case, for example, that if T holds a right on trust for B, and then transfers that right to C, it may be possible for B to assert a right against C. In that case the relevant 'property' that has 'come into the hands of' C is T's *right*: the right initially held on trust for B. Our point is that such a third-party effect can be recognized without allowing B's right to be prima facie binding on *any* third party whose action may affect the trust property.[38] It may be the case that a third party has the potential to come under a duty to B *if* that third party acquires a particular right, as the third-party's assertion of that right may then be restrained. As a result, B can be seen as having more than a merely personal right against T. This does not mean, however, that all third

[35] See eg Lord Diplock in *Ayerst v C & K (Construction) Ltd* [1976] AC 167, 177: 'Upon the creation of a trust in the strict sense as it was developed by equity the full ownership of the trust property was split into two constituent elements … the "legal ownership" in the trustee, what came to be called the 'beneficial ownership' in the cestui que trust.' It is worth noting that such a view of the trust, as involving a division of entitlements on the same plane (rather than a generation of new rights, existing on a different second-order plane) seems to reflect Lord Diplock's broader view of the relationship between common law and equity, at least as expressed in *United Scientific Holdings Ltd v Burnley Council* [1978] AC 904, 925 ('the waters of the confluent streams of law and equity are surely mingled now'). That view, like Lord Diplock's analysis of the trust, is of course at odds with the model adopted in this chapter.

[36] See the discussion above of Webb v Webb (n 31).

[37] See eg *Spartan Steel Alloys Ltd v Martin & Co* [1973] 1 QB 27 (CA): D's careless act in severing a power cable, and thus interrupting the electricity supply to C's factory, caused physical damage to ingots owned by C that were then being processed in the factory. D was liable for such damage to C's property without ever having taken possession of that property.

[38] See J Penner, 'Duty and Liability in Respect of Funds' in J Lowry and L Mistelis (eds), *Commercial Law: Perspectives and Practice* (Butterworths 2006) 207–225, distinguishing between successor and trespassory liability.

parties are under a general, prima facie duty to B as soon as the trust is established. Indeed, rather than imposing a primary, general duty of non-interference, an equitable property right may be seen instead as imposing a second-order liability on third parties: one that serves only to regulate the enforcement of a particular *right* by such a third party. The liability of T's successor in title, identified by Lord Sumption, does not show that B's right has the same *in rem* quality as a legal property right: a third party, C, does not owe a primary duty of non-interference to B. Rather, equity again operates in a specific second-order fashion: it regulates C's acquisition and enforcement of a right, by recognizing that C may come under a duty to B in relation to the right acquired from T. The (limited) third-party effect of an equitable property right can thus be recognized without undermining the point that it is T, rather than B, who has a primary entitlement to the subject matter of the trust.[39]

This point can best be seen by considering two examples. In the first, T holds her right to a physical thing on trust for B, and X, a stranger, then deliberately or carelessly damages that physical thing. If X does so without the permission of T, or any other lawful authority, then of course T may bring a claim against X. Such a claim is a product of T's right to the thing and so T will be under a duty to use that right (and any proceeds acquired) to B's benefit.[40] In such a case, common law defines the primary rights and duties of T and X, and equity again plays a second-order role, controlling T's exercise of such rights for B's benefit. The relationship between X and B is not primary or direct,[41] but is mediated via the rights of T. The key point for our analysis is that B does not have a direct claim against X, as X has not breached any duty owed to B;[42] certainly, there is no sense in which B can seek to control the acquisition or exercise of any right of X. This point is consistent with Lord Sumption's idiosyncratic definition of B's right as a right *in rem*, as X is not of course a party into whose hands any property or its traceable proceeds has come.

In the second example, T transfers the trust property to C, who provides no value in return. Initially, C is unaware of any trust and, before gaining such awareness, C disposes of the property without retaining any traceable proceeds of it.[43] Here, C *is* a party

[39] See eg P Matthews, 'The Compatibility of the Trust with the Civil Law Notion of Property' in Smith (ed) (n 13) 313–339.

[40] If T refuses to bring such a claim, B can sue T, joining X, so that the two distinct claims (that of B against T and T against X) can be heard together. This procedural device does not however mean that B has a direct claim against X, as noted by Lord Collins in *Roberts v Gill* [2011] 1 AC 240, [62]. See the discussion of the effect of equitable assignment in section II.

[41] See eg *The Lord Compton's Case* (1587) 3 Leo 197; *Leigh & Sillivan Ltd v Aliakmon Shipping Co Ltd* [1986] AC 785, 812.

[42] In *Shell UK Ltd v Total UK Ltd* [2011] QB 86, the Court of Appeal allowed B, if joining T, to recover from X consequential loss caused to B as a result of X's having carelessly damaged property, where T held title to that property on trust for B. It is significant to note that, despite describing B as the 'equitable owner' of the property (at [132]) the court regarded B as having suffered purely economic loss (at [133]) and thus distinguished B's position from that of a party with legal title to the property. There is also a clear flaw in the court's reasoning, as the existence of the trust was said at [134] to 'constitute a special relationship of the kind required [to allow recovery of pure economic loss]'; such a special relationship must however be between the claimant and the defendant and in *Shell* the relationship identified was of course between B and T, not B and X. The best available justification for the result is that the pipeline was possessed by the claimants through the operators as their agents. Such possession of the pipeline gave the claimants a right *in rem* exigible against all others, sufficient to justify a claim for the economic loss they suffered as a result of the damage to the pipeline.

[43] As would be the case if eg C made a gift of the property to C2 before becoming aware of the trust.

'into whose hands the property' has come, and C is *not* a bona fide purchaser for value without notice; yet it is clear that B has no claim against C.[44] This might appear to be inconsistent with the statement of Lord Sumption cited above; but it aligns perfectly with a point he makes later in the same judgment and which addresses the specific issue:[45]

> [E]quitable interests arise from equity's recognition that in some circumstances the conscience of the holder of the legal interest may be affected. When the asset is transferred to a third party, the question becomes whether the conscience of the transferee is affected.

As has been pointed out, extrajudicially, by Lord Briggs,[46] conscience thus plays an important role in Lord Sumption's analysis.[47] This provides a further important way in which the operation of an equitable property right, such as a right under a trust, differs from the standard model of a right *in rem*. Liability in trespass and conversion, for example, is of course strict, in the sense that there is no requirement for the defendant to have been aware that she was dealing with the property of another. In equity, in contrast, it seems that B has to show specifically *why* it would be contrary to conscience for C to be free to assert a right in a particular way. The introduction of the idea of conscience, of course, provides an opportunity for the court to consider particular substantive principles which may then be seen as distinctively equitable. To understand such principles, however, it is crucial to note that they are used not to answer a general question as to C's behaviour, but rather to answer the specific question of whether C's acquisition or enforcement of a right can be controlled in B's favour. This can be seen by considering our second example, where C, a donee, no longer holds the trust property or its traceable proceeds, and never held such a right with knowledge of the initial trust in B's favour. If C retains any enrichment as a result of the receipt of the trust property (as when C has used the trust property in meeting an expense C was in any case bound to meet), then it could plausibly be said that it would, in a general sense, be unconscionable for C to retain that benefit, now that C is aware of its source.[48] In such a case, however, as B cannot make a claim in relation to a specific right held by C, it is not possible to say that there is a reason why C's acquisition or enforcement of a particular right can be controlled in B's favour, and so no claim can be made in equity.

Our conclusion on this point, therefore, is that Lord Sumption's description of B as holding a 'true proprietary right' depends simply on his adoption of a particular meaning of 'proprietary'. More importantly, his acceptance that it is possible to have a trust where the *lex situs* knows no such concept, like his description of the effect of a trust on third parties, is consistent with our analysis of the trust. On that analysis,

[44] See eg *BCCI v Akindele* [2001] Ch 437 (CA); Farah Constructions Pty Ltd v Say-Dee Pty Ltd (2007) 230 CLR 89.
[45] *Akers* (n 25) [89].
[46] Chancery Bar Association Annual Lecture, April 2017.
[47] See S Agnew and B McFarlane, 'The Paradox of the Equitable Proprietary Claim' in B McFarlane and S Agnew (eds), *Modern Studies in Property Law* (Hart 2019) vol X, 303–320.
[48] See eg JB Ames, 'Purchaser for Value Without Notice' (1887) 1 Harvard Law Review 1, 3.

B's protection depends not on equity's recognizing additions to the list established by common law of rights that prima facie bind the rest of the world, but rather on equity's characteristic intervention to control in favour of the claimant the assertion of a primary right held by the defendant.

3. Beneficial interests and dispositions

The two aspects of *Akers* considered thus far (the validity of a trust of Saudi property, and the fact that B's right under the trust counts as 'property' for the purposes of s 127 of the 1986 Act) were thus each resolved in favour of B's liquidators. It was on the third point, however, that their claim failed.[49] The Supreme Court found that a transfer of trust property to a third party against whom no claim can be made, such as a bona fide purchaser for value of the trust property without notice of the trust, is not a 'disposition' for the purposes of s 127. There is thus a clear difference between the transfer (eg by a director) of a right vested in a company and the transfer by a trustee of a right held on trust for a company.[50] The practical effect of each transaction—the loss of a company's right—may be the same, but the legal analysis differs as each transaction has a distinct formal structure.

In reaching this conclusion, the Supreme Court relied on an earlier judgment of Lloyd LJ. It was noted there that, while, from C's point of view, a transfer by the trustee to a bona fide purchaser 'is as effective as it would be if [the trustee] could vest the beneficial title in the purchaser', it does not transfer B's beneficial interest to C.[51] While C then has title to the property, and is free to use that property for C's own benefit, this is not because previously separate legal and beneficial interests have been reunited. It is rather because C has acquired a right from T and, given the bona fide purchase, there is no grounds on which equity can impose a restriction, in B's favour, on C's use of that right.[52] There is, therefore, no disposition from B to C.[53]

The Supreme Court's confirmation that the acquisition of trust property by a bona fide purchaser does not involve a transfer or disposition of B's equitable interest is inconsistent with the idea that a party holding an unencumbered legal title has both a legal and an equitable interest in the property. It is true that C, the bona fide purchaser, is free to use the property for her own benefit, can declare a new trust of the property, and has rights that are recognized in equity. But those consequences flow simply from C's acquisition of the rights that formerly comprised the trust property and do not depend on any particular equitable intervention. There is no independent equitable title

[49] This decisive point had not in fact been considered in the courts below, nor in oral argument before the Supreme Court, but was noted by the justices only after that point, so that written submissions were invited: see *Akers* (n 25) [9].

[50] As noted by eg Lord Mance at [53]–[55].

[51] *Independent Trustee Services Ltd v GP Noble Trustees Ltd* [2013] Ch 91 (CA) [106].

[52] *Akers* (n 25) [51] (Lord Mance) and [88] (Lord Sumption). See too *Pilcher v Rawlins* (1872) 7 Ch App 259, where B's inability to bring a claim against C in such a case is seen as depending on a lack of equitable jurisdiction to reach C.

[53] Although this point is not mentioned by the Supreme Court in *Akers*, such an analysis accords precisely with the interpretation of the phrase 'disposition of an equitable interest' given by the House of Lords in *Vandervell v IRC* [1967] 2 AC 291 when considering s 53(1)(c) of the Law of Property Act 1925. There, similarly, the transfer of legal title to shares by T to C, with the permission of B, did not involve any disposition of the beneficial interest of B to C.

that needs to be located in relation to property; rather, such rights arise only if a party holds a right and is subject to a duty in relation to that right. If there are no grounds for regulating C's assertion of a right, then no equitable title arises.[54]

Our argument is thus consistent with the Supreme Court's analysis in *Akers*, and with Lord Sumption's focus on the role of conscience as the means by which B can assert a right against successors in title to T. In Hohfeldian terms, the bona fide purchaser defence can be seen as providing an immunity to C: even if C later acquires knowledge of the trust in B's favour, C's conscience will not be deemed affected, as C is protected by the circumstances in which C acquired the right from T. Given that, on our view, a precondition of C's liability to B is C's acquisition of a particular right, it is perhaps no surprise that the circumstances in which C acquired such a right are relevant to, and can even prevent, C's liability. In contrast, when considering the impact on a third party of a right that is *in rem* in the usual sense (ie it is prima facie binding on the rest of the world), it is only in relatively rare cases[55] that a bona fide purchaser defence is available. In such cases, the duty owed by strangers (eg the duty of X not to deliberately or carelessly interfere with a physical thing owned by O) is neither defined by any particular right, nor dependent on X's acquisition of any particular right, so it is also unsurprising that the circumstances in which X may have acquired a right give X no general defence to O's right *in rem*.[56] The fact that many equitable claims are claims that the acquisition or enforcement of the defendant's right can be controlled in favour of the claimant thus has implications not only for the grounds on which such claims arise, but also for the defences available against such claims.

4. The distinctiveness of beneficial interests

The aim of the foregoing argument has been to show that, in recognizing beneficial interests, equity has implemented a specific form of second-order intervention: it has controlled, in favour of B, A's acquisition and enforcement of a particular right or rights. As a result, B is recognized as having a particular type of right: a right that relates to a right of A. The distinctiveness of such intervention would, however, be reduced if such rights can also be generally found at common law. Certainly, some legal property rights may, in a broad sense, be said to be second order, or linked to other rights. A lease, for example, is linked to a reversion, and an easement must be 'appurtenant' to a dominant tenement. In such cases, however, the key characteristic of a beneficial interest is absent: the content of B's right is not defined by A's being under a duty to B in relation to a particular right of A. This can be seen by considering which third parties are prima facie bound by B's right. If A, a freehold owner, grants B a legal lease, then B has a right that is capable of binding not only A, and a successor in title of A, but also any stranger who interferes with the land. The same is true of a legal easement granted by A to B, and, if the easement is appurtenant to an estate at all, it is the estate of *B* to which it is attached.

[54] See eg *Westdeutsche Landesbank Girozentrale v Islington LBC* [1996] AC 669 (HL) 705 (Lord Browne-Wilkinson).

[55] For example, the acquisition of money used in currency: see eg *Miller v Race* (1758) 1 Burr 452.

[56] See eg *Farquharson Bros v King* [1902] AC 325.

Of course, if A has only a lease of land, and grants B an easement, that easement will be limited in its duration, but this is simply a consequence of the *nemo dat* rule: as A has a right to exclusive possession of the land for only a limited period, A cannot grant B a property right in that land of greater duration.

There are perhaps two forms of right recognized at common law that come closest to sharing the particular nature of a right that relates to another right. First, where A grants B a lease, it is possible for particular duties in that lease (leasehold covenants) to bind not only A and B, but also later parties in 'privity of estate' ie assignees of A's freehold or of B's lease.[57] Such effect is of course necessary to enable key aspects of the landlord–tenant relationship (eg B's duty to pay rent and A's duty to afford B quiet enjoyment of the land) to endure through changes in ownership.[58] The impact of such leasehold covenants on third parties is limited to those in privity of estate, and so is narrower not only than that of a standard legal property right, but also of a beneficial interest. So a sublessee, for example, is not bound by a leasehold covenant in a head lease, as such a sublessee is not in privity of estate with the head landlord; whereas if A holds a freehold on trust for B, and grants a lease to C, B's beneficial interest may affect C. That is because B's beneficial interest can bind any party who acquires a right that depends on A's right, whereas a leasehold covenant can bind only a party who acquires the same estate as A or B. Further, while there are restrictions on what types of duty can count as leasehold covenants and thus bind by privity of estate,[59] those limits are not based on asking if A is under a duty to B in relation to a specific right. Indeed, under English law, *any* promise by A, as landlord, made to B as tenant in a lease entered into after 1995, if not expressed to be personal, is capable of being a leasehold covenant and thus may bind C, A's assignee.[60]

Second, where B transfers a right to A as a result of A's fraud, or duress, then B is recognized as having a common law power to set aside that transfer. The transfer of the right to A is valid, so B does not deny that A has that right; however, B's exercise of the common law power can lead to the immediate revesting of title in B.[61] This contrasts with the position where B has an equitable power to set aside a transfer. B's exercise of the power does not then lead to an immediate revesting of title, but rather has the effect that A is under a duty to transfer A's right back to B. So, the common law rule does not have as its aim the restriction, in B's favour, of A's enjoyment of a particular right: it rather allows B to revoke a transaction directly. Nonetheless, it would be foolish to deny that there are some similarities between the common law power to rescind and equitable intervention: in particular, that common law power cannot be invoked against a

[57] See eg *Spencer's Case* (1583) 5 Co Rep 16a; Landlord and Tenant (Covenants) Act 1995.

[58] See eg *City of London Corporation v Fell* [1994] 1 AC 458, 464 (Lord Templeman).

[59] See eg *P&A Swift Investments v Combined English Stores Group plc* [1989] AC 632 (HL) 642 (Lord Oliver).

[60] Landlord and Tenant (Covenants) Act 1995, ss 2 and 28(1).

[61] See eg *Load v Green* (1846) 15 M & W 216. Note of course that requirements for acquiring legal title operating in particular contexts (eg the need for registration) may mean that B's exercise of the power does not lead to any automatic revesting of title in B. If A transfers the right to C, before B exercises the power, and C is a bona fide purchaser, it may then be too late for B to revest title: see eg Sale of Goods Act 1979, s 23 and UCC, §2-403.

bona fide purchaser from A who has no notice of A's fraud or duress.[62] As has been noted,[63] this makes the common law power to rescind a very unusual form of legal right and it seems to be of relatively recent origin, and to have been developed by the courts by analogy to longer-established equitable rules.

5. Justifying the recognition of beneficial interests

Our argument is that, once we have understood the form of equitable proprietary rights, we are in a position to understand the kind of reasons that can justify their recognition. Examining those reasons in detail must be the subject of future work, but the key point to be made now is that the formal difference between legal and equitable property rights has very important consequences when considering the reasons for which such rights arise. In particular, the distinctive nature of beneficial interests means that it would be a mistake to expect the grounds justifying those rights to be as limited as the grounds justifying the acquisition of legal property rights. Compare the following two examples:

> Example 1: *D* steals *C*'s mobile telephone and exchanges it in *X*'s shop for a knife.
> Example 2: *T* holds title to a Rembrandt painting on trust for a number of beneficiaries, of whom *B* is one. *T* exchanges his title to the Rembrandt for a jade chess set.

In Example 1, there is no comprehensible method by which C can claim legal title to the knife. X has a power to choose to whom to convey title to the knife, and clearly intended to convey that title to D. X does not intend to exercise any power in favour of C. The effect of acquiring legal title is that third parties are subject to an immediate, strict duty to the holder of legal title: the interests of such parties are therefore very important when considering the rules governing the acquisition of legal title. Certainly, none of the standard means of acquiring such title (eg taking possession; manufacture) can be relied on by C. This is not to deny, of course, that, as between C and D, it may be thought unjust for D to take the benefit of his legal title. It may therefore be possible for C to claim that D holds his title to the knife on constructive trust for C;[64] but in such a case the reason for recognizing the trust (eg to prevent D's unjust enrichment;[65] to respond to D's wrongful taking) is distinct from the reason for recognizing C's initial title to the telephone.

In Example 2, by contrast, it is possible to understand how the subject of B's right may change from T's title to the painting to T's title to the chess set. If the disposition

[62] As discussed in eg *Car & Universal Finance Ltd v Caldwell* [1965] 1 QB 525 (CA).
[63] W Swadling, 'Rescission, Property, and the Common Law' (2005) 121 LQR 123.
[64] The wording of §55(1) of the Restatement (Third) of Restitution and Unjust Enrichment is broad enough to allow for the imposition of a constructive trust in favour of C of D's right to the knife; see too the *obiter dicta* of Lord Browne-Wilkinson in *Westdeutsche Landesbank Girozentrale* (n 54) 716. The difficulty facing the constructive trust argument is that there was no pre-existing fiduciary relationship between D and C, and, as D had no power to give X good title to the telephone, C has not lost title to it. For discussion of the point, see A Nair, *Claims to Traceable Proceeds* (OUP 2018) ch 8.
[65] See §55, Illustration 10 of the Restatement (Third) of Restitution and Unjust Enrichment.

of the Rembrandt was authorized, the title to the chess set is caught by the terms of the trust. But what if the disposition is not authorized? Is T free to use the newly acquired right for his own benefit, or does the original reason for which he was under a duty not to use the Rembrandt for his own benefit entail that he is now similarly obliged in relation to its substitute?

The better view is that the reason for the original duty does not disappear when perfect compliance with it is no longer possible. We would argue that, in this case, the original reason now entails that T must do the next best thing to perfect compliance.[66] Does he get to choose whether he can use the chess set, or does B have the choice? Whatever the original reason for the duty to hold a right on trust, this reason is sufficient to require that the trustee holds unauthorized substitutions on the same basis.[67] The crucial point is that the new right was acquired by T's exercise of powers of title to the original right, and T was under a duty to B in relation to those powers. No fresh reason needs to be provided: it is the original reason for the original duty that requires the recognition of the new duty in relation to the substitute. Just as T was under a duty to B in relation to the original right, T can now be under the same duty to B in relation to the substitute right. There is thus an important element of truth in the much-criticized view of the House of Lords[68] that a claim to traceable proceeds flows naturally from the existence of B's initial equitable interest.

It is for this reason that the cases have traditionally distinguished between 'tracing rules' at common law and in equity, and have required the identification of a 'fiduciary relationship' (more accurately a duty not to use a particular right for one's own benefit) before permitting a claim to any identifiable substitute.[69] Once a trust has arisen, for whatever reason, that reason will suffice to capture substitute rights. We do not need to invoke a new reason, such as unjust enrichment, to provide an explanation. Nor do we need to adopt an explanation that is capable of applying in each of Example 1 and Example 2: the distinctive formal nature of beneficial interests means they may arise for reasons that do not justify the acquisition of legal property rights.

This point is of general importance in relation to other trusts that arise by operation of law. Such trusts are often treated with some suspicion,[70] and this is due in part to the fact that there are only very limited grounds on which a legal property right may arise by operation of law. However, the distinctive form of equitable proprietary rights

[66] This is an application of the broader argument made by J Gardner, 'What Is Tort Law for?' (2011) Law and Philosophy 30, 33.

[67] As the beneficiaries thus have the power to deny T any freedom to use the right for T's own benefit, there can also be no objection if the beneficiaries instead choose to impose a lien on the right to secure T's duty to pay money to remedy the breach of trust: see *Foskett v McKeown* [2001] 1 AC 102 (HL) 131 (Lord Millett).

[68] See *Foskett v McKeown* [2001] 1 AC 102 (HL).

[69] A Televantos, 'Losing the Fiduciary Requirement for Equitable Tracing Claims' (2017) 133 LQR 492 argues that the 'fiduciary relationship' requirement rests on a misunderstanding of earlier uses of that term, but our argument is rather that there is in any case an ongoing justification for a similar requirement for claims in relation to substitutes.

[70] See eg W Swadling, 'Explaining Resulting Trusts' (2008) 124 LQR 72 and 'The Fiction of the Constructive Trust' (2011) 64 CLP 399.

means that it is no surprise that their acquisition may be justified by reasons which do not apply to legal property rights. Consider the following example:

> X wishes to purchase C's asset and so enters into negotiations with D, C's agent. To persuade D to deal with her on good terms, X makes a gift to D of a jade chess set worth £1m. D proceeds to bind C to the sale to X. After the contract of sale is performed, C discovers the bribe.

The issue of whether there is a trust of D's right to the chess set turns upon the nature of the duties of D. Is D obliged to transfer to C the monetary equivalent or value of the chess set, so as to remain free to use that right for his own benefit? Or is C entitled to require, if she so chooses, that D does not use for his own benefit the very right with which he has been bribed? For many years, the answer to this question as a matter of the positive law was unsettled. However, D is under a duty to subordinate his interests to those of his principal. It seems right that it should be his principal who gets to choose whether D can keep the very right with which D has been bribed. In which case, if C does choose to impose such a duty, D is under a duty not to use the bribe for his own benefit: a trust.[71] The point is not simply that D should never have acquired the bribe; D could be deprived of the bribe in a number of different ways, eg through confiscation by the state. It is rather that equity restrains D's ability to acquire such a right because, *as against* C, D is not free to use his position as agent for his own benefit. As Lionel Smith has argued, the trust of the bribe follows naturally from this limit on D's powers to acquire a particular right:[72] equity does not deny that D acquired the bribe, but controls, in favour of C, D's use of that right.

The key point in relation to our bribe example is that there is a reason why D comes under a duty to C in relation to a specific right: the bribe itself. The fact that the content of D's duty to C relates to a specific right held by D is, on our analysis, a necessary condition of the recognition of D's beneficial interest. This also explains why a trust may arise where C transfers a right to D under a contract, but later exercises an equitable power to rescind that contract. Where the reason for the transfer of a particular right no longer applies, D ought to return what he has received. If he ought to return that right, he is not free to use it for his own benefit. If he is not so free, there is a trust.[73] Compare, however, the following case:

> C agrees to buy two green sofas from D for £1,000. A deposit of £200 is paid by C in cash in advance. D goes into bankruptcy.

[71] *FHR European Ventures LLP v Cedar Capital Partners LLC* [2015] AC 250 (SC).

[72] L Smith, 'Constructive Trusts and the No-Profit Rule' [2013] CLJ 260.

[73] Note that, consistently with the role of conscience as discussed by Lord Sumption in *Akers* (n 25) [89], it seems a trust can arise only if and when D holds the relevant right with awareness of the reason for which the right should be returned: see eg *Westdeutsche Landesbank Girozentrale* (n 54) 705 (Lord Browne-Wilkinson) and Wambo Coal Pty Ltd v Ariff [2007] NSWSC 589. It is difficult before that point to regard D as being under a duty to return the right. The possibility of D's later gaining such awareness, however, justifies regarding C as having a 'mere equity' and thus more than a merely personal right against D: for discussion, see B McFarlane, 'Trusts and Knowledge: Lessons from Australia' in J Glister and P Ridge (eds), *Fault Lines in Equity* (2012) 169–192.

Let it be assumed that C can identify the very notes he paid with in D's cash register. Is D obliged to transfer the right to those notes back to C, thereby giving rise to a trust?

This depends upon the agreement. Clearly there was a good reason for the payment of the deposit: that is what had been agreed. Had it been agreed that the *right* to the cash was conditional, or only the *performance* rendered? As far as restitution is concerned, is D obliged to reconvey those identifiable rights, or merely to pay back £200? As it was clearly intended that D should be free to use the cash after it had been paid, it is impossible to conclude that the parties were agreeing that the transfer of any particular rights was conditional. Without some agreed ring-fencing, the transfer of the rights was unconditional. C therefore only has a personal claim for restitution of the value of the performance made. The point is that C cannot show any grounds to restrict D's enjoyment of a *specific* right. The form of beneficial interests thus provides an important limit on the grounds on which such rights can be recognized. Certainly, the mere fact that D has behaved unconscionably, or that we have sympathy for the plight of C, cannot justify the recognition of a beneficial interest in C, as it cannot overcome the need to locate a particular right to which D's duty to C relates.[74]

B. Equitable Assignment

At one time, almost all contractual debts and other claims could not be assigned, by which in English we mean transferred, at all.[75] So, in order to acquire a contractual right against another it was necessary to establish that you had both been promised something by that person, and that you had provided consideration in exchange for that promise. A purported assignee of a contractual right could satisfy neither of these requirements and could not therefore make a claim. The prohibition on assignment followed from the justification for privity of contract, which itself follows from the reasons why contractual rights are acquired.[76] At common law, the only mechanism available to achieve the same effect as an assignment is an agreement by way of novation. Commercially, such a restrictive rule against transfers is extremely inconvenient. For most businesses, a large (frequently the largest) portion of their wealth is tied up in the claims they have against other parties. If these cannot be bought and sold, they may face significant financing problems.[77]

Equitable assignment of a contractual right, despite its name, does not involve the transfer of the right, but rather the creation of a new right in the 'assignee', the subject

[74] *re Goldcorp Exchange Ltd* [1995] 1 AC 74 (PC) provides a clear example of this formal limit on beneficial interests.

[75] There are long-standing exceptions for eg debts owed to or by the Crown.

[76] See CH Tham, 'Notice of Assignment and Discharge by Performance' [2010] LMCLQ 38. See too CH Tham, *Understanding the Law of Assignment* (CUP 2019) ch 3.

[77] See eg H Beale, L Gullifer, and S Paterson, 'A Case for Interfering with Freedom of Contract? An Empirically-Informed Study of Bans on Assignment' (2016) JBL 203, noting the problems caused in practice for small and medium enterprises by express 'bans on assignments'. Note that regulations have now been introduced under the Small Business, Employment and Enterprise Act 2015, s 1 to nullify such clauses in particular contracts.

matter of which is the assignor's contractual right against the promisor.[78] Where therefore a claim is (in England but not the United States) brought by an equitable assignee it is necessary to ensure that the assignor is before the court as a party (as claimant if he was willing to be joined, as defendant if not).[79] This is because there are two claims (and two rights) in play: assignee vs assignor; assignor/promisee vs promisor. Commercially, but not legally, the overall effect is the same as a transfer of the right, mainly because the assignee is secure against the assignor's bankruptcy. The doctrinal barrier to transfer had been overcome because of the form of equitable rights.

An equitable assignment is therefore very similar to a trust:[80] the subject matter of the equitable assignee's right, like the subject matter of a beneficiary's right, is a right held by another: in an equitable assignment, it is the right of the assignor against the debtor. One difference[81] is that a trustee, unlike an assignor, is under no duty to transfer or convey the right he holds or its proceeds to the beneficiary (unless and until, under a bare trust, the beneficiary exercises his power[82] to demand a transfer of the trust property). The similarity between an equitable assignment and the existence of a trust means that the language of assignment is misleading: an equitable assignor, like a party declaring a trust of a right, does not divest himself of any right; he rather retains the right and comes under a duty to another in relation to it.

Statutory assignment is quite different. It involves the actual transfer of the right being assigned and it was therefore necessary for this change to be made by legislation.[83] There are at least five differences between equitable and statutory assignment. These differences appear arbitrary, until it is realized that despite sharing a name, the form of equitable assignment is quite different from that of statutory assignment, and the different form justifies the substantive differences.[84]

[78] See eg CH Tham, 'The Nature of Equitable Assignment and Anti-Assignment Clauses' in J Neyers and R Bronaugh (eds), *Exploring Contract Law* (Hart 2009) 283–318; McFarlane and Stevens (n 19) 6–8; J Edelman and S Elliott, 'Two Conceptions of Equitable Assignment' (2015) 131 LQR 228; see too Tham (n 76) ch 4.

[79] *Roberts v Gill* [2011] 1 AC 240 (HL) [62]–[71]. Lord Collins states at [71] that: 'It is plain that, other than in the most exceptional circumstances such as existed in [*Brandt's Sons & Co v Dunlop Rubber Co Ltd* [1905] AC 454], even in the case of an equitable assignment the assignee cannot proceed to judgment without joining the assignor.' For more detailed discussion, including variations where the proceedings brought by the assignee are equitable, see Tham (n 76) chs 7–9.

[80] We would not however go as far as J Edelman and S Elliott, 'Two Conceptions of Equitable Assignment' (2015) 131 LQR 228, who suggest that an equitable assignment is no more and no less than the creation of a trust. The model adopted by Tham (n 76) chs 4–6, is of 'trust plus agency', whereby the (irrevocable) agency gives an equitable assignee the ability to invoke some of the assignor's powers directly.

[81] An equitable assignment is not identical to a trust: note, for example, that the courts have allowed a trust to be declared of a right even if there is a prohibition on making an equitable assignment of that right: see eg *Don King v Warren* [2000] Ch 291 317–19; *Barbados Trust Co v Bank of Zambia* [2007] EWCA Civ 148 [43]. A further difference is that an equitable assignee, unlike a beneficiary of a trust, is able to give the debtor a good discharge by accepting payment: a point discussed by Tham (n 76) 39 and Tham (n 76) 142–146. See too P Turner, 'Prohibitions on Assignment: Intellectualism v Law' (2018) 134 LQR 532, 535–36.

[82] The power acknowledged in English law in *Saunders v Vautier* (1841) 4 Beav 115. The position in the United States is different as discussed by eg P Matthews, 'The Comparative Importance of the Rule in *Saunders v Vautier*' (2006) 122 LQR 266.

[83] See Law of Property Act 1925, s 136. Note that Tham (n 76) ch 13 takes a different view, arguing that the provision does not transfer the debt or thing in action itself, but rather only the 'three sets of entitlements' set out by s. 136(1). As Tham states at eg 439, on that view, '"statutory" assignments *are* equitable assignments, but with a limited statutory overlay in respect of certain entitlements'.

[84] The substantive differences also show the danger of the view, expressed by Gloster LJ in *First Abu Dhabi Bank PJSC v BP Oil International Limited* [2018] EWCA Civ 14, [37], that 'the equitable assignee is owner of the chose'.

First, a statutory assignment must be made in writing.[85] Formal requirements such as these are common for the transfer of many types of rights (eg title to land,[86] equitable rights,[87] intellectual property rights).[88] The only types of rights that can be transferred by agreement alone, without any formality or registration requirement, are rights to goods.[89] Equitable assignment requires no formality[90] because it involves no transfer. Second, statutory assignment requires that notice (in writing) is given to the debtor.[91] A debtor must know to whom his obligation is owed so that he can perform with respect to the correct party. Again, equitable assignment does not require any notice to be given to the debtor,[92] any more than does the declaration of a trust over a debt, because it involves no transfer of the obligation owed by the debtor.

Third, a statutory assignee can, indeed must, sue in his own name.[93] The right is now vested in him, and so he is the proper party. In contrast, the requirement that an equitable assignee join the assignor, noted above, is not a procedural quirk,[94] but reveals the structure of what has been done.[95] Fourth, the statute requires that the assignment must be absolute.[96] A partial transfer of a debt is not absolute, and cannot constitute a statutory assignment. If a debtor disputes a debt, it would prejudice him if a debt could be split up into the hands of multiple different creditors, each of whose claims he would then have to resist individually.[97] Again, this may be contrasted with an equitable assignment. An equitable assignment involves the transfer of nothing. The debtor is not prejudiced by an assignee creating many different rights in third parties, and so partial 'equitable' assignment of a debt, to as many parties as is desired, is unobjectionable. Finally, we cannot transfer what we do not have. A statutory assignment of future property is therefore not possible. By contrast, as an equitable assignment involves the imposition of a duty in relation to a right, a duty can arise immediately and bite in relation to a right when that right is later acquired. The willingness of equity to recognize this effect of an ongoing duty allowed the creation of charges over future property.[98]

[85] Law of Property Act 1925, s 136(1).

[86] See eg Land Registration Act 2002, ss 4 and 27.

[87] Law of Property Act 1925, s 53(1)(c).

[88] See eg Copyright, Designs and Patents Act 1988, s 90 (assignment of copyright); Trade Marks Act 1994, s 24 (assignment of a registered trade mark); Patent Act 1977, s 30(1) (assignment of a patent).

[89] See Sale of Goods Act 1979, s 17.

[90] See eg *Brandt's Sons & Co v Dunlop Rubber Co Ltd* [1905] AC 454, 462 (Lord Macnaghten).

[91] Law of Property Act 1925, s 136(1).

[92] See eg *Gorringe v Irwell India Rubber and Gutta Percha Works* (1886) 34 Ch D 128 (CA).

[93] Law of Property Act 1925, s 136(1) (a) and (b).

[94] We would therefore disagree with Gloster LJ's *obiter* characterization of joinder of the assignor as 'a matter of procedural practice' only in *First Abu Dhabi Bank* (n 84) [37].

[95] See eg *MH Smith (Plant Hire) v DL Mainwaring* [1968] 2 Lloyds Rep 244, 246 where (in a case of an insurer's subrogation where equitable assignment was considered by way of analogy), Kerr LJ stated that it would be 'untenable' to suggest that the requirement of joining the equitable assignor is simply a question of form rather than substance.

[96] Law of Property Act 1925, s 136(1). This also means that a conditional assignment cannot take effect as a statutory assignment, as this would 'leave the debtor in uncertainty as to the person to whom the legal right is transferred': *Durham Bros v Robertson* [1898] 1 QB 765 (CA), 773 (Chitty LJ).

[97] *Deposit Protection Board v Barclays Bank* [1994] 2 AC 367 (HL) 392 (Lord Browne-Wilkinson).

[98] See *Tailby v Official Receiver* (1888) 13 App Cas 523 (HL). It also allowed for the recognition of a trust in *Pullan v Koe* [1913] 1 Ch 9.

III. Conclusion

We have examined two areas in which equitable principles continue to play an important practical role. In each of those areas, one common form of analysis is to say that equity has supplemented the common law, addressing the same questions but providing different answers by applying different moral principles which allow for a more flexible approach. So it might be said, for example, that by recognizing the beneficial interest, or by regarding a chose in action as capable of transfer, equity has gone beyond the common law, expanding the situations in which a property right is recognized or when assignment is possible. On this model, it is difficult to see what merit there is in continuing to divide the common law and equitable rules, or what specific contribution equitable doctrines have made to the law as a whole.

We have argued that such a model should be rejected, as it fails to describe the special contribution of equity. In each of the areas examined, a careful analysis of the precise form of equitable intervention shows that it does *not* consist of simply recognizing an equitable shadow of a common law doctrine, or of bringing different values to bear when answering the same question posed at common law. Rather, in each case, equity answers a *different* question. Moreover, in each case, that question is of the same type: it asks whether B has acquired a right in relation to a right of A. The unifying feature of equitable intervention in these areas is the *form* of that intervention: equity asks if there is a good reason why a restriction should be recognized, in B's favour, on A's acquisition or enforcement of a specific right. This is the *specific* form of second-order intervention performed by equity in the areas examined and it is, we claim, the feature that explains the distinctive and special characteristic of much of modern equity. In such cases, when we look for the philosophical foundations of equity, we are in fact looking for justifications for doctrines that regulate, in favour of B, A's acquisition or enforcement of a specific right.

10

Fusion of Law and Confusion of Equity

*Henry E Smith**

I. Introduction

Sometimes controversies seem deep because we have dug a hole for ourselves. Such is the case with the role of equity in the legal system. Many seemingly intractable and philosophically interesting debates have origins in a central feature of recent legal history: the fusion of law and equity. We are told that contract has died and been swallowed up by tort, that standards and rules compete on the terrain of altruism and individualism, and that everyday disputes implicate the relation of law and morality at the deepest level.

That such weighty matters should depend on what seems like mundane traces of history—equity?!—might come as a surprise, for several reasons. To begin with, the fusion of law and equity is a fait accompli, and so invoking it in connection with contemporary problems or debates might seem like refighting the last war. And fusion is not only largely complete but is regarded as uncontroversial. The fusion of law and equity happened over a period extending from the mid-nineteenth to the early mid-twentieth century.[1] At the time fusion was taking place, many thought the elimination of an extra court system would solve the major problems in the administration of justice. And although we have not actually reached nirvana after the fusion of law and equity, very few would advocate turning the clock back on the jurisdictional merger of law and equity. To top things off, in the fusion of law and equity, equity seems to have won. From the flexible procedural devices like joinder, discovery, and notice pleading to substantive matters like unconscionability, equity is everywhere. Statutes effecting merger of law and equity uniformly provided that where the rules of law and equity conflict, the equitable one would win. In the United States, equity started becoming a lost art, and elsewhere it lost some of its distinct character. With fusion, equity triumphed, even in death.

* I would like to thank Lionel Smith and participants at the conference on philosophical foundations of the law of Equity for their helpful comments. All errors are mine.

[1] For the United States, see Fed R Civ P (1938); New York Code of Procedure of 1848, NY Laws ch 379 (Field Code); Ralph E Kharas, 'A Century of Law–Equity Merger in New York' (1949) 1 Syracuse Law Review 186. For England, see Supreme Court of Judicature Act 1873, 36 & 37 Vict, c 66; Supreme Court of Judicature Act 1875, 38 & 39 Vict, c 77; JH Baker, *An Introduction to English Legal History* (3rd edn, Butterworths 1990) 108–09; Stephen Waddams, 'Equity in English Contract Law: The Impact of the Judicature Acts (1873–75)' (2012) 33 Journal of Legal History 185.

Henry E Smith, *Fusion of Law and Confusion of Equity* In: *Philosophical Foundations of the Law of Equity*. Edited by: Dennis Klimchuk, Irit Samet, and Henry E Smith, Oxford University Press (2020). © The several contributors.
DOI: 10.1093/oso/9780198817659.003.0011

Perhaps most importantly, those carrying out the fusionist project did not see anything special in equity beyond the procedural devices it made available. On this view, there was nothing distinctive to preserve in the process of merger—as fusion tends to be called in a procedural context. It should then come as no surprise that equity would lose its character, aside from a few pockets where constitutional requirements for jury trial prevent its full submersion in a unified law. At the end of this process, a distinctive equity seems to have been effaced to the extent that it can't do much of anything, much less cause jurisprudential misunderstandings and analytical distortions.

We should not let this tidy picture of the fusion of law and equity mislead us. Instead, we need to ask what functions were associated with traditional equity and what became of them.

In this chapter, I will argue that a misunderstanding of certain dimensions of equity have indeed led to jurisprudential problems with real-world effects in the law. I will argue that equity was not merely a historical jurisdictional artefact but that it correlated imperfectly with an important function. This equitable function was neither purely procedural nor exclusively substantive. Instead, it was a second-order aspect of the legal system, law about law, or 'meta law'. This role is clearest when equity overrides the normal legal result, as where a court enjoins a suit or imposes a constructive trust, but also where a court withholds relief on grounds of unconscionability or disproportionate hardship. This equitable function need not correspond to a separate court, but it did dovetail with certain procedural devices. Second-order devices are familiar in complex systems: all manner of control modules and feedback mechanisms are examples. And yet a second-order function is a powerful device that should be used sparingly, especially if it can be misused. It is suited for dealing with certain kinds of problems—problems of great variability and uncertainty.

Because of variability and uncertainty, three kinds of problems (and perhaps more besides) are suited for meta-level treatment: polycentricity, conflicting rights, and opportunism. First, polycentric tasks are complex in the sense of involving multiple interacting entities.[2] Lon Fuller gives the example of the problem of a court allocating paintings left under a will to two museums; the problem is complex, because the value of a painting depends on the other members of the set to which it belongs. Likewise, multiparty litigation may present many interlocking issues. Traditionally equity courts were called upon to deal with these problems, and part of their intervention was to adjust the first-order law that governed such interactions in order to produce a globally sensible result.[3] Second, problems of conflicting rights require courts to reconcile conflicting uses, as in the law of nuisance or situations of coming to the nuisance.[4] Solving

[2] Lon L Fuller, 'The Forms and Limits of Adjudication' in Kenneth I Winston (ed), *The Principles of Social Order: Selected Essays of Lon L. Fuller* (Hart 2001) 101, 126–36 (introducing the concept of polycentric tasks); see also Michael Polanyi, *The Logic of Liberty; Reflections and Rejoinders* (University of Chicago Press 1965) 171.

[3] Polycentricity is also a rationale for administrative regulation, and the parallels between equity and administration have long been apparent. See Henry E Smith, 'Equity and Administrative Behavior' in PG Turner (ed) *Equity and Administration* (CUP 2016) 26.

[4] John CP Goldberg and Henry E Smith, 'Wrongful Fusion: Equity and Tort' in John CP Goldberg, Peter Turner, and Henry E Smith (eds), *Equity and Law: Fusion and Fission* (CUP 2019) 309, 315–19, 324.

them required making reference to first-level potential rights and duties and regulating their interaction. Notably, courts sometimes performed this equitable function even on the law side of the jurisdictional divide. Finally, opportunism was a familiar theme of equity, under the heading of 'constructive fraud'.[5] As I have argued and as courts and commentators were aware in an earlier era, opportunism is inherently difficult to define *ex ante*: opportunists will anticipate the rule and find new ways around it. In a pithy quotation borrowed from Lord Hardwicke, Story notes that '"[f]raud is infinite" given "the fertility of man's invention"'.[6] Thus, it may be necessary to go *ex post* and one level up to meet opportunists on their more comprehensive field of operation.

Needing to intervene in problems of high complexity and uncertainty is consistent with the constant Aristotelian theme in equity: equity intervenes in law where law fails owing to its generality.[7] Complexity and uncertainty are reasons for such failure. In particular, an opportunist who tries to take unfair advantage of the law is, as Aristotle would have it, a 'stickler in a bad way'.[8] What unifies problems of polycentric tasks, conflicting rights, and opportunism is the difficulty of dealing with them without going to a higher level.

In fusing law and equity, this equitable function was *flattened* out of the legal system. Because those carrying out fusion ignored the second-order safety valve function of equity, the process led to a host of problems. In theory, legal reasoning could be structured in a two-step fashion, with equity triggered by proxies for the kinds of highly variable and uncertain problems for which it is most suitable. The safety valve function could be served through a series of further presumptions, such as those that traditionally governed the granting or withholding of equitable relief. That is not how fusion happened. The view underlying the actual process of fusion was primarily procedural: equity mainly afforded a different decision-making procedure. Equity was associated with certain remedies and even substantive doctrines, but to the fusionists any of these aspects of historical equity with continuing value could be carried over unproblematically into the new unified law. In the United States, the procedural focus of fusion was coupled with a focus on results and a scepticism about the special status of equity. This outlook led fusion to be a powerful broom, which swept away not only separate jurisdiction but also an important function that was entwined with, but in principle separable from, jurisdiction: equity as meta law.

To solve the tough problems that equity addressed, but at a single flattened level, the law in the United States gravitated away from bright-line *ex ante* rules and towards vague *ex post* standards, especially in the form of multifactor balancing tests. Elsewhere in the common law world, the attempt at doing law and equity at one level gave rise

[5] 1 Joseph Story, Commentaries on Equity Jurisprudence: as Administered in England and America (Hillard, Gray & Co, Boston, 1836) §§ 334, 439.

[6] ibid § 186 (quoting a Letter from Lord Hardwicke to Lord Kames (30 June 1759)). *Stonemets v Head*, 154 SW 108, 114 (Mo 1913). See also LA Sheridan, *Fraud in Equity: A Study in English and Irish Law* (Pitman & Sons 1957) 1–9.

[7] Aristotle, *The Nicomachean Ethics* (JL Ackrill and JO Urmson eds, David Ross tr, OUP rev edn, 1980) 133.

[8] Aristotle (n 7); see also Dennis Klimchuk, 'Equity and the Rule of Law' in Lisa M. Austin and Dennis Klimchuk (eds), *Private Law and the Rule of Law* (OUP 2014) 247; Klimchuk, this volume Chapter 2.

to more complicated single-level doctrine. Thus, shifting presumptions about constructive fraud give way to an all-things-considered fairness analysis, even if both can be shoehorned under the rubric of 'unconscionability'. Either way, fusion was a form of flattening.

In this chapter, I focus on philosophically and jurisprudentially inflected problems stemming from a flattening of equity through fusion. I begin in section II by isolating a function of equity as a second-order safety valve, and the tendency of fusion to flatten the legal system. Section III will identify the structural aftershocks of fusion in the modern debate between formalism and contextualism and the choice between rules and standards. Section IV will then take up substantive jurisprudential issues that trace back to the effacement of a structurally articulated equity. These more content-based instabilities include supposed broad shifts in private law like the 'death of contract' and the floodtide of tort, as well as the interpretation of the choice between rules and standards as reflecting a battle of large notions like autonomy and fairness. And finally even much of the debate between positivists and moralists can be seen as aftershocks of the flattening out of equity from the law. The chapter concludes with some conjectures about why the flattening of equity has had such profound consequences for law and legal philosophy.

II. The Equitable Dimension of the Legal System

'Equity' carries many meanings, many of which are associated in some way with the old equity jurisdiction and the law that it generated. As time went on and the equity administered by these special courts became rule-like, the idea took hold that the division between the courts was not only inconvenient but also arbitrary and counterproductive. Equitable notions—the substance of equity, such as fairness or discretion—could be found in parts of the common law as well, and many believed that they should apply more widely.[9] And by the late nineteenth century, the natural law and natural rights underpinnings of law and especially equity were increasingly called into question, making it seem less likely that a special court devoted to dispensing justice based on conscience made much sense.

'Fusion' has many meanings. In the first instance the merger of law and equity simply eliminates the dual court system. The single court is called upon to apply both law and equity, and invariably where the two courts would have given different answers the single court was to follow equity. Where does this leave the second-order safety valve function of equity, to the extent that traditional equity tended to serve it? In theory there need be no change; a single court could reason in multiple steps, through a stage

[9] *Dursley v Fitzhardinge Berkeley*, 6 Ves 251, 260 (1801; *Lord Eldon's Anecdote Book* (Anthony LJ Lincoln and Robert Lindley McEwen eds, Stevens & Sons 1960) 162 (Lord Eldon reporting Lord Chief Justice De Grey as saying that 'he never liked Equity so well as when it was like Law', and Lord Mansfield as saying that 'he never liked Law so well as when it was like Equity'); 3 Bl Comm 431 (arguing that the common law did not ignore equitable considerations).

of first-order law and then a possible second stage of 'meta law' that might alter the result from the first stage. However, without a high degree of self-consciousness, such an articulated kind of reasoning would be difficult to maintain—as it turned out to be. Instead, without a clear sense of how equity as meta law functions, the temptation is to streamline—and flatten—the law. I have argued elsewhere that in common law jurisdictions, and especially the United States, the fusion of law and equity has turned out in fact to be a process of ironing the equity—in the functional sense—out of the legal system.[10]

If allowed to operate, equity will give a different answer from the law's some of the time. And so those like Hohfeld and later the realists who focus on results will see a conflict. On the other hand, if we restrict ourselves to the first-order law, then equity does not conflict with law. Remove equity and the legal result would spring back. As with many paradoxes, there is a hidden problem of domain, especially domains at different levels, lurking in the background.[11]

Returning to fusion, those advocating and those carrying out fusion have overlooked the second-order equitable function. This did not mean that the special types of problems that call for second-order intervention disappeared. Nor does it mean that commentators and judges were unaware that something higher order than the ordinary law comes into play in legal reasoning and the development of the law. What is missing is the association of second-order conceptual structure with equity—equity as meta law.

In both the United States and the Commonwealth, there is certainly an awareness that there is more to law than the operation of first-order rules. In the United States, the approach to meta law is shaped by general realist-style scepticism about conceptualism. For the realists, concepts tended to be shallow and close to particulars.[12] Where adjustment was needed, the realists saw this as coming from freewheeling legal reasoning, informed by policy considerations outside the law. The idea that legal conceptual structure would itself contain a metalevel and that the relation of the second to the first level would be constrained by limited triggers would be needlessly confining to the realists. And the substance of equity probably carried too many associations with natural law to be congenial to the realists.

Instead, the realists emphasized other second-order aspects of the law and it is only here that we find traces of equity—shorn of its structure and limiting devices. Thus, the realists achieved a revolution in procedure that drew heavily on equity.[13] The idea was

[10] Henry E Smith, 'Fusing the Equitable Function in Private Law' in Kit Barker, Karen Fairweather, and Ross Grantham (eds), *Private Law in the 21st Century* (Hart 2017) 173.

[11] This is one tack taken in resolving the liar paradox. See eg Bradley Dowden, 'Liar Paradox' *Internet Encyclopedia of Philosophy* <www.iep.utm.edu/par-liar/#SH3b> accessed 27 April 2018; JC Beall, Michael Glanzberg, and David Ripley, 'Liar Paradox' *Stanford Encyclopedia of Philosophy* <https://plato.stanford.edu/entries/liar-paradox> accessed 27 April 2018. See also Margaret Cuonzo, *Paradox* (MIT Press 2014) 116–18.

[12] Henry E Smith, 'On the Economy of Concepts in Property' (2012) 160 University of Pennsylvania Law Review 2097, 2100–106.

[13] See eg Douglas Laycock, 'The Triumph of Equity' (Summer 1993) 56 Law & Contemporary Problems 53, 53 ('The distinctive traditions of equity now pervade the legal system. The war between law and equity is over. Equity won'); Thomas O Main, 'Traditional Equity and Contemporary Procedure' (2003) 78 Washington Law Review 429; Stephen N Subrin, 'How Equity Conquered Common Law: The Federal Rules of Civil Procedure in Historical Perspective' (1987) 135 University of Pennsylvania Law Review 909.

to free litigation from the straitjacket of the vestiges of the writ system and its associated procedure. Equity containing a strong strain of meta law might help explain why many fusionists gravitated to the idea that equity was merely procedural. As we will see, the realists had reason to overplay the notion of the formalism of their predecessors, and substantive equity did not fit with this caricature. Why procedure, though? Procedure is a kind of meta law: it governs the operation or carrying into effect of substantive law. The operation of procedure has substantive consequences and over time there is a noted tendency for procedure to shape substantive change, especially in the common law.[14] Thus, one could half-capture the idea of equity as meta law while playing down (but not entirely ignoring) its substantive aspect simply by calling it procedure.

Likewise, for the realists, purposive interpretation was the servant of the rise of the administrative state, and its proponents dusted off the 'equity of the statute'—equitable interpretation as applied to statutes—in order to give this looser, less formal style of statutory interpretation a historical pedigree.[15] Finally, societal values were associated with public law; and the constitution, legislatures, and even the administrative process could modify and modulate the law.[16] Constitutions are power conferring, and have been identified as 'meta law'.[17] Consistently with a 'principles-based' view of constitutional law, the post-realist paradigm tends to regard meta law as coming from outside the law. Again, the idea is that this higher-order aspect is not conceptual and not 'internal' to something called private law. Instead, it is all mixed together in one complex system, with the conceptual component a relatively shallow sideshow. On the one hand we have narrow shallow legal concepts and on the other a power in courts to fashion and refashion law in light of external policy considerations. In such an atmosphere, the more constricted sense of equity that found historical expression in the dual-court system would appear to be superseded.

Outside of the United States, realist anti-conceptualism has not held sway and so did not shape the path that fusion took. And yet fusion has strong proponents who express scepticism about the distinctiveness of equity.[18] Whereas in the United States we find multifactor tests and an emphasis on public law, Joshua Getzler finds an increased use of discretionary standards coupled with elaborated *ex ante* doctrines.[19] I would conjecture that these effects in English law stem from the difficulty of dealing with highly variable and uncertain problems like opportunism and multipolar interactions using a single-level conceptual structure.[20]

[14] Henry Sumner Maine, *Dissertations on Early Law and Custom* (Holt 1883) 389 ('[I]n the infancy of Courts of Justice ... substantive law has at first the look of being gradually secreted in the interstices of procedure').

[15] See eg JM Landis, 'Statutes and the Sources of Law' in *Harvard Legal Essays* (Harvard UP 1934) 213, 215, reprinted in (1965) 2 Harvard Journal on Legislation 7.

[16] Smith (n 3).

[17] Laurence H Tribe, *Constitutional Choices* (Harvard UP 1985) 246.

[18] Andrew Burrows, 'We Do This at Common Law But That in Equity' (2002) 22 OJLS 1; Sarah Worthington, *Equity* (2nd edn, OUP 2006) 323; Sarah Worthington, 'Integrating Equity and the Common Law' (2002) 55 CLP 223, 243–61.

[19] Joshua Getzler, 'Patterns of Fusion' in Peter Birks (ed), *The Classification of Obligations* (Clarendon Press 1997) 157, 192–93.

[20] Smith (n 10). Chaim Saiman theorizes that English and American law distribute doctrinal complexity differently in response to concerns about legitimacy: In the United States courts have developed elaborate public law doctrines of standing, immunity, federalism, and state action, and in England the complexity can be found

There is an irony at the heart of this revised story of fusion. Those engaged in the fusion project, particularly in its realist-inspired culminating phase in the United States, believed they were clear-eyed functionalists, who would not be swayed by stodgy tradition or sentimental history. And yet by overlooking an important functional aspect, they flattened it in a way that created a new set of troublesome consequences, including the need for a more cumbersome single-level law. A truly functional approach would lead us to re-evaluate fusion. A re-evaluation of something as seemingly technical as fusion should lead us to rethink or at least reframe some of the most familiar and enduring debates in legal theory.

III. Structural Effects

Effacing equity has contributed to the misframing of some fundamental dichotomies in legal theory. Their very status as 'dichotomies' is likely a symptom of the flattening of equity. Formalism versus contextualism and rules versus standards bear the tell-tale marks of the flattening of equity through hyper-fusion.

A. The Formalism Debate

Equity as meta law makes possible a certain hybrid between formalism and contextualism. Formalism versus contextualism is certainly a perennial debate in the law. In this section, I will suggest that our current debate was profoundly shaped by the fusion of law and equity and its consequent effacing of the hybrid system containing an equitable safety valve. The downplaying of equity or its identification with boundless discretion was sometimes calculated, sometimes inadvertent, but always consequential.

The conventional story sets fusion against a background of an eighteenth- and early-nineteenth-century freewheeling and moralistic 'Grand Style', being replaced by legal science and formalism, supplanted in its turn by waves of progressivism and legal realism.[21] Let me suggest that misunderstanding or ignoring the role of equity has caused this history to seem tidier than it was.

Recently, some have pointed out that the formalist era was not as formalist as is sometimes claimed.[22] Nevertheless, equity does not play much of a role in this discussion.

in private law doctrines such as those relating to restitution. Chaim Saiman, 'The Domain of Private Law: An Anglo vs. American Comparison' (draft, Sept 2018). The argument in the text dovetails with Saiman's theory: the flattening of equity in fusion led to complication in the characteristic parts of the law, in both the United States and England.

[21] See eg Grant Gilmore, *The Ages of American Law* (Yale UP 1978); Morton J Horwitz, *The Transformation of American Law, 1870–1960: The Crisis of Legal Orthodoxy* (OUP 1992); Duncan Kennedy, 'Form and Substance in Private Law Adjudication' (1976) 89 Harvard Law Review 1685, 1725–40.

[22] See eg Anthony J Sebok, *Legal Positivism in American Jurisprudence* (CUP 1998); Brian Z Tamanaha, *Beyond the Formalist–Realist Debate: The Role of Politics in Judging* (Princeton UP 2010); but see Brian Leiter, 'Legal Realism and Legal Doctrine' (2015) 163 University of Pennsylvania Law Review 1975, 1980–81 (arguing that nineteenth-century judges were not vulgar formalists or natural lawyers and providing sympathetic reconstruction of realist

'Classical Legal Thought' looks a lot more 'deductive' and formalistic when equity is left out of the picture.[23]

James Barr Ames saw equity as a vehicle for the law to incorporate morality and as an avenue for reform. For Ames, equity contributes to a hybrid system, and he was quite sensitive to the way equitable rights and remedies potentially impacted third parties: his work on the good faith purchaser was among his most important.[24] And in 'Law and Morals', he claims in an anti-Holmesian vein that:

> Enough has been said to make plain that much as our law owes to the action on the case for its ethical quality, it is to the principles of the court of equity, acting upon the conscience of the defendants and compelling them by decrees of restitution and specific performance to do what in justice and right they ought to do, that we must look to justify our belief that the English and American systems of law, however imperfect, are further on the road to perfection than those of other countries.[25]

More surprising still is that Ames's ally in moral and policy-oriented equity was none other than supposed arch-formalist and proponent of 'legal science' Christopher Columbus Langdell. Tony Sebok argues that Langdell was not the formalist in the familiar portrayal by Holmes and later by the realists.[26] To this we can add that, contrary to his image as the ultimate in deductive formalists,[27] a view tracing back to Holmes himself,[28] Langdell wrote extensively on equity and famously taught a course on it at the Harvard Law School.[29] His view of equity was anything but formalistic or rigid, even though, like Ames, he was aware of its limits. About equity, Langdell had this to say:

> [T]he object of equity, in assuming jurisdiction over legal rights, is to promote justice by supplying defects in the remedies which the courts of law afford ... [T]he jurisdiction is co-extensive with its object; that is, equity assumes jurisdiction over legal rights so far, and so far only, as justice can be thereby promoted.[30]

views on formalism without distortions of realism in Critical Legal Studies). See generally 'Forum: Once More unto the Breach: Late Nineteenth Century Jurisprudence Revisited' (2002) 20 Law & History Review 541.

[23] See eg Thomas C Grey, 'Langdell's Orthodoxy' (1983) 45 University of Pittsburgh Law Review 1, 13–14 (minimizing the significance of Langdell's work on equity). Kennedy uses the term 'equitable' to mean fair and does not discuss equity in terms of law versus equity, despite his concern with the history of nineteenth- and twentieth-century legal ideologies. Kennedy (n 21) 1685, 1700–01, 1710, 1726, 1728, 1743, 1751, 1775. See generally Horwitz (n 21).

[24] James Barr Ames, 'Purchase for Value without Notice' (1887) 1 Harvard Law Review 1, 9–10.

[25] James Barr Ames, 'Law and Morals' (1908) 22 Harvard Law Review 94, 108–109 (1908).

[26] Sebok (n 22) 60–103.

[27] See eg Thomas C Grey, 'Modern American Legal Thought' (1996) 106 Yale Law Journal 493, 493, 496.

[28] Oliver Wendell Holmes, 'Book Review' (1880) 14 American Law Review 233, 234. This caricature has been challenged, but not from the point of view of equity. Bruce A Kimball, 'Langdell on Contracts and Legal Reasoning: Correcting the Holmesian Caricature' (2007) 25 Law & History Review 345, 373–94; see also Bruce A Kimball, 'The Langdell Problem: Historicizing the Century of Historiography 1906–2000s' (2004) 22 Law & History Review 277.

[29] Franklin G Fessenden, 'The Rebirth of the Harvard Law School' (1920) 33 Harvard Law Review 493, 512 ('[Langdell] did not teach equity until 1873–74. His course in this subject brought the best results ever achieved by him, and was as successful as his treatise is enduring').

[30] CC Langdell, 'A Brief Survey of Equity Jurisdiction II' (1887) 1 Harvard Law Review 111, 116.

For the Langdellian equity judge, the question of jurisdiction itself is infused with morality and policy, requiring in cases of preventive injunction to ask: 'Will more perfect justice be done by preventing the tort than by leaving the plaintiff to his remedy at law? This, however, is a very complex question, depending partly upon the nature of the tort, and partly on other considerations.'[31] Langdell then goes on to discuss what we would call disproportionate hardship and extortion, and notes that there are limits to system in this area of law:

> Questions of jurisdiction do not receive the same careful and constant attention which is bestowed upon questions of substantive right; and therefore, in dealing with such questions, the elements of haste, accident, caprice, the habits of lawyers, the leanings of individual judges, and the ever-changing temper of public opinion, have been factors of no inconsiderable importance.[32]

Nowhere does Langdell suggest that this is fatal or requiring a formalistic remedy. Indeed, he notes that *ex post* contextualism is inherent in many of the wrongs for which equity intervenes:

> But an act which is in itself rightful, and which is wrongful only because of some effect which it produces, or some consequence which follows from it, can seldom be proved to be wrongful by *a priori* reasoning, or otherwise than by actual experience; and even when it does sufficiently appear that a given act done in a given way will be wrongful, it does not follow that some part of it may not be rightfully done, or even that the entire act may not be done in such a way as to be rightful. For these and similar reasons a court of equity frequently finds it impossible to interfere in case of a nuisance until the act which constitutes the nuisance is either fully completed, or at least far advanced towards completion; and, in either of the latter events, it will often be found that the damage to the defendant which the interference of the court will cause will be out of all proportion to the damage to the plaintiff which it will prevent.[33]

This is not formalism; it is closer to anti-formalism.[34] Nor was this a matter of mere remedy, as some of the proponents of a supposed classical Langdellian orthodoxy wrongly claim.[35] Moreover, Langdell was no opponent of moralism in the law, at least in the limited way that traditional equity allowed. All in all, the portrait of a Langdellian

[31] ibid 121.

[32] ibid 122.

[33] ibid 125–26.

[34] It certainly would not count as formalism according to the discussion in Duncan Kennedy, 'Legal Formalism' in Neil J Smelser and Paul B Baltes (eds), *Encyclopedia of the Social and Behavioral Sciences* (Elsevier 2001) vol 13 8624.

[35] Thomas Grey claims that '[i]t is fair to say that these arguments of justice and policy do not bulk large in the Langdellian corpus' (n 23) 15, and that '[a]pplying that distinction [of substantive law versus procedure and remedies], they [the 'classical scientists'] treated the distinction between law and equity, potentially an ideologically charged clash of governance by rule with judicial discretion, only as an aspect of the peripheral law of remedies' (citing CC Langdell, *A Summary of Equity Pleading* (2nd edn, Sever 1883) 27–40). This could hardly be more wrong. In the passage cited by Grey, Langdell had this to say:

legal system that emerges is one of a sophisticated hybrid, not the caricature familiar from the later progressive and legal realist eras.

Langdell and Ames did have an opponent in their view of equity at the time—none other than Oliver Wendell Holmes, Jr. Holmes is taken to be the pragmatist and proto-realist hero who started the process of slaying the formalist dragon. Holmes was not hostile to all morality in the law but opposed traditional and a priori-sounding moral notions and sought to put them on a more objective footing.[36] In particular, he was anti-equity. In one of his earliest articles, he argued that equity had not really contributed anything substantive to the law and that any signs to the contrary in earlier law were unimportant relics that had hung on a little longer through clerical influence.[37] Even more interestingly, Holmes did his best to leave out equity from his book *The Common Law* and his famous article, 'The Path of the Law'. His treatment of contracts as a promise to perform or pay damages, which has been taken as a precursor to the theory of efficient breach, was predicated on a dismissal of equity:

> Nowhere is the confusion between legal and moral ideas more manifest than in the law of contract. Among other things, here again the so called primary rights and duties are invested with a mystic significance beyond what can be assigned and explained. The duty to keep a contract *at common law* means a prediction that you must pay damages if you do not keep it,—and nothing else. If you commit a tort, you are liable to pay a compensatory sum. If you commit a contract, you are liable to pay a compensatory sum unless the promised event comes to pass, and that is all the difference. But such a mode of looking at the matter stinks in the nostrils of those who think it advantageous to get as much ethics into the law as they can.[38]

Whether Holmes really thought there was always an option to breach is open to question,[39] but Holmes did identify with the common law. He continued after the quoted passage in the same vein with a further discussion of an opinion by that champion of common law and foe of equity, Lord Coke,[40] and then with this disclaimer:

> Of course, however, it must not be supposed that equity in modern times is simply a different system of remedies from those administered in courts of law; for there are many extensive doctrines in equity, and some whole branches of law, which are unknown to the common-law courts. Indeed, it may be said without impropriety that equity is a great legal system, which has grown up by the side of the common law, and which, while consistent with the latter, is in great measure independent of it. But what should be clearly understood is, that the whole of this growth has its root in the system of remedies adopted. It has often been said that it is the office of chancery to mitigate the rigor of the common law, to supply its deficiencies, to relieve against its technical rules, and to decide controversies according to equity and good conscience; but it is because of its system of remedies that it is enabled to do this.
>
> CC Langdell, *A Summary of Equity Pleading* (2nd edn, Sever 1883) § 45, 40–41

[36] See eg Oliver Wendell Holmes, Jr, *The Common Law* (Little, Brown, and Company 1881) 130–40; David Rosenberg, *The Hidden Holmes: His Theory of Torts in History* (Harvard UP 1995) 42–68 (discussing the 'new jurisprudence').

[37] OW Holmes, Jr, 'Early English Equity' (1885) 1 LQR 162, 173–74.

[38] Oliver Wendell Holmes, 'The Path of the Law' (1897) 10 Harvard Law Review 457, 462 (emphasis added).

[39] Joseph M Perillo, 'Misreading Oliver Wendell Holmes on Efficient Breach and Tortious Interference' (2000) 68 Fordham Law Review 1085, 1086–87.

[40] *Bromage v Genning* (1616) 81 Eng Rep 540 (KB) (denying specific performance for a covenant to grant a lease). Holmes had this to say about the case:

> I have spoken only of the common law, because there are some cases in which a logical justification can be found for speaking of civil liabilities as imposing duties in an intelligible sense. These are the relatively few in which equity will grant an injunction, and will enforce it by putting the defendant in prison or otherwise punishing him unless he complies with the order of the court. But I hardly think it advisable to shape general theory from the exception, and I think it would be better to cease troubling ourselves about primary rights and sanctions altogether, than to describe our prophecies concerning the liabilities commonly imposed by the law in those inappropriate terms.[41]

To Holmes, equity was marginal and anomalous, as opposed to law, which was better understood as 'a body of dogma enclosed within definite lines'.[42]

Interestingly, in playing up the objective common law and downplaying equity, Holmes treated the common law and all of law as *always* aimed at the opportunist—in a sense a clever version of the Holmesian 'bad man'.[43] In other words, Holmes could delink equity and anti-opportunism by assuming that everyone is in bad faith. The law would do the best it could in light of the bad man and not wring its hands over behaviour that could not be reached. Indeed, Holmes's attitude towards opportunism is echoed in versions the rational actor paradigm that see nothing special in opportunists simply responding to incentives.[44]

Holmes was a violent opponent of natural rights and natural law, and the bigger picture here is that when fusion happened, opponents of these earlier ways of understanding rights had to do something with equity. It is true that in the mid-nineteenth century equity had been formulated in a natural rights framework, and some of its most famous proponents in the United States, Joseph Story and James Kent, were federalists of a pragmatic and mildly natural law bent.[45] But anti-opportunism has been

> In *Bromage v. Genning*, a prohibition was sought in the King's Bench against a suit in the marches of Wales for the specific performance of a covenant to grant a lease, and Coke said that it would subvert the intention of the covenantor, since he intends it to be at his election either to lose the damages or to make the lease. Sergeant Harris for the plaintiff confessed that he moved the matter against his conscience, and a prohibition was granted. This goes further than we should go now, but it shows what I venture to say has been the common law point of view from the beginning, although Mr. Harriman, in his very able little book upon Contracts has been misled, as I humbly think, to a different conclusion.
> (n 81) 462 (fn omitted)

See also Perillo (n 39) 1086 n 6 (noting that Holmes mentions this case as having been earlier law in an opinion for the United States Supreme Court and quoting Holmes as saying '[t]he old law seems to have regarded it as technically in the election of the promisor to perform or to pay damages. Bromage v. Genning, 1 Roll. R. 368; Hubert v. Hart, 1 Vern. 133'), citing *Globe Ref Co v Landa Cotton Oil Co*, 190 US 540, 543 (1903).

[41] Holmes (n 38) 462–63.

[42] ibid 459.

[43] ibid.

[44] See Yoram Barzel, 'Transaction Costs: Are They Just Costs?' (1985) 141 Journal of Institutional and Theoretical Economics 4, 10–11 (arguing that because it is costly to tell whether someone is acting in a self-seeking manner and not 'as he should', the concept of opportunism does not help in understanding behaviour and only confuses); Peter Klein, 'Does Transaction Cost Economics Need Opportunism?' 6 October 2006 <http://organizationsandmarkets.com/2006/10/06/does-transaction-cost-economics-need-opportunism>; see also Oliver E Williamson, 'Opportunism and Its Critics' (1993) 14 Managerial & Decision Economics 97 (defending usefulness of notion of opportunism against social science critics); Leo Katz, 'A Theory of Loopholes' (2010) 39 Journal Legal Studies 1.

[45] Calvin Woodward, 'Joseph Story and American Equity' (1988) 45 Washington & Lee Law Review 623, 627–30 (noting Story's approval of natural law but the small role it played in his approach to equity).

a theme of equity as it has gone through many shifts, from overtly religious roots in canon law, to secularized natural law, to a more pluralistic version—or whatever to call the equity espoused by those like Langdell and Ames—during the process of fusion. Equity as anti-opportunism can even be analysed in a law-and-economics framework as well.[46]

Judges and commentators of the twentieth century could have formulated equity in a fashion consistent with a wide range of schools including pragmatism and utilitarianism, but instead equity was treated as an embarrassment. The moral overtones of equity were now unwelcome, but equally importantly, equity stood in the way of regarding the law as hopelessly rigid and outdated. In particular, if the account of equity as a second-order safety valve has merit, it was equity—to the extent it served this function—that allowed the common law to be relatively formal without causing undue rigidity in the legal system overall. Thus, by focusing on the formalism of the common law, realists and others of like mind were not presenting the legal system in its best light or even presenting an accurate picture. The caricature of late nineteenth-century legal thought as woodenly formalistic required the erasure of equity.

This standoff over formalism lives on today. Because courts and commentators have partially effaced the second-order equitable function that makes a special hybrid between formalism and contextualism possible, the two positions tend to be exaggerated. It's all equity all the time or extreme cabining or attempted abolition. I have shown elsewhere how this polarization plays out in the new formalism in contract law as a reaction to post-realism.[47] In corporate law, formalism versus contextualism is at the centre of the debate over the role and merits of Delaware corporate law, which is the province of one of the few remaining American equity courts.[48] It can also be found in debates over statutory interpretation,[49] and even in the Supreme Court's equity jurisprudence.[50] On the one side formalists will look to whether equity jurisdiction in 1789 covered a particular device like the asset-freezing injunction, and on the other contextualists give unqualified praise to an unconstrained generative power of equity.[51] Neither position does justice to the possibility of an intermediate hybrid of law and equity, with the latter as a second-order safety valve on the former.

[46] Henry E Smith, 'Equity as Second-Order Law: The Problem of Opportunism' (15 January 2015) (unpublished MS) <http://ssrn.com/abstract=2617413>

[47] Henry E Smith, 'The Equitable Dimension of Contract' (2012) 45 Suffolk University Law Review 897; Henry Smith, 'Is Equitable Contract Law a Pipe Dream? <http://blogs.harvard.edu/nplblog/2016/06/09/is-equitable-contract-law-a-pipe-dream-henry-smith>

[48] See Andrew S Gold and Henry E Smith, 'The Equity in Corporate Law' (MS).

[49] See eg Guido Calabresi, *A Common Law for the Age of Statutes* (Harvard UP 1982) 5–7; William N Eskridge, Jr, *Dynamic Statutory Interpretation* (Harvard UP 1995); Richard A Posner, *The Problems of Jurisprudence* (Harvard UP 1990) 247–309; Adrian Vermeule, *Judging under Uncertainty* (Harvard UP 2006); Antonin Scalia, *A Matter of Interpretation* (Princeton UP 1998); Abbe R Gluck, 'The States as Laboratories of Statutory Interpretation: Methodological Consensus and the New Modified Textualism' (2010) 119 Yale Law Journal 1750; John F Manning, 'Textualism and the Equity of the Statute' (2011) 101 Columbia Law Review 1, 22–23; Caleb Nelson, 'What Is Textualism?' (2005) 91 Virginia Law Review 347.

[50] Samuel L Bray, 'The Supreme Court and the New Equity' (2015) 68 Vanderbilt Law Review 997.

[51] *Grupo Mexicano de Desarrollo, SA v Alliance Bond Fund, Inc*, 527 US 308 (1999). See generally Stephen B Burbank, 'The Bitter with the Sweet: Tradition, History, and Limitations on Federal Judicial Power—A Case Study' (2000) 75 Notre Dame Law Review 1291 (analysing *Grupo Mexicano* case).

B. Rules versus Standards

Related to the formalism debate is the question of *ex ante* rules versus *ex post* standards. Indeed, the debate over equity often devolved into a referendum on rules, with defenders of the common law disparaging equity for its excessive discretion. Today rules find able defenders among philosophers.[52] Seeing traditional equity as partially reflecting an equitable function of second-order adjustment casts the rules versus standards debate in a new light. In the US legal literature rules are distinguished from standards based on factors like the timing of decision-making, the degree of discretion at the point of application and the amount of contextual detail of the situation at hand that is treated as relevant.[53] Speed limits versus mandates to drive reasonably under the conditions are the prototypical example. Through this lens, equity is often taken to embody—or consist of—standards as opposed to rules. On the account offered here, this sells equity short: equity can accomplish at a second level what sometimes cannot be handled well—by either rules or standards—at the primary level of the law.

Emily Sherwin argues that equity has to be either self-defeating or deceptive.[54] The danger is that equity will undermine the benefits of rules. A good rule is one which gives better results if followed over the long run, even if it leads to mistakes in given cases. The problem is that deviating from the rule when it seems like a good idea means the rule cannot save the decision maker from the mistakes it was designed to prevent.[55]

This is a real concern and it is at its greatest when all decision-making occurs on a single level. The mistakes the rule is designed to prevent and the departures all happen on the same level, and the one will bleed into the other. If, however, the presumption is for a first-order rule, which can only be overcome through a proxy for special problems requiring the second order. The combined system can partake of the advantages and disadvantages of both systems. If the triggers are good ones, the benefits from specialization overcome the errors of both systems and the cost of two-level decision-making.[56] Whether this is so and under what circumstances is a good question.

[52] See Larry Alexander and Emily Sherwin, *The Rule of Rules: Morality, Rules, and the Dilemmas of Law* (Duke UP 2001); Fred Schauer, *Playing by the Rules: A Philosophical Examination of Rule-Based Decision-Making in Law and in Life* (Clarendon Press 1991); E Sherwin, this volume Chapter 12.

[53] Louis Kaplow, 'Rules versus Standards: An Economic Analysis' (1992) 42 Duke Law Journal 557; Kathleen M Sullivan, Foreword: The Justices of Rules and Standards (1992) Harvard Law Review 22.

[54] Emily Sherwin, 'Equity and the Modern Mind' in Goldberg, Turner, and Smith (eds) (n 4) 353, 368–70.

[55] Alternatively, Sherwin notes that equity might relay on acoustic separation, in which legal directives are disseminated though the common law and equity acts in a covert fashion such that the rules are not undermined for primary actors (ibid). See Meir Dan-Cohen, 'Decision Rules and Conduct Rules: On Acoustic Separation in Criminal Law' (1984) 97 Harvard Law Review 625. I would argue that the equity reflects a different kind of acoustic separation. Equity is not secret or deceptive; it sends the same message to good faith and bad faith actors, while the message is taken as reassuring by the former and as a threat by the latter. Yuval Feldman and Henry E Smith, 'Behavioral Equity' (2014) 170 Journal of Institutional & Theoretical Economics 137.

[56] For a discussion of triggers and specialization in the context of two modes of dealing with the evaluation of corporate sale transactions, see Einer Elhauge, 'The Triggering Function of Sale of Control Doctrine' (1992) 59 University of Chicago Law Review 1465. Tellingly, the doctrine in that context is an equitable one applied by a separate court of equity.

It exceeds the scope of this chapter to theorize about how the triggers for equity evolved, but it is worth pointing out that the equitable structure is not unlike that involved in moral reasoning. Philip Pettit argues that our moral reasoning should be guided by general dispositions until warned by certain 'contextual cues', 'red lights', or 'alarm bells'. At this point 'stand-by guide'-style general principles of right kick in.[57] He offers the humorous (in a way) example of the saying that a good friend will help you move an apartment but only a very good friend will help you move a body.[58] Automatic loyalty to friends is appropriate until a red light—like a possible murder—triggers a different set of principles. This structure and the kind of morality—general and approximate versus principled in tailored fashion—is quite reminiscent of the equitable safety valve I am proposing. Interestingly, when it comes to the triggers themselves, Pettit views the use of cues in moral psychology as being like Aristotle's 'phronesis' and Aquinas's 'prudentia'.[59] There is no doubt that equity requires a kind of prudence or wisdom in its application.

More generally, the relationship of rules to standards is more complex than is usually thought. While the choice does have to do with the timing of decision-making,[60] the nature of the hybrid—here first versus second level—also matters. The relation between rules and standards need not be mono-level, and the possibility of meta law potentially solves some of the concerns equity raises. The key to combining rules and standards is what the triggers are for moving from one to the other.

In this, equity is more like a metarule, another familiar device from philosophy and computer science.[61] Equity overrides the law but not vice versa. There is no conflict at any given level. And it is only relevant to ask whether the output of the entire system is consistent. As with many paradoxes, the problem is one of domain. Indeed, a classic method to avoid paradoxes is to distinguish language and metalanguage.[62] Law and equity have different domains, and to some extent the former is the domain for the latter, such that equity operates at a metalevel.

IV. Substantive Effects

The possibility of metalevel equity allows us to see many jurisprudential controversies, especially those relating to formalism versus contextualism, in a new and clearer light. Modern theories of altruism and fairness in the law, of very different stripes, need to be

[57] Philip Pettit, *The Robust Demands of the Good: Ethics with Attachment, Virtue, and Respect* (OUP 2015) 221.

[58] ibid.

[59] ibid 222. Aristotle (n 7) 142–44; St T Aquinas, *Summa Theologiae* (Fathers of the English Dominican Province trs, Christian Classics, 1981) IIaIIae 47.2 ad 1, IIaIIae 47.4.

[60] See eg Kaplow (n 53).

[61] Metarules play a crucial role in the system of the great Indian grammarian Pāṇini of the fourth century BC. In his system, some rules will turn other rules on or off. See George Cardona, *Pāṇini: A Survey of Research* (Mouton 1976) 193–95; SD Joshi and Paul Kiparsky, 'The Extended *siddha*-Principle', Annals of the Bhandarkar Oriental Research Institute 2005, 1–26 (2006), <http://web.stanford.edu/~kiparsky/Papers/siddha.new.pdf>.

[62] See (n 11) and accompanying text.

supplemented by the possibility of a law-equity hybrid. The theory of equity as meta law furnishes in part just such a theory.

A. Death of Contract and Rampant Tort Law

In a self-conscious echo of Nietzsche, realist Grant Gilmore declared the death of contract.[63] At the same time, the law of torts started growing profusely in response to policies pointing to expanded liability. Tort was even said to have swallowed contract, and even in England Patrick Atiyah argued that contract's brief and artificial separation from tort in the late nineteenth and early twentieth centuries had come to an end.[64] The flattening of equity leaves its traces here too.

Exhibit A for Gilmore was promissory estoppel. He saw the adoption of section 90 of the First Restatement of Contract as the application of tort principles in order to expand liability in the area of contracts.[65] Although the roots of promissory estoppel are complex, they do include equity and equitable-style thinking.[66] Indeed, some reliance on pre-contractual promises can be the result of the kind of opportunism that would have gone under the equitable heading of 'constructive fraud'.

For Gilmore, the death of contract happened at the hands of tort, because the former was being reabsorbed into the latter: 'Classical contract theory might well be described as an attempt to stake out an enclave within the general domain of tort. The dykes which were set up to protect the enclave have, it is clear enough, been crumbling at a progressively rapid rate.'[67] Although he allowed for the possibility of resurrection, he concluded that 'the fate of contract to be swallowed up by tort (or both of them to be swallowed up in a generalized theory of civil obligation)'.[68]

This is a more general pattern. Tort serves as the post-equity version of a no-holds-barred equity.[69] Post-realist tort is an all-purpose tool, in contrast to a competing older tradition of torts as a law of wrongs. Recasting equity decisions as sounding in tort was one method of implementing the realist programme of contextualized policymaking and change in private law.

Flattening equity made equity decisions more usable in this supercharged tort that expanded and swallowed parts of contract and is giving rise to new torts like interference with inheritance.[70] These new torts displace traditional more equity-style approaches based on restitution.[71] Thus, misguided fusion of the flattening sort has fed a whole new way of thinking about private law.

[63] Grant Gilmore, *The Death of Contract* (Ohio State UP 1974) ('We are told that Contract, like God, is dead. And so it is.') 3.

[64] PS Atiyah, Contracts, 'Promises and the Law of Obligations' in *Essays on Contract* (Clarendon 1986) 10.

[65] Gilmore (n 63) 72.

[66] Eric Mills Holmes, 'The Four Phases of Promissory Estoppel' (1996) 20 Seattle University Law Review 46.

[67] Gilmore (n 63) 87.

[68] ibid 94.

[69] Goldberg and Smith (n 4).

[70] See John CP Goldberg and Robert H Sitkoff, 'Torts and Estates: Remedying Wrongful Interference with Inheritance' (2013) 65 Stanford Law Review 335, 351–53.

[71] ibid 368–74.

B. Altruism and Fairness

Casting equity as a second-order safety valve permits us to defuse some of the stark dichotomies sometimes attributed, knowingly or not, to the law–equity divide. One such dichotomy is altruism versus individualism.

Duncan Kennedy in a landmark article set out two world views reflected in the rhetoric of the law and aligned them with rules versus standards.[72] For Kennedy, rules promote and reflect an individualistic outlook: one can exercise one's freedoms up to the point at which they bump against someone else's rights, and one can exercise rights without regard to others' interests—as long as the activity in question falls within the right. By contrast, standards, according to Kennedy, promote and reflect an altruistic world view: the standard is applied *ex post* with regard to the fairness of the situation as it has developed. In Kennedy's view, standards are applied in a way that fosters concern for others.

The alignment of formalist rules with individualism and contextualist standards with altruism can be questioned.[73] For one thing, clear rules can form the basis for norms of sharing. And under some circumstances a rule of strict liability might encourage greater sharing of misfortunes than a contextualized standard of negligence, which allows an injurer to avoid liability when the standard of reasonable care has been met.

And yet, Kennedy's dichotomy has an intuitive appeal. For one thing, as we have seen, equity has to some extent been reinterpreted as unbounded contextualism in the service of breaking down the baselines of private law in favour of a supposedly more social approach. Indeed, Kennedy's intellectual history of nineteenth- and twentieth-century jurisprudence in terms of individualism and altruism can be seen as an example of exactly this. On a more micro level, Kennedy can certainly point to numerous examples of *ex post* standards being at least couched in terms of *ex post* fairness. Not coincidentally, many of these examples stem from historic equity. Nevertheless, Kennedy does not treat them as falling under a category of equity; indeed, he barely mentions 'equity' at all. Sifting the rhetoric of judicial opinions through a lens of individualism and altruism, as he does, has its severe limits. Equity had a defined role, both during the period of the 'Grand Style' earlier in the nineteenth century and in the supposed classical legal thought later in the century, and that role is not exhausted by its effects of promoting altruism. And, when it comes to explaining developments in equity at the turn of the last century, we should look to the breakdown of natural rights and the contemporaneous fusion of law and equity against a background of rapid social change.[74]

[72] Kennedy (n 21).

[73] See eg Anthony J Duggan, 'Is Equity Efficient?' (1997) 113 LQR 601, 628–29. In his discussion of rules and standards, Mark Kelman does note that 'the rules position is associated with the traditional common law domain, the standards position with the traditional equity domain', and notes that modern commentators see no reason to keep decisions from the two types of court apart. Mark Kelman, *A Guide to Critical Legal Studies* (Harvard UP 1987) 38. Also, the vast literature on rules and standards in law and economics provides a very different take on the dichotomy. See Kaplow (n 53).

[74] Henry E Smith, 'Custom in American Property Law: A Vanishing Act' (2013) 48 Texas International Law Journal 507.

Equity as a second-order safety valve allows us to capture what is appealing in Kennedy's theory, without going as far as seeing the constant clashing of opposing world views in the law–equity divide. Kennedy recognizes that rules promote selfish behaviour in the form of 'walking the line' in order to comply with the rule while violating its spirit.[75] This classic form of opportunism requires in response not only standards but a move to meta law. Equity as meta law by the nature of its function needs to be ex post and is non-accidentally framed in moral terms, especially when it comes to fraud. It does, in a limited way, promote altruism, in the sense that opportunistic advantage taking—an act of selfishness to be sure—is singled out for unfavourable treatment.

C. Law and Morality

The flattening of equity through fusion has implications for the relationship of law and morality. At the most basic level, the second-order equitable safety valve allows for a kind of combination of two kinds of morality, one reflecting the fairness of general rules and the other the attempt at greater accuracy of contextualized justice. Removing this combination makes the problem of reconciling law and morality more difficult.

By eliminating the second-order equitable function, the choices in the moral arena are similar and related to those discussed under the heading of formalism and contextualism. If equity is not a separate mode that is triggered some of the time, the choice devolves into one where equity is operative or at least available in principle all of the time or it is ruled out most or all of the time. As with formalism and contextualism, the debate becomes more polarized than it otherwise would be.

It is well recognized that equity traditionally served as a conduit for natural law thinking to make its way into the law.[76] When equity could apply the standards of conscience, it would often make reference to natural law. Today a philosophical commitment to natural law is far from universal among those who seek to reconstitute equity in current law. Perhaps given the structure of the equitable safety valve, the more limited invocation of moral considerations can allow an overlapping consensus or incompletely theorized agreement to license the use of context in this more limited domain.[77]

Likewise, equity traditionally invokes custom and commercial morality when it intervenes in the law. This use of custom and commercial morality is far different from the attempt by the realists—including Llewellyn in the Uniform Commercial Code and various Restatement reporters—to adopt commercial custom as a legal standard.[78] The use of custom and commercial morality *ex post* in an environment of presumptive opportunism to defeat a suspect transaction is different from attempting to define *ex ante*

[75] Kennedy (n 21) 1695–96.

[76] RH Helmholz, *Natural Law in Court: A History of Legal Theory in Practice* (Harvard UP 2015) 37–38.

[77] John Rawls, 'The Idea of an Overlapping Consensus' (1987) 7 OJLS 1; Cass R Sunstein, *Legal Reasoning and Political Conflict* (OUP 1997) 35–38.

[78] See eg Lisa Bernstein, 'The Questionable Empirical Basis of Article 2's Incorporation Strategy: A Preliminary Study' (1999) 66 University of Chicago Law Review 710; Alan Schwartz and Robert E Scott, 'The Political Economy of Private Legislatures' (1995) 143 University of Pennsylvania Law Review 595.

obligations in detail. Because it is specialized in this fashion, equity can be far less informationally demanding. Indeed, the demands of information are often invoked as a drawback to Dworkin's interpretivist theory.[79] Interestingly, Dworkin often draws on equitable principles,[80] but needless to say not structured as a second-order safety valve.

Conversely, equity as meta law offers a potentially more constrained version of the morality of law. Elsewhere I argue that because legislatures and courts can themselves act opportunistically in trying to evade the requirements of the rule of law, a macro version of equity may be necessary to support any system of law.[81] Equity as meta law allows a range of unexplored combinations of formalism and open texture, some of which may be better at or even required for serving the rule of law. Overall, if the possibility of equity as meta law is left out of the picture, we are bound to distort a range of jurisprudential debates.

As a cautionary tale in many ways, consider the *über*-chestnut case of *Riggs v Palmer*.[82] The case illustrates how the flattening of equity in the fusion process leads to problematic results and to a host of jurisprudential interpretations that need to be rethought in the light of equity as meta law.

In *Riggs*, the court was faced with a grandson claiming an inheritance from a grandfather he had killed with the purpose of preventing him from changing his will. Under the existing will, Francis Palmer, a widower, provided for bequests to his daughters with the rest of his estate going to grandson Elmer and for support of Francis's mother, Susan Palmer.[83] Upon remarriage, Francis entered into a prenuptial agreement that required him to amend the will to include a provision of lifetime support for his new wife, Mrs Bresee (in lieu of dower).[84] Elmer poisoned his grandfather to prevent the changes and to get his property. After Elmer was convicted of second-degree murder, the deceased's daughters sued to prevent title to the assets from passing to Elmer.

The court per Judge Earl held for the daughters, invoking a 'fundamental maxim[] of the common law' that '[n]o one shall be permitted to profit by his own fraud, or to take advantage of his own wrong, or to found any claim upon his own iniquity, or to acquire property by his own crime'.[85] The court also applied equitable interpretation to the Wills Act to prevent its operation in Elmer's favour. In the end, the court held the transfer to Elmer void and vested title in the daughters as qualified by the interests of Francis Palmer's mother and his wife. Judge Gray's dissent countered that the Wills Act

[79] See eg Steven J Burton, 'Particularism, Discretion, and the Rule of Law' in Ian Shapiro (ed), *The Rule of Law* (NYU Press 1994) 178; Robert Justin Lipkin, 'Beyond Skepticism, Foundationalism and the New Fuzziness: The Role of Wide Reflective Equilibrium in Legal Theory' (1990) 75 Cornell Law Review 811, 841–49.

[80] Frederick Schauer, 'The Jurisprudence of Reasons (Review of Law's Empire, by Ronald Dworkin)' (1987) 85 Michigan Law Review 847, 863–65.

[81] Henry E Smith, 'Property, Equity, and the Rule of Law' in Lisa M. Austin and Dennis Klimchuk (eds), *Private Law and the Rule of Law* (OUP 2014) 224.

[82] 22 NE 188 (NY 1889).

[83] ibid 188. The will also provided that if Elmer predeceased the daughters, they would receive the estate subject to the support of Mrs Palmer.

[84] ibid 189.

[85] ibid. The court labelled the principle a 'common law' one in order to promote the fusion of law versus equity begun in New York in the Field Code in 1848. See Note, 'Can a Murderer Acquire Title by His Crime?' (1891) 4 Harvard Law Review 394, 395 (attributing decisions like *Riggs v Palmer* to the confusion of law and equity as a result of their jurisdictional fusion).

made no exceptions and that punishment for Elmer was provided for and had been applied through the criminal law.

Let's start with the case as an exemplar of equity. The maxim invoked is one of the traditional maxims of equity (and equitable reasoning in common law),[86] but it is here relabelled one at common law, possibly as an attempt to implement fusion in the New York Field Code. The substance of the reasoning is indeed equitable: taking stock of the entire situation to prevent opportunism and going beyond the letter of the will and the statute. Moreover, the Wills Act was probably passed against a background of equitable intervention that would have covered the so-called slayer problem.[87] The remedy, however, exhibits a flattening of equity. As James Barr Ames and a number of student note writers pointed out, the alternative to declaring the transfer to Elmer void would be to recognize the transfer (legally) but subject it to an (equitable) constructive trust in favour of the daughters.[88] By contrast, the flattening of equity in *Riggs* here has significant negative consequences, for example if Elmer had sold the property to a good faith third party.[89] As among an identified group of claimants and an indefinite set of potential good faith purchasers, the equitable solution shows great promise.

Interestingly, *Riggs* has launched a thousand jurisprudential theories, or at least served as the ultimate 'old jurisprudential chestnut'.[90] But its status as a jurisprudential chestnut stems in part from the flattening of equity in fusion. Theorists who invoke *Riggs* are attracted by the dichotomy between regularity and particularity, between certainty and morality, and the like. Among such treatments are those of renowned judges and scholars including Pound,[91] Cardozo,[92] Dworkin,[93]

[86] Peter W Young, Clyde Croft, and Megan Louise Smith, *On Equity* (Lawbook Co 2009), 203 (discussing maxim as equitable but with origins in both equity and law).

[87] The Wills Act was passed against a backdrop of equitable, and in particular English ecclesiastical law, which likely would have reached the same result as in *Riggs*. See Robert Ludlow Fowler, *Decedent Estate Law of the State of New York* (Ulan Press 1911) 52. Generally, states have since passed statutes dealing with the slayer problem. Robert H Sitkoff and Jesse Dukeminier, *Wills, Trusts, and Estates* (10th edn, Aspen 2017) 133; see also Restatement (Third) of Restitution and Unjust Enrichment § 45 (2011) ('A slayer's acquisition, enlargement, or accelerated possession of an interest in property as a result of the victim's death constitutes unjust enrichment that the slayer will not be allowed to retain'); Nili Cohen, 'The Slayer Rule' (2012) 92 Boston University Law Review 793.

[88] James Barr Ames, 'Can a Murderer Acquire Title by His Crime and Keep It?' (1897) 45 American Law Register 225; Note, 'Can a Murderer Acquire a Title by His Crime?' (1890) 4 Harvard Law Review 394; Note, 'Can a Murderer Acquire a Title by His Crime?' (1894) 8 Harvard Law Review 170; Note, 'Can a Murderer Acquire a Title by His Crime?' (1896) 9 Harvard Law Review 474.

[89] See Note, 'Vesting Title in a Murderer: Where Is the Equity in the Georgia Supreme Court's Interpretation of the Slayer Statute in Levinson?' (2011) 45 Georgia Law Review 877; Grant Gilmore, 'The Commercial Doctrine of Good Faith Purchase' (1954) 63 Yale Law Journal 1057, 1059–62 (describing the consequences for third parties who acquire void versus voidable title in fraudulently transferred property—the latter privileges good-faith purchasers for value over true owners). Proponents rationalize this policy as promoting finality in commercial transactions. See Andrew Kull, 'Rationalizing Restitution' (1995) 83 California Law Review 1191, 1234.

[90] Posner (n 49) 105.

[91] Roscoe Pound, 'Spurious Interpretation' (1907) 7 Columbia Law Review 379, 382–83 (arguing that spurious interpretation by courts in cases like *Riggs* used to be unavoidable but would become less needed in an era of increased legislation); Pound seems to have come later to agree with Ames that the constructive trust is a simple solution to the problem in cases like *Riggs*. Roscoe Pound, 'The Progress of the Law—Equity' (1920) 33 Harvard Law Review 420, 421 ('If one bears in mind the purely remedial nature of constructive trust, the results which courts have reached in this sort of case are attained with much less difficulty.').

[92] Benjamin N Cardozo, *The Nature of the Judicial Process* (Yale UP 1921) 40–43 (treating *Riggs* as evidence of the need for judges to choose among competing principles).

[93] Ronald Dworkin, *Taking Rights Seriously* (Harvard UP 1977) 17–45.

Posner,[94] Calabresi,[95] Farber,[96] and Leiter.[97] *Riggs* forms the basis of chapter I of Hart and Sacks's *Legal Process*,[98] and is taught in basic statutory interpretation.[99] It is the central example in Dworkin's morally oriented jurisprudence of right answers.[100] Most of these theories and the related cases key off the majority opinion and reflect a post-fusion equity that is at once mono-level and pervasive, and not confined to the types of problems like opportunism and conflicting rights that call for two-level treatment. Arrayed against them are formalists who also see the choice in stark terms and, inspired by the dissent in *Riggs*, regard the opinion as a cautionary tale in judicial overreach.[101] These approaches all overread *Riggs*, because a more genuinely equitable version of *Riggs* need not raise this stark dichotomy.[102] Instead, the jurisprudential treatment of *Riggs* is a symptom of the hole that flattening by fusion has left in the jurisprudential toolbox.

Why has fusion led to this flattening of the law? It is tempting to see the American version of fusion as partaking of the legal realists' wish to trivialize the law, the better to replace it with something more to their liking. Legal realists thought they were being pragmatic and even invoked contemporary philosophical positivism in order to rid law of the metaphysical. Felix Cohen's disdain of legal concepts as transcendental nonsense may have been extreme,[103] but even more moderate legal realism put a heavy thumb on the scale for shallow concepts.[104] And yet fusion has led to a significant amount of flattening in other common law jurisdictions, where realism never took hold. Thus, although something travelling under the heading of 'equity' may appear to feature strongly in English and Commonwealth law, it often reflects a flattening of a different sort: the replacement of second-order adjustment with elaborate first-order standards and highly detailed *ex ante* rules.[105]

[94] Posner (n 49) 105–07.

[95] See eg Calabresi (n 49) 5–7.

[96] Daniel A Farber, 'Courts, Statutes, and Public Policy: The Case of the Murdering Heir' (2000) 53 SMU Law Review 31 (analysing *Riggs* in terms of the Hart–Dworkin debate); Schauer (n 95) 196–206 (discussing the role of the statute in Dworkin's approach to *Riggs*).

[97] Brian Leiter, 'Explaining Theoretical Disagreement' (2009) 76 University of Chicago Law Review 1215, 1217–20, 1232–36, 1240–47 (arguing that *Riggs* was about punishment and more consistent with positivism than Dworkin's theory).

[98] Henry M Hart, Jr and Albert M Sacks, *The Legal Process: Basic Problems in the Making and Application of Law* (10th edn 1958) 75–110. This is true of the current edition as well. See also William N Eskridge, Jr and Philip P Frickey, 'The Making of *The Legal Process*' (1994) 107 Harvard Law Review 2031, 2043.

[99] John F Manning and Matthew C Stephenson, *Legislation and Regulation* (3rd edn, Aspen 2017) 36–44 (presenting excerpt of *Riggs* and discussing the opinion as an example of a court allowing the spirit of a law to trump its letter); Caleb E Nelson, *Statutory Interpretation* (Foundation Press 2011) 5–27.

[100] Dworkin (n 93) 17–45 (analysing *Riggs* as a case of a principle determining a legal result); Ronald Dworkin, *Law's Empire* (Harvard UP 1986) 15–20, 122–23 (analysing *Riggs* as a search for legislative intent); Ronald Dworkin, 'Reflections on Fidelity' (1997) 65 Fordham Law Review 1799 (seeing in *Riggs* a judicial search for law).

[101] Not everyone is a formalist or contextualist in this debate. For example, Leiter criticizes the majority in *Riggs* for in effect increasing the criminal punishment, a concern which equity as meta law might partially defuse.

[102] Recognizing equity as meta law thus opens the possibility for partial convergence between jurisprudential approaches at the level of doctrine. cf Andrew S Gold and Henry E Smith, 'Sizing Up Private Law' (forthcoming) University of Toronto Law Journal <https://muse.jhu.edu/article/742434/pdf>.

[103] Felix S Cohen, 'Transcendental Nonsense and the Functional Approach' (1935) 35 Columbia Law Review 809.

[104] Karl N Llewellyn, 'A Realistic Jurisprudence—The Next Step' (1930) 30 Columbia Law Review 431, 438–51; Henry E Smith, 'The Persistence of System in Property Law' (2015) 163 University of Pennsylvania Law Review 2055.

[105] See Getzler (n 19) 192–93.

V. Conclusion

In the book *Flatland*, the main character, A Square (a country lawyer!), recounts how difficult it is to explain what a world of higher dimensions is like to one who has only inhabited a world of fewer dimensions.[106] Perhaps something similar has happened with equity in our legal system. The effect of fusion has been to flatten equity such that it is harder to explain a second-order safety valve conception of equity. Equity has become confused.

The pro-fusionists of yesterday were right. Fusing law and equity was indeed earth-shaking. Whether deliberately or indeliberately, fusion and its flattening out of the second-order equitable function profoundly shaped post-fusion law. Unfortunately, it took a special hybrid of relatively formal and general rules and tailored contextualized intervention off the table. No longer employing two specialized levels, the legal system found it more difficult to manage Aristotelian equity. Greater use of standards and multifactor tests, as in the United States, or more elaborate *ex ante* law, as in England, became the predictable result.

Flattening out equitable meta law has caused related jurisprudential aftershocks as well. Without the special hybrid made possible by two levels, debates over formalism versus contextualism and rules versus standards take on a more extreme character, because the remaining alternatives do not allow for specialization over subdomains. All-or-nothing victory appears to be required for one or the other pole in these debates. Similarly, in terms of the substance of law, jurisprudential discussion also tends towards extremes: contract is dead, tort is rampant, and altruism and individualism battle it out in rules and standards within individual doctrines. The idea that different moral considerations might be implicated in different domains in the law is out the window and in its place grand uniform theories reach into every corner of a flattened law.

All of which is not to say that philosophical theories are not relevant to doctrine and vice versa. On the contrary, recognizing equity as meta law will allow us to theorize better about the full range of possibilities. We can ask what the proper domain of elements in more pluralistic theories could be. Even a problem as specific as that involved in *Riggs v. Palmer* illustrates both where fusion went off the rails mechanically—voidness rather than constructive trust as a remedy—and how the flattening-though-fusion it represents has fed into larger philosophical quandaries.

Legal philosophy has an important role in getting us out of this mess. It is too late to rethink merging law and equity courts, and reversing merger would resurrect all the procedural inconveniences and anomalies it was meant to solve. Instead, if there is a second-order equitable function, it is for legal philosophers to bring out the equitable function as a conceptual if not a procedural component of our legal system. Legal concepts have consequences, and equity is no exception.

[106] Edwin A Abbott, *Flatland: A Romance of Many Dimensions* (first published 1884, Rosemary Jann (ed), OUP 2006).

11

Form and Substance in the Fusion of Law and Equity

Samuel L Bray[*]

I. Introduction

The metaphor of translation has been often used by scholars in the law.[1] It is a peculiar metaphor for legal scholars to choose, however, because there is little agreement about exactly what translation is or how it should be done.[2] Only after one has a view of translation, of its kinds and possibilities and virtues, is it really possible to use the metaphor well. And, for the metaphor to work, the legal scholar using the metaphor must have the same understanding of translation as the reader. If they do not—well, the communication failure has an irony that is certainly delightful.

In this chapter, to illuminate the 'fusion' of law and equity I draw on critical thinking about translation, ranging from the seventeenth-century poet and translator John Dryden to contemporary scholars in the field of translation studies. The aspiration is not only to understand the existing state of fusion, but also to gain a better sense of what the options might be for the future.

I am not quite using translation as a metaphor.[3] I am instead using it as a fiction. The question is not 'How is the fusion of law and equity an act of translation?' but rather 'What can we learn if we think of fusion *as if* it were an act of translation?'

The text which is to be translated, as it were, is independent equity—the doctrines, principles, practices, procedures, and institutions that are characteristic of equity. The

[*] For comments and criticisms I am grateful to Nathan Chapman, Andrew Gold, John Goldberg, Allison Hoffman, Douglas Laycock, Mark Leeming, Jason Oh, Richard Re, Henry Smith, Peter Turner, participants in a faculty workshop at UCLA, and participants in 'Law and Equity: Fusion and Fission', a conference at St Catharine's College, Cambridge.

[1] eg Máximo Langer, 'From Legal Transplants to Legal Translations: The Globalization of Plea Bargaining and the Americanization Thesis in Criminal Procedure' (2004) 45 Harvard International Law Journal 1; Lawrence Lessig, 'Fidelity in Translation' (1993) 71 Texas Law Review 1165. For criticisms of the translation metaphor, see Sanford Levinson, 'Translation: Who Needs It?' (1997) 65 Fordham Law Review 1457; John O McGinnis, 'The Inevitable Infidelities of Constitutional Translation: The Case of the New Deal' (1999) 41 William & Mary Law Review 177.

[2] cf Kwame Anthony Appiah, 'Thick Translation' in Lawrence Venuti (ed), *The Translation Studies Reader* (3rd edn, Routledge 2012) 339 ('[T]he reason why we cannot speak of the perfect translation here is not that there is a definite set of desiderata and we know they cannot all be met; it is rather that there is no definite set of desiderata').

[3] For warnings that 'the language of metaphor and simile serves to confuse and confound' any discussion of fusion, see Anthony Mason, 'Fusion' in Simone Degeling and James Edelman (eds), *Equity in Commercial Law* (Lawbook Co 2005) 339.

Samuel L Bray, *Form and Substance in the Fusion of Law and Equity* In: *Philosophical Foundations of the Law of Equity*. Edited by: Dennis Klimchuk, Irit Samet, and Henry E Smith, Oxford University Press (2020).

DOI: 10.1093/oso/9780198817659.003.0012

question is what we should make of these in a contemporary legal system.[4] In the terms of this fiction, 'equity' must be translated, not merely transposed, because of the passage of time and changes in legal rules, cultures, and institutions. It must be translated, not merely ignored, because of rules that require the consideration of equity as well as the more general norm of continuity in judicial decision-making.[5]

Many issues regarding translation are not discussed here. There is no discussion of authority, legitimacy, connotation, implicature, culture, appropriation, status, power, or the reader.[6] And some points of contact between translation and fusion are so obvious that no consideration needs to be given to them: both are hard, both demand skill, and so on. Similarly, some divergences between translation and fusion are not considered here. For example, a translation can be considered a commentary on the original, but the fusion of equity with law in the present is not a commentary on the equity of an earlier moment.

What then, are the insights gained from thinking of the fusion of law and equity as if it were an exercise in the translation of equity from the past to the present? For legal scholars interested in fusion, this fiction reveals agreements that we did not know we had, as well as disagreements we did not know we had. Those legal scholars who support more fusion and those who resist it may seem to be disagreeing about whether the past of equity is relevant. But they are not. They may seem to be disagreeing about whether the past of equity needs to change in the present. Again, they are not. Instead they have a deeper, less examined disagreement. It is, in essence, a disagreement about which model of translation should be used for taking equity and conveying it—or something from it—into the present.

The literature on translation invoked here distinguishes between two dimensions along which translations can be arrayed: past versus present, and form versus substance. Once these are distinguished, it becomes clear that some disagreements between legal scholars that appear to be about past and present are really disagreements about something else—about whether there is value not only in equity's substance but also in its form. As discussed below, this chapter uses 'form' for the following three aspects of equity: *edge*, a sharp line between what is and is not equitable; *hierarchy*, equity supplements law and is subordinate to it; and *texture*, a mode of decision-making marked by shifting presumptions, maxims that express moral principles, and a higher than usual ratio of standards to rules. Thinking about translation also reveals a broader range of possibilities for the fusion of law and equity than scholars have previously recognized.

[4] In most (but not all) jurisdictions in the United States there has been procedural fusion (or 'merger'), including a fusion of legal and equitable courts. But the distinction between law and equity persists in a number of areas, especially the law of remedies and the substantive fields that developed in equity's exclusive jurisdiction, such as trusts.

[5] On the continuing debate over fusion, see John CP Goldberg, Peter Turner, and Henry E Smith (eds), *Equity and Law: Fusion and Fission* (CUP 2019); Joshua S Getzler, 'Patterns of Fusion' in Peter Birks (ed), *The Classification of Obligations* (Clarendon Press 1997) 157. On US law requiring distinctions between law and equity, see Samuel L Bray, 'The System of Equitable Remedies' (2016) 63 UCLA Law Review 530, 542–44. On continuity, see Allan Beever, 'The Declaratory Theory of Law' (2013) 33 OJLS 421.

[6] A sketch of the field can be found in José Lambert, 'Prelude: The Institutionalization of the Discipline' in Carmen Millán and Francesca Bartrina (eds), *The Routledge Handbook of Translation Studies* (Routledge 2013) 7.

This is a time when interdisciplinary studies are common in the legal academy, but serious engagement with the field of translation studies has not yet occurred. Perhaps the reader expects an apology that will justify that choice. But the proof is in the pudding, and instead of more talking it is time to serve it up.

II. Before Starting Out: Only in America?

I should note at the outset that the fiction of translation may be unusually apt for the federal courts of the United States. In common parlance, though not always in scholarly discourse, translation is the carrying of something from one language to another. In the fiction used here, equity is not translated between languages. The transference is largely temporal: independent equity (the original, the source text) is being translated from past to present.

In England and Australia, equity is praised and condemned, but what is being praised or condemned is something living. In the United States, at least in the federal courts, equity is often seen as something from the past, something to be retrieved rather than developed.[7] It is not clear why this is so, but among the likely causes are the following. First, the Seventh Amendment of the US Constitution 'preserve[s]' the constitutional right to a jury trial and is interpreted as preserving the jury trial right as it existed in 1791.[8] Second, the Judiciary Act of 1789 is interpreted as giving federal courts the equitable jurisdiction that Chancery had in 1789.[9] Third, there was the demise of *Swift v Tyson* and its replacement with the *Erie* doctrine—which requires, in diversity jurisdiction cases, that federal courts use the common law developed by state courts. The *Erie* shift has limited the development of federal common law, including the federal common law of equity and equitable remedies.[10] The cumulative result of these interpretive choices is that when the federal courts do equity, they are often doing someone else's equity.

Thus, it may be that the fiction of translation is more apt for equity in the federal courts of the United States, than it is for state courts and the courts of Australia, Canada, and England.

[7] cf Samuel L Bray, 'Equity: Notes on the American Reception' in Goldberg, Turner, and Smith (eds) (n 5) 37, 43.

[8] eg *City of Monterey v Del Monte Dunes at Monterey, Ltd*, 526 US 687, 708 (1999).

[9]

> The Judiciary Act of 1789 conferred on the federal courts jurisdiction over 'all suits ... in equity.' We have long held that the 'jurisdiction' thus conferred ... is an authority to administer in equity suits the principles of the system of judicial remedies which had been devised and was being administered by the English Court of Chancery at the time of the separation of the two countries.
>
> *Grupo Mexicano de Desarrollo, SA v Alliance Bond Fund, Inc*, 527 US 308, 318 (1999) (citation, alteration, and internal quotation marks omitted)

[10] Whether principles of equitable remedies are regarded as 'substantive' or 'procedural' for *Erie* purposes, the point still holds: if substantive, in diversity cases federal courts are not in a living tradition of equity but are asking about other people's equity; if procedural, the label might encourage federal courts to make only technical revisions of doctrines about equitable remedies.

III. Starting Out: Dryden's Typology of Translation

The practice of translation is ancient, and so is critical reflection on that practice. 'Over some two thousand years of argument and precept, the beliefs and disagreements voiced about the nature of translation have been almost the same. Identical theses, familiar moves and refutations in debate recur, nearly without exception, from Cicero and Quintilian to the present-day.'[11] One of those familiar moves is a good place to begin.

John Dryden was a translator as well as a poet, and in the preface to his translation of Ovid's *Epistles* he reflected on the practice of translation.[12] His reflections summed up the existing tradition of thought and to this day are treated as insightful.[13] Dryden contrasted three kinds of translation. They should be understood as ideal types in the sense that every actual translation (unless trivially short) is made up of elements of all three.

The first is '*Metaphrase*, or turning an Authour word by word, and Line by Line, from one Language into another.'[14]

The second is '*Paraphrase*', which is a middle way between the extremes. It is 'Translation with Latitude, where the Authour is kept in view by the Translator, so as never to be lost, but his words are not so strictly follow'd as his sense, and that too is admitted to be amplyfied, but not alter'd.'[15] George Steiner calls Dryden's paraphrase 'faithful but autonomous restatement.'[16]

The third is '*Imitation*', in which the translator freely chooses to keep or discard what the original says. In this ideal type, 'the Translator (if now he has not lost that Name) assumes the liberty not only to vary from the words and sence, but to forsake them both as he sees occasion.'[17] In an imitation, the translator takes only 'some general hints from the Original.'[18]

Dryden's typology 'has been found widely useful and it seems to fit broad realities of theory and technique' for translation.[19] The exact terms Dryden used, however, have taken on other senses. Now 'paraphrase' is often used for a free rendering instead of

[11] George Steiner, *After Babel: Aspects of Language & Translation* (3rd edn, OUP 1998) 251.

[12] John Dryden, 'From the Preface to Ovid's Epistles' in Venuti (n 2) 38.

[13] eg Steiner (n 11) 266–70; Theodore J Cachey, Jr, 'Between Hermeneutics and Poetics: Modern American Translation of the "Commedia"' (1990) 8 Annali d'Italianistica 144, 146–49. The *locus classicus* in Dryden was cited by Lawrence Lessig and Maximo Langer in their respective works deploying the metaphor of translation (n 1).

[14] Dryden (n 12) 38 (emphasis added). Even with such a technique (and sometimes especially with such a technique), it is impossible to carry every element of the original into the receiving language fully intact. The equivalence between the original and the translation is always a matter of 'the balance between what has been kept invariant and what has undergone transformation.' Gideon Toury, *Descriptive Translation Studies—And Beyond* (rev edn, Benjamins 2012) 113.

[15] Dryden (n 12) 38. Dryden's description of paraphrase, and his application of the term to his own work, should be read as having some mixture of rhetoric and aspiration. For critique of Dryden's rewriting in the guise of translating, see Maria K Greenwood, 'What Dryden Did to Chaucer's *The Knight's Tale*, or Translation as Ideological Input' in Rosalynn Voaden and others (eds), *The Medieval Translator/Traduire au Moyen Age* (Brepols 2003) vol 8, 189–200.

[16] Steiner (n 11) 266.

[17] Dryden (n 12) 38.

[18] ibid.

[19] Steiner (n 11) 266. A similar division can be found in writing on translation by a fifteenth-century humanist and once famous translator. Giannozzo Manetti, *A Translator's Defense* (Mark Young tr, Myron McShande ed, Harvard UP 2016) 241: 'For there are three kinds of translation: one is word for word; a second is, as it were,

being, as it was for Dryden, the middle category.[20] 'Mimetic' is now sometimes used for a translation that follows the original closely, not one that follows it loosely.[21] Nevertheless, 'metaphrase', 'paraphrase', and 'imitation' will be used in this chapter with the sense that Dryden gave to each.

It is not difficult to organize positions about equity according to Dryden's typology. Almost all judges are in the middle, in the realm of paraphrase, invoking equitable doctrines from the past while inevitably adjusting them in the present, following the sense more exactly than the words. Even so, there is one case from the US Supreme Court where it is possible to find Dryden's positions of metaphrase and imitation. In *Grupo Mexicano de Desarrollo, SA v Alliance Bond Fund, Inc*,[22] the Court considered whether a plaintiff could obtain a preliminary injunction when the defendant was dispersing assets, but the plaintiff's ultimate claim was for a legal remedy (damages). The majority opinion by Justice Scalia can be read as insisting that federal courts today can apply only the equitable remedies known to the Chancellor in 1789. The dissenting opinion by Justice Ginsburg can be read as suggesting that all the courts must take from equity's past are abstract values such as adaptability and flexibility.[23] If the opinions are read in these ways—and note that other, less extreme readings are possible—then Justice Scalia was urging the rigors of metaphrase and Justice Ginsburg the freedom of imitation.

Yet *Grupo Mexicano* is the exception. Almost every view of fusion expressed by judges and scholars falls within Dryden's paraphrase. Those who seek a greater degree of fusion want to draw from equity more than just general hints or abstract values. Those who resist a greater degree of fusion also recognize the impossibility of a perfect rendering of equity's past into the present.

So far, the foray into translation has only told us what we knew already. Yet Dryden's typology was not merely for instruction, but for argument. He was justifying his own approach (the middle course, paraphrase), and critiquing the choices made by other translators of classical verse. One could say that Dryden was on the march with straw men to the left of him and straw men to right of him. Of course, a judge deciding how to apply an old demarcation of equity's bounds must not merely take inspiration from that

according to sense; and a third occurs when some things are sometimes omitted because they are purely ornamental, while other things are added at the discretion of the translator.'

[20] Dryden himself anticipates this.

[21] eg Michael V Fox, 'Translation and Mimesis' in Frederick W Knobloch (ed), *Biblical Translation in Context* (UP of Maryland 2002) 207, 208; Peter Newmark, *About Translation* (Multilingual Matters 1991) 3–4, 9.

[22] 527 US 308 (1999). See Stephen B Burbank, 'The Bitter with the Sweet: Tradition, History, and Limitations on Federal Judicial Power—A Case Study' (2000) 75 Notre Dame Law Review 1291; Samuel L Bray, 'The Supreme Court and the New Equity' (2015) 68 Vanderbilt Law Review 997, 1010, n 61.

[23] *Grupo Mexicano*, 527 US 308, 336–37 (Ginsburg J, dissenting). Note that there are two ways to read the Ginsburg dissent, and these two ways correspond to the difference between a paraphrase and an imitation. First, her dissent could be taken as saying that the preliminary injunction should remain as it is except for one crucial change needed to bring it into the present: it should be available regardless of whether the plaintiff's claim is legal or equitable. That would be a paraphrase. Second, her dissent could be taken as saying that not merely the availability of the preliminary injunction but everything about it is up for grabs—the only duty owed to its equitable past is that the judge must take to heart the virtues of flexibility and adaptability. On that second, more radical reading, she is calling for imitation. Similarly, in *Petrella v Metro-Goldwyn-Mayer, Inc*, 134 SCt 1962 (2014), Justice Breyer's dissent can be given a paraphrastic or an imitative reading.

line (as in imitation), nor must that judge hew to the old line with the same exactitude as an old-time English Chancellor (as in metaphrase). But to say the judge must avoid imitation and metaphrase does not resolve questions judges regularly have to make that are related to fusion, such as whether to apply the traditionally equitable defence of laches to a legal claim for damages.[24] The middle space is large. It is 'the great central area of "translation" '[25]—an area too great unless further distinctions are made. Thus, we turn next to ways of translating within Dryden's middle course.

IV. Further in: Critiques of the Scholars and Philologists

Once the extremes of metaphrase and imitation are set aside, there are still vigorous debates about the task of the translator. No effort is made here to survey those debates—after all, translation is being used as a fiction. But we will eavesdrop on two critiques of translators made in the last half century or so.

In one critique, the offending translators were tarred with the label 'scholars'; in the other, with the label 'philologists'. In both critiques, a better way was suggested. The pairing of the two critiques is especially helpful. At first glance they are entirely incompatible, but on inspection they have an insight that can be borrowed for thinking about the fusion of law and equity. This insight is that two dimensions can and should be distinguished: past versus present, and form versus substance. Once these are distinguished it will become clear that there are more possibilities for the fusion of law and equity than has been previously realized, and the points of agreement and disagreement between different scholarly positions will be clarified.

The first critique, by William Arrowsmith and Roger Shattuck, is aimed at 'scholars', those translators who seek to recover a past text and transmit it, unmodified, to their readers.[26] By contrast, they praise the 'poets' who think of translating as 'the *re-creation* of the past; by rendering an ancient or an alien experience contemporary or familiar, the translator renews it, and this renewal is the heart of his labor'.[27] '[T]o the acute distress of scholars', these poets are 'often careless of the literal words of their originals' and 'attentive to the spirit (by which is often meant the meaning of the original to the translator's time rather than its meaning to its own)'.[28]

Thus, poets give priority to the present, and scholars to the past. In this formulation, *past* and *present* are a shorthand for distance between the translation and the original.

[24] eg *SCA Hygiene Products Aktiebolag v First Quality Baby Products, LLC*, 137 S Ct 954 (2017).

[25] Steiner (n 11) 266.

[26] William Arrowsmith and Roger Shattuck (eds), *The Craft and Context of Translation: A Critical Symposium* (Anchor 1964). Arrowsmith and Shattuck's essay introduces a volume of symposium papers on translation that was once widely read. The symposium preceded the existence of a recognizable field of translation studies, and it primarily considered the problems and methods of literary translators—a relatively narrow range of concern. Nevertheless, three decades later it could still be called a 'landmark' and the resulting volume 'the most complete expression of the problematics of literary translation'. Sidney Monas, 'Luminous Translation' (1994) 38 Slavic and East European Journal 5, 5.

[27] William Arrowsmith and Roger Shattuck, 'Introduction' in Arrowsmith and Shattuck (n 26) xvii–xviii.

[28] ibid xviii.

There may be a significant temporal distance, as when a new English translation is made of the *Iliad*. Or the temporal distance may be slight, as when a new English novel is promptly translated into French. Even so, there are other gaps a translator might have to bridge, including geography and culture.[29] All such kinds of distance are meant by distinguishing 'past' and 'present'.

The authors making this critique, Arrowsmith and Shattuck, leave no doubt about their loyalties: the better translation is that of the poet, the renewal that competes with the original, not the crib that reproduces it. That choice of sides does not have to be accepted; my own view is that there is much to be said on the side of the scholars.[30] At any rate, there is value in having multiple translations of a given work, some by poets and some by scholars.[31] But the critique is still useful because it identifies a way translations differ, a dimension of variation.[32]

The second critique, made by Robert Alter, is aimed at 'philologists'.[33] 'For the philologist, the great goal is the achievement of clarity', but clarity 'can quickly turn into too much of a good thing'.[34] The philologist works microscopically, considering each individual instance of a word or construction in the source text and trying to explain each one in the receiving language—without attending to the form of the original, including its register, rhythm, parallelism, and patterns of lexical and syntactic repetition.[35]

[29] Viggo Hjørnager Pedersen, 'Accuracy in Translation' in Gunilla Anderman and Margaret Rogers (eds), *Word, Text, Translation: Liber Amicorum for Peter Newmark* (Multilingual Matters 1999) 47–48.

[30] Samuel L Bray and John F Hobbins, 'To the Reader' in *Genesis 1-11: A New Old Translation for Readers, Scholars, and Translators* (GlossaHouse 2017).

[31] Arrowsmith and Shattuck do recognize, but grudgingly, that each kind of translation has its own limitations, Arrowsmith and Shattuck (n 26) xviii ('Both genres possess the deficiencies appropriate to their basic purposes and chosen loyalties').

[32] I have cited Arrowsmith and Shattuck because they express the differences sharply. Many others have expressed one or another of these two views, or presented them as a choice, or advanced an intermediate position. For example, compare RJC Horan, 'Literary Translation' (1978) 8 J European Studies 217, 219 (noting that many speakers at a large conference on translation 'saw as a basic right of the translator (whom they regarded as sharing some of the privileges of the creative artist), the right of imposing his own style on the original. ... [I]f Pope's *Homer* is not *Homer* it should at least be *Pope*') with André Lefevere, 'The Translation of Literature: An Approach' (1970) 16 Babel 75, 77 ('[The literary translator] is not allowed to impress the stamp of his own originality on the work he is creating anew. His task is to become the author's mouthpiece; never to distort the author's voice'). Manetti had the view that each kind of translation was appropriate for different works: something like the rendering of 'poets' for translating poets, orators, and historians (such as Thucydides), and something like the rendering of 'scholars' for translating philosophers and theologians ((n 19) 239, 241, 263, 299 n 46).

[33] Alter is a comparative literature scholar at the University of California-Berkeley and an accomplished translator. The critique invoked here is found in Robert Alter, 'Introduction to the Hebrew Bible: I. The Bible in English and the Heresy of Explanation' in *The Hebrew Bible: Volume 1, The Five Books of Moses* (Norton 2019) xiii– xlii. I have cited Alter because his contrast is clear and can be put to use in thinking about fusion. Another division could be form, purpose, and substance. Kirsten Malmkjær, 'Meaning and Translation' in Kirsten Malmkjær and Kevin Windle (eds), *The Oxford Handbook of Translation Studies* (OUP 2011)108, 113–14 (summarizing Katarina Reiss's distinction between '*expression (Ausdruck), appeal (Appel)* and *representation*'—roughly speaking, form, purpose, and substance—with the relative importance of each aspect depending on the type of text). Note that the premise for these divisions—namely that a translation should be analysed in terms of its equivalence to the original—is not held by all scholars in translation studies (ibid 114).

[34] Alter (n 33) xv. Alter is not condemning philologists like Vico and Nietzsche but rather is using the term in a relatively narrow sense. In his words: 'To be fair to the broad enterprise of philology, which has included some great literary critics, I use the term here as shorthand for "biblical philology," a discipline that, especially in its Anglo-American applications, has often come down to lexicography and the analysis of grammar.' ibid xiv.

[35] ibid xxvii ('A suitable English version should avoid at all costs the modern abomination of elegant synonymous variation, for the literary prose of the Bible turns everywhere on significant repetition, not variation'). Alter's critique of translators of the Hebrew Bible resembles Douglas Hofstadter's critique of machine translation, Douglas R Hofstadter, *Le Ton beau de Marot: In Praise of the Music of Language* (Basic Books 1997) 118–21; and

Such a translation is 'form-blind'.[36] Ignoring these aspects of form, the philologist is intent on one goal: expressing clearly the substance of the original.

Although Alter provides a term for the translator who cares about substance and not form ('philologist'), he does not provide a term for the obvious alternative: the translator who cares about both form and substance. For that translator, the term used here will be one that aptly describes Alter himself, 'critic'.[37] As applied to translation, then, a 'philologist' seeks to carry over to the receiving language only the substance of the original, while the 'critic' seeks to carry over the form and substance.

Now if we think of translations only in terms of being more or less 'literal', then these two lines of critique will seem incomprehensible or else entirely opposed. It might seem that the 'scholars' are criticized for being too literal, while the 'philologists' are criticized for not being literal enough. But there is a schema that makes both of these criticisms intelligible, and it is this schema that can aid our thinking about the fusion of law and equity.

Imagine that on the horizontal axis there is a distinction about who has creative control—whose stamp the work primarily bears, whose experiences give it shape, whose voice is heard in its distinctive eloquence or lisp.[38] That person could be the author or the translator.

If the author is given creative control, then the translator is relatively deferential. Of course, translation requires creativity, and the constraint of deference can demand of the translator even more ingenuity. Yet such translators would bend their own language towards that of the original.

But if the translator is given creative control, then the translator may remake the original. There would still be a sense of fidelity, but not of deference; the relationship between author and translator would be one of joint responsibility and co-making. Indeed, the translator must be careful to be careless of details in order to recreate the original for a new time, a new cultural moment.[39]

This axis of creative control and deference is the one on which 'poets' and 'scholars' are distinguished. On this axis, the poets are to the left and the scholars are to the right.[40] As a poet's translation moves further left on this axis it shades into Dryden's

Milan Kundera's critique of translators of Franz Kafka, Milan Kundera, 'A Sentence' in *Testaments Betrayed: An Essay in Nine Parts* (Linda Asher tr, HarperCollins 1995) 108.

[36] David Daube, 'Lecture III: The Form is the Message' in *Ancient Jewish Law: Three Inaugural Lectures* (Brill 1981) 91.

[37] Of course, 'critic' can be used in many senses. I have especially in mind Cleanth Brooks's insistence on the unity of form and content and his rejection of 'the heresy of paraphrase'. Cleanth Brooks, *The Well Wrought Urn: Studies in the Structure of Poetry* (Harcourt Brace 1947) 192–214.

[38] Arrowsmith and Shattuck (n 26) xix. Day-Lewis describes this 'co-operation' between the author and the translator-as-poet, and says that such a translator uses the process of translating as 'an exercise, a way of developing his own style', a way 'to mediate between his own imagination and some field of experience hitherto unexplored or unsatisfactorily worked over—to clarify his own ideas'. C Day-Lewis, *The Second Jackson Knight Memorial Lecture: On Translating Poetry* (Abbey 1970) 6; ibid 5–6, 15–17.

[39] Arrowsmith and Shattuck (n 26) xix.

[40] This should go without saying, but 'left' and 'right' are used without political valence.

imitation. As a scholar's translation moves further right on this axis it shades into Dryden's metaphrase.

On the vertical axis is a distinction about form and substance. Is the form of the original—its parallelism, rhythm, repetition, and so on—something that can be put to one side so the translator can get at the substance? Or does form have its own meaning, and so need to be carried over, as much as possible, into the translation?[41] The 'philologists' are those who would give up the form to more successfully render the substance in a particular instance—for example, not trying to use a consistent word or construction in the receiving language to show a pattern of repetition, but only trying to show the exact shade of meaning for a lexical or syntactic element *here*. Those who would try to hold on to such a pattern of repetition are critics, not philologists.

On this axis there is also one other choice. Writing about translation, and in particular the translation of West African proverbs, Kwame Anthony Appiah has noted that 'we may choose, rightly, to translate a term in a way that is unfaithful to the literal intentions, because we are trying to preserve formal features that seem more crucial.'[42] In this way, the translator of a proverb might try to carry over *only the form*—remaking the point of the proverb, while taking care to preserve the formal features that identified it as a proverb.[43] This third choice is rare for literary translation. It is common enough, however, for the 'translation' of a text into a movie. The screenwriter might preserve certain aspects of the form, such as place, pacing, and genre cues, even while letting go of the substance, perhaps replacing the author's point with one that is quite different.[44] This translator, attending to the form but not to the substance, could be called an 'aesthete'.

Recognizing these two dimensions leads to several possibilities. All are within Dryden's middle course of paraphrase, but at the outer bounds they shade into imitation or metaphrase.

These possibilities for translation—six possibilities distinguished along the poet-scholar and philologist-critic-aesthete axes—are shown in Figure 11.1. To repeat: all six boxes are instances of paraphrase. But as a translation by 'scholars' becomes more exact in following the original it shades into Dryden's metaphrase, and as a translation by 'poets' becomes more free in naturalizing the original it shades into Dryden's imitation.[45]

[41] cf Gideon Toury, 'How Come the Translation of a Limerick Can Have Four Lines (or Can It)?' in Anderman and Rogers (n 29) 161.

[42] Appiah (n 2) 339. See Hofstadter (n 35) 146–47.

[43] That can be done in different ways: a scholar might take care to preserve the features that marked the expression as a proverb in the source language, while a poet might take care to give the expression the features of a proverb in the receiving language.

[44] See Katy Waldman, 'How Disney's New *Jungle Book* Subverts the Gross Colonialism of Rudyard Kipling' *Slate* (19 April 2016).

[45] What Alter approves of is box 4: a relatively strict paraphrase of both form and substance. What Arrowsmith and Shattuck approve of is a translation the 'poet' has remade in her own language, but they take no position on whether the translator should have regard to the form: thus box 1, 3, or 5.

	POETS (naturalize)	SCHOLARS (follow closely)
PHILOLOGISTS (substance)	The translator naturalizes the substance of the original, but discards the form (1)	The translator follows the substance of the original closely, but discards the form (2)
CRITICS (substance and form)	The translator naturalizes the original, both form and substance (3)	The translator follows the original closely, both form and substance (4)
AESTHETES (form)	The translator naturalizes the form of the original, but discards the substance (5)	The translator follows the form of the original closely, but discards the substance (6)

Figure 11.1 Translation in two dimensions.

V. Form and Substance in Equity

These distinctions can now be brought to bear on the fusion of law and equity. It is not conventional to distinguish equity's form and substance, however, and I need to say what I mean by each term. By referring to equity's 'form', I mean three things.[46]

First, *edge*: the sharp line between what is and is not equitable. This line is maintained, at least in the United States, by a number of legal authorities and practices, such as the constitutional right to a civil jury trial, which requires a court to determine whether a claim is legal or equitable; the requirement that a court may give an equitable remedy only if legal remedies are inadequate; and various statutes that authorize 'equitable relief' and thus require a court to determine whether the relief sought is legal or equitable.[47]

Second, *hierarchy*: the sense that equity is supplementary and can come into play only if there is some defect in the law. The doctrine that embodies this hierarchy is the requirement of no adequate remedy at law.[48]

Third, *texture*: the distinctive mode of decision-making that is characteristic of equity.[49] It has sometimes been said that equity has more 'discretion', though this basis of distinction has often been criticized.[50] A better way to describe the equitable mode of decision-making is to say that it is characterized by a preference for standards over rules;[51] by an emphasis on moral conduct, expressed in equitable maxims and found in

[46] The three features discussed in the text are not conventionally called 'form'. This description is therefore new but not intended to be tendentious. The continued vitality and wisdom of each of these features remains contested among legal scholars.

[47] Bray (n 5) 542–44.

[48] For criticism, see Douglas Laycock, *The Death of the Irreparable Injury Rule* (OUP 1991). For a qualified defence, see Bray (n 5) 580–81. For a more general defence of equity as a second-order system, see Henry E Smith, 'Fusing the Equitable Function in Private Law' in Kit Barker, Karen Fairweather, and Ross Grantham (eds), *Private Law in the 21st Century* (Hart 2017).

[49] On texture, compare Duncan Kennedy, 'Form and Substance in Private Law Adjudication' (1976) 89 Harvard Law Review 1685, 1687–89.

[50] Douglas Laycock, 'The Triumph of Equity' (1993) 56 Law & Contemporary Problems 53, 71–73; Andrew Burrows, 'We Do This at Common Law But That in Equity' (2002) 22 OJLS 1.

[51] eg Mark Leeming, 'Common law, Equity, and Statutes: Limitations and Analogies' (Private Law Seminar, University of Technology, Sydney, November 2014) 7 ('There is the immediately striking difference that damages at common law which are available as of right after 5 years and 11 months become unavailable after, say, 6 years; a very different approach obtains in equity'). Note that Duncan Kennedy's work on rules and standards also tended

a recurrent concern with conscience;[52] and by an emphasis not so much on the content of rights as on how those rights may be used and abused.[53]

By equity's 'substance' I mean almost everything else. The substance of equity includes, for example, the *injunction*, an all-purpose remedy for ordering the defendant to do or not do something; *laches*, a defence that the plaintiff waited too long to bring the suit even though the period of time specified by the statute of limitations has not run;[54] *non-enforcement of penalties*, an unwillingness to enforce harsh liquidated-damages provisions; and *depositions*, a procedure for taking party testimony before a trial.[55]

Note that I am stipulating what counts as form and what counts as substance. The distinction is impressionistic and intuitive. That is, edge, hierarchy, and texture seem to me the most obvious analogues to literary features such as parallelism, register, and repetition. Moreover, there seems to be an affinity between edge, hierarchy, and texture: a legal scholar is likely to adopt the same stance towards all three.

Most of those writing about fusion, at least in the United States, have thought in terms of a past–present distinction, a distinction between those who want to keep the division between law and equity established in the past, and those who would like to remake it in the present. That distinction suggests that those writing on fusion can be divided into 'scholars' and 'poets'. The 'scholars' would tend to follow closely the received equitable doctrines, at least about equitable remedies and equitable substantive areas.[56] The 'poets', by contrast, would remake the traditional distinction between law and equity, naturalizing it in the present.

But the contrast between 'scholars' and 'poets' becomes more subtle when Alter's criticism of 'philologist' translators is added. The philologist (in Alter's sense) ignores the form, the structure, of the original and seeks only its substance.[57] How does this distinction reveal new options for the fusion of law and equity?

Begin with the 'scholars', those who would try to follow more closely the traditional distinction between law and equity. They may take either side of Alter's choice. One

to associate standards with equity. Of his 'two opposed modes for dealing with questions of the form in which legal solutions to the substantive problems should be cast', one 'supports the use of equitable standards producing ad hoc decisions with relatively little precedential value' ((n 49) 1685).

[52] On equitable maxims as focal constraints for judges, see Bray (n 5) 582–83, 584–86. On conscience, see Richard Hedlund, 'The Theological Foundations of Equity's Conscience' (2015) 4 Oxford Journal of Law & Religion 119; Irit Samet, 'What Conscience Can Do for Equity' (2012) 3 Jurisprudence 13.

[53] cf Ben McFarlane and Robert Stevens, 'The Nature of Equitable Property' (2010) 4 Journal of Equity 1.

[54] Laches illustrates the interpenetration of equity's form and substance. This defence corresponds to the maxim 'Equity aids the vigilant, not those who slumber on their rights'.

[55] With procedural merger, depositions are of course generally available.

[56] eg Bray (n 5) (equitable remedies); Henry E Smith, 'Why Fiduciary Law Is Equitable' in Andrew S Gold and Paul B Miller (eds), *Philosophical Foundations of Fiduciary Law* (OUP 2014) 261–284 (fiduciary law).

[57] My own view is that Alter's critique is correct, at least for a text with literary, legal, or religious significance. 'Because all human speech consists of arbitrarily selected but intensely conventionalized signals, meaning can never be wholly separated from expressive form' (Steiner (n 11) 252). On literary texts, see eg Vladimir Nabokov, 'Foreword' in *Eugene Onegin: A Novel in Verse by Aleksandr Pushkin Translated from the Russian, with a Commentary, by Vladimir Nabokov* (rev edn, Bollingen Series 72, Princeton UP 1975) vol 1, vii–xii; on legal texts, Charles Donahue, Jr, 'On Translating the Digest' (1987) 39 Stanford Law Review 1057; on religious texts, Fox (n 21).

could want a relatively strict translation of the substance of equitable doctrines without any attention to the form. Or one could seek to carry over not only the substance but also the form of equity—on the view that equity's edge, hierarchy, and texture are intrinsic to it, with the interlocking of form and substance being crucial to equity's effectiveness.

The best example of keeping the substance but not the form of equity comes from a surprising source: Douglas Laycock. It might be expected that Laycock would oppose any close following of traditional equitable doctrines. But consider carefully *The Death of the Irreparable Injury Rule*, and in particular the chapter in which he proposes a restatement that could be adopted to replace the irreparable injury rule, also called the 'no adequate remedy at law' requirement.[58] In that chapter, Laycock aims to recreate the results that courts arrive at when they invoke the 'no adequate remedy at law' requirement, but to do so with a different and more rational set of principles. For example, courts sometimes find an adequate remedy at law when the requested injunction would be difficult to administer. Laycock restates the point this way:

> § 4 *Impracticality*
> A court should deny permanent specific relief if:
> (a) the relief would be impractical to implement or burdensome for the court to supervise, and
> (b) these problems outweigh the disadvantage to plaintiff of receiving only substitutionary relief.[59]

Laycock's restatement—seventeen sections in all—can be seen as a very close translation of the substance of the irreparable injury rule. (To be sure, Laycock himself does not see it this way: because he considers the 'no adequate remedy at law' requirement to be gibberish, there is no substance to translate.) Moreover, Laycock expressly rejects some aspects of equity's form. For example, the following section is a rejection of the hierarchy of legal over equitable remedies:

> § 1 *General Rule*
> A plaintiff who has prevailed on the merits is presumptively entitled to choose either a substitutionary or specific remedy. A Court should refuse plaintiff's choice of remedy only when countervailing interests outweigh plaintiff's interest in the remedy he prefers.[60]

[58] Laycock (n 48) 265–86.

[59] ibid 269. Intriguingly, though, Laycock does not quite entirely discard the form of equity. Running through his entire restatement is a crisp distinction between substitutionary remedies and specific remedies. That distinction could be considered a naturalizing translation of one aspect of equity's form, namely edge. Nevertheless, he rejects 'hierarchy' and the proposed restatement is not in keeping with equity's 'texture'. The proposal is therefore best seen as a translation of substance.

[60] ibid 266. Another example of a strict paraphrase of substance with a discarding of form is Leigh Anenson's work on equitable defences: she wants the traditional equitable defences to be carried over into the present, seemingly preserving their requirements and effects (substance) while jettisoning their limitation to equitable claims (form). eg T Leigh Anenson, 'Treating Equity Like Law: A Post-Merger Justification of Unclean Hands' (2008) 45 American Business Law Journal 455.

Thus, Laycock's proposed restatement can be seen as preserving the substance, but not the form, of that most traditional of traditional equitable doctrines, the 'no adequate remedy at law' requirement.

By contrast, other 'scholars' (again using Arrowsmith and Shattuck's terminology) would follow the law–equity distinction closely, not only with respect to substance but also with respect to form. A notable example is Henry Smith. In a number of pieces, he has explicated the value of traditional equity as a way of constraining opportunism.[61] In doing so, he looks to the substance of equitable rules. But he also considers the form of equity and finds it valuable. He finds a sharp distinction between law and equity ('edge') useful because it allows a 'two-system' mechanism for resolving disputes and constraining opportunism.[62] He has argued for a sequence in the application of those two systems, with equity as the backup system, or safety valve ('hierarchy').[63] And in work with Mark Gergen and John Golden, he has sharply criticized the US Supreme Court's *eBay* decision for imposing a multi-part test instead of using an analysis more characteristic of equity (*eBay*'s neglect of equity's 'texture').[64]

Interestingly, Smith's embrace of form shows that equity's formal characteristics can have ecumenical appeal. It may be obvious that equity's form can be valued by those who adopt an internal perspective on the law, evaluating the law by reference to its own structures and categories of thought.[65] Yet equity's form can also be valued by those who adopt an external perspective, evaluating the law by reference to consequences.[66]

Thus, the scholars, those who offer a close translation of equity, might take the substance and discard the form (Laycock), or keep both substance and form (Smith). What might have seemed to be a fault line among American scholars about attitudes to fusion turns out to be a difference in attitudes to form. The third option for 'scholars', that of following equity's form and discarding the substance, has not yet been advanced in the legal literature.

And what of the poets, those who want a creative remaking of equity? Again, the distinction between form and substance will prove illuminating. Poets might abandon equity's form—its edge, hierarchy, and texture—and instead try to naturalize only the substance of equitable doctrines.

A good example is Owen Fiss's argument in *The Civil Rights Injunction*.[67] Fiss sets out to defend the structural injunction, which he describes as 'the initiation of a relationship between the judge and an institution—a declaration that the judge will henceforth

[61] eg Smith (n 56); Henry E Smith, 'Property, Equity, and the Rule of Law' in Lisa M Austin and Dennis Klimchuk (eds), *Private Law and the Rule of Law* (OUP 2014) 232–237.

[62] Smith (n 48).

[63] Kenneth Ayotte, Ezra Friedman, and Henry E Smith, 'A Safety Valve Model of Equity as Anti-Opportunism' (draft paper of 30 March 2013).

[64] Mark P Gergen, John M Golden, and Henry E Smith, 'The Supreme Court's Accidental Revolution? The Test for Permanent Injunctions' (2012) 112 Columbia Law Review 203. See also Bray (n 5), finding value in equity's edge, hierarchy, and texture.

[65] Conversely, an internal perspective can lead to the rejection of an aspect of equity's form if it is thought no longer to fit the law's structures and categories of thought.

[66] On these perspectives and the possibilities for convergence, see Andrew S Gold and Henry E Smith, 'Sizing Up Private Law' (forthcoming 2019) University of Toronto Law Journal.

[67] Owen M Fiss, *The Civil Rights Injunction* (Indiana UP 1978).

manage the reconstruction of an ongoing social institution'.[68] He clearly values the substance of equity, and he praises the transformation of the federal injunction in the twentieth century. In other words, he is a poet.

But what is Fiss's position on the form of equity? On one aspect of its form he leaves no doubt: fully half the book is a sustained attack on the remedial hierarchy. As for edge, he does not offer a critique of distinguishing between law and equity. But there is abundant evidence that he does not consider the distinction to be important, for he repeatedly declines to give any force to it.[69] With regard to the texture of equity, Fiss does not object to standards and judicial discretion.[70] But there is no evidence that Fiss thinks there are or should be relatively more standards in equity. Fiss creatively remakes equity's substance, and jettisons its form.

Those who try to remake equity do not have to abandon its form; poets do not have to be philologists. They might translate the edge between legal and equitable remedies into some other division of remedies into two fundamental categories, such as specific and substitutionary relief, or monetary and non-monetary relief. Whatever the two new categories are, there could be a hierarchical relationship between them. For example, substitutionary relief might be available only if specific relief were defective, or conversely, specific relief might be available only if substitutionary relief were defective.

An example of the naturalization of equity's form may be Guido Calabresi and Douglas Melamed's 'One View of the Cathedral'.[71] Calabresi and Melamed draw no distinction between legal and equitable remedies.[72] But they do keep a fundamental distinction between two kinds of remedies, or regimes of protection for entitlements, namely 'property rules' and 'liability rules'. To that extent they are keeping the 'edge' of equity, not following it closely but instead recreating it freely. And much of the vast secondary literature on property rules and liability rules is concerned with hierarchy: which kind of rule should be the default? Calabresi and Melamed also naturalize the substance of equity, keeping remedies like the injunction even while changing them quite dramatically (and perhaps unwittingly).

The positions just described are mapped in terms of the poet-scholar and philologist–critic–aesthete axes in Figure 11.2.

Now there is some artificiality in these assignments, since an author or a case can fall into more than one box. An example is the *eBay* decision about permanent injunctions.[73] In *eBay*, the US Supreme Court laid out a four-part test for a plaintiff seeking an injunction in patent cases and perhaps other cases brought in federal

[68] ibid 92.

[69] For example, he argues that if the US Supreme Court is going to be committed to federalism, it should compare a federal injunction to all state remedies, not merely to legal ones (ibid 67–68), and he aligns the legal remedy of habeas with the injunction instead of with damages (ibid 105 n 19).

[70] Fiss concludes the book by professing his belief that 'courts have a unique capacity to create the terms of their own legitimacy' (ibid 95).

[71] Guido Calabresi and A Douglas Melamed, 'Property Rules, Liability Rules, and Inalienability: One View of the Cathedral' (1972) 85 Harvard Law Review 1089.

[72] That is one reason Calabresi and Melamed misdescribe the law of remedies. Samuel L Bray, 'Remedies, Meet Economics; Economics, Meet Remedies' (2018) 38 OJLS 71; Douglas Laycock, 'The Neglected Defense of Undue Hardship (and the Doctrinal Train Wreck in *Boomer v. Atlantic Cement*)' (2012) 4 Journal of Tort Law 1.

[73] *eBay Inc v MercExchange, LLC*, 547 US 388 (2006).

	POETS (naturalize)	SCHOLARS (follow closely)
PHILOLOGISTS (substance)	Owen Fiss on structural injunctions (1)	Douglas Laycock's proposed restatement of the 'no adequate remedy at law' requirement (2)
CRITICS (substance and form)	Guido Calabresi and Douglas Melamed on property rules and liability rules (3)	Henry Smith on equity (4)
AESTHETES (form)	?	?

Figure 11.2 Illustrations of translation in two dimensions.

court.[74] The test itself is not traditional (in saying it was, the Court was wrong), but each of its four factors is quite traditional. If the test is thought to be exhaustive of the considerations for the grant of an injunction, *eBay* would be a 'poetic' remaking of the equity tradition. But if it is not exhaustive (which is the better reading), then *eBay* is 'scholarly' in its adherence to the substance of equity.

With respect to form, *eBay* respects the edge between legal and equitable remedies. But it does not respect the texture of equity inasmuch as it replaces a series of more fine-grained and contextually varied equitable doctrines with a crude multi-part test.[75] A scholar-critic would say this is where *eBay* went wrong: it should have followed the form closely instead of naturalizing it. Others faulted *eBay* for keeping the 'no adequate remedy at law' requirement (ie for being 'critical' in keeping equity's edge and hierarchy)[76] or for pretending to follow traditional equity but in reality not doing so (ie for pretending to be 'scholarly' while really being 'poetic').[77]

Even so, despite the way a single author or case can cross over these lines, there is a striking disparity in how these views treat equity's form. Consider the hierarchy between legal and equitable remedies. This is something Fiss and Laycock strongly reject. Not only does Laycock reject the hierarchy of legal over equitable remedies, but even when he offers the alternative categories of specific and substitutionary remedies, he rejects any hierarchy between them. By contrast, many of the scholars who have written in the wake of Calabresi and Melamed have made arguments for hierarchy, for having either property rules or liability rules be the default that is set aside only if it is in some way inadequate. And in contrast to both of those perspectives, Smith's work argues that there is value in the

74

> According to well-established principles of equity, a plaintiff seeking a permanent injunction must satisfy a four-factor test before a court may grant such relief. A plaintiff must demonstrate: (1) that it has suffered an irreparable injury; (2) that remedies available at law, such as monetary damages, are inadequate to compensate for that injury; (3) that, considering the balance of hardships between the plaintiff and defendant, a remedy in equity is warranted; and (4) that the public interest would not be disserved by a permanent injunction.
>
> (ibid 391)

75 Gergen, Golden, and Smith (n 64).

76 eg Caprice L Roberts, 'The Restitution Revival and the Ghosts of Equity' (2011) 68 Washington & Lee Law Review 1027, 1034.

77 eg Doug Rendleman, 'The Trial Judge's Equitable Discretion Following *eBay v MercExchange*' (2007) 27 The Review of Litigation 63, 76 n 71.

hierarchy between law and equity, with equity serving a gap-filling, backup role that prevents people from taking advantage of legal rules. The ability of equity to serve that role, while still keeping a crisp legal rule in most cases, depends on equity's being supplementary and extraordinary and not in play in every case.[78]

VI. Lessons for Fusion

The dimensions given above—past and present, form and substance—offer a number of lessons for thinking about fusion.

First, there is no metaphrase position. (Recall that 'metaphrase' is Dryden's term for an excessively close translation, 'turning an Authour word by word, and Line by Line, from one Language into another'.) Those who support keeping something distinctively equitable do not favour keeping every jot and tittle of equity from some moment in the past. When Smith argues for equity as a constraint on opportunism, he is careful to note that his concept of equity is functional and does not perfectly correspond to equity as it could be defined historically or doctrinally.[79] (That is, a remedy or doctrine that is historically legal could be effectively 'equitable' in Smith's analysis, and vice versa.) In my own argument that equitable remedies in current American law are a coherent and rational system, I recognize points of difference between equity in the present and equity in the past.[80] Nor are the opponents of the 'fusion fallacy' in Australia and elsewhere arguing for a fixed and settled equity; they want equity to develop and change, but using its own principles and methods of decision-making (that is, its own 'texture').[81]

Second, the vigorous disagreement between the supporters and critics of fusion may seem to be about the present versus the past. For example, one might expect Laycock's position to be that the past of equity has no claims on us, and Smith's position to be that the past of equity has considerable rationality and should not be lightly jettisoned. But Laycock and Smith are both offering fairly strict translations of traditional equitable doctrines; both turn out to be 'scholars' in Arrowsmith and Shattuck's sense (and, for that matter, in any sense of the word). Where the disagreement really lies is about whether the form of equity—its edge, hierarchy, and texture—has any value.[82] Put

[78] Alexander Hamilton, 'The Federalist No 83' in Jacob E Cooke (ed), *The Federalist* (Wesleyan UP 1961) 558, 569 (fn omitted): 'The great and primary use of a court of equity is to give relief *in extraordinary cases*, which are exceptions to general rules. To unite the jurisdiction of such cases with the ordinary jurisdiction must have a tendency to unsettle the general rules and to subject every case that arises to a *special* determination.'

[79] For example, Smith (n 48) refers to 'Equity in a functional sense'.

[80] Bray (n 5). Equity in the past was of course not monolithic. On the artificial history of equity relied upon by US courts, and also by legal scholars, see Bray (n 22).

[81] Thus, in JD Heydon, MJ Leeming, and PG Turner (eds), *Meagher, Gummow & Lehane's Equity: Doctrines and Remedies* (5th edn, LexisNexis Butterworths 2015) 65–66, ss 2-380–2-395, one finds a critique of 'fusion by analogy' as well as a frank recognition that 'neither common law nor equity is frozen' and 'in an appropriate case both may be developed'.

[82] The general question of the effect of form in the law has been given too little attention. Exceptions include Shyamkrishna Balganesh and Gideon Parchomovsky, 'Structure and Value in the Common Law' (2015) 163 University of Pennsylvania Law Review 1241, and Jeremy Waldron, '"Transcendental Nonsense" and System in the Law' (2000) 100 Columbia Law Review 16. There has also been scant consideration of whether a doctrine is different if given in the form of a case or of a restatement, or whether a test has different results if it is sequential or multi-factor.

differently, right now scholars tend to talk past each other (I have done this myself), responding to a position on one dimension (form/substance) by taking a position on the other dimension (past/present). But by attending to these distinctions, we can better understand each other, and we can agree and disagree more precisely.

Third, the range of possibilities for fusion is broader than we realize. There can be variation, over time and across jurisdictions, not only with respect to the *degree* of fusion[83] but also with respect to the *kind*, that is, to whether equity's substance or form (or both) is thought to have something worth preserving. In the United States, the debates about fusion have been, surprisingly, the intramural disagreements of 'scholars'. There has been a remarkable absence of any attempt to creatively redesign the inherited difference between law and equity. There is of course the distinction between property rules and liability rules, but that might be considered an accidental translation: Calabresi and Melamed did not set out to translate the distinction between law and equity for their time and place. Twenty years ago, Laycock urged the development of new rules to replace the ones that separate legal and equitable remedies.[84] The invitation has not yet been accepted. Nor has any state creatively remade the distinction between law and equity.[85]

Fourth, thinking of fusion as translation requires us to ask exactly what is valuable about our equitable inheritance. Is it the substance, the form, or both? The answer to this question will determine whether we approach the problem of fusion as philologists, critics, or aesthetes.

Fifth, and relatedly, this fiction of translation requires us to ask how far removed we are from equity before fusion. If there were no gap—or even if the difference in legal rules, culture, and institutions were relatively small—then a very close translation would be possible. Dryden's metaphrase might even be achievable.[86] Equity could be transposed in the style of Pierre Menard.[87] But what if the gap between us and traditional equity were a chasm? Then Dryden's imitation might be the sincerest and only form of translation. But if we are in between those two—if there have been profound changes in legal rules, culture, and institutions since the time of, say, the eighteenth-century Chancellors, yet also many enduring legal phenomena (eg judges, juries, injunctions, pleadings)—then we are in the vast middle area of translation. We must paraphrase.

Yet the scope of the achievable paraphrase may shift over time. It may be that where legal rules or habits seem like something to be recovered from the past, as that past recedes there may be a gradual shift from metaphrase and paraphrase towards paraphrase and imitation.[88]

[83] Burrows (n 50).

[84] Laycock (n 50) 81–82.

[85] The civil jury trial right in the Seventh Amendment of the US Constitution is one of only a very few provisions of the Bill of Rights not 'incorporated' against the states. The result is that it does not constrain states; they have a freer hand than the national government in redrawing the distinction between law and equity.

[86] See (n 88).

[87] See Jorge Luis Borges, 'Pierre Menard, Author of the *Quixote*' in *Labyrinths: Selected Stories & Other Writings* (Donald A Yates and James E Irby eds, New Directions 1964) 36–44.

[88] cf DS Carne-Ross, 'Translation and Transposition' in Arrowsmith and Shattuck (n 26) 3: 'Transposition ... occurs when the language of the matter to be translated stands close enough to the language of the translator—in age, idiom, cultural habits and so on—for him to be able to follow the letter with a fair hope of keeping faith with

Moreover, how exactly we are inclined to paraphrase—more creatively remaking, or more closely following—will depend on considerations that go beyond this chapter. These include: the degree of value we attribute to (traditional) equity, the degree of distance we perceive between (traditional) equity and our present, our view of the traditionality and systematicity of law, our view of the kinds and degrees of judicial expertise, our view of the relative merits and legitimacy of statutory and common law, our view of the 'conformity conditions' imposed by our present legal norms on any translation from equity's past,[89] whether we have a temperament that favours conserving the good or one that favours experimenting in pursuit of the better, how exactly we are inclined to avoid risk,[90] and so on. These sorts of considerations will incline us towards ceding more creative control to the past, or grasping more of it in the present.

Given the answers to these questions, how should we think about equity and fusion today? Answering the question about what is valuable determines whether we are philologists, critics, or aesthetes; answering the question about distance determines whether we are poets or scholars. Yet these answers are only a beginning. Of the six possible compound answers—poet-philologist, scholar-philologist, poet-critic, scholar-critic, poet-aesthete, scholar-aesthete—each offers shape to the task of doing something with equity. Each still leaves the task.

VII. Conclusion

Fusion, and carrying something from independent equity over into contemporary law, require creativity, patience, and revision, just like the task of translation. Susan Bernofsky, an acclaimed translator and scholar of translation, has said, 'There is rarely a single perfect solution to any given translation problem, and so the process of revising involves trying out dozens of potential solutions until one of them begins to shimmer in that peculiar way that marks it as the best possible choice.'[91] Perhaps the experience of other common law countries is different, but, speaking from the vantage point of the United States, it would be impossible to say that we have tried out dozens of potential solutions to the problem of fusion and that one, or even two or three, have started to shimmer.

the spirit.' See also Toury (n 14) 206–07. Note that the translation may also alter the translator's own language, bending it towards the language of the original.

[89] In Gideon Toury's definition, '**literary translation** involves the imposition of "conformity conditions" beyond the linguistic and/or general-textual ones, namely, to models and norms which are deemed literary at the target end. It thus yields more or less well-formed texts from the point of view of the *literary* requirements of the recipient culture, at various possible costs in terms of the reconstruction of features of the source text' (ibid 202). By analogy, the translation of equity from the past must comply with the models and norms for legitimacy in a jurisdiction's present.

[90] cf Anthony Pym, 'On Toury's Laws of How Translators Translate' in Anthony Pym, Miriam Shlesinger, and Daniel Simeoni (eds), *Beyond Descriptive Translation Studies: Investigations in Homage to Gideon Toury* (Benjamins 2008) 311–328.

[91] Susan Bernofsky, 'Translation and the Art of Revision' in *In Translation: Translators on Their Work and What It Means* (Columbia UP 2013) 225.

12
Equitable Correction of Law

Emily Sherwin

Maitland suggested that following the procedural merger of law and equity, the only common characteristic of the various rules and remedies associated with equity is their shared history.[1] Although this is strictly true, courts have continued to administer many formerly equitable rules and remedies in ways that are distinct from their administration of ordinary rules of law. In this essay, I will suggest one possible reason why this is so. I will also consider what effect legal realism has had on the role of equitable rules and remedies in the American legal system.

One feature of judicial administration of historically equitable rules and remedies is that courts have used these rules and remedies, and particularly the special defences applicable to equitable remedies, to correct unsatisfactory outcomes that sometimes result from the application of general, determinate legal rules of law. In other words, courts have used historically equitable devices to accomplish equity in the Aristotelian sense.[2] General, determinate rules serve a number of important legal and social purposes, the foremost of which is to enable individuals to coordinate their actions with the actions of others. Yet, generality and determinacy build unacceptable outcomes into the administration of law. Strictly applied, a general, determinate rule may invite opportunism, or it may impose undeserved hardship on one party to a dispute.

Traditionally, another distinguishing feature of the judicial administration of equity has been the subordinate position courts assign to equitable rules and remedies. Courts have treated equity as a branch of law that comes into play only when the resolutions offered by legal rules and remedies are objectionable in one way or another. Although the extent to which courts continue to adhere to traditional standards, giving priority to legal remedies, is a subject of debate, courts still tend to speak of equity as a secondary component of the legal system.[3]

[1] Maitland defined equity as 'that body of laws administered by our English courts of justice which, were it not for the operation of the Judicature Acts, would be administered by courts that would be known as Courts of Equity'. FW Maitland, *Equity and Also the Forms of Action at Common Law* (JH Chaytor and J Whittaker eds, CUP 1929) 1.

[2] See Aristotle, *Nicomachean Ethics* (Terence Irwin ed and tr, Hackett 1985) 1138b25 ('And this is the nature of what is decent—rectification of law in so far as the universality of law makes it deficient'). Although Maitland argued that equity did not follow a set of specifically equitable principles, he did view equity as a supplement or 'gloss' on the common law, which softened the operation of common law rules. See Maitland (n 1) 18–19 ('if the legislature had passed a short act saying "Equity is hereby abolished", we might still have got on fairly well, in some respects our law would have been barbarous, unjust, absurd, but still the great elementary rights ... would have been decently protected').

[3] Douglas Laycock has argued at length that although courts continue to cite the rule that equitable relief is not available if the plaintiff has an adequate legal remedy, they do not in practice withhold equitable relief unless there are functional reasons to do so. See Douglas Laycock, *The Death of the Irreparable Injury Rule* (OUP 1991).

Emily Sherwin, *Equitable Correction of Law* In: *Philosophical Foundations of the Law of Equity*. Edited by: Dennis Klimchuk, Irit Samet, and Henry E Smith, Oxford University Press (2020).
DOI: 10.1093/oso/9780198817659.003.0013

Another traditional feature of equity, both before and after their procedural merger, is that equity has operated relatively obscurely within the legal system. Legal rules are comparatively easy to grasp, and courts tend to refer first to legal rules before turning to equitable exceptions. Further, corrective equity often takes the form of defences that apply only to historically equitable forms of relief.[4] The result is to decrease the perceived effects of equitable correction on legal rules: correction appears to be confined to one limited form of legal redress.

The combined effect of these three features of the administration of equitable rules and remedies is to maintain a precarious but useful balance between the benefits of determinate legal rules and the attraction of leniency. For reasons I will describe below, a system of law must provide in some way for corrective equity. At the same time, too much equitable correction can undermine rules and consequently threaten other important ends of the legal system.[5] The result is that determinate rules, which allow for coordination, and corrective equity, which allows for leniency, cannot easily coexist unless equity remains both subordinate to law and relatively obscure.

The legal realists who shaped American law in the last century were sceptical of rules and enthusiastic about particularized, fact-based decision-making. They also disliked obscurity in law and insisted that the grounds of legal decisions should be clear: only through clarity can law be harnessed effectively to social scientific objectives. The result of this combination of attitudes was a programme that altered the relation between law and equity by placing corrective equity front and centre in the legal system. Pleading and procedure were geared towards facts rather than law and substantive rules were supplemented or replaced by explicitly particularistic doctrines such as unconscionability.[6]

If the realists were wrong about rules, the strategies they pursued may be costly over time. By enlarging and spotlighting equity, they dispensed with the protective cover that once surrounded equitable decision-making and limited the effects of equity on general, determinate rules. When rules and equitable correction are equally open to view in a public system of law, the reliability of rules is significantly, and progressively, diminished.

This is not to suggest that equity can or should be hidden deliberately from public view. At least in a system that aspires to maintain the allegiance of its citizens, deceptive tactics will backfire. My objective is simply to explain the need for equity and the dilemma that it poses for law.

[4] Examples of equitable defences appear below in the text accompanying (nn 30–34).

[5] In a public legal system, each act of leniency in applying a rule will reduce the perception, by actors and judges, that the rule is regularly enforced, and in so doing will reduce the coordination and other values of the rule. Consequently, leniency decreases the weight of first order reasons for actors and judges to follow the rule. See Larry Alexander and Emily Sherwin, *The Rule of Rules: Morality, Rules, and the Dilemmas of Law* (Duke UP 2001) 81–83.

[6] See n 41.

I. Rules

One way to look at legal decision-making is from the forward-looking perspective of a benevolent lawmaking authority. I assume for this purpose that the lawmaking authority aims to serve the interests of those who are governed by law. I assume also that it approaches this task in a competent way.

From the authority's vantage point, legal rules[7] perform a number of important functions. If the authority has better information about the consequences of behaviour than most of its subjects have, it can guide decision-making by enacting rules to govern conduct or transactions. Whether or not the authority has superior information, it can enact rules that will enable private actors to coordinate their behaviour.[8] In the absence of reliable rules, self-regulation may be difficult, and, in any event, individual actors cannot anticipate what others will do. Once a set of rules is in place and regularly followed, it becomes easier to anticipate what others will do and so to plan around the predicted conduct. Finally, regularly followed rules settle controversy and uncertainty that might otherwise consume individual and social resources.

To provide these benefits, rules must be general in application and reasonably determinate.[9] Generality allows the rule-maker to provide for similarly situated parties and like cases that cannot be fully specified in advance in a single rule. Determinacy enables the rule to provide effective guidance, to serve as a basis for coordination, and to settle controversy in terms that do not revive the dispute when the rule is interpreted and applied.

General and relatively determinate rules, however, will sometimes prescribe outcomes that are incorrect, all things considered. General language chosen in advance will cover unanticipated cases in which the rule's prescription is out of place. Determinate terms will sweep in some situations that a more open-ended inquiry would exclude.

If the errors brought about by a general, determinate rule are too frequent or too great, the rule should be discarded or revised. In at least some cases, however, the benefits a rule provides through guidance, coordination, and settlement are more significant than the errors it periodically generates. In that case, the rule is a good rule and should

[7] The most comprehensive source on the benefits of determinate rules and the problems they pose is Frederick Schauer, *Playing by the Rules: A Philosophical Examination of Rule-Based Decision-Making in Law and Life* (Clarendon Press 1991). The points made in this subsection are also discussed at length in Alexander and Sherwin (n 5) 53–95.

[8] On the coordination effects of rules, see, eg, Gerald J Postema, 'Coordination and Convention at the Foundations of Law' (1982) 11 Journal of Legal Studies 165, 172–86.

[9] See Schauer (n 7) 53–68. The arguments made here assume that rules have a core of determinate meaning, even if their meaning is uncertain in some contexts. See generally Kent Greenawalt, *Law and Objectivity* (OUP 1992) 34–89; HLA Hart, *The Concept of Law* (Clarendon Press 1961) 122–38; Schauer (n 7) 53–68; Jules L Coleman and Brian Leiter, 'Determinacy, Objectivity, and Authority' (1993) 142 University of Pennsylvania Law Review 549; Lawrence B Solum, 'On the Indeterminacy Crisis: Critiquing Critical Dogma' (1987) 54 University of Chicago Law Review 462.

be retained.[10] I will assume for the purpose of this essay that the rules at issue are good rules in this sense, despite some flawed results.

It might be thought that the flawed results of justified rules can be eliminated by adding a general exception for all cases in which, as a result of a rule's generality and determinate language, the rule prescribes a wrong result. The exception, in other words, would instruct the rule-applier to follow the rule 'except whenever, all things considered, the rule dictates the wrong result in a particular case'. A general equitable exception of this kind would come into play at the time the rule is applied to a particular set of facts, when more is known about the likely consequences of following the rule. If it appeared at the time of application, after taking into account the damage that a violation of the rule will cause to values such as future guidance, coordination, and settlement, that following the rule is a mistake, then an equitable modification would be called for; otherwise, it would not.

The difficulty with this solution, from the point of view of a benevolent lawmaking authority, is that a general equitable exception must be applied by human agents, who are not omniscient and do not reason flawlessly from the evidence they have. The rule-applier may be a rule-subject deciding whether to obey, or a judge deciding whether to enforce the rule according to its terms. Either way, she is likely to have incomplete evidence about the consequences of breaking or following the rule. Moreover, the rule-applier will be subject to common reasoning biases. Like most human agents, she will tend to overvalue relatively immediate and salient facts, as compared to facts about long-term consequences of violating the rule such as diminished capacity for interpersonal coordination.[11] As a result, the rule-applier is likely to undervalue reasons to follow the rule in a systematic way. For example, she may focus on the cost or unfairness of following the rule in this case, omitting to consider that violating the rule, or failing to enforce the rule, may affect general perceptions that the rule is regularly followed, and so reduce its usefulness as a source of coordination.[12] Accordingly, the rule-applier is likely to err in favour of corrective equity more often than she errs in favour of following the rule.

Another possible compromise solution is to add both a general exception for recalcitrant cases and a presumption in favour of following the rule unless it appears that there are reasons of considerable magnitude to violate the rule.[13] Presumptive rule-following, however, is also subject to error at the point of application. A general practice of presumptive rule-following may also tend to erode over time: a presumption in

[10] If the rule is a good rule, but revisions could reduce the number of bad results, then ideally the rule should be revised. In the law–equity debate, however, this is a secondary problem.

[11] For overviews of the problem of cognitive biases and studies documenting the availability heuristic and similar patterns of human reasoning, see Daniel Kahneman, Paul Slovic, and Amos Tversky (eds), *Judgment under Uncertainty: Heuristics and Biases* (CUP 1982) 163; Daniel Kahneman, Paul Slovic, and Amos Tversky (eds), *Heuristics & Biases: The Psychology of Intuitive Judgment* (CUP 2002).

[12] The rule-maker might build an exception into the rule, for cases with special features. To avoid the reasoning errors the rule is designed to prevent, however, the exception must be stated in fairly objective terms. Consequently, an exception of this type is really just an additional term of the rule.

[13] This is Schauer's preferred solution. See Schauer (n 7) 202–05 and Frederick Schauer, 'Rules and the Rule of Law' (1991) 14 Harvard Journal of Law & Public Policy 645, 674–79.

favour of compliance assumes that subjects will weigh the immediate reasons to break a rule against reasons to follow the rule, such as the potential harm to coordination and other benefits of the rule. Each decision to violate the rule slightly decreases the perception that the rule is generally followed, and therefore slightly decreases the weight that other potential rule-followers will assign to the benefits associated with the rule. For these reasons the best resolution, from authority's point of view, is for all persons to follow the rule in all cases.

Thus if, on average, the benefits of the rule outweigh the errors it will cause, the rule is justified. And if, on average, the rule outperforms individual judgment at the point of application, a general equitable exception is unwarranted. Another way to put this is that, from the authority's point of view, it is best that all those who apply the rule should treat the existence of the rule as an exclusionary reason for action.[14] An exclusionary reason is one that functions both as a first-order reason to act in a certain way and as a second-order reason not to consider, or at least not to act on, a range of possible contrary reasons for action.[15] Treating rules as exclusionary reasons for action solves the problem of error, and preserves the benefits of the rule, by blocking evidence of special particular circumstances, as least if they fall within the general range of circumstances the lawmaker considered in designing the rule.

II. Equity

A strict approach to rules, in which rules function as exclusionary reasons for action, has significant practical benefits as long as the rules are good rules and perform better on average than human judgment at the point of application. Why, then, might there be a need for corrective equity?

A. Opportunism

One answer, proposed by Henry Smith, is that equity allows judges to police the opportunism that determinate rules inevitably attract.[16] Relatively sophisticated players can profit through bad behaviour that is accidentally allowed, or not quite covered, by the

[14] On exclusionary reasons for action, see Joseph Raz, *The Morality of Freedom* (OUP 1986) 57–62; Joseph Raz, *The Authority of Law* (OUP 1979) pp 16–19, 22–23, 30–33.

[15] See Joseph Raz, 'Promises and Obligation' in PMS Hacker and J Raz (eds), *Law, Morality, and Society* (Clarendon 1977) 221–23 (indicating that the exclusion is limited).

[16] For Smith, policing opportunism is a prominent function of equitable defences, although not the only role that equity plays in modern legal systems. See, eg, Henry E Smith, 'Why Fiduciary Law Is Equitable' in Andrew S Gold and Paul B Miller (eds), *Philosophical Foundations of Fiduciary Law* (OUP 2014) 261; Yuval Feldman and Henry E Smith, 'Behavioral Equity' (2014) 170 Journal of Institutional and Theoretical Economics 137; Henry E Smith, 'Equity as Second-Order Law: The Problem of Opportunism' <http://papers.ssrn.com/sol3/papers.cfm?abstract_id=2617413> (15 January 2015); Henry E Smith, 'Equitable Defenses as Meta-Law', in Paul S Davies, Simon Douglas, and James Goudkamp (eds), *Defences in Equity* (Hart forthcoming).

terms of the rule. Corrective equity allows judges to intervene after the fact and eliminate unfair gains obtained in this way.

This is an appealing argument, which assigns a function to equity in a procedurally merged legal system without endorsing the sort of open-ended correction that does most damage to the value of rules. The opportunism argument, however, raises several questions. One of these is empirical. From the point of view of the lawmaking authority, it may or may not be the case that the instrumental benefits of penalizing opportunists counterbalance the loss of rule-based benefits such as coordination that occurs when rules are not enforced according to their terms. Moreover, if judges can recapture enough opportunistic gain to outweigh the benefits of full enforcement, then the rule probably is not a good rule and its terms should be amended. Another problem that enters into the empirical balance is the possibility that judges may fail to distinguish accurately between deliberate advantage-taking and innocent reliance on rules that generate losses for one party.

Smith characterizes the anti-opportunism function of equity as a second-order function in a system that otherwise enforces the rules. Equity, in other words, is a type of law about law, distinct from the ordinary business of enforcing legal rules. This characterization seems designed in part to limit the effects of equity on rules. The distinction between first-order and second-order law, however, is not likely to affect actors' practical assessments of their legal reasons for action unless equity is not only second order but also hidden from full view. In a legal system in which all judicial decisions, legal and equitable, are publicly accessible, what matters is which set of reasons ultimately will prevail. To the extent that equity wins, legal rules are inert.[17]

B. The Rules Gap

My argument for equity is somewhat different, and depends on gap between the point of view of the rulemaking authority and the point of view of those who act under rules.[18] Rule subjects and rule-appliers encounter rules in the context of a particular case, in which adverse consequences of a general, determinate rule are likely to be both evident and salient. From this perspective, correction will sometimes seem necessary, and limited correction based on opportunistic behaviour may not be enough.

Consider the position of a conscientious actor who confronts a case governed by a general rule. The actor agrees with the rulemaking authority that the rule is a good

[17] This seems to have been Hohfeld's view. In his work on equity, Hohfeld said that when law and equity come into conflict, 'the so-called legal rule in every such case has, *to that extent*, only an apparent validity and operation as a matter of *genuine* law. Though it may represent an important stage of thought in the solution of a given problem ... as regards the very relation in which it suffers direct competition with a rule of equity, the law is, *pro tanto*, of no greater force that an unconstitutional statute.' Wesley Newcomb Hohfeld, 'The Relations Between Law and Equity' (1913) 11 Michigan Law Review 537, 543–44.

[18] Frederick Schauer has used the term 'asymmetry of authority' to describe this difference in perspective ((n 7) 128–44). Larry Alexander refers to the problem as the 'Gap'. Larry Alexander, 'The Gap' (1991) 14 Harvard Journal of Law & Public Policy 695. For further discussion, see Alexander and Sherwin (n 5) 54–95.

rule and understands the various reasons why, from the authority's point of view, she should follow the rule in this case. She understands that rules yield important practical benefits when regularly followed. She also understands that individual reasoners are prone to errors, especially when confronted with the salient facts of a single situation. Consequently, she understands that in the long run, the sum of outcomes will be best if all actors, including her, follow the rule in all cases that fall within its terms.

Yet, the actor may still believe that she should not follow the rule in this case. The authority's position is a position that holds on average, subject to the further understanding that any general and determinate rule will sometimes dictate the wrong result for a particular case. A reflective actor will consider not only which action best fits the circumstances, but also whether others are likely to observe her conduct and if, so, what effect a violation would have on the coordination value of the rule. She must also consider the likelihood that her own reasoning is biased or otherwise faulty and the chance that authority possesses special expertise that exceeds her own. Nevertheless, after taking all these considerations into account, the actor may conclude that it is best to violate the rule in this case.

In these circumstances, the perspective of the actor diverges from that of the rule-making authority. From the actor's point of view, following the rule will seem irrational and wrong. In fact, the actor may be incorrect: she may have underestimated the probability of harm to the rule and overestimated her reasoning abilities. Nevertheless, if she complies with the rule she is acting against her own best understanding of current reasons for action.

This dilemma can be restated in terms of practical rationality. Practical rationality is the rationality of agents in choosing and taking action.[19] I assume a primarily instrumental understanding of practical rationality, in which it is rational for an agent to choose the action that will best advance her ends.[20]

Traditionally, practical rationality is evaluated in terms of the agent's current reasons for action.[21] More recently, a number of writers have suggested that it is a mistake to think about practical rationality solely in terms of present reasons for action. Instead, practical rationality is a condition that extends over time: actors often can achieve greater instrumental benefits by forming intentions and sticking with them over time than by focusing exclusively on current reasons for action.[22] Thus, if the actor will do

[19] A classic discussion appears in Derek Parfit, *Reasons and Persons* (Clarendon Press 1984).

[20] See, eg, Michael E Bratman, *Intentions, Plans, and Practical Reason* (Harvard UP 1987) 52. Instrumental benefit can be defined broadly to encompass moral values of the agent.

[21] Edward McClennen calls this the principle of 'Separability' and illustrates with a decision tree in which each new decisional node starts fresh with current forward-looking reasons. A decision tree of this type separates rationality into slices of time and rationality at each slice tied to current reasons for action. See Edward F McClennen, 'Pragmatic Rationality and Rules' (1997) 23 Philosophy & Public Affairs 229.

[22] See Bratman (n 20) 2–3, 83–91; David Gauthier, 'Intention and Deliberation' in P Danielson (ed), *Modeling Rationality, Morality, and Evolution* (OUP 1998) 13; David Gauthier, 'Assure and Threaten' (1994) 104(4) Ethics 690; Edward F McClennen, 'Pragmatic Rationality and Rules' (1997) 26(3) Philosophy & Public Affairs 210, 230; Edward F McClennen and Scott J Shapiro, 'Rule-Guided Behavior' *New Palgrave Dictionary of Economics and the Law* (Palgrave 1998) vol 3, 367; Scott J Shapiro, *Legality* (Harvard UP 2011) 122–24; and Scott J Shapiro, 'The Difference that Rules Make' in Brian Bix (ed), *Analyzing Law: New Essays in Legal Theory* (Clarendon 1998) 33.

better in the long run by always following the rule than by always exercising her best judgment, then the rational choice is to follow the rule.

There are difficulties with this temporally extended approach to rationality, particularly in the context of rule-following. First, rationality seems to presuppose the possibility of a reasoned change of mind when the agent confronts circumstances that she did not specifically anticipate when she formed her intention.[23] Sticking doggedly to a plan when current reasons for action appear to support a change in course may be a practical mistake. Second, it is hard to explain the cognitive mechanism that would allow a rational actor to act on a prior intention in the face of a contrary belief about what she now should do. Arguably, deliberation can only conclude in action when the action is supported by the agent's will.[24] Once the actor forms a belief about reasons for action, based on current evidence, she will lack the will necessary to support the act.

One possible way to explain the rationality of acting on prior intentions is to argue that once the actor has settled on a plan, rationality does not require further reflection at the time of action. In other words, although it might not be rational for an actor to act against her present reflective understanding of reasons for action, it can be rational to act on prior intentions without reflection at the point of action. Michael Bratman, in particular, has argued that it is rational to act unreflectively on prior intentions as long as the actor is guided by practically reasonable general dispositions towards intentions, meaning dispositions that achieve good results over time. In Bratman's view, intentions are special cognitive states that carry with them an element of 'volitional commitment' as long as they remain in place. As a result, unless the actor pauses to reconsider, her prior intention will support current action without the need to form new beliefs about current reasons for action.[25] In this way, the actor can obtain the benefits of making and acting on stable plans without sacrificing rationality.

Bratman's account of temporally extended practical rationality provides a cognitive explanation for adherence to rules, and for the idea that legal rules provide exclusionary reasons for action. A rational actor can form an intention to follow a set of good rules, then act directly on her intention without considering contrary reasons for action, based on her prior volitional commitment to follow the rules. It seems to follow that rationality does not require equitable exceptions to rules. If it is rational over the long run to follow the governing rules, rational actors can and should adopt the authority's point of view and follow the rules unreflectively in particular cases.

Yet, the argument that it is always rational to act on a prior intention to obey sound rules has several weaknesses. One is that nothing other than the force of habit requires actors to follow or apply rules without reflection. At least according to Bratman's account of rationality, the volitional commitment associated with rules dissipates if the

[23] This is most clear in Bratman's discussion. See Bratman (n 20) 60 (suggesting that whenever an agent spontaneously reflects on reasons for an action, she effectively reconsiders prior intentions relating to that action).

[24] Raz, for example, argues that deliberation does not lead directly to action but instead requires the assistance of both intention and an element of will. See Joseph Raz, *From Normativity to Responsibility* (OUP 2011) 131–37.

[25] See Bratman (n 20) 15–16, 64–65, 811–83. Bratman's approach also provides an answer to Raz's point that deliberative action depends on will. Volitional commitment can be understood to carry the element of will and so to satisfy the requirement of will. See text to (n 25).

actor chooses to reflect. As a result, there may still be cases in which the actor reflects, reconsiders, and then must face a conflict between the demands of the rule and what she perceives to be the rational choice of action.

A second problem is this. Assume the actor does not reflect before complying with a rule, and assume that it is practically rational for her to do so, in the sense that regular unreflective compliance with rules will be instrumentally beneficial over time. In this type of case, practical rationality appears to lead the actor into epistemic irrationality. A very plausible understanding of epistemic rationality holds that individuals must advert to evidence in their possession that defeats beliefs they currently hold.[26] This standard of responsibility can easily be extended to the case of the rule-follower who believes that it is generally best follow a rule but has evidence suggesting that she should not follow the rule in a particular case. The evidence does not defeat her belief that is it is generally best to follow the rule, but it indicates that her belief is misplaced in her current circumstances and that she should adjust her belief to suit the case. Thus, although the practically rational course may be to treat the rule as an exclusionary rule and follow it without reflection, an actor who does this may not be epistemically rational.

III. Judicial Equity

Equity enters in because the foregoing observations about discomfort and irrationality in particular cases apply not only to actors who are called on to follow rules but also to judges who must apply rules to individual actors after the fact. Judges often act as rule-makers, and so are likely to understand the long-term benefits of regular application of rules. Yet judges are also rule-appliers, who confront rules in the setting of particular cases and face difficulties similar to those that actors face when a general rule produces a result that seems unintended or wrong. Moreover, judges are human reasoners, who are similarly susceptible to the type of cognitive bias in favour of immediate, salient facts that affects any fallible reasoner.[27]

From the point of view of the rulemaking authority, it is best that judges apply good rules according to their terms, even when the judge believes the outcome the rule calls for is wrong. Because judges are not perfect reasoners, regular enforcement of the rule according to its terms often will produce better results over time than particularistic decision-making by judges. Moreover, when judges err, the risk of harm to rule values is especially high. If actors perceive that judicial decisions do not regularly conform

[26] See Richard Feldman, 'The Ethics of Belief' in Earl Conee and Richard Feldman (eds), *Evidentialism: Essays in Epistemology* (OUP 2004) 186–88 (beginning with a very limited view of epistemic responsibility but later qualifying it by requiring agents to take account of defeating evidence); Alvin Goldman, 'Toward a Synthesis of Reliabilism and Evidentialism' in Trent Doherty (ed), *Evidentialism and Its Discontents* (OUP 2011) 23 (writing from a process reliabilist point of view, but adding a standard of epistemic responsibility to process defeating evidence).

[27] See Jeffrey J Rachlinski, 'Bottom-Up and Top-Down Lawmaking' (2006) 73 University of Chicago Law Review 933, 942–43 (discussing the effects of affect and availability biases in judicial decision-making); Frederick Schauer, 'Do Cases Make Bad Law?' (2006) 73 University of Chicago Law Review 883, 895 (observing that judges, as rule-makers, are subject to the availability bias).

to rules, they will not expect other actors to follow the rules and can no longer rely on them as focal points for coordination. From the point of view of the judge, however, enforcing the rule when the judge believes the outcome is wrong will appear irrational and unfair to the parties affected.

In cases involving equitable defences, judges often self-consciously invoke the corrective function associated with the equity side of law. For example, in *Panco v Rogers*, Panco agreed to sell his house to Rogers.[28] Mr Panco, a retired carpenter who had built his own house, agreed to sell the house to the Rogers. After discussing the transaction with Mrs Panco, who was not a native English speaker, Mr Rogers prepared an agreement naming a price of $5,500. Panco, who was elderly and deaf, signed the agreement without reading it, then later refused to convey.

Panco testified that he intended to ask for $12,500 for the house and the court found the house was worth at least $10,000. The court found no evidence that Rogers had engaged in fraud, concealment, or undue influence, and determined that Panco had breached the contract. It nevertheless denied Rogers's claim for specific performance, saying that

> an application for specific performance is directed to the sound discretion of a court of equity… [T]he court must be satisfied that the claim is fair, reasonable, and just, and in judging of its fairness, the court will look not only at the terms of the contract itself, but at all of the surrounding circumstances, including the relations the parties.… Where the enforcement of a contract for the sale of land would be harsh, oppressive or manifestly unjust to one of the parties thereto, its specific performance will not be decreed, but the parties will be left to their remedy at law.[29]

This is a classic example of corrective equity, applied to deny equitable relief. The applicable rules did not recognize unilateral mistake as a ground for rescission, so the contract was valid and Panco theoretically was liable for breach. In fact, the equitable defence probably was conclusive. A damage claim would require Rogers to incur additional expense, and in any event a jury fixing damages for the value of the Rogers' lost bargain would likely fix a low sum based on the same considerations that led the court to deny an equitable remedy. Therefore, the decision amounts to an exception to the court-stated rule, that a unilateral mistake is not a defence to contract obligation.

Panco v Rogers can be viewed as a case of opportunism. Rogers had reason to believe that the Pancos were not experienced bargainers, may have known the price was low, and may have suspected that Panco had not read the contract. If so, the case fits well with the view that corrective equity operates, or should operate, as a mechanism by which courts can detect and penalize parties who have taken advantage of general, determinate rules to obtain unjustified gains.

The potential for equitable correction, however, goes beyond opportunism. Suppose instead that, on the best understanding of the facts, Rogers acted in good faith: he was

[28] *Panco v Rogers* 87 A.2d 770 (NJ Ch Div 1952).
[29] *Panco* (n 28) 773.

an inexperienced buyer who was not familiar with prices, he believed that Mrs Panco stated and intended a price figure of $5,500, and he did not realize that Panco was mistaken about the contents of the written agreement. Although there are no signs of opportunism in this case, the bargain is one-sided and there is no reason to believe that the exchange is efficient. Thus, the judge in this revised case would still be under rational and sympathetic pressure to depart from the rules and deny full enforcement of the contract.

Another example is *Patel v Ali*.[30] Mrs Ali, a young mother, agreed to sell her home to the Patels in what appears to have been a fair transaction. Closing was significantly delayed for various reasons that were not attributable to the Patels, including a claim by Mr Ali's bankruptcy trustee that eventually was dismissed. In the interim, Mrs Ali had a second and third child. She also developed bone cancer, which resulted in amputation of a leg. By the time of the closing, she was dependent on help from her sister, who lived nearby, and other sympathetic neighbours in a close-knit Muslim community.

In these circumstances, the court refused to grant specific performance and limited the Patels' remedy to damages for loss of bargain (to be financed by helpful friends). As in the case of Mr Panco, it seems unlikely that the plaintiffs would choose to press a claim for damages or that, if they did, the jury would award substantial damages. So, in effect, the judge made an exception to the normal rules of contract obligation.[31] The ambivalence he felt in doing so is evident in his opening remarks:

> The circumstances of [this] case are unusual and it has caused me some anxiety. The argument for the defendant ... necessarily arouses so much sympathy that I felt for a long time that any exercise of discretionary jurisdiction in her favour would probably be unfair to her opponents, just because of the force of such sympathy.[32]

In the end, however, sympathy in light of Mrs Ali's circumstances prevailed over fidelity to the rules.

In each of these cases, it might be better from the authority's point of view to enforce the rule, both to preserve its value as a guide to contracting parties and to contain judicial error over the long run. But this approach is unsatisfying from the vantage point of the particular case. The two viewpoints at work are fundamentally different: they cannot be reconciled or averaged, because they pit long-term practical rationality against epistemic rationality, human sympathy, and human error. Both viewpoints are important to a legal system that depends in part on the loyalty of both actors and judges. Corrective equity gives recognition to the second, particularized point of view.

[30] *Patel v Ali* [1984] 48 P & CR 118.

[31] The court stated that subsequent personal hardship is not normally a defence to contract obligation; the seller takes the risk of unexpected events. It reasoned that in the case of Ms Ali, she never bargained for a situation in which years would pass before closing. Arguably, however, delay can also be a risk the buyer assumes by signing a contract (ibid 123–24).

[32] ibid 119.

IV. Equity and Legal Realism

Modern American law has been much influenced by the legal realist movement that began in the first half of the twentieth century. Although the American legal realists took various views on judicial decision-making, they converged on several general ideas. First, most were sceptical about the value of general, determinate rules. They argued that judges typically have a choice among eligible but conflicting rules and that in any event, rules are subject to conflicting interpretations. Consequently, rules exert no real force on judicial decisions.[33]

A closely related idea was that judicial decisions respond primarily to the facts of particular cases. Judges may be moved by the impact of their decisions on the parties involved, or by the social and economic consequences of their decisions, or simply by their own 'hunches' about the dispute before them.[34] It follows that operative 'law' is located not in rules but in the facts and outcomes of individual disputes or empirical judgments about the impact of decisions.[35]

This understanding of nature of law and legal decision-making led to several prescriptions. Pleading and procedures should be oriented towards the fullest possible discovery of facts and legal doctrine should be stated in open terms that lead judges to investigate the facts of cases before them.[36] Legal theory should be empirical rather than analytical and legal reform should work from the premise that decision-making turns on facts.[37] Finally, judges should state the grounds of their decisions as forthrightly as

[33] Even Karl Llewellyn, principal drafter of the Uniform Commercial Code, took this view, saying that 'every single precedent, according to what may be the attitude of future judges, is ambiguous, is wide or narrow at will'(*The Bramble Bush: Some Lectures on the Law and Its Study* (Oceana 1930) 64–69) (emphasis omitted); see also Karl N Llewellyn, 'A Realistic Jurisprudence—The Next Step' (1930) 30 Columbia Law Review 431, 447–48 (discussing the difference between 'paper rules' and the 'real rules' that govern decisions). See generally Brian Leiter, 'American Legal Realism' in Dennis Patterson (ed), *A Companion to Philosophy of Law and Legal Theory* (2nd edn, Blackwell 2010) 249, 253–54 (discussing realist endorsement of 'rational' indeterminacy).

[34] See, eg, Jerome Frank, *Law and the Modern Mind* (Brentano's 1930) 111 ('The peculiar traits, dispositions, biases and habits of the particular judge will, then, often determine what he decides to be the law); Joseph C Hutcheson, 'The Judgment Intuitive: The Function of the "Hunch" in Judicial Decision' (1929) 14 Cornell Law Quarterly 274, 278 ('I, after canvassing all the available material ... wait for the feeling, the hunch—that intuitive flash of understanding that makes the jump-spark connection between question and decision'); Llewellyn, *Bramble Bush* (n 33) 69 (advocates must build an inductive case for their desired result); Herman Oliphant, 'A Return to Stare Decisis, Pt. 2' (1928) 14 ABA Journal 159, 159 ('we see that courts are dominantly coerced not by the essays of their predecessors but by a surer thing—by the intuition of fitness of solution to problem—and a renewed faith in judicial government is engendered').

[35] Frank, *Law and the Modern Mind* (n 34) 276 ('Law is what happened or will happen in concrete cases'); Llewellyn, *Bramble Bush* (n 33) 2–4 ('to my mind the main thing is seeing what officials do. . .; and seeing that there is a certain regularity in their doing—a regularity which makes possible prediction'). See generally Leiter (n 33) 257 ('the Core Claim of realism' is that 'judges respond primarily to the stimulus of the underlying facts of the case').

[36] Stephen N Subrin, 'How Equity Conquered Common Law: The Federal Rules of Civil Procedure in Historical Perspective' (1987) 135 University of Pennsylvania Law Review 909, 962–74 (relating the history of Charles Clark and the Federal Rules of Civil Procedure); Llewellyn, 'Realistic Jurisprudence' (n 33) 452 (lawmakers 'must so shape [the rule] as to induce its application'); Oliphant (n 34) 160 (proposing 'reclassification of most of law in terms of the human relations affected by it').

[37] See, eg, Llewellyn, 'Realistic Jurisprudence' (n 33) 442–43 (the focal point of legal thought should be 'the area of contact between judicial (or official) behavior and the behavior of laymen') (emphasis omitted); Walter Wheeler Cook, 'The Logical and Legal Bases of the Conflict of Laws' (1924) 33 Yale Law Journal 457, 460 (proposing to 'observe concrete phenomena first and form generalizations afterwards').

possible, so that these can be studied and understood by all actors in the system. 'Covert tools are never reliable tools.'[38]

Steven Subrin has argued persuasively that in the realm of procedure, legal realism brought about a fundamental shift from traditional common law methods to fact-oriented methods associated with equity.[39] Subrin does not advocate a return to rigid common law procedures, but he suggests that the realist-inspired Federal Rules of Civil Procedure may have gone too far in the direction of unstructured and particularized decision-making. Lawsuits often lack focus, costs are high, outcomes are unpredictable, and the system consequently is not as effective as it might be in vindicating rights.[40]

The realist programme brought about similar changes in the substantive law, favouring fact-specific equitable doctrines over the more technical rules of the common law. A leading example is Karl Llewellyn's Uniform Commercial Code, which makes liberal use of equitable terms such as 'unconscionability' and 'good faith' that are virtually impossible to define outside the setting of a particular dispute.[41] Broad defences of this kind are no longer confined to equitable relief, but applied to legal remedies as well.[42]

Thus, in many places, Mr Panco could now rescind his contract with the Rogers, based on a unilateral mistake with unconscionable consequences.[43] Mrs Ali's defence of subsequent hardship remains unusual. When allowed, however, it is likely to be a full defence to contractual obligation, rather than a special defence to equitable relief. Thus, in the post-realist legal system, equity no longer operates in the background as a way for judges to act on their best judgment that a rule has misfired, by selectively denying remedies. Instead, corrective equity is built into the primary law: contracts shall be enforced unless there are good reasons not to enforce them.

In each of these cases, there was a legal rule in force that may have been a good rule from the general, forward-looking perspective of the rule-maker: a unilateral mistake about the terms of a written contract does not invalidate the contract; unanticipated difficulties arising after an agreement is made do not excuse performance; a bargained-for benefit is sufficient to support a contract. In any event, the courts were not prepared to

[38] Karl N Llewellyn, *The Common Law Tradition: Deciding Appeals* (Little Brown 1960) 365, quoting Karl N Llewellyn, 'Book Review' (1939) 52 Harvard Law Review 700, 703. See Oliphant (n 34) 159 ('With eyes cleared of the old and broad abstractions which curtain our vision, we come to recognize more and more the eminent good sense in what courts are wont to do about disputes before them').

[39] See Subrin (n 36) 973 ('the major theme [of the Federal Rules of Civil Procedure] was that procedures should step aside and not interfere with substance'), 1000 (in this way, 'equity procedures have swallowed those of common law').

[40] ibid 986–91.

[41] See UCC §§1–304 (good faith in performance and enforcement), (2–302) (unconscionability). Arthur Alan Leff was highly critical of the unconscionability provisions of the UCC and also distinguished Code unconscionability from the more modest unconscionability defence previously recognized in equity. See Arthur Allen Leff, 'Unconscionability and the Code: The Emperor's New Clause' (1967) 115 University of Pennsylvania Law Review 485. Unconscionability and similar terms were also incorporated into realist-inspired Restatements. See, eg, Restatement (Second) of Contracts §§ 153 (unilateral mistake), 205 (good faith and fair dealing) (American Law Institute, 1979).

[42] For example, the UCC's provision on unconscionability provides judges with a broad array of remedies in response to unconscionability, including refusal to enforce the contract by any means, legal or equitable. UCC § 302; see also Restatement (Second) of Contracts §208 (1981).

[43] Restatement (Second) of Contracts §153(a) (1981).

overrule the governing rules or amend them to exclude a defined set of circumstances. Instead, each court made an equitable exception based on the particular facts of the case before it and denied equitable relief without rescinding the contract or denying damages. Practically speaking, the result may have been that the contracts at issue were unenforceable by any means, but this effect was not explicit in the courts opinions and might not be apparent to observers who lack sophisticated understanding of law and legal remedies. Thus, in each case, particularized justice prevailed over a general rule, but in a roundabout and non-obvious way.

V. Clarity about Equity

Legal realism not only pushed law in the direction of particularistic decision-making, but also made the equitable component of legal decision-making more open and explicit. Traditionally, the main vehicles for corrective equity were equitable defences of the type applied in *Panco v Rogers* and *Patel v Ali*, which may not be immediately evident at the planning stage of actions and transactions. Although the existence of equitable defences has long been publicly accessible in judicial reports, parties—even those acting with professional legal advice—may not comprehend the importance of equitable relief or the special defence that may apply if an equitable remedy is needed. As a result, the effect of traditional equitable defences on the level of public confidence in the rules governing legal obligation is considerably muted. Judges deciding cases after the fact may understand that allowing an equitable defence creates an exception to the governing rules, but parties acting under rules may not fully grasp this point. In this way, the comparative obscurity of equitable defences provides a partial solution to the dilemma of general rules and equitable correction: judges perceive the effects of their decisions, but actors may not fully comprehend the unreliability of the rules.[44]

In addition to widening the scope of equitable correction, realist reforms placed equitable correction in a more visible role. The role of equity in modifying the outcome of rules has been codified, restated, and extended beyond the traditional, less visible realm of defences to equitable relief. Whatever cover the features of subordination and obscurity may once have provided to equitable correction is now largely gone.

VI. Conclusion: the Place of Equity in Modern Law

Corrective equity is inevitable in a legal system because actors and judges must apply general rules in the context of particular facts that cannot be fully specified when the rule is formulated. Even given a set of rules such that the sum of outcomes over time

[44] See generally Meir Dan-Cohen, 'Conduct Rules and Decision Rules: On Acoustic Separation in Criminal Law' (1984) 97 Harvard Law Review 625. See also Feldman and Smith (n 16) (considering the possibility of acoustic separation of messages aimed at good and bad actors in the legal system).

would be better if all people followed the rules in all cases, it will sometimes appear wrong, irrational, and unfair to enforce a rule. Corrective equity, however, impairs the reliability of, and so decreases the benefits of, determinate rules.

As a consequence of realist reforms, the effect of corrective equity on rules is no longer limited by the obscurity of equitable doctrines and defences and their seemingly secondary role in the system. Nor can this type of obscurity be reinstated. In a public system of law, obscurity cannot be engineered: proposal for deliberate obfuscation of corrective equity would surely be rejected as a form of manipulation practiced on judges and citizens. Thus, obscurity can only arise by an accident such as the separation of common law courts and chancery courts in much of Anglo-American legal history.

In the current legal world, the only available answer is that judges must do their best to understand the effects that relief from the errors of rules may have on the value of rules. This is not an ideal answer. It requires that judges, in making their decisions, must bear in mind the coordination benefits and other advantages of regularly enforced rules, try to calculate at least roughly the cumulative effects that exceptions in the current case and other similar cases will have on those benefits, and take account of the possibility that their own reasoning will be mistaken. It requires, in other words, that they must not take too seriously the realist faith in the accuracy of judicial 'hunches' and particularistic situation sense.

13

What Can 'Equity's Darling' Tell Us about Equity?

Aruna Nair and Irit Samet

I. Introduction

'The black market in stuff that just might have fallen off the back of a lorry predates lorries and probably the invention of the wheel.'[1] According to the Office of National Statistics, there were 5,066,000 incidents of crime against property in 2016 in the UK; of these, 59 per cent had the potential to generate stolen goods that could be resold as new or 'preloved'.[2] In the previous year, 1 per cent of mobile phone owners (equivalent to 446,000 people), experienced a theft. With the ubiquity of electronic commerce, and mega websites like eBay which allow people to sell used items in relative anonymity, competition between the original owners of property and purchasers from unauthorized sellers is highly likely to erupt.[3] But the new electronic platforms are just a new foil for one of property law's oldest chestnuts: the conflict between an owner of assets (FO), a purported purchaser of those assets under an unauthorized transfer (P), and the community that has a stake in the outcome of the dispute. It is, and has always been, a conflict that engages a particularly complex and varied smorgasbord of values and interests. Every system for the allocation of property rights must therefore make a choice as to the values and interests the solution it offers will cater for.[4] In this chapter, we take a close look at the particular legal dilemma of priority conflict, at law and in Equity. Our aim is to use this dilemma as a prism to examine the unique character of Equity's contribution to property law, highlighting how the central concept of conscience shapes both the content and structure of equitable rights to assets.

The choice Equity has made—to prefer the purchaser for value without notice over a first-time equitable owner—may look like a straightforward use of the usual building

[1] Mark Easton, 'Can You Persuade People Not to Buy Stolen Goods?' (*BBC News Magazine*, 31 October 2013) <www.bbc.co.uk/news/magazine-24745784>.

[2] Office for National Statistics, 'Focus on Property Crime: Year Ending March 2016' (2016). Vehicle-related theft comprised 17 per cent of the total, other theft of personal property—15 per cent, domestic burglary—14 per cent, and other household theft—13 per cent.

[3] See for example, Maya Rhodan, 'Feds Say Family Sold Millions in Stolen Goods on eBay' (*TIME Magazine*, 7 March 2014) <http://time.com/15678/feds-say-family-sold-millions-in-stolen-goods-on-ebay>.

[4] We define a system for the allocation of property rights in a broad sense, as including any system that allocates control of, and access to, items of social wealth to private individuals to the exclusion of others. Debates about whether equitable rights are property rights in any narrower sense are not, therefore, relevant for our purposes. On this point see further (n 10).

Aruna Nair and Irit Samet, *What Can 'Equity's Darling' Tell Us about Equity?* In: *Philosophical Foundations of the Law of Equity*. Edited by: Dennis Klimchuk, Irit Samet, and Henry E Smith, Oxford University Press (2020).

DOI: 10.1093/oso/9780198817659.003.0014

blocks of property law to construct a solution to a specific permutation of this age-old conflict. This is not so. In this chapter, we argue that the choice made by Equity on this occasion reflects its distinctive nature as a body of law that is highly responsive to interpersonal morality. At the same time, its flexibility allows Equity to locate the fine point at which patterns of moral responsibility coincide with efficiency considerations. As a result, Equity is able to develop a solution that is sensitive, so far as is possible, to the incommensurable values that are at play in such an intricate conflict. The distinctive nature of Equity's solution is particularly clear against the background of the current (ie post-1994) English common law, which treats these conflicts in a different way from civil systems or the UCC in the USA. The English common law solution represents a legitimate, albeit slightly unusual, choice from both efficiency and moral perspectives. However, we wish to argue, its framework does not fit the paradigm situation to which Equity responds, namely that of a competition between a beneficiary under a trust and a purchaser of assets from a trustee acting ultra vires. In a setting of trust, considerations of justice and efficiency call for a different solution from that offered by the common law; and Equity—with its habit of fastening on the purchaser's conscience, and probing into the special circumstances of every transaction—is particularly well suited to accommodate these considerations.

The chapter proceeds as follows. We first set out the array of justice and utility considerations that provide a metric for assessing different solutions to the conflict between first owners and purchasers (henceforth FO–P conflicts). In section III, we compare and contrast Equity's solution (ie the protection of Equity's darling) with the approach adopted by the common law. We then move to examine, in section IV, how the differences between the two approaches reflect the unique features of Equity, first and foremost its engagement with the defendant's conscience. These characteristics, we argue, enable Equity to weave an array of values and social goals into a successful strategy for coping with the challenge of incommensurable values we set out in section II.

II. What We Need to Consider

A 'winner takes it all' battle between innocents, which is played out in the crossroad between property and commercial law, is bound to be fiendishly difficult to solve. Some, indeed, believe that property law does not have the resources to offer a satisfactory solution to FO–P conflicts: a (largely) rule-based body of norms like property law, which is dominated by zero-sum games, can be perceived as lacking the nuance necessary for a satisfactory solution to such intricate conflicts.[5] But even if this is true, Equity, we argue, has at its disposal some unique tools it can employ in order to do a better job than other property law regimes. In that respect, the issue of FO–P conflicts is an excellent

[5] Allen Schwartz and RE Scott, 'Rethinking the Laws of Good Faith Purchase' (2011) 111 Columbia Law Review 1332. For the goals served by the zero-sum approach of property law, as compared to those promoted by the more context-specific approach of tort law, see Carol M Rose, 'The Shadow of the Cathedral' (1997) 106 Yale Law Review 2175.

test case for assessing the potential of Equity to utilize its unique features in order to construct solutions to perplexing problems. But before we can assess the merits of the way Equity tackles FO–P conflicts, we need to draw a conceptual map of the values and social goals that any good answer to the conundrum should address, and the different principled ways in which those values can be reconciled.

A. Protecting Entitlement to Property

The question 'what is property for?' or 'how can we be justified in allocating control over scarce resources to individuals who will not necessarily put them to the best possible use?' has intrigued the best minds in political philosophy. Those who believe that such justification can be found have come up with a highly diverse range of opinions about where we can find it, and which uses of private property it can sanction. However, while scholars differ on the ends, goods and values that private property serves, there is a wide consensus that title must come with the authority to decide not only what use the property will be put to, but also over whether, when and to whom it will pass (or the right to have these questions answered in a manner that promotes one's individual interests).[6] As Charlie Webb puts it, without the assurance to the owner that 'the dispositions he wants are the dispositions he gets ... an owner's claim to his assets would be no greater than my claim to the seat I happen to take on the bus: "mine" to enjoy while I am in occupation, but free to all comers the moment I am not'.[7] Whether ownership is designed to enable us to 'act in relation to others in accordance with self-chosen purposes', express our humanity, shield us from arbitrary state power, or incentivize people to work and create, it cannot do so on the 'bus seat' model.

In an FO–P conflict, the first owner did not voluntarily transfer her rights to the purchaser; the decision to do so is not made in accordance with either her will or her interests. When the common law has to decide whether (a full) title nevertheless passed, it therefore contemplates an exception to a principle that stands at the foundation of positive property law—*nemo dat quod non habet*—and the justifying principle behind this law (whatever it may be).[8] When FO–P conflicts flare up in Equity, the legal structure of the parties' rights is different. If the trustee sells a trust asset, the question is not whether he transferred the equitable interest of the beneficiary (he cannot), but whether the equitable interest disappeared as a result of the transfer of the legal title.[9]

[6] Jim Harris's definition of private property as involving 'authorised self-seekingness' is wide enough to cover this type of beneficial ownership as well (James Harris, *The Idea of Property: Its Meaning and Power* (OUP 2003) 76.

[7] Charlie Webb, 'Property' *Reason and Restitution* (OUP 2016) 90.

[8] On the cultural and economic roots of the *nemo dat* rule in Roman law and society, see Boris Kozolchyk, 'Transfer of Personal Property by a Nonowner: Its Future in Light of Its Past' (1987) 61 Tulane Law Review 1453, pt II.

[9] '[The trustee] simply transferred his legal ownership of the shares to [the purchaser], and, on the assumption that Samba was a bona fide purchaser for value without notice, the equitable interest effectively disappeared' (*Akers & Ors v Samba Financial Group* [2017] UKSC 6 (UKSC) per Lord Neuberger at [65]).

But the *normative* question remains importantly similar to the one we find at common law: under which conditions are we willing to say that an owner—a person to whom the law has allocated the right to have an asset used for her benefit—[10]has lost her rights because of an unauthorized transfer to a third party?

A decision that P gets a good title despite the involuntary nature of the transfer lands a blow to the FO's autonomy.[11] But since, as between the P and FO this is a zero-sum game, a decision that title does *not* pass means that respect for the FO's autonomy will come at the expense of P. And as Dennis Klimchuk points out (in the context of unjust enrichment claims arising out of similar circumstances of involuntary transfer), if the purchaser did not bring about the compromise of the first owner's autonomy, why should she account for it? [12] In FO–P conflicts, the responsibility for the setback to FO's autonomy lies squarely with the thief or embezzler.[13] The purchaser's responsibility is, at best, indirect: the maximum we can say is that if purchasers were *very* careful to investigate the title, thieves would lose much of the incentive to steal (assuming that very few steal or embezzle property for their personal use). This is not enough to justify treating P as responsible for the injury to FO's autonomy. Moreover, where purchasers are constantly exposed to the risk that first owners will come after them, their autonomy, as expressed in the ability to enjoy one's possessions and make plans for them, is also compromised. It seems therefore that, while a rule that overwhelmingly prefers the purchaser would indeed fail to properly take into account the owner's autonomy, a strong pro-FO priority rule cannot be justified purely on the basis of the need to protect entitlement to property.[14]

[10] One might think that the beneficiary in a FO–P conflict is to be treated differently by virtue of lacking this status of an 'owner', due to the quasi proprietary/personal, rather than fully proprietary, nature of the beneficiary's interests (for an account of the beneficiary's interest in trust assets as intermediate between a property and personal right, see McFarlane and Stevens, Chapter 9 in this volume). However, this explanation of the difference between common law and Equity on FO–P conflicts puts the cart before the horse. For the way to answer the question 'what is the nature of the beneficiary's interest', is to look into the different incidents of this particular relationship (like possession, right to exclude or use) in order to find out whether they support a property or *in personam* analysis: see, for instance, the exchange between JE Penner, 'The (True) Nature of a Beneficiary's Equitable Proprietary Interest under a Trust' (2015) 27 Canadian Journal of Law & Jurisprudence 473 and Ben McFarlane and Robert Stevens, 'The Nature of Equitable Property' (2010) 4 Journal of Equity 18 about the importance of 'possession' as an indicator of the proprietary nature of the relationship. If so, it is the law on how the BO–P conflict is resolved that explains the nature of the beneficiary's interest, not the other way around. In other words, one's view about whether the beneficiary's interest is proprietary or personal *follows from* one's interpretation of the legal norms that apply to the right (like Equity's darling, the ability to sue a thief directly, or the way the right behaves in bankruptcy), rather than explains it.

[11] See, for example, Dagan, 'Property's Structural Pluralism: On Autonomy, the Rule of Law, and the Role of Blackstonian Ownership' (2014) 3 Brigham–Kanner Property Rights Conference Journal 27.

[12] Dennis Klimchuk, 'The Normative Foundations of Unjust Enrichment' in Robert Chambers, Charles Mitchell, and JE Penner (eds), *Philosophical Foundations of the Law of Unjust Enrichment* (OUP 2009) 95–96.

[13] Although, as the judiciary often note, such 'rogues' are often practically very difficult to hold to account, or in the more colourful language of Lord Salmon, 'usually, the rogue ... is not worth powder and shot' (*Moorgate Mercantile Co Ltd v Twitchings* [1977] AC 890, at 907).

[14] The Italian law which prefers the purchaser in a number of respects may succumb to this criticism (see Giuseppe Dari-Mattiacci, 'Law and Culture: A Theory of Comparative Variation in bona fide Purchase Rules' (2015) 35 OJLS 543; see especially the table at 555).

B. Corrective Justice

In the context of FO–P conflicts, corrective justice answers the questions 'whether and to what extent and in what form and on what ground [property] should now be allocated back from one party to the other, reversing a [faulty] transaction that took place between them'.[15] If before the transaction the parties were equal, in the sense that each of them had what lawfully belonged to him or her, an injustice occurs 'when, relative to this baseline, one party realises a gain and the other a corresponding loss. The law corrects the injustice when it re-establishes the initial equality'.[16] However, tackling FO–P conflicts from a corrective justice perspective faces a serious difficulty. For corrective justice, as Weinrib explains, 'conceptualizes the parties as the active and passive poles of the same injustice'.[17] But, in an analogy to Dennis Klimchuk's contention in the context of unjust enrichment claims, the parties in FO–P conflicts are not really linked as doer and sufferer of the same wrong.[18] For even if the purchaser was not careful enough in examining the title (more on that below), the wrong which brought about FO's misery, and which links the parties together, is first and foremost the theft/embezzlement, and this is not a wrong committed by P. P is in fact also a victim of that wrong. And so, it seems to us that the transfer of property from FO to P cannot really be analysed as a transaction which is constituted on a wrong and must be reversed in order to correct it.

But perhaps corrective justice is after all the right perspective from which to explore the morality of FO–P conflicts if we replace the analogy to unjust enrichment with an analogy to accidents. For some, the conceptual relationship between FO–P conflicts and accidents is very intimate; according to Mautner, for example, '[t]riangle conflicts may well be viewed as accidents, while accidents may be viewed as events involving priority conflicts'.[19] The idea is, presumably, that since neither P nor FO intended the result (ie involuntary transfer), and can, at most, be blamed for carelessness, their status is similar to that of parties in tort lawsuits concerned with cases of accidental loss. Corrective justice is (at least) a prominent explanatory principle behind one idea of tort law, namely, that one may be made to bear the cost of a loss to which she has a causal connection even if she never intended to cause it.[20] And if conflicts between first owners and purchasers are indeed a kind of accident, one could argue that a successful solution will run along the lines of corrective justice. Alas, the analogy between FO–P conflicts and accidents can only be of limited assistance in helping us to solve the question who should be the new owner of the property in dispute. If the analogy with tort law is to work, we need to establish some kind of fault which can be pointed out as the

[15] John Gardner, 'What Is Tort Law For? Part 1. The Place of Corrective Justice' (2011) 30 Law and Philosophy 1 10.

[16] Ernest Joseph Weinrib, *Corrective Justice* (OUP 2012) 16.

[17] ibid 2.

[18] Klimchuk (n 12) 87.

[19] Menachem Mautner, '"The Eternal Triangles of the Law": Toward a Theory of Priorities in Conflicts Involving Remote Parties' (1991) 90 Michigan Law Review 95 102; see also Schwartz and Scott (n 5).

[20] See for example Gardner (n 15).

cause of the other party's woes (unless, that is, you want to invoke the highly controversial concept of strict liability as a basis of responsibility).[21] But in many cases of FO–P conflict no fault can be identified (except that of the thief, of course). When we look at these cases, a deep structural difference between negligence law and property law comes to light. In negligence law, we have a person who suffered a loss, and the assumption is that unless she can show that someone else must bear the cost of repairing it, she has to pick it up herself. In property law, in contrast, the FO who suffered the loss of theft or embezzlement is assumed to be entitled to the property since she never passed her title voluntarily. The burden of proof is *on P* to show that the title nevertheless ought to be transferred (or considered as transferred) to him.

We have already shown (section A) that the *nemo dat* rule—according to which the thief/embezzler could not transfer to the purchaser a title he never held—embodies values that underlie any regime of private property. And, so, while it need not be an exception-less, or even a very strong rule, it makes a lot of sense to use it as a baseline for asking questions about transfer of title to property.[22] Thus, if we want to remain within the framework of property law as we know it, the question we should ask is 'under which conditions ought FO to be deemed to have given up her title, even though the transfer was not voluntary?'. This question assumes a very different allocation of burdens from the one underlying the negligence model, namely, that FO will not have the loss repaired, ie the property returned, unless she can show that P is negligent. The legal analysis of FO–P conflicts therefore runs on lines that are materially different from accidents. Consequently, corrective justice does not seem to be the right prism through which to view FO–P conflicts. In the Aristotelean typology, FO–P conflicts are better understood as problems of distributive justice, to which we turn now.

C. Distributive Justice

Principles of distributive justice provide 'moral guidance for the political processes and structures that affect the distribution of economic benefits and burdens in societies'.[23] When these principles apply to legal disputes, 'instead of linking one party to the other as doer and sufferer [as corrective justice does, they] link all the parties to the benefit or the burdens they all share'.[24] The two parties to FO–P conflicts, who have fallen a victim to the wrongs of the thief/embezzler, both have a good claim to a scarce resource—the property that FO was wrongly deprived of and P paid to buy. The judge, qua 'animated justice', is thus called upon by principles of distributive justice to offer a fair distribution

[21] On the problems of deciding FO–P conflicts in accordance with the standard of negligence, and a suggestion on how to solve them, see Schwartz and Scott (n 5).

[22] See text to (n 8). For a criticism of this baseline, see, for example, D Stevens, 'Restitution, Property, and the Cause of Action in Unjust Enrichment: Getting by with Fewer Things Part II' (1989) 39 University of Toronto Law Journal 325, 329, describing the rule as perhaps representing 'merely a remnant of a more superstitious age'.

[23] Julian Lamont, Christi Favor, and Edward N Zalta (eds), 'Distributive Justice' *Stanford Encyclopaedia of Philosophy* (Winter edn, 2017) <https://plato.stanford.edu/archives/win2017/entries/justice-distributive>.

[24] Weinrib (n 16) 18.

of the burdens created by the wrongdoing.[25] While the model of distributive justice also differs from the doctrinal property law (*nemo dat*) paradigm, in that it treats the parties as having an equal claim to the property, it offers, we think, a neutral position from which to examine the automatic preference given to FO in the doctrinal framework.

Distributive justice is traditionally analysed as responding to various bases. Here we look at two that are most relevant to FO–P conflicts: need and desert.

1. Need

'The core idea of the concept of needs may be generalized to imply that scarce resources should be allocated to avoid excessive hardship and suffering, i.e., to parties who would undergo a great amount of suffering if they were deprived of such resources.'[26] According to Mautner, 'need' is therefore one of the most relevant bases of justice for resolving FO–P conflicts.[27] This may be so in theory, but the practical difficulties of using a need standard for solving FO–P conflicts in a court of law are daunting: it is not easy to decide which human needs should be taken into account in resolving the dispute. Psychological attachment to the property is difficult to weigh against economic factors, such as each party's ability to internalize the loss, or the importance of the use being made of the particular thing (eg a set of tools that FO uses for her craft). Even if we agree on which needs are to be taken into account, it is impossible to determine *ex ante* who is likely to be in more need: a typical FO or an archetypal P. If so, a 'need' criterion will have to see the judges doing the balancing work on an *ad hoc* basis—a decision-making process which will rob the parties of a certain and predictable baseline for further negotiations. Such formidable rule-of-law considerations suffice, we believe, for ruling out 'need' as a basis for a just distribution of the burdens created by FO–P conflicts.

2. Desert

Sidgwick's remark that '[m]en ought to be rewarded in proportion to their deserts'[28] strikes many people as a truism. In a just state, so the thought goes, 'in every case in which a citizen ... deserves—in virtue of his or her political economic desert bases—to have some political economic desert, he or she gets it'.[29] Views as to which features secure desert are varied. Some believe that to be deserving, one must be responsible for having the feature on which the desert claim is based. In the context of FO–P conflicts, Locke's claim that God gave the world to the 'industrious and rational', and the great emphasis he places on the value of labour is highly relevant. [30] The argument that one deserves the fruit of one's labour favours FO—at least, if she produced the stolen/embezzled property. But in most cases, both FO and P will have acquired the property

[25] Term used by Aristotle in Aristotle and WD Ross, *The Nicomachean Ethics* (OUP 2009) IV.
[26] Mautner (n 19) 105.
[27] ibid 26.
[28] Henry Sidgwick, *The Methods of Ethics* (repr 1907, Palgrave Macmillan 1962) Bk III, ch 5.
[29] Fred Feldman, *Distributive Justice* (OUP 2016) 27.
[30] John Locke, *Second Treatise on Civil Government* (first published 1668, Hackett 1980) ch 5, ss 34 and 40–44.

simply by spending money to purchase it, so that the special relationship between labourer and the fruit of her labour will not help us find who is more deserving. A very different picture of the basis of desert is drawn by consequentialists who believe that someone deserves something if giving it to her would lead to the best possible outcome overall. Below, we discuss efficiency-based solutions to FO–P conflicts which follow this route. Justice, in this solution, is no longer a matter as between the parties to a specific dispute (as corrective justice would have it), but rather a large scheme of distribution that aims to maximize the satisfaction of preferences across the entire community.

But those who subscribe to the 'Autonomy of Desert', ie, the view that desert claims cannot be justified by appeal to claims about any other normative notion, will not stray into such considerations of overall utility but consider the inherent features of the parties to the dispute.[31] Vulnerabilities which hamper human flourishing and can only be remedied by some sort of collective effort are good examples of such a desert-generating inherent feature. Our defencelessness as individuals in the face of natural disasters immediately comes to mind.[32] Vulnerability to crime is another case in point, and gets us closer to FO–P conflicts. Owners are susceptible to falling victim to crimes against their property, and it is unreasonable to expect them to fend this risk off all by themselves. Helping them to reclaim stolen property can be one element in a package of property-defence measures which owners deserve to receive from the state. The other side of the coin is that an FO who did not do what can be expected of an individual to minimize her exposure to harm does not deserve the state's help in repossessing the property. Yet, the human susceptibility to being cheated arguably places the purchaser in a position of no lesser claim to desert: a title-transfer mechanism can then be conceptualized as part of the protection from fraud we deserve from the state. However, unlike the need base, in some permutations of the FO–P conflicts it is definitely possible to tell *ex ante* which party displays a greater vulnerability. And as we will see below, this fact will enable a good lawmaker (the Courts of Equity as it happens) to take the desert basis on board when designing a solution to FO–P conflicts.

Other types of justice like retributive justice have been mentioned by some writers as a possible framework for solving FO–P conflicts.[33] But we will leave the prism of justice here, and focus in the rest of this part on the social goals that may be promoted or thwarted by the way we formulate the priority rule for FO–P conflicts. We will accept here, without arguing for it, the view that such considerations can play a legitimate role in the array of considerations in favour, or against, a solution to disputes in private law.[34]

[31] See for example, Feldman (n 29) s 2.1.

[32] ibid 77.

[33] See Mautner (n 19) 103–04.

[34] Contra Weinrib's view that 'no distributive consideration can serve as a justification for holding one person liable to another' ((n 16) 19), but in alliance with legal economists, and pluralists like Ḥanoch Dagan, *Property: Values and Institutions* (OUP 2011) ch 3. See also Matthew Harding Chapter 16 in this volume, for the argument that a wider view that takes into account the effect of the court's decision on the robustness of the social institutions that stand at the background of the claim (like the trust) is typical of Equity.

D. Efficiency

Space limits do not allow us to explore the efficiency of different solutions to the FO–P conflicts in any detail. Instead, we sketch a few of the goals, sometimes incommensurable, that the literature suggests an efficient solution ought to achieve, and highlight the difficulties in realizing these goals, or in determining what it would take to do so.

1. Security in entitlements and flow of commerce

When parties to FO–P conflicts appear in court, their interests are diametrically opposite—one's gain is the other's loss. But, from a bird'-eye point of view, a pro-P priority rule reduces the value of ownership *for all owners*, as it renders this right prone to the risk of being lost to a third party. As a result, everyone's incentive to labour, in order to be able to afford ownership or to improve what one already owns, is reduced under such a rule.[35] The flipside is that where potential purchasers worry about the security of transfer and must invest in checking the title to a property they are interested in, the flow of commerce slows down and it is harder for goods to end up in the hands of the person who values them most.[36]

But is such a chilling effect really a necessary consequence of a pro-P rule? After all, if any advantage given to P is also a disadvantage to the same person when he becomes an owner, why should the rule of priority (either way) affect the flow of commerce?[37] Those who insist that the priority rule we pick *does* have a chilling effect on the market point out that the risk to the owner, lest her property is stolen and sold off to a purchaser with a defence, is lower than the risk that an item one contemplates purchasing may be located by its original owner.[38] And if the risks do not cancel each other out, purchasers will need to pay a 'premium' to move to a lower risk position (ie, that of an owner), and their reluctance to do so will hold back the flow of transactions. One factor that makes it relatively easy to incorporate the goal of 'flowing markets' into the rule we choose is our ability to predict, at least in some cases, whether the rule will have the desired effect. Thus, with regard to some assets, like notes and bills, the power to transfer is central to their function; with idiosyncratic exceptions, it is unlikely that owners value the possession of such assets just as such, and apart from their potential to be subsequently transferred to others for value.[39] With regard to them, therefore, purchasers should get

[35] Barak Medina, 'Inducing Investment in Gathering Information by Settling Conflict of Rights between a Bona Fide Purchaser and the Original Owner [Hebrew]' (2000) 5 HAMISHPAT 117 50. On the instrumental value of property as promoting work, investment and other beneficial behaviours and institutions, see JW Harris, *Property and Justice* (Clarendon Press 1996) ch 15.

[36] On the origins of the *nemo dat* rule in Roman law as protecting the *res mancipi*—the type of property that is inextricably tied to the status of the *paterfamilias*, see Kozolchyk (n 8) 1462–45.

[37] WM Landes and RA Posner, 'An Economic Analysis of Copyright Law' 18 Journal of Legal Studies (1989) 325.

[38] Medina (n 35) 50

[39] cf *Moss v Hancock* [1899] 2 QB 111, where the owner of a stolen gold piece had always kept it in a cabinet in his drawing room, never having let it into circulation as currency, and valued it primarily as a curiosity. As a result, the purchaser of the coin from a thief did not have any defence against the original owner. We might justify this result on the basis that the owner's valuation of his security of title, in the case of that particular coin, outweighed any gain that could result from security of transfer.

priority;[40] the disadvantage to an owner in being unable to easily transfer such assets to a willing purchaser is likely to outweigh any advantage of security from loss of title.

2. Clear and predictable rules

There is no need to repeat the benefit to all members of the community of a clear and predictable rule which minimizes the costs of litigation, and forms a baseline for negotiations following which the party who values the property most will become its owner. To fulfil this rule-of-law ideal, the legal norms of priority ought to be 'typical situations' rules, rather than case-by-case principles, a structure that saves the court the need to bring the thicket of considerations we are exploring here to bear on each novel situation.

3. Prevent the conflict from arising in the first place

The first and foremost state-induced disincentive to stealing and handling stolen goods is, of course, the criminal law.[41] Alas, the criminal law system is not nearly strong enough to uproot theft or the market for selling and buying the loot: in the UK, just 7 per cent of stolen goods were recovered from the £2 billion of valuables taken from homes and businesses in two million break-ins between 2011 and 2016.[42] From the perspective of the law enforcement authorities, any help they can get from private law would therefore be welcome. Legal economists actually disagree about whether theft is a 'social cost' in and of itself, as some prefer to analyse it as just another means by which property is transferred from one person to another.[43] But they do seem to agree that the phenomenon of theft is utility-reducing as it 'increases transaction costs in the transfer of property relative to other modes of transfer by imposing huge costs on individuals, in particular on potential victims who invest in protection measures'.[44] And, so, even without committing ourselves to intricate arguments about the immorality of theft, we can agree that if forming the priority rule in a particular way will affect the players' structure of incentives, so as to reduce the chance that FO–P conflicts ever arise, there is value in following this formula. Nipping FO–P conflicts in the bud can be achieved by tackling one (or both) of the events that lead to them, namely, the theft and the sale of the stolen/embezzled goods. Alas, a formulation of the rule that affects FO in the right direction may have the opposite effect on P, while potential thieves/embezzlers may be deterred by yet another way of devising the rule. Let us see how.

40 Medina (n 35) 51.

41 For some commercially significant assets, such as land, state-run registries of transactions and/or rights also provide an important mechanism for pre-empting fraud.

42 Steven Hopkins, 'Nine Out of 10 Burglaries Unsolved and 7% of Stolen Goods Recovered' (*Huffington Post*, 31 March 2017) <www.huffingtonpost.co.uk/entry/nine-out-of-10-burglaries-unsolved-and-7-of-stolen-goods-recovered_uk_58de0a03e4b08194e3b8e41d>.

43 Steven Shavell, 'Individual Precautions to Prevent Theft: Private Versus Socially Optimal Behavior' (1991) 11 International Review of Law and Economics 123 125; Richard L Hasen and Richard H McAdams, 'The Surprisingly Complex Case against Theft' (1997) 16 International Review of Law and Economics 367.

44 Omri Ben-Shahar, 'Property Rights In Stolen Goods: An Economic Analysis' (1999) University of Michigan Working Paper 2.

(a) Before the theft

A Press Association analysis of Home Office data shows that in 2014/15, forces in England and Wales closed 80.2 per cent of investigations into break-ins without identifying a suspect. The prevention of burglaries is so low on the agenda, that in the same year, Leicestershire Police revealed they had not fully investigated break-ins at odd-numbered houses as part of an experiment to look at ways of saving money.[45] Surely the most eye-catching of all crimes against property is art theft: the global market for stolen art is worth $6bn. With an appalling rate of recovery—between 10 per cent (according to the optimists) and 2 per cent (as per the sober)—the consensus is that 'once art is stolen, there's an abysmally small chance of getting it back'.[46] Prevention seems to be the best strategy for reducing the social price of theft. Can the priority rule in FO–P conflicts create the conditions in which prevention is encouraged? From a socially optimal perspective, the owner ought to invest in precautions against theft until 'the marginal reduction in the probability of theft times the goods' value to her equals the marginal precaution cost'.[47] A pro-FO priority rule enhances the chances that FO will be able to retrieve the property if it is stolen or misapplied; as a result, where that is the case, investment in protecting it in the first place is less expedient from FO's perspective. Thus, a priority rule which prefers FO, especially if it does not sanction a careless owner, incentivizes a suboptimal investment by owners in guarding their property.

A pro-FO priority rule would affect the chances of the theft taking place in another way: if purchasers know that their chances of retaining property they are thinking of buying are lower—because the priority rule would give it back to their original owner if she finds the property—they will be reluctant to buy it or will offer a lower price for it. That would disincentivize thieves, and bring about a further reduction in the amount of precautions by owners.[48] An eighteenth-century observer already had this advice for theft prevention: 'deprive a thief of a safe and ready market for his goods, and he is undone'.[49] If you are after reducing thievery across the community, you would be happy with this result. But if you think this is only a worthwhile cause if done efficiently, ie, inter alia, when owners make the optimal investment in precautions, you will see this as an unwelcome result of a pro-FO priority rule. And here is another cause for scepticism about the effect of the priority rule formulation on the thievery: the belief that thieves can be incentivized to stop by manipulating the law is based on a highly contested assumption that criminals act rationally, ie choose the best means to promote their ends.[50] But behavioural economics demonstrates that people make systematic mistakes in decision-making, and criminals, in particular, may not use objectively verifiable

[45] 'Leicestershire Police "Ignore" Attempted Burglaries at Odd-Numbered Houses' (*BBC News*, 5 August 2015) <www.bbc.co.uk/news/uk-england-leicestershire-33788264>

[46] James Tarmey, 'What Happens to Stolen Art after a Heist?' (*Bloomberg*, 15 June 2015) <https://www.bloomberg.com/news/articles/2015-06-15/what-happens-to-stolen-art-after-a-heist->.

[47] Schwartz and Scott (n 5) 1339.

[48] Ben-Shahar (n 44) 25.

[49] Patrick Colquhoun, 'A Treatise on the Police of the Metropolis' (1796) 29 European Magazine and London Review 386.

[50] Definition of rationality for legal economics purposes in Richard A Posner, 'Rational Choice, Behavioral Economics, and the Law' (1998) 50 Stanford Law Review 1551 1551.

evidence of the frequency and severity of the punishment for the offences they consider committing.[51] In addition, criminal activity is a prime example of 'bounded self-control', ie, activity in which poor control of impulses explains severe deviations from rationality (the problem is particularly acute with criminals who are addicted to substances, as many offenders against property are).[52] That said, sophisticated thieves, eg, those who target specific art works or other valuable goods, are more likely to engage in a cost–benefit calculation and take into account their chances of selling the stolen goods for a profit. Still, with regard to the vast majority of thefts, all arguments that a certain formulation of the priority rule can reduce their occurrence should be taken with a pinch of salt.

(b) After the theft

Once property is stolen, we might reduce the chances of a FO–P conflict by incentivizing the owner to search for her property, in the hope that she finds it before it is sold on. In the face of public authorities' unwillingness to spend on recovering stolen goods, private owners can invest their own resources in searching, by hiring private detectives, filing a complaint with the police, searching online markets like eBay. Under an FO-favouring rule, FO gets a better chance of retrieving the property if she only manages to find it after it was sold to a third party. Such a rule therefore incentivizes her to invest more in searching for the misappropriated goods, as she knows that even if it was sold on, the investment may bear fruit.[53]

But a more likely way of reducing the amount of FO–P conflicts at this stage is to encourage potential purchasers to investigate the title of goods they contemplate buying. The purchaser should ideally invest in ensuring that he is getting a good title until 'the marginal increase in the probability of receiving a good title times the goods' value to him equals the marginal inquiry cost'.[54] Yet, purchasers will spend less than this ideal sum on scrutinizing the title because they know that there is a fair chance that the real owner (if there is one) will never find her property. Can the way we formulate a priority rule further detract from the ideal investment, or improve it? Some writers are doubtful about the ability of a priority rule to influence the behaviour of purchasers, especially if exchange of misapplied goods is a relatively small fraction of the trade in merchandise of this type, and where goods are unidentifiable so the purchasers can do very little to investigate the title.[55] Others believe that purchasers can, if they want, notice shady features in a deal they are being offered, and invest in substantiating or

[51] For a critical review of the literature, see Richard H McAdams and Thomas S Ulen, 'Behavioural Criminal Law and Economics' in Boudewijn Bouckaert and Gerrit de Geest (series eds) and Nuno Garoupa (volume ed) *Encyclopedia of Law and Economics* (2nd edn, 2009) vol 3.

[52] See more in Glenn D Walters, 'The Decision to Commit Crime: Rational or Nonrational?' (2015) 16(3) Journal of Criminology, Criminal Justice, Law & Society 1.

[53] Schwartz and Scott (n 5) 1350.

[54] ibid 1339.

[55] Ben-Shahar (n 44) 3. Indeed, according to Mautner, purchasers (under the UCC) are subject to a narrow standard of actual knowledge, rather than negligence because 'generally purchasers of assets or rights in assets are unable to take any meaningful precaution- any measures to verify whether a prior conflicting claimant exists', see Mautner (n 15) 117.

refuting the suspicion.[56] If so, lawmakers should be worried by the adverse effect which a pro-P priority rule may have on the purchaser's incentives to investigate the title. A rational maximizer of utility will calculate what minimum investment will be sufficient for proving to the court that he fulfilled the conditions for getting priority according to the rule, eg, bona fides. The result of this calculation may be very different from the ideal investment.[57] This consideration would be a real drawback for a pro-P rule of priority, unless the court has tools to tackle it (as, to foreshadow, the Court of Equity has).

In section III, we move to look more closely at the solution offered by Equity to FO–P conflicts that arise between a beneficiary and a purchaser of a legal title to the subject matter of the trust. Against a foil of highly pro-FO rules of the kind offered by the common law, the special attributes of the 'Equity's darling' solution to FO–P conflicts come to light. In section IV, we build on the insights of section II and III and ask how the Chancery Court employs the distinctive *modus operandi* of Equity to reach a good enough solution to a complicated permutation of FO–P conflicts.

III. Equity's Darling and *nemo dat* Exceptions at Common Law

In his *Lectures on Equity*, Frederic Maitland proposed that the distinctive character of equitable interests can be understood by reference to two examples, 'which in the eyes of the moralist may seem closely similar but between which the lawyer will see a vast difference'.[58] Both are classic FO–P conflicts. In the first, there is a clash between a legal owner of land and X, who has paid money to a third party to buy that land in reliance on a forged deed. In the second example, the clash is between a beneficiary under a trust and Y, who has paid money to a trustee to buy the trust land in reliance on a forged deed concealing the existence of the trust. Both X and Y have diligently inspected the forged deeds and found nothing suspicious, and both have given value. Nevertheless, Maitland says, X will undoubtedly lose to the freeholder in the first scenario and Y will likely win against the beneficiary in the second. This is because 'X has had the misfortune to buy from one who had nothing to sell';[59] by contrast, Y, 'having come to legal ownership bona fide for value and without notice, actual or constructive, of [the beneficiary's] rights', is unaffected by those rights. [60] In other words, the common law solves the priority conflict by applying the *nemo dat* principle: FO keeps her land because she has done nothing to give it away, and the purchaser's innocence and diligence are irrelevant, as is the fact that he has given value. Meanwhile, Equity solves the priority conflict very differently, by asking whether the purchaser has become a legal owner and, if so, whether he has given value and how he has behaved. This difference between common

[56] See for example advice in Keith, 'Stolen Goods Online: 8 Red Flag Warning Signs' (*Scambusters.org*) <www.scambusters.org/stolengoods.html>

[57] Schwartz and Scott (n 5) 1351.

[58] Frederic William Maitland, *Equity: A Course of Lectures* (2nd edn, CUP 1936) 129.

[59] ibid 130.

[60] ibid.

law and Equity, according to Maitland, captures a fundamental distinction between legal and equitable rights and provides an important plank of his argument that equitable rights are importantly different from common law property rights.

This argument is, however, complicated by the existence of bona fide purchase defences at common law. Maitland himself noted that 'sales in market overt', and sales that complied with section 9 of the Factors Act 1889, could destroy a common law owner's title to the thing sold and confer a good title on the purchaser—where the purchaser was bona fide, had given value, and did not have notice of the problem with the seller's title.[61] While the market overt exception—a narrower version of which is still an important exception in the UCC—was abolished in England in 1994,[62] the solution to FO–P conflicts offered by the common law has retained the structure Maitland is grappling with. The baseline preference is for FO over P, subject to a cluster of specific and context-defined exceptions that favour 'bona fide purchasers'. For example, in the context of sales of goods, P, like his American counterpart, can win where FO has entrusted someone else with possession of the goods she has purchased and where the owner is estopped from denying the ownership or authority of a seller by her own representations or negligence.[63] Another standard exception to the pro-FO rules is specific to chattels which perform the functions of money, such as negotiable instruments and cash. Here, again, a purchaser who can show he was bona fide can get good title.[64]

Maitland acknowledges that these common law defences 'at first sight ... may seem analogous to the case of the person with an equitable estate who loses it when a *bona fide* purchaser obtains the legal estate for value and without notice'.[65] Nevertheless, he insists, the analogy is misleading: there is really a 'marked difference' between the two cases.[66] This conspicuous disparity comes down to the structure of the argument made by P in the two scenarios. In the case of a common law defence, like that of a sale in market overt, P gets ownership but does not get it from FO, who does not have it to give. His argument, against FO, is that he has somehow obtained the very rights that were once held by FO, despite FO's lack of consent to the transaction. In the case of the sale by a trustee, P need not say that he has obtained the very rights of the beneficiary to the trust property; having obtained the trustee's own title to the trust property, he can

[61] Section 9 of the Factors Act provides a defence where the owner has agreed to allow a prospective purchaser of goods to take possession and that purchaser deals with the goods before the owner's title has actually passed to her; it has been substantively re-enacted by the Sale of Goods Act 1979, s 25. The 'market overt' rule has been explained in an early seventeenth-century KB case as stating that 'if plate be stolen and sold openly in a scrivener's shop on market day, this shall not alter property; otherwise if it had been in a goldsmith's shop' (77 Eng Rep 180, cited by Kozolchyk (n 8) 1499).

[62] The thought being that in light of changing social and economic conditions, most people are no longer dependent on local markets and the rule no longer serves a useful purpose. See Sale of Goods (Amendment) Act 1994, cf UCC § 2-403.

[63] Sale of Goods Act 1979, s 24 (buyer in possession) and 25 (seller in possession), and s 21. For the limited meaning of negligence in this context, see *Moorgate Mercantile Co Ltd v Twitchings* [1977] AC 890, discussed at n 82. Some exceptions are specific to kinds of goods, for example, where a car is let on hire-purchase, there is a defence in favour of a private purchaser of such a car (Hire-Purchase Act 1964, s 27). See UCC § 2–403(2) (the entrustment rule).

[64] Bills of Exchange Act 1882; *Miller v Race* (1758) 1 Burr 452; See also UCC § 3-401–20.

[65] Maitland (n 59) 139.

[66] ibid.

point to the consent of the trustee as the source of his ownership, and argue, as against the beneficiary, that 'there is no reason for taking away … the legal right which has thus been transferred to him'.[67] As Lord Mance explains in the recent Supreme Court decision of *Akers & Ors v Samba Financial Group*

> [I]f the trust rights are overridden, it is not because they have been disposed of by virtue of the transfer of the legal title. It is because they were protected rights that were always limited and in certain circumstances capable of being overridden by virtue of a rule of law governing equitable rights, protecting in particular … bona fide third-party purchasers for value (Equity's 'darling').[68]

It is not clear, however, how this formal and structural difference between the operation of the defences at common law and in Equity reflects any significant normative difference between the choices made by the two jurisdictions. Both appear, in some circumstances, to favour a purchaser for value in good faith.

In his *Reading on the Statute of Uses*, Francis Bacon is baffled by the same conundrum. In discussing the nature of the use (the medieval form of trust),[69] Bacon notes that a purchaser for value of stolen goods who buys in market overt can acquire a good legal title to those goods. Like Maitland, he compares this with the Equity's darling defence, and argues for a fundamental distinction between the two cases, albeit on somewhat different grounds. He contends that the reason why a purchaser in market overt will get a clean title with or without notice, while a use will bind any purchaser who takes with notice, is that 'chancery looketh farther than the Common Law, namely, to the corrupt conscience of him that will deal with the land, knowing it to be in equity another's … so that consideration, or no consideration, is an issue at the common law; but notice, or no notice, is an issue in the chancery'.[70]

As with Maitland's account, it is not immediately clear what this analysis is getting at that is of any normative importance. Bacon could not have meant that a purchaser who actually knew that his seller lacked title would get a clean title in market overt; this is not how the archaic defence worked at common law.[71] Meanwhile, as Bacon himself notes, a purchaser of land from a feoffee to use (equivalent to the modern trustee) could only escape liability to the cestui que use (the beneficiary) if he had given consideration; both in Equity and at common law, no defences were available to mere donees who had not given value.[72] Both the common law and Equity seem, then, to have been interested

[67] Maitland (n 59) 140.

[68] *Akers* (n 9) per Lord Mance at [51], see also Lloyd LJ in Independent Trustee Services Ltd v GP Noble Trustees Ltd [2012] EWCA Civ 195.

[69] For a comparison between the medieval use and the modern trust, see NG Jones, 'Uses, Trusts, and a Path to Privity' (1997) CLJ 175, 176–82.

[70] Francis Bacon, *The Reading Upon the Statute of Uses of Francis Bacon* (WH Rowe ed, Stratford 1806) 16.

[71] 2 Co Inst 713: 'If the buyer doth know whose goods they were, and that the seller thereof hath at most a wrongful possession, this shall not bind him that right hath.'

[72] See WS Holdsworth, *A History of English Law: Volume 4* (3rd edn, Methuen 1945) 432; and 2 Co Inst 713: 'It must be a sale and not a free gift, without any valuable consideration; for fairs and markets were not instituted for gifts but for sales[.]'.

in 'notice, or no notice' *and* 'consideration, or no consideration'. What is the basis for Bacon's view that notice—which goes to conscience—is in some sense the special concern of Equity, while the common law maintains more of a focus on consideration? We believe that despite their surface opaqueness, these arguments made by Maitland and Bacon do point to substantive differences in Equity's approach, both to the availability of purchaser-protective defences and to the 'without notice' standard that a purchaser must satisfy to avail himself of such a defence.

A. Availability of Purchaser Protection

The general approach of the common law to the bona fide purchaser is well illustrated by the decision in *Dyer v Pearson*.[73] The claimants had authorized one Smith to buy thirty bags of wool on their behalf. Smith took delivery of the wool and the bill of lading, and hired the first defendants, who were warehouse keepers, to store it. Nothing in the bill of lading revealed the claimants' ownership of the wool, and Smith was entered in the warehouse keepers' records as its owner. He subsequently borrowed £528 from them for his own purposes on the security of the wool, and sold ten bags of it to the second defendant, Clay, for £579. Clay paid off the £528 debt and the first defendants duly delivered the wool to him, although by then they had been notified of the claimants' title. The claimants sued all the defendants in trover. On the first hearing of the claim, Abbott CJ instructed the jury to determine 'whether Clay had purchased under circumstances which would induce a reasonable, prudent, and cautious man to believe that Smith … had authority to sell' or if, contrariwise, he had purchased under circumstances 'which ought to excite his suspicion'.[74] He directed them to find for the plaintiffs if the circumstances were suspicious, and otherwise to find for the defendants. Obeying these instructions, the jury found in favour of the defendants: they had transacted with Smith under circumstances that led them to believe he had the authority to sell the wool, and would have led any 'reasonable, prudent and cautious man' to believe the same. An appeal against the decision succeeded, on the grounds that the jury had been misdirected. Abbott CJ agreed that he had asked the jury the wrong question, since 'the general rule of the law of England is that a man who has no authority to sell, cannot, by making a sale, transfer the property to another'.[75] There was only one exception, market overt, which was not engaged on the facts. Thus, 'even if there was an unsuspicious purchase by the defendants', they were unable to defend themselves against the claim in trover—unless, 'perhaps', if the claimants had 'by their own conduct enabled Smith to hold himself forth to the world as having not the possession only, but the property'.[76] The question whether they had done this was the

[73] (1824) 3 B & C 38, 107 ER 648.
[74] ibid.
[75] ibid 650.
[76] ibid.

most favourable way of putting the case for the defendant, and the dispute was sent back for a new trial on that issue.

Contrast the position in Equity. Suppose that Smith, instead of being an agent, had been a trustee of the legal title to the bags of wool and Clay had purchased that title from him. The conduct of the claimants, as beneficiaries under a trust, would have been irrelevant. The important question would have been the one put to the jury the first time around—had Clay purchased 'under circumstances which would induce a reasonable, prudent, and cautious man to believe that Smith, of whom he purchased, had authority to sell'? If so, he would have won: 'from such a purchaser, a Court of Equity takes away nothing which he has honestly acquired', 'however hardly it may operate on the persons on whom ... fraud has been committed'.[77] Equity's starting point, therefore, is different from that of the common law. A purchaser, however innocent and cautious, cannot defeat a legal owner's title unless there are some special circumstances that justify a subordination of the legal owner.[78] By contrast, an owner in Equity, however unfortunate or needy, cannot defeat a purchaser of a legal title, unless there are some special circumstances that justify a finding that the purchaser has not acquired the asset with clean conscience.[79]

The common law's approach cannot be explained as built upon a general quest after the person who can most efficiently minimize the utility costs arising from a fraudulent transaction.[80] This is because it does not adopt a broad principle that allocates loss to the person who, as between owner and purchaser, bears more causal responsibility for the loss.[81] Nor does the common law generally penalize owners for failing to avoid loss of this kind, even in circumstances where the potential loss-avoidance measures are cheaper for owners than for purchasers.[82] It adopts a much narrower strategy, limiting the circumstances in which an owner will bear the loss to a discrete set of situations that do not straightforwardly map either on a cost/benefit analysis or on ideas of desert based on carelessness or irresponsibility. A causal link between the owner's carelessness and the purchaser's loss is neither sufficient nor, always, necessary for the purchaser to have a defence at law. In the sale of goods context, the law is attentive to situations

[77] *Taylor v London and County Banking Company* [1901] 2 Ch 23; *Thorndike v Hunt* (1859) De GF & J, 44 ER 138.

[78] For a detailed overview of these situations in the context of sales of goods, see L Merrett, 'The Importance of Delivery and Possession in the Passing of Title' (2008) 67 CLJ 376.

[79] cf *Bassett v Nosworthy* (1673) Fin 102, 104; 23 ER 55, 56: 'Precedents of this Nature are very antient and numerous, *viz* where the Court hath refused to give any Assistance against a Purchaser either to an Heir, or to a Widow, or to the Fatherless, or to Creditors, or even to one Purchaser against another.'

[80] See section II.D.3.

[81] Contra the well-known dictum of Ashhurt J in *Lickbarrow v Mason* (1787) 2 D & E 63, 70; 100 ER 35, 39 that English law recognizes 'a broad general principle, that, wherever one of two innocent persons must suffer by the acts of a third, he who has enabled such third person to occasion the loss must sustain it'. As has been pointed out, the dictum has most often been cited to criticise it or to deny its general application and only rarely applied: see M Bridge, *Benjamin's Sale of Goods* (9th edn, Sweet & Maxwell 2016) 7-008 and authorities cited there.

[82] In *Farquharson Bros & Co v C King & Co* for example, Lord Macnaghten emphasized that carelessness on the part of an owner and diligence on the part of a purchaser would not displace the normal preference of the common law for the owner: 'unless there has been a sale in market overt', an owner who loses his chattel to a finder will be able to recover it from a purchaser from the finder, and this right 'is not prejudiced or affected by his carelessness in losing the chattel, however gross it may have been' ([1902] AC 325). The application of this principle by the majority of the House of Lords in *Moorgate Mercantile Co Ltd v Twitchings* illustrates the apparent irrelevance of the cost of loss-avoidance as between owner and purchaser ([1977] AC 890).

where the owner has allowed the property to be out of her possession, or where she is responsible for the seller's apparent ownership or apparent authority to sell.[83] Thus, it has refused to provide a defence to a purchaser, however innocent, from a seller who is in a position to sell goods without any consent at all on the part of the owner, even if the owner has been careless.[84] By contrast, where transactions involving negotiable instruments and money are concerned, the law is interested in neither consent nor carelessness on the part of the owner; it prefers the purchaser in good faith who lacks notice.[85] This very specific exclusion is, apparently, justified on the efficiency consideration (what the judges abstractly call 'policy') that preferring the owner in this context would seriously hamper the flow of commerce, and undermine the expectation of the parties.[86] Thus, it is difficult to reduce the patchwork of protections that the common law offers to certain purchasers, in certain situations, to any single principle of loss-allocation or account of moral desert.[87]

If we turn to the approach of Equity, can we identify a more coherent underlying principle? In Equity, we saw, we do not find a parallel structure of special exceptions to a general rule preferring equitable owners against subsequent purchasers. When a competition arises between P who purchased a legal interest and an FO who is a beneficiary, the rule gives priority to P who satisfies a set of conditions. The traditional language of the courts of Equity is that they lack the power, or jurisdiction, to reach a purchaser for value of a legal estate unless she has notice of the equitable interest. In *Stanhope v Earl Verney*,[88] Lord Northington LC described the principle 'that a purchaser for a valuable consideration [without notice] ... cannot be hurt by a court of equity' as 'the polar star of equity'.[89] This raises the question, which both Maitland and Bacon found perplexing, why a purchaser in Equity is in any different situation from an apparently identical purchaser at common law. In his comparative analysis of different solutions offered to FO–P conflict in various legal systems, Saul Levmore notes that '[t]he relevant incentives that the different rules can place on the owner and the purchaser are of uncertain magnitude and cut in opposite directions ... Variety, or diversity in outcomes, is [therefore] explained by the difficulty of the problem'.[90] But the case of Equity and common law, we want to argue, is different. For here, the different solutions respond to different considerations of interpersonal morality, efficiency, and justice that apply to the version of the conflict we find in each system.

[83] eg Sale of Goods Act 1979, s 24 (seller left in possession by a buyer) and s 25 (buyer in possession); Factors Act 1889, s 9 (mercantile agent in possession with the owner's consent). A very similar entrustment exception can be found in the UCC s 2-403(2); Sale of Goods Act 1979, s 21(1).

[84] *National Employers Mutual Assurance v Jones* [1990] 1 AC 24.

[85] eg *Chichester v Hill & Son* (1882) 52 LJQB 160.

[86] In *Miller v Race* (1758) 1 Burr 452, 459; 97 ER 398, 402 Lord Mansfield says: 'A bank-note is constantly and universally, both at home and abroad, treated as money, as cash; and paid and received, as cash; and it is necessary, for the purposes of commerce, that their currency should be established and secured.'

[87] As noted by A Tettenborn, proposing that the current 'incoherent mess' be replaced by a broad principle of 'entrustment': see A Tettenborn, 'Transfer of Chattels by Non-Owners: Still an Open Problem' [2018] CLJ 1.

[88] (1761) 2 Eden 81, 28 ER 826.

[89] (1761) 2 Eden 81, 85; 28 ER 826, 828.

[90] Saul Levmore, 'Variety and Uniformity in the Treatment of the Good-Faith Purchaser' (1987) 16 Journal of Legal Studies 43 48.

One reason for the difference, we think, is that a purchaser can be unaware of the existence of equitable rights in a sense that is quite special to the institution of the trust and parallel equitable rights. While members of the public need not know who owns a piece of property at common law, they can expect, and be expected, to know *that* it is owned;[91] thanks to the *numerus clausus* principle, they can also make a reasonable prediction as to the shape of any legal property right that might affect that particular piece of property, and tailor their conduct accordingly. Common law rights are, in that sense, public. Trusts and other equitable interests, by contrast, are often private arrangements.[92] Unless an official registry of equitable interests is in place—and it is notable that, where such registers have been introduced, statutory defences have superseded[93] the Equity's darling defence—it is hard to know whether any equitable interests in some asset exist at all. In addition, the law leaves a legal owner free, within certain very broad limits, to create—in the form of a trust or an equitable charge—an idiosyncratic structure of rights and powers in Equity that would be hard for an individual purchaser to predict. A purchaser who buys a legal title from an ostensible owner, who happens to be a trustee, cannot be expected, by default, to predict the possibility or effect of an unknown trust. This may also explain why Equity extends its protection only to purchasers of common law rights, and does not grant the status of 'Equity's darling' to a person who has given value but is seeking to invoke Equity's more flexible and more secret institutions by purchasing (only) an equitable interest.[94]

B. Notice at Common Law and in Equity

In addition to the difference in availability of purchaser-protective defences, the *content* of the defence in Equity differs significantly from analogous 'good faith'-based exceptions to the common law rule. This, we argue, is down to the distinctive concept of notice used by Equity. The difference is best captured by the notion of 'constructive notice'. A purchaser with 'constructive notice' is 'deemed to know the answers to questions that a reasonable person in his conditions would have asked, even if he does not actually know the answers because he did not in fact ask the questions'.[95] Some dicta suggest that constructive notice does not apply in the context of commercial transactions.[96]

[91] Property law places owners under a duty to publicize their rights in various ways, see Carol M Rose, 'Possession as the Origin of Property' (1985) 52 University of Chicago Law Review 73.

[92] For an account of this 'private' and hidden character of the trust, and its implications for our understanding of the beneficial interest under a trust as a right in *rem*, see Wai Lau, Ming, 'The Nature of the Beneficial Interest: Historical and Economic Perspectives' available at <https://ssrn.com/abstract=2213055> 38–41. See also, B McFarlane and R Stevens, 'The Nature of Equitable Property' (2010) 4 Journal of Equity 1, 2, where the authors note the variety of unpredictable ways in which different equitable interests can arise by operation of law and the absence of any *numerus clausus* principle limiting their content.

[93] eg Land Charges Act 1972, s 4; Land Registration Act 2002, s 29; Companies Act 2006, s 859H.

[94] *Phillips v Phillips* (1861) 4 De Gex, Fisher & Jones 208, 45 ER 1164.

[95] Charles Mitchell and David J. Hayton, *Hayton and Mitchell: Commentary and Cases on the Law of Trusts and Equitable Remedies* (13th edn, Sweet & Maxwell 2010) 1–137.

[96] eg *Eagle Trust plc v SBC Securities Ltd* [1992] 4 All ER 408, 507 (Vinelott J), and *Polly Peck International plc v Nadir (No 2)* [1992] 4 All ER 769, 782 (Scott LJ).

However, recent authority has made it clear that, although precise expectations of a purchaser's behaviour will vary according to the context in which he finds himself, a purchaser may still be bound in Equity if he has failed to discover facts in circumstances where his failure to inquire is unconscionable in the broad sense, ie motivated not only by actual dishonesty but also by laziness or selfishness.[97] Meanwhile, the common law defences operate a laxer standard, under which a purchaser will lose his right to keep the property only if he possesses *actual* knowledge or if the circumstances justify an inference of a deliberate decision to abstain from inquiry, with the specific motive of defeating FO's rights.[98]

Unlike the common law defences, P will not be bound in Equity only where the facts are such that she *must* have been aware that there was something inherently improper or dishonest about a transaction or that it is probable that a third-party right exists somewhere.[99] If P fails to appreciate the risk that the property she is buying is held on trust, because she did not bother to make the inquiries that a reasonable person would have made in the circumstances, she will be fixed with constructive notice of the trust.[100] In this context, the reasonable person is the person who possesses all the attributes of the purchaser herself but lacks her *motive* for being unaware of the facts—whether she intentionally avoided seeking the information, or hid it from herself by resorting to self-deception. *Papadimitriou v Crédit Agricole Corpn & Investment Bank* provides a good example.[101] P was a bank which received the proceeds of a fraudulent sale of FO's art-deco collection; the thief used the proceeds, which were held on trust for FO, to settle a debt he owed to P. The payment was made via a series of complex transactions, involving various different legal entities, which had no discernible commercial purpose. The Privy Council held that, in the circumstances, a reasonable bank with the attributes of the defendant bank would have made inquiries or sought advice about the reasons why the seller had gone to the trouble and expense of using such 'a web of legal entities', since the transaction raised a risk of money laundering or tax evasion that a reasonable bank would have investigated. This subjective standard of prudence—the test is what a reasonable P *with the attributes of the actual P* would have done—suggests that Equity's concern is to capture P who, if his own interests alone were at stake, would have made more detailed inquiries into potentially dubious features of the transaction but who is willing to close his eyes to risk where the rights of others might be at stake: the purchaser who, as Lord Sumption JSC puts it, is willing to tell himself that 'there might well … be an honest explanation' for unusual facts surrounding the transaction in his favour, and then does not objectively investigate the evidence for and against this probability. This focus on what P would have done if he lacked a self-regarding motive is distinctive to Equity's concept of notice.

[97] *Papadimitriou v Crédit Agricole Corpn and Investment Bank* [2015] UKPC 13.
[98] See eg *English and Scottish Mercantile Investment Co Ltd v Brunton* [1892] 2 QB 700, 707–08.
[99] See *Jones v Gordon* (1877) 2 App Cas 616.
[100] Sinclair Investments (UK) Ltd v Versailles Trade Finance Ltd [2012] Ch 453, per Lord Neuberger MR at [97].
[101] *Papadimitriou* (n 97).

Thus, Equity handles the competition between FO (the beneficiary) and P (the purchaser of a legal interest) differently from the common law, in respect of who is preferred (P), how the purchaser gets a good title (FO's beneficial ownership disappears), and what state of mind is required of him (lack of actual or constructive notice). The next part shows that this distinctive solution to FO–P conflicts is expressive of Equity's character as a body of rules and principles that follows the matrix of the parties' *moral* accountability fairly closely, and pays close attention to the specific circumstances of the parties to the dispute.

IV. Is Equity's Darling Equitable?

In one important sense, the solution offered by Equity to FO–P conflicts follows the common law (and most other legal systems): it is binary. At the end of the day, either FO or P takes the property home. In another sense, however, we saw that Equity greatly departs from the common law—beneficial owners do not get the same protection as a 'normal' owners. In what follows, we argue that Equity's solution can be interpreted as a measured response to the melange of values and social goals that ought, ideally, be served by a solution to FO–P conflicts. Given the diversity and incommensurability of these values and goals, the 'Equity's darling' solution cannot fully address each one of them. However, in our view, Equity can be seen to employ its unique tools to achieve a result that reflects the moral merits of the case and creates an efficient incentive structure. This enables Equity to strike a good balance between the conflicting ideals that are at play in FO–P conflicts.

A. Justice

Let us look first at the way Equity's darling is expressive of the relevant distributive justice considerations. While a priority rule that fully accounts for the parties' needs (psychological, economic, and other) would have to leave room for unacceptable levels of judicial discretion, 'Equity's darling' is a feasible solution that takes into account a significant aspect of what each party deserves. To begin with, unlike a standard P, purchasers from a trustee are highly likely to have a special vulnerability, namely, ignorance as to the existence of (or the terms of), a trust. Due to the private character of the trust, sketched above, it is very hard for a purchaser to know that the legal owner's rights do not include one of the most basic attributes of ownership, namely, the right to benefit from the asset.[102] A purchaser who buys a legal title from an ostensible owner, who happens to be a trustee, deserves

[102] See, for example, Lord Neuberger explanation on why s 127 of the Insolvency Act 1986 (which avoids property dispositions in the run up to liquidation) does not apply to transfer of legal ownership by a trustee to the company to an Equity's darling in *Akers* (n 9) [76].

protection from this risk as a player in the market who has relied on the public dimension of ownership.[103]

Moreover, as the benefits to society from a system that allows a beneficial interest to be engrafted unto legal ownership are significant, it makes sense to demand that the vulnerability that is created by the sotto voce nature of the trust should be redressed by communal action—here, in the form of enacting a pro-P rule. Further, it seems only fair that the person who benefits directly from the secretive arrangement (viz. the beneficiary) will be the one made to answer for this vulnerability. Indeed, beneficiaries are also highly vulnerable to being cheated by their trustees; for this reason, a particularly stringent duty of loyalty is placed on the latter. From a distributive justice point of view, however, the innocent purchaser who never benefited from the trust arrangement is more deserving of protection than the beneficiary who enjoyed the various freedoms arising from the equitable nature of her right (eg freedom from the restrictions of *numerus clausus* and registration requirements). Obviously, all that is true only if the purchaser indeed displays this vulnerability, namely, if he is indeed truly ignorant of the trust. Equity is highly attuned to the temptation to exploit the shelter it offers to the vulnerable, and its attempt to subvert such abuse is captured by the notions of notice and clean conscience to which we now turn.

B. Conscience

The bona fide purchaser for value features in various solutions to FO–P conflicts—from the UCC's voidable title and entrustment exceptions, to civilian systems with strong 'market overt' protection. But when Equity resorts to this formula it adds a unique element: conscience.[104] When the Court of Chancery seeks to resolve FO–P conflicts, as Bacon explains, it 'looketh . . . to the corrupt conscience'.[105] Is there more to this reference than a linguistic frill? We have seen that the answer is a firm 'yes'. The requirement of conscionability has an important role to play in explaining why the Courts of Equity think it their business to force some purchasers, but not others, to return the property so as to reconstitute the trust. As is the case with other Equitable doctrines where conscience is invoked, it does not grant judges a licence to resolve the FO–P conflict on a basis of their gut feeling as to which party holds the higher moral ground. The reference is rather to objective moral standards, which are transparent and accessible to anyone who is willing to engage with the moral dilemma at stake with honesty and integrity.[106] In equitable FO–P conflicts, we saw, the limelight is on P—if he can show that his state of mind when making the purchase is such that Equity does not have authority

[103] On the duty of owners to shout about their right, and the sanctions for not doing so, see Carol M Rose, 'Possession as the Origin of Property' (1985) 52 University of Chicago Law Review 73.

[104] One of us has set out her views about the role of the conscience category in Equity in Samet Irit, *Equity: Conscience Goes to Market* (OUP 2018) ch 1.

[105] (n 70). On the way Equity supplements the UCC in the US, see TW Merrill and HE Smith, *Property* (OUP 2010) 173.

[106] Irit Samet, 'What Conscience Can Do for Equity' (2012) 3 Jurisprudence 13.

to declare that the beneficiary's interest in the property affects him, he gets to hold on to the property. When asking themselves which state of mind indeed justifies intervention, the allusion to conscience guides the court to look into the moral merits of the purchaser's position at the time of the purchase.

One aspect of the concept of conscience that is particularly relevant for resolving FO–P conflicts, and that illuminates Equity's approach to constructive notice, is the way it engages with the phenomenon of self-deception. When a purchaser is offered a deal for a particularly excellent price, from someone who is not in the business of selling this type of property, or is not very likely to be the real owner of the property, he may get suspicious. He may then decide to ignore the suspicion and go ahead with the deal. But not everyone is hard-nosed enough to do this. Honest people will feel guilt and shame for taking advantage of the owner's misfortune. Prudent people will be scared of being found out, losing what they paid plus transaction costs, and suffering public humiliation to boot. But such unpleasant feelings and concerns will not necessarily be enough to motivate everyone to give up on an excellent bargain. Instead of passing the deal they may convince themselves, against strong evidence to the contrary, that the deal is actually kosher. Such blissful ignorance can be achieved with the help of the psychological mechanism that fixes mismatches between the agent's desires, and her beliefs about appropriateness of pursuing this desire: self-deception.[107]

Closing oneself to reality via self-deception is extremely prevalent, for, as Demosthenes explains, 'nothing is easier than self-deceit. For what every man wishes, that he also believes to be true.'[108] Surely the fact that the agent is now genuinely unconscious of the wrong nature of her action does not exonerate her from responsibility for the wrongs she committed under the spell of self-deception.[109] But since the agent is (at least) not fully aware of the wrongfulness of his actions, his responsibility has to be 'pegged' to the earlier stage, ie, to the stage where he allowed himself to fall into the oblivion of self-deception. One suggestion on how to understand the backwards attribution is Linehan's: the self-deceived, he says, displays culpable ignorance: 'ignorance is culpable when the person could have, and should have, known; he should have known if the actions his ignorance allows have grave consequences for others'.[110] This echoes the language of constructive notice and shows how, in the circumstances of FO–P conflicts, it is the search for clean conscience that alerts the court to the very real possibility that P, who comes across as unaware of the existence of a trust, should nevertheless lose to FO when the responsibility for his false belief lies with him.[111]

[107] For a clear philosophical analysis of self-deception, see D Davidson, 'Deception and Division' in E LePore and B McLaughlin (eds), *Actions and Events* (Blackwell 2015) 138.

[108] Demosthenes, *Third Olynthiac* (Heinemann 1930) 3.19.

[109] Otherwise we fall into the paradox that 'trying to deceive oneself so as not to be responsible is bad (morally evil), but succeeding restores one to moral innocence' (EA Linehan, 'Ignorance, Self-deception, and Moral Accountability' (1982) 16 Journal of Value Inquiry 101–15, 109).

[110] ibid 102.

[111] For a law-and-economics perspective on the strength of the duty to inquire, see Richard A Epstein, 'Inducement of Breach of Contract as a Problem of Ostensible Ownership' (1987) 16 Journal of Legal Studies 1. The author argues there that the tort of inducement of breach of contract is best understood as a manifestation of the problem of ostensible ownership of an individual's labour.

Thus, in the circumstances of FO–P conflicts, the search for clean conscience alerts the court to the very real possibility that P who comes across as telling the truth when claiming he was unaware of the trust, should nevertheless lose to FO when the responsibility for the ignorance lies with him. In this context, Equity introduces a reasonable person standard for deciding whether a purchaser genuinely lacks constructive notice.

C. Efficiency

At the end of his discussion of the preference awarded in some systems to the bona fide purchaser, Menachem Mautner arrives at the conclusion that formulating the defence in accordance with justice principles will also generate the most efficient result.[112] A fairly similar blissful overlap can be found in the case of Equity's darling—a result that would not surprise those who believe that finding the cheapest cost avoider plays a part in deciding desert claims in distributive justice. In departing from the strong pro-FO solution of the common law, the Courts of Equity designed a solution that fits the efficiency considerations that are particular to situations where FO is a beneficiary, and the unauthorized sale is performed by a trustee.

At the pre-theft stage, a beneficiary can do precious little to guard the property over which she has rights. She can insist that the trustee submits reports, and call him to account promptly whenever she has a reasonable suspicion that he is mishandling the trust assets. But, at the end of the day, trusts are created in order to separate the ownership of an asset from its daily management. The person who can be incentivized to make efficient investment at the pre-theft stage is therefore the *settlor*: a pro-P rule can drive her to gather more information on the prospective trustee, as she knows that the wrong person may cause (intentionally or negligently) a complete loss of the trust property.[113] Heightened attention to the identity of the trustee would also promote the reputation of the trust as a social institution one can have faith in. But what about the argument according to which a pro-FO priority rule would disincentivize *thieves* by chilling the market for stolen property? Unlike the burglar who is after his next fix, a trustee who contemplates a misapplication of trust property may indeed respond to a pro-FO rule as a rational maximizer of wealth, taking into account the reduction in people's willingness to buy property from suspicious sellers. But Equity has a more powerful tool for disincentivizing embezzlement in the form of the severe sanctions for breach of trust, including profit-stripping remedies for breach of fiduciary duty by express trustees and claims based on tracing against constructive as well as express trustees. Meanwhile, trustees who misapply the property by *mistake* will be blind to any incentive provided by a pro-FO priority rule. Efficiency considerations that support an FO rule are

[112] Mautner (n 19) 126

[113] Or, in jurisdictions where this is an option, to appoint a trust protector to monitor performance of the trust duties.

therefore particularly weak when it comes to the pre-theft stage with respect to an FO who is a beneficiary of a trust.

Let us move then to the post-theft stage. What effect will the pro-P Equity's darling rule have on the actions of potential Ps and upset FOs? It may be that once she learns of the misapplication, the beneficiary can invest in identifying the misapplied property, or at least in asking the court to appoint a new trustee who will so act. Her incentive to do so will be stronger if a pro-FO rule increases her chances of retrieving the property. But again, given the beneficiary's distance from the everyday management of the asset, crucial time is likely to be lost until she finds out about the misapplication; if a new trustee has to be appointed, the start of the search will be delayed even further. Her chances of finding the property before a conflict with a purchaser arises are even lower than in the case of an ordinary FO, and so a major push for a pro-FO priority rule is largely inapplicable to Equity's take on FO–P conflicts. Almost everything that can be achieved by way of prevention is, therefore, dependent on dissuading P from buying the property from the trustee. But won't a pro-P rule—which considerations of justice and promoting the flow of the market support—create an incentive for *underinvestment* in title investigation? Recall that Schwartz and Scott raise the worry that a rational maximizer of utility will only invest at the minimum level that is sufficient for proving to the court that he fulfilled the conditions for getting priority according to the rule, instead of following the formula of optimal investment (ie 'invest until the marginal increase in the probability of receiving a good title times the goods' value to you equals the marginal inquiry cost'). In the context of the UCC 'good faith'-based exceptions to the *nemo dat* rule (such as the voidable title or entrustment), this worry makes a lot of sense, as it defines 'good faith' as 'honesty in fact and the observance of reasonable commercial standards of fair dealing in the trade'.[114] While the reference to a 'good faith' standard in the UCC can be interpreted as an equitable mitigation of a fairly rigid pro FO rule, Equity (as a body of law) offers a unique formula that tackles the problem in a particularly appealing way.

By prioritizing on the basis of conscience, Equity makes working one's way around the exception harder. For the Courts of Equity have at their disposal a particularly sensitive set of tools for gauging the real state of mind of the purchaser. While proxies like 'reasonable commercial standards of fair dealing in the trade' can do some important work, the conscionability requirement encourages the judge to look for the very specific circumstances of the transaction by which P (allegedly) acquired the property. Even if P has, for example, immaculately followed the rules of a respectable online market in order to purchase an item of jewellery, low-quality photos, reduced price in comparison with same designs on other websites, and reluctance/inability of the seller to answer questions about the pieces in details can be interpreted as tell-tale signs that P chose to ignore in bad

[114] At § 2-103. The comment explains further that '"[F]air dealing" ... is concerned with the fairness of conduct rather than the care with which an act is performed. This is an entirely different concept than whether a party exercised ordinary care in conducting a transaction.' For a clear exposition of the good faith requirement, see *Kotis v Nowlin Jewelry INC* 844 SW 2d 920—Tex: Court of Appeals 1992.

conscience.[115] Other types of goods, and even specific types of the same goods, may have different giveaways that would trigger a well-functioning conscience to sound an alarm. Fastening on the defendant's conscience means that the court will also pay full attention to P's behaviour before and after the purchase.[116] Did he make reasonable enquiries as to the nature of the deal, or does it look like he is trying to have as little as possible to do with the seller? Does he display the work of art in the living room/wear the jewellery in public/use the equipment in his front office, or does it look like he is trying to avoid unsolicited inquiries from people who might see it in his possession? This power granted to the Court of Equity to conduct a highly refined investigation into the state of mind of P undermines the purchaser's ability to peg his investment into the title to the inefficient minimum required for proving his innocence; to be found conscionable, he would actually need to *be* conscionable, and that means investing, roughly, at the efficient level for the particular subject matter.[117] Of course, this judicial power comes with a price tag: reduced predictability, increased risk of a judicial mistake, and an increase in litigation costs. However, at least the purchaser who suspected something dodgy and managed to dismiss his suspicion cannot be heard to complain about the uncertainty. Others will have to take it as a price worth paying for approximating an elusive ideal balance between the interests and deserts of two innocent parties and the community in which they act.

V. Conclusion

Equity's stance on the perplexing dilemma of FO–P competition sheds a bright light on Equity's self-perception as a court of conscience. In a sharp distinction from the priority rule at common law, which comprises a core tenet of property law (*nemo dat*) and a string of pragmatic exceptions, Equity's point of departure is a refusal to engage defendants whose conscience is clean. Relegating the structure of property rights to a secondary place, the frame of reference that Equity adopts is built around the notion of conscionability.

Some will say that this change of focus—from the power of ownership to the mindset of the purchaser—shows that beneficiaries do not have ownership rights in the trust property. Without taking a position on this question, we have argued that Equity has taken a typically independent path on the question of when ownership should be limited for reasons of justice or efficiency. In using a conscionability standard to resolve the standoff between FO and P in favour of Equity's darling, Equity devised a solution

[115] See in more details https://pages.ebay.co.uk/safetycentre/help.html. In *Kotis v Nowlin Jewellery* ((n 114) 924) for example, P contacted FO after the sale to ask whether the seller/thief has given good payment for the watch before the latter learnt that the cheque would not be honoured. Nevertheless, the extremely low price, of which P was aware, was enough to rob him of purchaser in good faith status.

[116] See, for example, the courts' detailed analysis of every step of the purchaser's conduct in *Gray v Smith* [2013] EWHC 4136.

[117] For an analysis of Equity as tackling the opportunism that navigating the priority rules to make a lower-than-efficient investment exemplified, see Henry Smith in this volume Chapter 10.

that tracks the pattern of the parties' moral responsibility for the predicament they now face, and at the same time serves the communal goal of encouraging owners and purchasers to make efficient investment in preventing it. The situations in which Equity is prompted to resolve an FO–P conflict are unique in that they involve a social institution that, while it enables people to manage their wealth in creative ways, also puts the public aspect of property under a great strain.[118] The needs which deserve to be accounted for by a social action are therefore different from what we find in FO–P conflict outside the equitable context, and finding a good balance between them requires subtle work on the question who should bear the burden of a third-party's wrongdoing. Due to the unique position of equitable right holders, the question of moral responsibility for the conflict hangs almost entirely on P's state of mind. Happily, an efficiency-oriented analysis yields a similar conclusion as to the importance of ascertaining P's state of mind for an optimal solution of the conflict. The ad hoc retroactive standard of conscionability, which empowers the court to investigate P's position in all its particularity and subtlety, is therefore particularly suitable for arriving in a successful resolution that is responsive both to interpersonal justice and the interest of the community at large.

[118] Thus, in contexts where equitable interests have relinquished their historic advantage of secrecy as a result of statutory registration regimes, the distinctive 'Equity's darling' defence has also vanished, to be replaced by simpler and more predictable statutory defences: see, generally, L Gullifer (ed), *Goode on Legal Problems of Credit and Security* (5th edn, Sweet & Maxwell 2013) 2-22–2-33. As a result of the introduction of such registration regimes for many classes of equitable interests in land, and for equitable charges over company assets, the defence now plays its traditional role of protecting a purchaser with a clean conscience from a hidden interest primarily in cases involving equitable interests affecting personal property and trusts of unregistered land. These are the main contexts in which the defence remains available in modern English law.

14

From *Riggs v Palmer* to *Shelley v Kraemer*

Judicial Power and the Law–Equity Distinction

John CP Goldberg and Benjamin C Zipursky[*]

I. Introduction

American legal scholars like to point out that judges are governmental officials, not oracles. They do so in aid of the claim that common law adjudication is no less 'state action' than any other mode of lawmaking. Like other realist formulations, this one distorts as much as it illuminates, for it treats officials' actions as a monolith. Leave aside familiar interbranch differences. Judges themselves wear different hats: sometimes they apply law; other times they do equity. To understand Anglo-American legal systems, one must be attentive to the differences between these two modes of adjudication.

An important body of recent scholarship has argued that the law–equity distinction is neither a mere historical artefact nor bad jurisprudence.[1] While we are not equity experts, we aim in this chapter to add to that literature by means of a dialectical account. We start with a deliberately stark contrast between two kinds of judicial authority—the authority to apply law and the authority to do equity. Although there probably is some historical grounding for this contrast, we do not offer it as an accurate description of the precise domains of 'law' and 'equity' at any particular moment in Anglo-American legal history. Law and equity, on this understanding, are two distinct modes of judicial decision-making.

Next we explain how certain features of the relationship of law and equity will tend to cause (and almost certainly have caused) the lines between these two forms of judicial authority to shift and blur. The upshot of this second stage of the argument, however, is not that the distinction between law and equity should be abandoned. Quite the opposite, it provides a set of tools that, we hope, will generate greater understanding of its significance and its subtleties.

To be more specific: section II maintains that a theoretical approach to private law we have developed under the banner of 'civil recourse theory' can shed light on the

[*] Thanks for excellent comments to Andrew Gold, Dennis Klimchuk, Bharath Palle, Steven Schaus, and Henry Smith. Remaining errors are ours.

[1] In offering an account of equity as structurally distinct from law in a way that complements it, we follow a path staked out long ago by Aristotle. Aristotle, *The Nicomachean Ethics* (JL Ackrill and JO Urmson (eds), tr David Ross, rev ed OUP 1980). Aristotle's cryptic account has been developed by a number of sophisticated theorists from whose works we have benefited greatly, including Henry Smith, as well as Andrew Gold, Larissa Katz, Dennis Klimchuk, Ben McFarlane, Paul Miller, Irit Samet, and Robert Stevens.

John CP Goldberg and Benjamin C Zipursky, From *Riggs v Palmer* to *Shelley v Kraemer* In: *Philosophical Foundations of the Law of Equity*. Edited by: Dennis Klimchuk, Irit Samet, and Henry E Smith, Oxford University Press (2020).
DOI: 10.1093/oso/9780198817659.003.0015

law–equity distinction. A plaintiff who sues in tort, or breach of contract, and who seeks compensatory damages, is best understood as claiming to be legally entitled to recourse from the defendant (and to judicial assistance in obtaining recourse). A claim for equitable relief is a different beast. The claimant does not assert an entitlement to judicial enforcement of a right of recourse but instead petitions the court to block or alter the ordinary operation of the law, or to provide relief to which the claimant has no legal entitlement based on an allegation of some deficiency in the operation of the law.

Section III elaborates our account of the distinctive nature of courts' equitable authority by cataloguing its applications in famous decisions such as *Riggs v Palmer*[2] and *Meinhard v Salmon*.[3] Section IV then harnesses our rendition of the law–equity distinction to help make sense of two prominent but perennially controversial American decisions—*Moore v Regents of California*[4] and *Shelley v Kraemer*.[5] Both, we contend, are best understood as instances of courts doing equity rather than enforcing legal rights. These examples suggest that an appreciation of the differences between a court decision vindicating a claim of legal right and a decision granting equitable relief can help courts and commentators make better decisions even in the modern, 'post-fusion' world.

Section V explains why, even though law and equity are distinct, the lines between them have tended to shift and to become subtler over time, and why these tendencies are bound to continue. On the one hand, in applying and developing the law, courts sometimes incorporate equitable doctrines, concepts, or ways of thought. On the other hand, for good reasons, the judicial administration of equity has a tendency to become more routinized, and in that sense more law-like. Moreover, the granting of equitable relief to fill gaps in the law sometimes has led courts to eliminate those gaps, thereby moving certain matters from the equitable to the legal side of their dockets. The courts' application of the law, and their exercise of equitable authority to respond to problems generated by the law, is an iterative phenomenon. An adequate understanding of Anglo-American law requires an appreciation of this dynamic.

II. Law vs Equity

Historically and theoretically, equity has operated as a supplement to law. If a plaintiff has a claim predicated on a legal right, the court will ordinarily resolve the case by applying the law. Legal causes of action have, in this sense, a kind of priority over equitable causes of action, even though, as we will see, equity also claims a certain kind of authority over the operation of law. We thus begin with an account of law—private law, more specifically. This account, building on earlier work, analyses Anglo-American

[2] 115 NY 506 (1889).
[3] 164 NE 545 (NY 1928).
[4] 793 P2d 479 (Cal 1990) (In Bank).
[5] 334 US 1 (1948).

private law as a scheme of civil recourse. We then offer a contrastive account of what it means for courts to grant equitable relief.[6]

A. Civil Recourse

In areas of private law such as tort and contract, if a complaint is properly pleaded and its allegations proven, the plaintiff is *entitled* to have a judgment against the defendant. This entitlement is a composite of two rights enjoyed by the plaintiff. First, it consists of a Hohfeldian *claim right against government*, correlative to a *duty owed by government to individuals* that it afford them recourse against persons who have, under applicable legal rules, wronged them. Second, it consists of a Hohfeldian *power* that correlates to a *liability* in the defendant. This power—the plaintiff's capacity to alter legal relations by commencing and proving a lawsuit—is often called 'a right of action'.

In providing citizens with courts and rights of action, the state satisfies the principle of civil recourse, which is a principle of both law and political morality. According to it, persons who are prevented by the state from responding directly to conduct deemed by the law to be a mistreatment of them must be given an avenue of civil recourse against those who have mistreated them. Tort law provides a clear illustration of private law operating as civil recourse. A person at the 'victim end' of what a court or legislature has deemed to be a tort is entitled to redress from the person who injuriously wronged her, typically in the form of money damages. The provision of a right of action to plaintiffs complies with the principle of civil recourse. Through tort law, the state empowers a victim to redress a wrong done to her by obtaining damages payments from a person who has been determined to have committed the wrong against the victim.

Much of the common law of contract fits within a similar framework. Although the primary obligations of contract are distinct from those of tort by virtue of being largely defined by agreement, the state supplies the breach-of-contract plaintiff with a legal power akin to the power enjoyed by a tort plaintiff—ie, the power to change legal relations by having a court issue a judgment that the defendant owes compensation to the plaintiff. In this area of private law, compensation amounts not so much to 'redress' (as we use that term) as to the provision of an equivalent to performance. Hence, damages are typically awarded in an amount sufficient to put the plaintiff in the position she would have been had there been performance. In granting a right of action for damages for breach of contract, the state is again satisfying the duty it owes to persons under its authority to enable them to invoke judicial procedures to obtain recourse.

Beyond tort and contract, Anglo-American legal systems contain various bodies of law that confer rights of action. Replevin confers a power on plaintiffs to have officials seize personal property owned by the plaintiff that is in the possession of another.

[6] We thus share with Andrew Gold the view that an adequate grasp of the law–equity distinction requires attention to the 'tripartite relation of plaintiff, defendant, and state', and, in particular, to when a court does or does not owe it to a claimant to lend its assistance. See in this volume Chapter 4.

Because criminal and tort law severely constrain the use of self-help to repossess property, the state instead provides a right of action to obtain such assistance. A decedent's legal designee—an executor—has a duty to probate a will in accordance with the decedent's instructions. Anglo-American law provides them with a legal power to do so through the courts. Certain civil rights statutes provide individuals with rights of action that allow them to obtain recourse for statutory wrongs. And so on.

We have developed civil recourse theory in part by distinguishing it from corrective justice theory. Both theories accept that legal claim rights (such as the rights recognized in tort law not to be defamed or negligently injured) are correlative to legal duties (such as the duties not to defame or negligently injure). But they part ways over the characterization of the legal relations that arise when primary rights are violated and primary duties are breached.

Consider the situation of a tort victim. Corrective justice theorists regard the victim as enjoying a legal claim-right to compensation correlative to a duty owed by the defendant to compensate. In other words, a person's duty to refrain from negligently injuring or defaming someone is seen as continuous with her duty to pay damages to one whom she negligently injures or defames.[7] On this view, courts presiding over tort claims see to it that a plaintiff's claim right (that the defendant compensate her) is satisfied and that the defendant's duty (to compensate the plaintiff) is performed. In this sense, *justice* is done—a normative disequilibrium is *corrected*.

By contrast, we deny that a tort victim (*qua* tort victim) is the bearer of a legal claim right that the defendant compensate her, and that a tort defendant is under a legal duty to the plaintiff to compensate her. Instead, as noted, the victim enjoys a legal power that correlates to a liability. A tortfeasor who has not yet been sued might be under a moral duty compensate his victim, but he is not under a legal duty to do so. Instead, he faces a vulnerability to having his legal relations altered at the behest of the victim. There are certainly situations, outside of tort law, in which an actor does incur a legal duty to pay a plaintiff prior to being sued. For example, an insurer has a legal duty to pay a covered claim properly submitted by an insured, and a government is sometimes under a statutory duty to pay benefits to eligible beneficiaries. In these instances, the law, by granting rights of action to insureds and beneficiaries, really is empowering them to enlist the courts to enforce a pre-existing legal duty to pay. Tort law operates differently. So too does contract law.

The question of whether to characterize private law as instantiating the principle of civil recourse or the principle of corrective justice is theoretical, but it has normative implications. On the corrective justice view, when the courts resolve tort, contract, and other private law claims, they are by definition seeing to it that justice is done. By contrast, while our approach grants that there is *some* connection between a state providing for civil recourse and the pursuit of justice, it takes this connection to be indirect. The institutions of private law no doubt reflect a governmental aspiration or obligation to provide a just political and legal order. It hardly follows that tort and contract law

[7] A Ripstein, *Private Wrongs* (HUP 2016) 233–62.

aim for the doing of justice in each case. Rather, when tort and contract law operate properly in cases where claims have been made, persons are being empowered to obtain recourse—as they are entitled to be empowered—regardless of whether the terms on which recourse is provided amount to the doing of justice as between plaintiff and defendant.

As our use of the word 'entitled' in the previous sentence indicates, civil recourse theory, like corrective justice theory, is deontological. But it is deontological on a roughly contractarian model, rather than a justice-seeking or teleological model. Part of what earns a legitimate state the allegiance of the governed is its being structured on terms, and operating in ways, that demonstrate a certain degree of solicitude for the interests of each member of the governed. Law that provides civil recourse is one way in which a state can demonstrate such solicitude. A body of law such as tort law is concerned to vindicate rights of individual empowerment. In this context, the judge's role is to serve (along with the jury) as adjudicator of the authenticity of such demands, and to provide the anchor of authority that render such demands enforceable. In tort and contract law, justice is respected by ensuring a kind of empowerment, not by seeing to it that just results are realized in each case.

Finally, to reiterate and emphasize a point made earlier that will be important for subsequent discussion, although legal right holders are entitled to court-ordered remedies for violations of these rights, under the scheme of civil recourse instantiated in Anglo-American common law, the right holder's remedies are, overwhelmingly, limited to awards of money damages. (Court judgments such as those requiring the return of personal property are relatively rare, and do not involve an order enjoining the defendant to perform or refrain from performing some action on pain of court sanction.) To be sure, courts and legislatures enjoy leeway to choose among different rules for determining appropriate damages awards, so long as the rules provide for damages in amounts that plausibly can be understood to amount to genuine redress. They need not limit tort plaintiffs to 'make-whole' damages, for example. Still, recourse at law has historically been limited to damages.[8]

B. From Law to Equity

While civil recourse theory can plausibly claim to fit Anglo-American tort and contract law, it seems to offer little purchase on equity, at least under standard conceptions of what it means for a court to do equity. This is no coincidence. Indeed, it is precisely because the theory does a good job of capturing the terms on which courts exercise their authority to make and apply private law that it does not capture the terms on which courts exercise their authority to do equity. In particular, three distinguishing features of courts' equity jurisdiction jump out as not fitting the civil recourse model.

[8] We take no position in this chapter on whether some or all declaratory judgments amount to the provision of recourse.

The first is that individuals who bring claims in equity do not, strictly speaking, possess rights of action. In other words, they do not come to court claiming an *entitlement* to relief. Rather, in the manner of a petitioner, they *request* it. Instead of asserting a legal power over the defendant that the court is bound to authenticate, equity claimants ask the court to act for their benefit.

The second and related departure from the model of private law, understood on a civil recourse view, is that equity courts enjoy leeway that courts of law do not. In deciding whether to grant equitable relief, courts assert a power and indeed a responsibility to exercise substantial discretion. Courts of law make neither of these assertions. This is because any claim to discretion of this sort is fundamentally inconsistent with the idea of a plaintiff being entitled to have a court heed its institutional duty to enforce her demand for recourse once the basis for the demand is proven. Conversely, the discretionary aspect of equity fits hand in glove with the petition-like character of complaints in equity. Here, complaints set forth reasons why a court should choose to exercise its power. In law, the plaintiff demands that the defendant pay a certain amount and asks the court to authenticate the legitimacy of, and enforce, that demand.[9]

It is important not to overstate the foregoing pair of contrasts. It would be silly to claim—and we do not claim—that suits seeking to vindicate legal rights involve some sort of automatic or mechanical judicial ratification. Even plain-vanilla tort and contract cases call on judges (and sometimes juries) to make judgment calls on various issues of law and fact. Likewise, in hard cases, judges must craft rules defining causes of action and affirmative defences on the basis of contestable arguments of precedent, principle, and policy. Moreover, legislatures and courts obviously have adopted procedural, evidentiary, and remedial rules that both empower and constrain claimants at law: a claimant who fails to bring her breach-of-contract claim within the relevant limitations period is not entitled to any relief.

These qualifications notwithstanding, there is a regulative ideal for claims sounding in private law that does not apply to claims for equitable relief. When, in accordance with applicable procedural, evidentiary, and substantive rules, a plaintiff establishes that the defendant's conduct amounted to a violation of her legal right, the plaintiff is entitled to a remedy. It is not open to a court of law to conclude that the plaintiff has proven her tort claim, and that the defendant has no affirmative defences, yet then withhold judgment.[10] Claims in equity, as we are defining it, do not operate under such an ideal, and claimants in equity enjoy no equivalent entitlement. Even if they establish that they have suffered harm as a result of a certain kind of injustice done to them, they may still be denied relief.

[9] As we explain in the text, our point is not that equity is to be distinguished from law on the ground that courts of equity operate in a completely discretionary manner, such that they are entitled to dismiss a complaint for any reason, or no reason. S Worthington, *Equity* (2nd edn, OUP 2010) 328–29 (noting and criticizing the claim that the law–equity distinction should be drawn on this basis). Certainly today the exercise by courts of their equitable powers is constrained by various rules and standards.

[10] Of course a court might rule, for example, that a tort claimant has proven that she was the victim of a tort, yet also conclude that she failed to prove tangible or intangible compensable losses, and thus is entitled only to an award of nominal damages.

A third difference pertains to the remedies granted by courts of equity. An injunction is a command from a court, and the failure to comply with that command constitutes contempt of court. Back when there were separate courts of equity, those courts 'would tell people what to do—*exactly* what to do, on pain of imprisonment or contempt'.[11] By contrast, a money judgment entered by a court of law is an authentication of the defendant's legal position as a debtor. A court's authority to do equity remains a discretionary power. When courts apply law, they are following through on a standing commitment to maintain legal relations in accordance with an equality-based allocation of legal powers to those who have been wronged, or to whom contractual duties have been breached, or from whom property has been taken.

Again, a caution is in order. For purposes of exposition, we are at the moment envisioning law and equity operating in completely separate spheres: either a claimant proceeds with her legal claim, or she seeks relief in equity. In reality, as we discuss below, the two modes of judicial decision-making overlap. In certain instances, for example, a court might, on equitable grounds, deny relief to a claimant who proves that she has suffered a legal rights violation. In these cases, equity intervenes into the domain of law, blocking the law from operating on its own terms. The courts' authority to apply and make law provides them with no basis for denying valid legal claims. However, their equitable authority authorizes them (on certain occasions) to decline to enforce valid legal claims in the name of avoiding an injustice between or among affected parties.

When these three features of equity are taken together, it becomes somewhat less surprising that, initially, the officials charged with doing equity were different from those who adjudicated claims at law, and that the former acted on terms more in keeping with what today would be called the 'executive' branch of government than did the officials charged with applying law.[12] Sitting in equity, a court does not adjudicate claims between two private parties in the way that courts hearing private law disputes do. It entertains requests for appropriate governmental interventions in favour of the 'petitioner'—exercises that require the intervening actor to possess a certain kind of authority. Arguably, that is what the Chancellor was, and the Chancery was a place for hearing such requests.

III. Types of Equitable Claims

Thus far, our account of the distinctiveness of court's equitable authority has operated at a high level of abstraction. We now elaborate it by considering some familiar

[11] SL Bray, 'Equity: Notes on the American Reception' in JCP Goldberg, HE Smith, and P Turner (eds), *Equity and Law: Fusion and Fission* (CUP 2018) 31, 34 . In an internal citation omitted from the above quotation, Professor Bray thanks Professor Andrew Kull for the quoted formulation.

[12] Equity, of course, was originally administered by the Chancellor, who was 'primarily an officer of state and a minister of the Crown' and frequently functioned in the manner of a prime minister. JH Baker, *An Introduction to English Legal History* (4th edn, Butterworths 2002) 99. In her contribution to this volume, Larissa Katz emphasizes in different ways the sense in which the doing of equity is more an exercise of an executive power to see to it that injustices are addressed than an adjudication and enforcement of legal rights (see Chapter 8).

examples of courts doing equity. These cases hardly exhaust equity's domain. But they are central cases, and thus appropriate examples on which to focus. In each, we argue, the claimant does not assert a legal entitlement to recourse, but instead seeks to invoke the court's equitable authority to address an injustice that arises out of the operation of law, and that has resulted, or stands to result, in a particular hardship for the claimant. Of course, equity cases remain *cases* in which courts are required to adjudicate between two or more parties. And, indeed, with doctrines such as unclean hands and laches, equity courts are quite attentive to the posture of the litigation and the status of the litigants before them. Still, their role in these cases is not to validate the plaintiff's demand but to see what ought to be done according to equitable principles.

A. Ordering the Unwinding or Reformation of a Transaction That, While a Valid Exercise of Legal Powers, Works an Injustice against the Claimant

The chestnut of *Riggs v Palmer* nicely illustrates a category of equity case.[13] *Riggs* is famous for the majority's morally infused interpretation of New York's inheritance statutes. Less commonly noticed is the posture of the litigation. The plaintiffs were the daughters of the testator, Francis Palmer. They sued the murdering heir, Elmer Palmer (Francis's grandson), along with the administrator of his grandfather's estate, to have the will 'cancelled and annulled'.

Although the majority and dissenting opinions are not as clear as they might have been,[14] it seems quite likely that the plaintiffs sought relief as a matter of equity.[15] Their suit did *not* challenge the validity of the will under statutes defining the procedures for executing a will.[16] There was no claim, for example, that Francis's will, under which Elmer inherited, had been secured by fraud, or that Francis was incompetent at the time his will was executed. More to the point, it was clear that the daughters, as mere intended beneficiaries of a planned will that Francis never had a chance to execute, were not entitled to have a court recognize their *legal* right to inherit—they had no such right.[17] Nonetheless, the daughters sought relief, arguing, among other things, that

[13] 115 NY 506 (1889).

[14] Some of the difficulty in isolating the nature of the plaintiffs' claims stems from the fact that, by the time of *Riggs*, the New York courts' law and equity jurisdictions had been merged for almost fifty years.

[15] While maintaining that *Riggs* itself was an instance of a court reaching a result on the basis of unconvincing legal reasoning, James Barr Ames argued that denial of inheritances to murdering heirs was best understood as the doing of equity. JB Ames, 'Can a Murderer Acquire Title by His Crime and Keep It?' in *Lectures on Legal History and Miscellaneous Legal Essays* (Harvard UP 1913) 310, 321–22. We differ from Ames only in suggesting that a charitable reading of *Riggs* would permit one to view the court as doing what Ames said it should have done—namely, apply equitable principles. Thanks to Henry Smith for pointing us to Ames's essay. See also W Farnsworth, *Restitution: Civil Liability for Unjust Enrichment* 74 (University of Chicago Press 2014) ('the difficulties associated with *Riggs* merely illustrate the limits of law as distinct from equity').

[16] The action does not seem to have been commenced in Surrogate's Court, in which challenges to wills were entertained. Rather, it appears to have been filed in the New York Supreme Court, General Term, which court referred the matter to a referee.

[17] Indeed, under New York law of the time, even the beneficiary of a properly executed will was deemed to have no right to inherit until the death of the testator. *Hutchins v Hutchins*, 7 Hill 104 (NY Sup Ct 1845) (prior to the

'Elmer Palmer is estopped by his own conduct from claiming the title to his property, or [from claiming] that the condition upon which he takes has, in contemplation of law, happened.'[18] In short, they maintained that it was a crucial fact that the concededly valid will was only triggered by an act of heinous misconduct by Elmer, seeking to secure for himself assets that otherwise would have gone to them. This fact provided grounds for a court sitting in equity to do justice by, in effect imposing a constructive trust on Elmer's inheritance.

The Court, of course, accepted the invitation, invoking its authority to give the state's inheritance statutes an 'equitable construction'.[19] Indeed, the majority opinion cites Blackstone for the proposition that a court in equity is 'at liberty' to act *as if* the statute did not address the question at hand, thus leaving it free to order a transfer of assets from Elmer to the daughters.[20] Needless to say, the relief provided by the court—an injunction—attests to the equitable posture of the case.[21]

In short: the claim in *Riggs* invoked the Court's equitable jurisdiction rather than its legal jurisdiction. The claimants could not and did not assert a legal right to inherit and did not ask the court merely to authenticate and enforce such a right. Rather, they alleged that Elmer stood to benefit unjustly, and at their expense, from a perverse invocation of applicable legal rules. As New York's inheritance statute contained only general language (and thus said nothing specific about the case at hand), the Court concluded that it could grant the plaintiffs' request and order ownership transferred without violating the law. The relief it provided thus consisted of an order invalidating a transfer effected by an otherwise valid exercise of legal powers.

Another New York chestnut—*Meinhard v Salmon*—provides an example of an equity case that falls within the present category.[22] Meinhard provided funds to Salmon for use in improving commercial space that Salmon had arranged to lease for a period of twenty years from Gerry. Meinhard was essentially a passive investor; Salmon was in charge of renovating the space and putting it to profitable use. The two were to share profits according to a formula. Towards the end of the lease period, Salmon, without informing Meinhard, negotiated a new lease between himself and Gerry's successor. When Meinhard discovered that Salmon had entered into the new lease solely on his own behalf, Meinhard sued to have Salmon's interest in the lease held in trust as an asset of their joint venture.

testator's death, a will beneficiary has only a 'naked possibility' of inheriting, and thus has no cause of action against a defendant who fraudulently induced the testator to revoke the will).

[18] *Riggs* (n 2) 507 (the quoted text is from the reporter's summary of the argument of plaintiffs' counsel). In making this argument, plaintiff's counsel cited treatises on estoppel as well as Joseph Story's equity treatise.

[19] ibid 510–11.

[20] ibid 511. In the face of a valid statute explicitly stating that murdering heirs were entitled to inherit, the Court presumably would have concluded that there would be no occasion for equitable construction of this sort.

[21] While Ames may have been correct to argue that the most appropriate equitable remedy for the case was a constructive trust, it hardly follows that the remedy actually provided was not equitable. Ames (n 15) 311. On the centrality of judicially imposed trusts to the development of equity, see Worthington (n 9) 63–64.

[22] 164 NE 545 (NY 1928).

Writing for the Court of Appeals, Chief Judge Cardozo affirmed lower court rulings in favour of Meinhard. Cardozo granted that Salmon had not acted with 'a conscious purpose to defraud'.[23] Indeed, he suggested that Salmon had probably acted in good faith in supposing that he, as the active party in the co-venture, was entitled to negotiate a new lease for himself. Nonetheless, because Salmon was a fiduciary with respect to Meinhard, he owed him 'undivided loyalty'—a demanding standard that he had not met.[24]

> Here the subject matter of the new lease was an extension and enlargement of the subject matter of the old one. A managing coadventurer appropriating the benefit of such a lease without warning to his partner might fairly be expected to be reproached with conduct that was underhand, or lacking, to say the least, in reasonable candor, if the partner were to surprise him in the act of signing the new instrument. Conduct subject to that reproach does not receive from equity a healing benediction.[25]

Accordingly, the Court imposed a constructive trust—'the remedial device through which preference of self is made subordinate to loyalty to others'[26]—by which Meinhard was deemed to own half the value of the new lease.

Cardozo has sometimes been criticized for projecting dated notions of chivalry and honour onto an ordinary commercial relationship.[27] And it is possible that he overstated the duty Salmon owed Meinhard, given their expectations of one another and the customary norms governing a business deal of the sort that they struck. Regardless, the case was decided on the basis of an equitable principle: namely, that—separate and apart from whether it constitutes the violation of a legal right—it is an injustice as between co-venturers for one of them to keep for himself a business opportunity that relates to their venture, and to which he gained access only by virtue of the legal powers he exercised as a co-participant in the venture.

B. Ordering a Transfer of Assets to Rectify an Unjust Pattern of Holdings

Equity courts sometimes act to prevent or unwind certain transactions that are defective—that should never have taken place—and that have generated an unjust pattern of holdings. Certain claims seeking to undo a conveyance based on a mistake fit

[23] ibid 548.
[24] ibid.
[25] ibid.
[26] ibid (citing *Beatty v Guggenheim Exploration Co*, 122 NE 378 (1919)).
[27] RB Thompson, 'The Story of *Meinhard v. Salmon*: Fiduciary Duty's Punctilio' in JM Ramseyer (ed.), *Corporate Law Stories* (Foundation Press 2009) 105, 124–26 (suggesting that Cardozo's opinion relied on high-minded generalizations rather than close attention to the actual terms of the business relationship between the parties).

this description.[28] In such cases, the recipient of the property might claim legal possession. But the courts of equity nonetheless would order the transaction undone to avoid an injustice.

Other instances of this category include actions for contribution. The notion of contribution is fundamentally equitable, involving as it does the idea of the fair sharing of a common burden.[29] Consider, for example, actions for contribution between or among tortfeasors. *Merryweather v Nixan*, a King's Bench decision from 1799, arguably ruled that one of two tortfeasors who is made to pay a plaintiff's entire damages has no legal right to contribution from the other.[30] However, subsequent decisions rendered by courts of equity in the US maintained that such a rule was inconsistent with the equitable nature of contribution, which calls for a judgment as to whether the equities in a particular case were aligned so as to warrant contribution. In the language of an 1823 Virginia decision, 'courts of equity ... admit contribution whenever the parties were originally subject, jointly, to the burthen, and are *in aequali jure*, and where the party claiming the assistance of the court is not precluded, from his own turpitude, from receiving it'.[31] Writing in 1879, Melville Bigelow supposed that contribution between tortfeasors was available in equity unless they 'engaged in some offense *malum in se*, or some directly intended, or actually known, breach of the law'.[32] Although by the time Bigelow was writing, courts of equity had developed rules of thumb as to when a tortfeasor's claim for contribution would be granted, because his 'right' to contribution turned on the court's assessment of the equities as between defendants, contribution remained equitable in nature.

C. Ordering Dismissal of a Valid Suit at Law on the Ground That Enforcement Would Amount to Abuse

A claimant can seek relief in equity when the application of prevailing legal rules stands to work an injustice with significant deleterious consequences for the claimant. As Henry Smith has trenchantly argued, many cases in this category involve appeals to courts of equity to block opportunistic exercises of legal powers.[33] In modern times,

[28] D Ibbetson, *A Historical Introduction to the Law of Obligations* (OUP 1999) 273–74 (noting that eighteenth-century equity courts would grant relief for certain transfers of land and for certain payments based on mistake, fraud, or duress).

[29] J Story, *Commentaries on Equity Jurisprudence, As Administered in England and America* (Hilliard, Gray & Co 1836) vol 1, 78 (where allowed, actions for contribution instantiate the equitable maxim 'Equality is Equity'); MM Bigelow, *Elements of Equity for the Use of Students* (Little, Brown 1879) 246 (contribution actions allow for the correction of an unfairness consisting of a person paying more than his fair share of a debt also owed by others).

[30] (1799) 8 TR 186.

[31] *Thweatt's Admin v Jones*, 1 Randolph 328, 334 (Va Sup Ct 1823) (Green, J).

[32] Bigelow (n 29) 247.

[33] HE Smith, 'Fusing the Equitable Function in Private Law' in K Barker, K Fairweather, and R Grantham (eds), *Private Law in the 21st Century* (Hart 2017) 173–196; HE Smith, 'Equity as Second-Order Law: The Problem of Opportunism' (unpublished MS, 15 January 2015) <http://ssrn.com/abstract=2617413>

decisions of this sort often take the form of a court refusing to lend its aid to a plaintiff notwithstanding that the plaintiff has a legally valid claim. A powerful (though controversial) example of this phenomenon is found in another well-known Cardozo opinion: his dissent in *Graf v Hope Building Corp.*[34]

An employee of the mortgager, a corporation owned and controlled by one Herstein, miscalculated a monthly payment, such that it was $402 shy of the $6,120 owed. Herstein made out checks for the incorrect amount to be delivered to the mortgagee, then left for a business trip. The employee discovered the computational error, but because Herstein was unavailable and the payment date had arrived, and because no one else was authorized to issue checks for the corporation, the employee submitted the checks to Graf, the mortgagee, with a note pointing out the error and indicating that it would be corrected promptly when Herstein returned from his trip four days after the due date for the payment. However, the employee forgot to bring up the matter with Herstein upon his return, and Graf, after waiting for the twenty-day cure period specified in the loan documents, without warning or demand, accelerated the loan and commenced foreclosure proceedings. Immediately upon receipt of the notice of the foreclosure, Herstein tendered payment of the shortfall, which tender Graf rejected.

A majority for the Court of Appeals ruled that Graf was entitled to foreclose. Cardozo's dissent did not dispute this conclusion. Rather, it suggested that the judicial enforcement of legal rights created by covenants to a mortgage, as is true of all legal rights, is subject to equitable limitations. True, the law—and associated interests in stability and predictability—requires courts to enforce valid acceleration clauses according to their terms, especially when the relevant agreement provides a grace period to protect mortgagors against 'inadvertence and improvidence'.[35] Nonetheless, this case was sufficiently distinct as to warrant the trial court in 'refusing to co-operate with the plaintiff in the effort to collect the accelerated debt'.[36] It would allow Graf to take an 'unconscionable advantage of the letter of his bargain' for the courts to assist him in the exercise of his legal power to foreclose.[37]

> The omission to pay in full had its origin in a clerical or arithmetical error that accompanied the act of payment, the very act to be performed. The error was not known to the debtor except in a constructive sense, for the secretary, a subordinate clerk, omitted to do her duty and report it to her principal. The deficiency, though not so small as to be negligible within the doctrine of de minimis, was still slight and unimportant when compared with the payment duly made. The possibility of bad faith is overcome by many circumstances, of which not the least is the one that instantly upon the discovery of the error, the deficiency was paid, and this only a single day after the term of grace was at an end. Finally, there is no pretense of damage or even inconvenience ensuing to the lender. On the contrary, and this is the vital point, the inference is inevitable that the lender appreciated the blunder and was unwilling to avert it. From his

34 171 NE 884 (NY 1930).
35 ibid 887 (Cardozo, CJ, dissenting).
36 ibid 886.
37 ibid 888 (quoting *Console v Torchinsky*, 116 A 613, 614 (Conn 1922)).

> conduct on the day immediately succeeding the default, we can infer his state of mind as it existed the day before.[38]

In sum, the courts were entitled to refrain from ordering foreclosure, and should have refrained from ordering it, because doing so would work a substantial injustice by allowing the plaintiff to 'lay in wait', then opportunistically demand enforcement of his legal rights.

D. Ordering Actions Necessary to Vindicate the Legal Rights of the Plaintiff

In this familiar class of cases, a claimant enjoys an entitlement at law to money damages, yet, because of special circumstances, damages fail adequately to vindicate her legal right. Accordingly, the claimant seeks alternative or supplemental relief in the form of an injunction.

While it is commonplace today for courts to issue injunctions in certain classes of tort and contract cases, this pattern should not obscure the fact that injunctions are equitable in nature. When a court orders specific performance of a contract for the sale of land, or enjoins a nuisance, it is not, strictly speaking, fulfilling its obligation to provide the plaintiff with an avenue of civil recourse. It is doing equity. This is why, if the equities point strongly against the grant of an injunction, a court can decline to issue it, notwithstanding that the plaintiff has proven herself to be the victim of a breach of contract for the sale of land, or a nuisance. By contrast, if the plaintiff has proven her case (including her losses), no comparable judicial discretion exists with respect to the question of whether to award compensatory damages: the fact that a damages award in a breach-of-contract suit will work a massive hardship on the defendant, and confer only a modest benefit on the plaintiff, provides no ground for the court to decline to enter judgment on that award.

Even today, doctrinal evidence for this characterization abounds. An order of specific performance ordinarily issues only upon a finding that legal remedies are inadequate, and even then can be withheld if it granting it would work a significant injustice.[39] Likewise, an injunction that promises to work an undue hardship on the defendant will not be granted.[40] As noted, there is no comparable discretion at work when courts entertain claims as a matter of law.

[38] ibid 889.

[39] EA Farnsworth, *Contracts* (4th edn, Wolters Kluwer 2004) 739–57 §§12.4–12.8.

[40] D Laycock, 'The Neglected Defense of Undue Hardship (and the Doctrinal Train Wreck in *Boomer v. Atlantic Cement*)' (2012) 4 Journal of Tort Law 1. Of course Professor Laycock famously argued elsewhere that the courts have abandoned the requirement of inadequate legal remedies as a necessary condition for the grant of injunctive relief. D Laycock, *The Death of the Irreparable Injury Rule* (OUP 1991). For the suggestion that Laycock's 'death' imagery is overblown, see GR Shreve, 'Book Review: The Premature Burial of the Irreparable Injury Rule' (1992) 70 Texas Law Review 1063.

IV. Recognizing Equity

Our effort to isolate the distinct nature of courts' authority to do equity is not simply a fanciful intellectual exercise or a flirtation with legal history. It has practical payoffs in terms of the ability of courts and commentators to understand and apply law. Or so we now claim. Two controversial American decisions—*Moore v Regents of California* and *Shelley v Kraemer*—exemplify the explanatory value of the law–equity distinction, as we have cast it.

Moore was litigated in the California Supreme Court at a time when that court was famous for taking a flexible and pragmatic approach to tort law. Yet, in a fractured decision, even it struggled to identify what, if any, tort had been committed. The majority ultimately 'fudged' the result by simultaneously recognizing a claim for the informed-consent variety of medical malpractice and a claim for breach of fiduciary duty. In light of the framework we have sketched above, however, *Moore* is arguably more cleanly cast as granting equitable relief (rather than providing redress for the violation of the plaintiff's legal rights).

According to the pleadings in *Moore*, Dr Golde, while treating Moore for leukaemia, determined that cells produced by Moore's body might have commercial value. Thus, throughout the treatment, which included a splenectomy followed by years of post-operative care, Golde saved blood and tissue that he removed from Moore. During this time, Golde joined others in a profitable business venture that developed clinical applications from the cells. Golde never informed Moore of his research and commercial interests.[41] Moore later brought suit against Golde, as well as the researcher with whom Golde was working and the university that owned and operated the medical centre out of which Golde practised.

Moore's complaint asserted thirteen causes of action ranging from fraud and conversion to the performance of medical procedures without informed consent ('informed consent'), breach of fiduciary duty, and unjust enrichment. A majority of the justices ruled, confusingly, that Moore's informed consent and breach of fiduciary duty claims, though pleaded separately, amounted to two assertions of a single and valid claim.[42] In so ruling, the majority also rejected Moore's conversion claim, reasoning that his cells and tissue were not property that was taken from him. Separate

[41] Moore became suspicious and hired a lawyer to investigate the situation in part because, after he moved his residence and balked at the expense associated with travelling for additional treatments, Golde agreed to fund his travel expenses and indeed paid for him to stay at a 'posh Beverly Hills hotel'. MJ Burke and VM Schmidt, 'Old Remedies in the Biotechnology Age: *Moore v. Regents*' (1992) 3 Risk, Issues in Health & Safety 219, 222–23. Several years into the treatment, Golde also presented Moore with a form to sign—which he described as a mere formality—according to which Moore agreed to grant rights in his cell line to the University of California (ibid 222).

[42] *Moore* (n 4) 483 (Moore's allegations concerning Golde's failure to disclose 'state a cause of action' that 'can properly be characterized either as the breach of a fiduciary duty to disclose facts material to the patient's consent or, alternatively, as the performance of medical procedures without first having obtained the patient's informed consent').

concurring and dissenting opinions primarily took issue with the majority's rejection of the conversion claim.

Like many notable judicial decisions, *Moore* is fascinating because it raises issues at the intersection of multiple legal domains: contract, tort, restitution, and—we would submit—equity. Part of why *Moore* lends itself to being described as equitable is a matter of timing. It was a case of first impression, which is why the complaint offered more than a dozen grounds for liability. The Court thus found itself attempting to make a judgment about certain questions of interpersonal justice at a moment when academic medicine was just becoming increasingly associated with commercialization. Given the situation in which the decision was rendered, as well as the terms in which it is expressed, it seems plausible to conclude (for reasons elaborated below) that the Court essentially granted Moore equitable relief rather than finding an actionable tort.

To be sure, the majority purported to hold that Moore had a claim tantamount to a malpractice claim based on a physician's failure to obtain his patient's informed consent to a course of treatment. However, as noted, the Court also maintained that this malpractice claim could alternatively be described as a claim for breach of fiduciary duty. Moreover, an informed-consent theory does not map neatly onto the facts alleged in *Moore*. Ordinarily, an informed-consent plaintiff must prove that the physician's failure to provide information about the risks of a procedure induced her to undergo an injury-generating procedure that she otherwise would have foregone. There may not have been any such inducement in *Moore*, and in any event the majority did not specify such inducement as a condition of recovery.[43] Instead, it seemed to treat the nondisclosure itself as wrongful.[44]

In sum, the problem with treating *Moore* as a tort case is that, although it involved wrongful conduct—a doctor, for reasons of material self-interest, knowingly withholding information from a patient about certain dimensions of his treatment—there was nothing that amounted to an injuring of Moore by Golde. And where a wrongful act with the potential for injury does not ripen into injury, there is no right of redress. Golde's wrongful conduct, one might say, ripened into profits for Golde, not a setback for Moore.

But tort—and private law more generally—is not the only basis on which a claimant can seek relief. There is also equity. Like *Riggs* and *Meinhard*, *Moore* is a case in which the defendant profited by acting wrongfully in relation to the plaintiff. Moore's complaint thus had less to do with his having suffered the violation of a recognized legal

[43] It is unclear whether in his desire to harvest cells and materials, Golde subjected Moore to post-operative treatments that were medically unnecessary or questionable. A separate opinion in the case, with which we have some sympathy, suggests that Moore could have made out an informed consent claim if he were able to establish that he would not have undergone certain treatments had he known they were being performed primarily or exclusively for Golde's economic benefit (ibid 500) (Broussard, J, concurring and dissenting). The discussion in the text leaves aside this possible basis for recovery.

[44] It is thus understandable that Moore also pressed a conversion claim, because the taking of his cells, and their being harnessed for use in a commercial product, carries with it the feel of an injury. Yet the majority did not buy this argument, reasoning that Moore had no property interest in cells that were removed from his body as part of a proper course of medical treatment. (One cannot imagine a court being willing to recognize a conversion claim when, for medically sound reasons, blood cells are removed and stored but never used commercially or otherwise.) In dissent, Justice Mosk was willing to overlook this problem, but the majority was not.

right and more to do with Golde's having inequitably used the occasion of his (appropriate, authorized) treatment of Moore as an opportunity to exploit. As courts of equity have always done, the *Moore* court responded to a claimant seeking to undo an injustice involving an exploitation of legal powers and privileges. Moreover, in classic equitable fashion, it did so in effect (though not in word) by imposing a constructive trust on profits gained by the exploiting party at the expense of the exploited. Judges who were more attuned to courts' distinct authority to do equity would have been better able to explain the basis of its decision, and to fend off the conversion issues that dominated Judge Mosk's dissent and have been debated by scholars ever since. Although the Court obviously recognized there was a fiduciary duty aspect to the case, it could not bring itself fully to embrace the equitable nature of its decision, and thus offered an unstable law-equity hybrid, rather than announcing clearly that the plaintiff's claim sounded in equity, and that a constructive trust (or disgorgement) was the appropriate remedy, not damages.

The United States Supreme Court's opinion in *Shelley v Kraemer* presents a still-more famous and more freighted puzzle for jurists.[45] We suggest that, like *Moore*, its puzzling aspects dissipate when it is viewed as a decision in equity.

The Equal Protection Clause of the Fourteenth Amendment to the United States Constitution bars discrimination on the basis of race. However, this right against racial discrimination is a right against government—discrimination by private actors acting in a private capacity does not violate the Equal Protection Clause. There must be 'state action', ie, discriminatory treatment imputable to an official or a private individual acting in something like an official capacity. The operation of a privately owned business, even a business that clearly benefits from public services (police, fire, roads, the enforcement of trespass laws, etc), ordinarily will not count as state action.

Although the state action doctrine is longstanding, in 1948—six years before *Brown v Board of Education*—the Court issued *Shelley*, a decision that seemed either to ignore the doctrine or to portend its demise. The plaintiffs, residents of a neighbourhood of St Louis, brought suit to enjoin the sale of a property in the neighbourhood to an African-American buyer. In a companion case from Michigan, *McGhee v Sipes*, the plaintiffs went further, seeking a judicially ordered ejection of the African-American buyers of a home that the buyers had already occupied.[46] In both cases, the basis on which plaintiffs argued for judicial intervention was a restrictive covenant specifying that the properties in question could not be occupied by non-whites.

Before the Supreme Court, the buyers argued that an order enjoining the sale and purchase of property on the basis of a racially restrictive covenant amounted to state action in violation of the Equal Protection Clause. Doctrinally, it was certainly open to the Court to reject this argument. Indeed, the 1926 case of *Corrigan v Buckley* had refused to invalidate racially restrictive covenants applicable to land located in the District of Columbia.[47]

[45] 334 US 1 (1948).
[46] ibid 7.
[47] 271 US 323 (1926).

In *Shelley*, however, the Court overturned the respective decisions of the Missouri and Michigan high courts ordering injunctive relief. The apparent relaxation of the state action requirement in *Shelley* and *McGhee*, followed by decades of decisions insisting that the application of the Equal Protection Clause is limited by a robust state action requirement, has struck some commentators as incoherent or unprincipled.[48]

A detailed reconstruction of the state action doctrine is beyond the scope of this chapter. Yet, on the narrower question of whether that issue merited special treatment in *Shelley*, the Court adopted an entirely defensible position. In both *Shelley* and *McGhee*, private actors had, through the exercise of facially valid legal powers, imposed restrictions on the alienability of properties in formal legal documents, thereby creating a basis for the plaintiffs to claim that the sellers were under a legal duty to refrain from selling their lands to non-whites. Yet the plaintiffs had called upon the courts to do something special in these cases, namely, to enjoin (and indeed undo) private transactions. In short, the plaintiffs were asking the courts to exercise their equitable authority, not their legal authority. This makes all the difference in the world, and not simply because a court sitting in equity is entitled to look to see whether claimants have clean hands, and to conclude that a claimant who seeks assistance to maintain a blatantly racist practice has unclean hands.

As we noted above, the power of courts when doing equity includes a distinctly executive dimension. The *Shelley* and *McGee* plaintiffs did not have a *legal* power to stop private land sales from whites to non-whites. Instead, they had only the ability to request that a court of equity intervene to that effect. In turn, for a court to enjoin such a transaction is for it to decide whether to issue a *command* rather than deciding whether to ratify or validate a claim of right. Because this special mode of judicial action has the flavour of an executive branch action, it can credibly be treated as state action without requiring the conclusion that *all* judicial decisions concerning private interactions amount to state action. As *Shelley* expressly recognized, the restrictions built into the relevant covenants could only be realized through 'the active intervention of the state courts, supported by the full panoply of state power'.[49] As such, the judicial action requested and granted 'b[ore] the clear and unmistakable imprimatur of the State'.[50]

[48] See eg G Peller and M Tushnet, 'State Action and the Birth of a New Freedom' (2004) 92 Georgetown Law Journal 779, 789. In defence of *Shelley*'s holding, Henry Smith and Tom Merrill have suggested that, given the judicial norm of declining to enforce agreements that violate public policy, the withholding by Missouri's and Michigan's courts of a policy-based waiver could fairly be deemed state action. HE Smith and TW Merrill, *The Oxford Introductions to U.S. Law: Property* (OUP 2010) 81–82. Carol Rose has alternatively suggested that the judicial enforcement of racially restrictive covenants constitutes state action because it amounts to judicial recognition of a community norm of racial disparagement, thereby risking its conversion into a legal rule. Carol Rose, 'Property Stories: *Shelley v. Kraemer*' in G Korngold and A Morriss (eds), *Property Stories* (2nd edn, Foundation Press 2009) 199, 215–16.

[49] *Shelley* (n 5) 19. As the Court also explained, *Corrigan v Buckley* was distinguishable because there 'the only constitutional issue before this Court... was the validity of the covenant agreements as such' (ibid 8–9).

[50] ibid 20. In a companion case to *Shelley*, Justice Frankfurter highlighted the equitable aspects of suits seeking to enforce racially restrictive covenants. *Hurd v Hodge*, (1948) 334 US 24, 36 (Frankfurter, J, concurring) ('In these cases, the plaintiffs ask equity to enjoin white property owners who are desirous of selling their houses to Negro buyers.... Equity is rooted in conscience. An injunction is, as it always has been, 'an extraordinary remedial process, which is granted, not as a matter of right, but in the exercise of sound judicial discretion.' In good conscience,

Understood to hold that *a court doing equity* amounts to state action, *Shelley* makes a good deal of sense.[51]

V. Blurred Lines

We have argued that a court's authority to apply law is distinct from its authority to do equity. And we have given examples designed to convey what, on our view, it means for a court to do equity. However, law and equity have always interacted in complicated ways. In certain respects, law has claimed primacy over equity, as for example, when the adequacy of available legal remedies provides a ground for denying equitable relief. In other respects, equity has claimed primacy over law—the very point of Cardozo's *Graf* dissent.[52] With the fusion of courts' law and equity jurisdictions, the distinction has become even more difficult to track. In fact, various features of law, equity, and our court system have operated to blur the lines. This is part of what makes the task of isolating equity's distinctiveness so difficult.

Today, of course, a court can entertain and validate assertions of legal right that are pressed through procedural devices born of equity. And the same court can provide both legal redress and equitable relief. In such a world, it is difficult to maintain a robust sense of the difference between a claim that sounds in law and one that sounds in equity. Difficult, but not impossible. The judges of Cardozo's time, after all, operated in a post-merger world but managed to keep sight of the distinction. That judges today have a harder time seeing it is in part attributable to changes in how lawyers and legal scholars think about law. In particular, with the waning of the idea that private law forms a circumscribed domain of legal rights and duties, the space for a separate domain called 'equity' threatens to disappear.[53]

A further difficulty is that law and equity operate in partially overlapping spheres. Just as certain conduct might fit the definition of two torts (for example, some forms of medical malpractice arguably amount both to a battery and to negligence), there is a good deal of conduct that can be described both as a violation of legal rights *and* an injustice of a sort to which equity might well attend. This overlap explains why there is a need for meta-rules governing the relation between them. And this body of meta-rules is itself complex, ranging from the hoary 'adequate-remedy-at-law' rule to the notion that a court sitting in equity will sometimes decline to enforce a valid legal claim.

it cannot be 'the exercise of a sound judicial discretion' … to grant the relief here asked for') (quoted authority omitted).

[51] In a decision subsequent to *Shelley*, the Supreme Court ruled that the judicial enforcement of damages awards for breach of racially restrictive covenants also violates the Equal Protection Clause. We discuss this decision below.

[52] Although Cardozo obviously did not convince his colleagues that they ought to have invoked their equitable authority to decline to grant relief to the plaintiff on his legally valid claim, the idea that such an authority exists and can be exercised in appropriate cases was not in dispute.

[53] At a deeper level, it is probably impossible to make sense of the distinction between a remedy obtained as a matter of legal right and a remedy obtained as a matter of equity from within the sort of Holmesian jurisprudence to which American legal scholars are unduly attracted. (On the Holmesian view, what it means for there to be a legal right or duty is for someone to have the ability to obtain court-ordered relief against another, regardless of the court's basis for granting that relief.)

There are two subtler reasons why it is difficult to distinguish law and equity in the manner we have described. First, something like a 'law of equity' has naturally emerged as courts have done equity in particular cases.[54] Like courts of law, courts of equity have established procedural and substantive rules, along with maxims and presumptions. No doubt they have developed these out of a notion of fundamental fairness—of treating like cases alike. A court that grants a petition for relief on a certain set of facts will rightly feel some pressure to grant a petition based on comparable facts. For these reasons, there has emerged a law applied by courts sitting in equity. This is in part why it makes sense today to speak of 'equitable wrongs', 'equitable defences', and 'equitable remedies'. Reasons of even-handedness tend, over time, to strengthen the assertion of future equity claimants that they have something like an entitlement to judicial intervention.

Second, even as equity bends towards law, law bends towards equity. Common law legal rights and duties evolve. And they sometimes do so in a manner that reflects reasons characteristic of equity. This occurs at the level of kinds and at the level of particularized judgments. The doing of equity, in other words, can give rise to new law. When it does so, it closes off gaps in which equity operated (though it might also conceivably open up new ones).

One example of an evolution from equity to law involves the emergence, in the early twentieth century, of the tort of appropriation of likeness—a legal cause of action that was later identified by William Prosser as one of four privacy torts.[55] In the standard case, a plaintiff alleging this tort asserts that the defendant has, without her permission, used her image or likeness in advertising a product or service. The defendant's wrong is to associate the plaintiff with a commercial venture with which the plaintiff does not wish to be associated, and to have given the plaintiff public visibility that she does not wish to have, thereby interfering unduly with her ability to control when and how she presents herself to the public.

Among the first decisions to recognize the appropriation-of-likeness tort is the Georgia Supreme Court's 1905 decision in *Pavesich v New England Life Insurance Co*.[56] Without permission, the defendant used a photograph of the plaintiff in a newspaper ad for its life insurance policies, adding a fabricated quotation stating that the plaintiff was grateful to have purchased one of its policies. The plaintiff sued for damages, alleging defamation and invasion of privacy. Conceding that it had not previously recognized invasions of privacy as tortious, the Court nonetheless allowed the claim, concluding that the defendant had violated the plaintiff's right to 'be let alone',[57] ie, his right to determine, within limits, when and how he would 'exhibit his person in [a] public place'.[58]

[54] Bray (n 11) ('Over time, as the Chancellor saw a number of similar cases and resolved them the same way, one could identify the equitable rule'); R Pound, 'The Decadence of Equity' (1905) 5 Columbia Law Review 20. Pound argued that modern equity had been corrupted by excessive formalization. We do not endorse or reject this claim, and instead are content to note that a certain amount of formalization is consistent with the idea of a court doing equity.

[55] WL Prosser, 'Privacy' (1960) 48 California Law Review 383.

[56] 50 SE 68 (Ga 1905).

[57] ibid 71.

[58] ibid 70.

Although entering new legal territory, *Pavesich* took its cues from equity, which had long been available to remedy breaches of confidence. In particular, it noted English and American cases in which courts had enjoined the publication of information or images on the ground that the defendant had obtained them with the condition that they be kept confidential, including the well-known English case of *Prince Albert v Strange*.[59] More directly on point was *Corliss v EW Walker Co*,[60] in which the defendant published a biographical sketch of the plaintiff's deceased husband and sought to sell it along with a photograph of the husband. A federal court in Massachusetts declined to enjoin the publication of the book, but enjoined publication of the photograph on the ground that it would violate a confidence placed in the photographer not to distribute the image except as specified by his subject.

As articulated in the later English decision of *Coco v AN Clark Engineers*,[61] an equitable action to enjoin a breach of confidence has much in common with breach of fiduciary duty claims of the sort discussed above in cases such as *Meinhard* and *Moore*. The gist of the complaint is that the relationship of confidence between defendant and plaintiff—a relationship that the law, by empowering enforceable agreements, helped to shape—limited the defendant's freedom of action with respect to the subject matter of the confidential relationship, and that actions taken outside of those limits, if they work an injustice to the plaintiff, can be enjoined at the behest of the plaintiff or can generate for the plaintiff an entitlement via a constructive trust to an interest in any transactions or arrangements emerging out of the unauthorized action.

In *Pavesich*, by contrast, the focus is not whether unauthorized conduct by the defendant can be blocked, nor whether the effect of the exercise of legal rights and powers must be revised. Rather, the defendant's conduct is deemed to be a wrongful injuring of the plaintiff, for which the plaintiff can seek and obtain redress in the form of compensatory damages. The complaint asserts that there has been a breach of a primary duty and a violation of primary right recognized by tort law—the duty to refrain from publicly displaying, without permission, another's image in aid of one's commercial venture and the right not to have one's image so displayed. Today, a century after *Pavesich*, misappropriation of likeness is the name of a well-established tort. With the recognition of this tort, the boundaries of the line between law and equity shifted, as they have done repeatedly throughout Anglo-American legal history.

While decisions in equity sometimes serve as a springboard for the emergence of a new legal wrong, equitable decisions sometimes generate legal change in a more focused and forced manner. Here, the courts recognize that the provision of equitable relief in a particular scenario practically necessitates modification of legal rules addressing that scenario. The United States Supreme Court's opinion in *Barrows v Jackson*,[62] decided five years after *Shelley v Kraemer*, nicely illustrates how the doing of equity can sometimes necessitate changes in law.

[59] 2 De G & Sm 652, (1849) 64 ER 293 (VC), aff'd, 1 Mac & G 25, (1849) 41 ER 1171 (Ch).
[60] 57 F 434 (CCD Mass 1893).
[61] [1969] RPC 41, [1968] FSR 415.
[62] 346 US 249 (1953).

Like *Shelley*, *Barrows* addressed the issue of racially restrictive covenants. However, the question was not whether to enjoin a sale to non-whites in violation of such a covenant, but instead whether a state court could award damages to one white signatory to a covenant for breach of the covenant by another white signatory. Some state courts had concluded that *Shelley* did not rule out such liability, while others had reached the opposite result. For its part, the Court in *Barrows* was unwilling to draw what it regarded as a conspicuously fine line that promised to generate something close to an incoherent body of law. Just as in *Bolling v Sharpe*,[63] for example, the Court could not permit *de jure* segregated schools in DC after forbidding it in the states,[64] so in *Barrows*, it could not permit damages actions for breach of racially restrictive covenants to achieve what would have been achieved had *Shelley* gone the other way.

That *Barrows* was prepared to deem a damages award grounded in a claim of legal right—as opposed to injunctive relief grounded in equity—as 'state action' might seem to cast doubt on our explanation of why the Supreme Court ruled as it did in *Shelley*. After all, *Barrows* comes out the same way as did *Shelley* even though it did not present the issue of whether courts should exercise their quasi-executive equitable powers so as to enforce racially restrictive covenants. But these doubts are misplaced. One of the central claims in this part of our analysis is that the judicial grant of equitable relief sometimes supplies reasons for subsequent courts to adjust legal rules so that the legal system as a whole better comports with basic desiderata of coherence, even-handedness, and justice. It is not so much that there is the sort of direct 'state action' in *Barrows* that one finds in *Shelley*. It is rather that judicial decisions that properly count as 'state action'—including, in some circumstances, decisions involving the power to grant injunctive relief—can exert a gravitational force on nearby legal rules.[65]

VI. Conclusion

Private law recognizes legal rights that, when violated, generate in victims an entitlement to judicial assistance in obtaining redress from the rights violator. When operating

[63] 347 US 497 (1954).

[64] *Brown v Board of Education of Topeka*, 347 US 483 (1954).

[65] An intriguing analogue to the treatment of state action in *Shelley* and *Barrows* can be found in Supreme Court decisions setting out federal constitutional limits on defamation liability. No less than *Shelley*, *New York Times v Sullivan*, 376 US 254 (1964) raised a state action issue. Moreover, as was also true in *Shelley*, certain features of *Sullivan* aided the Court in resolving that issue in favour of the party claiming to have suffered a constitutional rights violation. In *Sullivan*, the crucial feature was not the presence of a claim for equitable relief. Rather, it was that the plaintiff was a public official essentially seeking to punish the defendant for statements allegedly made about the official's performance of his duties. Given the identity of the plaintiff, the overtly political nature of the allegedly defamatory statements, the jury's award of punitive damages, and the freighted context in which the suit was brought, the Court quite reasonably concluded that Sullivan's nominally civil action was close enough to a criminal prosecution for seditious libel to count as state action. When the Court was subsequently faced with libel cases that did not so straightforwardly involve public officials suing to punish defendants for criticism of their official conduct, the analogy to a seditious libel prosecution no longer fit, and the issue of state action became more problematic. The Court nonetheless concluded—roughly in the manner of *Barrows*—that it could not tenably draw the constitutional line at suits for statements about public officials in their official capacities. It therefore extended its constitutional restrictions on libel law to public figures (and, perhaps more questionably, to certain private citizens). See, eg, *Curtis Publishing Co v Butts*, 388 US 130 (1967).

as private law tribunals, courts, in accordance with the principle of civil recourse, adjudicate the question of whether the plaintiff has proven herself to be the victim of a legally recognized wrong. If she has, the court—so far as the law is concerned—must validate her demand for redress.

Equity is not a scheme of rights and duties in the same sense. To be sure, a court operating in this mode entertains complaints. But the complainant is not demanding something from the court to which she is entitled. She is instead requesting that the court intervene to rectify a certain kind of injustice perpetrated through the law.

So understood, equity is not a magic wand available to courts whenever any manner of injustice is brought to its attention. Nor is it merely a carefully honed counterbalance to the exercise of law. It is a distinct head of judicial authority. When private law by its own terms misfires—when it leaves a void, when legal rules of ownership give rights in property to persons who clearly should not have them, when legal powers are abused or exceeded, or when legal remedies fall well short of protecting or vindicating that which they purport to protect or vindicate—there is a basis for requesting equitable relief.

Although law and equity are thus fundamentally distinct, over time they inevitably become entangled. Law incorporates rules and doctrines developed in equity. This is why modern private law includes doctrines such as equitable tolling and equitable estoppel. And, as certain fact patterns are recognized as warranting equitable relief, equity becomes more law-like. The development of these patterns of equitable relief in turn encourages courts to recognize new *legal* rights, duties, powers, and liabilities.[66] None of this is to say that the law–equity distinction has vanished or is vanishing. It is merely to explain why it is often difficult to isolate when, within a complex legal system, a court is exercising its authority to apply law and when it is exercising its authority to do equity.

By enabling courts to respond to instances in which law—a set of rules and principles established to help ensure the maintenance of something approximating a just social order—unjustly works a hardship on the person seeking relief, equity serves a gap-filling role, moves the law forward, and sometimes create occasions for new equitable interventions. To lose sight of equity is thus to have an incomplete understanding of Anglo-American legal systems, to deny individuals the range of opportunities for obtaining judicial relief available to them, and to ignore an important driver of the growth of the law.

[66] PB Miller, Chapter 5 in this volume; JCP Goldberg and HE Smith, 'Wrongful Fusion: Equity and Tort' in Goldberg, Smith, Turner (eds) (n 11) 309–330.

15

Some Varieties of Consent in Equity

Enhancing and Protecting Autonomy?

Simone Degeling[*]

I. Introduction

This chapter considers the consent of the claimant in particular equitable domains, where it seems that such parties enjoy a limited or bounded ability to make decisions. These domains include the categories of trustee and beneficiary, and fiduciary and principal, since in both instances the trustee or fiduciary holds factual or legal decision-making power to be exercised for the ends of the object of that power. Of interest are equity's requirements for obtaining the informed consent of the beneficiary or principal to a breach of duty by the trustee or fiduciary. This chapter similarly considers equitable relief for undue influence and unconscionability, since the consent of the principal or claimant is structurally insinuated into each of these claims in which the claimant similarly has a constrained ambit of decision-making.

In determining whether or not the claimant has consented, for example to a breach of duty or a transfer of value, this chapter argues that equity examines the antecedent conditions to that decision. Equity is concerned with the situation in which the claimant finds herself, the context framing the apparent consent, in order to determine whether or not the claimant will be bound by that decision. This is most strongly expressed through a requirement that the claimant's decision be independent. By contrast, equity responds in varying degrees to whether the claimant has a range of options available in making her decision. Nonetheless, despite a variable commitment to the need for options in decision, this chapter argues that in this limited sphere, equity operates to recognize and protect the autonomy of the claimant.

At the outset it must be acknowledged that breach of fiduciary duty and breach of trust on the one hand and claims for undue influence and unconscionability on the other, are different categories of dual relationship. Undue influence and unconscionability are not breaches of a duty in any conventional legal sense of that word. Even in relation

[*] I am grateful for the comments of the other participants at the Philosophical Foundations of Equity Conference held at King's College London in 2017, and I thank the organizers of the conference for inviting me to participate in a wonderful event. I am also indebted to my colleagues Michael Crawford and Jessica Hudson, for discussing some of the ideas in this chapter with me, and to the members of the Obligations Group at Melbourne Law School who gave feedback on an earlier version of this chapter. Finally, I thank Whittens & McKeough for their financial support of private law research at the Faculty of Law, University of New South Wales. All remaining errors are my own.

Simone Degeling, *Some Varieties of Consent in Equity* In: *Philosophical Foundations of the Law of Equity*. Edited by: Dennis Klimchuk, Irit Samet, and Henry E Smith, Oxford University Press (2020).
DOI: 10.1093/oso/9780198817659.003.0016

to fiduciary duty, Lionel Smith has argued that although there is a legal requirement of loyalty, properly understood this is not a legal duty in the strict Hohfeldian sense.[1] However, despite the particular formal legal characteristics of these categories and the doctrinal silos into which they fall, this chapter places these examples in parallel since all have at their centre the limited factual or legal power of the claimant to make decisions and the potential for an abuse of the relationship by the defendant. As stated by Lord Selborne LC in *Earl of Aylesford v Morris* '[equitable] [f]raud does not here mean deceit or circumvention; it means an unconscientious use of the power arising out of these circumstances and conditions'.[2]

We are concerned with the claimant's consent. At the doctrinal level, consent in equity refers to the claimant's fully informed and freely given assent. It thus has two components: information and freedom. In general terms, equity asks whether the claimant has sufficient information to hand as will enable her fully to appreciate her own interest in the matter, including the nature and extent to which her interest has or may be compromised by the conduct or interest of the other party. In relation to freedom, equity asks whether there is any impediment to the exercise of the claimant's will in giving or withholding consent. For example, is the claimant in virtue of an incapacity or the influence of another unable to appreciate her own concerns? In such cases, the giving of consent may be illusory, and equity will not hold the claimant to any permission granted.

Consent is an artefact of the whole private law landscape, not only in equity. This chapter does not set out to examine consent in equity by situating the analysis alongside a common law or indeed a statutory comparator. Rather, the analysis assumes that we may sensibly interrogate equity on its own terms. Further, it is important to notice that while this chapter considers consent to a breach of trust, consent to a breach of fiduciary duty and claims arising from undue influence and unconscionability, there are broader senses *not* considered here in which equity also examines the claimant's consent.

A prominent example is a mistaken voluntary disposition, such as a gift or settlement, which is vulnerable to rescission on the ground of mistake. The Supreme Court of the United Kingdom in *Pitt v Holt*[3] confirmed that where there has been a causative mistake of sufficient gravity,[4] such that it would be unconscionable to refuse relief,[5] rescission of the transaction may be granted. Mistakes which will normally satisfy the test are those as to the legal character or nature of the transaction, or as to a matter of fact or law which is fundamental to the disposition.[6] An argument may be made

[1] L Smith, 'Can We Be Obliged to Be Selfless' in Andrew S Gold and Paul B Miller (eds), *Philosophical Foundations of Fiduciary Law* (OUP, 2014) 153.

[2] *Earl of Aylesford v Morris* (1873) LR 8 Ch App 484, 490–91 (Lord Selborne LC).

[3] *Pitt v Holt* [2013] 2 AC 108.

[4] ibid [122] (Lord Walker).

[5] ibid [126], [128] (Lord Walker).

[6] *Pitt v Holt* raises further questions. For example: to explain why actionable mistake is more limited in equity than at law and how the principles articulated in the case integrate with the existing framework of restitution for unjust enrichment; whether the equity described encompasses all gifts and all subject matter; whether the only remedy is a monetary reversal of a disposition via a personal restitutionary remedy. See, eg: B Häcker, 'Mistaken Gifts after *Pitt v Holt*' (2014) CLP 1; S Watterson, 'Reversing Mistaken Voluntary Dispositions' (2013) CLJ 501.

that such cases also fall into the category for examination in this chapter, to the extent that a claimant whose decision to transfer value is vitiated by a spontaneous mistake arguably does not truly consent to the transaction. However, the claimant's decision-making ambit in such cases arguably is not constrained in the same manner as one who is affected by undue influence or unconscionability, or who is the object of a fiduciary or trustee's power. While it must be conceded that this is a fine line, such broader conceptions of consent or agreement fall outside this chapter. This chapter therefore examines such expressions of consent as it operates to exculpate the defendant across express breach of trusts, fiduciary duty,[7] and in undue influence and unconscionability.

II. Autonomy

This chapter notices that in scrutinizing the claimant's consent, equity is concerned with the situation in which the claimant finds herself. Equity looks to the existence of any antecedent conditions impacting or surrounding the claimant's consent in determining whether or not the claimant ought to be bound by that consent. This chapter argues that in this limited sphere, equity operates to recognize and protect the autonomy of the claimant. In order to advance this argument, it is necessary to set out what is meant by autonomy.

The analysis is informed by the perspective that autonomy or the 'autonomous life'[8] of an individual is a question of degree, and reflects the extent to which that person 'is the author of [her] own life'[9] or 'exercises her will in self-determining ways',[10] such that the three components of autonomy identified by Professor Raz are met: appropriate mental abilities, an adequate range of options in decisions, and independence.[11] Each of these are further elaborated as follows. First, in relation to a person's mental abilities or 'inner capacities',[12] a person must, in relation to a particular transaction or decision, have the necessary state of physical and mental health and well-being, intellectual ability, and emotional capacity.[13] Secondly, a person 'must actually use these faculties to choose what life to have ... there must be adequate options available for him to choose from'.[14] According to this view, the role of the liberal state is therefore to 'enable individuals to choose valid conceptions of the good' by proactively providing 'a multiplicity of valuable options'.[15] What constitutes an adequate range of options will depend on the variables surrounding a person and what is necessary to sustain well-being. Third,

[7] In relation to a breach of trust or fiduciary duty, the claimant may do so either before (authorization) or after (confirmation or ratification) the conduct in question.
[8] J Raz, *The Morality of Freedom* (OUP, 1986) 372.
[9] ibid 372.
[10] M Harding, *Charity Law and the Liberal State* (CUP, 2014) 50.
[11] Raz (n 8) 372–78.
[12] ibid 372.
[13] ibid 373.
[14] ibid.
[15] H Dagan, 'The Challenges of Private Law' in K Barker, K Fairweather, and R Grantham (eds), *Private Law in the 21st Century* (Hart 2017) 72.

a person must be independent. She must live a life 'free from coercion and manipulation by others'.[16] On this understanding, both coercion and manipulation interfere with a person's will, albeit in different ways. Coercion interferes with free choice by reducing a person's options by forcing them down a particular path. By contrast, manipulation does not (directly) interfere with a person's options.[17] Instead, it operates on a person's preferences and goals, shaping the internal arbiter of their choices and in this way distorting the exercise of their will.[18]

The question therefore arises: to what extent do equitable models of consent meet these conditions for autonomy? The next sections of the chapter consider these elements in relation to consent to a breach of fiduciary duty or trust and the finding of an equity for relief in undue influence or unconscionability.

III. Fiduciary Obligations and Trusts

The fiduciary must 'not ... obtain any unauthorised benefit from the relationship and not ... be in a position of conflict'.[19] The fiduciary must avoid placing herself in a position of conflict between duty and personal interest and similarly must not take on conflicting engagements as 'by reason of the multiple engagements, the fiduciary must be unable to discharge adequately the one without conflicting with [her] obligation in the other'.[20] Equity determines that actionable conduct arises on actual or potential conflict, such that the fiduciary must avoid a position of a conflict, or real or substantial possibility of conflict between duties, or between their self-interest and duty to the principal.[21] A fiduciary may obtain effective consent to a breach of fiduciary duty to the

[16] Raz (n 8) 373.

[17] ibid 377.

[18] ibid 377–78.

[19] *Breen v Williams* (1996) 186 CLR 71, 113 (Gaudron and McHugh JJ), approved in *Pilmer v Duke Group Ltd (in liq)* (2001) 207 CLR 165, [74] (McHugh, Gummow, Hayne and Callinan JJ) and *Youyang Pty Limited v Minter Ellison Morris Fletcher* (2003) 212 CLR 484, [41] (Gleeson CJ, McHugh, Gummow, Kirby and Hayne JJ); see also *Bristol & West Building Society v Mothew* [1998] Ch 1, 18 (Millett LJ); *Bray v Ford* [1896] AC 44, 51 (Lord Herschell). In the common law of Australia and England/Wales, fiduciary obligations are said to be proscriptive norms. See eg: *Breen v Williams* (1996) 186 CLR 71, 82–83 (Brennan CJ) and 113 (Gaudron and McHugh JJ); *ASIC v Citigroup No 4* [2007] FCA 963, [375] (Jacobson J); *Friend v Brooker* (2009) 239 CLR 129, [84] (French CJ, Gummow, Hayne and Bell JJ); *Howard v Commissioner of Taxation* (2014) 253 CLR 81, [56] (Hayne and Crennan JJ). This stands in apparent contrast to Canada, where fiduciary obligations are described as prescriptive: *McInerney v McDonald* [1992] 2 SCR 138, 150 (La Forest J). However, as stated by Getzler: '[o]ne may put to one side the idea ... that fiduciary relationships are merely proscriptive. This model is questionable both historically and analytically; for one, the line between proscriptive and prescriptive duties is as hazy as between omission and commission.' J Getzler, 'Rumsford Market and the Genesis of Fiduciary Obligations' in A Burrows and Lord Rodger of Earlsferry (eds), *Mapping the Law Essays in Memory of Peter Birks* (OUP 2006) 580. There is also a debate beyond the scope of this chapter as to whether or not the profit principle stands separately to the conflict principle. See, eg: *Chan v Zacharia* (1984) 154 CLR 178, 198 (Deane J); *Warman v Dwyer* (1995) 182 CLR 544, 557–58 (Mason CJ, Brennan, Deane, Dawson and Gaudron JJ); M Conaglen, *Fiduciary Loyalty* (Hart 2010) 114–20; R Nolan, '*Regal (Hastings) v Gulliver*' in C Mitchell and P Mitchell (eds), *Landmark Cases in Equity* (Hart 2012) 519–27.

[20] *Commonwealth Bank of Australia v Smith* (1991) 42 FCR 390, 392 (the Court).

[21] ibid 392 (the Court); *Breen v Williams* (n 18) 135 (Gummow J); *Birtchnell v Equity Trustees and Agency Co Ltd* (1929) 42 CLR 384, 408 (Dixon J); *Boardman v Phipps* [1967] 2 AC 46, 124 (Lord Upjohn); *Hospital Products v USSC* (1984) 156 CLR 41, 103 (Mason J); *Pilmer v Duke Group* (n 19), [79] (McHugh, Gummow, Hayne and Callinan JJ); *Australian Careers Institute Pty Ltd v Australian Institute of Fitness Pty Ltd* [2016] NSWCA 347, [3]–[5] (Bathurst CJ); [132] (Sackville AJA with whom Meagher JA agreed).

extent that all information relevant to the principal's decision whether or not to consent is provided. Information such as the nature and extent of any conflict, the nature of existing legal rights between the parties and any secret profits should be disclosed. As stated in *Re McGrath & Anor (In their capacity as liquidators of HIH Insurance Ltd)* 'the task of explanation inherent in a request to be excused from a fiduciary requirement is an onerous and exacting one'.[22]

In addition to their fiduciary obligations, trustees may be in breach of trust. Leaving to one side debates about which obligations do or do not comprise the irreducible core of trust obligations,[23] the primary obligation of the trustee is to properly execute the trusts of the trust. A beneficiary may consent to a breach of trust, thus releasing the trustee from responsibility. In determining the validity of this consent, a court must be satisfied that the beneficiary is *sui juris*, has had proper legal or other advice as necessary and possesses the requisite degree of knowledge. The knowledge requirement is expressed such that 'he or she had full knowledge of all the material facts'.[24] As such 'it is not necessary that [the beneficiary] should know that what he is concurring in is a breach of trust, provided that he fully understands what he is concurring in, and that it is not necessary that he should himself have directly benefited by the breach of trust'. Handley JA in *Spellson* also emphasized that '"[u]nderstanding" can involve at least some matters which are not expressed or communicated'.[25] In the trusts context, consent is only a prima facie defence. The court must also examine all the circumstances in which the consent is given to determine whether it is 'fair and equitable' that, despite having given her consent, the beneficiary should afterwards be permitted to complain of the breach.[26]

Returning now to the conditions identified by Raz, we ask to what extent does equity in this domain respect the principal/beneficiary's autonomy? Leaving to one side for the moment the overriding question in trusts relating to 'just and equitable', breach of trust and breach of fiduciary duty essentially have the same requirements for good consent in equity. Equity asks whether the claimant has given fully informed consent to the breach of duty. This standard is not itself directed to ensuring that the claimant possesses the necessary inner capacities or ability to consent or excuse the party in breach. Rather, the application of the informed consent framework largely presumes the claimant possesses the necessary capacity to consent.[27] As such, informed consent may

[22] [2010] NSWSC 404, [37] (Barrett J) referring to the decision of the NSWCA in *Winthrop Investments Ltd v Winns Ltd* [1975] 2 NSWLR 666.

[23] *Armitage v Nurse* [1998] Ch 241, 253–54 (Millett LJ, with whom Hutchinson LJ and Hirst LJ agreed).

[24] *Spellson v George* (1992) 26 NSWLR 666, 670 (Handley JA). See also *Re Pauling's Settlement Trusts* [1962] 1 WLR 86, 106–08 (Wilberforce J).

[25] *Spellson* (n 24) 675 (Handley JA), adopting the test in *Re Pauling's* (n 24) 108 (Wilberforce J). See also *Byrnes v Kendle* (2011) 243 CLR 253, [25] (French CJ), [77] (Gummow and Hayne JJ); *Pourzand v Telstra Corporation* [2014] WASCA 14, [60] (McLure P); *Corporate Systems Publishing Pty Ltd v Lingard* [2009] WASCA 158, [87], [94] (Owen J).

[26] *Spellson* (n 24) 669 (Handley JA); *Re Pauling's* (n 24) 108 (Wilberforce J). See also *Byrnes v Kendle* (n 25) [25] (French CJ); *Crossman v Sheahan* [2016] NSWCA 200, [366] (Ward JA); *Pourzand* (n 25) [110] (Pullin JA). *Re Pauling's Settlement* is discussed in J Payne, 'Consent' in P Birks and A Pretto (eds), *Breach of Trust* (Hart 2002) ch 10.

[27] A claimant who is not capable will likely be subject to the Court of Protection.

be seen as being concerned with securing the conditions necessary for the claimant to exercise this capacity in a meaningful way, such that the claimant's choice is freely exercised. Informed consent therefore appears most consistent with the third of Raz's requirements, that the claimant's decisions should be independent. As noted below, the second condition for autonomy, that the claimant have an adequate range of options in decisions, receives less protection in this domain, albeit in the trusts category the requirement of 'fair and equitable' may accommodate an absence of options in decision.

Equity's concern to ensure the claimant exercises her decision-making abilities is reflected in the fact that courts have an ambit of discretion in determining the adequacy of disclosure by the fiduciary or trustee. Depending on the particular claimant, too much information may be as irrelevant as too little:

> [w]hat is required for a fully informed consent is a question of fact in all the circumstances of each case and there is no precise formula which will determine in all cases if fully informed consent has been given.[28]

Further, 'the requisite disclosure may be given at different times and in different ways, and sufficiency of disclosure can depend on the sophistication and intelligence of the persons to whom disclosure must be made'.[29] On the facts of *Farah Constructions v Say-Dee Pty Ltd*, the court described the principals of Say-Dee as 'shrewd and astute'[30] rather than 'babes in the woods'[31] holding that any disclosure was sufficient and that 'the consent which Say-Dee expressed was informed consent'.[32]

A contrasting example is *Maguire v Makaronis*[33] in which the mortgagors executed a mortgage in favour of their solicitors to secure bridging finance. Their solicitors did not advise the mortgagors to obtain independent legal advice about the bridging finance transaction nor draw to their attention that the solicitors were to be the mortgagees.[34] In the face of a breach of fiduciary duty by the solicitors, who had a personal interest in the mortgage transaction, the question arose whether the mortgagors had given informed consent to the conflict.[35] The High Court of Australia confirmed that 'the [solicitors] had [not] taken the necessary steps ... to answer the charge of breach of fiduciary duty'.[36] The solicitors had not disclosed their interest, had not advised the mortgagors to seek independent counsel and the Court was satisfied that, taking the claimants as they really were, the mortgagors did not understand the legal nature and incidents of the relationships described in the mortgage.[37] Equity's commitment to the

[28] *Maguire v Makaronis* (1997) 188 CLR 449, [466] (Brennan CJ, Gleeson, McHugh and Gummow JJ).
[29] *Farah Constructions Pty Ltd v Say-Dee Pty Ltd* (2007) 230 CLR 89, [107] (the Court).
[30] ibid [108] (the Court).
[31] ibid (the Court).
[32] ibid (the Court).
[33] *Maguire* (n 28).
[34] ibid 461–62 (Brennan CJ, Gaudron, McHugh and Gummow JJ) (referring to the findings of the trial judge).
[35] ibid 466.
[36] ibid 467.
[37] This conclusion was reached even after taking account of the fact that the primary judge had a poor view of the veracity of the mortgagors, finding that they had exaggerated their poor understanding of transactions and that

independence of the claimant's decision is also evident in the requirement that the consent cannot itself be the product of undue influence. Undue influence is dealt with in section IV.

However, there are limits to equity's concern for the claimant's autonomy in this sphere. In particular, the model for claimant consent does not strongly align with a requirement that the claimant have a range of options in decision. The ambit of decision-making available to the principal or beneficiary may as a *practical* matter be curtailed such that her ultimate choice may in reality be binary, being to consent or not.[38] It is unclear the extent to which equity's model for consent in this sphere anticipates negotiation. Despite providing information as is relevant to a particular claimant's decision whether or not to agree to the breach, this information is not directed to informing the commercial or legal *terms* on which the claimant's consent may be given. Equity's role is limited to informing the very specific decision to consent or not. Similarly, the specific legal context of breach of duty means that there is only one monopoly party with whom the claimant may deal, the trustee or principal. Thus, for example, while as a matter of commercial reality a principal may in theory demand terms for the release of the fiduciary obligation,[39] the fiduciary's obligation to disclose the nature and extent of their breach does not of itself appear to arm the claimant principal to negotiate with the fiduciary a particular basis for giving consent, or to obtain any reasonable alternatives to the terms being offered.[40] Information which would *not* likely be disclosed as part of the fiduciary's obligation of the 'fullest of disclosure' might, for example, include the price the same or similar fiduciaries in the market have had to pay their principals in order to obtain consent for similar breaches.

This observation should not surprise us. While the giving of consent may well operate to narrow the scope of a fiduciary duty, and thus alter the relationship such that the conduct in question is no longer a breach of duty, once established the relationship is not an exchange or bargaining relationship in the same sense as a contractual relationship.[41] Therefore, equity's settings are apparently only to provide information as will meet the fiduciary's or trustee's breach of duty.

We now return to the overriding requirement, at least in the express trusts context, of whether notwithstanding her consent, it would be fair and equitable nonetheless to

each read and wrote English better than they had testified to be the case. Nonetheless, the claims for breach of duty were made out (ibid 455–56).

[38] This should not be taken to suggest, for example, that a trustee may escape liability by simply putting the beneficiary to an election of 'object or acquiesce' to the relevant breach. See, eg *Spellson* (n 24) 672 (Handley JA). Rather, the point is to notice that subject to the beneficiary being fully informed of the circumstances of the legal effect of their acts, equity models the choice available to the beneficiary ultimately as being one of consent or not.

[39] See generally: JD Heydon and MJ Leeming, *Jacobs' Law of Trusts in Australia* (8th edn, LexisNexis Butterworths 2016) [22–33], '[p]urely equitable rights may be released under seal, for consideration and (unlike legal rights) even under hand or orally and without consideration'.

[40] See, eg: B Bix, 'Contract' in F Miller and A Wertheimer (eds), *The Ethics of Consent: Theory and Practice* (OUP 2009), 254.

[41] Even contracts, which are often assumed to be entirely voluntary relationships, commonly have terms that cannot be said to have been voluntarily assumed: see A Robertson, 'The Limits of Voluntariness in Contract' (2005) 29 Melbourne University Law Review 179.

permit the beneficiary to complain of the breach.[42] The possibility arises that, through the additional requirement in the trusts context that notwithstanding the beneficiary's consent it be 'fair and equitable' that the beneficiary afterward be permitted to complain of the breach, substantive recognition of the claimant's position may be eroded. This escape route may provide a warrant for equity nonetheless to cut back on the protection for the claimant's autonomy. However, 'fair and equitable' may also be a mandate for the court to consider all relevant circumstances, including whether the claimant had adequate options in decision making.[43]

An example is *Byrnes v Kendle*.[44] Kendle held on trust for his wife Byrnes an interest in a house which was leased to his son from a previous marriage. The son paid only a small amount of rent and for a substantial period Kendle made no attempt to collect from his son any rent at all. Kendle and Byrnes later separated. All members of the High Court of Australia highlighted that '[f]or the sake of matrimonial harmony, Mrs Byrnes ... [had not pressed] Mr Kendle to insist upon payment of the rent owed by his son'.[45] French CJ held that her failure to insist on Kendle pursuing his son for rent did not mean 'it was not fair and equitable for Mrs Byrnes to be permitted to complain of a breach of trust [by Kendle]'.[46] She took no action for the sake of matrimonial harmony and was on the facts not held to her apparent consent. Thus, notwithstanding her consent, it would be fair and equitable to permit Byrnes as the beneficiary to complain of the breach of trust. Arguably Byrnes's independence in decision making, and her range of options in decision, in relation to pursuing Kendle's son for rent, had both been compromised during her relationship to Kendle. 'Fair and equitable' was on these facts capable of accommodating the second and third conditions for autonomy.

IV. Undue Influence

The equitable doctrine of undue influence *inter vivos* is concerned with transfers of value between an ascendant or influencing party and the transferor.[47] As pointed out by Edelman and Bant, undue influence may occur where the claimant is unable to appreciate her own interest in an impugned transaction, or where the influence of the other may be 'benign, welcome or otherwise'.[48] Apex courts in the United Kingdom and Australia appear to have steered undue influence away from a preoccupation

[42] *Spellson* n (24).

[43] *Barescape Pty Limited as trustee for the V's Family Trust v Bacchus Holdings Pty Limited as trustee for the Bacchus Holdings Trust (No 9)* [2012] NSWSC 984, [171] (Black J). See Payne (n 26) 318.

[44] (2011) 243 CLR 253.

[45] ibid [24], [28] (French CJ), [75] (Gummow and Hayne JJ), [127] (Heydon and Crennan JJ) (where the reference is less specific, being to the 'unwilling cooperation' of Mrs Byrnes in her husband's decision not to press for rent).

[46] *Byrnes* (n 44) [30] (French CJ). See also [129] and [131] (Heydon and Crennan) (who found there was no consent by Byrnes) and [77]–[79] (Gummow and Hayne JJ) (indicating there was insufficient evidence to establish a consent).

[47] The recipient may be a third party who receives from the transferor under the influence of the ascendant party. This chapter does not consider third-party liability.

[48] J Edelman and E Bant, *Unjust Enrichment* (2nd edn, Hart 2016) 231.

with categories and subcategories of influence[49] to refocus on the essential matter of whether or not the claimant's act is 'free'[50] such that despite their consent it 'ought not to be treated as the expression of a person's free will'.[51] A majority of the High Court of Australia in *Thorne v Kennedy* explained that there are different ways to prove undue influence. One method is by 'direct evidence of the circumstances of the particular transaction'.[52] Another method is by evidential presumption, such as arises 'where common experience is that the existence of one fact means that another fact also exists'.[53] As stated by the plurality:[54]

> Common experience gives rise to a presumption that a transaction was not the exercise of a person's free will if (i) the person is proved to be in a particular relationship, and (ii) the transaction is one, commonly involving a 'substantial benefit' to another, which cannot be explained by 'ordinary motives', or 'is not readily explicable by the relationship of the parties'. Although the classes are not closed ... the relationships that could give rise to the presumption [include] parent and child, guardian and ward, trustee and beneficiary, solicitor and client, physician and patient, and cases of religious influence. Outside recognised categories, the relationship can also be raised by one party occupying a similar position of ascendency or influence, and the other a corresponding position of dependency or trust. In either case, the presumption is rebuttable by the other party proving that the particular transaction or transfer, in its particular circumstances, was nevertheless the result of the weaker party's free will.

In undue influence equity demonstrates a strong commitment to ensuring that the endeavours are the claimant's own and that her autonomy is both protected and vindicated. Returning to the conditions of autonomy identified by Raz, undue influence does not of itself guarantee the inner capacities that are necessary for autonomy. However, as discussed below, undue influence may be relevant in securing a range of options for the claimant to choose from and also in ensuring a life free from manipulation and coercion. The different methods of proving influence suggest a concern to ensure that there are not underlying structural causes or preconditions determining the claimant's choice. Similarly, the equitable framework is concerned to determine whether on the facts the claimant is emancipated from any influence and may thus satisfy the court that the claimant's choice is self-determined. The discussion below considers undue influence proved on the facts of the case and emancipation from influence.

[49] See, eg: *Royal Bank of Scotland plc v Etridge (No 2)* [2002] 2 AC 773, [92] (Lord Clyde) and [17] (Lord Nicholls), referring to the confusion caused by the schema of dividing undue influence into 'actual undue influence' and 'presumed undue influence', the latter category itself divided into a special class of established relationships of presumed influence (2A) and relationships outside these categories in which the claimant proves a relationship of influence (2B).

[50] *Thorne v Kennedy* [2017] HCA 49, [32], [34] (Kiefel CJ, Bell, Gageler, Keane and Edelman JJ); [85], [87] (Gordon J).

[51] *Etridge* (n 49) [7] (Lord Nicholls).

[52] *Thorne* (n 50) [34] (Kiefel CJ, Bell, Gageler, Keane, and Edelman JJ). Historically this was labelled actual undue influence. See also *Etridge* (n 49) [8] (Lord Nicholls).

[53] *Thorne* (n 50) [34] (Kiefel CJ, Bell, Gageler, Keane and Edelman JJ).

[54] ibid [34] (Kiefel CJ, Bell, Gageler, Keane and Edelman JJ).

In *Thorne v Kennedy*[55] the claimant proved undue influence and successfully obtained rescission of highly prejudicial prenuptial and postnuptial agreements. She did so through direct evidence of the circumstances and did not rely on a presumption.[56] The claimant travelled from her home country to Australia in order to marry the defendant. She had no substantial assets compared to the defendant's estimated assets of between $18 million and $24 million. She spoke poor English and relied on her relationship with the defendant for the continuation of her legal right to remain in Australia. She wanted a child, which was one of her prime motivations in marrying. A few days prior to the intended wedding date, the defendant instructed a solicitor to prepare a prenuptial agreement. The defendant informed the claimant that if she did not sign the agreement, the wedding would not proceed. The defendant took the claimant to an independent family law solicitor in order that the claimant might receive independent legal advice on the prenuptial agreement, and waited in the car outside during this appointment. From the solicitor, the claimant first discovered the contents of the prenuptial agreement, but by this time the claimant's family had been flown to Australia for the wedding ceremony. All other wedding preparations had also been completed: her dress had been made, the ceremony and reception had been booked, and the wedding guests had been invited.

The solicitor advised the claimant not to sign the prenuptial agreement, pronouncing it 'the worst agreement that [the solicitor] had ever seen'.[57] Depending on the circumstances, the terms of the agreement provided for either no amount for the claimant, or a 'piteously small' payment. The prenuptial agreement required the claimant to execute a postnuptial agreement on the same terms following the marriage. Against the solicitor's emphatic advice, the claimant executed both agreements. Approximately four years later, the claimant and defendant divorced, and the defendant sought to enforce the agreements against her. The claimant resisted, and the matter came to court. The defendant died during the proceedings and was substituted by his executors and trustees. The claimant sought equitable relief seeking to set aside the agreements.

In upholding the primary judge's finding that the claimant had been the subject of undue influence in her entry into the agreements, the plurality held that 'it was open to the primary judge to conclude that [the claimant] considered that she had no choice or was powerless other than to enter the agreements',[58] pointing to factors such as her lack of financial equality with the defendant and her lack of permanent residential visa status in Australia.[59] In the specific context of prenuptial and postnuptial agreements,

[55] ibid [54]–[62] (Kiefel CJ, Bell, Gageler, Keane and Edelman JJ), confirming at [2] that the 'findings and conclusion of the primary judge should not have been disturbed. The agreements were voidable due to both undue influence and unconscionability'.

[56] The High Court of Australia held that the relationship of fiancé and fiancée does not give rise 'to a presumption that either person substantially subordinates his or her free will to the other'. ibid [36] (Kiefel CJ, Bell, Gageler, Keane and Edelman JJ). Hence the claimant could not rely on a presumption that the transaction was not the exercise of her free will. Note that even if the relationship had been one to which the presumption applied, the claimant would also have had to demonstrate that the transaction was one 'commonly involving a "substantial benefit" to another, which cannot be explained by "ordinary motives", or "is not readily explicable by the relationship of the parties"' (ibid [34] (Kiefel CJ, Bell, Gageler, Keane and Edelman JJ)).

[57] ibid [12] (Kiefel CJ, Bell, Gageler, Keane and Edelman JJ).

[58] ibid [59] (Kiefel CJ, Bell, Gageler, Keane and Edelman JJ).

[59] ibid [62] (Kiefel CJ, Bell, Gageler, Keane and Edelman JJ).

the following factors were identified as being relevant to the matter of whether a transaction is subject to undue influence: whether the agreement was subject to negotiation; the surrounding emotional circumstances, including whether there was a threat not to marry if the agreement was not signed; whether there was time allowed for reflection and whether any independent advice was received (and whether there was time to consider that advice); the relative financial position of the parties and the nature of the parties' relationship.[60] These factors align with the second and third conditions for autonomy identified by Raz. Returning to the idea that undue influence entertains the possibility that the claimant may vehemently consent to a transaction, precisely because of the influence, equity in this sphere takes seriously Raz's concern that a person's will may not be independent. The will may be coerced or moulded such that 'the way that [a] person reaches decisions, forms preferences or adopts goals'[61] is manipulated. Undue influence therefore attempts to be sensitive to the means by which the claimant's consent to a transaction is procured. Additionally, the model appears to permit recognition of the range of effective options open to the claimant. Obviously, the analysis will be highly fact dependent, but the plurality specifically identified as relevant whether or not a pre/postnuptial agreement was subject to negotiation and, in relation to the claimant in *Thorne*, that she had no choice but to enter the agreement or else experience the shame and embarrassment of calling off the wedding.

A narrower conception of autonomy is taken in *Thorne v Kennedy* by Gordon J, who did not find the evidence proven before the primary judge supported a conclusion of undue influence. Despite agreeing that in general there may be circumstances surrounding the 'weaker' party which impairs their autonomy to a 'serious and exceptional degree',[62] and that the focus of undue influence is the 'free exercise of an independent and voluntary will',[63] Gordon J emphasized that the claimant was well advised, intelligent, and signed the agreements despite knowing and understanding their disadvantageous nature and effect. Gordon J's model aligns with Raz's requirement for independence to the extent that both contemplate that the exercise of free will may be impacted, for example, by information asymmetries, a lack of comprehension, and pressure. However, Gordon J states in relation to the apparently limited choice the claimant had of either not signing and not marrying or signing and marrying (both involving consequences), the claimant's paucity of options did not indicate that her decision was not free. On Gordon J's model, a limited or even 'eliminated'[64] range of options is not the concern of undue influence: 'equity does not aspire to resolve philosophical questions about whether it is meaningful to speak of "free will" when one's zone of autonomy has been bounded'.[65] This position is in part sought to be justified on the ground that 'undue influence does not protect against bad deals'[66] as, since the

[60] ibid [60] (Kiefel CJ, Bell, Gageler, Keane and Edelman JJ).
[61] Raz (n 8) 377–78.
[62] *Thorne* (n 50) [93] (Gordon J).
[63] ibid [94] (Gordon J).
[64] ibid [107] (Gordon J).
[65] ibid (Gordon J).
[66] ibid [103] (Gordon J).

claimant was independently advised and chose the transaction, she should be bound by it. On Gordon J's view, therefore, the claimant's autonomy was vindicated as equity permits the possibility that the claimant may have entered (an apparently inexplicable)[67] transaction through the free exercise of her independent will.[68]

Returning to Raz's conditions for autonomy, how do these engage with Gordon J's view? We might argue that the conditions identified by Raz as necessary for securing the claimant's autonomy are arguably not met since the requirement for a range of options in decisions is absent. However, the extent to which this minority view aligns with the conditions identified by Raz as necessary for securing the claimant's autonomy largely turns on the circumstances and context surrounding the claimant's absence of alternative options in deciding to sign and marry. Respecting autonomy can sometimes mean allowing us to bear the burden of our choices.

The means by which equity identifies or construes emancipation are similarly a barometer of equity's posture towards autonomy in this sphere. For example, in a case of undue influence proved by presumption, the possibility exists that despite the presumption, the defendant may demonstrate emancipation. Thus, where a gift passes from a child to a parent, the presumption that the gift is not the exercise of the claimant's free will is established if the claimant is proved to be in a particular relationship (here parent–child) and the transfer cannot be explained by ordinary motives.[69] However, '[t]he existence of a proper feeling of respect and regard for the parent does not necessarily indicate the continued existence of the parental influence which gives rise to the presumption in question'.[70] The child may be emancipated.

An example is *Tillett v Varnell Holdings Pty Ltd*[71] where the presumption of undue influence was rebutted in relation to a son's transfer of residential property to a company which was partially controlled by his mother. The son suffered from various illnesses including alcohol addiction.[72] The property had been purchased by the family in the name of the son to preserve the son's feeling of independence, with the mortgage and purchase price to be provided by the company. The son was to make some contribution to outgoings according to his ability. The son was registered as owner and apparently signed as mortgagor (mortgagee was the company). However, the company would have effective control.

Despite earning some income, the son could not service the mortgage[73] and he executed documents discharging the mortgage and selling the land to the company.[74]

[67] Or at least one in which there was an 'explanatory gap' (ibid [104] (Gordon J)).

[68] ibid [106] (Gordon J). Note that as discussed below, the lack of choice in decision is also identified by Gordon J ([107, [116], [123]) as relevant to the claimant's disadvantage in finding for her in unconscionability.

[69] ibid [34] (Kiefel CJ, Bell, Gageler, Keane and Edelman JJ).

[70] *Lamotte v Lamotte* (1942) 42 SR (NSW) 99, 103 (Roper J).

[71] [2009] NSWSC 1040.

[72] The son also pleaded unconscionability, but this claim failed. The court held that the son was not unable to conserve his own interests, nor at a relevant special disadvantage or vulnerable to exploitation. Further, the lack of independent advice was not in the factual context significant (ibid [76] and [103] (Brereton J)).

[73] Brereton J specifically found that the exercise of power under the mortgage by the company was an exercise of a legal right [84] which was itself not tainted by influence, albeit that it did involve some pressure on the son. However, this pressure was the inevitable consequence of the conditions on which the land had been purchased in the son's name.

[74] ibid [44] (Brereton J).

The son argued that a relationship of presumed undue influence arose between him and his mother in relation to this transaction. Brereton J held that the son was emancipated from his mother and that there was no presumed relationship of undue influence.[75] In relation to determining emancipation, Brereton J stated:[76]

> At what point a child becomes emancipated is not fixed. While some authorities have focused on the age of the child, and assumed that a child becomes emancipated in the years shortly after attaining majority … the better view is that emancipation is to be determined by reference to the ongoing nature of the relationship between parent and child … depends upon each particular case. However, where the parent is elderly and the child is in middle age—having left home years before—it is unlikely that there will be an ongoing relationship of undue influence.

Tillett illustrates that the key question in determining emancipation is whether or not the claimant is independent. In the parent–child example, the substance of the relationship is examined to determine whether, for example, the child is free from manipulation and has an adequate range of options in decision or must choose from those presented by the parent. Equity asks whether on the facts the claimant is sufficiently able to exercise free will.

An important, but not determinative, factor in determining emancipation is whether or not the claimant has received independent advice. As stated in *Re Coomber*:[77]

> some independent person, free from any taint of the relationship, or of the consideration of interest which would affect the act, should put clearly before the person what are the nature and consequences of the act. … the advice shall be removed entirely from the suspected atmosphere; and from the clear language of an independent mind, [the claimant] … should know precisely what they are doing.

Thus, in *Inche Noriah v Shaik Allie Bin Omar*,[78] an illiterate, feeble, elderly, and socially isolated woman made a gift *inter vivos* to her nephew of all her real estate. She received legal advice about the transaction prior to execution of the deed. However, the lawyer advising her did not know that the claimant was parting with nearly all her property, and that by doing so she would be left without any rental income. Further, the lawyer did not advise her that she could devise her property to her nephew by will, and the lawyer seemed to have obtained much information about his client from the nephew. On these facts, the advice of the lawyer was not competent nor independent,[79] and was not sufficient to rebut the presumption of undue influence since it did not '[bring]

[75] ibid [85] (Brereton J).
[76] ibid [80] (footnotes omitted) citing *Lamotte v Lamotte* (1942) 42 SR (NSW) 99, 102–03 (Roper J). See also *Anderson v McPherson [No 2]* [2012] WASC 19, [249] (Edelman J); *Kwan v Kwan* [2008] NSWSC 465, [71] (Macready AsJ); *Powell v Powell* [2002] WASC 105, [131] (McLure J).
[77] [1911] Ch 723, 730 (Fletcher Moulton LJ); approved by Lord Nicholls *Etridge* (n 49) [60].
[78] [1929] AC 127 (PC).
[79] It was not doubted that the lawyer acted in good faith (ibid 136).

home to her mind the consequences to herself of what she was doing [or inform her about alternative strategies, eg transfer by will]'.[80]

Apart from a requirement of independence, the provision of information may also arguably inform the range of options available to a claimant. In *Inche Noriah*, the claimant did not receive competent independent advice which would have revealed other choices open to her. In this sense, by demonstrating that she was *not* emancipated and that the influence remained, her autonomy was protected. However, as shown by the interpretation of the facts taken by Gordon J in *Thorne v Kennedy*, the presence of independent advice may also confirm and vindicate the claimant's exercise of free will.[81]

V. Unconscionability

The equitable doctrine against unconscionable transactions permits equitable relief where the recipient attempts to enforce a transaction or keep a benefit obtained through an unconscionable dealing with a claimant under a special disadvantage or disability.[82] Intrinsic to the claimant's equity for relief is that equity looks to the circumstances surrounding the claimant's apparent consent to the transaction or transfer. As stated by Deane J in *Commercial Bank of Australia Ltd v Amadio*:[83]

> The jurisdiction . . . generally [extends] to circumstances in which (i) a party to a transaction was under a special disability in dealing with the other party with the consequence that there was an absence of any reasonable degree of equality between them and (ii) that disability was sufficiently evident to the stronger party to make it *prima facie* unfair or 'unconscientious' that he procure, or accept, the weaker party's assent to the impugned transaction in the circumstances in which he procured or accepted it. Where such circumstances are shown to have existed, an onus is cast upon the stronger party to show that the transaction was fair, just and reasonable.

The claimant must be under a special disadvantage or disability to the knowledge of the defendant and the defendant must exploit the disadvantage or disability in order to obtain the claimant's consent to the transaction. The special disadvantage includes as set out by Fullager J in *Blomley v Ryan*:[84]

[80] ibid.
[81] *Thorne* (n 50) [104], [123] (Gordon J).
[82] *Commercial Bank of Australia Ltd v Amadio* (1983) 151 CLR 447, 474 (Deane J).
[83] ibid.
[84] (1956) 99 CLR 362, 405. Subsequent cases have decided that a 'pathological interest in gambling' was not on the facts a special disadvantage (*Kakavas v Crown Melbourne Ltd* (2013) 250 CLR 392, 432 (the Court)) and that a plaintiff's romantic infatuation, his (Diprose) 'extraordinary vulnerability . . . in the "false atmosphere of crisis" in which he believed that the woman with whom he was "completely in love" and . . . emotionally dependent was facing eviction from her home and suicide unless he provided the money for the purchase of the house' would qualify: *Louth v Diprose* (1992) 175 CLR 621, 638 (Deane J) with whom Mason CJ, Brennan J and Dawson, Gaudron and McHugh JJ agreed. Toohey J at 651 dissented pointing to the fact that Diprose was a solicitor who must have appreciated the consequences of his actions.

> poverty or need of any kind, sickness, age, infirmity of body or mind, drunkenness, illiteracy or lack of education, lack of assistance or explanation where assistance or explanation is necessary. The common characteristic ... [is] that they have the effect of placing one party at a disadvantage vis-a vis the other.

In demonstrating that the exploitation of the claimant's disadvantage is unconscientious, the defendant must act with knowledge of the claimant's special disadvantage.[85] What is required is 'proof of a predatory state of mind.... not ... mere inadvertence or ... indifference, to the circumstances of the other party to an arm's length commercial transaction. [These] ... fall ... short of the victimisation or exploitation with which the principle is concerned.'[86] Victimization in this context is a broad concept and may include so called 'passive' receipt of a benefit in unconscientious circumstances.[87]

Unconscionability is clearly concerned with the conduct and conscience of the defendant in victimizing the claimant. However, this rests on an anterior matter: the extent to which the claimant is able to 'make a judgment as to [their] own best interests'.[88] The will of the innocent party, 'even if independent and voluntary, is the result of the disadvantageous position in which he is placed and of the other party unconscientiously taking advantage of that position'.[89] Therefore, the unconscionability silo is also relevant in considering the extent to which equity protects and promotes the claimant's autonomy.

The first thing to notice is that unlike the other categories examined in this chapter, unconscionability *does* identify matters which may impact the claimant's inner capacities for intention, planning, and commitments that are necessary for autonomy. However, any protection for this condition of autonomy in this category is indirect, since the claimant's equity for relief does not arise on the mere existence of the claimant's disadvantage or disability to the knowledge of the defendant. A finding of unconscionability also requires the defendant to exploit the claimant's vulnerability.

As shown by *Thorne v Kennedy*, the facts which demonstrate the necessary vulnerability may also extend beyond matters of 'inner capacity', and encapsulate the second and third of Raz's conditions for autonomy. In *Thorne*, the plurality found the claimant to be unable to make a judgement in her own best interests, since a situation of manufactured urgency surrounded her signing the agreements and receiving legal advice. She had been given an ultimatum by the defendant, her family had been brought to Australia only for the purpose of attending the wedding, and no offer to assist to pay for their return journey had been made.[90] Further, there was gross inequality between the

[85] *Kakavas* makes clear that this is not a principle of constructive knowledge. Equity does not ask that the defendant know or ought to have known of the plaintiff's special disability. What is required is actual knowledge, which encompasses wilful ignorance. *Kakavas* (n 84) [150]–[155], [162] (the Court).

[86] ibid [161] (the Court).

[87] *Wu v Ling* [2016] NSWCA 322, [14] (Leeming JA) (referring to *Bridgewater v Leahy* (1998) 194 CLR 457, [76] (Gaudron, Gummow and Kirby JJ)). In *Wu* Leeming JA held [15] that 'there was neither active extortion nor passive acceptance of a benefit by Mr Ling'. See also *Hart v O'Connor* [1985] AC 1000.

[88] *Thorne* (n 50) [38] (Kiefel CJ, Bell, Gageler, Keane and Edelman JJ).

[89] ibid (Kiefel CJ, Bell, Gageler, Keane and Edelman JJ) approving *Amadio* (n 82) 461 (Mason J).

[90] *Thorne* (n 50) [65] (Kiefel CJ, Bell, Gageler, Keane and Edelman JJ).

claimant and defendant. These factors of 'special disadvantage' were not only known to the defendant, but had been in part created by him. The plurality held that the defendant took advantage of the claimant's vulnerability to obtain her signature to the agreements which were 'entirely inappropriate and wholly inadequate',[91] and therefore the agreements were also vitiated on the ground of unconscionability. Thus, the finding of vulnerability was itself a function of the claimant's lack of options in decision and lack of independence in decision. Similarly, Gordon J found the claimant was unable to 'make a rational judgment to protect her own interests'.[92]

However, the evidence may also indicate the claimant's *ability* to make an independent judgement. The object of the unconscionability doctrine is not 'to protect people from the consequences of their own mistakes'.[93] Equity gives some credence to the 'values of privacy and autonomy'[94] which lie behind our individual decisions to transfer wealth, 'to say [the transfer] is no one else's business'.[95] Thus the appellant in *Wu v Ling* was denied relief in unconscionability since she exercised her own judgement:[96]

> The appellant [was effectively warned about the risk of fraud] but decided that her judgment about the people with whom she was dealing was sound when it was not. The appellant ... [was] ... a person who is able to make a judgment, but fail[ed] to make a sound one. She could still make a judgment (as unsound as it was) about whether she borrowed money at a particular rate of interest to continue to pay it to the fraudster.

VI. Autonomy Enhancing Equity?

Despite some doctrinal fragmentation between the above silos, there is an overarching unity.[97] Equity examines the antecedent conditions to the claimant's consent, the context framing the apparent consent, in order to determine whether or not the claimant will be bound by that consent. In determining that consent is fully informed and freely given, equity is not simply concerned with an absence of overt interference by others, but is also concerned with the situation in which the claimant finds herself. Returning to Raz's conditions for autonomy, unconscionability may, depending on the facts grounding the relevant 'special disability', engage with whether the claimant has

[91] ibid.
[92] ibid [81].
[93] *Anderson v McPherson (No 2)* [2012] WASC 19, [255] (Edelman J). See also *Louth* (n 84) 638 (Deane J).
[94] *Kakavas* (n 84) [28] (the Court).
[95] ibid (the Court).
[96] *Wu* (n 87) (Bergin CJ).
[97] This claim should not be overstated. It is not contested, for example, that the category undue influence may be an instantiation of unjust enrichment, and may also contain examples properly located as equitable wrongs. *Thorne v Kennedy* certainly lends weight to the view that, consistently with unjust enrichment, undue influence is an event which is a function of the claimant's vitiated intention to transfer wealth. Similarly, unconscionability clearly responds to the conduct and conscience of the recipient and may thus be said to be about wrongdoing. The underlying basis of fiduciary obligations is also the subject of debate. However, the fact of these differences does not derogate from the possibility of identifying other similarities between the categories.

appropriate physical and mental abilities in relation to a particular decision or transaction. However, as has been said, any protection for this aspect of autonomy is incidental and is also conditioned on the defendant exploiting the claimant's disability. All other categories examined in this chapter assume that the claimant has the relevant inner capacity to respond to reasons.

In relation to the other conditions for autonomy, the strongest commitment is to the requirement of independence in decision. Equity models decision-making as being free when those decisions are made without pressure and with relevant information, including independent advice. Less secure is the notion that a range of options in decisions may be relevant. As shown by the division of views in the High Court of Australia in *Thorne v Kennedy*, and the decision model for consent to breach of fiduciary duty, a range of decisions available to the claimant is not always considered necessary for autonomous decision-making in the equitable domains considered.

In the fiduciary and express trusts category, the inquiry as to consent is open-textured. Equity considers all relevant circumstances, including the positional factors surrounding the claimant, in determining if consent is validly given. Recall that the sufficiency of fiduciary disclosure is said to be calibrated to the sophistication and intelligence of the principal, and that there is no precise formula to determine whether on any set of facts fully informed consent has been given.[98] The same inquiry of antecedent conditions occurs in undue influence albeit that equity's decision-making is more structured. This is arguably because part of the difficulty in undue influence is that the claimant's awareness of self-interest may be paralysed such that their 'perceptions, cognitions and preferences'[99] are shaped to influence their desires, thoughts and ultimately decision to enter an impugned transaction.[100] Thus, it is useful in undue influence to ask about relationships of ascendancy or trust presumed to carry excessive influence or about personal and situational factors which will demonstrate that excessive influence is present. Independent advice operates across all categories as a potential circuit breaker in showing that the claimant's choice is truly self-determined and thus binding.[101] The evidence allows a limited conclusion that the liability model incorporates recognition that decisions or choices may be self-determined (eg by informed reason, religious belief) and also potentially informed by wider or antecedent factors which may make any consent illusory. In undue influence equity places a high value on respecting each person 'as they really are'.[102]

Subject therefore to the particular differences in the extent to which equity in these silos appears to value independence and an adequate range of options in decision,

[98] *Maguire v Makaronis* (n 28) [466] (Brennan CJ, Gleeson, McHugh and Gummow JJ).

[99] S Lukes, *Power: A Radical View* (2nd edn, Palgrave Macmillan 2005) 28.

[100] Arguably, undue influence in this respect illustrates Lukes's third dimension of power, which is typified by an absence of conflict or grievance, and in which the plaintiff or transferor does not question the legitimacy of the relationship. There is an appearance of consensus between the ascendant and the other party. See S Degeling, 'Undue Influence and the Spiritual Economy' in K Barker and others (eds), *Private Law and Power* (Hart 2017) 169–70.

[101] See, eg: Ms Wu's receipt of independent advice in an improvident transaction was a factor counting against a finding of special disadvantage: *Wu* (n 87) [19] (Leeming JA) and [108] (Bergin CJ); *Aboody v Ryan* [2012] NSWCA 395, [80] (Allsop P).

[102] Dagan (n 15) 73.

we may therefore tentatively conclude that equity's approach to consent is autonomy enhancing. What consequences flow from this observation? The first is that we hopefully obtain a more nuanced view of equity's approach to autonomy. For example, accounts of the trustee–beneficiary or fiduciary relationship may notice that the trustee's or 'fiduciary's personal autonomy is [by that relationship] ... constrained'.[103] Yet the purpose of this chapter has been to demonstrate that in the categories identified, which includes trustee and beneficiary and the fiduciary relationship, equity also has concern for the principal or beneficiary's autonomy. Autonomy is relative and interdependent.

The second is to make explicit the differing conditions for autonomy adopted or implicit in equitable doctrines. Clarity to further doctrinal development may be assisted when the embedded normative positions to autonomy are exposed. Of particular relevance is the extent to which equity considers, at least in the domains identified, the need for a range of options in decision making as being necessary for the claimant's decision to be regarded as free. This issue is prominent in *Thorne v Kennedy*. Recall that the plurality held that the claimant did not exercise free will and found undue influence, since the claimant was not independent and had no choice in making the decision to sign the agreements. In the same vein, the plurality held the claimant was unable to make a judgement in her best interests. This inability of judgement was held to be a vulnerability exploited by the defendant establishing unconscionability. Gordon J differed on the finding of undue influence, holding that the absence of the claimant's available options in decision *did not* on the facts indicate an absence of free will. However, the same lack of choice was relevant to establishing unconscionability. Similarly, in the express trust context, *Byrnes v Kendle* is an example where a lack of independence in consenting to a particular breach of trust, and a paucity of options in relation to that decision, were factors relevant in permitting the conclusion that the beneficiary's apparent consent was not binding.

The third is that we may work towards a deeper understanding of the capacity of a court to excuse a breach of duty. Specifically, in relation to the defence of informed consent given by the principal after fiduciary disclosure of the nature and extent of the conflict. Fidelity to an approach which recognizes the autonomy of the *principal* suggests that, absent very special circumstances, not only may the fiduciary be released by the consent of the principal, but importantly it is *only* the principal who is competent to do so, at least where the permission sought is prior to fiduciary breach.[104] In contradistinction to the position of a trustee, in which a court drawing on the general jurisdiction of equity to secure the administration of estates may give authority to enter conflicted transaction,[105] the fiduciary category is arguably much more constrained. Examples in

[103] S Worthington, *Equity* (2nd edn, OUP 2006) 131.

[104] See generally: S Degeling, 'Breach of Fiduciary Duty: Consent and Prior Court Authorisation' in J Goudkamp and others (eds), *Defences in Equity* (Hart 2018). See also M Conaglen, 'The Extent of Fiduciary Accounting and the Importance of Authorisation Mechanisms' (2011) 70 CLJ 548.

[105] A court has particular inherent and statutory jurisdiction which may be relevant. For example: (1) s 63 Trustee Act 1925 (NSW) (trustee may seek judicial advice and direction); (2) order for general administration, *In re Duke of Norfolk's Settlement Trusts* [1982] 1 Ch 61 (CA) 78 (Fox LJ); *In re Drexel Burnham Lambert UK Pension Plan* [1995] 1 WLR 32 (Ch); (3) jurisdiction to vary trust powers, including conferring power on a trustee to do acts which place fiduciary duties under pressure. See *Re New* [1901] 2 Ch 534 (CA); *Chapman v Chapman* [1954]

which a court could give a non-trustee fiduciary permission to act in breach of fiduciary duty can be found in cases concerning solicitors,[106] and also receivers. Notably however, both solicitors and receivers are officers of the court and thus might in any case have been subject to court supervision. In addition, the Court of Chancery had an inherent power to appoint receivers and to receive and preserve assets.[107] So it is perhaps not surprising that additional normative concerns enter the equation in these instances.

Outside these categories, an exceptional case in which a court *may* authorize in advance a breach of fiduciary duty is in the protective jurisdiction. The court has an inherent jurisdiction which supervises the administration of estates of incapable persons. In exercising this jurisdiction, the paramount consideration for the court is to determine the best interests of the protected person. Relevantly, the court may authorize conflicted remuneration to be received by a manager of the protected person's estate, where the manager occupies a fiduciary position but is not a trustee. This is shown by *Ability One Financial Management Pty Ltd v JB by his Tutor AB*[108] in which the court authorized in advance the manager's remuneration from the fund as was just and reasonable, noting:[109]

> [T]he office of a manager of the estate of a protected person ... [is] ... unique, but taking colour from the terms of ... appointment, governed by the Court's protective jurisdiction and informed by the nature, purpose and historical origins of that jurisdiction.... The relationship ... is 'a fiduciary relationship with particular characteristics'.

In this instance, the fiduciary's remuneration is authorized by the court, not the principal. The principal cannot do so since she is incapacitated. In addition to the requirement of 'best interests' of the incapacitated person, the court is enjoined to decide 'not only what may directly benefit him or her but what, if he or she were capable of self-management, he or she would, as a right minded and honourable person, desire to do'.[110] Thus the court in giving consent to a breach of fiduciary duty is only to a very limited extent standing proxy for the principal in releasing the fiduciary. Rather, the substitute consent to which the principal is being held is that given, in all of the circumstances, by a properly instructed conscience.

AC 429 (HL); *Tickle v Tickle* (1987) 10 NSWLR 581 (SC), 586 (Young J) (inherent jurisdiction to confer power on trustees) and s 81 Trustee Act 1925 (NSW) (statutory power to confer power on trustees).

[106] *Sidny v Ranger* (1841) 12 Sim 118 (Ch) 120; 59 ER 1076, 1077. See also *Popham v Exham* (1860) 10 Ir Ch Rep 440, solicitor permitted to continue in the transaction subject to an order which removed the substance of the conflict. In *Ex Parte James* (1803) 8 Ves Jr 338; 32 ER 385, 352 Lord Eldon denied a solicitor permission to bid at the auction of the property of an estate of the bankrupt. See also *Guest v Smythe* (1870) LR 5 Ch App 551 (CA) 556 (Giffard LJ).

[107] For a modern analogue, see, eg, s 67 Supreme Court Act 1970 (NSW).

[108] [2014] NSWSC 245.

[109] ibid [174] (Lindsay J) (references omitted).

[110] *C v W (No 2)* [2016] NSWSC 945, [45] (Lindsay J). See also [7] 'Consideration should be given to what the particular person incapable of self-management would be likely to do (acting with wisdom and prudence) if he or she possessed the capacity to act.'

VII. Conclusion

In asking about our consent to a breach of fiduciary duty or trust, or in holding us to a transfer of value unless there is undue influence or unconscionability, there is some evidence that equity looks to our embedded histories and our antecedent conditions. We are held only to permissions given freely, and equity's strongest commitment is to ensure independence in decision making. There is some evidence that the claimant must have a relevant choice in decision. The claimant's 'inner capacities', or mental and physical abilities to make a decision are largely assumed. However, this commitment to autonomy may cut both ways. Having demonstrated independent judgement, the claimant may well be held to it.

16

Equity and Institutions

*Matthew Harding**

I. Introduction

Much recent scholarship in private law theory has sought to explore the senses in which private law is a site of remedial justice.[1] Thus, debates have focused on the extent to which private law realizes or instantiates corrective justice, understood in one or another sense;[2] theorists have also concentrated on the deontological structure of rights and duties that gives form to much private law doctrine, and the implications of this structure for private law remedies.[3] This focus on remedial justice has been true of scholarship about equity no less than scholarship about the law of torts or the law of contracts, to the extent that equity has been the subject of theoretical attention at all.[4] The focus is appropriate: there can be no doubt that questions of remedial justice are central to private law, especially to the extent that private law is practised in the setting of disputes calling for adjudication and resolution by courts. Nonetheless, my starting point in this chapter is the conviction that the horizon of private law extends beyond such questions, and the related conviction that equity demonstrates this well. My general aim is to explore aspects of equity that challenge and unsettle the proposition that private law is invariably focused primarily on remedial justice.

More specifically, in this chapter I seek to show that in a range of situations, equity takes an interest in what I call 'institutions'. By 'institutions' I mean arrangements or frameworks for human action that have some distinctive normative identity and are oriented to some purpose or goal.[5] When I say that equity 'takes an interest' in institutions, what I mean is that equity is concerned to ensure that institutions are formed, well governed and viable; more generally, equity's interest in institutions is an interest

* My sincere thanks to Dennis Klimchuk and Irit Samet for their thoughtful and perceptive comments on a draft of this chapter.

[1] According to one tradition, associated with Hume and exemplified recently in the work of Michael Sandel and John Gardner, justice is in its nature remedial: see further Michael J Sandel, *Liberalism and the Limits of Justice* (2nd edn, CUP 1998); John Gardner, 'The Virtue of Justice and the Character of Law' in his *Law as a Leap of Faith* (OUP 2012) 238. I tend to align with this tradition, but my arguments in the text do not turn on this.

[2] Two leading examples are Ernest J Weinrib, *The Idea of Private Law* (2nd edn, OUP 2012); John Gardner, 'What Is Tort Law For? Part 1: The Place of Corrective Justice' (2011) 30 Law and Philosophy 1.

[3] See, eg, Robert Stevens, *Torts and Rights* (OUP 2007).

[4] In his contribution to this volume, Paul Miller discusses in detail the various strands of theoretical work on equity that take a remedial perspective, understood in one or another sense (see Chapter 5).

[5] See *Oxford English Dictionary* <www.oed.com>. A note of caution is in order here. In law, 'institutions' are sometimes defined in opposition to trusts: see, eg, *Minister of National Revenue v Trusts and Guarantee Co Ltd* [1940] AC 138, 149–50 (Lord Romer). In this chapter, I conceive of institutions as including trusts, and so I should emphasize that my conception is both broad and extralegal.

Matthew Harding, *Equity and Institutions* In: *Philosophical Foundations of the Law of Equity*. Edited by: Dennis Klimchuk, Irit Samet, and Henry E Smith, Oxford University Press (2020). © The several contributors.
DOI: 10.1093/oso/9780198817659.003.0017

in ensuring that institutions flourish as arrangements or frameworks for human action. In cases where equity takes an interest in institutions in this way, its primary concern may not be questions of remedial justice. Rather, in such cases, equity might be interested primarily in considerations affecting the parties to a dispute irrespective of remedial implications, it might be interested in considerations affecting parties before the court even though there is no dispute, and it might even be interested in considerations affecting people who are not before the court at all. In section II, I explore some ways in which equity's focus seems to be on developing institutions for people to utilize in ordering their affairs. In section III, I consider the ways in which equity takes an interest in the governance of institutions. In section IV, I consider equity's role in facilitating institutional change. And finally, I conclude in section V by considering what might be said about equity's institutional interest in light of normative, justificatory, arguments in private law theory.

II. Developing Institutions

As is true of the law of property and, in a different way, the law of contract, one of equity's signal contributions to private law lies in the facilities that it makes available to people who seek to utilize the law to achieve their various goals.[6] Many of these facilities are given shape and content by the law of trusts, and this body of law is therefore a rich source of guidance about ways in which equity develops institutions.[7] The history of the law of trusts reveals judges in equity working out remedial law that enables trust beneficiaries to gain relief in circumstances where trustees have fallen short of the standards expected of them or where trust assets have been misapplied in one way or another. But that history tells another story as well. It shows judges in equity developing the trust as a distinctive institutional type; moreover, that history shows judges in equity seeking to individuate trust types for settlors with different sorts of goals. In this section, I consider some key ways in which judges in equity have worked to develop distinctive trust types, before considering how equity's longstanding commitment to the trust itself as a distinctive institutional type has been challenged lately by increasing settlor demand for tailored, individualized, trust arrangements. I address the normative ramifications of such a shift in section V.

Perhaps the clearest example of equity developing a distinctive trust type is to be found in the law of charity. As is well known, over hundreds of years, judges exercising equitable jurisdiction have crafted and refined a body of jurisprudence spelling out

[6] This insight is well developed in the law and economics literature on aspects of equity: see, eg, John Langbein, 'The Secret Life of the Trust: The Trust as an Instrument of Commerce' (1997) 107 Yale Law Journal 165; Robert H Sitkoff, 'An Economic Theory of Fiduciary Law' in Andrew S Gold and Paul B Miller (eds), *Philosophical Foundations of Fiduciary Law* (OUP 2014) 197.

[7] James Penner, 'An Untheory of the Law of Trusts, or Some Notes Towards Understanding the Structure of Trusts Law Doctrine' (2010) 63 CLP 653, 668, writes 'Both bridges and the law of trusts are primarily facilitative things, ways of allowing us to achieve goals which are not themselves dictated either by physics or morality, respectively.'

the circumstances in which a trust may be viewed legally as constituted for a charitable purpose.[8] In doing this, those judges have given shape and content to a particular institutional type: the charitable trust. This institutional type is distinctive in several important ways. To begin with, as was confirmed in the great case of *Morice v Bishop of Durham*,[9] the purpose for which a charitable trust is formed must be analogous to one of the purposes set out in the preamble to the Statute of Charitable Uses of 1601.[10] The purposes that count as analogous to the preamble were classified helpfully by Lord Macnaghten in *Commissioners for Special Purposes of Income Tax v Pemsel* in a way that has shaped our understanding of the institution of the charitable trust ever since: relief of poverty, advancement of education, advancement of religion, and other purposes beneficial to the community, not falling within the first three 'heads'.[11] Moreover, the purpose of a charitable trust must stand to benefit the public in some way, and since the nineteenth century judges in equity have developed a detailed jurisprudence spelling out both the 'public' and the 'benefit' elements of this requirement.[12]

Thus, the institution of the charitable trust is oriented to the pursuit of public benefit purposes within the spirit and intendment of the Elizabethan preamble, and only to those purposes. And while the history of charity law, at least in the twentieth century, has been one of exponential growth in the range of purposes that are recognized in law as charitable,[13] judges in equity continue to exercise control over the boundaries of the institution.[14] Indeed, they do so even when explicitly invited to relax that control.[15] In doing so, they maintain an institutional type as a defined and demarcated object of choice for those who seek to utilize the law's facilities in planning and ordering

[8] For an authoritative description of this jurisprudence, see Hubert Picarda, *The Law and Practice Relating to Charities* (4th edn, Bloomsbury Professional 2010).

[9] (1804) 9 Ves Jun 399; (1805) 10 Ves Jun 522. The best discussion of the historical importance of this case is Joshua Getzler, '*Morice v Bishop of Durham* (1805)' in Charles Mitchell and Paul Mitchell (eds), *Landmark Cases in Equity* (Hart 2012) 157.

[10] The preamble, rendered in modern English, makes reference to the following purposes: the relief of the aged, impotent, and poor people; the maintenance of sick and maimed soldiers and mariners, schools of learning, free schools, and scholars in universities; the repair of bridges, ports, havens, causeways, churches, sea banks, and highways; the education and preferment of orphans; the relief, stock, or maintenance of houses of correction; the marriages of poor maids, the supportation, aid, and help of young tradesmen, handicraftsmen, and persons decayed; the relief or redemption of prisoners or captives, and the aid or ease of any poor inhabitants concerning payment of fifteens, setting out of soldiers, and other taxes. For discussion of the preamble, and the development of the case law before *Morice v Bishop of Durham*, see Gareth Jones, *History of the Law of Charity 1532–1827* (CUP 1969).

[11] [1891] AC 531, 583. This taxonomy has also been adopted, to a greater or lesser extent, in statutory definitions of charitable purpose around the common law world: see, eg, Charities Act 2005 (NZ) s 5; Charities Act 2011 (England and Wales) s 3(1).

[12] Some key cases include *Verge v Somerville* [1924] AC 496, *National Anti-Vivisection Society v Inland Revenue Commissioners* [1948] AC 31, *Gilmour v Coats* [1949] AC 426, *Oppenheim v Tobacco Securities Trust Co Ltd* [1951] AC 297. The best academic treatment of the public benefit requirement of charity law is Jonathan Garton, *Public Benefit in Charity Law* (OUP 2013).

[13] See further GE Dal Pont, 'Charity Law: "No Magic in Words"?' in Matthew Harding, Ann O'Connell, and Miranda Stewart (eds), *Not-for-Profit Law: Theoretical and Comparative Perspectives* (CUP 2014) 87.

[14] See, eg, *Royal National and Agricultural and Industrial Association v Chester* (1974) 48 ALJR 304. See also, in the tax setting, *Vancouver Society of Immigrant and Visible Minority Women v Minister of National Revenue* [1999] 1 SCR 10, and *AYSA Amateur Youth Soccer Association v Canada Revenue Agency* [2007] 3 SCR 217.

[15] See, eg, the decision of the Supreme Court of New Zealand in *Re Greenpeace of New Zealand Incorporated* [2015] 1 NZLR 169, in which the Court rejected the proposition that public benefit purposes should be presumed charitable in the absence of evidence to the contrary. The Court confirmed that such purposes are charitable only where they are within the spirit and intendment of the Elizabethan preamble: at [27]–[31].

their affairs. Those whose purposes do not count as charitable in law may not utilize this institutional type and must find other ways of achieving their goals.[16] I return to the interesting question of why equity might engage in such a boundary-setting exercise in relation to the charitable trust in section V. For now, I simply note that the boundary-setting has been core to the project of charity law from its early days and continues today.

Because charitable trusts are expressed to be for purposes, it is relatively straightforward to view them as 'institutions' in the sense I am using in this chapter, namely, arrangements with a distinctive normative identity that are oriented to some purpose or goal. But in thinking about equity's interest in institutions, we should not confine ourselves to trusts that are expressed to be for purposes; we should also consider trusts that are on their face expressed to be for the benefit of named persons or described classes of objects. Such arrangements may also be viewed as institutions to the extent that they are purpose- or goal-oriented notwithstanding that they are expressed to be for the benefit of named persons or classes.[17] And we find equity taking an interest in institutions precisely to the extent that judges, when dealing with trusts for persons, seek to craft and develop an institutional type with an eye to some purpose or goal underpinning such trusts.

Arguably, this is exactly what happened in the well-known case of *McPhail v Doulton*.[18] A question arose as to the validity of a discretionary trust for the benefit of a class of objects that included employees and former employees of a company along with their relatives and dependants. According to the law as it then stood, the test for certainty of objects in relation to discretionary trusts was the same as that in relation to fixed trusts; thus, the discretionary trust should have been struck down because it was not possible for the trustees to compile an exhaustive list of the members of the class of objects in question.[19] However, the House of Lords was urged to align the test for certainty of objects in relation to discretionary trusts with that in relation to mere powers of appointment, so that the discretionary trust in *McPhail v Doulton* itself would be valid if, as a conceptual matter, it could be said of any person that they were either within or not within the class of objects as described.[20] In his leading judgment, Lord Wilberforce declared that the test for certainty of objects of mere powers of appointment should apply also to discretionary trusts, and the question of the validity of the discretionary trust in view was referred back to a Chancery judge to be determined in accordance with that test.[21]

[16] *Re Astor's Settlement Trusts* [1952] Ch 534. Note, though, that in certain exceptional circumstances non-charitable purpose trusts are permitted in equity; see the discussion by Roxburgh J in the *Astor* case at 542–46. And note also the decision of Goff J in *Re Denley's Trust Deed* [1969] 1 Ch 373.

[17] Indeed, it seems arguable that even certain trusts that on their face seem remedial have an institutional character in the sense that they are planned for and serve particular goals: the trust in *Barclay's Bank Ltd v Quistclose Investments Ltd* [1970] AC 567 might be offered as a good example.

[18] [1971] AC 424.

[19] *Inland Revenue Commissioners v Broadway Cottages Trust* [1954] 1 Ch 20.

[20] In relation to mere powers of appointment, see *In re Gestetner Settlement* [1953] 1 Ch 672; *Re Gulbenkian's Settlement Trusts* [1970] AC 508.

[21] *McPhail v Doulton* [1971] AC 424, 447–457 (Lord Wilberforce). The discretionary trust was ultimately upheld as valid, although for reasons that remain obscure, by the Court of Appeal in *Re Baden's Deed Trusts (No 2)* [1973] Ch 9.

For present purposes, what is of most interest is the extent to which Lord Wilberforce's judgment in *McPhail v Doulton* reveals equity developing an institutional type for trust settlors to use in ordering their affairs. In reasoning that a list test was excessively demanding in determining certainty of objects for a discretionary trust, Lord Wilberforce was mindful of the general purpose that underlay an arrangement such as the one in *McPhail v Doulton*. So much is clear from his dicta addressing the duties of trustees of such an arrangement when exercising their dispositive powers:[22]

> A trustee of an employees' benefit fund, whether given a power or a trust power, is still a trustee and he would surely consider in either case that he has a fiduciary duty: he is most likely to have been selected as a suitable person to administer it from his knowledge and experience, and would consider he has a responsibility to do so according to its purpose.... [A] trustee with a duty to distribute, particularly among a very large class, would ... examine the field, by class and category; might indeed make diligent and careful inquiries, depending on how much money he had to give away and the means at his disposal, as to the composition and needs of particular categories and of individuals within them; decide upon certain priorities or proportions, and then select individuals according to their needs and qualifications.

In these passages, Lord Wilberforce made clear that in his conception a trust of the type in view in *McPhail v Doulton* serves the purpose of constituting a large-scale distributive scheme to be operated in a principled but ultimately discretionary fashion.[23] A trust for that purpose demands that trustees discharge certain relatively diffuse responsibilities in localized distributive justice, and such responsibilities may be discharged adequately in the absence of exhaustive knowledge of the identity of every member of the class of objects. In contrast, in the case of a fixed trust, trustees' responsibilities are much more carefully circumscribed by the settlor and demand that the identity of each and every beneficiary be known.[24]

In ruling in *McPhail v Doulton* that an 'in or out' test of certainty of objects applies to discretionary trusts as well as to mere powers of appointment, the House of Lords helped to develop a trust type. This trust type may be distinguished from fixed trusts on the one hand, and mere powers of appointment on the other. It provides a particularly valuable facility to settlors who wish to establish large scale distributive and discretionary schemes such as the one in *McPhail v Doulton*; prior to the decision of the House of Lords in that case, settlors with such goals were constrained in what they could achieve using the tools of trusts law.[25] It has been observed that this institutional type is likely not often utilized by settlors;[26] equally, it has been said that the

[22] *McPhail v Doulton* [1971] AC 424, 449.

[23] Note also that in *In re Baden's Deed Trusts (No 2)*, Sachs LJ described the settlor as 'forward-thinking' and his arrangement as one for 'furthering the welfare of the employees and those connected with them': [1973] Ch 9, 17. The settlor had been the managing director of the company whose employees were among the class of objects.

[24] Although even here courts may be willing to relax the list test: see *West v Weston* (1998) 44 NSWLR 657.

[25] The pre-*McPhail* case of *Oppenheim* demonstrates some of the difficulties: *Oppenheim v Tobacco Securities Trust Co Ltd* [1951] AC 297.

[26] See Lionel Smith, 'Massively Discretionary Trusts' (2017) 70 CLP 17, 24 (observing that discretionary trusts are 'rarely created' and that the more commonplace arrangement is a fixed trust coupled with a very wide power of appointment).

type generates difficulties in relation to enforcement that remain to be overcome in the jurisprudence.[27] Nonetheless, the trust type that was recognized and enabled in *McPhail v Doulton* is both available to settlors and distinctive, and its development in that case represents a key moment at which judges in equity took an interest in institutional design.[28]

Cases such as *Morice v Bishop of Durham* and *McPhail v Doulton* suggest that one element of the history of trusts law has been judges in equity developing institutional types to facilitate settlor goals. In part that development has entailed an expansion in the range and scope of trust types that are available to settlors, but in part it has entailed some degree of control being maintained over those institutional types. In recent years, equity's commitment to this blend of liberalization and control has been challenged by increasing settlor demand for tailored, individualized trust arrangements.[29]

In order to understand and evaluate this trend, it is important to recall that, at a high level of abstraction, the 'trust'—understood now in a broad sense to include modular arrangements composed of combinations of fixed trusts, discretionary trusts, mere powers of appointment and other powers and duties conferred on trustees or others—is itself an institutional type.[30] The distinctive normative identity of this institutional type depends on what has sometimes been called the 'irreducible core' of the trust, which is the duty of the trustee to apply the trust assets for the benefit of the trust beneficiaries (or for the trust's constitutive purpose, if it is a purpose trust).[31] An arrangement in which this duty does not figure is not, according to orthodox doctrine, recognized as a trust. The distinctive normative identity of the trust as an institutional type is also closely connected with norms of stewardship and trustee accountability, and with fiduciary norms at least in cases where trustees exercise discretionary powers. Underpinning the trust's irreducible core, along with norms of stewardship, trustee accountability and fiduciary responsibility, is a distinctive sort of purpose, which helps to lend unity to the trust as an institutional type: the purpose of holding, managing, and applying assets for the benefit of others.

Evidence suggests that settlor demand for tailored, individualized, trust arrangements has in recent decades entailed efforts to minimize and even extinguish the core norms of stewardship, trustee accountability, fiduciary responsibility, and, in extreme cases, the trust's irreducible core itself.[32] For example, in *Citibank NA v MBIA Assurance*

[27] See James Penner, *The Law of Trusts* (9th edn, OUP 2014), [3.66] (observing that the objects of a discretionary trust are not well situated or incentivized to enforce the trust).

[28] The significance of *McPhail v Doulton* for trusts practice is addressed in Jessica Palmer and Charles Rickett, 'The Revolution and Legacy of the Discretionary Trust' (2017) 11 Journal of Equity 157.

[29] '[T]he forms and functions of settlements have changed to a degree which would have astonished Lord Eldon': *Schmidt v Rosewood Trust Ltd* [2003] 2 AC 709, [34] (Lord Walker of Gestingthorpe).

[30] For discussion of the difference between 'trust' in this broad sense, and 'trust' in the narrower sense of an 'obligation with respect to the benefit of property', see Smith (n 26) 19–20.

[31] *Armitage v Nurse* [1998] Ch 241, 253. Much has been made of Millett LJ's reference in that case to standards of honesty and good faith as part of the irreducible core, but those standards cannot exhaust the trust's irreducible core because they apply to legal actors other than trustees: Tobias Barkley '*Clayton v Clayton*: The Court of Appeal on the Concepts of Property and Trusts' [2015] New Zealand Law Journal 164. See also JE Penner, 'Exemptions' in Peter Birks and Arianna Pretto-Sakmann (eds), *Breach of Trust* (Hart 2002) 241, 250.

[32] See Adam Hofri-Winogradow, 'The Stripping of the Trust: A Study in Legal Evolution' (2015) 65 University of Toronto Law Journal 1; Smith (n 26).

SA, a trust instrument authorized a third party to direct the trustee in the exercise of various powers, thus overriding the norm of fiduciary responsibility that usually applies to a trustee.[33] In *JSC Mezhdunarodniy Promyshenniy Bank v Pugachev*, the settlor of a discretionary trust held unfettered non-fiduciary powers as trust protector that, according to Birss J, enabled him to exercise 'complete control over the [trust] assets'.[34] The trust's irreducible core, along with norms of trustee accountability, were considerably weakened by the arrangement. And in each of *Clayton v Clayton*[35] and *Webb v Webb*,[36] a settlor set up an arrangement in which, as sole trustee and trust protector, he held wide unfettered powers of appointment and other powers enabling him to appoint all the capital and income of the arrangement to himself at any time without even considering other claims on those assets. In *Clayton* and *Webb*, the settlor's intention to engage the trust's irreducible core by assuming a duty to apply assets for the benefit of trust beneficiaries seemed inchoate at best.

These cases raise a difficult question for equity, insofar as equity takes an interest in institutions: at what point do arrangements cease to be recognizable as examples of the general institutional type that is the trust, understood in a broad sense? At what point should equity refuse to recognize such arrangements as trusts in order to preserve the coherence and unity of that institutional type? In *Pugachev* and *Webb*, the courts that determined the cases thought that a line had been crossed. In *Pugachev*, Birss J found that the powers the settlor had reserved to himself as trust protector stood at odds with trust norms to such an extent that the settlor had not created the discretionary trusts that his trust instrument purported to create; he had instead created a bare trust for himself.[37] In *Webb*, a strong Cook Islands Court of Appeal found that, once all the terms of the settlor's trust instrument were interpreted from an objective standpoint, the arrangement described in that instrument as a 'trust' could only be understood to be an 'objective nullity' because of lack of certainty of intention to put the trustee under a duty to apply assets for the trust beneficiaries.[38] In *Citibank*, on the other hand, Mann J found that the fact that a third party could direct the trustee in the exercise of the trustee's dispositive powers did not undermine trust norms in any fundamental sense.[39] And in *Clayton*, the Supreme Court of New Zealand recognized that the case raised the difficult question whether the arrangement under scrutiny was a trust,[40] but declined to provide an answer to that question, and determined the appeal on other grounds.[41]

33 [2006] EWHC 3215.

34 [2017] EWHC 2426, [245].

35 [2016] NZSC 29. The case is discussed critically in Mark Bennett, 'Competing Views on Illusory Trusts: The *Clayton v Clayton* Litigation in Its Wider Context' (2017) 11 Journal of Equity 48, 54–59; Palmer and Rickett (n 28) 178–83.

36 [2017] CKCA 4.

37 [2017] EWHC 2426, [245], [265]–[278], [436], [452]–[455]

38 [2017] CKCA 4, [53]–[65]; the reference to 'objective nullity' is at [56].

39 [2006] EWHC 3215, [48].

40 [2016] NZSC 29, [118]–[127].

41 ibid [127] and [85]–[98]. The trusts law questions in *Clayton v Clayton* arose against the backdrop of a dispute between Mr and Mrs Clayton as to the distribution of the trust assets on the breakdown of their relationship. The Supreme Court ruled that the trust assets were 'relationship property' within the meaning of s 8 of New Zealand's Property (Relationships) Act 1976 and determined the appeal on that basis. See also the analogous Australian case *Kennon v Spry* (2008) 238 CLR 366.

The differing approaches taken in the cases reveal that courts experience as difficult the question whether an arrangement sufficiently exemplifies the trust as an institutional type. Each case seems to turn on its facts and, in particular, on a careful and objective interpretation of the provisions of a written trust instrument where such an instrument is present. And underpinning this difficulty is a further challenge. Even if it is accepted that in a particular case an arrangement is not an instance of the trust as an institutional type, whether because it is not characterized by the trust's irreducible core or lacks other central norms associated with the trust, it might still be argued that the trust as an institutional type should be recrafted and expanded to accommodate the arrangement in view.[42] After all, if the attraction of trusts is to be found in their facilitative capacity, then why not facilitate a broader rather than a narrower range of settlor aims? Indeed, if the very concept of the trust itself has to give way to some broader, more inclusive, concept to enable this liberalization to occur, then why should that move not be made? I think the answer to this question lies in a normative argument for individuating and maintaining the distinctiveness of institutional types in law, and I will return to this argument in section V.

III. Governing Institutions

Equity's interest in the governance of institutions is profound and pervasive, and helps to explain large parts of equitable doctrine.[43] That interest takes many forms. In some respects, courts in equity participate directly in institutional governance. So much is clear from the court's supervisory jurisdiction over trusts, a jurisdiction with equitable origins but many of the elements of which are now spelt out in statutory provisions. For example, the court may remove trustees and replace them, although the circumstances in which this is likely to occur are not extensive.[44] The court may vary the terms of a trust, although again the circumstances in which this may occur are circumscribed both by case law and by statute.[45] On one authoritative view a trust beneficiary's right to seek disclosure of trust documents is an aspect of the court's supervisory jurisdiction as well.[46] And trustees are always free to approach the court to seek direction in relation to the administration of a trust. In one sense the purpose of judicial direction is to protect trustees who might worry about liability for actions taken in circumstances of uncertainty; this suggests that equity has an eye to potential remedial concerns in the exercise of the supervisory jurisdiction. But in another sense, the purpose of judicial direction

[42] In *Clayton v Clayton*, this was the move that found favour in the New Zealand Court of Appeal. There, it was thought that the core of trusteeship was composed of duties of honesty and good faith and that these duties were present in the arrangement in view: see *Clayton v Clayton* [2015] 2 NZLR 293, [51]. For the reasons referred to in (n 31) above, this cannot be right.

[43] This is a key theme of the important collection, PG Turner (ed), *Equity and Administration* (CUP 2016).

[44] See Penner (n 27) [10.48]–[10.57].

[45] ibid [10.66]–[10.77].

[46] *Schmidt v Rosewood Trust Ltd* [2003] 2 AC 709. For insightful analysis of this case and its implications, see Lusina Ho, 'Trustees' Duties to Provide Information' in Elise Bant and Matthew Harding (eds), *Exploring Private Law* (CUP 2010) 343.

does not engage remedial considerations; it is rather to ensure the due administration of the trust itself, as was recognized by Lord Oliver of Aylmerton in *Marley v Mutual Society Merchant Bank and Trust Co Ltd*:[47]

> [I]n exercising its jurisdiction to give directions on a trustee's application the court is essentially engaged solely in determining what ought to be done in the best interests of the trust estate and not in determining the rights of adversarial parties.

This statement suggests that an important objective of the supervisory jurisdiction is to provide the guidance that might be needed if an institution is to be viable and succeed. Moreover, there is authority to suggest that this objective remains important even in cases where the jurisdiction is invoked against the backdrop of a dispute that calls to be adjudicated.[48]

More commonly, equity's interest in institutional governance is indirect and expressed in the rules and duties that equity imposes on those who are responsible for managing and directing institutions. In key ways, these rules and duties have been developed so as to ensure the integrity of institutions themselves, as opposed to bringing about remedial justice in the setting of adjudication, and this simply serves to reinforce the sense that equity's interest in governance is institutionally oriented. The rules that spell out the ways in which trustees are accountable to their beneficiaries for their dealings with trust assets provide a good example. Take the account of administration in common form. On the traditional view of this species of account, trustees are liable as custodians of trust assets and therefore must ensure that the assets in question are preserved and maintained.[49] To the extent that trustees fail in this custodial role, by disbursing the trust assets in ways that are not authorized by the mandate given to them by the settlor, the trustees are required to restore to the trust value equal to the value of the misapplied assets. The liability here is not to meet the claim of any particular beneficiary; it is a liability to preserve the integrity of the institutional structure within which beneficiary claims fall to be considered and dealt with. None of this is to suggest that equity is indifferent to beneficiary claims to trust assets; given that the whole point of the trust as an institutional type entails giving beneficiaries such claims, such indifference would be incoherent. But in common account cases, equity's interest in beneficiary claims is expressed via rules that have as their primary concern the structure of the trust itself; to that extent, equity's way of showing interest in beneficiary claims is to worry over institutional governance.

[47] [1991] 3 All ER 198, 201. See also Macedonian Orthodox Community Church St Petka Inc v His Eminence Petar, the Diocesan Bishop of the Macedonian Orthodox Diocese of Australia and New Zealand (2008) 237 CLR 66, [71]–[72] (Gummow ACJ, Kirby, Hayne and Heydon JJ).

[48] As was the case in the *Macedonian Orthodox Community Church* case (n 47); there, it was held that an 'adversarial' setting was no impediment to seeking judicial direction ([97]–[116] (Gummow ACJ, Kirby, Hayne, and Heydon JJ).

[49] The traditional view is expressed in *Ex parte Adamson* (1878) 8 Ch D 807; *Libertarian Investments Limited v Hall* (2013) 16 HKCFAR 61 (Lord Millett); *Agricultural Land Management Ltd v Jackson [No 2]* [2014] WASC 102 (Edelman J).

Recent developments in English law have weakened equity's traditional institutional focus in relation to the common account. In the case of *Target Holdings Ltd v Redferns*, the House of Lords ruled that in cases where trusts have been used to facilitate commercial transactions, upon the completion of the transaction there is no case for maintaining the integrity of the trust structure and, to the extent that trust assets have been misapplied during the transaction, compensation for losses caused by the misapplication is a sufficient remedy for an aggrieved beneficiary.[50] This change in focus was endorsed by the Supreme Court of the United Kingdom in the recent case of *AIB Group (UK) Plc v Mark Redler & Co*,[51] and as a result the law of the United Kingdom now seems to be that the common account demands an inquiry into the extent to which the misapplication of trust assets has caused loss to the beneficiaries of the trust. The arguments for and against this legal development have been well rehearsed elsewhere.[52] For present purposes I simply emphasize one point in relation to the common account. The institutional focus of the traditional view, concerned as it is with the integrity of the trust structure itself, is not to be found in the decisions in *Target Holdings* and *AIB*. Rather, the focus in those decisions is on achieving satisfactory, but not excessive, remedial outcomes for trust beneficiaries. The decisions are less about institutional governance than they are about remedial justice;[53] they reveal that equity's interest in institutions sometimes gives way to other concerns.

In recent work, Lionel Smith has highlighted a sense in which a fiduciary's liability to account for profits may also be understood as having an orientation that is better described as institutional than as directed at remedial justice.[54] On Smith's view, the account of profits is not optimally conceived as an equitable remedy that is awarded against a fiduciary who has acted in breach of duty. Rather, it is best understood a species of 'primary' liability that is entailed in the very 'logic' or 'nature' of the fiduciary relationship.[55] For Smith, a fiduciary relationship establishes what he calls a 'sphere of fiduciary management' within which all profits are to be attributed to the principal;[56] thus the requirement that, in the words of Deane J in *Chan v Zacharia*, the fiduciary disgorge 'any benefit or gain obtained or received by use or by reason of [the] fiduciary position or of opportunity or knowledge arising from it'.[57] If Smith is right, and

[50] [1996] AC 421.

[51] [2014] UKSC 58.

[52] See, eg, Matthew Conaglen, 'Equitable Compensation for Breach of Trust: Off *Target*' (2016) 40 Melbourne University Law Review 126; James Edelman, 'An English Misturning with Equitable Compensation', James Penner, 'Falsifying the Trust Account and Compensatory Equitable Compensation', and Lusina Ho, 'Causation in the Restoration of a Misapplied Trust Fund: Fundamental Norm of Red Herring?' all in Simone Degeling and Jason Varuhas (eds), *Equitable Compensation and Disgorgement of Profit* (Hart 2017) at 91, 143, and 159 respectively.

[53] Elsewhere I argue that this remedial focus is apt to generate commercial uncertainty in circumstances where trusts are used to facilitate transactions: Matthew Harding, 'Equity and the Value of Certainty in Commercial Life' in Peter Devonshire and Rohan Havelock (eds), *The Impact of Equity and Restitution in Commerce* (Hart 2018) 143.

[54] Lionel Smith, 'Deterrence, Prophylaxis and Punishment in Fiduciary Obligations' (2013) 7 Journal of Equity 87; Lionel Smith, 'Fiduciary Relationships: Ensuring the Loyal Exercise of Judgement on Behalf of Another' (2014) 130 LQR 608; Lionel Smith, 'Can We Be Obliged to Be Selfless?' in Gold and Miller (eds) (n 6) 14.

[55] Smith, 'Fiduciary Relationships' (n 54) 628 ('primary', 'nature'); Smith, 'Can We Be?' (n 54) 150 ('logic').

[56] Smith, 'Can We Be?' (n 54) 150.

[57] (1984) 154 CLR 178, 198. See also *Regal (Hastings) Ltd v Gulliver* [1967] 2 AC 134, 144 (Lord Russell of Killowen), talking of '[t]he rule of equity which insists upon those, who by use of a fiduciary position make profit, being liable to account for that profit'.

a fiduciary's liability to account for profits is not dependent on any wrongdoing but is instead a species of primary liability entailed in the sphere of fiduciary management, then that liability, just like the trustee's liability to the common account, seems to have as its primary concern institutional integrity and not remedial justice. The institutions that in law entail a sphere of fiduciary management are various, ranging from the trust, to the corporation, to the partnership. On Smith's view, equity's no profit rule may be viewed as bolstering those institutions by ensuring that they are governed in accordance with the fiduciary norms embedded in them. And, on that view, even in cases where fiduciary relationships arise in non-institutional settings,[58] the concern of the no profit rule is not principally remedial justice but rather the governance of arrangements, even if those arrangements have not risen to a level that warrants describing them as institutions.

The rules relating to the accountability of trustees and other fiduciaries are arguably examples of equity taking an indirect interest in institutional governance through imposing rules that are designed to preserve the integrity and viability of institutional structures. Equity's indirect interest in institutional governance is manifested in other, more subtle, ways as well. Take, for example, the principles that spell out the duties of trustees when exercising administrative powers to invest or otherwise deal with trust assets.[59] In key cases, courts in equity have indicated that, in order to discharge such duties, trustees must be mindful of the purpose for which the trust has been formed; in this way, equity exhibits a concern that governance be faithful to institutional settings within which it takes place.[60] In some cases, the purpose for which a trust has been formed may be apparent from the terms of the trust, but in other cases it may lie behind those terms, and this may generate complications for trustees.

One good example of equity's sensitivity to purpose when giving content to the investment duties of trustees is *Cowan v Scargill*.[61] The British Mineworkers' Pension Scheme was overseen by a board of trustees, half of whom were appointed by the National Union of Mineworkers. The Union trustees refused to sign off on an investment plan that was proposed for the scheme, on the basis that it was Union policy to oppose industries that might compete with British coal and that the investment plan entailed investments in some such industries. The matter was referred to Megarry V-C for resolution. In his view, the purpose of the scheme was straightforwardly to 'provide financial benefits for the beneficiaries'.[62] Given that the scheme had this purpose, the duty of the trustees was to act in the best financial interests of their beneficiaries,

[58] As, for example, where they arise in the setting of commercial contracts.

[59] In many jurisdictions these equitable rules have been supplemented and modified by statute; see, eg, Trustee Act 2000 c 29.

[60] *Cowan v Scargill* [1985] 1 Ch 270, 288 (Megarry V-C); *Harries v Church Commissioners* [1992] 1 WLR 1241, 1246 (Nicholls V-C); *Re Merchant Navy Ratings Pension Fund* [2015] All ER (D) 298, [228]–[229] (Asplin J). Note that courts have done this whether the trust is expressed to be for a purpose or for persons. Thus, the overall picture may be more complicated than that presented by Paul B Miller and Andrew S Gold, 'Fiduciary Governance' (2015) 57 William & Mary Law Review 513, who distinguish between purpose-oriented fiduciary mandates and fiduciary duties to act in the best interests of individual persons.

[61] [1985] 1 Ch 270.

[62] ibid 287. Megarry V-C also noted that a trust would 'usually' have this purpose.

irrespective of their own political objections or commitments.[63] Megarry V-C ordered the trustees to reach a resolution among themselves in relation to the plan, in light of the law as he had declared it in the case.[64] Interestingly, though, in obiter dicta Megarry V-C noted that in a case where all the beneficiaries of a trust have very strict moral or political views, a trustee might discharge her duty by taking this into account in choosing investments.[65] In these dicta, Megarry V-C affirmed his view that trustees' duties in exercising administrative powers must be sensitive to the institutional settings in which those powers are exercised.

Cowan v Scargill may be contrasted with the more complex case of *Harries v Church Commissioners*.[66] The trust in the latter case was for charitable purposes connected with the provision of economic support to retired Anglican clergy. The trustees adhered to an investment strategy, which was impugned by the Bishop of Oxford and others on the basis that certain investments contemplated by the strategy were contrary to Christian belief and practice. In *Harries*, the purpose of the trust was not to produce financial returns for beneficiaries; the trust was for charitable purposes.[67] Nonetheless, as Nicholls V-C recognized in deciding the case, the charitable purposes of the trust were best served by generating financial returns, and so it was not open to the trustees to eschew financial returns in order to adhere to strict moral views.[68] Rather, Nicholls V-C seems to have thought that a balance must be struck, a balance that on the one hand recognized the importance of financial returns to the trust qua wealth management arrangement, but on the other hand was sensitive to some degree to Church teachings and commitments.[69] Nicholls V-C was satisfied that the trustees had struck a satisfactory balance by excluding certain investments that were at odds with Anglican commitments, but he did not think that their duties demanded the more austere investment strategy urged by the Bishop of Oxford.[70] In *Harries* the institutional settings in which the trustees acted were complex, entailing a wealth management scheme for charitable purposes connected with a Christian community. The approach taken by Nicholls V-C in determining the case was one that sought to reflect those institutional complexities in working out what the trustees were required to do. It was an institutionally oriented approach.

Equity's approach to institutional governance in cases such as *Cowan v Scargill* and *Harries* has been criticized for failing to achieve sufficient sensitivity to the institutional settings within which trustees must exercise their administrative powers. On the one hand, it has been argued that equity leaves trustees too little scope to choose

[63] ibid 287–88.
[64] ibid 296–97.
[65] ibid 288.
[66] [1992] 1 WLR 1241.
[67] ibid 1248–49. Nonetheless, it must be said that the distinction between charitable purposes connected with providing economic support to retired Anglican clergy and the purpose of producing financial returns for beneficiaries is a fine one.
[68] ibid 1246 and 1250.
[69] See the discussion at ibid 1246–50.
[70] ibid 1250.

investments on ethical or social grounds connected with the fundamental purposes of their trusts.[71] And on the other hand it has been argued that, especially in trusts with substantial funds to invest, taking into account considerations other than financial returns for beneficiaries may place trustees at odds with sound investment strategies and to that extent must be viewed as inconsistent with the wealth management purpose of trusts.[72] Putting to one side the merits of the different arguments, the important point to note for present purposes is that the arguments point to aspects of the institutional settings in which trustees exercise administrative powers. They, like the equity jurisprudence to which they respond, take an interest in institutions and view questions of governance in that light, and so, presumably, will any law reform to which the arguments might give rise.[73]

IV. Changing Institutions

The history of equity reveals an ongoing interest in facilitating institutional change, sometimes to ensure that institutions remain viable over time notwithstanding changing circumstances, and sometimes to render institutions consistent with prevailing social and political norms. Earlier, in discussing the court's supervisory jurisdiction in relation to trusts, I mentioned some ways in which equity might facilitate institutional change in that setting; these include courts varying trust terms or removing and replacing trustees. However, in the limited space available, I want to concentrate on a different, and especially striking, means by which equity has expressed its interest in facilitating institutional change: the cy-pres doctrine that applies to charitable trust. According to this doctrine, courts in equity may order that trust assets be applied for a purpose other than the purpose for which the trust was constituted by the settlor.[74] The original purpose must be impossible, impracticable or illegal to carry out, and there must be a general charitable intention on the part of the settlor.[75] If these conditions are satisfied, the court may effectively disregard the expressed terms of the trust to enable application of the trust assets for a purpose that is closely analogous to the original purpose.

The cy-pres doctrine is in a sense the most far-reaching manifestation of equity's interest in institutions. Earlier, I argued that courts in equity develop institutional types for people to choose in ordering their affairs. That aspect of equity is consistent with the general facilitative project that underpins and helps to justify private law. So

[71] See, eg, Susie Daykin, 'Pension Scheme Investment: is it always just about the money?' (2014) 28 Trust Law International 165.

[72] Rosy Thornton, 'Ethical Investments: A Case of Disjointed Thinking' (2008) 67 CLJ 396.

[73] Such reform occurred recently in England and Wales, where s 15 of the Charities (Protection and Social Investments) Act 2016 explicitly permits charity trustees to make investments that aim at both financial return and 'mission benefit'. In *Fiduciary Duties of Investment Intermediaries* (LawCom 350, 2014), the Law Commission declined to recommend broader reforms that would affect trustees generally.

[74] The cy-pres doctrine now has a statutory overlay as well: see, eg, Charities Act 2011 (England and Wales) s 62.

[75] See generally Picarda (n 8) ch 30.

is the core of the cy-pres doctrine; to the extent that judges invoke that doctrine to adjust a charitable trust to render it possible or workable, the doctrine may be viewed as a practical contribution to private law's general facilitative project. However, in some cases where courts in equity have utilized the cy-pres doctrine, they have shown themselves willing to go well beyond rendering trusts workable within an overall facilitative outlook; they have instead effected changes to trusts, with an eye to prevailing social and political norms, that render those trusts clearly at odds with settlor intention.[76] At first glance, the normative justification for such far-reaching use of the cy-pres doctrine seems elusive; however, in section V I will suggest a way in which we might reconcile an expansive cy-pres doctrine with private law's general facilitative project.

The use of the cy-pres doctrine to override settlor intention in the service of social and political norms is amply demonstrated in case law from the pre-toleration era in the United Kingdom.[77] In several reported cases, assets settled on trust for purposes that advanced religions other than Anglicanism were applied instead for purposes relating to the established religion.[78] For example, in *Attorney-General v Baxter*, a trust for the maintenance of non-conformist clergymen was declared to be a 'superstitious use' and the assets applied cy-pres to the maintenance of an Anglican chaplain because of the general charitable intention that lay behind the trust in question.[79] In the well-known case of *Da Posta v Da Paz*, a similar move was made in relation to a trust to support a Jewish school.[80] And in *Cary v Abbott*, a trust for educating children in the Roman Catholic faith was declared to be a superstitious use, and the assets applied cy-pres.[81] In the last case, Sir William Grant MR articulated clearly the extent to which the courts of that time felt free to craft institutions at odds with settlor intention, using the cy-pres doctrine:[82]

> [W]henever a testator is disposed to be charitable in his own way, and upon his own principles, we are not to content ourselves with disappointing his intention, if disapproved by us; but we are to make him charitable in our way and upon our principles. If once we discover in him any

[76] John Picton goes further, arguing that public policy is the courts' priority across the whole range of application of the cy-pres doctrine: 'Donor Intention and Dialectic Legal Policy Frames' in Matthew Harding (ed), *Research Handbook on Not-for-Profit Law* (Edward Elgar 2018) 189.

[77] Historically there have been two cy-pres jurisdictions in Chancery: one judicial; and one prerogative, exercised on behalf of the monarch as *parens patriae*: see Rachael Mulheron, *The Modern Cy-Pres Doctrine: Applications and Implications* (UCL Press 2006) 23–30. To the extent that the pre-toleration cases were instances of prerogative cy-pres, they could be viewed as resting on a distinctive jurisdictional basis and therefore not illustrative of trends in equity per se. Nonetheless, the history of prerogative cy-pres shows that it was integrated into equity (see Jones (n 10) 72–87, 151–53), and in any event as I argue in the text the pre-toleration cases have counterparts in what can fairly be described as modern equity.

[78] I discuss these cases in detail in Matthew Harding, 'Trusts for Religious Purposes and the Question of Public Benefit' (2008) 71 MLR 159, 161–62.

[79] (1684) 1 Vern 248; 1 Eq Cas Abr 96. The decree was reversed by the Charity Commissioners after the passage of the Act of Toleration 1689. See *Attorney-General v Hughes* (1689) 2 Vern 105.

[80] (1754) 1 Dick 259.

[81] (1802) 7 Ves Jun 490. Jones (n 10) 143 n 7 notes that it is not known where the assets were ultimately applied.

[82] (1802) 7 Ves Jun 490, 495.

charitable intention, that is supposed to be so liberal as to take in objects, not only within his intention, but wholly adverse to it.

The advent of religious toleration removed the pressure for courts to apply the cy-pres doctrine in the way it was applied in the pre-toleration cases. However, to the extent that the pre-toleration cases illustrate a general willingness in Chancery to change trusts contrary to settlor intention, those cases find counterparts in the twentieth and twenty-first centuries. In particular in more recent times courts have shown themselves willing to utilize the cy-pres doctrine to change trusts that, in their terms, discriminate against groups on grounds such as sex, race, and religion. For example, in *In re Dominion Students' Hall Trust*, Evershed J approved a scheme permitting the trustees of a racially discriminatory charitable trust to administer that trust on a non-discriminatory basis; in doing so, he noted that social understandings of racial discrimination had changed since the trust was first settled.[83] And in *In re Lysaght*, Buckley J approved a scheme to render a racially discriminatory charitable trust non-discriminatory, although he was careful not to do so on grounds of public policy;[84] instead, he reasoned that rendering the trust non-discriminatory was the only way to ensure that the settlor's chosen trustee would carry out the trust.[85] *In re Lysaght* therefore reflects an interesting equitable strategy in relation to institutional change: the strategy of permitting trustees themselves to force such change by refusing to administer a trust on its terms and requesting a cy-pres scheme to bring into being an institutional framework that conforms to prevailing social and political norms.[86]

Perhaps the best-known example of a court in equity invoking the cy-pres doctrine to change a discriminatory charitable trust is *Canada Trust Co v Ontario (Human Rights Commission)*.[87] The trust, the Leonard Foundation, had been settled in the 1920s to provide a scheme of educational scholarships.[88] The terms of the trust were clearly and unmistakeably discriminatory; the benefits of the scheme, along with participation in its administration, were restricted to white Protestants of British nationality or parentage. Women were also excluded from some of the trust's benefits.[89] The trustees had administered the scheme for many years but in the face of considerable public attention and pressure had sought direction from the court in relation to the trust's discriminatory aspects. The Ontario Court of Appeal ordered a cy-pres variation of the terms of the scheme to ensure that the scheme could be lawfully administered on a non-discriminatory basis. In *Canada Trust*, a court in equity fundamentally changed the character and orientation of a trust with an eye to prevailing social and political norms,

[83] [1947] 1 Ch 183, 186.

[84] [1966] 1 Ch 191, 206.

[85] ibid 209. Note that in the United Kingdom, the Equality Act 2010 now contains provisions that vary racially discriminatory charitable trusts: see further *In re Harding* [2007] EWHC 3.

[86] This strategy does not invariably work: see eg (against a statutory rather than an equitable backdrop) *BoE Trust Limited NO* [2010] ZASCA 136.

[87] (1990) 69 DLR (4th) 321.

[88] For the history of the trust, see Bruce Ziff, *Unforeseen Legacies: Reuben Wells Leonard and the Leonard Foundation Trust* (University of Toronto Press 2000).

[89] The terms of the trust are set out at (1990) 69 DLR (4th) 321, 326–29.

and in doing so it overrode the expressed intention of the trust's settlor. Interestingly, in Canadian cases since *Canada Trust* was decided, Canadian courts have refused to invoke the cy-pres doctrine in this far-reaching way; those courts have sought to distinguish the bigotry of the Leonard Foundation with the more benign types of discrimination that underpin trusts to provide educational scholarships to, say, Roman Catholics or women, and they have upheld such trusts.[90] Equity takes an interest in institutional change, even where this entails prioritizing prevailing social and political norms over expressed settlor intention, but the case for change must be well established before cy-pres orders will be made.

V. Concluding Thoughts

What are we to make of this brief overview of equity's interest in institutions? In concluding, I want to offer some thoughts that aim to establish a connection between that interest and normative, justificatory, arguments in private law theory. My starting point is a particular version of liberalism according to which a measure of the justification of state action lies in the contribution of that state action to an overall social, economic, and political order in which people are able to live autonomous lives.[91] The conditions of this autonomy are various. For example, in order to live autonomously people must possess and develop certain capacities and dispositions such as literacy, numeracy, and the cognitive ability to think about the choices that they make. In addition, autonomous people must be free to some sufficient degree of coercion and manipulation in deliberating about their options and choosing among them. And, of most interest for present purposes, people must have available to them a sufficient range of options from which to choose in realizing a self-determining path in life. The state plays a role in securing and promoting these various conditions of autonomy, using a range of techniques from direct provision of public and private goods, to incentivizing and encouraging action on the part of others, to refusing to facilitate and even coercively suppressing action that stands to harm autonomy by interfering with the conditions on which it depends.

Against the backdrop of this version of liberalism, I think something may be said about equity's interest in institutions with the imperative that people enjoy a sufficient range of options in view. A sufficient range of options demands that options be individuated one from another so that they are available to people as distinct objects of choice. Thus, the ways in which options are so individuated is of interest from a liberal point of view centred on the value of autonomy. One way in which options might be

[90] See *Re Ramsden Estate* (1996) 139 DLR (4th) 746; *University of Victoria v British Columbia (AG)* 2000 BCSC 445; *Re the Esther G Castanera Scholarship Fund* [2015] 7 WWR 191. Perhaps ironically, the *Canada Trust* case has been more often relied on in Canada to strike down 'private' trusts that discriminate: see *McCorkill v Streed* 2014 NBQB 148; *Spence v BMO Trust Company* 2015 ONSC 615.

[91] The *locus classicus* is Joseph Raz, *The Morality of Freedom* (Clarendon Press 1986). My account in this and subsequent paragraphs owes much to Raz's analysis.

individuated is on the basis of the values and normative commitments that underpin them;[92] another is on the basis of the purposes and goals that they might enable people to realize; yet another is on the basis of the modes of interaction that they reflect and promote. To the extent that options are individuated in these ways, they enable people to make genuine choices based on their sense of the values and commitments with which they wish to engage, the purposes and goals that they wish to pursue, and the modes of interaction that they seek to participate in. The processes by which options are individuated on these and other grounds are complex, a function of history and culture, and to be found in family and private life, civil society, and the market economy. They are also to be found in state action; through law and in other ways the state plays a key role in giving content and shape to the options on which autonomy depends.

To the extent that private law is facilitative, its justification in light of political ideals and values may lie, at least in part, in an argument along the lines just described. For example, the institutions of private property may have value insofar as they reflect distinctive ways of valuing and regulating relations with the resources of the world.[93] Thus, the options of holding title as joint tenants or tenants in common may enable people to choose between different models of sharing that ultimately rest on different values. And the law of contract may perform valuable service insofar as it facilitates the market as a distinctive mode of interaction.[94] It may also have value insofar as it establishes distinct contract types that appeal and are available to differently situated people depending on their purposes and goals.[95] In these and others ways, the institutions of private property and the law of contract play their role in constituting, maintaining, and refining options and in individuating those options so that people may choose among them in self-determining ways.

Insofar as it is facilitative, equity plays a similar role. Because equity's interest in institutions is an expression of its facilitative dimension, it is therefore arguable that equity's interest in institutions reveals it contributing to a broader state project that seems normatively justified and desirable when viewed in light of the political ideal of autonomy. So, for example, the development of the charitable trust as an institutional type reveals equity constituting an individuated option characterized by a highly distinctive mode of interaction: a mode organized around a particular conception of altruism whose content is given by charity law itself.[96] Arguably, without equity's past support this option simply would not have developed and civil society might have been poorer for it;

[92] '[L]aw should facilitate (within limits) the coexistence of various social spheres embodying different modes of valuation': Hanoch Dagan, 'Pluralism and Perfectionism in Private Law' (2012) 112 Columbia Law Review 1409, 1424. For the relation of autonomy and value pluralism, see Raz (n 91) 161, 398–99 and Isaiah Berlin, 'Two Concepts of Liberty' in Henry Hardy (ed) *Liberty* (OUP 2002) 166, 216–17.

[93] See Hanoch Dagan, *Property: Values and Institutions* (OUP 2011).

[94] On ways in which contract law facilitates the market: Nathan Oman, *The Dignity of Commerce: Markets and the Moral Foundations of Contract Law* (University of Chicago Press 2017).

[95] See Hanoch Dagan and Michael Heller, *The Choice Theory of Contracts* (CUP 2017). Raz's own view of the relation of autonomy and contract law is presented in Joseph Raz, 'Review: Promises in Morality and Law' (1982) 95 Harvard Law Review 916, esp 933–38.

[96] I argue at greater length in support of this proposition in Matthew Harding, *Charity Law and the Liberal State* (CUP 2014) esp ch 3.

moreover, without equity's future support the option may die and with it a distinctive mode of interaction may be diminished or even extinguished.[97]

Similarly, equity's interest in maintaining the trust itself as a distinctive institutional type is arguably appealing in light of the demands of autonomy. Insofar as the trust is a particular facilitative mode—characterized by its irreducible core and associated norms of stewardship, accountability, and fiduciary responsibility—the trust enables settlors to achieve their desired purposes and goals in a certain way that is not otherwise available to them. Moreover, the activation of trust norms opens up possibilities for people autonomously to engage with further individuated options, such as options associated with the social role of trusteeship. The option that is the trust itself, and allied options such as those bound up in trusteeship, are potentially undermined when the trust ceases to be identifiable with sufficient clarity and precision as a distinctive institutional type. For example, settlors who lack certainty about what is entailed in choosing the trust as a particular facilitative mode may elect vehicles other than the trust to pursue their chosen purposes, rather than incur transaction costs associated with gaining the desired certainty. And trustees may cease to have a sense that they occupy a particular social role, viewing themselves instead as something akin to agents of their settlors.[98] From a liberal point of view centred on autonomy, then, there are reasons to maintain the trust as a distinctive institutional type, notwithstanding settlor demands for bespoke arrangements such as those on display in cases such as *Citibank*, *Pugachev*, *Clayton*, and *Webb*.

Not every aspect of equity's interest in institutions seems immediately reconcilable with the proposition that equity contributes to the conditions of autonomy by contributing to the development and maintenance of individuated options that may be the subject of autonomous choice. Earlier, I described equity's interest, manifested in the cy-pres doctrine, in changing institutions where those institutions do not conform to prevailing social and political norms. Clearly, the early illiberal uses of that doctrine to divert assets away from religions that were not tolerated and into the hands of the established church are indefensible from the perspective of a liberalism centred on the political ideal of autonomy. However, more recent uses of the cy-pres doctrine to reform charitable trusts that entail discrimination on grounds such as race, sex, and religion may be reconcilable with an overall project to contribute to the conditions of autonomy. The value of autonomy does not demand that people have a limitless number of options from which to choose, and in particular it does not require the availability of options that are inconsistent with fundamental liberal commitments.[99] It is arguable that the

[97] There is evidence that the distinctive mode of interaction that is charity in the legal sense is currently under substantial pressure, thanks to the phenomenon of 'social enterprise' and the widespread delivery of government policy agendas and programmes by charities with government funding: see respectively Anup Malani and Eric A Posner, 'The Case for For-Profit Charities' (2007) 93 Virginia Law Review 2017 and Debra Morris, 'Paying the Piper: The "Contract Culture" as a Dependency Culture for Charities?' in Alison Dunn (ed), *The Voluntary Sector, the State and the Law* (Hart 2000) 123.

[98] In this regard, consider the interesting discussion of the evidence relating to the trustee, Mr Patterson, in the *Pugachev* case: [2017] EWHC 2426, [299]–[358].

[99] See further Raz (n 91) 410–12.

conditions of autonomy include a public culture in which people are able to form and maintain self-respect in view of elements of their personal identity; such self-respect itself seems an important element of the conditions under which people enjoy the capacities and dispositions to be autonomous.[100] The state plays an important role in contributing to the necessary public culture, and arguably to the extent that it facilitates and endorses arrangements that single out people for unfavourable treatment based on elements of personal identity, it fails in discharging that role.[101] By reforming charitable trusts that discriminate impermissibly, then, the state may be viewed as contributing to the conditions of autonomy even if at first glance such interferences seem at odds with the maintenance of the charitable trust as an institutional type that facilitates settlor goals and altruistic interaction.

Much more could be said about the normative justification and desirability of equity's interest in institutions. But for now, it will suffice to underscore a few key points that I hope have emerged from this chapter, and that may have resonance in broader debates in private law theory. First, while equity, like all private law, is undeniably interested in achieving remedial justice in the setting of adjudication, there is another story to be told as well, one in which equity takes a keen interest in the institutional arrangements within which parties operate. Whether equity is distinctive insofar as it takes this interest in institutions, or in the extent to which it expresses such interest, are questions on which this chapter has not offered a view, even though they are questions worth exploring in light of the survey presented here. What I think I have shown, however, is that equity's interest in institutions stands in striking contrast to accounts of private law that locate its normative concerns wholly or even largely in considerations of remedial justice. A second point: by taking an interest in the development, governance, and reform of institutions, equity contributes to the development and maintenance of individuated options that might be the subject of autonomous choice, whether these options be distinguished by their underpinning values and commitments, the purposes and goals that they facilitate, or the modes of interaction that they enable and embody. And, finally, to the extent that equity makes that contribution, equity, like the whole body of facilitative private law, seems appealing when measured against fundamental liberal commitments, at least from the perspective of a liberalism centred on the political ideal of autonomy.

[100] I discuss this further, with reference to the philosophical literature on discrimination, in Harding (n 96) 226–36.

[101] This thinking suggests that, at least in jurisdictions where constitutional commitments entail anti-discrimination norms, something like the 'state action' doctrine applied in the celebrated case of *Shelley v Kraemer* 334 US 1 (1948) might be justified across private law, and arguably the justification is strengthened in the case of trusts because of the court's supervisory jurisdiction.

17

The Equity of the Statute

James Edelman

I. Introduction: the Two Meanings of the Equity of the Statute

In Blackstone's *Commentaries*, he cited an example of statutory interpretation, which he attributed to Cicero. The example concerned a law which mandated that those who abandoned a ship in a storm would forfeit all property on the ship. In a storm, all of the mariners abandoned the ship except for one passenger who was too sick to escape. The ship, by fluke, drifted into port. The sick man claimed that he was entitled to all the property on the ship. But Blackstone said that all agreed that the sick man was not entitled to the property. He said that from this method of interpretation 'arises what we call *equity* . . . the correction of that, wherein the law (by reason of its universality) is deficient'.[1] This equity, he said, depends essentially 'upon the particular circumstances of each individual case'.[2] Blackstone explained that there are two limbs to this doctrine of the equity of the statute. (1) Cases 'out of the letter, are often said to be within the equity', and (2) 'cases within the letter are frequently out of the equity'.[3] This equity of the statute approach had much support when Blackstone wrote. The technique was also supported by St German,[4] Viner,[5] Bacon,[6] Coke,[7] and Wood.[8] But there is controversy about what it involved.

This chapter is about the history and philosophical foundation of this doctrine of the equity of the statute. The primary focus is upon statutes, which is where this role of 'equity' has received the greatest attention. But the doctrine is not limited to statute. A similar doctrine applies to all written documents that create legal rules and norms. The legal rule created might be of narrow application, such as a private Act of Parliament applying to a single corporation, a contract between two persons, or a will with a single beneficiary. Or the legal rule created might be widespread and in the public interest, such as a general statute, a treaty between many nations, or a large trust or will with

[1] Sir W Blackstone, *Commentaries on the Laws of England* (1st edn, 1765) bk 1, s 2, 61 (quoting Grotius, *De Aequitate*).
[2] ibid.
[3] ibid bk 3, c 27, 431.
[4] C St Germain and W Muchall, *Doctor and Student* (17th edn, 1787) Dialogue 1, c 17, 49.
[5] Viner, *A General Abridgement of Law and Equity* (2nd edn, 1791) 513.
[6] M Bacon, *A New Abridgement of the Law* (5th edn, 1786) 649.
[7] Sir E Coke, *The First Part of the Institutes of the Laws of England* (9th edn, 1684) c 2, s 21, 24ff.
[8] T Wood, *An Institute of the Laws of England* (10th edn, 1772) 9.

James Edelman, *The Equity of the Statute* In: *Philosophical Foundations of the Law of Equity*. Edited by: Dennis Klimchuk, Irit Samet, and Henry E Smith, Oxford University Press (2020).
DOI: 10.1093/oso/9780198817659.003.0018

many trust powers, beneficiaries, and legatees. In each case, there can be a role for the equity of the instrument to be applied. The focus of this chapter is upon two, opposed meanings of this notion of equity. One is much more legitimate than the other.

On one view, likely to have been the original view, the equity of the statute is an invitation to apply an external principle of justice that involves changing the meaning, and therefore the effect, of statutory words. It is not 'interpretation'. The 'equity', in this sense, involves justice beyond the meaning of the words of the statute, even though the justice is limited by that which the judge considers that a reasonable and just lawmaker might have enacted had he or she considered the issue.[9] The equity here is truly a 'correction' or rectification of the statutory words 'to be applied in contradiction to the positive law'.[10] It respects neither the intended meaning of the words nor the application to the facts that is required by that meaning. Rather, it involves *not* applying the meaning of the law that is actually enacted.

The other, more modern, view might have evolved, with the recognition of a separation of powers, as a transformation of the original conception of the equity of the statute. That other view of the equity of the statute is little more than what is commonly described as modern purposive and contextual interpretation and construction.[11] The equity of the statute in this sense can operate in two ways. First, in this modern sense, it can operate in the process of interpreting the meaning of the statutory words. The 'equity' of the statute requires preference to be given to a meaning that is consistent with the purpose of the statute even if that meaning is contrary to the semantic, literal meaning of the words of the statute. Second, the doctrine also operates in the process of applying the meaning to the facts by construction. If the meaning of the statutory words leaves scope for different possible applications to the facts (such as an open-textured provision that depends on notions such as 'offensive', 'unfair', or 'unconscionable') preference must be given to a construction that would apply most consistently with the statutory purpose. In both cases, the concern with the 'equity' of the statute is really just a concern with its context and purpose. Equity, in this sense, does not describe a principle of justice at all. It is a misnomer to describe as 'equitable' these techniques of interpretation and construction that are similar to techniques that apply to all speech acts.

II. An Early Example of the Equity of the Statute: the Statute of Frauds

In order to illustrate the two possible meanings of the equity of the statute it is helpful to begin with a well-known example of the doctrine before turning to the two different approaches to that example. In 1677, the Cavalier Parliament passed An Act for Prevention of Frauds and Perjuries. The Act was said to be designed to prevent fraud

9 For which reason Klimchuk in this volume argues that it is 'not quite' an external account: (see Chapter 2).

10 G Spence, *The Equitable Jurisdiction of the Court of Chancery* (1846) 326–27.

11 See DR Klinck, *Conscience, Equity and the Court of Chancery in Early Modern England* (Ashgate 2010) 49 who suggests that this view might be attributed to St German.

and perjury in oral testimony. The Statute of Frauds is a useful case study in the application of the equity of the statute because Holdsworth described it as the most important of the older private law statutes.[12] And at the end of his life, Lord Kenyon described it as 'one of the wisest laws in our Statute Book'.[13]

A short-lived example of the application of the equity of the statute approach to the Statute of Frauds is the decision of Lord Mansfield in *Simon v Motivos*.[14] In that case, Lord Mansfield suggested that the Statute of Frauds might not apply to a sale by auction. There was nothing in the meaning of the words of the statute which could have revealed this exclusion. But Lord Mansfield said that 'many cases, though seemingly within the letter, have been let out of it'.[15] In the same case, Wilmot J remarked that '[h]ad the Statute of Frauds been always carried into execution according to the letter, it would have done ten times more mischief than it has done good, by protecting, rather than preventing, frauds'.[16] Ultimately, this view of sale by auction did not prevail.[17]

A more lasting example of the equity of the statute approach to the Statute of Frauds is the decision of the English Court of Appeal in *Rochefoucauld v Boustead*.[18] That case considered section 7 of the Statute of Frauds, which provided that 'all Declarations or Creations of Trusts or Confidences of any Lands ... shall be manifested and proved by some Writing signed by the Party who is by Law entitled to declare such Trust ... or else they shall be utterly void and of none Effect'. The litigation concerned the Delmar coffee estates in what was then Ceylon. The Comtesse de la Rochefoucauld owned the estates and mortgaged them. When she could not meet the mortgage repayments, and fearing that her recently divorced husband would enforce his interest recognised by the Divorce Court by buying the titles from the mortgagee, she arranged for the defendant to buy the titles from the mortgagee. She alleged that the defendant had orally declared a trust of the estates for her, subject to her promise to repay to him the purchase price which he had paid to the mortgagee.[19] The defendant subsequently mortgaged, and then sold, the land without her knowledge. She sought to recover the price received by him less the amount which she said was owed to him. The trial judge, Kekewich J, heard the oral evidence of the declaration of trust but, consistently with the words of section 7 of the *Statute of Frauds*, refused to admit that evidence.[20]

The Court of Appeal was not merely referred to the oral testimony of the Comtesse. It was also referred to written correspondence prior to the creation of the trust. But the judges considered that they did not need to determine whether the trust was manifested and proved by some writing. They considered that the trust would not be void even if

[12] Sir WS Holdsworth, *A History of English Law* (2nd edn, Sweet & Maxwell 1937) vol 6, c 7, 379.

[13] *Chaplin v Rogers* (1800) 1 East 192, 194 [102 ER 75, 76].

[14] (1746) 1 Black W 599 600–01 [96 ER 347 347–48].

[15] ibid 600 [96 ER 347, 347].

[16] ibid 601 [96 ER 347, 348].

[17] See *Kenworthy v Schofield* (1824) 2 B & C 945 [107 ER 633] and the discussion of Lord Blackburn in *Maddison v Alderson* (1883) 8 App Cas 467, 488.

[18] [1897] 1 Ch 196.

[19] The trust was an express trust, as Swadling explains: see W Swadling, 'The Nature of the Trust in *Rochefoucauld v Boustead*' in C Mitchell (ed), *Constructive and Resulting Trusts* (Hart 2010) 95.

[20] The first instance proceedings are not reported on this point, but this is discussed in the Court of Appeal at [1897] 1 Ch 196, 199.

it had not been manifested and proved in writing. This was because, 'notwithstanding the statute',[21] oral evidence was 'admissible in order to prevent the statute from being used in order to commit a fraud'.[22] The so-called 'fraud' was for 'a person to whom land is conveyed as a trustee, and who knows it was so conveyed, to deny the trust and claim the land himself'.[23] The Court of Appeal relied upon an earlier decision in which it was said that the general principle that a statute is not to be used as an instrument of fraud 'has long been recognised by Courts of Equity'.[24]

Rochefoucauld was not an uncontroversial decision. In 1760, in *Bartlett v Pickersgill*, the Lord Keeper had reached the opposite result without even calling upon the defendant. Henley LK (later Northington LC) explained that to allow the evidence 'would be to overturn the statute'.[25] Although doubts had been expressed about the decision in *Bartlett*,[26] it had been upheld on nearly identical facts in *James v Smith*.[27] Curiously, the trial judge in *James v Smith* was the same trial judge (Kekewich J) who later decided *Rochefoucauld* and the Court of Appeal in *James v Smith* included Lindley LJ who sat in the Court of Appeal in *Rochefoucauld*.[28] However, in *Rochefoucauld*, Lindley LJ dismissed *James v Smith* as inconsistent with the modern decisions which had held that the Statute of Frauds cannot be used as an instrument of fraud.[29]

The decision in *Rochefoucauld* prevailed in England and the Commonwealth. It was anticipated by, and consistent with, the decision of the majority of the Supreme Court of Canada in *Barton v McMillan*.[30] In contrast, in *Barton*, Strong J, in dissent, borrowing from Sir Edward Sugden, said that to allow oral evidence would be 'directly in the teeth of the Statute of Frauds'.[31] In Australia, where *Rochefoucauld* has been approved by the High Court of Australia,[32] White J reiterated that the reason 'the Statute of Frauds does not stand in the way is that it would be to use the Statute as an instrument of fraud to deny enforcement of the true transaction'.[33] These explanations use 'fraud' in a sense other than actual fraud. There was no suggestion that the defendant in *Rochefoucauld* was deceitful or dishonest merely by relying upon the statute. Perhaps for this reason Glass JA preferred to say that the doctrine in *Rochefoucauld* was said to rest upon the proposition that the 'trust is enforced, because it is unconscionable of the legal owner to rely on the statute to defeat the beneficial interest'.[34] But it is difficult to know what

[21] *Rochefoucauld v Boustead* [1897] 1 Ch 196, 206 per Lindley LJ (giving the judgment of himself, Lord Halsbury LC, and A L Smith LJ).

[22] ibid 207.

[23] ibid 206.

[24] *In Re Duke of Marlborough; Davis v Whitehead* [1894] 2 Ch 133, 141 per Stirling J.

[25] *Bartlett v Pickersgill* (1760) 1 Eden 515, 516 [28 ER 785, 786]; 1 Cox 15, 15 [29 ER 1041, 1041].

[26] *Heard v Pilley* (1869) LR 4 Ch App 548.

[27] [1891] 1 Ch 384 (Kekewich J).

[28] [1891] WN 175.

[29] *Rochefoucauld v Boustead* (n 21) 206.

[30] (1892) 20 SCR 404.

[31] *Barton v McMillan* (1892) 20 SCR 404, 413.

[32] *Cadd v Cadd* (1909) 9 CLR 171, 178 per Griffith CJ, 187 per Isaacs J; [1909] HCA 59; *Bloch v Bloch* (1981) 180 CLR 390, 403 per Brennan J; [1981] HCA 56.

[33] *Ciaglia v Ciaglia* (2010) 269 ALR 175, 191 [69]; [2010] NSWSC 341. See also *Dalton v Christofis* [1978] WAR 42 (Smith J). There have been some attempts to evade the obvious words of the statute by attaching the label 'constructive' to the trust which is recognized. See the discussion in Swadling (n 19) 95.

[34] *Allen v Snyder* [1977] 2 NSWLR 685, 693.

is meant by the reference to 'unconscionable'. As has been said in the High Court of Australia, 'the statement that enforcement of the transaction would be "unconscionable" is to characterise the result rather than to identify the reasoning that leads to the application of that description'.[35]

The equity of the statute was also applied to the Statute of Frauds in relation to the doctrine of part performance. The doctrine permitted the enforcement of a parol contract for the sale of land that had been partly performed despite the plain terms of the Statute of Frauds[36] including the prohibition that 'no action shall be brought' to charge a person for a contract for the sale of land unless the agreement upon which the action is brought, or memorandum or note of it, is in writing and signed. However, by the late eighteenth century the doctrine of part performance had been narrowed and confined.[37]

The leading nineteenth-century case was *Maddison v Alderson*.[38] Thomas Alderson promised his housekeeper, Elizabeth Maddison, that he would leave her a life estate in his land in his will. On the faith of this promise, she continued as his housekeeper. But Alderson's will was not attested. Alderson's heir demanded the title deeds. Ms Maddison pleaded that there was an agreement that she be entitled to a life interest. The difficulty for Ms Maddison was that the agreement was oral. It fell squarely within section 4 of the Statute of Frauds, which broadly provided that no action shall be brought to charge any person upon any contract or sale of lands unless the agreement, or a memorandum or note of it, is in writing and signed by the person to be charged or his or her agent.

Various of their Lordships expressed concerns with the doctrine of part performance that had been the product of the equity of the statute. Lord Selborne, the Lord Chancellor, referred to the technique discussed above of justifying the doctrine of part performance on the basis that it rested on the principle of 'fraud', although he immediately noted the inadequacy of this basis as a general explanation.[39] Lord O'Hagan said that previous 'bold decisions' on part performance were 'prompted no doubt by a desire to defeat fraud and accomplish justice'.[40] And Lord Blackburn said that he had 'not been able to discover to my satisfaction what is the principle which is involved in the numerous cases in equity'.[41] He said that the principle involved a construction of the statute 'as if it contained these words, "or unless possession of the land shall be given and accepted"'.[42] Ultimately, the House of Lords held that although there was no

[35] *Garcia v National Australia Bank Ltd* (1998) 194 CLR 395, 409 [34] per Gaudron, McHugh, Gummow, and Hayne JJ; [1998] HCA 48. See also *Australian Competition & Consumer Commission v CG Berbatis Holdings Pty Ltd* (2003) 214 CLR 51, 73 [43]; [2003] HCA 18 (Gummow and Hayne JJ saying that the use of terms like unconscionable and unconscientious 'may have masked rather than illuminated the underlying principles at stake'); *Tanwar Enterprises Pty Ltd v Cauchi* (2003) 217 CLR 315, 325–26 [23]–[26] per Gleeson CJ, McHugh, Gummow, Hayne & Heydon JJ; [2003] HCA 57.

[36] An Act for Prevention of Frauds and Perjuries 1677 (UK) ss 4(4) and 4(6).

[37] See, for instance, the rejection of the sufficiency of payment of money as an act of part performance: *Clinan v Cooke* (1802) 1 Sch & Lef 22, 40–41; *Hughes v Morris* (1852) 2 De G M & G 349, 356; 42 ER 907, 910; *Britain v Rossiter* (1879) 11 QBD 123, 130–31.

[38] (1883) 8 App Cas 467.

[39] ibid 474.

[40] *Maddison v Alderson* (n 17) 485.

[41] ibid 488.

[42] ibid 489.

memorandum in writing the agreement might still have been enforceable if the defendant had performed acts of part performance that were unequivocally referable to an agreement of the general nature as that alleged. However, continuing in the service of Alderson without wages was not an act that was unequivocally so referable.

III. The Modern Meaning of the Equity of the Statute

In 1839, Lieber drew a distinction between interpretation and construction.[43] The words are today sometimes used interchangeably and sometimes used differently from Lieber's terminology. Nevertheless, that terminology helpfully illustrates two different concepts that are in play. 'Interpretation', he said, involves determining the meaning conveyed by the text itself.[44] Therefore, an interpreter from one language to another is involved in determining the best meaning of the words. When words are interpreted contextually, they are not limited to the range of their literal semantic meanings. Even 'black' can mean 'white' in the process of contextual interpretation.[45] An example is French legislation that, read literally, would have made it an offence for passengers to get on or off a train when it was *not* moving. This, and other obvious examples, are instances of 'simple, grammatical, drafting errors which if uncorrected would defeat the object of the provision'.[46] Despite the diametrically opposed literal meaning, the correction of such 'thumping, obvious error[s]' in the course of interpretation is still a 'contextualist' approach to the meaning of the statute.[47] Of course, statutes are generally expected to be carefully drafted instruments so the more that their words are said to depart from the range of their literal semantic meanings, the more closely that the proffered interpretation must be examined.

In contrast with 'interpretation', Lieber used 'construction' to mean 'the drawing of conclusions respecting subjects, that lie beyond the direct expression of the text, from elements known from and given in the text'.[48] Construction, in this sense, requires the application of interpreted meaning. The interpreted meaning is applied to the subject matter to reach a conclusion about its legal effect. Construction generally requires the application to the facts of the statutory words as contextually interpreted. An open-textured word, such as 'offensive', 'unfair', or 'unconscionable' might not present great difficulty for interpretation but the process of applying that meaning may be very difficult.

[43] F Lieber, *Legal and Political Hermeneutics* (Little, Brown 1839). See also the different distinction in *Life Insurance Company of Australia Ltd v Phillips* (1925) 36 CLR 60, 78; [1925] HCA 18 explaining *Chatenay v Brazilian Submarine Telegraph Co* [1891] 1 QB 79, 85 per Lindley LJ.

[44] Lieber (n 43) 55.

[45] *Mitchell v Henry* (1880) 15 Ch D 181.

[46] *Taylor v Owners—Strata Plan No 11564* (2014) 253 CLR 531, 548 [38] per French CJ, Crennan and Bell JJ; [2014] HCA 9.

[47] Siegel, 'What Statutory Drafting Errors Teach Us about Statutory Interpretation' (2001) 69 George Washington Law Review 309.

[48] Lieber (n 43) 56.

A modern view of the 'equity of the statute' is that it is a label that describes a contextual approach to interpretation and construction. In other words, it relies upon context and purpose in interpretation to supply a meaning to the words that may be different from their literal semantic content or to supply an application of the meaning where different applications are open. In each case, the context or purpose is derived from the ascertained intention of the notional speaker, Parliament from the objective perspective of a notional reasonable reader.

This meaning of the 'equity of the statute' renders 'equity' a misnomer. Blackstone, with whom this chapter began, apparently favoured this modern meaning of the equity of the statute. He gave the example of the ship's sick passenger as an illustration of discovering the 'true meaning' of the law when 'the words are dubious'.[49] He did not explain how the words of the law should be interpreted, by their expression or by implications, to deny property to the sick man. But he saw the question as being one of giving the best meaning to the statutory words based upon the intention of Parliament. Blackstone observed that if 'the parliament will positively enact a thing to be done which is unreasonable, I know of no power that can control it'.[50] The unreasonableness of one interpretation of a law can be a factor which militates against that interpretation because it is unlikely that a reasonable person would perceive the reasonable notional speaker, Parliament, to have meant that. But, as Blackstone emphasized, if that interpretation is the intention of Parliament then for judges to reject it would 'set the judicial power above that of the legislature, which would be subversive of all government.'[51]

There are, of course, large questions concerning the 'intention of Parliament'. For some, like Sir John Laws and Professor Andrew Burrows, it is nonsense to speak of the intention of Parliament because courts are not concerned with the subjective intentions of Members of Parliament, individually or even if their intentions could be aggregated.[52] This approach, requiring focus on the intention of Parliament, is also favoured by some modern commentators. This view is correct in that courts are not concerned with identifying the subjective intention of Parliamentarians any more than they are concerned with identifying the intention of the parties to a contract, the author of a will, or the person declaring a trust. In each case, the references to intention are a shorthand description for what a reasonable, informed person (the listener or reader) would understand to have been the intended meaning of the person making the utterance (the speaker). In each case, the relevant speaker, like the relevant reader, is a construct. We are not concerned when construing legal instruments with the actual, subjective intentions of any person involved in the utterance. Hence, in contract, we ask what a reasonable, informed person would understand to be the intended meaning of contractual words uttered by a person in the position of *both* of the parties. It does not matter

[49] Blackstone (n 1) bk 1, s 2, 61.
[50] ibid s 3, 91.
[51] ibid.
[52] Laws, 'Publication Review: The Nature of Legislative Intent' (2016) 132 LQR 159; A Burrows, *Thinking about Statutes* (CUP 2018) 17–18. Compare the force of R Ekins and J Goldsworthy, 'The Reality and Indispensability of Legislative Intentions' (2014) 36 Sydney Law Review 39; F Bennion, *Bennion on Statutory Interpretation* (5th edn, Butterworths 2010) 463.

that no such person actually exists. So too, we ask what a reasonable, informed person would understand to be the intended meaning of statutory words uttered by a person in the position of Parliament without concern that this intention is conceptual.

On the modern view of the equity of the statute the 'intention of the Parliament' applies to determine the meaning of the words used even if that meaning involves a large departure from the semantic literal meaning of the words. For some, this view was controversial. It was disputed by those who would limit words to their literal, semantic meanings in all but the most extreme cases. Towards the end of the eighteenth century, Jeremy Bentham pleaded that 'such a degree of comprehension and steadiness might one day perhaps be given to the views of the legislator as to render the allowance of liberal or discretionary interpretation on the part of the judge no longer necessary'.[53] Hence, a large or liberal departure from the literal semantic meaning of statutory words is sometimes deprecated, even if that departure involved giving a meaning to the words, in context, as the notional Parliament intended.

For the same reasons, even if some of the cases concerning the Statute of Frauds could be understood as applying the modern view of the equity of the statute, they would still have been controversial. Lord Kenyon lamented that 'if the Courts had at first abided by the strict letter of the Act it would have prevented a multitude of suits that have since been brought'.[54] Lord Cowper LC emphasized that he had 'been always tender in laying open that wise and just provision the parliament had made' and refused 'to obviate the pretence of such and such cases being out of the mischief of the statute'.[55] Lord Macclesfield LC said in response to a submission that signature was unnecessary: 'to put a different construction upon the Act, would be to repeal it'.[56] And in one of the first texts written on the Statute of Frauds, William Roberts, an iconoclastic barrister, and a prolific writer and editor whose views may have expressed the prevailing opinion at the Middle Temple at the time, introduced his book with a plea that:[57]

> An administrator of the laws ought not to aim *phainesthai philanthropoteros tou nomou*;[58] for the true compassion of the law is to prevent cases of compassion from recurring. That indulgence is but treacherous lenity, which, by departing from known rules, leaves men in uncertainty as to means of their security, and destroys confidence by the misdirection of feeling.

These criticisms of the modern approach to the equity of the statute invite two possible responses. One powerful response is to acknowledge the criticisms but to use them merely as a basis to take care when applying the equity of the statute to depart from literal, semantic meaning of the words or to take care when applying an interpretation

[53] J Bentham and HLA Hart, *Of Laws in General* (OUP 1970) 240.
[54] *Chater v Beckett* (1797) 7 TR 201, 204 [101 ER 931, 933].
[55] *Bawdes v Amhurst* (1715) Prec Ch 402, 403 [24 ER 180, 181].
[56] *Hawkins v Holmes* (1721) 1 P Wms 770, 771 [24 ER 606, 607].
[57] W Roberts, *A Treatise on the Statute of Frauds* (1805) xxvi–xxvii.
[58] An approximate translation of the Greek, which itself may be a paraphrase from Paul in Romans, is 'to be more charitable than the law'.

to particular facts. In the leading modern work on the Statute of Frauds, Williams cautiously explained that 'fraud' was a 'very broad term' and although in 'its broadest sense the principle under discussion might well amount to a complete negation of the Statute', the principle could be confined to cases of part performance and intentionally preventing the execution of a sufficient writing.[59] In other words, the historical anomaly that used 'fraud' as a technique to evade the statute should be confined to historically developed doctrines but not extended. This response also seems to underpin the approach of the Lord Chancellor in *Maddison v Alderson* whose focus was to preserve the doctrine of part performance as based upon history and his attempt to justify that history by what the 'statute ... has in view'.[60] In an attempt to marry the language of the statute with the doctrine, albeit one that was not without difficulty, the Lord Chancellor said that a defendant was '"charged" upon the equities resulting from the acts done in execution of the contract, and not ... upon the contract itself'.[61]

The second response to the concern that the equity of the statute involves departure from the meaning of Parliament's words is to deny that construction must give effect to the interpreted meaning of the statutory words. The second response is that statutory construction permits the words to be applied contrary to their meaning. This is truly to apply principles of justice that are external to the statute. This response involves a different, and much older, conception of the equity of the statute, considered below. Without a statutory mandate to depart from the meaning of words in construction[62] and without the legal practice and precedent that is applied in adjudication, that conception is much harder to justify today.

IV. The Older Meaning of Equity of the Statute

The classic story of the history of equity as a different conception of justice begins with Aristotle, particularly his excursus in Book V of *Ethics*.[63] With the subtitle 'A digression on equity, which corrects the deficiencies of legal justice', Aristotle wrote:[64]

> For equity, though superior to one kind of justice, is still just, it is not superior to justice as being a different genus. Thus justice and equity coincide, and although both are good, equity is superior. What causes the difficulty is the fact that equity is just, but not what is legally just: it is a rectification of legal justice. The explanation of this is that all law is universal, and there are some things about which it is not possible to pronounce rightly in general terms; therefore in cases where it is necessary to make a general pronouncement, but impossible to do so rightly, the law takes account of the

59 J Williams, *The Statute of Frauds Section Four in the Light of Its Judicial Interpretation* (CUP 1932) 221–23.
60 *Maddison v Alderson* (n 17) 476.
61 ibid 475, 478 per Lord Selborne LC.
62 See, for instance, Human Rights Act 1998 s 3.
63 Aristotle and JAK Thomson, *The Ethics of Aristotle: The Nicomachean Ethics* (rev ed, Penguin 1976).
64 ibid 199, 200 [1137b5–1137b20, 1137b30–1138a1].

majority of cases, though not unaware that in this way errors are made. And the law is none the less right; because the error lies not in the law nor in the legislator, but in the nature of the case; for the raw material of human behaviour is essentially of this kind ... This also makes plain what the equitable man is. He is one who chooses and does equitable acts, and is not unduly insistent upon his rights, but accepts less than his share, although he has law on his side. Such a disposition is equity: it is a kind of justice, and not a distinct state of character.

Following Aristotle, the first sentence of Justinian's Digest began with Celsus's statement that *ius est ars boni et aequi* ('law is the art of the good and the equitable'),[65] borrowing the *aequitas* from Aristotle's ἐπιείκεια ('equity'). The Roman notion of two autonomous systems of justice was controversial. In the Republican period, the *praetor's* role of 'correcting' the *ius civile* was circumscribed and contentious. Similarly, in the Empire, Capitolinus explained how even the equitable imperium of the Emperor was questioned. In his biography of Opilius Macrinus, Capitolinus said that Macrinus wanted to abolish rescripts and establish a system of lawmaking by General Edict, because he could not bear the thought of individual discretion being exercised by rulers like Commodus or Caracalla.[66] From Rome, through to the Middle Ages,[67] Aristotle's views on justice remained controversial.

Adjudication in the early development of English law is generally described as bifurcated in the same manner. Courts of common law usually dispensed a strict or generalized form of justice. General legal rules governed cases so that a claimant usually needed to bring a claim within an existing writ. In contrast, the Lord Chancellor allowed a claimant to bring a petition to the Chancellor based on the facts of the claimant's individual case. A claimant's petition was a supplication seeking whatever mercy the Chancellor, and his judges, might dispense. The Court of Chancery would restrain the enforcement of a judgment at common law if it considered the result to be contrary to conscience. As Henderson observed, by the sixteenth century the injunctions occurred so frequently that people must have assumed that there was something wrong with the common law.[68]

With the advent of legally trained Chancellors and law reporting the Chancery courts began to develop general legal rules and the exercise of an individual, unrestrained discretion became less and less common. Prior to his appointment, the first legally trained Chancellor, Sir Thomas More, argued passionately that if judges 'rule by the leading of their own nature ... then the people will in no way be freer, but, by reason of a condition

[65] *Digest* 1.1.1.pr.

[66] A Birley, *Lives of the Later Caesars* (Penguin 1976) 268.

[67] Responding to Augustine's objection that *epikeia* (equity) is a vice rather than a virtue because 'seemingly *epikeia* pronounces judgment on the law, when it deems that the law should not be observed in some particular case', Aquinas responded with an example of a madman demanding his legal entitlement to the return of his sword while he was mad: 'on these and like cases it is bad to follow the law, and it is good to set aside the letter of the law and to follow the dictates of justice and the common good. This is the object of "*epikeia*" which we call equity' (see Aquinas, *Summa Theologica* II.II, Q120, art 1).

[68] EG Henderson, 'Relief from Bonds in the English Chancery: Mid-Sixteenth Century' (1974) 18 American Journal of Legal History 298, 306.

of servitude, worse, when they will have to obey, not fixed and definite laws, but indefinite whims changing from day to day'.[69] By the start of the nineteenth century, the Lord Chancellor, Lord Eldon, remarked that '[n]othing would inflict on me greater pain, in quitting this place, than the recollection that I had done any thing to justify the reproach that the equity of this Court varies like the Chancellor's foot'.[70]

Equitable principles were also sometimes applied at common law.[71] Applying Chancery's discretionary, equitable form of justice was the common law approach to the equity of the statute by which the common law judges relied upon externally imposed principles of justice, independently of the intention of the legislature as deduced from the words used by Parliament. However, the common law approach would rarely involve a purely external principle of justice. That external principle was usually constrained by the purpose of the statute. In other words, although the equity of the statute approach permitted words of the statute to be applied despite their meaning, the approach could not be used if to do so would be contrary to what the hypothetical legislator of that law would have considered appropriate.

One of the most famous discussions of this version of the equity of the statute thesis is by Plowden in his lengthy note to the report of *Eystone v Studd*.[72] Plowden considered many cases involving numerous different statutes and explained the meaning of the *Eystone* decision as follows:[73]

> From this judgment and the cause of it, the reader may observe, that it is not the words of law, but the internal sense of it that makes the law, and our law (like all others) consists of two parts, viz. of body and soul, the letter of the law is the body of the law, and the sense and reason of the law is the soul of the law, *quià ratio legis est anima legis*.... And equity, which in Latin is called *equitas*, enlarges or diminishes the letter according to its discretion, which equity is in two ways: The one Aristotle defines thus, (which is touched by Catline, Chief-Justice, in Stowell's case) *Equitas est correctio legis generatim latae qua parte deficit*, or, as the passage is explained by Perionius, *Equitas est correctio quaedam legi adhibita, quia ab ea abest aliquid propter generalem sine exceptione comprehensionem*, both which definitions come to one and the same thing. And this correction of the general words is much used in the law of England ... in these cases the general words of the law are corrected and abridged by equity.

The same approach, relying on principles of justice rather than a consideration of the intended meaning of the words that were used, was taken by St Germain, who spoke of the leaving the 'words of the law' to follow that which 'reason and justice requireth' as 'an exception of the law of God, or the law of reason'.[74] It was also the approach taken by

[69] St Thomas More, '*Responsio ad Lutherum*' in J Headley (ed), *The Yale Edition of the Complete Works of Thomas More* (Yale UP 1969) vol 5, 277.

[70] *Gee v Pritchard* (1818) 2 Swans 402, 414 [36 ER 670, 674]. Harman LJ once commented that "since the time of Lord Eldon ... equitable jurisdiction is exercised only upon well-known principles": *Bridge v Campbell Discount Co Ltd* [1961] 2 WLR 596, 605.

[71] *Roxborough v Rothmans of Pall Mall Australia Ltd* (2001) 208 CLR 516, 550 [88]; [2001] HCA 68 (Gummow J referring to the 'common counts' of *indebitatus assumpsit* which Lord Mansfield described as being in the nature of a bill in equity: *Clarke v Shee* (1774) 1 Cowp 197, 199–200 [98 ER 1041, 1042]).

[72] *Eystone v Studd* (1574) 2 Plow 459, 465–469 [75 ER 688, 695–700].

[73] ibid 465 [75 ER 688, 695–96].

[74] St Germain and Muchall (n 4) Dialogue 1, c 16, 45.

Pufendorf, where he observed that in contrast with the meaning of the statute derived from the words used by Parliament, the 'equity' could permit a law to be 'restrained' if, 'although it be not absolutely unlawful to stick to the Letter ... upon weighting the Thing in Candour and Prudence, it appears to be too grievous and burdensome'.[75]

The approach taken by Sir Edward Coke was less clear. In his famous report of *Heydon's Case*,[76] he described the decision that the Acts of Dissolution by Henry VIII[77] did not invalidate a grant of copyhold, despite the apparent words of the statute, as arising because 'the office of all the Judges is always to make such construction ... according to the true intent of the makers of the Act, *pro bono publico*'.[78] This, it seems, was an approach that allowed departure from the intended meaning of the words used by Parliament in favour of a 'true intent' independent of the words but only based upon what the judge considered that the makers of the Act would have decided. However, an apparently stronger approach was taken by Coke CJ, while still Chief Justice in Common Pleas, when he spoke in *Bonham's Case*[79] of a statute being adjudged void and controlled by the common law because it is 'against common right and reason'. That view was used against Coke, and relied upon as an application of the older approach, in *The Earl of Oxford's Case*, when the Lord Chancellor, arguing for equity to prevail, asserted that 'the Judges themselves do play the Chancellors Parts (upon Statutes, making Construction of them according to Equity ... and enlarging them *pro bono publico*, against the Letter and Intent of the Makers, whereof our Books have many Hundreds of Cases'.[80] The Lord Chancellor referred to the approach of Sir Edward Coke, in the Court of King's Bench the orders of which the Lord Chancellor had restrained from execution. The Lord Chancellor said that Sir Edward Coke's decision and report of *Bonham's Case* had applied that doctrine of the equity of the statute despite the intention of Parliament.[81]

The more constrained approach to the equity of the statute was sometimes seen in relation to the *Statute of Frauds*. When Lord Mansfield applied the equity of the statute approach in *Simon v Motivos*, he did so without focus upon the meaning of the words of the statute but he accepted that the construction would be constrained by the 'key' which was 'the intent of the Legislature'.[82] But, in contrast, when Pratt LCJ (later Lord Camden), in a dissenting opinion in 1765, differed from Lord Mansfield's conclusion in *Wyndham v Chetwynd*,[83] the Lord Chief Justice said pointedly that 'it is not my business to decide cases by my own rule of justice, but to declare the law as I find it laid down; if the statute of frauds has enjoined this determination, it is not my opinion, but the judgment of the legislature'.[84]

[75] SvP Pufendorf, *Of the Law of Nature and Nations* (5th edn, (1749), bk 5, 550.

[76] *Heydon's Case* (1584) 3 Co Rep 7 [76 ER 637].

[77] 31 H VIII, c 13.

[78] *Heydon's Case* (n 76) 7b [76 ER 637, 638]. See also Coke (n 7) s 21.

[79] (1610) 8 Co Rep 113b, 118a [77 ER 646, 652].

[80] (1615) 1 Chan Rep 1, 12 [21 ER 485, 488]. See further the comprehensive discussion of this case in this volume by D Klimchuk (Chapter 2).

[81] (1615) 1 Chan Rep 1, 11 [21 ER 485, 487].

[82] *Simon v Motivos* (1746) 1 Black W 599, 600 [96 ER 347, 347].

[83] (1757) 1 Black W 95 [93 ER 53].

[84] *Hindson v Kersey* (1765) in R Burn, *The Ecclesiastical Law* (9th edn, 1842) vol 4, 116, 118.

V. The Decline of the Older Approach

The older approach to the equity of the statute might not be thought surprising in the era in which it occurred. As Postema explained, Coke's view of the law was that 'legislative change represented degeneration of the law from its pristine purity in ancient times'.[85] For this reason, Frederick Pollock remarked that the doctrine of the equity of the statute 'cannot well be accounted for except on the theory that Parliament generally changes the law for the worse, and that the business of the judges is to keep the mischief of its interference within the narrowest possible bounds'.[86]

The older approach to the equity of the statute lost its legitimacy for three reasons. First, in early English law statutes were also sometimes drafted by the very judges who were called upon to interpret them.[87] A judge who had drafted a statute could correct a statute by saying, in effect, 'this statute objectively means x but for reasons of equity I am going to apply meaning y because I know what I had meant to say'. As Professor Manning observed, 'one would hardly expect the medieval English judge to have a sense of usurping the responsibilities of a different branch, with distinct competence and legitimacy, when interpreting a clear statute contrary to its terms'.[88] But by the mid-eighteenth century the judges who construed a statute were rarely the same persons who had drafted it. Even the draftsmen of the Statute of Frauds had been forgotten. It was thought by some that Sir Matthew Hale had drafted the statute.[89] But when, in *Wyndham v Chetwynd*,[90] counsel relied on the stature of Lord Hale as part of a submission that the word 'credible' would not have been used in a superfluous sense, Lord Mansfield pointed out that Hale had died the year before the Act was drafted.[91] The notion of independent, objective judicial construction on this approach to the equity of the statute therefore required it to be based upon the notional construct of the reasonable intention of Parliament.

Second, the rise of notions of separation of powers did not permit real equity in this sense of judicial rectification of the meaning of a statute.[92] As Deane and Gummow JJ observed in *Nelson v Nelson*,[93] the doctrine of the equity of the statute 'fell deeply into disfavour in England and the United States with the rise of legal positivism in the last century'. The process of creating new law by reference to considerations of justice independent of the statute was recognized as one that can cross the line of constitutional

[85] GJ Postema, *Bentham and the Common Law Tradition* (Clarendon Press 1986) 15.

[86] Sir F Pollock, *Essays in Jurisprudence and Ethics* (Forgotten Books 1882) 85.

[87] SE Thorne, 'The Equity of a Statute and *Heydon's Case*' (1936) 31 Illinois Law Review 202, 203.

[88] J Manning 'Textualism and the Equity of the Statute' (2001) 101 Columbia Law Review 1, 42–43.

[89] John Campbell described Hale as 'not merely by far the best Common Law Judge, but by far the best Equity Judge of his time'. The great Lord Nottingham regarded Hale as 'his great master': *The Lives of the Chief Justices of England* (rev edn, Forgotten Books 1979) vol 1, 551–52.

[90] (1746) 1 Black W 96, 97 [93 ER 53, 54].

[91] The likelihood is that the first draft was written by Lord Nottingham: CD Hening, 'The Original Drafts of the Statute of Frauds and Their Authors' (1913) 61 University of Pennsylvania Law Review 283.

[92] J Landis 'Statutes and the Sources of Law' in M Carlisle and others (eds), *Harvard Legal Essays* (Harvard UP 1934) 217–18.

[93] (1995) 184 CLR 538, 553; [1995] HCA 25.

settlement between adjudication and legislation. By the mid-nineteenth century, Sedgwick remarked of this approach to the equity of the statute:[94]

> The process, therefore, in these cases, is not obedience to legislative commands; it is not an effort to arrive at the legislative intention; it is not construction of a doubtful provision; it is a violation of the words of the statute, in order to make a rule according to the judicial notion of right. It is purely and strictly judicial legislation. And, fortunately, we are not without abundant authorities in our law which steadily, it may be sternly applied, will establish in its proper place the line that separates the judicial from the legislative functions.

Third, concerns about consistency with the rule of law may have contributed to the general rejection of the older approach to the equity of the statute. In *Burragubba v State of Queensland*,[95] I considered a submission that the 'equity' of the Native Title Act 1993 (Cth) concerning awards of costs should extend to judicial review proceedings, about which that statute was not concerned and about which there could be no basis to prescribe any parliamentary intention. As I observed in that case, a difficulty with the approach to the equity of the statute that applies a law in terms beyond what it means is that this contravenes the legislative principle, of which Barwick CJ spoke in *Watson v Lee*,[96] that a person should not be bound by a law the terms of which she has no means of knowing.

However, the doctrine of the equity of the statute in its older sense persisted in some cases. An example in 1889 is *Riggs v Palmer*.[97] In that case, a majority of the Court of Appeals of New York held that a legislative provision that apparently permitted a grandson to inherit most of his grandfather's estate would be construed as subject to an exception where the grandson had murdered the testator. At one point in his reasoning in the majority, the Chief Justice appealed to the maxim that a person shall not profit from his wrong, effectively suggesting that it was a background assumption to the meaning of the legislation. Whether or not it is plausible that such a wide and general background assumption could be given direct effect, as though it were an implication, independently of any statutory words, that approach is still an example of legitimate techniques of statutory interpretation.[98] Yet the Chief Justice did not rationalize the result on the basis of an implication from the words of the statute in their context, including their background. He said that that the equity of the statute permitted him to ask whether if the lawmakers had been consulted they would have permitted the passage of title to the grandson.[99] In this hypothetical consultation with the lawmakers the meaning to be given to the legislative provision was not derived from the meaning

94 *The Interpretation and Application of Statutory and Constitutional Law* (1857) 307.
95 (2015) 236 FCR 160.
96 (1979) 144 CLR 374, 381; [1979] HCA 53.
97 (1889) 22 NE 188.
98 *Welwyn Hatfield BC v Secretary of State for Communities and Local Government* [2011] 2 AC 304, [45]–[46].
99 *Riggs v Palmer* (1889) 22 NE 188, 189.

of the law that *was* passed. It was a concern with the law that *should* have been passed. For this very reason, Professor Dworkin argued in favour of the approach of the Chief Justice in *Riggs v Palmer.* He saw that approach as giving effect to extrinsic normative principles rather than any ascription of notional parliamentary intention based only on interpretation of the words used. For Dworkin, those principles were external considerations of justice, albeit ones which 'could not depend on the judge's own preferences amongst a sea of respectable extra-legal standards'.[100]

Although the persistence today of the older view of the equity of the statute, in cases like *Riggs v Palmer,* is rare, remnants of the older version of the equity of the statute remain present in two forms. The first remnant is the continued recognition of doctrines that were developed in the period of classical application of the equity of the statute. The proper, incremental development of the common law may not permit the eradication of doctrines forged upon an illegitimate premise, especially where those doctrines have persisted for hundreds of years and have been assumed to exist in the course of legislative developments.

An example is the continued recognition of the doctrine of part performance in Australia. In *Pipikos v Trayans,*[101] a central issue was whether the doctrine of part performance should be expanded so that there was no longer a requirement that the act of part performance be unequivocally referable to a contract of the general nature as that alleged. It was argued that the decision of the House of Lords in *Steadman v Steadman*[102] had paved the way for the doctrine to be expanded, until legislative intervention in the United Kingdom brought an end to that venture. The High Court of Australia refused to extend the doctrine.[103] The joint judgment of Kiefel CJ, Bell, Gageler, and Keane JJ explained that although Chancery judges of the late seventeenth century might not have regarded the Statute of Frauds as applying to proceedings in equity, by the time of *Maddison v Alderson* in the late nineteenth century it was 'unacceptable' for a court of equity to take itself outside the prescriptions of Parliament.[104] In my reasons for decision I considered that although the doctrine had been forged upon the older view of the equity of the statute, it was too late for it to be abolished. Indeed, part performance was expressly preserved by section 26 of the Law of Property Act 1936 (SA).[105] I reiterated the point made by Sedgwick in 1874 that the doctrine 'approaches so near the power of legislation that a wise judiciary will exercise it with reluctance, and only in extraordinary cases'.[106]

The second remnant of the equity of the statute is a weaker, but far more legitimate, form by which the common law is extended or modified by reference to the general

[100] R Dworkin, *Taking Rights Seriously* (Harvard UP 1977) 37.
[101] [2018] HCA 39.
[102] [1976] AC 536.
[103] Law of Property (Miscellaneous Provisions) Act 1989 (UK), ss 2(1), 2(8), 4, sch 2.
[104] [2018] HCA 39, [73].
[105] ibid [125].
[106] T Sedgwick and JN Pomeroy, *A Treatise on the Rules which Govern the Interpretation and Construction of Statutory and Constitutional Law* (2nd edn, Baker, Voorhis & Co 1874) 251, citing *Monson v Chester* 22 Pick 385, 387 (1839).

purpose of a statute rather than by direct extension of the particular provisions. In 1907, Roscoe Pound observed that there were four ways that the common law might respond to legislation.[107] The fourth of these was integrating statute and common law and giving superior status to legislative analogies in the development of the common law. This weak version of the older equity of the statute approach extends the reach of the statute by reference to considerations of justice and the general purpose of the statute. By this route it is possible to reach a result that the common law might not have reached without the legislation.[108] But the form is much weaker because that modification will generally only occur when it is consistent with basic common law norms.

An example of this approach is equity's application of limitation periods 'in analogy to the statute'[109] provided that no 'greater equity' outweighs it.[110] Extension by analogy is not confined to statutes of limitation. In *Esso Australia Resources v Commissioner of Taxation*,[111] Gleeson CJ, Gaudron, and Gummow JJ said:[112]

> Where over a period of years there can be discerned a steady trend in legislation which reflects the view of successive Parliaments as to what the public interest demands in a particular field of law, development of the common law in that part of the same field which has been left to it ought to proceed upon a parallel rather than a diverging course.

The reason why this is a weaker, and legitimate form of the equity of the statute is because it does not involve the direct application of statutory provisions outside their terms and also because the common law will not be extended or constrained by reference to statutory policy where to do so would be contrary to the deeper common law norms. An example is the decision of the High Court of Australia in *Brodie v Singleton Shire Council*.[113] In *Brodie*, the High Court considered whether to maintain a so-called immunity of public authorities for tortious liability based on nonfeasance rather than misfeasance. A roads and traffic authority had the powers and the immunities of a council in relation to a public road. It was held by a majority of the court (Gaudron, McHugh, and Gummow JJ, with whom Kirby J generally agreed) that the statutory powers of the authority gave it a degree of control that was thought to be sufficient to render it liable for nonfeasance. However, the common law was developed, by abolishing the so-called immunity despite the existence of state statute law that preserved the so-called immunity.

This weak application of the older approach to the doctrine of the equity of the statute can also be seen in the approach to illegality taken in the High Court of Australia. An example is the decision in *Equuscorp Pty Ltd v Haxton*.[114] In that case, the High Court

[107] R Pound, 'Common Law and Legislation' (1907) 21 Harvard Law Review 383.
[108] See also PS Atiyah, 'Common Law and Statute Law' (1985) 48 MLR 1, 7.
[109] *Sterndale v Hankinson* (1827) 1 Sim 393, 398 [57 ER 625, 627]. See also *Smith v Clay* (1767) 3 Bro CC 646 [29 ER 743, 744, 746]; *Re Greaves; Bray v Tofield* (1881) 18 Ch D 551, 553.
[110] *R v McNeil* (1922) 31 CLR 76, 100; [1922] HCA 33.
[111] (1999) 201 CLR 49, 62 [24]; [1999] HCA 67.
[112] Quoting *Warnink v J Townend & Sons (Hull) Ltd* [1979] AC 731, 743 per Lord Diplock.
[113] (2001) 206 CLR 512.
[114] (2012) 246 CLR 498; [2012] HCA 7.

considered whether a common law claim for unjust enrichment could be brought by a lender to recover money assumed to have been paid to investors under contracts which were unenforceable for illegality. The statute which made the contracts unenforceable did not bar any action for unjust enrichment, either expressly or impliedly. The statute also contained its own regime of penalties, including possible imprisonment. The majority held that the common law claim based upon unjust enrichment must fail because it would 'stultify' the statutory purpose.[115] All of the judges in the majority relied upon the earlier decision of Deane and Gummow JJ in *Nelson v Nelson*.[116] In that judgment, their honours explained that the origins of this 'third class of illegality' might be seen in the equity of the statute, 'a survival of an earlier school of statutory interpretation'[117] which was a 'doctrine [that] had the support of the common law judges led by Sir Edward Coke, who looked back to a time before the rise of the doctrine of parliamentary sovereignty and the subjection to it of the common law'.[118] In *Haxton*, Heydon J dissented. His Honour held that there was nothing express or implied in the language of the statute which had the effect of extinguishing an otherwise valid common law claim:[119]

> The contrast between direct legislative prohibition and the policy of the law is not a contrast between what the statute provides and some entirely extra-statutory doctrine. The 'policy of the law' is to be found in the 'scope and purpose' of the statute. The scope and purpose of the statute depend solely on the meaning of its language.

VI. Conclusion and Wider Application

If the equity of the statute is regarded merely as a technique by which statutory context and purpose moulds the interpretation and construction of statutes, then it should be uncontroversial. There is nothing unusual about an interpretation of a statute extending beyond the literal range of semantic meanings of the words to reach what the judge believes to be the meaning of the words intended by Parliament, as a notional speaker, to a reasonable person, as a notional reader. Nor is there anything unusual in construing the application of the words of a statute by reference to the statutory context and purpose particularly in cases where the words are vague, ambiguous or leave gaps in their application. However, in the usual circumstances where Parliament has used words deliberately and carefully, the more the interpretation of the meaning of words departs from the literal range of semantic choices for the words, and the more that the construction or application of the words strays from a direct application of that interpretation, the more difficult the result should be to justify.

[115] *Equuscorp Pty Ltd v Haxton* (2012) 246 CLR 498, 514 [25] per French, Crennan, and Kiefel JJ, 537–38 [96], 544 [111] per Gummow and Bell JJ; [2012] HCA 7. Compare the English approach in *Patel v Mirza* [2017] AC 467.

[116] *Nelson v Nelson* (1995) 184 CLR 538, 552; [1995] HCA 25.

[117] ibid 554.

[118] ibid 552.

[119] *Equuscorp Pty Ltd v Haxton* (2012) 246 CLR 498, 549 [124]; [2012] HCA 7.

Much more controversial is the older sense of the equity of the statute. This older sense seeks to supplement the statute with external principles of justice. This is a separate philosophical principle. The two approaches might coincide in the result where the reader of the legal text can reasonably assume from the words and their context that the principle of justice is not external but is one which was intended by the notional speaker as the meaning of the words used. But to apply 'equity' as an external principle of justice, without finding an express or implied warrant in the words themselves, would make the exercise of giving effect to an expression of democratic power an exercise of predominantly judicial power. For this reason, as I have explained, the only broad acceptance that remains for this approach is where the common law is expanded or constrained by judicial development based upon the equity of the statute.

Although this chapter is concerned only with the interpretation and construction of statutes, the same issues arise in relation to all legal documents. The modern approach to the equity of the instrument, is consistent with an approach that is ubiquitous in speech acts generally. In every speech act, the listener or reader must interpret and construe the words by reference to context and purpose in an attempt to understand the intended meaning of the speaker. Hence, there is a powerful argument that there is nothing fundamentally different between the way we interpret and construe a statute and the way we interpret and construe any other speech act. This is why, in 1889, Bowen LJ said that the 'rules for the construction of statutes are very like those which apply to the construction of other documents'[120] and, a decade later, Holmes J said that 'we do not deal differently with a statute from our way of dealing with a contract'.[121] This point has further force where the statute enacts a treaty or a contract, such as a state agreement. Most recently, in *A-G of Belize v Belize Telecom Ltd*,[122] Lord Hoffmann, giving the advice of the Privy Council, gave examples of statutes, written contracts and articles of association as all involving a construction of the meaning which is conveyed by the instrument to a reasonable reader. And in *Byrnes v Kendle*,[123] Heydon and Crennan JJ observed how 'matched' approaches applied to contractual and statutory construction.

The older, controversial approach is sometimes also applied to other instruments. One example will suffice to illustrate the controversy that elsewhere surrounds the application of the older approach to the equity of the instrument. Historically, in cases where the effect of words in a trust or will would be to cause a charitable gift to fail—for example, where the original purpose is impossible—courts developed a doctrine called cy-pres, which allowed the words to be given a meaning 'as near as possible' to the meaning that they would otherwise bear. As Dixon and Evatt JJ said in *A-G (NSW) v Perpetual Trustee Co (Ltd)*:[124]

120 *Curtis v Stovin* (1889) 22 QBD 513, 517.
121 OWH, Jr, Holmes, 'The Theory of Legal Interpretation' (1899) 12 Harvard Law Review 417, 419.
122 [2009] 1 WLR 1988, 1993 [16]; [2009] 2 All ER 1127, 1132.
123 *Byrnes v Kendle* (2011) 243 CLR 253, [95]–[116] per Heydon and Crennan JJ; [2011] HCA 26.
124 (1940) 63 CLR 209, 225; [1940] HCA 12.

> [T]he court will execute the trust by decreeing some other application of the trust property to the furtherance of the substantial purpose, some application which departs from the original plan in particulars held not essential and, otherwise, keeps as near thereto as may be.

The application of the doctrine was sometimes consistent only with the older approach to the equity of the statute, constrained only by the *general* charitable intention of the settler or testator: 'a general principle of piety in the testator'.[125] The possibility for complete reinterpretation of a will or trust was manifest. For instance, the doctrine of cy-pres was used in one case by the Lord Chancellor to apply a bequest for a house of Jewish study to a home to bring up children in the Christian faith.[126] Lord Eldon remarked wryly that '[i]t would have caused some surprise to the testator if he had known how his devise would have been construed.'[127] Unsurprisingly, like the 'equity of the statute', the doctrine of cy-pres was always controversial and liable to be abused. In *A-G v Lady Downing*,[128] the Lord Chief Justice, expressing the opinion of himself, the Lord Chancellor, and the Master of the Rolls, said that the doctrine would permit a situation in which 'the testator is made to disinherit [the heir at law] for a charity he never thought of; perhaps for a charity repugnant to the testator's intention, and which directly opposes and encounters the charity he meant to establish'. And in *A-G v Andrew*,[129] the Lord Chancellor referred to older cases which had suggested that the doctrine 'ought never again to be mentioned in this Court'.

[125] *Moggridge v Thackwell* (1802) 7 Ves Jun 36, 69 [32 ER 15, 26] per Lord Eldon.

[126] *Da Costa v De Paz* (1754) Amb 228 [27 ER 150]; 2 Swans 532 [36 ER 715]. See, further, the discussion in J Getzler, '*Morice v Bishop of Durham* (1805)' in C Mitchell and P Mitchell (eds), *Landmark Cases in Equity* (Hart 2012) 157.

[127] *A-G v Mayor of Bristol* (1820) 2 Jac & W 294, 308 [37 ER 640, 645].

[128] *A-G v Lady Downing* (1767) Wilm 1, 32 [97 ER 1, 13].

[129] *A-G v Andrew* (1798) 3 Ves Jun 633, 649 [30 ER 1194, 1202].

Index

Note: *For the benefit of digital users, indexed terms that span two pages (e.g., 52–53) may, on occasion, appear on only one of those pages.*

www.ingramcontent.com/pod-product-compliance
Lightning Source LLC
Chambersburg PA
CBHW081143110626
46430CB00005B/14
9780198817659